Exeter Studies in History

General Editors: Jonathan Barry, Tim Rees and T.P. Wiseman

WITCHCRAFT IN EARLY MODERN SCOTLAND

This volume provides an introduction to the key concepts of witchcraft and demonology through a detailed study of one of the best known and most notorious episodes of Scottish history. The series of trials and executions that took place in Edinburgh between 1590 and 1591, known as the 'North Berwick witch hunt', involved King James as alleged victim and as interrogator, judge and demonologist. Hitherto unpublished and inaccessible material from the legal documentation of the trials, as well as full texts of the pamphlet *News from Scotland* and James' *Demonology*, are presented in a readable, modernised, annotated form. The book also brings to bear on this material current scholarship on the history of European witchcraft.

Part One provides information about the contexts needed to understand the texts: court politics, social history and culture, religious changes, law and the workings of the court, and the history of witchcraft prosecutions in Scotland before 1590.

Part Two introduces the texts themselves. 'Witch Hunting': Examinations, Confessions and Depositions—18 documents recording the examinations of those suspected and charged with witchcraft and a treasonable conspiracy to kill the king; 'Records of the Witchcraft Trials': Dittays—8 surviving documents that are the court records of the trials of the main suspects; 'Witch Hunt Propaganda': *News from Scotland*—a sensational, lurid account of the interrogations of suspects; 'Theorising the Witch Hunt': James VI's *Demonology*—written by James himself, a general work on witchcraft that draws on the North Berwick witch hunt for some details and sense of authenticity.

Lawrence Normand is principal lecturer in English at Middlesex University. Until his death in 1999, **Gareth Roberts** was senior lecturer in the School of English, University of Exeter, where he was Course Director of the MA in The History and Literature of Witchcraft.

WITCHCRAFT IN EARLY MODERN SCOTLAND

JAMES VI's *DEMONOLOGY*
and the
NORTH BERWICK WITCHES

Edited by
Lawrence Normand
&
Gareth Roberts

LIVERPOOL UNIVERSITY PRESS

First published in 2000 by
University of Exeter Press
This reprint published by
Liverpool University Press
4 Cambridge Street
Liverpool L69 7ZU

www.liverpooluniversitypress.co.uk

British Library Cataloguing in Publication Data
A catalogue record of this book is available from the British Library.

Hardback ISBN 978-0-85989-680-1
Paperback ISBN 978-0-85989-388-6

Typeset in 10/12 and 10.5/13 New Baskerville
by Quince Typesetting, Exeter

Printed and bound by CPI Group (UK) Ltd, Croydon, CR0 4YY

For
W. L. Normand
and in memory of
Hilda Normand,
Kitty Roberts
and
Aileen Kelly

CONTENTS

The Texts

———

ILLUSTRATIONS

ACKNOWLEDGEMENTS

This book was made possible by the generosity of many individuals and several institutions over a number of years. We are grateful to the following institutions for supporting and funding work on this book by way of research leave, relief from teaching, travel and other research costs: the University of Exeter; the Panytfedwen Fund and the Research Committee of the University of Wales, Lampeter; the School of Humanities and Cultural Studies, Middlesex University; and the British Academy.

The following librarians and archivists, libraries and archives, have been generous with their help in finding and providing the many and various materials which have gone into the making of this book: Kathy Miles, Inter-Library Loans Librarian at the University of Wales, Lampeter; Heather Eva, Inter-Library Loans Librarian at the University of Exeter; Diana Webster, Map Librarian of the National Library of Scotland; Helen Watson and Susannah Kerr of the National Galleries of Scotland; Veronica Wallace and Chris Roberts of the Local History Section of Haddington Public Library; D. M. Abbott of the Scottish Record Office; the Bodleian Library, Oxford; the British Library; Edinburgh University Library; Glasgow University Library; Harvard University Library; the Huntington Library; Lambeth Palace Library; and especially the expert, courteous and extraordinarily efficient staff at the Scottish Record Office, General Register House, Edinburgh, where much of the manuscript work for this book was carried out.

It is a pleasure to acknowledge the help given by many colleagues in the preparation of this book: Michael Bath, Tom Bennett, Robin Briggs, Dermot Cavanagh, Mark Dooley, Gregory Durston, Erica Fudge, Marion Gibson, Julian Goodare, Todd Gray, Rune Hagen, Jonathan Hope, Colin Jones, James Knowles, Matthew McGuinness, Mike MacNair, Janet Marx, Sara Mendelson, Ted-Larry Pebworth, Jennifer Richards, Lyndal Roper, Claude J. Summers, Ian D. Whyte, Joanne Winning, Louise Yeoman. We are grateful to Jenny Wormald who sent a pre-publication copy of her essay on King James and the witches which provided valuable insights; and also to Brian Levack whose comments on one section saved us from many errors on Scots law. We would like to thank Stuart Clark who was exceptionally generous in agreeing to read and comment on a draft of this book. For the errors and shortcomings that remain the authors are of course responsible.

Students on the History and Literature of Witchcraft MA at the University of Exeter provided valuable comments on early drafts of the texts by suggesting what annotation and glossing readers would find helpful, and many of their suggestions have been adopted. The Masters dissertations of Lesley Mackay and Emma Wilby covered some of the material that found its way into this book.

We owe a special debt of gratitude to Jonathan Barry, one of the General Editors of *Exeter Studies in History*, who sustained this project from the start, and whose patience and tact helped see it to completion. As a lively reader and scrupulous editor he offered many valuable suggestions, most of which have been silently adopted.

Grateful thanks are extended to the production team: Mike Dobson, Sean Goddard, Peter Mitchell, Jane Raistrick and all of the staff at University of Exeter Press who have worked on the book. We wish to acknowledge the generous financial support received towards production costs from the School of Humanities and Cultural Studies, Middlesex University; the School of English, University of Exeter; and the Gareth Roberts Memorial Fund.

Introduction

HISTORY, WITCHCRAFT, TEXTS

The year 1585 may serve in two ways as the origin of events represented in the texts in this book. It was probably in 1585, the year of the first record of her magical practice, that Agnes Sampson foretold Isobel Hamilton's death, when Isobel's husband would not pay for raising the devil to heal her.[1] In that same year negotiations began for the marriage of the nineteen-year-old king of Scots to a Danish princess. Of these two moments, one is located in the career of a local cunning woman in Lothian, the other among the national and inter-national, political and dynastic negotations of a royal court. These moments come from the lives of people whose immediate societies, cultures and concerns may seem to us at first glance quite different, but can on closer inspection at times be startlingly alike. In some instances these people shared a common culture, belief system and indeed locality. All these areas were in a few years to meet, overlap and fuse in the examinations and prosecutions, some conducted and supervised by the recently married King James VI, of the women (and some men) accused of witchcraft who were to become known as the North Berwick witches.

Robin Briggs has surveyed the 'many reasons why' witch hunts occur.[2] A full explanation of the North Berwick hunt has to take into account that it was a complex social event in which popular and elite culture interacted, and that it was also a social crisis that evolved rapidly over a number of months from an outbreak of rural witchcraft, to a crisis of state, to a national witch hunt. In such a complex event the motivations of the upper-class, mostly urban participants are likely to be different from those of the lower-class, predominantly rural participants. Social and economic pressures are more likely to explain village accusations; political, religious and ideological pressures are more likely to explain prosecutions by ruling-class agents in urban Edinburgh. The difference between these areas of interest can be seen by comparing some of the earlier witchcraft depositions, and early items of John Fian's and Agnes Sampson's dittays, containing accounts of domestic concerns, local disputes and fears of *maleficia*, with *News from Scotland*'s account which shifts rapidly from a domestic dispute to a focus on elite fears of the devil and demonic conspiracy against the king.

This book is primarily about the series of examinations, trials and executions of witches that took place in Edinburgh between late November 1590 and December 1591, and which concerned alleged conspiracy and treason against the king and queen. These trials were part of a larger outbreak of witchcraft trials that had begun in East Lothian in the second half of 1590 and would spread into other parts of Scotland by the end of 1592, then abate for a few years, and then flare up again in 1595–7. Confusingly, the name 'North Berwick' is used by historians to refer both to the national witch hunt of 1590–7 and to the small number of state trials that took place in Edinburgh in 1590–1. The name is used in this book to refer to the Edinburgh trials of 1590–1.

Because the king and privy council took charge of the examination and trial of those accused of witchcraft and treason in the North Berwick cases, the surviving legal records are remarkably full. This book is primarily concerned with four cases, those of Agnes Sampson, John Fian, Barbara Napier and Euphame MacCalzean, and presents all the surviving legal records relating to those cases: pre-trial examinations and depositions, and the dittays, or formal court record, of the trials in the justiciary court. In addition, it presents the dittay of the trial of the earl of Bothwell, who was accused of being involved in witchcraft against the king. Some documents have not survived. We do not have any records from the very first stages of these witchcraft cases, when local people made accusations to the authorities, such as kirk sessions or baillies. Nor do we have the dittays from the justiciary court for the period immediately following Euphame MacCalzean's trial.[3] This lacuna in the legal records was already remarked upon by Bothwell when in February 1593 he defended himself against the accusation of witchcraft by saying that the king's council were so 'ashamed of the iniquity of that process of witchcraft, in my opinion they have destroyed the same, for neither is it extant in the books "adjurnall" nor to be found out in any "scrowlis" [drafts]'.[4]

This interconnected series of witchcraft accusations and trials generated a series of similarly interconnected texts: depositions, dittays, a pamphlet and a demonological treatise. Our approach is in consequence primarily textual. The texts here are edited and annotated, many of them for the first time, and that process of editing is itself necessarily an act of interpretation. This book presents texts and contextualises them, and interprets those texts and the witch hunt they record. In addition, one feature of our particular approach is to consider the texts as reporting a series of narratives and fictions. The following chapters present in chronological order the texts produced at the time of, or shortly after, the North Berwick witch trials. Examinations and depositions are a record by legal officials of interrogations of the accused, or statements made by them or others. Although these records are filtered through the minds and legal conventions of officials, they bring us as close as we can get to the worlds of the accused. Court dittays also take us into the world of professional lawyers where evidence is further processed in response to both legal conventions and educated notions of witchcraft. The account of the witches' supposed doings in *News from Scotland*, written while trials were continuing, seeks to intensify the horror of witchcraft as a threat directed specifically at James as king. The witch hunt's political significance is made explicit by this propaganda pamphlet, and is further developed in James's theorisation of witchcraft in his dialogue *Demonology*. This text's demonological reasoning may seem furthest from the accused women's experience and testimony, but its claim to truth and authority depends in part on James's detailed knowledge of witchcraft acquired in questioning some the witches himself. In this sequence of texts, women and men accused of witchcraft become increasingly subject to a rewriting, indeed reinvention, which serves the various interests of the writers.

Writing and narrative have particular significance in witchcraft studies,[5] but especially so in this witch hunt. Accusations of witchcraft appear generally in the form of stories—of disagreements, suspicions, magical healing or harm, divination, and malefice. A person accused of witchcraft is arraigned on the basis of a series of stories that hostile or frightened neighbours have reported to the authorities. But this particular witch hunt was constructed by creating a large-scale narrative out of the many and diverse stories of individual accusations and examinations. It was not constituted simply by the appearance of a large number of cases in one area over a short period of time, although this was indeed the case. The particular nature of the North Berwick hunt lay in the authorities' idea that individual cases were all interrelated parts of one larger witchcraft event. From the particularities of the evidence from individuals over a period of weeks and months a narrative was formed which concerned conspiracy and treason. This process, driven by state and church authorities, and enforced by the use of torture, compelled the accused to confirm and indeed contribute to the story. That fantastic story is recounted in *News from Scotland*. Narrative is also important in demonological treatises in that two narratives, those of Job's afflictions and Saul's consultation with the witch of Endor, constituted the most important biblical evidence for witchcraft. James's discussion of the witch of Endor occupies the first chapter of his *Demonology*.

Historians too almost invariably approach the subject of this witch hunt by telling a story,[6] which is itself a tribute to the appeal of the story of the North Berwick witches as told in the various texts which represent it. Such stories are themselves a form of interpretation, and in their tendency to focus on individuals and their actions they overemphasise the immediate and personal, and neglect the longer-term and impersonal forces at work in producing the witch hunt. Some of these stories, in many ways understandably, focus on James, and have contributed to the continuing historiography of prejudice against him. Many nineteenth-century accounts held the 'crazed' king more or less solely responsible not only for the prosecution of Scottish witches,[7] but for inaugurating 'the darkest period of the history of witchcraft in the southern parts of our island'.[8] Scotland was, after all, a country where witchcraft preserved its hold on the population 'much longer than in the more civilised south'.[9] Similar views can still be found in this century. But James was initially sceptical about the charges against the East Lothian women, and he was only persuaded to credit them by the belief of one of the women themselves that she had supernatural powers. When charges were laid against Bothwell, James also doubted their truth.

The late 1580s and early 1590s were crucial ones for James, and also stressful ones for the whole country. In 1587 he reached his majority, in August 1589 he was married by proxy and in November 1589 in person. In May James and Anne returned to Scotland after their marriage in Denmark, and in early 1594 their first son was born. These stages in James's life (achieving manhood, his marriage, fatherhood) were both personal and political as they helped establish and consolidate his authority as king, as well as the Stuart succession. Also, after the execution of his mother, Mary queen of Scots, in 1587, James was moving along a trajectory which would eventually bring him to the throne of England in 1603, accompanied by a queen and three royal children, and a Scottish court. In the year of his accession three of his works, *Basilikon Doron*, *The Trew Law of Free Monarchies* and *Demonology*, were published in London. This trajectory passes through Scotland's largest witch hunt in the sixteenth century, which involved allegations of conspiracy to kill the king by magic.

But responsibility for this witch hunt cannot be attributed to one man, even if he was a king. In the North Berwick witch hunt, as in most European witch hunts, there was also a 'coalescence between longstanding popular beliefs and the agencies for enforcing social and religious conformity'.[10] During the 1580s in Scotland social and ideological forces were focused and intensified which would combine in 1590 to spark the witch hunt. A presbyterian form of church government was spreading especially through the Lowlands and north-east, putting in place kirk sessions that functioned as a mechanism for social policing, and that used their power to investigate and pursue witchcraft accusations. The group of extreme presbyterians, centred on Andrew Melville, began to return from their English exile from 1586 onwards, determined to pursue the process of presbyterianisation. One of their leaders, James Carmichael, returned from London in 1587 to become minister of Haddington; and it was in Haddington that Agnes Sampson, who was to be cast in the role of chief agent in the alleged witchcraft conspiracy, first had witchcraft charges raised against her. Carmichael spent eighteen months actively engaged with King James in pursuing witches in Edinburgh and East Lothian, and was almost certainly the author of *News from Scotland*, the semi-official pamphlet justifying the witch hunt. In the 1580s and 1590s church intellectuals were developing ideas representing the relations between believers and God as a covenant, which would provide the framework of ideas in which the relations between witches and the devil were imagined.

A witch hunt is essentially 'a judicial operation'.[11] The 1563 Scottish witchcraft act was adequate for the witch hunt of 1568 in Angus and the Mearns, and for the first wave of witchcraft cases that emerged in 1590 in East Lothian. But the number and nature of the trials in East Lothian and Edinburgh in 1590–1 prompted changes in legal procedures to deal with them. Legal changes made in response to the large number of trials then in turn influenced the ways in which witchcraft accusations and arraignments were pursued. After the major figures in the North Berwick trials had been dealt with, the central authorities acted in October 1591 to control further trials. In 1597 the entire witch hunt was stopped by government action when central control of further prosecutions was established. It was only between June 1592 and 1597 that the central authorities lost their control of witchcraft prosecutions to the localities, and that was the result of political weakness and the need to placate a dominant kirk. In the Appendix readers will find the texts of the privy council orders that established different legal regimes in the phases of the 1590–7 witch hunt.

The meaning that witchcraft could have in Scotland in 1590 depended, for the elite, partly on European demonology, particularly in its protestant inflections. For a wider range of social groups it was shaped by forms of sixteenth-century Scottish cultural life. The North Berwick witch hunt did not come out of nowhere. Chapter 2 explores some features of late sixteenth-century Scottish history and society that went into the making of the 1590s witch hunt, and shaped its particular meaning. Through the legal processes of interrogation and torture stories were produced out of material drawn from historical memory and contemporary circumstances, and refashioned into a new configuration of witchcraft. It is a feature of this witch hunt that relatively uneducated peasant women talked with highly educated and sophisticated leaders of church and state. In this extraordinary exchange a narrative of witchcraft and treason was forged that drew on experiences of popular and learned culture. Although it remains unclear what popular magic might actually have meant to its practitioners, it seems clear that in the process of witch hunting aspects of popular culture that were previously regarded as comparatively innocuous became demonised.

This book could not have been written without Christina Larner's groundbreaking research in *Enemies of God: The Witch-hunt in Scotland* (1981). The approach and focus of this book are, however, different from hers, which was a general overview emphasising common features of Scottish witchcraft during the period of most intense witch hunting, roughly the mid-sixteenth to mid-eighteenth centuries. The present book is a micro-study of one witch hunt that lasted just over a year and involved a limited number of people. Its method is to focus on the contexts of the witch hunt, and on the texts it generated, which not only record in remarkable detail the processes involved in a witch hunt, but are themselves instrumental in various ways in forming that witch hunt. The texts are different in kind, from the apparently simply historical (in pre-trial examinations) to the predominantly literary (in *Demonology*, which as a dialogue is formally a work of fiction); and they form a continuous series running from pre-trial material to an elite theorisation. For those involved in the North Berwick witch hunt, witchcraft was a matter of meanings as well as acts. This book's approach involves reading all of these diverse records as texts shaped by the demands of representation, a method that is at least partly new historicist in that we believe, like Stephen Greenblatt, that a text 'is not the passive surface on which this historical experience leaves its stamp but one of the creative agents in the fashioning and re-fashioning of this experience'.[12]

To represent actual historical persons in texts is a kind of ventriloquism. Robert Grierson is a minor character in the story of the North Berwick witches, but he appears in all the texts representing them, apart from *Demonology* where none of the witches is named. He was a real historical agent, and we know that he died from torture on 15 April 1591. He is represented in the texts as present at many conventions; at North Berwick kirk it is the devil's naming him that caused the witches to run 'hirdy-girdy'. He is the obstreperous man who berated the devil for not producing the wax image of King James on time, and who uttered the shrewd political comment that any gold expected from England to fund the conspiracy against James would be long in coming. The figure of Robert Grierson, or 'Rob the Rower' to use his demonic nickname, is a mixture of fact and fiction composed of popular, political, cultural and demonological motifs, which raises problems of representation and history in the North Berwick witch hunt with which this book engages.

Notes

1. Sampson's dittay, document 20, item 19.
2. Briggs 1996b.
3. See Larner, Lee and McLachlan 1977: vi–vii.
4. *CSPS* xi 62.
5. See Purkiss 1996: especially 7–58.
6. See for example the narrative summaries of events in Stafford 1953; Maxwell-Stuart 1997; Wormald 2000.
7. See Kittredge 1929: 276–7.
8. Wright 1851: i 179.
9. Wright 1851: i 160.
10. Briggs 1996b: 60.
11. Levack 1995: 68.
12. Greenblatt 1988: viii.

Discussion of the Texts *and* Editorial Conventions

Documents 1–18: examinations, confessions and depositions

These documents, not previously published or edited, are to be found among papers relating to proceedings of the justiciary court at Edinburgh, now in the Scottish Record Office, General Register House, Edinburgh, in a box pressmark JC 26/2. They are mentioned by Larner, Lee and McLachlan, who had looked through this and other boxes of similar records when compiling *A Source-book of Scottish Witchcraft* (1977), and Larner also mentions them in *Enemies of God* (1981). Having examined only some of these papers, we would like to repeat Larner's words: 'there may well be more in these boxes'. The earliest dated documents are those recording an examination of Agnes Sampson on 4–5 December 1590; the latest record the recantation of Geillis Duncan, just before her execution on 4 December 1591, of her previous depositions against Euphame MacCalzean and Barbara Napier. It is not possible to date all the documents precisely as many are damaged at the very top where the date was written. Internal and external evidence, mainly correspondence of Robert Bowes, the English ambassador to Scotland, to Burghley, the English secretary of state, have been used in the attempt to arrange them in chronological order. With some documents this order remains conjectural.

Documents 19–26: records of the witchcraft trials (dittays)

The dittays are to be found in the Books of Adjournal, the manuscript minutes of trials and court decisions of the sixteenth and seventeenth centuries, which are now in the Scottish Record Office, Edinburgh. The surviving dittays are of John Fian, alias Cunningham (SRO JC 2/2, ff. 195–196^v); Agnes Sampson (JC 2/2, ff. 201–206^v); Barbara Napier (JC 2/2, ff. 213–221); and Euphame

MacCalzean (JC 2/2, ff. 221–226ᵛ). There is one previous edition of the dittays, by Robert Pitcairn in his *Ancient Criminal Trials*. The document recording evidence against the earl of Bothwell is SRO JC 26/2/5; the list of Bothwell's assizers is JC 26/2/7; and the record of Bothwell's trial is JC 26/2/6.

Document 27: *News from Scotland*

Manuscripts

There is a manuscript of the text in a late sixteenth-century hand in the British Library, BL Additional MS 5495, ff. 34–40ᵛ. It is in a clear secretary hand, with an italic script for proper names, corresponding almost exactly to those instances where the printed text uses black-letter and Roman type respectively. There are hardly any deletions or corrections. Spelling and punctuation do not correspond consistently with any of the early quartos, although paragraphing sometimes does. The scribe is fond of double s, as in 'disscourse', 'dissapointethe' and 'practisses', and indeed double letters generally, such as 'holly [holy]' and 'deallinge', all on f. 34.

Ferguson thought that we cannot be sure whether this manuscript was copied from the printed text or from another manuscript,[1] but there is some evidence that it was the latter. The scribe has made a nonsense of the name of one of the witches. The early quartos (see below) name her as 'Iennit Bandilandis' (*D*) or 'Iennet Blandilandis' (*G*). The manuscript (f. 35) gives us the garbled 'Grniutt Baueilomis', which must have been caused by a misreading of another manuscript, not by misreading the printed text. Another mistranscription, 'John bres' and 'John Bres' (f. 36ᵛ) for John Kers, points in the same direction. The regular use of 'church', rather than *Q*'s 'kirk', indicates an English scribe. This manuscript was copied either from the author's holograph, or from a scribal copy, or from a copy of either.

This manuscript version does not contain the printed text's preface 'To the Reader' and begins with the heading 'A true discourse of the apprehension of sundrye witches . . .', which might suggest both that it was copied from another manuscript and that the preface to *News* is the work of the publisher. If this is so, then the pious opening of this section ('God, by his omnipotent power, hath at all times and daily doth take such care and is so vigilant for the weal and preservation of his own . . .') might suggest James Carmichael's authorship of the work from this point on.[2]

Early printed editions

The original quarto exists in three different versions and in six copies in all:

(i)   STC 10841a. *Newes from Scotland, declaring the damnable life and death of doctor Fian* [E. Allde?] for W. Wright, A–D4 with D4 blank. Oxford, Bodleian Library, pressmark Douce F.210; Cambridge, Massachusetts, Harvard

University Library, pressmark STC 10841a (imperfect).[3] The readings of these quartos are collated in the textual notes as *D*.

(ii) STC 10842. *Newes from Scotland, declaring the damnable life and death of doctor Fian* for Thomas Nelson, A–D4 with D4 blank. London, Lambeth Palace, pressmark 1597.15 (4). This is a variant of STC 10841a. The readings of this quarto are collated in the textual notes as *L*.

(iii) STC 10842.3. *Newes from Scotland, declaring the damnable life of doctor Fian* [T. Scarlet] for W. Wright, A–C4. Glasgow, Glasgow University Library, two copies, pressmarks Al–a.36 and Al–a.30; San Marino, California, Huntington Library, pressmark RB 59699. The readings of these quartos are collated in the textual notes as *G*.

Where all these early quartos (i.e. *D*, *L*, *G*) agree, this agreement is indicated in the textual notes as *Q*.

Ferguson gives a full description of these quartos and an account of what is known of their earlier owners and histories. The Lambeth Palace copy was once owned by Richard Bancroft (1544–1610), who became archbishop of Canterbury in 1604 and whose initials are stamped on the cover of a volume containing *News* and other rare pamphlets on witchcraft. The Shakespearean editor George Steevens (1736–1800) once possessed one of the quartos and used it in annotating *Macbeth*. Ferguson himself at one point owned the two copies now in Glasgow.[4]

Later editions

(i) 'Remarkable Account of Witches in Scotland' in *The Gentleman's Magazine*, August and September 1779, 393–5 and 449–52. The pamphlet was communicated to the *Magazine* by a reader. This edition gives the title and modernises the spelling (apart from the proper names), orthography and punctuation, which is heavy. Since the title page tells us that it was printed for Thomas Nelson, the original must have been *L*. This edition is indicated in the collation as *Gent Mag*.

(ii) *Newes from Scotland declaring the damnable life of Doctor Fian* (London: from the Shakespeare Press by W. Bulmer and Co., 1816). This is a reprint prepared by H. Freeling for the Roxburghe Club. It reprints one of the copies of STC 10842.3, probably one of the copies now in Glasgow. This edition is indicated in the collation as *Rox*.

(iii) Charles Kirkpatrick Sharpe reprints most of *News* in the context of his tracing of 'our legends of wizardry and spectral appearances'[5] which is the prefatory notice to his edition of *Memorialls; or The Memorable Things that fell out within this Island of Brittain from 1638 to 1684 by the Rev Mr Robert Law* (Edinburgh 1818). Since the work's title as given by Sharpe ends 'Printed for William Wright', his reprint (xxx–xliii) must have been from one of the copies now in Glasgow (i.e. STC 10842.3). Sharpe excerpts from and paraphrases the prefaces and takes up the pamphlet at the words

'Within the town of Trenent . . .', and omits the paragraph containing what were clearly thought improper details about the devil licking witches in a privy part of the body, and the shaving of Agnes Sampson. He also omits or paraphrases some of the details of Dr Fian's amatory magic and the pamphlet's peroration in its final paragraph.

(iv)   David Webster, *A collection of rare and curious tracts on witchcraft and the second sight with an original essay on witchcraft* (Edinburgh 1820). *Newes from Scotland* is on 13–35. The original was a copy of *G*. This edition is indicated in the collation as *Web*.

(v)   A reprint was included by Robert Pitcairn in his *Ancient Criminal Trials in Scotland* (Edinburgh 1833), where it follows his transcription of Fian's dittay (I iii 213–23). Pitcairn noted that an abstract had already appeared in the prefatory notes to *Laws Memorialls*, ed. Charles Kirkpatrick Sharpe, who gave Pitcairn an accurate transcript (from the Roxburghe edition). Pitcairn notes that the tract is also 'in the late eccentric David Webster', *Collectanea Scotica*, 'but it is there very inaccurately edited'.

(vi)   *Newes from Scotland*, ed. G. B. Harrison (Edinburgh: Bodley Head Quartos, 1924, reprinted as Elizabethan and Jacobean Quartos, 1966). The text is that of *D* in Bodley Douce, although Harrison introduces some errors.

(vii)   *Witchcraft*, ed. Barbara Rosen (London: Stratford-upon-Avon Library no. 6, Edward Arnold, 1969), now reissued as *Witchcraft in England, 1558–1618* (Amherst, Mass.: University of Massachusetts Press, 1991), 190–203.

The readings of i–iv, but not v–vii, have been collated as they offer some illuminating, independent readings or modernisations of *News*.

Illustrations in *News from Scotland*

There are either three or four woodcuts in the early quartos. Their number and location differ in the different editions. Their nature suggests the popular appeal of this work.

(i)   One woodcut (plate 10) shows the devil as a monster preaching in a pulpit, some prosperously dressed women who appear to be listening to him, and a man (Dr Fian?) writing at a table. It also shows a shipwreck, a man sleeping in a cellar (the pedlar transported to Bordeaux?), and in the top right-hand corner a group of four women, one is whom is dipping a spoon into a cauldron. In *G* this takes up over half the page, is on sig. B4^v, and comes before the words 'bee brought before the Kinges Maiestie'. In one of the Glasgow copies, in which the title page is missing (Glasgow Al–a.36), it also appears at the beginning of the work. In *D* and *L* this cut comes in the middle of sig. C2^v.

(ii)   The second woodcut (plate 11) shows a gallows, Fian conjuring the heifer, Fian and another man on horseback, and a church. The woodcut of Fian and another man on horseback with flaming brands on the horse's head illustrates an incident not narrated in *News*. However, Fian's dittay, item 11, describes a ride to Tranent on a horse with four candles upon the horse's 'two lugs' produced by Fian's 'devilish craft'. In *G* this cut is on sig. C2ᵛ and comes before the words '[wick]ed wayes, acknowledging his most ungodly lyfe'. In *D* and *L* this cut comes in the bottom half of sig. C4ᵛ.

(iii) The third woodcut (plate 12) shows a figure seated in judgement and witnessing the submission of four kneeling women over whom another man brandishes a rod. This appears in *D* and *L* on sig. Bᵛ, but in the Huntington copy of *G*, a copy of the illustration from *D* has been inserted facing sig. A4. This illustration is often referred to, understandably enough given its nature and context, as 'the King with a councillor on a dais' or 'the examination of the witches, before King James'.[6] It could be argued that the context gives the image this significance in *News*. But it is an image that appears in an earlier witchcraft pamphlet for which it was clearly devised.[7]

(iv) In the fourth woodcut (plate 13) a man is led away (to prison) by another man identified as a jailer by the bunch of keys at his belt. His left ear is held by a woman. This appears at the end of *News* on sig. D3ᵛ in *D* and *L*, and only in them. Again the Huntington copy of *G* supplies a copy of this illustration from *D*. This too looks as though it has come from a previous printed work, but we have not discovered its source.

Document 28: James VI's *Demonology*

Manuscripts

There are two early manuscripts of all or part of *Demonology*. Bodley MS 165, ff. 76, 79ʳ, 78, 77, 80 contains two fragments of *Demonology* in the king's own hand. These comprise book I, chapters i and ii and part of iii, and the end of book III, chapter i. This manuscript does not contain the preface or the two speakers' first exchange as these appear in the first edition printed at Edinburgh in 1597, but begins with Philomathes' first question: 'quhat thinke ye of thir strainge neuis . . .'.[8] In the Bodleian manuscript the two speakers are not yet named, as they will be in 1597, Epistemon and Philomathes, but are distinguished from each other simply as Q[uestion] and A[nswer].

The manuscript in the Folger Shakespeare Library, Washington, Folger MS V.a.185, is a scribal copy of the whole of *Demonology*, complete with preface and arguments preceding the three books and their individual chapters.[9] This copy of the work has been annotated and revised. There are three hands in this manuscript: the italic hand of the scribe who wrote out the text,[10] another italic hand which supplied a few revisions and marginal notes, and the hand of James himself who made about 100 additions and corrections, and added the scriptural references which were printed in the margins of Waldegrave's 1597 edition.[11] The suggestion that 'there is every reason to believe that this is the actual manuscript used by the Edinburgh printer Robert Waldegrave for the first edition'[12] has not received acceptance. Scholars now think that this manuscript might be only indirectly the source of the printer's copy. The speakers are indicated at the beginning of I i as 'Ph.' and 'E.' and James wrote 'and raison the mater', which would become the headnote after the argument of I i in the 1597 quarto. The variations between these two manuscripts and from the first quarto are listed by Craigie.[13]

The early printed editions[14]

The first edition is *Daemonologie, in forme of a dialogue* (Edinburgh: Robert Walde-grave, 1597). On the king's accession to the English throne the work was printed in England in 1603, *Dæmonologie, in Forme of a Dialogue, Divided into three books: Written by the High and mightie Prince, Iames by the grace of God King of England, Scotland, France and Ireland*. There were two different editions in 1603, and later *Demonology* was included in the folio edition of *The Workes of the Most High and Mightie Prince, James* (1616). The early editions are as follows.

(i)   STC 14364. *Daemonologie, in forme of a dialogue* (Edinburgh: Robert Waldegrave, 1597). There are several copies extant in Britain and in the USA.[15] There are three different states of the title-page which vary in small details.

> [ornament] DAEMONOL-/OGIE, IN FORME / *of a Dialogue,* / Diuided into three Bookes./ [device of Royal arms] / EDINBVRGH / *Printed by Robert Walde-graue* / Printer to the Kings Majestie. An. 1597. / *Cum Priuilegio Regio*

This 1597 quarto is referred to throughout this edition as *Q1*. *Demonology* was originally written in Scots. The work opens in the Bodleian MS: 'quhat thinke ye of thir strainge neuis quilke nou onlie furnishis purpose to all men at thaire meiting I meane of thir uitchis?'[16] Waldegrave's quarto considerably anglicised the spelling of the original as we find it in the manuscripts, although a few Scottish forms remained. Craigie thinks this was done with the king's permission, perhaps with an eye on the English market, as in 1597 James was clearly Elizabeth's heir apparent. *Q1* exists in two states: 'corrected' and 'uncorrected'.[17] As Craigie notes, the substantial variations are in book III:

	uncorrected	*corrected*
	IERVSALEM	*Babell* and *Edom*
	sluiches	sloughes
	Sylo	*Siloam*

The 'corrections' can be explained as follows. The marginal biblical references in *Demonology* III i (Isaiah 13 and 34, Jeremiah 50) clearly indicate James's sources in Isaiah and Jeremiah, and there Edom and Babel, not Jerusalem, are mentioned; 'sloughes' rather than 'sluiches' is an anglicisation; 'Siloam' is the version in the Geneva bible, 'Sylo' that of the Vulgate. These afterthoughts were intended as improvements either in accuracy or for other reasons, and have been adopted in this edition.

(ii) When James came to the English throne in 1603, *Demonology* was printed in England (*Q2*). There were two separate editions in 1603, and two issues of one edition:

> STC 14365. [R. Bradock] for William Aspley and W. Cotton 1603
> STC 14365.5 another issue for W. Cotton and W. Aspley 1603
> STC 14366 Arnold Hatfield for Robert Waldegrave 1603

These editions corrected a number of errors in *Q1* and the text was further anglicised. Both contain the 'uncorrected' readings, 'Jerusalem', 'sluiches' and 'Sylo', and so these editions must have been printed from an 'uncorrected' *Q1*. There are some textual variants between the editions of Aspley and Hatfield and these are recorded in the textual notes as *Q2 (Hatfield)* and *Q2 (Aspley)*.

(iii) *Demonology* was printed in the folio of James's *Works: The Workes of the Most High and Mightie Prince, James by the Grace of God, King of Great Britaine* (1616), 91–136. The folio text followed either an 'uncorrected' *Q1* or a copy of *Q2*, as it contains those same readings: 'Jerusalem', 'sluiches' and 'Sylo'.

There were editions in Dutch (Amsterdam 1603) and Latin (Hanover? 1604; Hanau 1607; London 1619; Frankfurt am Main 1689).

Modern editions

There have been a few modern editions and reprints. *King James the First. Daemonologie* (with *Newes from Scotland*), edited by G. B. Harrison (London and New York: Bodley Head Quartos no. 9, 1924), is largely a reprint of the Bodleian copy of the 1597 edition, and was later reissued by Edinburgh University Press in 1966. A facsimile reprint of the Bodleian copy of the 1597 quarto was printed as *James I. Daemonologie* (Amsterdam and New York: The English Experience, no. 94, Da Capo Press, 1969). The only scholarly modern edition is that of James Craigie in *Minor Prose Works of King James VI and I* (Edinburgh: Scottish Text Society, 1982). The text of Craigie's edition is that of a copy of an 'uncorrected' Edinburgh quarto of 1597 (National Library of Scotland L.C. 1499). Craigie's reason for choosing this as his text was that, as he correctly notes, a quarto of this kind was the basis for all the reprints of *Demonology* in the king's lifetime. His edition is referred to in the textual notes as *Craigie*.

This edition

This edition offers the text of *Demonology* in modern spelling and with modernised punctuation. Greek words have been transliterated into the Roman alphabet. The basis of this edition is substantially that of the text of Craigie's edition, compared with the 1597 and 1603 quartos. However, and unlike Craigie, we have preferred the readings of the 'corrected' 1597 quarto, assuming that these were made with the king's authority. One of the British Library's copies of the 1597 quarto (BL C.27.h.1) has been annotated by two early hands, and both gloss words or phrases that these early readers found difficult or strange. These annotations provide useful glosses (e.g. 'neoteric theologues' as 'divines of these later times'), and sometimes lively ones (e.g. 'stupid pedants' as 'dull-headed word-mongers'), of words and phrases which readers of even a modernised text of *Demonology* may need explicating. Because of their contemporary authority and the liveliness of their paraphrases these glosses have often been included in the annotations, indicated by *BL*.

Editorial conventions

One of the aims of this book is to provide readers with the series of original surviving texts from the North Berwick witches in a modernised, readable and intelligible form, and to provide a critical apparatus and notes which will help in that reading and understanding. Most of the texts have been re-edited from their original sources (manuscripts and early printed editions), and some are edited here for the first time.

Transcription of manuscripts

Manuscripts (the dittays and the pre- and post-trial documents) have been transcribed from the originals, then edited, punctuated and modernised. There are words or passages in these texts which are difficult to decipher as some of the manuscripts are damaged or simply illegible. The following conventions have been used in the process of transcription and editing:

[ ]	square brackets with nothing between them indicate that the text is damaged or missing
i[t]	square brackets containing letters indicate a likely conjecture
[?er]	square brackets containing letters preceded by a question mark offer a conjecture
[?wachep?]	square brackets containing text between question marks record a conjecture which is not entirely satisfactory
[???]	square brackets containing only question marks indicate that no guess has been possible
( )	indicates a space left in the manuscript by the scribe

The following conventions occur in the textual notes:

/	end of line in the manuscript
{ }	indicates a deletion in the manuscript
| |	indicates an insertion or addition in the manuscript

There are marginal notes in some manuscripts of depositions and dittays, usually acting as *aides-mémoires* to interrogators or court officials. These notes appear in this edition set in italic on separate lines within the text.

Editing of manuscripts

There is no previous edition of the depositions and examinations (documents 1–18), so no collation of readings is possible. Our transcription of the dittays has been compared with Pitcairn's and any substantive differences from readings in his *Ancient Criminal Trials* are indicated as *P* in the textual notes. In textual notes to the examinations and depositions, and to the dittays, the first reading after the lemma, unless otherwise indicated, is always that of the manuscript.

Editing of printed texts

In the case of *News from Scotland* and James VI's *Demonology* there are a number of early and also later editions. The editorial process for *News from Scotland* and for *Demonology* is explained above.

Manuscripts and printed texts: notes and annotations

There are two series of notes to each text. The first series is annotations. These are indicated in the text by a dagger, and the notes appear at the bottom of the page, with the lemma in bold (e.g. **compeared**). They provide glosses or explanations for difficult words, or for words which have changed their meaning, or have a different meaning in Scots. However, frequently used words of this kind (e.g. 'nor', 'umwhile') may be glossed on their first occurence only. These notes also give additional information of various kinds to the reader: parallels with other texts in this book, or elsewhere, and historical, legal, demonological or other contexts which may be useful or illuminating.

The second series provides textual notes. These are indicated in the text by superscript numbers and the notes are recorded at the end of each section. The lemma (e.g. modewart]) is the modernised reading and is followed by other readings, from manuscripts or earlier editions, when these have been considered significant or interesting in some way, or when the change involved in modernisation is a large one.

In both textual notes and annotations, a word marked with an asterisk (e.g. **gulleis***, drowis*) indicates that *The Dictionary of the Older Scottish Tongue* cites this particular passage as an example, sometimes the only example, of the word's usage.

Names

Personal and place names have been modernised throughout, except in quotations from other contemporary writers, where the spelling of the edition used has been followed. There was no regularised spelling at this time in Scotland

and England, so devill, dewill and divel are all forms which may occur. This
means that the names of places and persons have many and wonderfully diverse
forms. The goodwife of Spilmersford mill appears in these texts as Meg
Begtounn, Meg Bogtoun and Meg Bekton. This different spelling of names
makes it probable that many accused witches actually appear twice in the lists
in Larner, Lee and McLachlan's *Source-book of Scottish Witchcraft*. The names
Meg Bogtoun and Meg Begtonne in the list for Prestonpans in 1591 are a case
in point.[18] One name is found in even more diverse forms in contemporary
sources: Effie Mccalÿan, Ewfame Mcalÿane, Ewphame Mccalÿeane, Eufame
Maccaillion and Effe Machalloun. Her surname was probably pronounced
'Maccallion', and MacCalzean is the modern form. We have regularised and
modernised names of people and places, where possible, except that we have
kept the use of diminutives such as Gillie (Geillis) Duncan and Annie (Agnes)
Sampson, as they are the forms used commonly in the dittays and depositions.

Abbreviations

Abbreviations such as *CSPS* (*Calendar of the State Papers Relating to Scotland*) and
DOST (*Dictionary of the Older Scottish Tongue*) may be found expanded and
explained in the bibliography. Other abbreviations are standard, such as *OED*
(*Oxford English Dictionary*).

Notes

[1] Ferguson 1899: 45.

[2] See below, pp. 291–5.

[3] This copy is too fragile to be reproduced and we have not seen it. It is missing sigs C, C4, D–D3 and many leaves are mutilated.

[4] Ferguson 1899: 45–9.

[5] Sharpe 1818: x.

[6] Ferguson 1899: 47, 48.

[7] Gibson 1997.

[8] Transcribed in Craigie 1982: 184–9.

[9] For what is known of the history of this manuscript since the late eighteenth century see Craigie 1982: 172–4.

[10] Perhaps King James's friend Sir James Semphill, who was educated with James by George Buchanan, and who helped him prepare *Basilikon Doron* for the press; see Dunlap 1975: 40; Craigie 1982: 174.

[11] Craigie 1982: 161–5 lists the changes.

[12] DeRicci 1935: i 371.

[13] Craigie 1982: 159–60.

[14] For full bibliographical descriptions see Craigie 1982: 176–81.

[15] In Britain these are in the British Library, London University Library, the Bodleian, the National Library of Scotland and Glasgow University Library. In the USA there are copies in the Folger Shakespeare Library, the Huntington Library, Harvard University, University of Illinois, Princeton University and elsewhere.

[16] Craigie 1982: 184.

[17] Craigie 1982: 169 says that he found only three copies of the 'uncorrected' *Q1*: National Library of Scotland, L.C.1499; Edinburgh University Library De.10.105; British Library G.19130 (Craigie actually has C.19130).

[18] Larner, Lee and McLachlan 1977: 6–9.

CHRONOLOGY

Items in italics are supposed witchcraft events that appear in the texts.

1557

Protestant lords sign First Band pledging to advance the reformed faith; four
more similar bands by 1562

1558

Accession of Elizabeth to English throne

1560

First Book of Discipline produced by protestant reformers

1563

Acts of parliament criminalising witchcraft and consulting witches in both
Scotland and England

Fifteen witchcraft accusations during the year

1566

19 June. Birth of Prince James, son of Mary queen of Scots and Lord Darnley

1567

Mary queen of Scots forced to abdicate

29 July. Coronation of James VI of Scots

1567–73. Civil war between protestant lords of the congregation and catholic
supporters of Mary queen of Scots

1568

Witch hunt of about forty people in Angus and the Mearns

1573

Euphame MacCalzean consults a witch in the Canongate about poisoning a man

1577

April. *Euphame MacCalzean paralyses a man by witchcraft*

1578

James assumes full power as king; seized in coups by opposing factions

Second Book of Discipline produced by the protestant kirk of Scotland

1579

Esmé Stewart arrives in Scotland; becomes duke of Lennox (1581); ascendancy
    until 1582

1581

1581–2. Spanish intrigues with Lennox for invasion of Scotland

1582

James seized in coup by protestant faction in 'Ruthven raid', led by earl of
    Gowrie

1582–3. *Agnes Sampson predicts a woman's death unless the devil is raised*

1583

James escapes from Ruthven raiders

Francis Stewart, earl of Bothwell, appointed lord admiral

1584

Gowrie executed; exile in England for Andrew Melville

May. Parliament passes 'black acts' asserting supremacy of prince over church,
    and opposing presbyteries

James Carmichael and other presbyterians go into exile in London

1585

Approach made for James's marriage with Elizabeth, elder daughter of Frederick II of Denmark

1584–5 *Agnes Sampson foretells Isobel Hamilton's death*

1586

Return from exile of some ministers including Andrew Melville

League between Scotland and England, including annual payments to James from Elizabeth of £4,000

1586–7 *Euphame MacCalzean consults Agnes Sampson about bewitched image to kill her father-in-law*

1587

Agnes Sampson makes wax image and has it bewitched by the devil to kill Euphame MacCalzean's father-in-law

Act of parliament confers right on the lord advocate independently to pursue 'odious crimes'

8 February. Execution of Mary queen of Scots

Further attempt to arrange marriage with Princess Elizabeth of Denmark

July. John Maitland of Thirlestane becomes chancellor

Agnes Sampson uses ground corpses to help Euphame MacCalzean's childbirth

December. James Carmichael returns from exile

1588

Failure of the Spanish armada sent by Philip II against England

1589

February. Letter discovered offering earl of Huntly's support for Spanish invasion of England; start of Huntly's feud with Moray

April. Uprising of northern catholic earls; Bothwell leads uprising in borders; encounter between Huntly's and James's forces at Brig of Dee; rebels withdraw

April. *Barbara Napier tells Ritchie Graham that the king will be harmed by toad's venom*

Easter. *Agnes Sampson treats a sick woman, who nevertheless dies*

May. James returns to Edinburgh having dispelled military threat

May. Bothwell declared a traitor but sentence suspended; rebel lords briefly imprisoned

June. Embassy to Danish court led by George Keith, Earl Marischal; arranges marriage with Anne, younger daughter of Frederick II

Summer. *Agnes Sampson cures Robert Dixon and sick boy in Prestonpans by touching and charming*

20 August. Marriage of James and Princess Anne, aged fourteen, with Earl Marischal as James's proxy, at Kronborg Castle, Denmark

Late August. News of marriage by proxy reaches Edinburgh; new queen expected in Scotland during September

1 September. Anne sails for Scotland from Copenhagen in fleet commanded by Admiral Munk; flagship leaks

September. *Agnes Sampson conspires at Leith to raise storms preventing Anne's sailing to Scotland, and also storm that sank ship sailing from Burntisland to Leith*

Early September. *John Fian knows of leak in ship bringing Anne from Denmark*

10 September. Danish fleet forced by leaks and storms to take refuge in Norway

Mid-September. News reaches Scotland of storms preventing Anne's voyage; James at Seton for two weeks awaiting her arrival

September. Witchcraft charge raised against Agnes Sampson in Haddington

29 September (Michaelmas). *Agnes Sampson told by the devil of impending storms*

1 October. Danish fleet forced by gales again to return to Norway

10 October. James receives letter from Anne with news that voyage to Scotland abandoned; she will spend winter in Oslo

19 October. James orders arrangements for government of Scotland during his absence in Denmark

22 October. James's fleet sets sail from Leith for Oslo; James absent from Scotland from October 1589 to May 1590

22–23 October. *John Fian and others raise storms to delay James's sea voyage to meet Anne*

28 October. James reaches Norway, despite contrary winds and gales during the voyage

31 October. *John Fian and others sail from Prestonpans to a ship, where they drink, sink the ship, and return home*

After 31 October. *Agnes Sampson cures the sheriff of Haddington's wife who had been bewitched on Hallowe'en*

November. Bothwell makes public repentance for his sins in kirk of St Giles after sermon by minister Robert Bruce

November. A woman tried and acquitted of witchcraft in Perth

23 November. James and Anne married in person in Oslo, Norway

15 December. James sends letter to council saying that he will be absent from Scotland until spring 1590

December. Robert Bowes sent to Scotland by Queen Elizabeth as English ambassador

22 December. James and Anne set out for Denmark

Winter 1589–90. Admiral Munk attributes storms to a Danish witch, wife of a citizen of Copenhagen

1590

Late January. James, Anne and entourage arrive in Denmark; spend winter and spring in Denmark

21 January. James and Anne married again in person at Kronborg, Denmark

Winter. James visits Niels Hemmingsen, author of *Admonitio de Superstitionibus Magicis Vitandis*, at his home in Roskilde

8 March. Earl of Bothwell's daughter baptised, with English ambassador Robert Bowes as sponsor

March. Band from kirk and state pledging support for reformed religion

26 April. James and Anne set sail for Scotland in another stormy voyage

28 April. Meg Dow found guilty and sentenced to be burned for witchcraft and child murder in Edinburgh

1 May. Arrival of James and Anne at Leith

7 May. Haddington synod investigates witchcraft charge against Agnes Sampson

17 May. Anne crowned in the abbey at palace of Holyrood

19 May. Queen Anne's entry into Edinburgh

May. About six Danish women executed for witchcraft, for allegedly causing storms to stop Anne's fleet reaching Scotland in autumn 1589

4 July. Woman arrives from Lubeck with prophecy for James

July. Witchcraft accusations against several Edinburgh women for bewitching a laird

22 July. Witchcraft trials in Ross-shire of Hector Munro and Lady Foulis; both acquitted by packed juries

23 July. News of Danish witch trials reaches Edinburgh

31 July (Lammas Eve). *Convention of witches and the devil at Acheson's Haven where Agnes Sampson proposes the king's destruction at Bothwell's request; devil suggests toad poison and wax image*

18 August. Barbara Keand executed for witchcraft in Aberdeen

August. Janet Grant and Janet Clark sentenced in Edinburgh to be burned for bewitching people to death and summoning the devil

September. Earl of Bothwell appointed lord lieutenant of the borders

9 September. *Euphame MacCalzean at a conventicle at North Berwick kirk and requests king's image bewitched by the devil*

October/November. James examining witches from this time

31 October (All Hallows' E'en). *Convention of c.140 witches with the devil at North Berwick kirk; the devil promises wax image of king to roast*

November. Geillis Duncan accused of witchcraft in Tranent

28 November. English ambassador Bowes writes to Burghley that king and privy council busy with witchcraft prosecutions

6 December. Bowes reports that witchcraft charges still claiming king's attention

December. Geillis Duncan and Ritchie Graham examined by this time

15 December. Duncan states that Barbara Napier's Edinburgh house used as meeting place for witches trying to kill the king

26 December. Trial and conviction of John Fian

1591

During the year *c.*20 people from around Prestonpans accused of witchcraft

January. Bothwell forcibly removes from Edinburgh tolbooth a witness in court case of a follower while king and court of session in building

Late January. John Fian strangled and burned on the castle hill, Edinburgh

27 January. Trial and conviction of Agnes Sampson

28 January. Agnes Sampson strangled and burned on the castle hill

5 February. David Seton sent by James to England in pursuit of escaped witches

23 February. Eight convicted witches burnt in Haddington (including Sampson's servant 'Grey Meal'), one in Dalkeith, and one in Dumfries; forty more imprisoned and awaiting trial

April. Geillis Duncan still testifying

15 April. Bothwell brought before king and council on charge of treasonable consulting with Agnes Sampson and Richard Graham against the king

16 April. Bothwell committed to ward in Edinburgh Castle; imprisoned till 21 June 1591

6 May. Convention of nobles called to try Bothwell; many send excuses; trial does not take place

8 May. Trial of Barbara Napier on charges including treason and witchcraft; convicted on charges of consulting with witches but acquitted of attending a convention

10 May. James's letter to assizers in Napier's trial demands guilty verdict; Napier convicted and sentenced to death; claims pregnancy to avoid burning

24 May. Proclamation against Ninian Chirnside, servant of Bothwell's

June. Geillis Duncan and three others still alive

5 June. James and council allow women, children and accomplices to be witnesses in treason trials

6 June. Sermon of Robert Bruce in king's presence rebuking him for lawlessness, including witchcraft, in country

7 June. James appears at trial of twelve assizers who acquitted Napier of treason and witchcraft; forgives their crime of wilful error in acquitting her

8 June. Bowes sends copy of James's speech to assizers to Burghley

9 June. Trial of Euphame MacCalzean starts

10 June. Trial of MacCalzean continues as her prolocutors argue in her defence

11 June. Trial of MacCalzean continues into third day as MacCalzean objects to evidence against her; assize remains in council house overnight

12 June. Trial of MacCalzean continues; assize convicts her on ten counts

15 June. Justices sentence MacCalzean to be burned alive

21 June. Bothwell escapes from Edinburgh Castle at 2 a.m.

25 June. Royal proclamation in Edinburgh against the earl of Bothwell as traitor and outlaw; armed levies summoned for his capture

25 June. Execution on castle hill of Euphame MacCalzean

1 July. Bothwell sends message to king offering submission, or negotiations with members of the council

2–13 July. General assembly of kirk in Edinburgh; petition from assembly to the king urging action on various social ills

26 October. Privy council establishes commission for the discovery of witches, with powers to six commissioners of examination and torture

27 December. Bothwell's unsuccessful raid on Holyroodhouse to seize James and kill Maitland; several of his followers hanged

1592

7 February. Earl of Huntley attacks Donibristle Castle and murders the earl of Moray; briefly imprisoned

29 February. Richard Graham, having been kept in prison, finally tried, strangled and burned

24 May–5 June. Parliament meets in Edinburgh

5 June. Parliamentary act passed to establish presbyterian system of church government (the 'golden acts')

June. Parliament ratifies Bothwell's forfeiture

8 June. Privy council establishes royal and kirk commissioners to distribute standing commissions in localities for prosecuting witches

28 June. Bothwell makes unsuccessful raid on Falkland Palace to capture James

December. Discovery of conspiracy of catholic earls, Huntly, Errol and Angus, with Philip II of Spain to invade Scotland (the 'Spanish blanks')

1593

February–March. James marches on Aberdeen against the catholic earls; Huntly remains at large

March. Lord Burgh replaces Robert Bowes as English ambassador

July. Bothwell's coup against James; dominates king and court for several weeks

10–21 July. Parliament declares Bothwell a traitor and confiscates all his lands; northern earls not forfeited by parliament

August. Bothwell tried and acquitted of witchcraft by his peers

7–13 September. Convention of estates at Stirling; James sends Bothwell into exile

15 October. Chancellor Maitland returns to court

25 October. Bothwell publicly denounced as traitor and rebel

November. Northern earls ordered into exile but retain their estates

1594

19 February. Birth of James and Anne's first child, Henry, in Stirling Castle

April. Bothwell raids Leith; met by forces led by James; Bothwell withdraws

August. Bothwell secretly joins with northern catholic rebel earls

7 September. Bothwell seeks support of Edinburgh ministers

30 September. James leads expedition against rebel northern earls

3 October. James's military lieutenant Argyle defeated in the battle of Glenlivet against Huntly

October. James enters Aberdeen; orders demolition of Huntly's and Errol's castles

November. James returns to Edinburgh

1595

18 February. Bothwell excommunicated by the presbytery of Edinburgh

18 February. Hercules Stewart, Bothwell's brother, executed at market cross, Edinburgh, for involvement with northern earls

26 March. Proclamation of Huntly's and Errol's banishment from the kingdom; they go into exile though retaining their estates

April. Bothwell goes into exile; his estates forfeited

October. Death of Chancellor Maitland

1596

1596–97 Second severe wave of witchcraft persecution mostly in Fife, Lothians and Aberdeenshire

June. Huntly and Errol return secretly to Scotland; come to terms with parliament, then the kirk

September. Huntly received by James at Falkland

19 August. Birth of Princess Elizabeth at Dunfermline

September. James meets delegation from kirk at Falkland; Andrew Melville calls James 'Gods sillie vassall'

November. Prosecution of minister of St Andrews who preached 'all kings are devil's children'

17 December. Riot in Edinburgh while king and lords of session in tolbooth; king acts against ministers and town council

1597

James's *Demonology* published in Edinburgh

14 April. James stops trial of two suspected witches in Aberdeen

June. Huntly and Errol received into protestant church

Beginning of August. Huntly, Errol and Angus proclaimed free men at market cross in Edinburgh

12 August. James disbands all crown–kirk standing commissions to try witchcraft, established in 1592

November. Huntly's and Errol's forfeitures revoked by parliament

1598

James's *The True Lawe of Free Monarchies* published in Edinburgh

1599

James's *Basilikon Doron* published in Edinburgh

1600

5 August. Gowrie conspiracy against James unsuccessful

19 November. Birth of Prince Charles

1603

24 March. Elizabeth dies; James accedes to English crown as James I; the court travels to London

Demonology, *Basilikon Doron* and *The Trew Law of Free Monarchies* published in London

1612

Earl of Bothwell dies in Naples

1625

James VI and I dies

PART 1

CONTEXT

Chapter 1

THE COURT AND POLITICS

Events connected with the marriage of James and Princess Anne of Denmark appeared from the start in the evidence of those accused of witchcraft in the North Berwick witch hunt. The personal, political and dynastic import of this royal marriage was not lost on the accused, nor were the details of the perilous journeys. The accused also clearly understood what the earl of Bothwell's relation to the regime was, for he too appears in their evidence from an early stage. The royal marriage and Bothwell form two dominant themes of this witch hunt, and generate other minor motifs (ships, journeys, letters, disguise). In the following sections they are approached mainly through events and documents.

The royal marriage

On 19 June 1587 King James VI celebrated his twenty-first birthday, and the question of the royal marriage and the succession became pressing. A year later an observer of the court wrote to Sir Francis Walsingham in England that James's thoughts were turning to marriage as a result of pressure from his councillors, but not, he noted, from any interest the king might have in women, for the king 'never regardes the company of any woman, not so muche as in any dalliance'.[1] James's most passionate attachment to date had been to his cousin Esmé Stuart, Sieur D'Aubigny, a French catholic who had arrived in Scotland in 1579, and gone on to win the thirteen-year-old king's love.[2] Marriage for a Renaissance monarch was primarily a political and dynastic matter rather than a romantic one. King James's eventual choice of a Danish princess was suitable since she came from a protestant country, and Scotland had important trading links with Denmark and the Baltic.

In October 1589 the king was 'desirous to have universale peax [peace] and quietnes throchoute his haill realme, and specialie betuix noblemen quha aucht to interteny [who ought to maintain] the same'.[3] In February 1589 peace had been threatened when letters were discovered from the earl of Huntly and others expressing regret at the failure of the Spanish armada of 1588, and promising help should a further invasion of England be launched. Huntly lost his position as captain of the guard, returned to his estates in the north, and then began a march on Edinburgh. The protestant earl of Bothwell joined the rebellion from the borders mainly out of hatred for James's chancellor Sir John Maitland of Thirlestane. James rode north to encounter Huntly and his followers, and at the Brig of Dee (mentioned in the assize of error against Barbara Napier's jurors) he faced down the rebels, and advanced into Aberdeen. While there, James asked to see a reputed witch associated with the Foulis family, two of whose members would themselves be tried for witchcraft in July 1590. This request presumably proceeded from James's general curiosity rather than any particular or personal interest. Three rebel leaders, Huntly, Crawford and Bothwell, were briefly imprisoned, but by September 1589 all were released. Bothwell was imprisoned in Tantallon Castle on the East Lothian coast a few miles east of the town of North Berwick.[4] This uprising began a series of challenges to royal power that were to punctuate the next five or six years, involving the catholic earls and the protestant earl of Bothwell. In the end James was to emerge from the challenges strengthened, but he was to find these years dangerous and unpredictable.

Negotiations for a Danish princess had begun in 1585, alongside negotiations for the protestant French princess Catherine of Bourbon, sister of Henry of Navarre, which came to nothing. James set his sights on Elizabeth, the eldest daughter of King Frederick II of Denmark, but had to settle for Anne, the fourteen-year-old younger sister, and in June 1589 he sent George Keith, the earl Marischal, to Denmark to finalise the marriage treaty. Denmark was to renounce its claim to the Orkney and Shetland islands and provide a modest dowry, and Anne was to receive the lordship of Falkland, and also of Dunfermline, which was James's personal gift.[5]

Once the marriage had been agreed, James tried to ensure that proper preparations were made, but resources were scarce. The English ambassador Asheby reported: 'Surely Scotland was never in worse state to receive a Queen than at present'.[6] In Denmark, however, lavish preparations were under way to provide suitably rich clothes, jewels and furnishings; and the coach which was being constructed for Anne was said to contain no iron but only silver.[7] The coach that Princess Anne brought from Denmark was welcome, for James was too impoverished to provide one. As a result of the years of famine of 1585–7, and also of mismanagement of the currency, the late 1580s saw the destruction of economic confidence and the 'disrupting [of] traditional relationships in every sector of the economy'.[8]

Anne's attempted journeys to Scotland, September – October 1589

The marriage ceremony took place by proxy in Copenhagen on 20 August

1589, with the earl Marischal standing in for the king, and on 28 August the news reached Scotland. James was now married in name but not in fact. He awaited Anne's arrival, and oversaw the elaborate ceremonies planned for her landing at Leith and entry into Edinburgh. But there was no sign of the Danish fleet carrying Anne. Fearful news reached Scotland in mid-September when Lord Dingwall reported that 'he had come in companie with the Quenis fleit thrie hundrethe myles, and wes separat fra thame be ane great storme: it wes feared that the Queine wes in denger upone the seas'. David Moysie reports that the 'King remained xvi or xvii dayis in Settoun, luiking for hir coming'.[9] James was staying with his friend Robert, 6th Lord Seton, at Seton House, from which he would have a clear view of the Firth of Forth and any ships approaching Leith from the east. Seton is situated in the middle of the group of towns and villages whence many of the accused came. James's presence at Seton for over two weeks in mid-September could hardly have gone unnoticed by the local people, and they would have known too that the reason for the king's presence was his anxiety to see his new wife safely complete her dangerous sea voyage. These motifs would later appear in the examinations of accused witches. But through the month of September there was no sign of her.

The courtier Sir James Melville noted the king's anxiety at this time: 'His Maiesty . . . was very impatient and sorowfull for hir lang delay'.[10] Further news reached Scotland of storms off the coast of Denmark which only increased the tension. The English ambassador sent notes to London on 27 September: 'The King very sorrowful at the Queen's long stay; a fast appointed for her safe arrival'; and again on 2 October, 'Expectation of the Princess of Denmark; contrary winds; the King's trouble; surmises; Colonel Stewart sent to search for the fleet'; and again on 6 and 8 October, 'Non-arrival of the Princess; the King's trouble; fear of disaster; omens; public fast and prayer; Colonel Stewart not returned'.[11]

What happened to Princess Anne and the Danish embassy as they tried to make their way to Scotland after the wedding is described by Thomas Riis.[12] The fleet sailed on 1 September but on 10 September the flagship, the *Gideon*, sprung a leak and the fleet had to take shelter in Norway, where repairs were made. The fleet's attempts to sail were thwarted by gales. On 28 September the fleet sailed for the third time but the flagship sprang another leak and the fleet again sought shelter in Norway on 1 October. Consultations took place with Denmark whether another attempt to sail should be made so late in the year with winds driving from the south-west. On 5 October Colonel Stewart, who had arrived from Scotland, and the earl Marischal decided to abandon the attempt to reach Scotland, and on 7 October a letter was sent informing James. Anne and the earl Marischal travelled to Oslo, while the fleet, with the *Gideon* still leaking, limped on to Denmark.

Meanwhile accidents as a result of storms were occuring in Scotland as well as in Denmark. Sir James Melville's sister-in-law, Jean Kennedy, sent for by the king to be one of Anne's gentlewomen, drowned when her boat, sailing between

Burntisland and Leith, sank in a storm. Melville noted, 'This the Scottis witches confessit unto His Maiesty to have done. Wher I tint [lost] also tua saruandis.'[13] Melville's later explanation that the accident was caused by witches came to be generally accepted, but at the time of the events they were explained in natural not supernatural terms. On 28 September James wrote to George Keith, the earl Marischal (addressing him as 'my little fat pork'), expressing anxiety at Anne's delays caused by 'the contrariousness of the winds'.[14] On 11 October, the day after definite news of the Danish ships at last reached Scotland, he attributed their delay to 'sindry contrarious [many opposing] windes, and at last sindrie of thame fallin lek [springing a leak] in sic sort as thay ar not able to serve this seasoun'.[15]

James's journeys to Norway and Denmark

Then James did something extraordinary; he decided to sail to Norway himself. He was staying in Craigmillar Castle, near Edinburgh, and 'culd sleip nor rest'[16] when he made a sudden decision: 'I upoun the instant, yea very moment resolvit to mak possible on my part, that quilk [which] wes impossible on hirs'.[17] In his 'Declaration' to the privy council he explained how he reached this decision alone and in private: 'The place that I resolvit this in wes Craigmillair, not ane of the hail [entire] counsale being present ther; And as I tuke this resolutioun only of myselff, as I am a trew Prince, sa advised with myselff onlie what way to follow ffurth the same'. He presented himself as an independent, decisive agent and not, as he wrote, 'ane irresolute asse, quha can do nathing of himselff'.[18] James was taking events into his own hands, for his present situation was slightly emasculating: he was a husband waiting patiently and safely for his wife, who was risking a dangerous sea crossing to reach him. The declaration also reveals something of James's subjective state. Anxiety over his marriage was partly dynastic, since not only the continuation of the Stuart line (shaky through the fifteenth and sixteenth centuries) depended on it, but also the strength of his claim to the English throne. James's enemies liked to question his legitimacy by saying that his father was not Darnley but David Rizzio, Mary queen of Scots' Italian secretary. And James seemed to voice other personal anxieties in the declaration to his subjects. Replying to complaints that he had delayed too long in getting married, he wrote,

> the ressonis [reasons] wer, that I wes allane, without fader or moder, bruthir or sister, King of this realme and air appeirand [heir apparent] of England; this my naikatnes maid me to be waik [nakedness made me weak] and my Inemyis stark [enemies strong], ane man wes as na man, and the want of hoip [hope] of successioun bread disdayne; yea my lang delay bred in the breistis of mony a grite jealosie of my hinhabilitie [great suspicion of my impotence], as gif I wer a barrane stok.

James had shown no evidence of strong heterosexual desires, as his letter went on to say: 'as to my awne nature, God is my witnes, I could have abstenit langair nor the weill of my patrie [than the welfare of my native land] could have permitted'. The letter gives insights into James's feelings at this moment of great stress. His reputation has been threatened by not getting married earlier— 'it is manifestlie knawne to all how far I wes generallie found fault with be [by] all men for the delaying salang [so long] of my mariage'[19]—and this suggested political as well as sexual weakness. James was facing a crisis which touched on several issues: completing the much-delayed marriage, proving his virility, continuing the royal line. In a public proclamation James declared that he had not been 'rashe passioned, or utherwayis further addicted [prone] then honnour and gude advise led ws—nather be [by neither] licentious lyffe and behaviour',[20] and stated that 'nathing can be mair hurtfull to us and oure estate nor giff [than if] the consummatioun of oure mariage and the transporting of the Quene oure bedfellow in oure realme salbe differred [shall be deferred]'.[21] It is worth emphasising these aspects because the theme of sexual anxiety reappeared in 1591 in the evidence of Agnes Sampson, one of the accused witches. According to *News from Scotland*, it was Agnes Sampson's telling James what passed between him and Anne on their wedding night in Norway that convinced him of the witches' genuineness. In the exchange between monarch and 'witch', the anxieties implicit in James's letter to the Scottish people were recognised and reiterated, and the woman's uncanny knowledge joined the personal with the political. In effect, Agnes Sampson was merely returning to James the very fears which his own letter manifested.[22]

James left detailed instructions on how the country was to be governed in his absence. The fifteen-year-old duke of Lennox was to be president of the council, and the earl of Bothwell was to be his deputy.[23] Not mentioned in the documents read before the council was the part to be played in government by Robert Bruce, the leading minister of Edinburgh, who would oversee government actions from the point of view of the kirk. These were shrewd moves on James's part: Bothwell might be restrained from acting in a disorderly way by these responsibilities, and Bruce might encourage the goodwill of the clergy by his involvement in the council. Bothwell was always a source of conflict. On 19 October 1589 an order was issued by the council to suppress the quarrel that had broken out between Bothwell and Lord Hume and their followers. Hume was ordered to remain in the south-east, and Bothwell was ordered to attend the council in Edinburgh and stay within Lothian until the king returned.[24]

Anxiety about Scottish government in James's absence was expressed by Burghley on 1 December 1589 when he sent instructions to Robert Bowes, the experienced Scotland watcher, who was to be the new English ambassador there.[25] Burghley need not have worried, for the six months of James's absence were remarkably peaceful and trouble-free. The leading cleric, Mr James Melville (not to be confused with the courtier Sir James Melville), noted in his diary that 'of the fawour of God, there was never a mair peaceble and quyet estet of a countrey nor [than] during that tyme of the King's absence'. Even more remarkable is Melville's account of the general assembly of the kirk in spring 1590 which could find nothing to complain of in the state of the nation: 'diligent tryell being taken, it was fund, that na steirage [stirring] at all was in the countrey of Papists, of thieffes, or anie troubelsome, inordinat persones'.[26] The assembly praised God and ordered a general fast. At least part of the reason for the general peace was that James had removed many of his courtiers to Denmark, and along with them the usual court factions and quarrels: 'the company that wer with his Maiesty [in Denmark]', reports Sir James Melville, 'held him in gret fascherie [trouble], to agre ther continuall stryf, pryd and partialities'.[27] Chancellor Maitland, the first chancellor, as Gordon Donaldson notes, who was neither a prelate nor a peer,[28] was to become the focus of aristocratic hostility, and an object of particular hatred to the earl of Bothwell. The social, political and ideological stresses that ran through the body politic seemed to disappear in the period of the king's absence, but when, on his return, power was restored to the political system, those stresses once more made themselves felt.

On 22 October 1589 James sailed from Leith accompanied by Chancellor Maitland and three hundred friends and dignitaries. For two days there were contrary winds and the ships were driven towards St Monans on the Fife coast, but on 24 October the fleet was able to sail for Norway, where it arrived on 28 October. On 29 October Burghley wrote to the English ambassador, 'I do conceave by the late westerly wyndes that the Scottish King is afor this tyme in Norwaye; but if the wyndes come not esterly befo Martillmas it will be hard for the King to retorn afor the spring'.[29] James had told his council that the journey to Norway and back would take no longer than twenty days, but Burghley was right. The fleet made slow progress along the coast of Norway, and finally on 11 November the party landed and made its way to Oslo. At long last James and Anne met. On 23 November they were married in the Bishop's Palace in Oslo, and a month of celebrations followed. The royal party then made its way to Denmark, arriving at Kronborg Castle, Elsinore, on 21 January, where they were met by the queen mother and young king Christian IV.

The king enjoyed his stay in Denmark, which lasted until late April. He visited Tycho Brahe, the astronomer, and Niels Hemmingsen, the theologian.[30] Hemmingsen was the author of 'the single most important Danish contribution to the witchcraft debate', his *Admonitio de Superstitionibus Magicis Vitandis* (Copenhagen 1575).[31] Some historians have taken this contact between the king and an expert on continental demonology to be the way continental demonological ideas found their way into Scotland.[32] In this meeting, it is assumed, James discussed the continental notions of the demonic pact and the sabbat, which had not featured in Scottish witch trials previously, and then imported them into the 1590s witchcraft prosecutions on his return. However, recent research has uncovered no evidence that James and Hemmingsen discussed demonology, and a closer examination of Hemmingsen reveals that his notion of witchcraft may be less 'continental' than previously supposed, especially concerning the sabbat.[33] In the meeting in Roskilde Cathedral, which may have taken place in public, James and Hemmingsen talked about predestination not about witchcraft,[34] hence there is no conclusive evidence that James was individually responsible for introducing the idea of the pact and the sabbat into the witch hunt that was to break out in 1590.

The ideas of demonic pact and sabbat that were believed by men who composed the political, religious and judicial elites of Scotland were more likely known to them before the witch trials of 1590 began. It is unlikely that even the king could have persuaded them to accept those ideas if there was not already some knowledge of them, and if they did not fit into existing beliefs about witchcraft, however vague or undefined. The contacts between Scots and Danes during the six months of James's Danish visit involved a large number of influential people. James travelled with Chancellor Maitland, the justice clerk Sir Lewis Bellenden, John Skene, and David Lindsay the minister of Leith, and 'sindrie other barons and gentlemen'.[35] Further opportunity for the dissemination of a wide range of ideas no doubt took place 'among the Scottish ruling classes during the return visit paid by the Danish Court in the month of May 1590'.[36] There had also been intellectual contact between both countries over many years, especially during Christian IV's regency, 1588–96: '[e]mbassies were so frequent that the learned envoys could hope to see their friends from time to time and at least to exchange letters fairly regularly through diplomatic channels. As central persons in this contact Peter Young [James's childhood teacher] and Niels Krag deserve a mention'.[37] Among the clergy, Andrew Melville's brother Richard had studied at the universities of Greifswald, Wittenberg and Copenhagen.[38] Merchants were also making frequent contact with Denmark and other northern European countries, and there were resident Scottish factors in the countries where Scots were trading most actively, in towns including Rotterdam, Veere, Bordeaux, Elsinore, London and Danzig.[39] Books and ideas passed to and from all these places at the same time as deals were struck and goods transported. In short, there were many channels through which continental ideas about witchcraft could flow into the minds of Scots in the late sixteenth century.

James and his entourage enjoyed their stay in Denmark till the spring of 1590. David Moysie wrote that 'his Majestie wes only occupied in making [wooing] of the Queine, and wes not myndit to come home befoir the spring of the yeir'. Another reason for staying on was no doubt, as Moysie observed, that 'the King wes thair interteined vpone the Queinis chairges'.[40] Orders were issued for various burghs to contribute to the fleet of six ships which was to bring the royal party home, including Edinburgh, Haddington and North Berwick.[41] The man to oversee the preparations for the return of the royal couple was the lord high admiral, the earl of Bothwell. Earls of Bothwell had held the office of admiral or vice-admiral since the first earl of Bothwell obtained the office in 1488.[42] It is worth noting that Bothwell, who was to be subject to witchcraft charges himself in 1591, was nominally responsible for the ships conveying James and Anne safely home from Denmark. One of the charges brought against the witches in Denmark and Scotland was that they tried to sink the royal fleets.

Bothwell's position as admiral made it easy to connect him with stories of witches trying to sink ships, and bring his loyalty into question.

The return of James and Anne to Scotland: Anne's coronation

James and Anne stayed at Elsinore for the marriage of Anne's elder sister to the duke of Brunswick. Finally, at the end of April 1590, the fleet once again set sail for Leith. As the time for their arrival in Scotland approached there was anxiety, punctuated by moments of panic and rumour, as people awaited the king and queen's return. On 29 April Bowes reported the rumour that English boats had been sent to surprise the Scottish fleet and been sighted off the coast at North Berwick.[43] The fleet arrived safely at Leith on 1 May, and the king and queen were met, according to David Moysie, 'command [coming] out of the boit be [boat by] the diuk of Lennox, lord Hamiltoun, erle Bothuel and a great number of the nobilletie, with sum honest men of Edinburgh'.[44] They stayed in Leith for six days and then moved to the repaired and renovated Holyroodhouse. The Danes included Admiral Peder Munk, commander of the *Gideon* which had sprung a leak the previous September. 'The number of the haill [Danish] trayne wes ij^c xxiij [223] personis, quhilkis [who] wer all interteined be the King and noblemen of Scotland, and bancketted daylie'.[45]

Certain ministers objected to the coronation and entry to Edinburgh taking place on a Sunday. Chancellor Maitland moved the ceremonial entry to the following Tuesday, but the coronation stayed on Sunday since, after reflection, the ministers decided that it was 'a mixed actioun, like mariage' in which 'a solemne oathe past mutuallie betuixt the prince and the subjects, and from both to God, and the minister was to blesse'. The ceremony was thus informed by the idea of a covenant, similar to that informing the witches' compact with the devil. The clergy reluctantly agreed to the coronation by pointedly omitting the numinous from their statement of how they understood it, but balked at James's plan for anointing. James had himself been anointed by a bishop at his coronation in 1567 when he was one year old, a ritual that had also been disputed. Knox and other preachers 'repyned at the . . . anointing',[46] but the protestant lords were determined 'to omit nothing whose absence might legally invalidate the deed'.[47] James's coronation plans for Anne may have been influenced by his stay in Denmark, where 'theocratic politics had become the strongest thematic element in the coronation ceremonies for the Danish kings'.[48] Certainly Anne's anointing represented an assertion of divinely bestowed rights rather than, as the ministers would have it, contractually agreed ones.

The dispute between ministers and crown centred on the meaning of the anointing ceremony: was it symbolic or efficacious? James was to discuss this issue in relation to witches' magical practices and the sacraments in *Demonology*.[49] This disagreement concerns the political question of the nature of kingship: whether supernatural power can be accessed by such ceremonies, and whether the monarch can receive supernatural power from God, questions with implications for political issues of legitimacy and power. In the witch hunt the same questions appear in inverted form: can witches receive supernatural power from the devil, and can their ceremonies access and appropriate it? James's answer in the cases of kings and witches was positive; and indeed in practice and theory a belief that witches might access and exercise supernatural power is predicated on believing the same thing for kings. The dispute over Anne's anointing is a clear indication of the nature of the religio-political terrain on which struggles between king and kirk were taking place, and on which the witch hunt would be located.

No doubt realising the implications of the anointing ritual of Queen Anne, some clergy objected that it 'was no part of the office of a minister' because it was 'a superstitious rite among Christians, borrowed from Jewes'.[50] In the Old Testament accounts of Saul, Samuel and David, 'coronal anointing' was 'God's own method of establishing kings, transmitting charisma to them, and (in the words of I Samuel 10.6) turning them into "other men"—that is, transferring them from the category of the profane to that of the sacred'.[51] It was to this idea that the ministers objected, and their objections were only overcome after James threatened to delay the coronation and find a bishop to anoint the queen, and a specially called convocation redefined anointing so as to remove from it all suggestion of charisma: it was to be merely 'a civill ceremonie' performed by a minister acting on the king's command as 'a civill persoun, providing declaratioun were made by the anointer in tyme of the actioun to that sense, that all opinioun of superstitioun be removed'.[52] The magic that the protestant hardliners were intent upon removing from the ceremony was what James was intent on having as the central action in the sacralisation of Anne. The outcome was ambiguous.[53]

On 17 May 1590 Anne's coronation took place in the abbey of Holyrood.[54] Robert Bruce declared that the coronation would follow the ceremony as directed by the king:

> The Countes of Mar immediatlie cumis to the Quenis Majestie, and taks hir richt arme, and openes the craige [neck] of hir gowne, and lyes bake [pulls back] ane certaine pairt of boithe. Mester Robert Bruce immediatly puires [pours] furthe upon thois pairtis of her breist and arme, of quhilk the clothes wer remowit, a bonye [generous] quantitie of oyll; quhilks pairtis efter the annoyntment therof, wer coverit with sum quhyt [white] silke. The same being done, the Quenis Majestie reteires hir selff to ane secret pairt [private place] prepared for that effect, to remaine ane certaine space . . . and hawing putt on ane princelie rob [robe], returnes againe to the former saite of the kirke.[55]

Anne's princely robe denotes her changed physical, spiritual and political state. Monarchy here uses the resources of theatre—ceremony, costume, action, words—to perform its power and demonstrate its legitimacy, but it is not theatre as illusion. The theatrical elements of the ceremony perform a kind of royal magic. The queen completes the ceremony by speaking the oath of allegiance

to, and entering into a covenant with, God, whose power, present in the ceremony, has effected her transformation into a consecrated queen. If Anne is
indeed assigned a semi-sacred status then royalty is enhanced in having been
seen to participate in divine mysteries. The need to construct such a ceremony
suggests James's anxiety about the legitimating of the royal marriage. When
later in 1590 witches were discovered, the conception of what they were was
also in terms of sacred rites and powers. Just as the coronation was a performance
of political power, so the witches' rituals were understood in political terms, as
treason. The worship of and covenanting with God, which Anne promised, was
a model for the witches' pact with the devil, as James would later explain in
Demonology (II iii).

Two days later, on 19 May 1590, Queen Anne made her triumphal entry into
Edinburgh, while the king remained in the palace of Holyrood. The celebrations
were lavish, and associated Anne's appearance with the promise of material
plenty. The style was courtly, with mythological figures surrounding the queen
and appearing in tableaux in the city, thus mixing popular carnival with the
idealised classical world of learned culture. The queen was accompanied by
'nymphs', and preceded as she passed through the city by 'xlij [42] young men
all cled in quhyt talfettie [clad in white taffeta], and wisseouris [visors] of black
cullour on thair faces lyk Mores [Moors], all full of gold chenyeis [chains], that
dancit befoir hir grace all the way'.[56]

Meanwhile, in Denmark in May 1590 the first witch was convicted of sorcery;
she confessed that she used sorcery to hinder the ships' second attempt to sail
to Scotland at the end of September 1589. She accused several others of involvement, and all were executed. It is possible, according to Riis, that the first court
proceedings against the Danish witches began *before* the Scottish party left
Denmark at the end of April 1590.[57] If that was so, however, we might expect
such trials to have been mentioned by the Scottish party before their return on
1 May 1590, and no such mention appears. Witchcraft charges emerged from a
series of actions which began with Admiral Peder Munk, the commander of the
Danish ships, attempting to clear himself of the charge of negligence for the
mishaps that had befallen the squadron during September 1589. He took legal
action against the governor of Copenhagen, whose responsibilities included
the maintenance of the royal navy, and who was blamed for the leaks that had
sprung in the *Gideon*. The supreme court tried the case and found 'the damage
suffered was caused by the gale although the captains could have done more to
limit its effects'.[58] The governor then tried to shift the blame by saying that
several people were currently being tried for witchcraft aimed at stopping Anne
from making a safe crossing from Denmark. Admiral Munk himself was still in
Scotland in May when the first Danish witch was convicted of sorcery, and the
first news to reach Scotland was not until July 1590.[59] As yet there had been no
mention of witchcraft in Scotland.

The earl of Bothwell

Bothwell and King James, 1589 – January 1591

Francis Stewart Hepburn, 5th earl of Bothwell, was James's first cousin.[60] He was the nephew of James Hepburn, the 4th earl of Bothwell, who had been the third husband of Mary queen of Scots after the death of her second husband Lord Darnley, James's father.[61] While James was bookish and machiavellian, Bothwell was intelligent and with an aristocratic pride comparable to James's sense of royal privilege. In 1589, on the eve of the witch hunt, James was twenty-three and Bothwell twenty-six, and the average age of the higher nobility was about twenty-nine; it was these young men 'who were to be at the centre of so much of the violence of the next few years'.[62] Bothwell's violence had been seen in 1584 when he attacked members of the Hume family, with whom he was at feud, 'killed all three, but hewed Davy Hume . . . all to pieces'.[63] Another feud, between Bothwell and the chancellor, John Maitland, intensified the factionalism at court.[64] Bothwell was an educated, cultured man who had travelled in Europe, and on his return home he added an Italianate façade to his castle of Crichton, an indication, in Wormald's words, 'of the aristocracy's image of itself as men of taste, travel, and culture'.[65] The witchcraft charge against him in 1591 was the first in a series of events that led to Bothwell's and his family's ruin. For much of the time after he was accused of treason and witchcraft in 1591 until his exile in 1595 he lived as an outlaw, attempting several violent assaults on the court, but also becoming a focus of opposition to the policies of the king and council. James took advantage of Bothwell's implication in the witch hunt of 1590–1 to assert royal authority, outmanoeuvring and finally exiling his most unpredictable rival, though only after a long-drawn-out, violent and dangerous struggle against a man on whom a few years earlier James had built if not an absolute, then at least a considerable trust.

Bothwell's entanglement with the witch hunt is perhaps best understood in the context of bloodfeud, the system of private justice depending on revenge and restitution and a code of honour.[66] The feud between Bothwell and Chancellor Maitland was believed by at least one contemporary to be behind the witchcraft charge against Bothwell, with James turning against Bothwell 'be [by] the malicious narrative of his Chanciller'.[67] While feuding was generally 'a traditional form of kin-based justice . . . adopted and institutionalised by the Scottish legal system',[68] it was rising to new levels of violence in the 1580s and 1590s, 'creating a situation that was seen as intolerable by James VI, the church and even a growing section of the nobility'.[69] Bothwell's behaviour, even against James, was sustained by the ideology of bloodfeud, and his defeat by James was a defeat for bloodfeud and a strengthening of official law and justice.

In late 1589, when James left Scotland for Norway and the feud between Bothwell and Maitland had temporarily subsided, he trusted his cousin sufficiently to appoint him second in command in the government. But relations between them were unstable. Ritchie Graham's evidence about Bothwell's consulting him shows that a story of Bothwell being eager to gain the king's favour by magic was plausible. Graham was examined by the king and Sir James Melville, who wrote that Graham

> was sent for be the Erle Bodowell, wha requyred his help to cause the Kingis Maieste his maister to lyk weill of him; and to that effect he gaif the said erle some drog or herb, willing him at some convenient tym to tuiche his Maiesteis faice therwith. Quhilk being done be the said erle, and fand him not the better, he delt again with the said Riche, to get his Maieste wracked [destroyed], as Riche allegit; wha said that he culd not do sic thingis him self, bot that a notable midwyf wha was a witche, callit Anny Sampsoun, culd bring any sic purpos till pass.[70]

Graham's evidence records the uneasy mix of closeness and conflict in Bothwell's relation to James. Had James not survived the hazardous journey to Denmark then Bothwell would have had some claim to the throne.

When Bothwell was appointed to the government in James's absence, the king was extending royal favour and patronage to a powerful magnate in traditional ways.[71] Bothwell's position as admiral made him responsible, at least nominally, for the ships and the royal couple. Among James's orders to the privy council was one that 'The earl Bothwell as admirall [was] to prepair the botis, that were appointed of before, and to pas with thame to the shippis to resave thair Majesties'.[72] During James's absence Bothwell found himself at odds with the kirk, because of his and his followers' violence, and found himself in the kirk of St Giles in Edinburgh on 9 November 1589 having to listen to a recital of his offences in Robert Bruce's sermon, and to repent on his knees before the congregation.[73] But he could act as statesman, visiting the general assembly of the kirk, and entertaining the English ambassador and important church ministers 'to guid cheir' at Holyroodhouse where he was living during that period.[74] Yet James's marriage would no doubt soon produce an heir, and extinguish any royal ambitions Bothwell might have. Margaret Murray wrote that Bothwell might 'claim to be the next heir male to the throne of Scotland . . . had James VI died without children',[75] and, true or not, this idea arises in the witchcraft examinations. Lodged in the popular imagination by 1591 was the notion of Bothwell as a challenger to James for the crown, evident in the record of the trial of Barbara Napier's assizers which records magical practices against the king with the intention 'that another might have ruled in his Majesty's place'. Murray was correct in identifying Bothwell as the 'devil' in North Berwick kirk, but only insofar as this was the way he might have been imagined by contemporaries, including James himself.[76] Bothwell's pride, arrogance and rebellion made elision with Satan imaginatively easy.

Accusations of witchcraft against Bothwell, January – December 1591

Bothwell was accused by some of the East Lothian witches of plotting against

James's person. In a deposition, probably from the end of January 1591, Agnes Sampson is reported as having 'said that there would be both gold and silver and victual gotten fra my Lord Bothwell'; and Janet Stratton said on 4 May 1591 that treasonable magic had been performed at the express command of the earl of Bothwell.[77] Bothwell was called to answer such charges before the privy council on 15 April 1591. Melville recorded the news in his memoirs:

> Specially ane renowned midwyf callit Anny Sampsoun, affirmed that sche, in company with nyn uthers witches, being convenit in the nycht besyd Prestounpannes, the devell ther maister being present standing in the midis of them; ther a body of wax schaipen and maid be the said Anny Sampsoun, wrappit within a lynnyng claith [linen cloth], was first delyverit to the devell; quhilk efter he had pronuncit his verde, delyverit the said pictour to Anny Sampsoun, and sche to hir nyxt marrow [companion], and sa every ane round about [in a circle], saying, 'This is K. James the sext, ordonit to be consumed at the instance of a noble man Francis Erle Bodowell'.[78]

Bothwell denied such charges but was imprisoned in Edinburgh Castle on 16 April 1591. According to Keith Brown, the 'entire episode looks deeply suspicious', but '[w]hatever the explanation, Bothwell had been ensnared'.[79] Charges of witchcraft against political enemies had long been familiar in Scottish politics.[80] Melville records that 'his Maieste [was] not willing to credit [Bothwell's] devellische accusers',[81] and it may be that Maitland exploited the accusations of witchcraft in order to ruin him. Robert Birrell, a contemporary diarist, records that the earl of Bothwell had been charged with 'alledgit witchcraft, and consulting with witches, especially with ane Richard Grahame, to conspyre the King's death'.[82] Graham was clearly maintained and provided for by the government on the understanding that he would testify against Bothwell.[83] Bothwell is supposed to have asked how long the king would live, a question directly affecting his own political future. He was convinced that his enemy Maitland was behind the witchcraft charge.[84] Indeed, he hinted as much when he was questioned by the chancellor before the king and council at the chancellor's house in April 1591: '[h]e alleged that this matter grew not only by Graham, but sprang from his enemies, . . . [and that] this practice with Graham was devised against him'.[85] Bothwell would later be far more explicit in his allegation of Maitland's manipulation of Graham in a 'Declaration' written in February 1593.[86]

Robert Bowes dutifully recorded the rumour on 27 April 1591 that Barbara Napier had sent a letter to Bothwell that told him to 'stand fast' and show that his enemies had invented the charge against him. 'Which letter', Bowes goes on, 'was delivered to a woman to take to one of Bothwell's servants to convey to Bothwell. Being open it was read by sundry, whereof one instructed Robert Bruce, who advertised the King. But the woman burnt the letter.'[87] Letters circulating in just such an elaborate way, through intermediaries, appear in several witchcraft depositions. This letter shows that Bothwell and Napier knew each other, possibly through the the earl of Angus: Bothwell was the 8th earl's brother-in-law, and Napier knew the earl's third wife.[88]

The council pursued its investigations into Bothwell's treasonable witchcraft against the king. Bothwell's servant, Ninian Chirnesyde, was ordered to give evidence about 'the perelling [imperilling]' of the king's person, crown and estate, but failed to appear, and on 7 May was denounced rebel.[89] During the weeks of Bothwell's imprisonment the trials of the accused witches were being relentlessly pursued. Barbara Napier's trial took place in May, and Euphame MacCalzean's in June, with MacCalzean's execution ordered for 25 June. These trials were of women who might be most convincingly associated with Bothwell in terms of class. This was the height of the witch hunt. But Bothwell did not stand trial in 1591. He was warded in Edinburgh Castle from 16 April but, four days before the execution of Euphame MacCalzean, he escaped and fled the city.

On 25 June 1591, the day that MacCalzean was burned alive on the castle hill, the privy council issued a proclamation denouncing Bothwell for giving himself 'ower altogidder in the handis of Sathan' and 'heiping tressoun upoun tressoun aganis God, his Majestie, and this his native cuntre'.[90] The proclamation declared that Bothwell had 'had consultatioun with nygromanceris, witcheis, and utheris wickit and ungodlie personis, bayth without and within this cuntre, for bereving of his Hienes lyff', and that this was part of a conspiracy that had been 'confessit be sum of the same kynd alreddy execute to the deid and sum utheris yit on lyve reddy to be execute for the same cryme'.[91] The council saw Bothwell as the leading conspirator in a plot involving many people, including Napier and MacCalzean. According to the proclamation, Bothwell had used witchcraft for deadly political ends, conspiring with people who were 'innemeis to God, [and] his Hienes' in order to achieve 'the subversioun of the trew religioun' in a 'tressonabill conspiracie aganis his Majesteis awin persoun'.[92] In the eyes of the council, Bothwell became the epitome of political, social and religious subversion. On the same day the council seized Bothwell's four properties.

Bothwell nevertheless had influential defenders. In June or July 1591, just after he had escaped from Edinburgh Castle, a letter addressed 'To the nobility' cast doubt on the evidence brought against Bothwell, and warned about the political dangers of the king's imprisoning one of the nobility. The writer defended Bothwell and denigrated his chief accuser, Ritchie Graham, declaring that the charge was an 'incredible and unnatural acusatioun led against a noble personage by an infamous persoun moved by the dispositioun and humeur of his divilish natur'.[93] 'If a Ritchie Grahame affirms', the writer continued, 'and Earl Bothwell denies, which—may I ask?—ought to be believed?' An earl was impugned by someone not only low-born but also infamous as a 'pretended nigromancer bot in effect a lyer and a false abuser ignorant of that art that men wald attribut unto him'.[94] The letter implies that officers of state manipulated Graham to set Bothwell up: Graham had been protected in return for making his accusations.[95] Although Maitland is not named, the letter says the court is under the control of evil counsellors who,'[i]n gilded and painted palaces . . . execute their power at the dictates of hatred and favour', and who 'obscure that great majestie that . . . is dew unto his sacred person'.[96] Blaming a monarch's counsellors is a regular way of criticising a monarch while not appearing to do so. This letter sees the accusations against Bothwell as the product of factional and class politics. Witchcraft as such is barely mentioned. Rather, Bothwell's fall is attributed 'not through any guyltines of the forged cryme bot through the in[i]quete of tyme [iniquity of the time]', and his enemies, fearing 'his pouer and revenge', wanting to see him dead. The letter's vague language makes it possible that the king is one such who fears Bothwell. Finally, an appeal is made to aristocrats against misdirected royal power: 'If [Bothwell] shall die because they fear him, then neither shall your lives be safe, for you also give them terror'.[97] Behind the charges of treasonable witchcraft lies political pressure: enemies at court, and Elizabeth's urging James that his life and religion are threatened by letting the earl live.[98] Witchcraft is merely a pretext for attacking Bothwell.

Bothwell contacted the king on 1 July 1591, offering his submission, or asking to deal with members of the council, but by that time James had ordered military pursuit. In a letter to James of August 1591 Bothwell sought to limit the damage to himself and his family, declaring that he was innocent of the 'supposed and devysed crymes' he had been charged with, and claiming that they had been trumped up by his enemies 'to induce the King to seek his ruin'. He tried to soften the blow of forfeiture that had been pronounced on 25 June by begging the king 'to take his wife and children under the royal protection during his absence, and not to suffer them to be dispossessed'.[99] But James was determined to assert royal power: he read the letter to the whole court 'that all the presence might know the contents and his evil acceptance thereof'; refused to 'promise favour to the children'; and left Bothwell 'to his own course as his rebel whom he would pursue'.[100] The proclamation accused him of 'tressonabill practizes', and though it did not accuse him directly of witchcraft, it did of consultation, and used demonological language in declaring that Bothwell had 'gevin himself ower altogidder in the handis of Sathan'.[101] Bothwell's position was rapidly weakening. On 6 August 1591 a band was signed in Edinburgh by lairds who promised to support the king in the 'pursuit of Frances, sometime Earl Bothuill . . . and other declared traitors'.[102]

On 27 December 1591 Bothwell struck back violently against the king and Maitland when he broke into Holyroodhouse attempting to seize James and kill Maitland. Calderwood describes how '[h]e and his complices came to the king's door, the queen's, and the chancellor's; at one tyme with fire to the king's doore, with hammers to the queen's doore'.[103] The attempt failed and Bothwell escaped, but seven or eight of his followers were seized, and later hanged at the market cross in Edinburgh. The horror and humiliation of that night confirmed James's hatred of Bothwell. In three sonnets, written 'when the King was surprised by the Earle Bothwell', James expresses his frustration at the attack: 'How long shall Furies on our fortunes feede / How long shall vice her raigne possesse in rest'; and he reflects bitterly that in these times, 'justice hath her hart infected sore'. James wished to impress justice upon rebellious subjects whether they were feuding subjects, defiant magnates or witches.[104]

A week after the assault at Holyrood James wrote to Sir James Melville, then his personal ambassador to England, with a version of events for Elizabeth.[105] The letter fuses witchcraft, Satan, catholicism, Bothwell, and political conspiracy and rebellion as interconnected threats to the established order that sustained both monarchs. The threats all spring from witchcraft, 'the bloodye counsellis of the enemeyis to God, his trew Religion and to all Monarchies professing the same', and the origin of witchcraft is Satan who 'ceases not daylie to stirre up thair suppostis [supporters] and desperat ministers to essay the taking away of laufull Princes be all unlaufull meanes'. Bothwell has led the conspiracy as 'the abhominable authour (who bewryeth him self guyltie of that sorcerye and witchecraft devised against our awin person)', and drawn into it other 'maist unnaturall subjectis . . . [who] have bene more easalye entised being of the Spanishe faction, and hes adventured so farre in this lait enterpryse as to be burreaux [hangmen] and executouris of their cruell deseingis [designs]'.[106] James was later in *Demonology* to think of the devil or fallen spirits as 'God's hangmen'.[107] Bothwell is elided with the devil, and witchcraft is seen as the type of all political and religious opposition: witchcraft is politicised, and politics demonised. James presents the fearful image of cosmic forces working through local agents to destroy and overturn the established order. In *Demonology* (II iii), James would discuss witches' efforts, under the devil's leadership, in 'the enlarging of Satan's tyranny, and crossing [impeding] of the propagation of the kingdom of Christ'. The idea of a personal Satan, a crucial part of the ideology of the witch hunt, and one that crystallised all James's fears, emerged as he struggled to come to terms with Bothwell's political violence.

Bothwell and King James, January 1592 – April 1595

Bothwell's eventual fate was to depend on shifting allegiances in the wider political scene. When Huntly murdered the earl of Moray at Donibristle on 7 February 1592, many blamed this horrific lawlessness on James's leniency towards the catholic Huntly. Support for Bothwell increased 'among the nobles and lairds, . . . driving even the Presbyterian clergy into some amount of sympathy with him, on the ground that a revolution even by *his* means might make matters better and could hardly make them worse'.[108] The king absented himself from Edinburgh to avoid the hostility against him and the chancellor.

Bothwell and witchcraft were kept to the fore by the execution of Bothwell's chief accuser, Ritchie Graham (whom Calderwood called 'the great sorcerer'), at the market cross of Edinburgh on 28 February 1592. Graham had been imprisoned for his own safety, but now with Bothwell an outlaw his usefulness was past. Nevertheless, at his death, a moment when words had special weight, he 'stood hard to his former confessioun tuiching Bothwell's practise against the king'. In his account, Calderwood discounted the story that 'the chancellor had some tables and images about his necke, and that he was sure [safe] so long as he used them so', but he recorded Graham's statements that 'Arran, Lord Farneyeere, was an inchanter; that the devill was raised at the Laird of Auchinfleck's dwelling-place, and in Sir Lewes Bellendine, the Justice-Clerk's yaird'.[109] With such rumours circulating it was difficult to distinguish political ally from supernatural subversive.

James's weakness was evident when the parliament met in Edinburgh from May to June 1592 'when public opinion was strongly against the king for his suspected complicity in the murder of Moray, he had to take the undignified step of sending for some ministers and requesting them to "clear his part before the people"'.[110] Calderwood records James's anger and frustration at Bothwell, as proceedings began:

> The first day of the Parliament the king had an harangue, wherein he layed to Bothwell's charge that he sought his destructioun, first by witchecraft, both when he was in Denmarke, and when he was at home, as the depositiouns of the witches would testifie, that he might succeed to the crowne, as the Erle of Atholl used against King James the First: Nixt, by violence, beating at his chamber-doores with hammers. 'And yett,' said he, 'he was but a bastard, and could clame no title to the crowne.' *Item*, That he had shed innocent blood, and had abused his bodie in adulterie; and sindrie other speeches he had to make Bothwell odious.[111]

The leading presbyterian Mr James Melville saw the king's weakness working to the kirk's advantage:

> The aw of Boduall's [fear of Bothwell's] remeaning alwayes within the Countrey, and often tymes hard about the Court, togidder with the horrour of the deid of Dinnibirsall [deed of Donibristle] . . . obteined (at the Parliament hauldin at Edinbruche in the monethe of Junie 1592, for better expeding of the forfaultrie of Boduall), by our expectation [for speeding up the confiscation of Bothwell's properties beyond our expectation], that quhilk haid cost us mikle pean in vean monie yeirs befor [great effort expended in vain over many years], to wit, the Ratification of the libertie of the trew Kirk.[112]

With the kirk and king both eager to get what they wanted from each other, the parliament confirmed Bothwell's forfeiture,[113] but also legalised presbyterian church government for the first time. The kirk seized the chance to push forward its moral and political agendas: witchcraft was prominent in the act that appointed royal and kirk commissioners to inquire into the state of the church, and to investigate various social miscreants, including those 'suspectit and dilaitit of witchcraft, or seikand responssis or help of thame'.[114] This crucial act (discussed in more detail in Chapter 5, sustained witch hunting and supplied the legal means for a national witch hunt that lasted until 1597.

Bothwell, stripped of his title and declared a rebel, continued to roam, posing a constant danger to the king. On 28 June 1592 with four hundred armed men he attacked Falkland Palace while James and Anne were in residence, but was beaten off. James informed Elizabeth on 5 July 1592 of this latest 'rare and rash attempt confirming now at Falkland that treason which in winter they committed at Holyroodhous', and asked that 'none of these traitors shall find refuge in any part of your dominions'.[115] But Elizabeth happily used Bothwell to pressure James to act against the rebellious catholic lords in the north-east.

In December 1592 the affair of the 'Spanish blanks' confirmed that those lords were still plotting. Blank papers were seized, signed by the earls of Huntly, Errol and Angus, that were to be filled with the terms agreed between them and Philip II of Spain for an invasion of Scotland. James marched north with an army in February 1593 and the earls fled before him. During 1593 James was engaged in dealing with two sets of rebellious subjects led by Bothwell and Huntly. At the same time witches continued to be pursued: on 19 May 1593 Katherine Muirhead was burnt for witchcraft in Edinburgh.[116]

In February 1593 Bothwell made public a passionate self-defence, attributing his misfortune to Chancellor Maitland's hatred. The charge of witchcraft, he wrote, was politically motivated:

> how partially and 'unformally' Chancellor Maitland with his accomplices 'caused feade' a process of witchcraft against me, most untruly alleging that I intended to destroy the King my sovereign. At the first he handled the matter so cunningly that even my dearest friends were put in suspicion of my sincerity; but immediately after . . . God of His mercy made my innocence so manifest that it were superfluous to make any mention thereof in this place.[117]

Bothwell points to the 'confession of the infamous witnesses at the hour of their execution that they were suborned and corrupted', presumably by Maitland's agents; and claims that Ritchie Graham's testimony, maintained 'to the hour of his death', was part of a deal with the government to save Graham's life.[118] The reference to the confession of witnesses at the hour of their execution may well be to the confessions of Geillis Duncan and Bessie Thomson, just before their execution on 4 December 1591, that they had slanderously accused Napier and MacCalzean of witchcraft, and had told 'leasings [lies]'.[119] The attempt to exonerate Napier and MacCalzean after their deaths might have been to clear Bothwell as well.[120] Bothwell further claims that 'Maitland with his accomplices' are 'ashamed of the iniquity of that process of witchcraft' so that 'in my opinion they have destroyed the same, for neither is it extant in the books "adjurnall" nor to be found out in any "scrowlis" [drafts]'.[121] He further asserts that his enemies' hatred is now behind the charge that he is conspiring with 'the Spanish faction' in 'an enterprise against his Highness'.[122] Bothwell represents witchcraft and catholicism as being merely the political tools that

Maitland used to destroy him. And he dismisses the latest charges against him, that their 'testimony should be more able to condemn me in religion than "Richie" Grame was to convict me of witchcraft'.[123] The declaration's fierce, self-justificatory rhetoric registers the pressures on Bothwell, but it also accurately defines the witchcraft charge as political.

But Bothwell was still dangerous. In July 1593 he staged a successful coup, effectively took control of the government and held the king in his power. With the connivance of some of James's courtiers, Bothwell entered Holyroodhouse and reached James's presence chamber, where the king found him 'offering his sword in surrender and loudly calling for the King's pardon'.[124] Bothwell requested recovery of his forfeited estates, and trial by his peers on the charge of witchcraft because, as a contemporary wrote, 'the originall caus of his truble was the suspicion of wichecraft',[125] James wrote to a supporter telling him to 'give no [ear]' to news that 'we are detained and pressed against our will and heart's liking',[126] and to raise no military force to rescue him. When Bothwell appeared in Edinburgh that same day he 'was received with exceeding great joy by the people'.[127] James agreed to a trial for witchcraft.[128]

James lost control of events for several weeks following the coup, and 'during the whilk season, to the 15 day of August, the king was in perpetuall greif of mynd, affferming that he was captive be Bothwell, and be the foresaidis noblis and gentilmen'.[129] Bothwell, however, faced the political dilemma of following the logic of his coup and killing the king, or yielding power to James and facing the king's anger.[130] He shrank from regicide, contenting himself instead with trying to clear his name of witchcraft, and recovering his lost estates. On 26 July 1593, two days after Bothwell's appearance in Holyroodhouse, his previous actions and those of his followers were condoned, and in August 1593 Bothwell was acquitted of the charges of witchcraft which had stood against him for more than two years since April 1591.

Bothwell's trial took place in Edinburgh on 10 August 1593 from 1 p.m. until 10 p.m. when his acquittal was announced. The assize consisted of two earls, seven lords, and eight barons. The king, having lost control of events, had been persuaded to come from Falkland for the trial, which Bowes described as consisting of the declarations of 'honest persons' that Ritchie Graham had been blackmailed into accusing Bothwell of witchcraft. Bowes wrote that

> The evidence against him was wholly grounded on the tales of 'Richy' Graham (executed for witchcraft), who before renounced the benefit of his baptism to serve the devil, and who was found 'variant in himself', and was disproved before the assise by the oaths and testimonies of honest persons . . . that he was entised to accuse the Earl, with hope of his life. By these and many other circumstances the assise was satisfied, and acquitted the Earl.[131]

This outcome was guaranteed by Bothwell's political dominance that was so great that the day after his trial the king was refused permission to return to Falkland because 'Bothwell and the rest would not like well of it'. James was subjected by Bothwell and others to a harangue on the 'many causes casting this estate into dangerous confusion', including 'the known boldness in the Papists, the effusion of innocent blood by murder committed in every corner without punishment (especially of the Earl of Murray), the great oppressions of the poor, the danger of breach of the amity with England, and the bareness of his estate; for which they prayed him to take order before his departure'.[132]

From the nadir of July–August 1593, however, James astonishingly managed to come out on top, and within two years had sent Bothwell into permanent exile in April 1595. Bothwell's 'insolence and presumption in his hour of victory' in July–August 1593 finally convinced many of his dangerousness; and that, combined with his 'grave error in agreeing to retire from court after his seizure of the King',[133] allowed the king to build support against Bothwell including from Maitland, who returned to court. Bothwell's alleged witchcraft conspiracy against the king had been eclipsed by the danger he posed to royal power and safety. James now felt 'extreme hatred' towards Bothwell, and in September 1593 the forced concessions of earlier in the year were reversed when the earl, his servants and dependents 'were discharged, by opin proclamatioun at the Mercat Croce of Edinburgh, to come neere the king within ten myles, unlesse they were sent for, under paine of treasoun'.[134]

James was notably conciliatory, by contrast, to the northern catholic earls. In November 1593 an act of oblivion for the conspiracy of the 'Spanish blanks' was obtained for them provided they conformed to the reformed church; otherwise they would be exiled. 'This was regarded', Donaldson concludes, 'with some justification, as the peak of the king's policy of concession to the "Roman Catholic" party'.[135] James's failure to crush Huntly's rebellion prompted a crisis with Elizabeth. She sheltered Bothwell in England, and used this military threat to pressurise James to act against the powerful catholic magnates. In April 1594, with English aid, Bothwell launched a final military assault, this time on Leith, but it failed, and Elizabeth finally withdrew her support. When Bothwell then switched his allegiance to the northern catholics, he appeared not as a principled defender of protestantism but as an unscrupulous political adventurer.

James's position strengthened when on 19 February 1594 Queen Anne gave birth to the couple's first child and royal heir, Prince Henry. In September 1594 James finally took military action against the earls of Huntly, Errol and Angus, who had continued to plot with Spain. He had promised the people in St Giles' kirk at the time of Bothwell's raid of Leith that 'If ye will assist me against Bothwell at this time, I promise to prosecute the excommunicated lords so that they shall not be suffered to remain in any part of Scotland'.[136] Andrew Melville accompanied the expedition, signalling the kirk's approval of an expedition against both catholic rebels and Bothwell, who by now had joined them. Like Bothwell, the rebels shrank from a showdown with the king, and thus avoided the fearful consequences that a royal defeat would have produced. Both the catholic earls and Bothwell were engaged not in rebellion aimed at overturning the monarchy but in the well-worn practice of seizing and maintaining power through court faction and feuding.[137] The king was magnanimous in victory. In March 1595 Huntly and Errol agreed to go into exile. They returned secretly to Scotland in June 1596; by June 1597 they had agreed to be received into the kirk; and in November 1597 parliament revoked their forfeitures. 'These proceedings', according to Donaldson, 'marked the extinction of Roman catholicism as a political danger'.[138]

Bothwell's political extinction was achieved by March 1595. Despite his pleas to the presbytery of Edinburgh that the desperate circumstance of losing a heritable earldom had forced him to 'conjoin with [Roman catholic] opposites',[139] the ministers agreed to the king's wish to have Bothwell excommunicated. In February 1595 the Edinburgh presbytery 'did cut off the said Francis from the company of the Kirk and deliver him to Satan, . . . and ordained intimation to be made hereof to all the brethren of the realm by every pastor'.[140] Ironically, Bothwell was returned to the satanic realm where the witchcraft charges imagined him to be. Bothwell was a ruined man; his 'lands and jurisdictions being granted to the Duke of Lennox, Lord Hume, and the baronial chiefs of the Scott and Kerr kindreds'.[141] Also in February 1595 his brother, Hercules Stewart, was hanged, in spite of considerable popular sympathy.[142] Exiled from Scotland in April 1595, he lived first in France, then Spain, and finally Italy where he had a reputation for 'suspected negromancie'.[143] He died in poverty in Naples in 1612.

Notes

[1] *CSPS* ix 655.

[2] For accounts of this episode see Bingham 1968, and Normand 1996.

[3] *RPCS* iv 423.

[4] *RPCS* iv 412n.

[5] For accounts of the marriage see Donaldson 1965: 185–93; Willson 1965: 85–95; and Stevenson 1997.

[6] Cited in Willson 1965: 88.

[7] Willson 1965: 87.

[8] Lythe 1960: 63.

[9] Moysie 1830: 79.

[10] Melville 1827: 369.

[11] *RPCS* iv 423n.

[12] A detailed account can be found in Riis 1988: 264–5.

[13] Melville 1827: 370. This incident is recorded in *News from Scotland*. Asheby said that James was impressed by the two bad omens of Kennedy's death and the explosion on the flagship (Riis 1988: 269).

[14] Akrigg 1984: 95.

[15] *Historie and Life of King James the Sext*, in *Papers Relative to the Marriage* 1828: 3.

[16] Melville 1827: 370

[17] *The Kingis Majesteis Declaratioun upoun the Causis of his Depairtur* in *Papers Relative to the Marriage* 1828: 13.

[18] *The Kingis Majesteis Declaratioun* 1828: 13–15.

[19] *The Kingis Majesteis Declaratioun* 1828: 12–13.

[20] *The Kingis Majesteis Declaratioun* 1828: 4.

[21] *RPCS* iv 424.

[22] This episode is discussed in Willis 1995: 145–6, who argues that 'Sampson's divinatory power is suggestive not only of the powers attributed to the childhood mother but also of Elizabeth's and Mary's [queen of Scots] surveillance of the young king', 146.

[23] See the texts of the three documents which

James had prepared, and which were read to the council the day after he had sailed in *RPCS* iv 423–30.

[24] *RPCS* iv 423.

[25] Read 1960: 455.

[26] Melville 1829: 186.

[27] Melville 1827: 372.

[28] Donaldson 1965: 188.

[29] *CSPS* x 182.

[30] For a full discussion of these meetings see Riis 1988: 121–5.

[31] Clark 1993: 67.

[32] See Larner 1984: 10–11, who notes that 'James himself was the principal, if not the sole, purveyor to his people of the concept of the demonic pact', and that it was 'James's first encounter with Continental thinkers and he must have been introduced to many new ideas then'. This view has been challenged by Maxwell-Stuart 1997, and Wormald 2000: 174.

[33] See, for example, Maxwell-Stuart 1997: 212–14; Johansen 1993: 362–3.

[34] Riis 1988: 121.

[35] *RPCS* iv 430n.

[36] Larner 1984: 11.

[37] Riis 1988: 137, mentions that Young and Krag 'had been ambassadors to the other country and could help others to establish contacts', and that Tycho Brahe and Chancellor Niels Kass were also very important in this respect. He notes, however, 'the almost total absence of theological concerns in the exchanges between Scottish and Danish scholars with James VI and Niels Hemmingsen as the exceptions', 125.

[38] Cameron 1993: 556.

[39] Smout 1972: 155.

[40] Moysie 1830: 81.

[41] *RPCS* iv 469.

[42] See Paul 1905: 151, for details of Sir Patrick Hepburne of Sunsyre, 1st earl of Bothwell's appointment as Great Admiral on 26 June 1488; see also 143, 153 for other Hepburns holding the office of admiral-depute.

[43] *CSPS* x 282.

[44] Moysie 1830: 83.

[45] Moysie 1830: 83.

[46] Calderwood 1842–9: ii 384.

[47] Cooper 1902: 18.

[48] Clark 1997: 613.

[49] Compare *Demonology* II v, 'even as God by his sacraments, which are earthly of themselves, works a heavenly effect though no ways by any cooperation in them . . . ; so the devil will have his outward means to be shows, as it were, of his doing, which hath no part of cooperation in his turns with him, how far that ever the ignorants be abused in the contrary'.

[50] Calderwood 1842–9: v 95

[51] Clark 1997: 620.

[52] Calderwood 1842–9: v 95.

[53] Cooper 1902: 23, concludes that 'the ministers' scruples had resulted only (1) in robbing such ceremonies as were retained—e.g., the Unction, of their sacred meaning, and (2) in representing the Queen's crown as coming to her not from God, but merely at her husband's will'.

[54] This account is drawn from *The Forme and Maner of the Coronatione of Anna, the Quenis Majestie of Scotland*, in *Papers Relative to the Marriage* 1828: 49–56.

[55] *Papers Relative to the Marriage* 1828: 53.

[56] Moysie 1830: 83–4.

[57] Riis 1988: 267.

[58] Riis 1988: 267.

[59] *CSPS* x 365.

[60] For accounts of Bothwell see Willson 1965: 96–115; Donaldson 1965: 190–2; Cowan 1983; Brown 1986: 126–30.

[61] James V (1512–42) was father of Mary, queen of Scots, and the illegitimate John Stewart, father of the 5th earl of Bothwell, as well as the illegitimate James Stewart, earl of Moray and regent 1567–70.

[62] Brown 1986: 20.

[63] Quoted by Brown 1986: 30.

[64] For details of the Bothwell–Maitland feud see Brown 1986: 128–9.

[65] Wormald 1981: 171.

[66] See especially Brown 1986.

[67] *Historie of James the Sext* 1825: 242, where the anonymous writer notes that 'the King had na just occasioun of greif, nor cryme to allege aganis him [Bothwell], bot onlie at the instigation of Chanciller Maitland'.

[68] Whyte 1995: 216. For useful summaries of bloodfeud see Whyte 1995: 216–18; Whyte 1997: 73–8.

[69] Whyte 1997: 76.

[70] Melville 1827: 397.

[71] Wormald 1981: 151–3, argues that James's

72 'Ordour Set Doun be his Majestie to be
Effectuat be his Hienes Secret Counsall,
and Preparit Aganis his Majesteis Returne
in Scotland. Feb 1589', in *Papers Relative
to the Marriage* 1828: 30.

73 See Bruce 1591: where Bothwell's offences are summarised as 'murther and
blood-shed, . . . taking the name of God
in vain; and for everie thing wherein he
hath abused himselfe; and for all his
offensiue and rash speaches: and generallie, for everie thing, wherein hee hath
offended the least of zou [you]'.

74 Melville 1829: 186–7, 'Boduell resorted
to that Assemblie, and keiping hous in the
Abbay in the Kings awin housses, he haid
the Quein of Eingland be hir Ambassator
ordinar (Mr Robert Bowes wha ley at
Edinbruche, a verie godlie man, and to
his uttermaist lowing and cairfull of the
peace and weill of the twa realmes of
Eingland and Scotland,) to be his commer,
and Mr Robert Bruce, my uncle, and me,
being Moderator of that Assemblie,
invited now and then to guid cheir,
haissing sum grait purpose and to luik in
hand; bot he wes neuer lukkie nor honest
to God nor man.'

75 Murray 1921: 56.
76 Murray 1921: 56.
77 Documents 5 and 8.

78 Melville 1827: 395. Melville gives a
detailed account of the accusations against
Bothwell, and of Bothwell's raid on
Holyroodhouse in December 1591, 395–
401.

79 Brown 1986: 155.

80 See Stafford 1953: 97, who mentions
twelve witches burned in 1479 for using a
wax image to kill James III; and Williamson 1979: 57, who notes that a witchcraft
charge 'seems in the 16th century to have
become a standard Scottish political
weapon', though 'only nobodies went to
their deaths'.

81 Melville 1827: 397.
82 Birrel 1798: 25.
83 Document 10.

84 See Cowan 1983: 131.
85 *CSPS* x 504.
86 *CSPS* xi 61–4.
87 *CSPS* x 506.
88 Cowan 1983: 130; *DNB sv* Archibald
Douglas, 8th earl of Angus (1555–88).
89 *RPCS* iv 614.
90 *RPCS* iv 643.
91 *RPCS* iv 644.
92 *RPCS* iv 643–4.
93 *Warrender Papers* 1931–2: ii 154.
94 *Warrender Papers* 1931–2: ii 155.
95 *Warrender Papers* 1931–2: ii 155n: 'Greyme
did never accuse Bothwell in any thing
till such tyme as he had a warrant under
the councelles handes , , . that if he wold
speake simply and trewly what he knewe,
his life should be preserved, and he should
lyve in Sterling castle, where he should
feare no manns mallice and have good
allowance' (also in *Border Papers* 1894–6: i
487).
96 *Warrender Papers* 1931–2: ii 157.
97 *Warrender Papers* 1931–2: ii 157.
98 *Warrender Papers* 1931–2: ii 162, '. . . the
English ambassador, who, having in his
mistress's name upbraided the King for
his long patience, concluded with her
Majesty's advice that he should no longer
"dandle offenders, that is to say, spare the
erle Bothuel." He persuaded the King that
his life and religion would both be
endangered if Bothwell lived, and that
sentence against him should be carried
out speedily.'
99 *Warrender Papers* 1931–2: ii 164.
100 *Warrender Papers* 1931–2: ii 165.
101 The proclamation can be found in *RPCS*
iv 643–4.
102 *RPCS* iv 666.
103 Calderwood 1842–9: v 140–1.
104 James VI 1955–8: ii 110–11.
105 *Warrender Papers* 1931–2: ii 167.
106 All quotations from *Warrender Papers*
1931–2: ii 168.
107 *Demonology* Preface; I vi.
108 *RPCS* iv lxiv.
109 Calderwood 1842–9: v 148.
110 Donaldson 1965: 193, quoting Calderwood 1842–9: v 145.
111 Calderwood 1842–9: v 160–1.
112 Melville 1829: 198.
113 Bothwell was no longer an earl and his

response to powerful magnates like
Bothwell was traditional, leaving their
local powers intact, involving them in
central government, and using non-
aristocratic officers of state.

estates were confiscated by the crown.

[114] *RPCS* iv 753.

[115] Akrigg 1984: 118.

[116] Birrel 1798: 30.

[117] *CSPS* xi 61–2.

[118] *CSPS* xi 62.

[119] See document 18.

[120] See chapter 7.

[121] *CSPS* xi 62. Indeed there is a gap in the books of adjournal immediately after the dittay of Euphame MacCalzean's trial.

[122] *CSPS* xi 62.

[123] *CSPS* xi 63.

[124] Akrigg 1984: 121.

[125] *Historie of James the Sext* 1825: 272.

[126] Akrigg 1984: 122.

[127] *CSPS* xi 133.

[128] James's public proclamation about the events of 24 July 1593 refers to Bothwell's 'protestacions that his intencions were as sincere and upright as the forme was suspitious and discommendabell, and therwithall craving exact tryall for the odious cryme of wytchcrafte objected against him, he faithfully promist to seperate frome him all his clientell and dependance . . . and to remaine our captyve and prisoner unto the tyme we should permyt him depart for preparing him self to his tryall forsaid', *CSPS* xi 133.

[129] *Historie of James the Sext* 1825: 272–3.

[130] See Brown 1986: 113: 'The coup was essentially a tool of minority politics, and became of decreasing use as the king grew older, a fact Bothwell failed to understand. Even his successful coup of 1593 could not last because the king could not accept it as a legitimating action, and Bothwell's only real option was to kill James'.

[131] *CSPS* xi 143–4.

[132] *CSPS* xi 143–4.

[133] Willson 1965: 113.

[134] Calderwood 1842–9: v 261.

[135] Donaldson 1965: 190.

[136] Willson 1965: 114.

[137] Brown 1986: 130, notes that 'The very intense factionalism and feuding in court politics which had characterised the years from the end of the Morton regency to the defeat of Huntly and Bothwell in 1594–5 was very much reduced thereafter by the growth in the king's own control over court politics'.

[138] Donaldson 1965: 194.

[139] *CSPS* xi 454.

[140] *CSPS* xi 544–5.

[141] Brown 1991: 62.

[142] Paul 1905: ii 169.

[143] See Cowan 1983: 139, who notes references to Bothwell being in the company of three Italian sorcerers in Brussels in 1598.

Chapter 2

Social Contexts and Cultural Formations

The witch hunt of the 1590s spread through central and east Scotland and the north-east, beginning at the same time as the North Berwick witch trials and continuing after they were over until about 1597. The conditions and causes of an early modern witch hunt are complex, and include ideology, law, religion, and the nature of the society where that hunt takes place. While none of these alone provides a complete explanation for a witch hunt, each contributes to the conditions necessary for accusations to be made, for prosecutions to be successful, and for a witch hunt to develop. These conditions are identified by Levack in his study of the European scene as 'conflict within communities, and, perhaps even more importantly, . . . a general mood of anxiety'.[1] Although sixteenth-century Scottish society was in many ways traditionalist and unchanging, social and economic changes were taking place that helped bring about witch hunting.[2] In addition, were there localised factors that would help explain the timing, location or personnel of the North Berwick witch hunt, or the kind of witchcraft they supposedly practised?

Levack distinguishes between witch hunts prompted 'from above', by members of the elite, and those started 'from below', out of quarrels among villagers.[3] If higher-class, educated men initiated prosecution then ideological and religious reasons may sufficiently explain their resort to laws against witchcraft; but if accusations came from lower-class accusers then social and economic factors are more likely to provide an explanation, and may indeed assume 'paramount importance'.[4] However, the sharp distinction between elite and popular witchcraft, although an essential conceptual difference, is often obscure in particular historical situations, where elite and popular notions actually blur, overlap, and influence each other. Recent research has shown how 'close and complex the relationships were between printed and oral media, urban and rural communities, and different levels of the local and national social hier-archy'.[5] The North Berwick witch hunt offers a striking example of a king's ideas being influenced by interviews with witchcraft suspects, while those suspects' confessions were being directed into accounts of treason and conspiracy that suited the elite's power politics. Judicial records show local wise women working their magic on an everyday level for members of the local gentry in the country and the towns. In Scotland at least, peasant magical practitioners and influential and wealthy people had many dealings with each other. The witch hunt involved prosecution by members of the ruling class, with David Seton a baillie depute initiating an early accusation, then the king supervising other accusations, and culminating in the action against the earl of Bothwell, and against Euphame MacCalzean and Barbara Napier, both associated with the ruling class. But it also involved accusations from lower-class villagers, especially as the hunt continued throughout Scotland in the years up to 1597. The events suggest a movement from local and non-elite accusations mainly in one local area (East Lothian) towards accusations at the centre by the crown and its agents (from late 1590 to 1593), and a simultaneous movement from 1590 out again (to other parts of the country) and down (in class terms) to a widespread witch hunt in several regions which lasted until 1597.[6] The complex-ity of this situation is increased still further by the fact that a politically motivated witchcraft accusation was brought against a member of the ruling class, the earl of Bothwell.

Witchcraft beliefs permeated every social and cultural level of late sixteenth-century Scotland.[7] All those involved in the witch hunt of 1590–1 in whatever way—as accused, accusers, jurymen, onlookers, or consumers of witchcraft publications—drew much of their understanding of what Scottish witchcraft was and how it worked from 'a pool of shared cultural meanings'.[8] However, the evidence for cultural meanings is asymmetrical, with more evidence available for elite than popular culture. Lawyers, ministers, diarists, historians, and James himself, were able to express interpretation of events more readily than the accused of whatever class. More information is needed about the social and cultural life of the lower social classes generally, particularly about what their cultural activities meant to them.[9] In what follows certain features of religion, politics and popular belief are identified as possible sources and forms of meaning of this Scottish witch hunt. What emerges are the ways that certain elements in the stories of the accused have a logic, meaning and significance in relation to the culture of late sixteenth-century Scotland.

One of the many remarkable things that emerges from the examinations and depositions of those accused of witchcraft, especially Agnes Sampson, is an interaction between peasant women and people from higher social classes. The Scottish witches demonstrate this exchange between different social and cultural worlds. The accused in this witch hunt are drawn from the lowest social levels ('Grey Meal' was a ploughman, Geillis Duncan a servant), from the peasantry (Sampson), from the lairds' wives who employed Sampson, from ruling-class women from legal and burgess families in Edinburgh (Napier and MacCalzean), and from the nobility (Bothwell).

Lyndal Roper has argued that witchcraft accusation and confession should not be thought of as being one-sided: as either an accused simply recounting events to a listening questioner, or a questioner simply imposing his fantasies on a compliant accused. Rather, she argues that accusation and confession involved a two-way traffic, with the accused sometimes collaborating with accusers to produce stories within a witchcraft scenario that satisfied the ideological needs of both interrogators and accused, what Larner calls 'an agreed story between witch and inquisitor'. In such circumstances, the interrogated person might be thought of, in Larner's words, as drawing 'through hallucination or imagination, on a common store of myth, fantasy, and nightmare'.[10] Or she might be thought of, according to Roper, as not merely 'a conduit . . . of the witch beliefs of her interrogators', but as creating her confessions 'out of the elements of fantasy available to her, from what her culture knew of the Devil and his ways', with what she selected having a logic.[11] Thus one might think of accusation and confession not only as transactions involving individuals, but also the communities and cultures which produced them. Roper's notion of logic shifts the emphasis from Larner's idea of fantasy towards the social. That logic is not only internal to the confessions themselves but also external, in their relationship to what has been called 'precise sociological forms'.[12] This relation is one of congruence between the ideological forms in the language recorded in the texts and produced through the processes of investigation, trial, propaganda and theorisation (represented in this witch hunt respectively by depositions, dittays, *News from Scotland*, and *Demonology*), and those forms as they appear in social, political and religious life—here collectively called culture. It would be a mistake to expect to find any particular cultural formation or context to be exactly identifiable or definable, since it will be subject to many variables, or to find exact correspondences between linguistic and cultural materials. Nevertheless, interrelations can be identified between what appears in the written records and what is in the culture. The surviving evidence of this witch hunt is textual, and reports actions and sequences of actions out of which stories gradually emerge that satisfy the listeners (examiners, assizers, or readers). These written records demonstrate how, in Natalie Zemon Davis's words, 'through narrative [speakers and listeners] made sense of the unexpected and built coherence into immediate experience'. But in addition they give evidence of how 'the rules for plot in these judicial tales . . . interacted with wider contemporary habits of explanation, description, and evaluation', and how 'possible story lines [were] determined by the constraints of the law . . . or derived from other cultural constructions'.[13]

Peasant insecurity

In the closing decades of the sixteenth century 'the Scottish economy passed through a critical and turbulent phase'.[14] Part of this turbulence was produced by the economic innovations of James's reign which made the period one of 'considerable economic dynamism'.[15] But the sense of change and crisis was also the result of the repeated natural disasters of harvest failure and plague that occurred during those decades throughout Scotland, and that led to widespread famine and poverty, including a subsistence crisis in the mid-1590s.[16] There were outbreaks of plague in 1568–9, 1574, 1584–8 and 1597–9.[17] These disasters occurred before and during the major witch hunt of 1590–7, increasing social instability and anxiety.[18]

Sixteenth-century Scotland was largely a rural, peasant society, with only about a quarter or a fifth of its population living in its small and scattered towns.[19] Peasant farm settlements in the Lowlands mostly consisted of a number of joint tenants working a farmtoun together, scattered hamlets dotted across arable land with rough ground separating them. Places named in the depositions and dittays, such as Gosford, Nether Keith or Saltoun, were probably no more than a few dwellings and perhaps a church. Smout describes 'the ground everywhere lying as open as moorland, studded with thickets of broom and gorse but unprotected from the sweeping winds by woods or planted rows of trees and seldom divided in any way by hedge, wall or dyke, apart from the broad earthen 'head dyke'.[20] It was over such a dyke that the devil was conjured on one occasion by Agnes Sampson.[21]

Poverty and distress intensified in the last quarter of the sixteenth century. Peasant farming was subsistence farming, with the result that 'smaller tenants must have lived their lives on the verge of poverty, terribly vulnerable to the effects of even a single poor harvest'.[22] In the second half of the sixteenth century 'there are 24 years of scarcity (local or national) mentioned in the sources, when people starved to death'.[23] Even as James's army was marching north against the rebel earl of Huntly in 1594, 'sundry of the King's army died for want of food'.[24] People in the country responded to acute food shortages by seeking poor relief from their parish, or abandoning their holdings and making for the towns. Famines and a growing population led to social dislocation in both rural and urban areas. For some poor country women the benefit they gained from witchcraft was not luxury but just absence of want, a low level material security that was unknown to them. The devil typically promised his servants 'ye shall never want', or specifically food for themselves and their bairns.

Edinburgh

While most towns in sixteenth-century Scotland were tiny, with populations in thousands, Edinburgh was growing fast, from 12,000 in 1560 to around 18,000 in 1600. Edinburgh's population included merchants whose wealth gave them social and political influence, and whose trade made Leith the major exporting centre. The city's lawyers, who included judges, advocates, clerks of court, and notaries, were an increasingly influential group in the sixteenth century. Legal dynasties were becoming established, including the families of David MacGill of Cranstoun Riddell, James's prosecutor in witchcraft trials, and of Chancellor Maitland. In 1565 Thomas MacCalzean, father of Euphame MacCalzean, was assessed for taxes, along with John Moscrop, at the highest band of £100, while David McGill was assessed at half that amount. These lawyers' surnames recur in the witchcraft records, for by the late sixteenth century lawyers 'possessed cohesion arising to some extent from the ties of kinship and to a greater extent from a considerable degree of homogeneity in social background'.[25] In Euphame MacCalzean James was accusing of witchcraft a wealthy heiress with powerful supporters among the lawyers.

Edinburgh itself was hardly one geographical unit: outside the limits of the old city walls lay the burgh of regality of the Canongate, which lay between the Netherbow and the abbey and royal palace of Holyroodhouse; and to the north lay the port of Leith.[26] The Canongate, as contemporary views of the city show, had a 'more spacious lay-out and relaxed atmosphere', and had become a 'residential suburb for courtiers and members of the central administration'. It had also become a 'safe haven, tantalisingly just outside Edinburgh's jurisdiction, for burgesses seeking to evade their civic duties and also for catholics'.[27] Edinburgh burgesses were one of several centres of power in the city, sufficiently independent-minded to acquit the Edinburgh woman Barbara Napier on three counts of witchcraft in 1591.

East Lothian and Catholicism

East Lothian society gives evidence of the uneasy coexistence of catholicism and protestantism among the peasantry, the laird class, and the nobility. That same mixture of old and reformed religious elements emerges in the witchcraft records. According to Larner, for witches the 'principal source of charms were the prayers of the pre-Reformation church'.[28]

In East Lothian 'the reformed ministry made slow headway',[29] and the reformation was received with little enthusiasm among ordinary people, many of whom clung to remnants of the old faith. When George Wishart appeared in Haddington in 1546 to preach the reform of religion, he attracted fewer than a hundred listeners after the then earl of Bothwell warned against heretical doctrine.[30] The spread of protestant ministers into this area was slow; in 1569 an East Lothian priest was summoned before the privy council to explain why the parishioners of Whitekirk had 'never heard the word twice preached, nor received the sacraments, since the Reformation';[31] in North Berwick in 1571 the minister was in charge of no fewer than four churches, and three years later two of those still did not have a minister.[32] Occasionally signs of anti-protestant feeling appeared openly in the area. Although Haddington and Tranent had a reformed ministry before 1562, in 1583, during the exile in England of the minister of Haddington, James Carmichael, the general assembly of the kirk dissolved the presbytery of Haddington 'be reasone of many enormities occurrand there—as rare [infrequent] convention of the brether [brethren], loathsomeness and contempt of the word in the people'.[33] In Haddington in 1593 the schoolmaster put on a play in which a pupil baptised a cat 'in derision of the kirk'.[34] Ideological incoherence, especially at the popular level, resulted from protestantism entering the locality in which attachment to the old religion was strong, and was supported by a powerful local family. Survivals of catholic rituals and belief, especially in decayed forms (such as some of the healing with prayers recorded in the depositions), were easily lumped together with older beliefs and practices, and categorised by the reformers as diabolic. Protestants campaigned against both cunning folk and catholics, though the distinction was often unclear.[35]

The Setons and Catholicism

Sanderson notes that indigenous catholicism in Scotland was on the wane in the 1570s, but thanks to 'Jesuit and other missionary priests from abroad and to the public protection of those known as the "Catholic Party", whose aims were often political' there was a resurgence of catholic practice in the 1580s and 1590s.[36] Reformers were frustrated in their attempts to win government support for the punishment of catholics. This odd situation is illustrated by the Seton family, one of whose members, David Seton, was credited in *News from Scotland* with starting the witch hunt. But although Seton Palace was used as a prison for accused witches, and depositions were taken there, and on 19 June 1591 Lord Robert Seton was present when a notary public took a statement from Janet Stratton that her previous testimony against Bothwell was false,[37] the Setons did not play a direct part in the witch hunt. The Setons' influence on the surrounding area was more general, for their recusancy inhibited the spread of protestant belief, offered protection to catholic proselytisers, and sustained the idea of non-conformity itself. In this and many similar locations the reformers' 'ideal of uniformity' turned out to be impossible.[38] Support for catholicism and resistance to reform came from Seton Palace where a catholic chaplain was maintained in the household during this period.[39] In 1573 in Tranent the benefice holder was deprived for failure to subscribe to the reformed Articles of Faith; and in Seton Palace clergy were reported to have celebrated the catholic mass.[40]

The Setons' influence may be gauged from the splendour of their family seat, and from their royal connections. Fynes Moryson, travelling in the 1590s, was impressed by 'the ancient and . . . stately Pallace of the Lord Seton beautified with faire Orchards and Gardens, and for that clime pleasant'.[41] The palace was 'during the sixteenth and seventeenth centuries . . . regarded as the most magnificent structure of the kind in Scotland', and was one of the places where James stayed in 1589 while anxiously awaiting the arrival of his bride from Denmark.[42] Setons held powerful positions in the courts of both Mary queen of Scots and James.

Although the parishes of Seton and Tranent were joined in 1580, Seton Palace still had its own chapel in 1589, and the presbytery of Haddington applied to Lord Seton to appoint a minister to it. Three years later the chapel still had no minister, and William Setoun, 'pretendit provist of Seton', appeared before the presbytery to explain.[43] Throughout the 1580s and 1590s Jesuit activity was reported in the Haddington area, as well as in Seton itself.[44] In East Lothian the national religious conflict was mirrored in the conflict of reforming ministers and the catholic Setons.

The North Berwick nunnery

Curiously, none of the 'North Berwick witches' came from North Berwick, yet its church features as the striking location of the convention reported in *News from Scotland* that was to give a name to the whole witch hunt. As the fragmentary stories extracted in judicial examinations were pieced together to form a grand narrative, so North Berwick emerged as the crucial locale.

North Berwick has a striking position overlooking the Forth estuary and is marked by a law, a conical volcanic hill that is topped with the ramparts of an iron age fort.[45] The law is visible as a dramatic landmark from the High Street in Edinburgh. In one of the earliest surviving examinations, Agnes Sampson's confession that 'she was on large law head'[46] suggests the importance of such a place in the popular imagination. In the town the old parish church, now in ruins, in which the witches supposedly gathered also has a striking setting, situated on a promontory, on which there was also a hospital and graveyard.

North Berwick had long-standing associations with the old religion in its Cistercian nunnery, as well as in being the point of embarkation for sea crossings for pilgrims *en route* to the shrine of St Andrew in Fife, with its relics of Scotland's patron saint. The ferry between North Berwick and Earlsferry in Fife was known as the pilgrim's ferry.[47] As early as the eighth century a chapel existed on what was then a small island a few metres off the coast that was later built up to form a promontory. When the annual flow of pilgrims reached about ten thousand in the fourteenth century, the landowner, the earl of Douglas, built a hospital on the island that was run by nuns. It was to this ferry landing and the church, both on the promontory, that the witches were supposed to have sailed. The story recalls the religiously inspired sailing which had gone on there for centuries, as well as memories of a women's community

North Berwick's Cistercian nunnery was founded about 1150. By the middle of the sixteenth century its income was second only to its larger sister house at Haddington.[48] In 1560 there were still sixteen nuns in North Berwick. Apart from their religious duties, the nuns were responsible for the hospital for the poor and pilgrims.[49] Such hospitals were administered by a secular priest, usually accorded the title of master, warden or prior, and inmates were normally addressed as 'brethren' or 'sisters'.[50] This communal structure offers an intriguing model for the social organisation of the witches' convention, as related in *News from Scotland*, with the male Fian supporting the women's activities by acting as register to the devil.

In Scotland there was no dissolution of the religious houses as in England; instead they faded away.[51] The North Berwick nunnery became the property of the Humes of Polwarth, with secular women of that family assuming the title of prioress;[52] as in other pre-Reformation religious houses the surviving religious were allowed to remain, and the house was finally dissolved when only one or two remained. In 1580 there were two remaining nuns. The priory buildings were said to be ruinous in 1587. In 1595 one nun was still alive, Margaret Donaldson, who was required to subscribe to the house's final dissolution in 1596.[53] When the women accused of witchcraft were producing their stories of the convention in North Berwick, they were drawing on the long history of a nunnery that was not yet quite extinct, though the property and income had passed into men's hands.

Women's lives

Women's legal status in sixteenth-century Scotland was more restricted than men's, though there were some areas of comparative freedom. A woman could inherit land and property from her father or husband if they had no male descendants, which seems to have been the case with Barbara Napier, whose father and husband had both died. According to Larner, 'women appear to have retained a considerable amount of independence on marriage, and the fact that they did not take on their husband's name may have been symbolic of such independence'.[54] Euphame MacCalzean is always referred to by this name: her husband is always referred to as Patrick Moscrop (e.g. 'Patrick Moscrop, your husband'), and her dittay is headed 'Euphame MacCalzean, spouse to Patrick MacCalzean alias Moscrop'. Euphame MacCalzean, as heiress of Lord Cliftonhall and wife of Patrick Moscrop, was a woman of considerable means, with 'lands, heritages, tacks, steadings, rooms, possessions, corns, cattle, goods and gear' that are recorded at the end of her dittay as forfeited. Women had no status in court, being placed in the same category as children and convicted felons, and were not allowed to give evidence. However, a decision of 1591 specifically allowed women's evidence in witchcraft cases.[55]

Recent research discloses a high degree of social mobility for some women at the lower as well as the higher levels of society, particularly among the young. Hired labourers and servants changed employers frequently; seasonal agricultural workers travelled from the Highlands to the Lowlands for harvests;

beggars were travelling throughout the year.[56] In East Lothian and Edinburgh there were particular reasons for poor women to travel as they brought produce from the country, or fish landed by their husbands at the villages along the coast, to sell in Edinburgh markets.[57] Town and country were closely interconnected, allowing exchange of news and gossip as well as produce for sale; and markets were largely women's places. The depositions and dittays of the witch trials record many journeys by women, especially Agnes Sampson, in East Lothian. And indeed in *News from Scotland* one aspect of witches' fearful power is supernatural travel, an intensification of women's usual freedom to travel.

Oral culture was more significant in most women's lives than men's, and certain places and activities were largely the preserve of women: 'the market, the household and the well, or the event of child-birth', as well as healing, medicine and magic.[58] The market was where women fashioned reputations for themselves and others, including men, further afield and beyond their social class. The knowledge women traditionally possessed involved areas where magic might operate: 'they watched over animals which could die mysteriously, prepared food which could become spoiled inexplicably, nursed the ill of all ages who could die without warning, and cared for children who were even more subject to disease and death than adults'.[59] Some women like Agnes Sampson developed their healing skills and earned extra income for such services. Women's lower educational levels largely excluded them from participation in political and cultural influence, and so made them more reliant on conservative, popular culture. Agnes Sampson's prayer is a popular version of the Roman creed, suggesting a continuing attachment to old catholic practices. As the social ambitions of the male, protestant intellectual elite shifted decisively towards the realisation of God's kingdom in Scotland through intensified moral control and a reformed religious polity, women's ways, whether as remnants of catholicism or as magical healing, were increasingly liable to come under suspicion of witchcraft.

Women themselves were often the accusers of other women, and arraignments cannot be simply explained as victimisation by male elites. Women's lives contained their own internal dangers and instabilities. Larner states that it 'is hard to overemphasise the importance of reputation in the production of a witch in Scotland', for the 'evidence' that created a women's reputation as a witch—the gossip exchanged at market, in the fields or the alehouse, or between mistress and servants—was the same evidence that convicted her in a legal trial.[60] Gossip policed the boundaries of the socially permissible or respectable, and created and sustained reputations. Men generally had access to a wider range of social action to create and protect their reputations—including physical violence, recourse to law, and economic or social power—and in any case were less dependent than women on sexual behaviour for their reputation.[61] But women trod a difficult line between conforming to their subordinate status in society and possessing enough forcefulness and independence to live successfully in precarious social and economic conditions.[62] Women's vulnerability lay in the difficulty of managing sexual reputation and social assertiveness; losing control of either and gaining a reputation as a sexually scandalous woman or a quarreller or scold could create the conditions in which a charge of witchcraft might emerge. Some women might have been happy to accept the roles of healer, promiscuous woman, or scold for the benefits they might bring. Women who were feared for their personal forcefulness, or their knowledge of their neighbours through dealing with them over matters involving magic, would be protected from attack by those very powers and knowledge. And such women might gain material benefit from their reputation: neighbours 'would be less likely to refuse assistance, and the wood, grain, or milk which she needed to survive would be given to her or paid as fees for her magical services such as finding lost objects, attracting desirable suitors, or harming enemies'.[63] But it was an unstable role, and if social antagonisms overcame fear, or social pressures redefined the witch as evil and dangerous, then women with such reputations became vulnerable. The oscillation in the relation between a wise woman and her patient, between helping and harming, can be seen in item 39 of Agnes Sampson's dittay.

A disciplinary regime

Pressure was exerted for changes in the moral, and particularly sexual, behaviour of a reluctant population through the local kirk sessions. The disciplinary powers of the reformers that aimed at establishing a godly society were founded on the 'recognition that a person excommunicated from the spiritual society of the church for persistent immorality was also an outlaw from the civil society of the state'.[64] However, the kirk's power to effect social change was not exercised uniformly: 'as the highest in society held aloof, and the lowest kicked against it, it was the middling classes, the lairds, burgesses, and ministers, who accepted discipline with enthusiasm'.[65] Sexual misdemeanours attracted much of the kirk sessions' attention.[66] In the process of acculturation, by which the religious elite with a clear ideological programme planned to effect social changes, witchcraft, magic and other traditional beliefs and practices came to represent activities of the devil. The kirk was notably successful in realising this programme of discipline, achieving what Cowan has described as 'an involvement between church and society that has never been surpassed', in which the 'indifference of the pre-Reformation church had been replaced by an intense interest in the lives of each individual member of society'.[67] Discipline worked in complex ways, ideologically, socially, subjectively. In the reformed church's long process of discipline moments of crisis occurred concerning the identification of the sinful. How do the godly recognise and punish the sinful; and can the sinful harm the godly? Witchcraft provided simple answers to these complex, elusive questions.

Pilgrimages

The assemblies' deliberations reveal that discipline was a persistent and protract-ed endeavour. Old catholic observances, such as pilgrimage, were condemned. But the church's difficulties in getting rid of pilgrimages is evident in its having to forbid its own ministers from supporting them: in 1583 it condemned ministers who supported 'the people repairing in pilgrimage to wells hard besyde their awne houses, not reproving them, but rather entertayning them with meat and drink in their houses'.[68]

The idea of witches' sailing to and from North Berwick recalls pilgrims' voyages of earlier decades. The pilgrims' ferry provides sufficient antecedent for witches sailing to North Berwick, but there are other possible sources for this motif. In seafaring villages witches are commonly accused of sailing and sinking ships. And the stormy voyages of King James and Queen Anne across the North Sea provided dramatic stories of dangerous sailing and leaky ships that reappeared in confessions. Pilgrims' voyages provide a prototype that associates sailing with spiritual intentions and hoped-for miraculous events. Pilgrimages, although forbidden, were still being undertaken, and the kirk repeatedly requested the crown to act more decisively against them.

Pilgrimages were not necessarily solemn or even virtuous affairs. They afforded pleasures away from the limits of ordinary life. People on pilgrimage enjoyed a festive release which, increasingly in the sixteenth century, prompted the criticism and hostility of moralists. Sir David Lyndsay, writing early in the century, describes young people joining a pilgrimage to Loretto for the fun and sexual opportunities it afforded:[69]

> I have sene pass one mervellous multytude,
>   Yong men and wemen, flyngand on thare feit,
> Under the forme of feynit santytude,
>   For tyll adore one image in Loreit.
>   Mony came with thare marrowis for to meit,
> Committand thare fowll fornicatioun:
>   Some kyst the claggit taill of the Armeit:
> Quhy thole ye this abominatioun?[70]

Lyndsay uses elements which recur in versions of the witches' convention in depositions and *News from Scotland*: a large group of men and women gather together from different places in high good humour ('flying on their feet') to a chapel or church. The pilgrims use the occasion to have sex, though the witches do not. The revelry of both groups involves crude physicality when the witches kiss the devil's arse and the pilgrims the hermit's. Lyndsay protests at the obscene kiss; but he does not object to the pilgrimage itself. He writes as a proto-reformer wishing to see a pious activity shorn of its 'abominatioun', and protests at carnival's temporary overturning of the decorous, moral everyday world. The protestant writer of *News from Scotland* does not countenance the idea of popular ritual at all. Instead, he presents the scene of festivity in *News*, with its drinking, music and dancing, as an inversion of the entire godly order, as a diabolic activity to be condemned in its entirety. What first emerge in the examinations and interrogations of witchcraft suspects are materials that draw on cultural memories including pilgrimages and their pleasures.

The reform of popular culture

A report in the kirk session records of Perth illustrates the objections the kirk made to certain popular social customs: it bans young men and women from going to a place with pagan associations, from processing through the town playing musical instruments, and expresses fear of the sexual activity the ritual involves:

> Because that the Assembly of Ministers and Elders understand, that the resorting to the Draggon Hole, as well by young men as women, with their piping, and drums striking before them, through the Town, has raised no small slander to this Congregation, not without suspicion of filthiness after to follow thereupon; for avoiding whereof in times coming, the said Assembly, with consent of the Magistrates of this Town, hes statute and ordained, that no person hereafter of this Congregation, neither man nor woman, resort nor repair hereafter, to the said Draggon Hole, as they have done in tymes bygone, namely, in the month of May; neither pass through the Town, with piping and striking of drums, as heretofore they have done, under the pain of twenty shillings to the poor to every person, as well man as woman that contravene hereof.[71]

The church tried to prohibit or restrict dancing, carol singing, plays, card-playing, drunkenness, gluttony, celebrations at weddings and burials, fine clothes, and 'filthie and bawdie speeches'.[72] That it had repeatedly to re-enact such prohibitions indicated widespread disregard or resistance to its puritan agenda. The king himself opposed the narrow moral agenda of the presbyterians and when he succeeded in reintroducing episcopacy into Scotland from 1600 their influence was for a time diminished. But in the last quarter of the century the reformers exerted pressure, particularly on the lower orders of society, for changes in behaviour.[73] Bans on customs such as those enjoyed at Perth offered the participants a choice between obedience and conforming to the values of the kirk, or defiance and continuing the custom secretly, thus overlaying social behaviour that was previously innocuous with political challenge and even subversion. It may be that *News from Scotland*'s representation of the meeting, drinking and dancing of women and men accused of witchcraft drew on no more than traditional popular pastime. In the context of general prohibitions such a meeting could easily be represented as political insubordination or subversion of the godly order.

The pursuit of protestant conformity in the later years of the sixteenth century involved charges against parishioners concerning what Sanderson calls 'the "popular" side of the old faith', including its elements of paganism: festivals, saints' days, pilgrimages, fire rituals, well dressing, guizers (people disguised), and magic.[74] The kirk repeatedly called on the king and council to act against 'enormities' which in 1591 included 'pilgrimagers' along with 'Jesuites, . . . profainers of the Sacraments; . . . idolaters, . . . papistical Magistrates, . . . publick mercatts upon the Sabbath day; violent invaders of Ministers be strikeing of them or shedding of thair blood; . . . Robein Hoodes playis; murderers and blood shedders quhilk overflow the land'.[75] But popular practices persisted. In other parts of Europe too certain feasts and vigils were accompanied by popular dancing, often carols or round dances, in the churchyards and sometimes even in the church itself. Peter Burke discovered churches and churchyards being used during the night prior to the feast of their patron saint for 'eating, drinking, singing and dancing', indicating popular understandings of the sacred 'more intimate, more familiar than they were later to become'.[76] The supposed dancing in North Berwick churchyard may have recalled such a gathering. In 1599 in Elgin twenty-two girls were charged with having sung carols in the ruins of the cathedral at Christmas.[77] Also in Elgin people visiting the shrine at Garioch were questioned about the names of other visitors, a situation that resembles accused witches being pressured to name their associates. Clandestine meetings with catholic priests dressed in black might easily be redescribed as meetings with the devil, as in the case of Elisabeth Burn in 1599 who, seeking to have her child baptised, 'met strangers whom she knew not, of whom one clad with a black plaid baptised the child'.[78] As Clark has indicated, the aim pursued by reformers was 'not merely for better doctrine or even improved morals, but for fundamental changes in popular culture'.[79] Clark identifies protestant demonology arising at this 'intersection of clerical and popular culture, with the result that . . . a very wide range of proscribed behaviour, most of it far removed from the classic stereotype of devil-worship' came to be included in 'witchcraft'.[80] When the kirk campaigned against witchcraft in the 1590s it found royal support. Witchcraft became the platform on which a wide range of popular beliefs and practices, including some catholic ones, could be pursued.

Traditional beliefs were seen as particularly the province of women. Healing consisted of traditional knowledge and practices that were a blend of religion, magic and medicine, depending on oral transmission. The beliefs of the women who 'went on pilgrimages to "Christ's Hole", a medieval holy place, to try to cure their illnesses' in sixteenth-century Stirlingshire, were a mixture of catholicism, magic and medicine.[81] The reformed kirk was zealous to reject those religious objects from catholic practice that seemed to involve magic (rosaries, crucifixes, images of saints) and practices that seemed to invoke even older pagan beliefs (bonfires, and pilgrimages to wells, trees, and old chapels).[82] It was ordinary parishioners, according to Wormald, 'who were far more vulnerable than the rich and powerful to this kind of onslaught'. Wormald mentions the case of Isabel Umphray, who was 'warned by the Elgin kirk Session not to frequent the Chanonry kirk (by the 1590s used only for private prayer), or "to pray on her bairn's grave"', and comments that such women were 'remote from the great doctrinal changes, conservative, confused in heart and mind, denied traditional, and, to them, harmless comfort'.[83] Popular customs could be assimilated by educated members of the elite into notions of witchcraft such as those found in *Demonology*, and practitioners of such customs could find their behaviour demonised. Such seems to have been the case with Agnes Sampson's magical healing and memories of catholic prayers.

Politics

The organisation of witchcraft that the North Berwick witch hunt of 1590–1 uncovered, or projected in fantasy, corresponded in certain features to familiar forms of religious and political organisation. The witches' meetings are referred to as 'conventions', a word used to denote one of the three major institutions of government, namely parliament, convention, and privy council.[84] A convention could be assembled at shorter notice, and involve fewer representatives than a parliament, but it still had wide powers. It is appropriate to the notion of political witchcraft that emerged from this witch hunt that the witches' meetings should be imagined as an assembly for decision and action. In this scenario the devil takes on a political role with the same relation to the witches' convention as James in relation to a convention of estates, and is even subject to criticism as James was. The notion of convention politicises witchcraft activity and moulds it into a form from national politics.

As part of Scotland's protestant movement in the early and mid-sixteenth century privy kirks were formed. Protestants at the end of the century might discover in witchcraft 'conspiracy' a repetition of a revolutionary strategy devised by a previous generation of protestants. Protestantism began as 'a clandestine, underground movement' in about 1525 until the Reformation in 1560 when, in John Knox's words, it 'took on a public face'.[85] In the 1550s privy kirks emerged in various towns in opposition to the established faith and as an alternative mode of religious organisation. Their organisation was cellular, and a 'strikingly radical feature of [them was] . . . the role played in them by men from humble origins'.[86] According to Lynch, the privy kirks 'promised the unprivileged masses an active stake in a godly future to come', and the people involved included 'apprentices and journeyman elected to office as elders and deacons',[87] though such privilege did not last long after 1560.

Privy kirks had analogies with the version of witchcraft organisation that emerges from the court cases and is explicated in *Demonology*. The privy kirks were 'a popular movement' in which people broke away from the established church to form 'their own separate communities of believers, worshipping in secret' in a 'shadowy underground world'. As heretics they risked hanging for attending their meetings. They came to see themselves as 'a congregation of believers', with groups existing in various parts of the country. Their preaching, like the witches' charming, took place, according to a hostile commentator, 'in chimlay nuikis [chimney nooks], secreit holes and sik privat places, to truble the hail cuntrie'.[88]

For the protestant accusers of witches the memory of the privy kirks might warn them of witchcraft as an alternative, subversive religion. Since the king responded to Roman catholic activity by downplaying and even ignoring it, catholicism could not figure as the major danger to protestantism. Instead, witchcraft is shaped as a conspiracy that repeats aspirations and long-term goals of protestantism's initiators: the overthrow of the established faith and its political protectors, and its replacement with another faith. The militant protestants who from the 1570s directed their attention to the establishment of a godly kirk and the discipline of the people, defined witches as one of their principal enemies.

Bands

When witches supposedly met the devil they pledged their allegiance to him by making 'oaths for their good and true service towards him'. This pact was first made between witch and devil alone and might later be collectively confirmed at a convention, and it is a version of the band made by men, individually or collectively, declaring their allegiance to a person or cause in a social or political context.[89] Bands had long been familiar enough in Scottish society[90] for this idea to emerge from the minds of the women interrogated or from the interrogators as a way of representing a group 'bound together by sworn pledges of fidelity'.[91] Bands provide an indigenous Scottish model for the satanic pact.[92]

In 1557 the reformation began with a group of protestant lords signing the First Band, pledging to 'maintain and forward, with all their might, the most blessed word of God and His Congregation and to forsake and renounce the Congregation of Satan'.[93] This band 'transformed the traditional concept [of the band] into . . . a pledge to fulfil the law of God irrespective of the wishes of the temporal power'.[94] Other religious bands followed. In March 1590 the general assembly cooperated with the privy council on a national band requiring nobles, barons and gentlemen to promise to defend the true religion against the 'present danger threatened', and 'to conveen and assemble ourselves publickly with our friends, in armes, or in quiet maner, at such times and places, as we shall be required by his Majesties proclamatiouns'.[95] Even the group of court poets and musicians whom James gathered round him in the 1580s were known as 'the Castalian band'. When the English agent Burgh arrived in Scotland in 1593 he tried to form an Anglophile faction by having men subscribe to a band, since, as he wrote, 'this manner of action is not strange in Scotland, for it is very usual there to make bands of mutual defence and offence'.[96] One of Chancellor Maitland's key policies in 1587–92 was 'a vigorous program of public banding'.[97] So the idea of the demonic pact was congruent with prevailing social practice. The witches pledging their obedience to Satan were imitating a political technique for the establishment of political solidarity and a shared purpose. The witches' interrogators 'discovering' the demonic band seemed to be discovering a familiar social practice.

This section has isolated certain features of the witch hunt as common aspects of a collective, cultural experience of the 1590s, and investigated how they might relate to the ordinary social world. The material in the witchcraft texts did not come from nowhere: much is drawn from historical memory, local experience, and political and religious ideology. The familiar method in witchcraft studies of distinguishing elite and popular cultures is useful to some extent in identifying where particular cultural forms have originated. Notions of convention and band are more likely to be elite understandings of supposed witchcraft activities than the accused's self-perception, though we cannot be sure. Details of magical healing practices are more likely to have originated from the accused than the educated interrogators. But the elite/popular distinction should not obscure the fact that there was exchange among different social levels concerning the cultural formations that found their way into accounts of witchcraft; and, more importantly, the accounts of witchcraft that finally emerged were meangingful to people from a wide social range, educated as well as uneducated. It was in the meaningfulness of witchcraft stories that their usefulness for the kirk lay in intensifying social control, and for the king in enhancing his authority.

The educated who pursued witchcraft prosecutions provided the ideological frame for the evidence of the accused, summarised in the dittays and theorised in *Demonology*. The details of sorcery, *maleficium* and magic produced by the accused were appropriated by the authorities and relocated within their ideological frame. That very frame was shaped to local conditions, however, as in the case of 'band', and indeed all the participants in the witch hunt responded to the local conditions of the culture, history and politics of 1590s Scotland.

Whether what they narrate is real is irrelevant to understanding the social force of the witchcraft texts. The important point is rather that once witchcraft stories emerge they should be meaningful; and this requires a set of common cultural contexts and formations of the kind described here.

Notes

1 Levack 1995: 127.
2 Detailed discussions of society and the economy in sixteenth-century Scotland can be found in the following items, from which this section of the introduction is largely drawn: Lythe 1960; Smout 1972; Lythe 1973; Larner 1981; Lynch 1981; Wormald 1981; Sanderson 1982; Sanderson 1987; Leneman 1988; Houston 1989; Whyte 1995; Whyte 1997.
3 Levack 1995: 126–7.
4 Levack 1995: 127. See also Briggs 1996b: 53, who states that 'Perhaps the most crucial distinction is that between the endemic trials of individual witches and more concentrated episodes of witch

hunting. These latter in their turn differ sharply when conducted by members of the ruling elite from outbreaks whose main inspiration lay among the people.'

5   Hutton 1995: 112.

6   See Larner, Lee and McLachlan 1977: 3–10, 61, 173–80, 238–9, 248, who note that the witch hunt of 1590–7 occured 'mainly in Aberdeenshire, Fife, and the Lothians', but the records of those trials 'are mainly lost or contained in family papers', v, vii.

7   The evidence of this witch hunt supports Burke's contention that the learned had their own culture, but 'they also participated in popular culture' (Burke 1982: 201).

8   This phrase is Annabel Gregory's 1991: 52.

9   A point made by Whyte 1997: 54.

10   Larner 1981: 136.

11   Roper 1994: 244.

12   Muchembled 1993: 141, 'Any myth [such as satanism], in fact, is subject to precise sociological forms and does not exist as a mere category of the mind'.

13   Davis 1988: 4.

14   Lythe 1960: 110.

15   Lythe 1973: 61.

16   Whyte 1995: 122.

17   Whyte 1995: 122.

18   Wormald 1981: 169, writes that 'Reaction to economic instability is perhaps the one factor that may be ascribed to all the periods of witch-hunts'.

19   Smout 1972: 135; Larner 1981: 47.

20   Smout 1972: 112.

21   See document 2, 'She passed to the garden herself to devise upon her prayer, at what time she charged the devil, calling him "Eloa" to come and speak to her; who came in over the dyke in likeness of a [   ] dog'.

22   Houston and Whyte 1989: 54.

23   Wormald 1981: 167.

24   *CSPS* xi 470.

25   Donaldson 1976: 16,18.

26   Lynch 1981: 5.

27   Lynch 1981: 5–6.

28   Larner 1981: 140.

29   Cowan 1982: 103, 165.

30   For an account of Wishart's capture and death see McNeill 1884: 185–7.

31   Cowan 1978: 32.

32   Cowan 1982: 165.

33   *Booke of the Universall Kirk* 1839: 283.

34   Cowan 1978: 32.

35   See Clark 1993: 62–9.

36   Sanderson, in McNeill and Nicholson 1975: 89.

37   See document 15.

38   Sanderson, in McNeill and Nicholson 1975: 89.

39   Cowan 1982: 16.

40   McNeill and Nicholson 1975: 89, 204–5.

41   'An Itinerary Written by Fynes Moryson', in Brown 1891: 82.

42   Brown 1891: 82n.

43   McNeill 1884: 194: He 'denyit that the college kirk of Seton was ane benifice of cure, or ane parish kirk; but yet quhatsomever service was done thair, competant to be done in ane parish kirk, was done thair be dispensation, at least be the permissioun or tollerance of the vicar of Tranent; and that if it war ane benifice of cure, he ought not to serve the same but the ordinarie'.

44   McNeill and Nicholson 1975: 207.

45   Whyte and Whyte 1988: 15.

46   Document 13.

47   Simpson and Stevenson 1981: 18. North Berwick had a ferry-boat and the St Andrews cross in the town coat of arms, Ferrier 1980: 14.

48   Cowan and Easson 1976: 144, 147–8; McNeill and Nicholson 1975: 46, 159.

49   Cowan and Easson 1976: 148, 186; McNeill and Nicholson 1975: 48.

50   For an overview see McNeill and Nicholson 1975: 47–8; Durkan 1962: 116–29.

51   Donaldson 1960b: 74.

52   Sanderson 1987: 172 mentions 'Alexander Hume, son of the laird of Polwarth, who built a "New Wark" on to the conventual buildings [of North Berwick] in the 1560s'.

53   *Carte Monialium* 1847: xvi.

54   Larner 1981: 51.

55   Larner 1981: 51; see also *CSPS* x 522.

56   Houston 1989: 126–7; Mitchison 1974: 19; Whyte 1995: 130.

57   Houston 1989: 125.

58   Houston 1989: 138–9.

59   Wiesner 1993: 223–5.

60   Larner 1981: 103.

[61] Amussen 1988: 99.
[62] Amussen 1988: 121.
[63] Wiesner 1993: 225.
[64] Smout 1972: 74.
[65] Wormald 1981: 137.
[66] Smout 1972: 75.
[67] Cowan 1982: 138.
[68] *Booke of the Universall Kirk* 1839: 284.
[69] Quoted in Fleming 1910: 155.
[70] Modernised as:

> I have seen pass a marvellous multitude,
>> Young men and women, flying on
>>> their feet,
> Under the form of feigned sanctitude,
>> For to adore an image in Loretto.
>> Many came with their marrows for the
>>> meeting,
> Committing there foul fornication:
>> Some kissed the clagged tail [shitty
>>> arse] of the hermit:
> Why thole [suffer] ye this abomination?

[71] From 'Kirk Session Records of Perth', *Chronicle of Perth*, 52–3, quoted by Cowan 1960: 72.
[72] Smout 1972: 78.
[73] Wormald 1981: 137.
[74] Sanderson 1970: 104; Whyte 1997: 54.
[75] *Acts of the General Assemblies* 1840: 784.
[76] Burke 1978: 109. He also notes that 'the church was especially important as a cultural centre in regions where people lived in scattered homesteads', such as Scottish farmtouns.
[77] Cowan 1982: 156.
[78] From *Extracts from the Records of the Presbytery of Ellon* (ed. T. Mair, p. 12), cited by Sanderson 1970: 97.
[79] Clark 1993: 71.
[80] Clark 1993: 62.
[81] Houston 1989: 145.
[82] Wormald 1981: 136.
[83] Wormald 1981: 136.
[84] Wormald 1981: 20.
[85] Kirk 1989: 1; Lynch 1987: 291. For accounts of the privy kirks see Kirk 1989: 1–15; and Lynch 1983: 85–96.
[86] Kirk 1989: 1; Lynch 1983: 93.
[87] Lynch 1987: 291.
[88] Kirk 1989: 1, 2, 10, 12.
[89] For discussions of bands see Cowan 1982; Wormald 1985.
[90] See Wormald 1985, who traces the change from the early bonds of manrent and maintenance to the religious and political bonds of the mid to late sixteenth century.
[91] Burrell 1958: 339.
[92] Williamson 1979: 61–2, noted that the idea of the demonic pact arose at a time when 'presbyterian leaders like [James] Carmichael, Bruce, and Davidson had variously initiated considerable discussions in Scotland about covenants and the process of covenanting', and central government began using bands.
[93] Quoted in McRoberts 1962: xix. For discussion of the First Band, or Common Band, in the context of religious reform see Mason 1983: 97–126.
[94] Mason 1983: 100, who adds that 'like Knox, its signatories viewed adherence to divine law as part of their "contract" with God which promised them in return the assurance of eternal salvation'.
[95] *Acts of the General Assemblies* 1840: 760.
[96] *CSPS* xi 45; quoted by Brown 1987: 140, who adds that 'the factions created by these bands were notoriously pragmatic and short-lived'.
[97] Williamson 1979: 73.

Chapter 3

THE KIRK

The witchcraft trials of the early 1590s can only be fully understood in relation to the Scottish reformation.[1] Witchcraft trials were a mechanism through which some of the ideological struggles between church and crown were articulated and realised, particularly in relation to questions of spiritual and political authority. Witchcraft too was involved in the protestants' campaign for the reform of morality and social life; it was used by the church to redefine as evil an inchoate and diverse range of beliefs and practices that were found mostly, but not exclusively, among the lower social classes. Scottish protestants participated with European counterparts in the formation of a distinctly protestant demonology, though their opportunity to practise what they preached was untypical. The vision of the godly state extended into secular politics at both the local and national levels, and also into the secular law. In practice, by the 1580s and 1590s religious and secular authority overlapped in lowland Scotland, and the secular–religious distinction was blurring. Robert Bruce, minister of St Giles in Edinburgh and sometime moderator of the general assembly, was a privy councillor from 1589, and was present when Janet Kennedy was examined before King James in June 1591.[2] By 1590 the agenda, particularly of the extreme presbyterians, permeated political and social life, with witchcraft among the things it sought to extirpate. In Scotland 'witchcraft [was] at the very heart of the reforming process'.[3]

In the witchcraft texts in this book the practices of witches are often imagined as the other of the godly community and the kirk. This is not only the way that King James discusses witches' conventions in *Demonology* (II iii), but also the way they are presented in many of the dittays. The centre of attention at the witches' meeting on All Hallows' Eve is, after all, the devil occupying the pulpit in North Berwick kirk.

The spread and success of reform

Witchcraft prosecutions were facilitated by the efforts of kirk sessions, consisting of minister and elders, in parishes, and the programme of moral reform spearheaded by the new kirk. The witchcraft act itself is one of the acts of 1563 intended to reform morality: parliament criminalised, among other things, witchcraft and adultery in 1563, fornication in 1567, sabbath breaking in 1579, and drunkenness in 1617.[4] The 1590s were a crucial decade for the church both in its struggle for presbyterian church government, and hence its relations with the crown, and in its campaign for moral reform.

Reformation of religion in Scotland did not happen in one convulsive moment. Although 1560 is usually given as the date marking the reformation, it really marks the start of a long process of change and conflict which continued until the settlement of 1690. The vision of a new church and society in *The First Book of Discipline* was in 1560 only a vision; but by 1589 and the eve of the witch hunts it seemed that many of those aspirations had been, or were about to be, realised. Church organisation along presbyterian lines had been gaining ground since the mid-1580s, although it was not yet recognised by parliament. In 1589 the kirk was enjoying one of its temporary periods of cooperation with the government, and seemed well placed to press on with the moral transformation of society.

The reformation swept away the mass and catholic institutions. In their place reformers wanted to see a religion with three distinguishing features: the preaching of the 'Word', the administration of the reformed sacraments, and the establishment of godly discipline. In 1566 John Knox was writing as if this vision had already been realised:

> As touching the doctrine taught by our ministers and . . . the administration of Sacraments used in our Churches, we are bold to affirm that there is no realm this day upon the face of the earth that hath them in greater purity; yea (we must speak the truth whomsoever we offend), there is none . . . that hath them in the like purity.[5]

Lairds and lawyers were particularly receptive to the kirk's teaching, and, along with the nobility, could fashion from it a new role for themselves as godly magistrates.[6] Burgesses, magistrates and, in rural areas, landlords supported the new church by sitting on local kirk sessions, thus creating a powerful 'interlock of church and state'.[7] But many groups, including powerful landowners and sections of the poorer classes, were hostile or indifferent and could disregard kirk sessions. It was middle groups, especially lairds and burgesses, who were the strong supporters, such as the depute baillie who in *News from Scotland* investigates his maidservant's behaviour, then charges her with witchcraft.

Many areas remained for years barely affected by the reformation: 'Protestant-ism originally took root most readily in the towns and . . . the Reformed kirk was not a significant presence in some rural areas before the early seventeenth century'.[8] One such area was East Lothian where most of the accused came from in the North Berwick witch hunt. In some regions there were catholic magnates whose influence hindered protestantisation, and who sheltered catholic kin and dependents. The Setons of East Lothian supported catholic missionaries and dabbled in catholic conspiracy in the 1580s. Wormald has written that 'the strength of Catholicism after 1560 is astonishing', with one estimate of 1602 putting the proportion of catholics among the nobility at one-third.[9] There was little persecution of catholics, and no general catholic counter-attack to protestant reform, according to Wormald, because loyalty to the old religion was intensely localised, and bound up with allegiance to the local magnate. Even within the royal household there were differences of religion after Queen Anne became a catholic. James's pragmatic response that she practise her faith quietly may well have been repeated in other households.[10] Scottish society was co-agnatic, with wives keeping their own names and kinship networks after marriage; consequently, '[m]arriage was a contractual convenience but not a merging of kin. As a result a resolutely Protestant household . . . might often conceal a second household, resolutely Catholic, within it.'[11] Catholicism was threaded through society in intimate ways and at too many levels to make it easy to extirpate or persecute. There was never a moment when catholics, scattered through the whole of Scotland, gathered together to challenge on a national scale the protestant hegemony. The last failed catholic regional uprising, led by Huntly, was in 1594.

Despite the reformers' ambitions the shift from old to reformed religion was gradual, and 'it was only from the 1590s . . . that the church began to receive sufficent money to expand its ministry throughout Lowland Scotland on a scale which started to realise many of the ideals of Knox and other early reformers'.[12] But the kirk's claim on all the old church's incomes was never realised. Instead of gaining control of the wealth and income of the old church, it became increasingly reliant on the support of laymen to forward its religious mission. When it came to decisions about religion, the reformers' vision of religious transformation competed with the crown's search for political advantage and great families' eagerness for aggrandisement.

In 1574 Andrew Melville returned from Calvinist Geneva with ideas that increased the pressure for the kirk to adopt a presbyterian polity in which bishops would be replaced by a hierarchy of church courts.[13] In the 1580s the influence of presbyteries increased. A presbytery was a church council above parish level, consisting of the ministers and elders of the kirk sessions, which became the alternative to the rule of bishops; but it came to signify a good deal more than this. Bishops drew much of their authority from being appointed by the crown, and were one means by which the government exerted its will on the church. Presbyteries, on the other hand, looked to God and the body of the kirk for their authority.

Two kingdoms

The church–crown conflict over which was the sovereign authority in the state had intensified by 1590, and its resolution in favour of the king was achieved partly through the North Berwick witch hunt. In March 1574 the general assembly, the kirk's highest authority, claimed that its right to exist came directly from God. There is no reference to the king's authorising the assembly's existence, simply a direct appeal to divine authority. *The Second Book of Discipline* in 1578 declared that 'the power ecclesiastical flows immediately from God . . . not having a temporal head on earth'.[14] The kirk was setting itself up as a sovereign religious institution, separate from and superior to the temporal power of nobles and crown. In the continuous century-long struggle between the presbyterians, determined to establish a fully fledged presbyterian system, and the crown, determined to assert some control over the national church, the 1590s were a crucial period. The witch hunts of that decade became an arena of ideological struggle between the church and the monarchy, which the king turned adroitly to his advantage by establishing himself as God's agent on earth and the witches' main enemy. An extraordinary moment in the examination of Agnes Sampson, 4–5 December 1590, registers this struggle of which the devil himself was supposedly aware: 'He said also to her that the ministers would destroy the king and all Scotland, but if he would use his counsel he should destroy them'.[15] The issues of spiritual and civil authority are played out in some of the North Berwick witches' direct dealings with the devil, which mime the protestant belief that the humblest member of the church can deal directly with God without benefit of bishop and ritual. The North Berwick convention seems a remarkably democratic meeting with little of the sense of hierarchy that characterises some continental sabbats.[16] The witches' actions have their full meaning in relation to a long history of contested authority between church and state.

The idea of the 'two kingdoms' held that state and church occupy two distinct and separate realms of activity, that the church was separate and superior to the temporal power, and even the monarch 'was only a member of the church, over which he was not permitted to exercise any authority'.[17] These ideas had less chance of being realised after James began to take control of state affairs in the 1580s, for he was consistently opposed to presbyterianism. James's 'earliest political and ecclesiastical memory', as Wormald notes, 'was of confrontation not with the Catholics but with the extreme Presbyterians'.[18]

In 1584 parliament passed the so-called 'black acts' declaring the king's power to be sovereign over all persons and estates, denounced presbyteries, and asserted the power of bishops.[19] Andrew Melville, with some twenty ministers, including James Carmichael who was to be involved in the witch hunt, went into temporary exile in England. Despite the black acts, presbyterianism spread in the 1580s, although without legal recognition. James's wish to see peace in his kingdom when he married Princess Anne encouraged friendly relations between himself and the kirk. Robert Bruce, minister of St Giles in Edinburgh, was one of the commissioners left in charge of the government when James left Scotland to marry; and Andrew Melville himself was allowed to recite a Latin poem at the queen's coronation in May 1590. The first half of the 1590s saw relations between church and state improve, and witchcraft prosecutions required their cooperation.

Witchcraft

Judging by the records of the general assembly, the church's attitude to witchcraft and magic fluctuated considerably in the decades before 1590.[20] The kirk saw witchcraft and sorcery as evils to be stamped out, but it was by no means always obsessed with them. At the same time, the kirk also imagined Satan as a personal presence actively at work in the country. But the assembly did not consider witchcraft to be the only way that Satan operated even in the 1590s during the witch hunt.

Witchcraft, sorcery and enchantment appeared among 'the horrible crymes as now abounds in the realme without any correction' that the general assembly of the kirk complained of to Queen Mary in June 1565, and called for judges in every diocese to punish.[21] That was two years after the passing of the witchcraft act, but when witchcraft prosecutions were still extremely rare.[22] Witchcraft, sorcery and enchantment were among sins by which the kirk depicted a state of lawlessness and moral disorder, along with 'idolatrie, blaspheming of God's name, manifest breaking of the Sabbath Day, . . . adulterie, incest, manifest whoredome, maintainance of Brodells, murther, reiffe, slaughter and spulzie'.[23] Magical activities were not connected with the devil. Moral outrage combined with dependence on the civil powers for action appear repeatedly in the assembly's addresses to the crown through the later sixteenth century. However, the assembly's attitude to those who consulted witches, which was a capital offence, could be surprisingly lenient: in 1573 bishops or superintendents were to interview anyone suspected of consulting witches, 'and if they have been found to have consultit with the said witches, that they cause them make publick repentance in sackcloth, upon an Sonday in tyme of preaching, under the paine of excommunication if they be disobedient'.[24] Consulting witches is a severe moral failing or error of belief, but not a sign of pact with the devil, tacit or explicit, or allegiance to demonic powers. The assembly's prescription of public repentance for consulting with witches is at odds with the 1563 act's imposition of the death penalty.

At times of political crisis the devil appeared in the assembly's discourse as an active, hidden presence. In 1566, during the civil war between the protestant lords and Queen Mary, the assembly warned the protestant nobility that 'Satan, be all our negligences . . . hes so far prevailed within this realme of late dayes, that we stand in extream danger not only to losse our temporall possessions, bot also be depryved of the glorious Evangell [gospel] of Christ Jesus, and so we and our posteritie to be left in damnable darkness'.[25] It imagined Satan aiming his malice directly at the kirk, warning that 'Satane, with his ministers, at every light occasion hath frustrate, in tymes past, the ministrie of [the faithfuls'] life and sustentation'; and that there were 'great labours taken be Satane and his members' trying to impede the kirk.[26] Once the civil war was over, however, Satan disappears from the minutes of the assembly's meetings, his place being taken by Roman catholics. But the personal devil is part of the kirk's imaginative repertoire, something that its preaching could reactivate and bring to the fore in other crises, as was to happen in the 1590s.

From 1587 the crown and the presbyterian party in the kirk moved into a period of cooperation, guided by Chancellor Maitland. Until 1596 an uneasy alliance of kirk and crown found common cause in suppressing witchcraft, catholic rebellion, and, despite phases of support for him, Bothwell. The presbyterian leaders who sought to influence James, and to whom he was attentive, included Andrew Melville, Robert Bruce, James Carmichael, and John Davidson of Prestonpans.[27] Carmichael returned in December 1587 from exile in London where he had worked as 'a kind of general secretary for the presbyterian party',[28] and was appointed in October 1589 'a judge of ecclesiastical causes'.[29] His return to Scotland would give him the chance once again to pursue his stated aim by which 'Sathan, Antichrist and his supporters may be quite houndit out of ther nests'.[30] As minister of Haddington he would have been involved in the appearance before the Haddington synod in September 1589 of Agnes Sampson on suspicion of witchcraft, a charge that was revived in May 1590.[31] By May 1590 Carmichael was writing an account of the coronation that, given the controversy surrounding it, probably had official approval.[32] By May 1590 Carmichael would have had first-hand knowledge of witchcraft in East Lothian, and may well have begun his period of collaboration with James. Certainly by June 1591 the king 'was much exercised' with Carmichael 'in Dalkeith in tryall of witchcraft and witches'.[33] Carmichael's probable part in writing *News from Scotland* in late 1591 is discussed below in the introduction to *News*.

Robert Bruce, along with Carmichael, 'did much to spearhead the attack on witchcraft',[34] and his sermons of 1591 focused attention on its pressing danger. The action he urged, rigorous application of the law against witchcraft, was intended to strengthen both crown and kirk as they asserted justice and righteousness. By June 1591 Bruce's sermons were registering the devil as a immediate, physical threat to individuals and to a country still struggling to achieve reform, and were urging James to do God's work 'concerning the purging of his country and the land from this gross devilry that never was in any reformed country'.[35] The presbyterian clergy were a major driving force behind the witch hunt of 1590–7, providing political support and ideological justification; and indeed, in Briggs's view, '[w]ithout the intellectual underpinning the Kirk provided there might well have been no witch-hunt of any significance in Scotland', for it influenced not only the king but also 'the lairds and lawyers [who] were deeply influenced by its teaching'.[36] The kirk's influence in 1592 led to the establishment of standing commissions for the prosecution of witches in local areas (see Chapter 5), and the temporary loss of central regulation of witchcraft prosecutions. In those circumstances Bruce's vision of 'gross devilry', and the law and order needed to suppress it, led to a national witch hunt that continued until the privy council regained control of witchcraft prosecutions in 1596.

Notes

[1] For discussions of issues relating to the kirk and witchcraft see Williamson 1979; Larner 1981; Larner 1984; Parker 1988; Kirk 1989; Wormald 1995; Clark 1997.

[2] See document 14.

[3] Clark 1993: 46–7.

[4] Whyte 1997: 52.

[5] Preface to Book 4 of Knox's *History of the Reformation in Scotland*, quoted in Lynch 1985: 232.

[6] Wormald 1981: 124; Briggs 1996a: 205.

[7] Parker 1988: 5.

[8] Whyte 1997: 54.

[9] Wormald 1983: 76.

[10] See Leith 1885: 264–5, for the letter of Fr. Robert Abercromby, S.J., describing Anne's conversion and claiming that Anne told him this story; cited in Wormald 1985: 148.

[11] Lynch 1987: 287.

[12] Whyte 1995: 102.

[13] See Donaldson 1960b: 190.

[14] Quoted by Donaldson 1960b: 203.

[15] See document 2.

[16] See McGowan 1977: 192–3, for Pierre de Lancre's accounts, recalling 'the late Valois court'.

[17] Donaldson 1960b: 186.

[18] Wormald 1985: 148.

[19] Donaldson 1965: 172–96, for an account of church–state relations from 1580 to 1596. Kirk 1980 puts an alternative view.

[20] See *The Booke of the Universall Kirk* 1839 for the general assembly's records.

[21] *Booke of the Universall Kirk* 1839: 29.

[22] Larner, Lee and McLachlan 1977: 238–9.

[23] *Booke of the Universall Kirk* 1839: 29.

[24] *Booke of the Universall Kirk* 1839: 138.

[25] *Booke of the Universall Kirk* 1839: 52.

[26] *Booke of the Universall Kirk* 1839: 62, 63.

[27] A detailed analysis of the changing political and ideological positions of the members of the ruling elite can be found in Williamson 1979, especially chapters 1–3, from which this section draws.

[28] Williamson 1979: 61.

[29] Williamson 1979: 66; Carmichael 1957: 36.

[30] Quoted by Williamson 1979: 61.

[31] Kirk 1977: 12, 22.

[32] Bowes sent a copy of 'the manner of the coronation, set forth by Mr. James Carmichael' to Burghley on 31 May 1590, *CSPS* x 307. See *The Forme and Maner of the Quenis Majesties Coronatioun at the Kirk of Holyrudhous, 17 May 1590*, in *Papers Relative to the Marriage* 1828: 49–56.

[33] Quoted by Williamson 1979: 55.

[34] Williamson 1979: 71.

[35] Quoted by Williamson 1979: 60.

[36] Briggs 1996a: 205, who qualifies this by adding that while 'doctrine was very powerful and represented an independent causal factor, . . . it was not enough on its own, unless it interacted with other social and political forces'.

Chapter 4

SCOTTISH WITCHCRAFT
BEFORE THE NORTH BERWICK
WITCH HUNT[1]

Larner believed that 'the beginning of witch-hunting in 1590 is unambiguous and the discontinuity with the previous era clear cut', and that the North Berwick witch trials stimulated a national witch hunt in 1591–7.[2] This section reconsiders whether there was such a clear break in 1590 by surveying the witch trials between the 1563 witchcraft act and November 1590. In addition it considers whether notions of magic and the supernatural, and especially of the devil, changed during the later sixteenth century. Larner thought it hard to see 'much development in beliefs about witchcraft' in the second half of the sixteenth century.[3] However, any generalisations on both counts must be tentative since the evidence that survives may be unrepresentative.

The witchcraft act allowed witchcraft prosecutions by civil authorities, but it was the kirk that regularly petitioned the government for more action on this issue. The number of cases, however, shows no sustained pattern of increase. There seems to have been an immediate increase in cases, or perhaps just an increased awareness of witchcraft: in 1563 four women were tried by the justiciary court, the highest criminal court, and at least one was executed. In 1563 also, one Dunfermline woman was convicted; two witches, one from East Lothian, were executed; and four women from Fife and Galloway are mentioned as witches in the records.[4] Larner noted that the surviving cases show more variation in the kinds of witchcraft prosecuted than appeared after 1590—murder, other kinds of malefice, invocation of spirits, and healing. On the evidence of the prosecutions which we know about, the general impression of witchcraft before 1590 is of a diffuse, heterogeneous jumble of healing practices, predictions, *maleficium*, and relationships with, and calling upon, various supernatural beings with whom the accused could form some relationship. Witches might operate in small groups, but were not thought of as gathering at large meetings. More significant was 'the developing relationship between church and state' in which moral and religious issues including witchcraft were increasingly contentious, with the kirk keen to act against such offences and secular powers largely indifferent.[5]

An important effect of the North Berwick trials and the publications it generated, *News from Scotland* and *Demonology*, was that it schooled people at various levels of society in a theory of witchcraft and a knowledge of its practices. Before 1590 Scottish witchcraft is more diffuse and various in idea and practice than after. Some cases seem eccentric even by the relaxed standards of pre-1590 witchcraft, such as that of Tibbie Smart who was tried in April/May 1586 and who claimed that she had transformed herself into a badger in the glen of Corloy.[6] The relation of the 1590s trials to those that went before is analogous to the relation of the dittays from the justiciary court to the surviving pre-trial material. In the pre-1590 trials and pre-trial examinations we see witchcraft motifs, themes and ideas in diffuse forms; in the trials themselves and the dittays that record them we see these themes fashioned and managed into coherent ideological forms.

Angus and the Mearns, 1568

The North Berwick witch hunt was not the first that had taken place in Scotland. In 1568–9 during the civil war the reforming churchman John Erskine of Dun led a witch hunt throughout Angus and the Mearns that lasted more than a year and involved more than forty accused. The number of those tried in 1568 is about the same as in 1590, and Erskine's motives in witch hunting to strengthen the new religious order can be compared to the motives of the leading clergy in 1590, and to James's desire to demonstrate the power and legitimacy of his regime as it entered a new phase after his marriage.[7] Neither was political witchcraft unknown in Scotland before 1590, especially in times of political stress. Sir William Stewart, Lyon King of Arms, was burnt in 1569 for conspiring to take the regent Moray's life by conjuration and witchcraft, an offence that anticipates the charges against Bothwell.

The case of Bessie Dunlop, 1576

In this case there are signs of elite examiners directing their questions in a way that suggests a more theoretical and religiously inspired notion of witchcraft. Pitcairn called this trial of 1576 one of the most extraordinary cases on record, especially in the 'very minute and graphic detail' of the accused's accounts to her interrogators of her meetings with a spirit, who introduced her to the magic realm of elf-hame (elf-home).[8] The dittay records two interrogations that give insights into Dunlop's mental and social worlds, and also into her interrogators' presuppositions about witchcraft. The case shows the encounter between popular supernatural belief and developing elite ideas. Dunlop's close relationship with a spirit, Thom Reid, and her meetings with the queen of fairy and her world reveal thriving, workable interactions between the peasant woman and super-natural realms.[9] Diane Purkiss notes how 'beliefs in fairies, or spirits of the countryside' were woven into witchcraft narratives 'often in troubling ways'.[10] Certainly in this case the lairds and churchmen who interrogated Dunlop tried to fit her country beliefs into the witchcraft notions of the educated, an attempt that Dunlop resisted.

Dunlop was a wise woman dealing with peasants and gentry in her locality, integrated into society through the magic she performed. Her magical skills were traditional for peasant wise women in Scotland and England: dealing with herbs and ointments, love, helping with child-birth, recovering stolen goods.[11] Behind Thom was the more powerful female figure of the queen of elf-hame and her spirits. Dunlop recounted how she met them:

> she had gone afield with her husband to Leith, for home-bringing of meal, and ganging [going] afield to tether her nag at Restalrig loch, where there came a company of riders by, that made sic a din as heaven and earth had gone together; and incontinent, they rode into the loch, with many hideous rumble. But Thom told [said], It was the good wights [the good people] that were riding in Middle-earth.[12]

Bessie Dunlop's claim, through Thom, that these were 'gude wichtis' corresponds to similar European popular beliefs in 'good people' or 'good fairies', which elites gradually transformed into evidence of witchcraft.[13] King James treats the 'kind of spirits called the fairy' in his *Demonology* (III v) in a chapter which shows that he was acquainted with the sort of belief held by Dunlop: fairies as good neighbours, the queen of fairy and her court, and fairy hills. For James's speaker, Epistemon, as for Dunlop's examiners, these sights were delusions caused by the devil, and those who claimed to prophesy by the aid of fairies ought to be punished as witches.

Her interrogators tried to extract from her stories evidence that proved renunciation of baptism,[14] copulating with Thom, prophecy, and, perhaps surprisingly, the future of the reformation. She described a magical realm which was neither devilish nor godly, but with an independent, enticing life of its own. What she recorded is a wish-fulfilment but also popular historical memory.

By 1590 any relationship between human and spirit, whether fairy or elf, could be seen only as evil. But Dunlop's spirit world included ordinary conversations with Thom about 'the evill weddir [bad weather] that was to cum'. In 1590 in Agnes Sampson's dittay a similar foreknowledge of bad weather is included as an accusation: 'Item, filed that she was made foreknown of the devil of the last Michaelmas storm and that there would be great scathe both by sea and land'. Fifteen years of theological indoctrination by protestant ministers, and the experience of other trials, stand between Dunlop's trial of 1576 and the first North Berwick trials. By 1590 interrogators, and perhaps uneducated people too, were familiar with the rudiments of protestant demonology. When the accused were questioned they had some idea of what was being asked of them.

Evidence of cases in the decades before 1590 shows no trends; there were about sixty in the 1560s, six in the 1570s, and fourteen in the 1580s, although these figures probably depend on incomplete records. In the 1590s there were 195.[15] Cases in 1590 started to appear while James was still in Denmark, and no doubt made witchcraft seem a more pressing issue. A witch hunt started in East Lothian some time before November 1590.

Robert Linkup and others in Leith, January 1590

On 14 January 1590 Robert Linkup, William Downie and John Watson, of Leith, were charged with the 'slaughter' of the passengers of a boat that sank on 7 September 1589. The boat was sailing from Burntisland to Leith in prep-aration for the arrival from Denmark of Anne, with those on board including Jean Kennedy who was to be one of Anne's ladies-in-waiting. Kennedy had been lady-in-waiting to Mary queen of Scots in England, and was married to James's master of household, Sir Andrew Melville, brother of Sir James Melville. According to *News from Scotland*, which was to attribute this sinking to witchcraft, there were on board jewels and other gifts for the royal princess. Although Sir James Melville mentioned in his memoirs the great storms raging at the time, he also noted that 'This the Scotis witches confessit to his Maieste to have done'.[16] This confession came later, however, in the course of the examinations of the North Berwick witches, among whom were the Linkups of Leith. This trial charges the three accused men of 'rinnand [running] of the said boit [boat] under sei'.[17]

The pursuers (prosecutors) in this case included Sir Andrew Melville, whose wife had drowned, and David McGill, the king's advocate, indicating that there was a state interest, in addition to a private interest, in this trial. The idea of sinking boats would figure prominently in the witchcraft examinations later in 1590.

John Boswell, laird of Auchinlek, March 1590

In March 1590 John Boswell of Auchinlek in Ayrshire was denounced rebel by the privy council for having failed to answer charges that he 'consultit with witchis, bot alswa be himselff practized witchecraft, sorcerie, inchantment and uthiris divilishe practizeis, to the dishonnour of God, sklender of his worde, and grite contempt of his Hienes, his authoritie and lawis'.[18] Ritchie Graham, the sorcerer whom Bothwell supposedly consulted and the chief witness against him, confessed in 1592 that he had raised the devil in Boswell's dwelling place.[19]

The council's denunciation names two of the three *dramatis personae* that were to appear in the North Berwick trials, God and the king. This document of March 1590, several weeks before the king returned to Scotland, uses a similar idea of witchcraft to the one that was to fuel the imminent witch hunt. The council's document imagines witchcraft as a challenge to the religious and political order, though the devil is not its personified adversary. This case suggests that the council was anxious about law and order, and confident enough to root out its disturbers.

Meg Dow and Janet Pook, April 1590

On 28 April 1590, three days before James and Anne landed at Leith from Denmark, Meg Dow of Gilmerton, along with Janet Pook, was 'wirreit [worried, strangled] at ane staik' on the castle hill of Edinburgh 'and thairefter hir bodie brunt in asses' for the crimes of witchcraft and child murder.[20]

Ross-shire trials, July 1590

On 22 July 1590 in Ross-shire, Catherine Ross, Lady Foulis, and her stepson, Hector Munro of Foulis, were finally brought to trial on charges involving witchcraft and attempted poisoning after a tangled family quarrel that had lasted fourteen years. Ross and Monro were acquitted thanks to juries in both trials being packed with family members and retainers. Pitcairn comments on Lady Ross's trial that the jury consisted of men of 'a very inferior rank and station of life to the pannel [the accused], contrary to the usual custom—and the private *prosecutor* is "Mr Hector Monro of Fowles," who was in a few hours to exchange places as pannel at the same bar for similar crimes!'.[21] Eleven other Ross-shire people, including four men, were also probably tried, and two were executed. These trials, unusually from a Gaelic part of Scotland, demonstrate the difficulty of gaining convictions in the face of kin loyalties, which would be repeated in June 1591 in Barbara Napier's trial. Mr David McGill, the king's advocate who would prosecute in the North Berwick trials six months later, was present at these trials, and his presence implies a state interest in them. Indeed, James himself, while in Aberdeen in 1589, had asked Munro to let him see and question one of the witches.[22] If there was a state interest, it might be witchcraft itself, or the issue of delivering state justice in the face of local kin and supporters' pressure. The latter issue was to be at stake in the king's attempts to bring Bothwell to trial.

Aberdeen trials, June – August 1590

The first Aberdeenshire witch to be burned was Barbara Keand (or Kaird) alias Leslie on 16 or 18 June 1590. Between 17 and 19 August three trials took place in which eight people were involved.[23] Janet Grant and Janet Clark were convicted for a range of malefice offences including the murder by witchcraft of five people, the attempted murder of several others, the killing of sixteen head of cattle, and the 'gewing and taking of power fra sindrie mennis memberis'. They were convicted, strangled and burned on the castle hill in Edinburgh. In their dittay the raising of the devil is casually mentioned: 'and als, of the rasing of the Dewill, and seiking of help to Duncan Rychie'.[24] It is the very casualness that is significant, for three months later, when the first suspects from the witch hunt that had broken out in full force in East Lothian were being examined, the devil was at the centre of the witches' activities. However, the devil that appears in the dittay against Janet Grant is that of traditional, popular belief, like Bessie Dunlop's, and Grant's maleficial powers derive simply from her witchcraft. The dittay does not present this act of devil-raising as the source of her power. The devil raised by Grant is an amenable, magical figure familiar in popular culture.

The three other Aberdeenshire witch trials that took place on 17, 18 and 19 August 1590 may constitute the start of the widespread witch hunt that lasted until 1597. That witch hunt itself was almost certainly made up of localised outbreaks of witch hunting with each particular outbreak lasting weeks or months rather than years. The North Berwick trials which involved James and the council may have been at their outset in late 1590 another such local outbreak springing from a particular set of tensions and anxieties. The surviving records from Aberdeenshire suggest that after the cluster of trials in 1590 there were no further outbreaks of trials and executions until 1596 and 1597, although trial records may have been lost. Two of the three 1590 trials were brought by a laird for the murder by witchcraft of his son in 1586. Bessie Roy, a nurse, whose trial took place on 18 August, was accused of complicity in the murder with Janet Grant and Janet Clark. Charged also with theft, she replied that 'ane blak manne came and gaif the samin to [her]', which the court dismissed as 'nothing but the illusioune of the Diuill'. Her dittay defined her in a familiar formula as 'ane notoriouse and commowne Wich in the cuntrie; and cane do all thingis, and hes done all mischeifis, that deuilrie or Wichcraft cane devyse', yet, surprisingly, the assize acquitted her and she survived.[25] The next day, 19 August, the laird pursued his attempt to pin responsibility for his son's death on someone by charging Williame Leslie of Crechie and Violet Auchinlek his spouse with murder by witchcraft, though their trial did not proceed partly because of the daunting array of powerful men willing to be '[p]reloquitouris [advocates] for the pannell', including the earls of Bothwell and Erroll, Lord Home, and two lairds.

These trials involved loyalties and conflicts among the laird's kin, like the Foulis trials in Ross-shire, and again we glimpse social and kin struggles being waged by means of witchcraft charges. Janet Grant and Janet Clark were sentenced to be executed in Edinburgh, and as they were transported from Aberdeen the stories of their supernatural deeds were no doubt told and retold.

Those stories would have conveyed two dominant messages: that witchcraft was taken seriously by the authorities, and that it could kill.

East Lothian trials, ?autumn 1590

There is evidence in depositions and dittays that a witch hunt was going on in East Lothian before the king and privy council became involved in late 1590. Action against Agnes Sampson began six months before she was first examined in Edinburgh, when in May 1590 she was investigated by the synod of Haddington on an accusation of witchcraft that had surfaced in September 1589. Sampson was among the first to be examined on witchcraft charges in Edinburgh in November 1590, and it is likely that she was being investigated in Haddington between May and November.[26] Her first deposition, taken some time before 4–5 December 1590, mentions her imprisonment in Haddington tolbooth before being brought to Edinburgh. In the same deposition, Sampson confesses to a convention with the devil about two years previously at Bara, with 'Kate Graw, Davie Steel, which were both burned sensine [since then]'. These executions must have taken place between the end of 1588 and December 1590. Sampson's later deposition of 4–5 December 1590 gives more information. There she mentions five people at the Bara convention, including Janet Campbell who also 'was burned thereafter'; and she names participants in the North Berwick convention on 31 October 1590 including Kate Gray (or Graw). In the dittay against Barbara Napier's assizers of June 1591, which contains the fullest account of the North Berwick convention, those named include Katherine Gray and Janet Campbell. This suggests that both Kate Gray and Janet Campbell were executed in the period between the date of the North Berwick convention, 31 October 1590, and Sampson's examination on 4–5 December 1590. Trials and executions were happening in East Lothian before the central authorities were involved. The trials of Gray, Steel and Campbell did not take place in the justiciary court, and no one has yet discovered their local trial records.

Conclusion

In 1590 witchcraft investigations, trials and executions were taking place in Edinburgh, East Lothian, Aberdeen and Ross-shire before the North Berwick outbreak began. Elements from some of these trials later combined in the North Berwick witch hunt from December 1590 onwards. The trial of Robert Linkup in January 1590 provided the motif of ships sinking. The conviction in Edinburgh of 'sundrie witches' on 22 July 1590 for killing a young laird by roasting a wax image so that 'the gentleman pined awaie by sweate as the wax melteth before the fier', provided the model for the North Berwick witches' planned attack on James. And also in July a woman from Lübeck, considered a witch, 'desired to see the mark in the King's side' before divulging his fortune discovered by 'magicians of the east': a bizarre inversion of searching a witch's body for the devil's mark that obsessed interrogators.[27]

The model for the creation of a state-run witch hunt out of an outbreak of local witchcraft can be found in England, where in 1578 four witches and a wise man in Windsor fashioned wax images of Elizabeth and stuck bristles into them,[28] although Jean Bodin says that the image was made by a priest 'd'un village qui s'appele Islinkton'.[29] The English privy council discovered this local witchcraft activity some months after it occurred, and investigated to discover if treason was involved in 'that device very likely to be intended to the destruction of Her Majesty's person'.[30] It decided that it was not, though the witches were executed anyway. This is very likely the same pattern of events as occurred in Scotland in 1590, with a localised outbreak of witchcraft in East Lothian producing evidence of treason that the central authorities investigated. In Scotland, unlike England, the king and privy council did take seriously the evidence of treason.

Notes

1. For accounts of pre-1590 witchcraft in Scotland see Pitcairn 1833; Black 1938; Larner, Lee and McLachlan 1977; Larner 1981; Williamson 1979; Whyte 1995.
2. Larner 1981: 65, 69.
3. Larner 1981: 67.
4. Larner, Lee and McLachlan 1977: 3, 172.
5. Larner 1981: 67–8.
6. See Scottish Record Office, JC 26/1/13.
7. Williamson 1979: 56; for a full discussion of witchcraft in relation to different strands of reforming thought see 48–9, 53–62.
8. Pitcairn 1833: I ii 49. The record of Dunlop's trial is to be found on I ii 49–58 of Pitcairn.
9. She described Thom as a dapper, rather old-fashioned figure: 'Declarit, he was ane honest wele elderlie [honest, quite elderly] man, gray bairdit [bearded], and had ane gray coitt [coat] with Lumbart slevis [Lombard sleeves] of the auld fassoun [fashion]; ane pair of gray brekis [breeks] and quhyte schankis [white stockings], gartanit abone [gartered above] the kne; ane blak bonet on his heid, cloise [close?] behind and plane befoir, with silkin laissis [laces] drawin throw the lippis [edges]

thairof; and ane quhyte wand in his hand', Pitcairn 1833: I ii 51.
10. Purkiss 1996: 159.
11. Thomas 1973: 252–300.
12. This text has been modernised as the original Scots is difficult. The original reads as follows: 'sche had gane afeild with hir husband to Leith, for hame bringing of mele, and ganging afeild to teddir hir naig at Restalrig-loch, quhair thair come ane cumpanye of rydaris by, that maid sic ane dynn as heavin and erd had gane togidder; and incontinent, thai raid in to the loich, with mony hiddous rumbill. Bot Thom tauld, It was the gude wichtis that wer rydand in Middil-zerd', Pitcairn 1833: I ii 57.
13. See Ginzberg 1983; Ankarloo and Henningsen 1993: 191–215.
14. See Pitcairn 1833: I ii 52.
15. Larner, Lee and McLachlan 1977: 239. Numbers quoted here include cases only mentioned; the figures from court records only are nine for 1560s, four for 1570s, nine for 1580s, and forty-six for 1590s, 238.
16. Melville 1827: 379–70.
17. Pitcairn 1833: I iii 185.

[18] *RPCS* iv 591.

[19] *RPCS* iv 729.

[20] Pitcairn 1833: I iii 186. For Janet Pook see Scottish Record Office, JC 26/2/27.

[21] Pitcairn 1833: I iii 191n. For the dittays of Catherine Ross's trial see Pitcairn 1833: I iii 191–201, and of Hector Munro's, 201–4.

[22] Wormald 2000: 171.

[23] The trials are those of Janet Grant and Janet Clark on 17 August 1590; Bessie Roy on 18 August 1590; and William Leslie and Violet Auhinlek on 19 August 1590, in Pitcairn 1833: I iii 206, 207–9, 209

respectively. Documents relating to the trials of Janet Clark (alias Spalding) and Janet Grant may be found in Scottish Record Office, JC 26/2/28–30.

[24] Pitcairn 1833: I iii 206

[25] Pitcairn 1833: I iii 207–8.

[26] See Kirk 1977: 12, 22.

[27] Letter from Bowes to Burghley, *CSPS* x 365, 348.

[28] See *A Rehearsall Both Straung and True* (1579), reprinted in Rosen 1991: 83–91.

[29] Bodin 1580: II viii ff. 116^v–17.

[30] Quoted by Rosen 1991: 83.

Chapter 5

THE LEGAL PROCESS

An accusation of witchcraft in early modern Scotland was usually brought against a woman by someone living in her neighbourhood. It often 'began with an insult [and] ended with a public burning'.[1] The steps along this tragic path were determined by men in authority and the institutions in which they operated. This section summarises the legal institutions and the processes of accusation, examination, trial and punishment which might be faced by someone charged with witchcraft in Scotland, and tries to trace a path through the 'confused and flexible system'[2] of criminal justice at that time.

The courts

In sixteenth-century Scotland there was a complex, loosely articulated, mostly localised set of jurisdictions.[3] On their lands landowners ran barony courts concerned mostly with minor disputes or criminal cases, but appeals and more serious cases went to the local sheriff court. Local custom as much as statute law shaped barony court judgements which were 'quite effective in maintaining good relations within the rural community as well as supporting the established order'.[4] Regality courts exercised judicial powers devolved from the crown to try crimes including the 'four pleas of the crown': robbery, rape, murder and arson. They were effectively independent jurisdictions, and covered about half of Scotland, with powers equivalent to the central court of justiciary. Until 1597 they could try cases of witchcraft; thereafter the privy council took back the right to decide if individual cases should proceed (though trials still usually took place locally). Sheriffs, as well as being the crown's agents in an area, had courts which had wide powers to deal with a range of civil and criminal cases. In towns burgh courts dealt with disputes involving property and debt, as well as criminal cases. The central criminal court was the court of justiciary that both sat in Edinburgh and sent out circuit courts. Witchcraft cases could be tried either centrally or at the justiciary court's regular justice ayres.

At the centre of the kingdom the privy council routinely performed legal functions when it issued orders concerning feuds between individuals and kin groups. It was a court of appeal for inferior courts which 'could, and did, intervene at every level of the judicial structure',[5] as is evident in the North Berwick cases where it directed interrogations of suspects who had been brought to Edinburgh, and, in the case of Barbara Napier, overturned her acquittal.

Legal rules concerning witchcraft

Sixteenth-century Scottish witchcraft trials took place under different legal rules at different periods of time:

before 1563	the church dealt with witchcraft in ecclesiastical courts, though punishment was enacted by secular powers
1563	the witchcraft act, which criminalised witchcraft
October 1591	the privy council established six commissioners to enquire into witchcraft cases, using torture if necessary, and consider whether the cases should go to trial
1592	commissioners from kirk and privy council empowered to distribute standing commissions in localities for enquiring into and prosecuting witchcraft
1597	the withdrawal of the 1592 standing commissions; thereafter the privy council considered individually each request for a commission to hold a witchcraft trial.

These changing legal settings were responses to changing ideas about witchcraft in Europe, and to the circumstances of actual witchcraft trials. The conduct of trials and the setting of legal rules were mutually influential. The witch hunt itself changed the procedures that governed trials.

There were at least two groups of trials in 1590–7. The first is the small number of trials held in the court of justiciary in Edinburgh of women and men from East Lothian and Edinburgh in 1590–1, and which were concerned with treasonable conspiracy against the queen and the life of the king, and subsequently involved the earl of Bothwell. These trials, for which some records survive and others are lost, are what we are referring to as the North Berwick trials, though the trial of Bothwell in 1593 by his peers should also be included. A much larger number of trials was also happening in 1590–7, mainly in Fife, the Lothians, and Aberdeenshire, and took place in local courts. The North Berwick witch hunt is sometimes thought of by historians as including all those local trials as well as those held centrally in the justiciary court. It is difficult to know what the relationship is between these local trials and the North Berwick trials, for as Larner has noted the records of the local trials have either been lost or not discovered.[6] There is evidence in one of Agnes Sampson's depositions[7] that local trials and executions had already taken place by the time she was examined on 4 December 1590, and if that is so then local trials, at least in East Lothian, may have have begun before those known as the North Berwick trials. In that case the trials concerned with treasonable conspiracy may be an outgrowth from this localised series of accusations and trials. That in turn raises the question, of course, of what started the larger, local witch hunt in 1590.

The witchcraft act of 1563

Before 1563 witchcraft was an offence in ecclesiastical law and also in common law, but very few cases are known in sixteenth-century Scotland before this date.[8]

The witchcraft act was one of several acts by which offences that before the reformation had been dealt with by church courts were transferred to the jurisdiction of the kirk and the secular courts. The act of 1563, 'Anent [concerning] the using of witchcraftis, sorsarie and necromancie',[9] ran in its entirety as follows [punctuation added]:

> Item, Forsamekill [forasmuch] as the Quenis Maiestie and three Estatis in this present Parliament, being informit that the havy and abominabill superstitioun usit be divers of the liegis [subjects] of this Realme be using of Witchcraftis, Sorsarie and Necromancie, and credence gevin thairto in tymes bygane aganis the Law of God. And for avoyding and away putting of all vane superstitioun in tymes tocum. It is statute [decreed] and ordanit be the Quenis Maiestie and thre Estatis foirsaidis that na maner of persoun nor persounis of quhatsumever [whatsoever] estate, degre or conditioun thay be of, tak upone hand in ony tymes heirefeter to use ony maner of Witchcraftis, Sorsarie or Necromancie, nor gif [give] thame selfis furth to have ony sic craft or knawlege theirof, thairthrow [by that means] abusand the pepill. Nor that na persoun seik ony help, response or consultatioun at ony sic usaris or abusaris foirsaidis of Witchcraftis, Sorsareis or Necromancie, under the pane of deid [death]. Alsweill [To the same extent] to be execute aganis the usar, abusar, as the seikar [seeker] of the response or consultatioun. And this to be put to executioun be the Justice Schireffis, Stewartis, Baillies, Lordis of Regalteis and Rialties, thair Deputis, and uthers Ordinar Jugeis competent within this Realme, with all rigour having powar to execute the samin.[10]

Clearly, this act was not meant to start a witch hunt, but was just part of a Reformation package of measures dealing with misbelief and misbehaviour.[11] As Wormald has noted, it is not clear why in 1563 witchcraft was included among the business that now had to be subsumed in the jurisdiction of either the state or the new kirk. The church's general assembly did not mention witchcraft when it petitioned the privy council to replace the old church courts.[12] Other legislation in 1563 gave the kirk the legal means to deal with 'sin crimes', as one writer has called them,[13] with which it became increasingly preoccupied, such as fornication, adultery, incest and bestiality.[14] A similar location of witch-craft among moral transgressions can be seen in the articles of the general assembly of 1583 presented to the king. There the general assembly complains 'That there is no punischment of incest, adulterie, witchcrafts, murthers abominable oathes, and uther horrible oathes'.[15]

In *Basilikon Doron* (1599) King James himself included witchcraft in a similar list of sins and crimes when he advised Prince Henry, 'there . . . [are] some horrible crimes that yee are bound in conscience neuer to forgiue: such as Witchcraft, wilfull murther, Incest, (especially within the degrees of consang-uinitie) Sodomie, poisoning, and false coine'.[16] Witchcraft was a *crimen exceptum* in that extraordinary procedures of examination, arraignment and trial were used to uncover and prosecute it, as James would remind the jurors who acquitted Barbara Napier. But such lists as those above may make us reconsider the place of witchcraft in sixteenth-century taxonomies of sin, transgression and crime, and see it as contemporaries did as merely one crime among others.[17] 'For the Reformed Kirk, witchcraft was all but invariably linked with the crimes of sodomy, incest, adultery, and wilful murder.'[18]

The wording of the 1563 legislation regards the practice of witchcraft, sorcery and 'necromancy' (which could mean magic or sorcery in general,[19] not just divination by the dead, as James would explain in *Demonology*, I iii) as a 'superstitioun', and belief in witchcraft and sorcerey as a sign of the 'credence [of] . . . tymes bygane'. Black and Larner regarded the wording of the act, and the use of words such as 'superstition', as indications of legislators' scepticism about witchcraft, and Larner even claimed that the act's language was 'as sceptical in its wording as the Witchcraft Act of 1735 which repealed it'.[20]

However, 'superstition' in the act signifies not a credulous readiness to believe, but rather erroneous belief on the part of the monarch's subjects. The act uses 'superstition' in a sense current in the sixteenth century, but now obsolete, of 'a false, pagan or idolatrous religion'.[21] The Danish protestant pastor Niels Hemmingsen, whose book was published twelve years after the Scottish statute was passed, wanted the prohibition of false and *erroneous* beliefs, not *groundless* beliefs, when he entitled his book urging the shunning of 'superstitions', *Admonitio de Superstitionibus Magicis Vitandis* (An admonition about magical beliefs to be avoided) (Copenhagen 1575). The 1563 act's reference to the 'credence gevin thairto in tymes bygane' is the language not of a newly enlightened and sceptical age looking back on an age of credulity, but of protestant reformers who are looking back and constructing previous papist times as those of 'gentilism' (heathen belief and practice), which fostered superstition, magic and misbelief. But although witchcraft, sorcery and necromancy are mentioned as being 'against the law of God', the emphasis in the act is less on their being challenges to God's rule than on their being temptations to wander from the path of true belief. After all, it is 'credence' in magic and witchcraft that the act declares against the law of God. The act's reference to the law of God must be an invocation of one of the Old Testament prohibitions of magical practices. The comprehensive list in Deuteronomy 18.10–12 of the magical and divinatory religious practices of other nations was often cited by demonologists as what was prohibited by God's law.

The act forbids anyone to practise any supernatural arts, or to claim to know about them, or to consult someone who did claim to know about them. Again, one should not be led astray by the expressions here: 'abusand the pepill' and 'abusars foirsaidis' more likely indicate the misleading and deception[22] of the people by magical practitioners who corrupted them with magic, rather than deception through empty trickery. The punishment was death for both those practising the 'superstitions' and those consulting them. As *The Historie of King James the Sext* points out, 'the municipall law of Scotland beris, That whasoever salbe fundin to consult with sorcerers, witches or suthesayers, thay sall dee the death'.[23] Although two weeks after the passing of the statute two witches were burned,[24] its passing does not seem to have resulted in any short-term increase in witch prosecutions.[25] However, this witchcraft act provided the legal basis for witch prosecutions in the sixteenth and seventeenth centuries when social conditions changed, and was the act under which the Edinburgh justiciary court tried Fian, Sampson, Napier and MacCalzean in 1590–1, and others in local courts in the 1590s.

The act's formulae may sometimes be heard echoed in the charges in the dittays of 1590–1. The final item in Agnes Sampson's dittay echoes the 1563 act in the phrase 'abusing the poor simple people'. Here 'abusing' clearly has the sense of spiritual seduction, not trickery:

> Item, for a common notorious witch, and user of sorceries and enchantments, with the invocation of the devil, her master, abusing the poor simple people therewith, drawing them from the leaning to the mercy of God and to believe in the support of the devil.

The sorcerer Ritchie Graham is several times referred to in the dittays as 'a necromancer and abuser of the people'. Barbara Napier is often accused of 'consulting with' Agnes Sampson and Ritchie Graham. Euphame MacCalzean is accused of similar consultations with Agnes Sampson and other witches. The dittays sometimes explicitly invoke the 1563 act in items like 'Item, for the haunting and consulting with a witch and necromancer against the tenor of the act of parliament made thereanent'. Indeed it is the alleged consulting with witches which made the two Edinburgh women Barbara Napier and Euphame MacCalzean liable to prosecution and is the accusation levelled at them early in the dittays, before the implication in treason against the king. It has also been suggested that one reason that Barbara Napier's assize was reluctant to convict her was that she would have been the first person in sixteenth-century Scotland known to have been convicted merely for consulting witches, although the 1563 act explicitly makes this punishable by death.[26]

A parliamentary act of 1587 made several legal reforms that affected witchcraft prosecutions. Twice yearly justice ayres were to be held in each shire with professional circuit judges presiding. Criminal courts could also be held to deal with specific crimes such as rebellions, feuds or witchcraft, with the king appointing unqualified judges with full judicial powers 'from the ranks of sheriffs, trusted noblemen, and provosts and baillies of burghs', 'a dangerous practice', according to Willock.[27] Witch trials could be held in such special courts authorised by the crown or, after October 1591, by a privy council commission. The lord advocate was empowered in 1587 to initiate prosecutions in the absence of the usual private prosecutor in cases where the state's interest was involved, such as treason.[28] The lord advocate was pursuer in all the North Berwick trials, as he had been the Ross-shire witchcraft trials of July 1590. The 1587 act also strengthened the jury in trials by requiring that all presentation of the evidence should be in the presence of the assize and accused,[29] a measure that may have raised the chances of acquittal.

The privy council commission of 26 October 1591

This act of the privy council was passed while witch trials were happening, as it specifically refers to persons 'alreddy convict, or utheris quhilkis ar detenit captive and hes confessit, and sum that hes not confessit, as alswa all sic utheris as ar dilaitit [charged], or that heireftir salbe accused'.[30] Four North Berwick witch trials had taken place, though other accused were still to be tried including Geillis Duncan and Bessie Thomson (executed December 1591, presumably tried then too), and Ritchie Graham (tried February 1592). The act named six commissioners—the lord advocate, the justice clerk, two ministers, including Robert Bruce, the lord provost and a burgess of Edinburgh—and gave them powers to make enquiries into all current and future cases of witchcraft, examine suspects, using torture if necessary, and report them to the king and privy council with a view to sending them to trial. The commissioners were authorised to use torture to find the truth: 'the personis wilfull or refusand to declair the veritie to putt to tortour, or sic uthir punishement to use and cause be usit as may move thame to utter the treuth'.

Historians are divided over the significance of this commission. Larner describes the commission as 'the most decisive instrument . . . in the maintenance of prosecutions', and 'the licence for an indiscriminate witch-hunt'.[31] She sees the North Berwick witch trials as having stimulated the general witch hunt of 1591–7, and this commission as evidence of the government's wish to maintain anxiety about witchcraft, and control the direction of prosecutions. She believes it had a potent political significance: for James, 'reminding the populace of the dangers of witchcraft, and taking responsibilty for rooting it out, [it] served to justify the recent episode and demonstrate his concern for the safety of the realm'.[32] But a different interpretation of the commission comes from Levack, who argues that 'it would be misleading to see the government as the inspiration of the large rash of witchcraft trials that took place between 1591 and 1597', because privy council action only came in response to requests to prosecute from particular areas.[33] The wording of the privy council act urges the commissioners to take an active role in pursuing and prosecuting, and it also assumes that witchcraft cases will keep on appearing. But it is possible that this commission was meant simply to deal with the outstanding North Berwick cases, and not primarily with cases from other parts of the country. Wormald sees it in this way as dealing with cases in Edinburgh and environs, and 'in that sense both "central" and also very local'.[34] Recent research by Levack also emphasises the limits of the 1591 commission in its giving power only to the six commissioners to investigate, torture, and refer prosecutions to the council. In relation to torture Levack considers the commission to be one of a series of attempts by the state to limit torture to the council, and notes that any torture that was used by local officials was simply illegal.[35] Since all evidence of the commissioners' deliberations has disappeared, however, the commission's precise effect on witch hunting is impossible to determine. Evidence from the justiciary court, in which trials authorised by the commission would presumably have taken place (either in Edinburgh or at its justice ayres), suggests that the commission may have been used to wind down the trials in and around Edinburgh. Indeed, Larner indicates that in the 'immediate aftermath [of the North Berwick trials] the number of trials may have diminished'.[36] Even if the central authorities were indeed trying to control prosecutions, in the following year that central control was decisively lost.

The kirk–state commission of 8 June 1592

In 1592 the privy council set up a joint body consisting of commissioners from kirk and government to tour the country and address a number of social and religious issues, including the finances and physical state of churches, and papists, beggars and witches.[37] With the church in the ascendant in 1592 and the king weak, this measure was passed in response to church pressure, as was the passing of a law three days earlier on 5 June 1592 legalising presbyteries. This act undoubtedly promoted witch hunting, as it sent commissioners round the country with blank commissions on which to inscribe the names of 'noblemen, baronis, gentilmen, and magistratis of borrowis'. These commissions made such men 'his Hienes justiceis and commissionaris' in their localities, and empowered them 'to inquire the names suspectit and dilaitit of witchecraft'. It was this commission, rather than the 1591 one, that was 'the licence for an indiscriminate witch-hunt'.[38] Witchcraft trials from June 1592 until 1597 could lie in the hands of local men who, armed with a privy council commission, were free to seek out and punish the witches in their area. These commissions provided a veneer of legality for widespread witch hunts for the next five years in towns and rural areas.

The abuses caused by providing standing commissions for local magistrates is illustrated in the case of Janet Finlayson in Burntisland. She was repeatedly subjected to a number of trials for witchcraft by two town baillies who sought to confiscate her property if she were found guilty. The privy council instructed the baillies to desist. Such devolved powers clearly posed a threat to local women and men. The period up to 1597 saw an unprecedented increase in witchcraft cases,[39] and in 1597 the council acted again to put a stop to local trials.

The privy council order of 12 August 1597

The period between 1592 and 1597 was unique in Scottish witchcraft prosecution. The unknown number of processes and trials that took place, conservatively estimated to have been around 195,[40] were based, if they were legal at all, on standing commissions authorised by the 1592 commissioners. This was a period of nationwide witch hunt, and it was ended by central government action by means of another order of the privy council of 12 August 1597.[41] The 1592 standing commissions were withdrawn from those to whom they had been granted, including, in the words of the order, 'sindrie noblemen, baronis, schireffis, stewartis, baillies, provestis and baillies of burrowis and townis and uthiris particulair personis'. Thereafter each request to prosecute a witch could proceed only with a privy council commission, and the council judged each case separately. The council no longer delegated its powers to individuals; instead it issued commissions only to groups of three or four men to safeguard against individuals acting prejudicially. But it required that those holding old commissions should provide the council with the names of consulters of witches in their area, which may have been a concession to the kirk. Anyone using an old commission to act against a witch would themselves be committing a crime.[42]

Again, historians disagree about the effects of this privy council decision. According to Larner, the 'immediate effect . . . was that the supply of witch suspects dried up', and more importantly in the long term 'that witchcraft became a centrally managed crime' that was situated firmly within the field of politico-religious forces.[43] Her emphasis on the social context of witch trials keeps in mind their interactive and multicausal nature, though her insistence that the central elite managed witchcraft prosecutions may attribute more intention to the state than was the case. Levack, on the other hand, sees Scottish witchcraft prosecutions generally as 'a reluctant government responding to pressure from subordinate authorities, in this case the clergy', and the post-1597 privy council commissions as the main tool in moderating that pressure.[44] He rejects the notion of witchcraft being used by a central state to augment its power, and argues that in Scotland after 1597 the council acted to put a brake on local pressure for prosecution. Levack's view may underestimate the political and cultural effects on the population of the period 1590–7 when witch panic was widespread, and state authorities promoted a witchcraft ideology that laid the foundations for individual cases and witch panics in the decades to come.

Again, it is important to distinguish carefully between phases in these trials and also to distinguish the trials of Fian, Sampson, Napier, MacCalzean, and eventually Bothwell, from the others. In the documents recording pre-trial examinations and depositions and in the dittays from the justiciary court, we can see the privy council and the king himself intervening ever more actively in the examinations and trials from December 1590 to June 1591, as treason increasingly becomes the central issue. Indeed what may distinguish these trials in the justiciary court from those conducted outside Edinburgh is the state's concern with the security of the king's person.

Accusation and examination

The North Berwick trials held in the justiciary court in Edinburgh must be distinguished from the many trials in local courts that were taking place from 1590. Although it is unclear whether the Edinburgh trials sparked off a witch hunt or were parasitic upon one, some trials had taken place in East Lothian before the king and the council became involved. The North Berwick trials were in a tradition in which aristocrats wishing to dispose of relatives, or even the monarch, commissioned witches to destroy them, often by image magic. In 1479 the earl of Mar was accused of practising magic against his brother, James III, and twelve witches and wizards, his accomplices, were burned in Edinburgh. In 1532 Janet Douglas, Lady Glamis, was accused and burned for trying to destroy James V by witchcraft or poison. The most famous story, and one told by Hector Boece, Buchanan and Holinshed (where Shakespeare found it), is of King Duff, whose image was roasted by hags.[45] Although the influence of the North Berwick trials may have been long-lasting among both the educated and uneducated, their particular formation of witchcraft was never repeated in Scotland. They emerged from local witchcraft and returned to deeply influence it. It is therefore important to consider how accusations and examinations took place in villages and towns, for those social processes remained much the same from the 1590s through the seventeenth century.

Larner has written that the 'process by which a witch was made was the same as that by which she was convicted'.[46] Incidents which led to a woman's acquiring a bad reputation among her neighbours, often over many years, became, once an accusation of witchcraft had been made, the evidence that the woman was indeed a witch. The creation of a witch was a social process in which 'it is hard to overemphasize the importance of reputation'.[47] At some point someone would accuse a neighbour of witchcraft.

The next step after accusation was the questioning of the accused by one or more men with a quasi-judicial function. In the case of Geillis Duncan, reported in *News from Scotland*, it is a baillie depute who first suspects her of witchcraft, and he is joined by a number of other unspecified men who then subject the girl to questioning: 'her master . . . did with the help of others' interrogate her. The questioning of the accused was supposed to take place as soon after a crime as possible, and depositions (written statements) taken from the accusers, and from the accused answering questions put by the investigators. An accused person was 'examined, confronted with the evidence against him, and asked for his explanation'.[48] If the woman could not be dealt with by the kirk session because the charges were too serious, then the investigators would seek a trial in a higher court, and depositions provided the evidence to back up that request as well as the main body of evidence at any subsequent trial.

An accusation of witchcraft was dealt with initially by local men with authority by virtue of birth or social position, and was in the first place a local event, with the accused, accusers and investigators all coming from the same locality and possibly being acquainted. The seventeenth-century jurist George Mackenzie wrote that a witch's accusers were likely to be her 'Masters, or Neighbours'.[49] The kirk session of a parish might first question a woman and, if the offence was not too serious, decide on a warning, fine or banishment.[50] Or a magistrate from a burgh or barony court might start proceedings. Kirk sessions had judicial powers to deal with sin offences, such as fornication, adultery, incest, and sabbath breaking. It was the kirk that first took action against Agnes Sampson on 7 May 1590 when the Haddington synod began to investigate a complaint of witchcraft against her that had been raised eight months before in September 1589.[51] If the kirk session wished to prosecute a case then it would need the support of the secular powers. Lairds, baillies or sheriffs would then bring the accused for trial before an assize. Meanwhile the suspected witch would be imprisoned in a local tolbooth, church steeple or barn. Agnes Sampson had been imprisoned in the tolbooth in Haddington.[52]

The procedure instituted in October 1591, by which a group of privy councillors considered if individual witchcraft cases should to to trial, had not yet come into force when the first trials took place in 1590. By October 1591 the interrogations and trials of the North Berwick witches were almost over. Dr Fian and Agnes Sampson had been tried in Edinburgh and executed, and Barbara Napier and Effie MacCalzean had been tried, and MacCalzean burned. The witches reported as having been tried and executed in Haddington[53] would have been charged under the 1563 witchcraft act in local courts or a travelling circuit court of the central justiciary court, though no records survive.

Legal proceedings could be initiated by those in authority mentioned in the 1563 act: sheriffs, stewards, baillies, lords of regalities, their deputies, and other ordinary judges. The overlapping of church and state meant that there was no clear distinction between the powers of church and state in the administration of justice. Minister, elders, schoolmasters, local nobility or chief tenants might be involved in legal proceedings at various stages of accusation, investigation, trial and punishment. An eighteenth-century observer wrote that 'inquisition concerning witchcraft was not confined to Magistrates and Judges . . . but was given, at least was permitted, almost to all persons in any sort of authority'.[54] Writing in the seventeenth century, Sir George Mackenzie was suspicious of commissions granted to 'Gentlemen and others in the Countrey', and noted that 'Most of these poor creatures are tortur'd by their keepers, who being perswaded that they do God good service, think it their duty to vex and torment poor prisoners'.[55] The same was true in 1590 when (as *News From Scotland* recounts) David Seton took it upon himself to examine Geillis Duncan, and then torture her with the pilliwinks. He was acting illegally in torturing her, although properly constituted authority and legal procedures were in practice vague. This case exemplifies Levack's observation that the 'elders and magistrates who conducted these local trials were acting as the rulers of their towns and villages, not as agents of the central government or as executors of a central governmental policy'.[56]

Examinations at Edinburgh, 1590–1

The legal procedures through which the North Berwick witches, Sampson, Fian, Napier and MacCalzean, passed to reach the Edinburgh court of justiciary in 1590–1 were exceptional. We know that examinations were conducted and depositions taken not just locally, or by a justice, but before the king and his privy council in Holyroodhouse. The privy council was acting as a court of law. Others closely associated with the alleged conspiracy and whose names appear repeatedly in the records were tried in local courts. What distinguished the witchcraft charges brought against the four main accused was treason against the king. The legal procedures that they were subject to once they reached Edinburgh and the jurisdiction of the privy council were more severe than those of local jurisdictions.

The North Berwick accused found themselves examined by the king and his council and considerable pressure was placed on them, including torture. Privy councillors were operating several overlapping judicial functions: interrogating the suspects; recording their evidence in written examinations; writing the accused's depositions; confronting accused with accusers; applying torture; and later in the justiciary court sitting as judges alongside professional judges; and joining in sentencing the accused. In the Barbara Napier case James acted as a higher judicial authority and rejected the jury's verdict. The king or council seem to have assigned to royal officials certain judicial tasks: the king's master of work conducted an examination of Sampson in January 1591.[57] And ministers of the kirk were present alongside privy councillors when depositions were taken.

In the interrogations of Sampson, Fian, Napier and MacCalzean personal and communal relationships between investigator and accused would not have existed as they did in local communities, such as between David Seton and Geillis Duncan in Tranent. But arguably some relationship already existed between king and accused witches, even before their examination, and certainly developed during those examinations. The accused women, like most Scots of the time, would have been well aware of James's marriage and the politics of the court. Indeed, if we are to believe the pre-trial examinations, Geillis Duncan deponed in January 1591 that Agnes Sampson had said 'Now the king is going to f[etch?] his wife but I shall be there before them'. Whatever this cryptic statement meant, it shows the king's doings were the subject of common talk. Any attempt at *maleficium*, even against a king, always presupposes some sort of relationship between witch and intended victim, and Agnes Sampson was, after all, accused of having been appointed to make a wax image of the king to destroy him. James's personal involvement in the examination of the supected witches can be seen in the pre-trial examinations, especially in his dealings with Agnes Sampson. The depositions taken in early December 1590 record him personally gathering together inconsistencies and contradictions in Sampson's testimony and then charging her 'straitly to confess the truth, which she did as after followeth'. The manuscript later records that Agnes Sampson had 'that same day resolved never to confess, were not his Majesty's speeches that had moved her, whereof she praised God that had wrought a repentance in her and a sense and feeling of her sins'. Such moments suggest a close inter-action between the suspect and her questioner,[58] even if the interaction finally re-establishes conventional relationships. There were moments of intimacy, the most remarkable, if we can believe *News from Scotland*, being when, 'taking his Majesty a little aside', Sampson told the king the words he had exchanged with Anne on their wedding night.

When a case came to trial the evidence consisted of depositions, obtained by whatever body of enquirers at whatever level, presented to the members of the assize. The depositions would often consist of neighbours' complaints and grievances against the accused. 'Where witchcraft was involved there was no limit to either the vagueness of the charges or the antiquity of their date.'[59] So the last item (53) in Agnes Sampson's dittay simply indicts her for 'a common notorious witch', while another (19) charges that she foretold Isabel Hamilton's death in 1584 or 1585.

As Larner discovered, evidence of malefice was not enough to convict, nor was having a bad reputation in the neighbourhood, though that 'was particularly useful in legal terms in that it could be made to imply a long-standing pact with the Devil'.[60] What established certainty of guilt was a confession. In theory, a confession required corroboration to lead to a conviction, but in witchcraft cases, as in others, confession alone could serve to convict.[61] In witchcraft trials evidence could be accepted from categories of witnesses usually assumed to be unfit to provide reliable evidence, namely women and *socii criminis* (partners in crime). A decision of June 1591, pushed through by James, specified that such evidence was valid in heresy and treason cases, and this allowed the crime of witchcraft to be aligned with treason, where similar special rules of evidence obtained.[62] The alignment of the rules of evidence for witchcraft and treason trials reflects the authorities' conviction in 1591 that both crimes were equally dangerous to the state. In fact in the dittays we witness the process of the two crimes being elided.

Torture

In the pre-trial investigations for the justiciary court trials of 1590–1, torture was used. Torture was only legal in Scotland if authorised by the privy council or parliament, which suggests that it might be used for reasons of state such as treason, rebellion, or witchcraft, which came to be understood (as a result of these trials) as conspiracy against the state.[63] Officially torture rarely entered the Scottish criminal procedure.[64] Even in witchcraft cases only two privy council warrants for torture were issued: one was the commission of October 1591, and the other was in 1610.[65] The torture applied to accused witches between December 1590 and June 1591 was not covered by a privy council warrant; it presumably took place simply by order of the king or other privy councillors. Such torture could be considered legal by virtue of an order having been given by word of mouth of the king or a councillor, though such sharply defined legal notions were anachronistic in the sixteenth century. The privy council authorised torture informally; it did not issue warrants to itself.

At local level investigators ignored the prohibition on torture completely and routinely applied it to witchcraft suspects, in the sense that they used harsh or cruel treatment that amounted to torture. When a local woman was taken into custody and examined, she might well suffer physical coercion as she was questioned and pressured to make a confession. Such torture was illegal. Its informality means that it is not recorded as part of the legal proceedings, and has to inferred from external evidence. *News from Scotland* exceptionally makes great play of the tortures suffered by the accused. In certain continental jurisdictions the applications of torture are sometimes detailed in terms of times, instruments, degrees of pain, and answers given. But there is no torture in the records of the examinations conducted at the Edinburgh tolbooth or at Holyroodhouse, nor in the dittays of the justiciary court.

At a local level, cruelty towards people accused of witchcraft included imprisonment in the town tolbooth, beating, sleep deprivation, shaving of head and body hair, and pricking for the devil's mark.[66] Torture was justified on the ground that 'the Devil had such a grip on his servants that only extreme pain could cause this grip to slip'.[67] Pricking, which was a kind of trial by ordeal, involved sticking a pin into several places on the body until a place was found which was insensible to pain. This was supposedly where the devil had sealed the pact with the witch by inflicting a wound which when healed would not register pain. Pricking sought to determine a person's criminality by 'an appeal to God, a miracle attesting the innocence or guilt of the accused'.[68] In practice there was little difference between torture and ordeal, and little possibility of *not* discovering an insensible spot on the body since by that stage the accused would be extremely disorientated. The meaning of the devil's mark is located more in demonological ideas than legal practice.

In an essentially imaginary crime the best evidence available to investigators was the confession of the accused. In most cases the pre-trial investigators 'were convinced of [the accused's] guilt beforehand . . . and directed their questioning to obtaining what they regarded as that "most secure" of all forms of proof, namely, a confession'.[69]

Privy council procedures

The four justiciary court cases of Fian, Sampson, Napier and MacCalzean followed procedures that were unprecedented and never repeated, and whose effect on later cases was considerable. It is the involvement of the king and council that makes the North Berwick trials so significant and unusual. The accused went through a legal procedure that in certain key respects resembled the inquisitorial system.[70] According to Unsworth, if informal, illegal actions against a witch 'are ranked most prejudicial to, and placing greatest pressure on, the accused, then, of the formal methods available, the inquisitorial mode must be ranked next'.[71] The king and privy council's approach to the accused was informal, even improvisatory, rather than systematic, but their assuming the functions of examiner in order to discover the facts of the case, employing official torture in that process, and having some of their members sit as judges at the trials, resemble aspects of inquisitorial law in which the legal process, from investigation to judgement, is performed by a legal official. Neither king nor councillor initiated proceedings against suspects, as far as we know, but once the suspects were held in the tolbooth the king and council directed their examinations and authorised their torture.[72] They took control of the pre-trial investigations, and extracted information and confessions from the accused to present at the trials. Had the king or councillors then acted as sole judges at the trials, the judicial process would have been taken over by officials. As it was all the trials took place before an assize which had to deliver the verdict. Even so, the procedures were exceptionally oppressive, and in the Napier trial the assize's verdict was overriden by the king's determination to have a guilty verdict. The lay assize was the judicial element that prevented the trials of the North Berwick accused being entirely subject to official direction and pressure.

Court procedure

In the trials of Napier and MacCalzean court procedures were used tenaciously to defend the panel. The procedures of the justiciary court are described by Willock.[73] The assize of usually fifteen men was chosen from a larger number summoned because they were 'sik persones as best knawis the veritie in the said matter'.[74] The indictment was read to the accused, who had to deny or affirm it, and its basis for a trial might then be debated. Then the assize was selected from those summoned, and put on oath. At this stage the assize might be threatened by either or both prosecution and defence laywers with wilful error should they acquit or convict the accused. After that the evidence was produced, first by reading the dittay aloud to the court, or by reading a confession previously recorded. In the latter case the accused would be asked to affirm its truth or to re-sign it, a part of the procedure thought to be a safeguard against the coercive effects of torture. After this the defence and prosecuting counsels could address the assize, often in a style, according to Mackenzie, 'firy, abrupt, sprightly and bold'.[75] After that the assize might raise questions before they left the court to decide the verdict. There was a ban on adjourning the proceedings, so the success of MacCalzean's advocates in stretching her trial out for four days was remarkable. It was possible for the assizers themselves to be charged with wilful error if their verdict flew in the face of the evidence, the charge that James brought against the assizers at Napier's trial.

The assize

Given that confessions were often obtained by torture, trial by an assize was 'a safeguard, though an inadequate one' against oppressive arraignment.[76] Each of the four North Berwick witchcraft trials was heard by an assize. The members of assizes usually came from the local area, thus intensifying the local nature of the legal process. Rumour, suspicion, gossip, allegation, and anything else which had not found its way into the offical depositions, would be circulating in the assizers' minds as they considered the case; and all these were considered fair for the jury to take into account.[77]

A proper verdict was sometimes blocked by assizers' kin or local loyalties. Lady Foulis and Hector Munro were found not guilty of witchcraft by assizes consisting largely of burgesses from Tain and Dingwall unwilling to convict fellow gentry.[78] It was not uncommon for nobles or lords to arrive for their trial with bands of retainers or allies to intimidate the assize. A letter from the earl of Bothwell to Sir Patrick Waus, laird of Barnbarroch and a senator of the court of justice, makes clear what response was expected from an ally:

> We ar sumound to underly [submit to] the law . . . for the slauchter of umquhile D[avid] H[ume]. Thairfoir we will maist ernistlie craue your l[ordship's] presens the said day, accompaneit with your l[ordship's] freindis and servandis, to the defence of our lyves, quhilk we sall nocht spair to hasard [avoid risking] for your l[ordship] quhensoever [whenever] the alyik occasioun sal be offerit.[79]

The assizers of Barbara Napier's trial shared the same city background as the accused.[80]

The procedure in the justiciary court was more developed than that in local courts. Accused brought to Edinburgh for trial would face an assize which contained fewer local people. In the unusual circumstances of the four North Berwick justiciary court trials, however, local loyalties entered the courtroom along with Napier and MacCalzean. Some members of the assizes of Fian's and Sampson's trials came from the accused's locality. Ten of the fourteen members of Fian's assize came from Tranent where he lived. At Sampson's trial, seven of the seventeen assizers were from Haddington, the nearest town to her village of Nether Keith, and the rest from villages in the area within the ambit of her extensive wanderings to practise her healing.

In local courts women and men charged with witchcraft were unlikely to be acquitted since the legal process merely repeated the social process by which the local community had already judged them guilty.[81] In the justiciary court after 1597 conviction rates were much lower at around 45 per cent, but in the special circumstances of the 1590–1 witch hunt all four defendants were convicted. In the seventeenth century the enlightened jurist George Mackenzie well understood the socially disastrous consequences of scapegoating as a witch, and wrote sympathetically of meeting one accused woman:

> I went when I was a Justice-Depute to examine some Women, who had confest judicially, and one of them, who was a silly creature, told me under secrecie, that she had not confest because she was guilty, but being a poor creature, who wrought for her meat, and being defam'd for a Witch, she knew she would starve, for no person thereafter would either give her meat or lodging, and that all men would beat her, and hound dogs at her, and that therefore she desired to be out of the world; whereupon she wept most bitterly, and upon her knees call'd God to witness to what she said.[82]

For those arraigned on witchcraft charges in local areas in the 1590s and throughout the seventeenth century there were few escape routes: counter-accusation, flight, banishment, death in prison, suicide.[83] Pregnancy delayed an execution. It was by claiming pregnancy that Barbara Napier may have escaped execution, for after the sentence of strangling and burning was pronounced against her, 'the said Barbara declared that she was with bairn, and therefore alleged that no execution of the said doom could be used against her while she was delivered of her birth'. The main line of defence, however, was to slander someone else as a witch, for that might divert the charge. This seems to have happened when the earl of Bothwell accused Ritchie Graham of witchcraft. Counter-accusations were the means by which a single charge of witchcraft turned into a witch hunt, and a social panic involving many people.

Punishment

Witchcraft carried the death penalty like murder, mutilation, aggravated theft, false coining, affording refuge to rebels, treasonable slaughter, bestiality, notorious adultery, sodomy and incest.[84] The court fixed a date for execution, normally a few days after the verdict. Agnes Sampson was sentenced on 27 January 1591 and executed the following day.[85] Euphame MacCalzean was sentenced on 13 June 1591, but had to wait until 25 June for execution. Dr Fian was convicted on 26 December 1590, but if we believe *News* he was not executed until late January 1591. Death was usually by strangling followed by burning. The sentence against Euphame MacCalzean, that she should be burned 'quick' (alive) was exceptionally severe. An execution was a great public event, with the convicted women and men being carted through the streets from their place of imprisonment in the tolbooth or church steeple to the place of execution. An execution might be accompanied by a day or more of general fasting and by a round of sermons from local ministers.[86] The execution was a communal event, and its meanings extended into the whole locality.

A witch's estate was automatically forfeit to the crown, as was that of someone convicted of treason.[87] The formula at the end of Agnes Sampson's dittay runs: 'and thereafter her body to be burned in ashes and all her moveable goods to be escheat and inbrought to our sovereign lord's use etc.'.

Notes

[1] Parker 1988: 13.
[2] Larner 1981: 36.
[3] Whyte 1995: 210–6, provides a convenient overview of the legal system.
[4] Whyte 1995: 211–12.
[5] Whyte 1995: 216.
[6] Larner, Lee and McLachlan 1977: v.
[7] See document 2.
[8] Black 1938: 21; Larner, Lee and McLachlan 1977: 172, 238–9; Larner 1984: 24.
[9] *Acts of the Parliaments* 1814: 539.
[10] Black 1938: 11.
[11] There seems to be no suggestion of any connection between the two witchcraft acts passed in both England and Scotland in 1563; see Kittredge 1929: 262–3.
[12] Wormald 1981: 168; Larner 1981: 66.
[13] Smith 1972: xii.
[14] Larner 1981: 66.
[15] *Booke of the Universall Kirk* 1839: 281.
[16] James VI and I 1994: 23.
[17] See Larner 1984: 35–67.
[18] Williamson 1979: 57.
[19] See *DOST* sv 'negramansy'.
[20] Black 1938: 11–12; Larner 1981: 66.
[21] *OED*, sb 2. On popular magic, and on superstition in this sense, see Clark 1997: 457–88.
[22] See *DOST*, abuse *v.* 2.
[23] *Historie of James the Sext* 1825: 242.
[24] Black 1938: 12.
[25] Larner 1981: 67.
[26] Larner 1984: 12.
[27] Willock 1966: 44.
[28] Smith 1972: v, notes that private prosecutions remained the norm, but the lord advocate (or king's advocate) could in exceptional circumstances supersede the private prosecutor. In cases of treason the lord advocate obtained the authority of the privy council to act, vi.
[29] Willock 1966: 197.
[30] The full text of the commission, passed at Holyroodhouse, 26 October 1591, is given in the Appendix.
[31] Larner 1981: 70.
[32] Larner 1981: 69.
[33] Levack 1996: 101.
[34] Wormald 2000: 177.
[35] Levack 1996: 106.
[36] Larner 1981: 69.
[37] The text is reproduced in *RPCS* iv 753.

38 Larner 1981: 70, a phrase Larner uses of the October 1591 privy council act.

39 Levack 1996: 101, refers to 'the large rash of witchcraft trials that took place between 1591 and 1597', and Larner 1981: 70, to 'an indiscriminate witch-hunt' of which 'the full extent . . . can never be known'.

40 Larner, Lee and McLachlan 1977: 238. Larner 1981: 61, gives a different estimate of 350.

41 The privy council order is reproduced in the Appendix.

42 Larner 1981: 71.

43 Larner 1981: 71–2.

44 Levack 1996: 101.

45 Law 1893: xii, xix, xxi; Wright 1851: 161; Sinclair 1871: 100–1.

46 Larner 1981: 103. This section draws on Larner's chapter 'The process from accusation to execution' (Larner 1981: 103–19).

47 Larner 1981: 103.

48 Smith 1972: x.

49 Mackenzie 1678: 87.

50 Larner 1981: 62.

51 Maxwell-Stuart 1997: 210.

52 See document 1.

53 *CSPS* x 467.

54 Hume 1797: ii 558.

55 Mackenzie 1678: 86–7.

56 Levack 1996: 103.

57 See document 4.

58 For some (sometimes disturbing) suggestions about the intimacy between an accused witch and her interrogators, and even torturers, see Roper 1994: 204–6.

59 Smith 1972: xxi.

60 Larner 1981: 107.

61 Smith 1972: xxx.

62 See Larner 1981: 180; Smith 1972: xxxvi.

63 See Smith 1972: xvii; Levack 1996: 105.

64 Langbein 1977: 149.

65 Levack 1996: 105–6.

66 Melville 1905: 235; Larner 1981: 107–13.

67 Larner 1981: 108.

68 Lowell 1897: 221.

69 Smith 1972: xv.

70 The most emphatic case for Scots law being inquisitorial in the seventeenth century is Smith 1972. Qualifications to his view are suggested by Willock 1966, who emphasises the role of the assize, and Levack 1996, who shows witchcraft trials springing from local pressure rather than central initiative. The case for the fairness of the inquisitorial mode is made by Tedeschi 1993.

71 Unsworth 1989: 87.

72 According to Lowell 1897: 228–9, 'It was strictly an inquisition, in which the judge attempted to detect a crime, and satisfy himself by his own efforts of the prisoner's guilt'.

73 Willock 1966: 191–209.

74 Willock 1966: 154.

75 Quoted by Willock 1966: 202.

76 Willock 1966: 197. He notes 'the strong feeling in the 16th and 17th centuries that trial by jury was of the very essence of criminal procedure', and quotes Skene, who wrote that 'be the law of this Realm, all crimes suld be decided and tryed be ane Assize, *Stat. Alex. c. 3*'. He adds that the assize was strengthened by the act of 1587.

77 For discussions of court procedure and the assize see Smith 1972: xlv–li (an account that emphasises inquisitorial aspects); and Willock 1966: 191–209.

78 Willock 1966: 179.

79 Willock 1966: 174–5.

80 Williamson 1979: 48.

81 Larner, Lee and McLachlan 1977: 237 (Table 2) estimate that the conviction rate in local commissioned trials is 95 per cent. For a discussion of rates of conviction see Larner 1981: 60–4; Levack 1996: 102–3.

82 Mackenzie 1678: 87. Mackenzie blamed ministers for many witchcraft accusations: 'And really Ministers are oft-times indiscreet in their zeal, to have poor creatures to confess in this: And I recommend to Judges that the wisest Ministers should be sent to them [suspected women], and those who are sent, should be cautious in this', 87.

83 For a discussion of ways of avoiding execution see Larner 1981: 116–19.

84 Smith 1972: lix.

85 Stafford 1953: 102.

86 Larner 1981: 113.

87 Larner 1981: 115

Chapter 6

AFTERMATH

The protracted witch hunt that lasted from 1590 until 1597 finally came to an end by state action but not before an unknown number of people had died. Scattered references indicate witch hunts, not just individual cases, breaking out in several areas. In June 1595 a letter recorded 'many witches are taken and burnt in the Merse, some for mean, some for greater matters'.[1] In Aberdeen in 1597 there was a particularly serious outbreak of trials and executions. The Aberdeen dean of guild was commended by the town council because he 'hes extraordinarlie takin panis [pains] on the birning of the gryt number of witches brint this yeir'.[2] In the trials in many parts of Scotland of 1596–7 signs appeared of 'disorderly legality' in which the trials, 'like the disorder of festivals . . . threatened to give rise to an institutionalized anarchy in which popular forces rather than state agencies set the norms of conduct'.[3] A Fife woman, Margaret Aitken, known as 'the great witch of Balwery', claimed to be able to spot another witch by simply looking in her eyes, and was 'carried from town to town to make discoveries in that kind'.[4] In Glasgow she sent many women to their deaths, until she was exposed as a fraud by being presented with the same person two days running, declaring them guilty one day and innocent the next. On 12 August 1597 the privy council acted to stop trials in local areas by revoking the commissions issued to local courts, and reclaiming its power to judge individual requests from towns and villages to prosecute for witchcraft. It was thought at the time that the Margaret Aitken scandal prompted James to revoke the post-1592 standing commissions, and indeed the 1597 commission alluded to complaints of innocent people being tried. The immediate effect of the 1597 order was that 'cases were reduced to isolated incidents'.[5] The witch hunt that began in 1590 was over.

Accusations made in the course of the North Berwick witch hunt were unravelling as early as 1591. Immediately after the execution of Euphame MacCalzean in June 1591 depositions were taken from people who had deponed against her in which they recanted their previous accusation. Geillis Duncan, with whom the hunt started according to *News*, declared, moments before she was executed in December 1591, that everything that she had said about Napier and MacCalzean had been lies. By the time Bothwell was tried for witchcraft against the king in August 1593 the urgency of this particular witchcraft charge had disappeared.

Demonology was published in London in 1603, the year that James became king of England. In 1604 the last of the three English witchcraft acts was passed. The first suggestion that James wished to see this English statute passed was Francis Hutchinson's in 1718, and in this he was followed by Walter Scott among others.[6] Notestein too thought too that the king influenced the passing of the 1604 act and was responsible for the increase of prosecutions in England after his accession to the English throne.[7] This idea of James's continuing enthusiasm for witchcraft prosecutions were, in Clark's words, 'comfortably disposed of some years ago'.[8] Kittredge has a long and detailed account of James and witchcraft, in which he claims that James did not start the witch hunt in 1590–1, but did become involved in it.[9] He exculpates the king from any blame, since James 'was only a mortal man, swept off his feet by the tide'.[10] This book cannot entirely support that view, as it contains evidence that James intervened personally in the examinations of the accused, and especially in Napier's trial. Larner found James 'relatively uninterested in demonology until 1590, intensely interested from the sorcery trials of 1590 until the publication of his *Daemonologie* in 1597, and slightly embarrassed . . . thereafter'.[11] Indeed, 'thereafter' in the course of his reign in England, James busied himself in detecting a series of pretenders to supernatural powers and afflictions.[12]

The pressure for witch hunting in Scotland in 1590 came not from the king but the kirk, which regarded the extirpation of witchcraft as part of its mission to found the godly society. Witchcraft was constituted, in Scotland as elsewhere in Europe, by aggregating a diversity of popular magical practices and the idea of the pact with the devil, material that was all to hand in Scottish culture by 1590. From January 1590 witch hunting was breaking out in various parts of the country.

In the year before *Demonology* was printed in Edinburgh, James was politically in the ascendant. The dangers in 1590 of catholic insurgency had been faced down, and Bothwell had been destroyed. The kirk continued to challenge royal authority, with the minister of St Andrews in 1596 daring to call all kings the children of the devil,[13] but in December 1596 an incident occured that James seized on to tame the ministers. While the king and the lords of session were in the tolbooth, and the ministers in a nearby church, a crowd gathered shouting about a papist uprising to kill the king and council. James blamed the ministers and ordered them to be warded in Edinburgh Castle, and threatened to abandon Edinburgh as the capital city. This marked the 'extinction of ultra-protestantism as a political danger',[14] and the revival of episcopacy in the next few years. The crown's temporary alliance with the kirk was ended since James no longer needed its support against Bothwell or the papists. And the crown no longer needed to support, or acquiesce to, the kirk's demands for prosecution of witches. In 1590 'a fearful state was willing to listen to the dictates of a determined Kirk, and turn to repression and violence'.[15] The privy council order of 12 August 1597 put a stop to the widespread witch hunting that was raging in several parts of Scotland. Even though James was not responsible for starting the 1590–7 witch hunt, his experience of examining the North Berwick witches found its way into *Demonology*, and that in turn articulated widespread Scottish witchcraft beliefs that would continue to appear in the next century.

Notes

1. *CSPS* xi 621.
2. See Ross 1962: 398, citing *Extracts from the Burgh Records of Aberdeen, 1579–1625* (Spalding Club, 1848).
3. Unsworth 1989: 76, quoting Hirst and Woolley 1982: 254.
4. Spottiswoode 1668: 448.
5. Larner 1981: 71.
6. Kittredge 1929: 289, 276–7; Wright 1851: i 179

7. Notestein 1965: 93–119.
8. Clark 1977: 161 and fn. 16, 178–9.
9. Kittredge 1929: 276–328.
10. Kittredge 1929: 279.
11. Larner 1984: 5, 10–12.
12. Kittredge 1929: 314–28.
13. Lee 1974: 53.
14. See Donaldson 1965: 194–5.
15. Wormald 1985: 164.

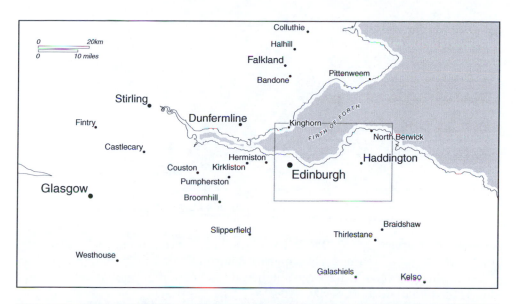

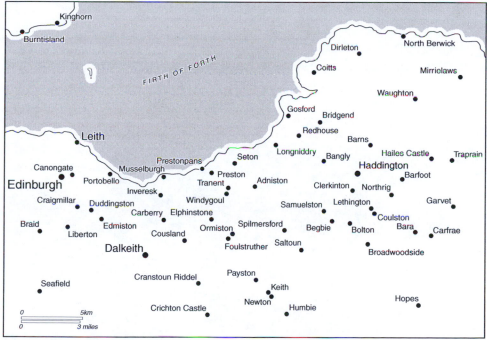

Edinburgh and central Scotland, showing locations mentioned in the documents.

Plate 1   An engraving of 1789 showing the ruins of the twelfth-century parish church of North Berwick, and possibly a pilgrims' hospital, on an offshore promontory. This was the place to which a large number of witches were supposed to have sailed for a convention with the devil.

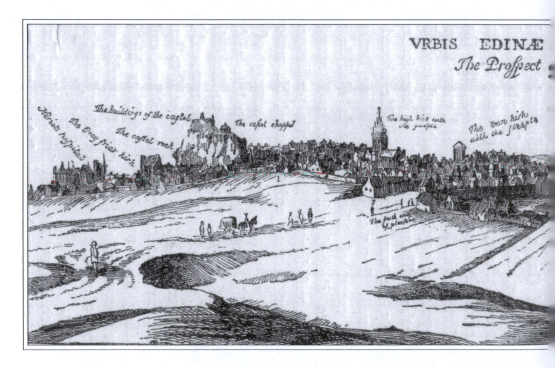

Plate 2   Edinburgh from the south, based on James Gordon of Rothiemay's 1647 drawing, showing the castle on the left and Holyrood palace and abbey on the right.

Plate 3 Seton Palace, on the estuary of the Forth, where James VI spent two weeks in September 1589, awaiting the arrival by sea from Denmark of Princess Anne. Many of the witchcraft accused came from surrounding villages, and some were imprisoned in Seton Palace.

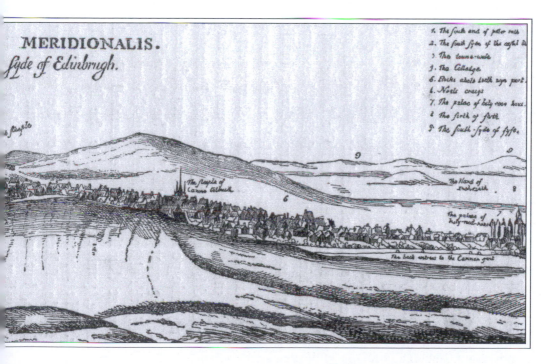

The steeple of St Giles church is clearly visible. The separate burgh of the Canongate lies between Edinburgh and Holyrood, marked by its larger houses and gardens.

Plate 4   The old Tolbooth of Edinburgh, adjacent to St Giles church, used as a prison for some of those accused of witchcraft.

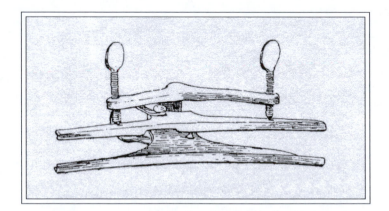

Plate 5   The pilliwinks, an instrument of torture used to squeeze the fingers. The maidservant Geillis Duncan, one of the first accused in the witch hunt according to *News from Scotland*, was subjected to this amateur, illegal torture by her master, David Seton.

Plate 6 James VI, aged twenty-nine, in a portrait of 1595 attributed to Adrian Vanson.

Plates 7 and 8   James VI and Queen Anne, aged nineteen, in a pair of miniature portraits of 1595 attributed to Adrian Vanson.

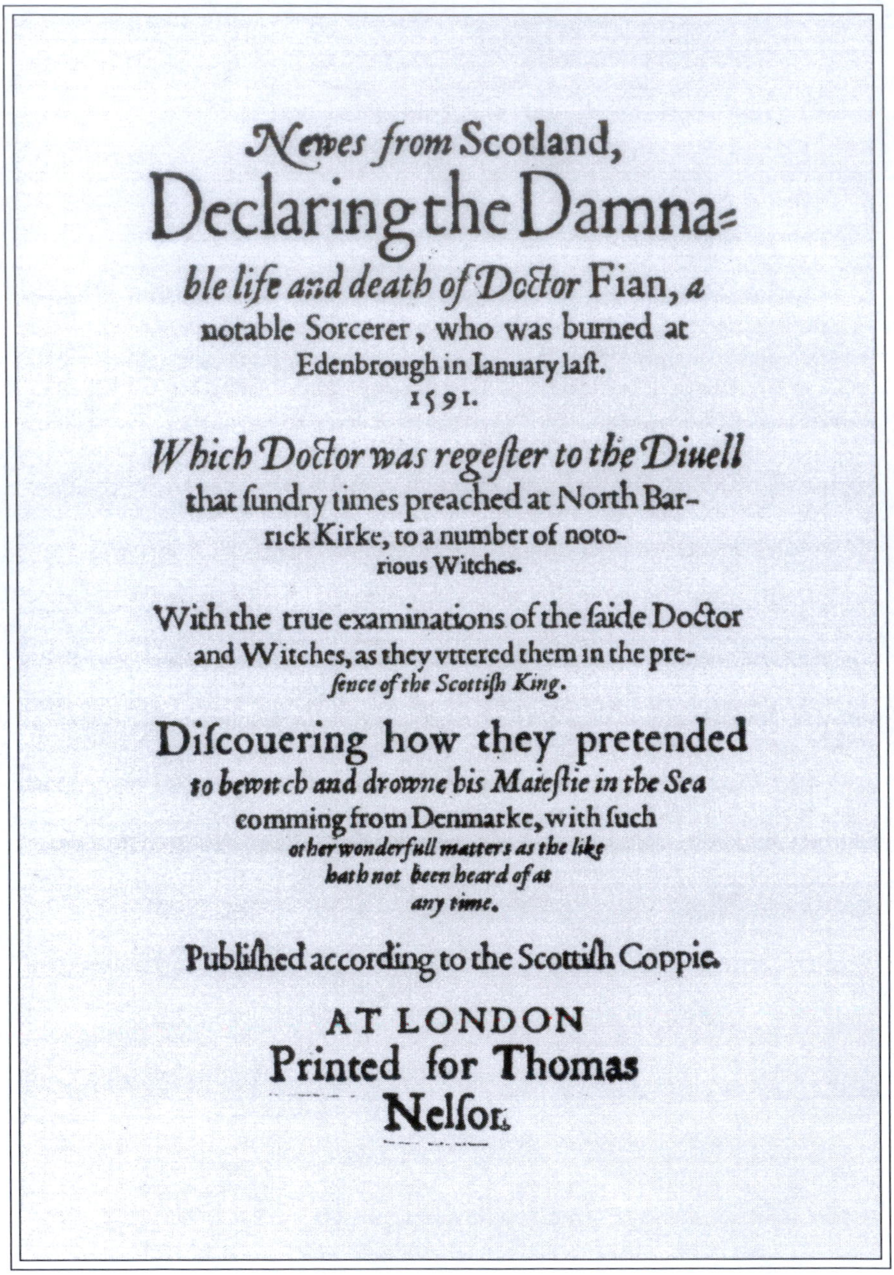

Newes from Scotland,
Declaring the Damna=
ble life and death of Doctor Fian, *a*
notable Sorcerer, who was burned at
Edenbrough in Ianuary laſt.
1591.

Which Doctor was regeſter to the Diuell
that ſundry times preached at North Bar-
rick Kirke, to a number of notorious Witches.

With the true examinations of the ſaide Doctor
and Witches, as they vttered them in the pre-
ſence of the Scottiſh King.

Diſcouering how they pretended
to bewitch and drowne his Maieſtie in the Sea
comming from Denmarke, with ſuch
other wonderfull matters as the like
hath not been heard of at
any time.

Publiſhed according to the Scottiſh Coppie.

AT LONDON
Printed for Thomas
Nelſon.

Plate 9   The title page of one of the early printed versions of the pamphlet *News from Scotland* issued in London. There is no date of publication given, but late 1591 seems likely.

Plate 10 A woodcut from *News from Scotland* with scenes loosely based on, or suggested by, the pamphlet.

Plate 11   A woodcut from *News from Scotland* with an image of Fian conjuring the heifer. The image of two men on horseback with flaming brands on the horse's head illustrates an image not in *News*, but in Fian's dittay (document 19).

Plate 12   A woodcut from *News from Scotland* often taken to show the king witnessing the submission of four women accused of witchcraft. However, the woodcut was first devised for an earlier witchcraft pamphlet, and must have been taken from the printer's general stock.

Plate 13   A woodcut from *News from Scotland* in a different style from the others, showing a man being led to prison by a jailor and a woman who holds his ear. Another woodcut from the printer's stock with a slight connection to a story in *News*, in this case Fian's imprisonment.

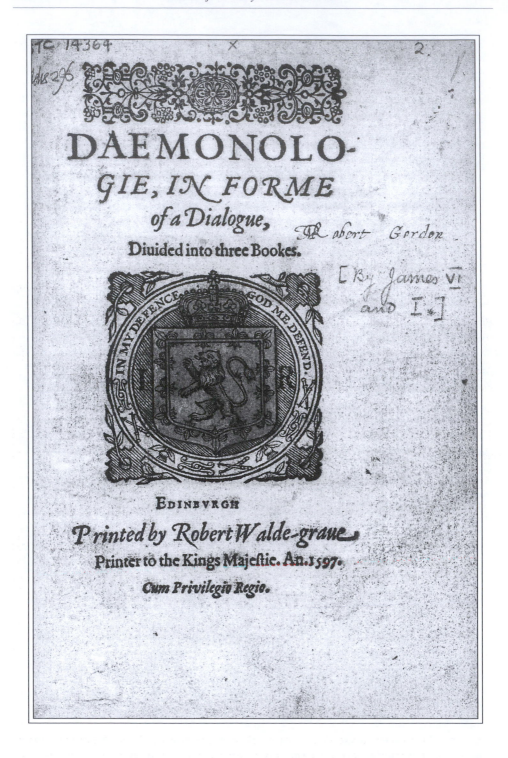

Plate 14   The title page of the first edition of *Demonology*, printed in Edinburgh in 1597 by Robert Waldegrave, with the device of the royal arms.

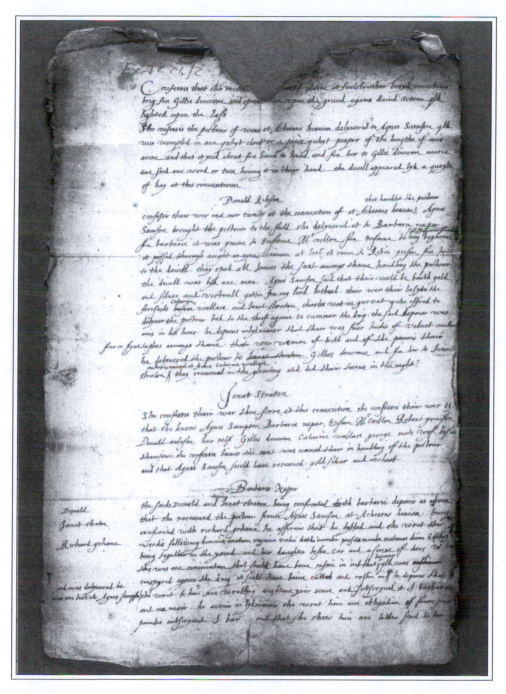

Plate 15 Manuscript page of JC 26/2/1 (document 5) recording the examinations and confessions of witchcraft suspects ?Bessie Thomson, Donald Robson, Janet Stratton and Barbara Napier, probably before members of the king's council in January 1591. The scribe has noted names mentioned in Napier's answers in the left margin.

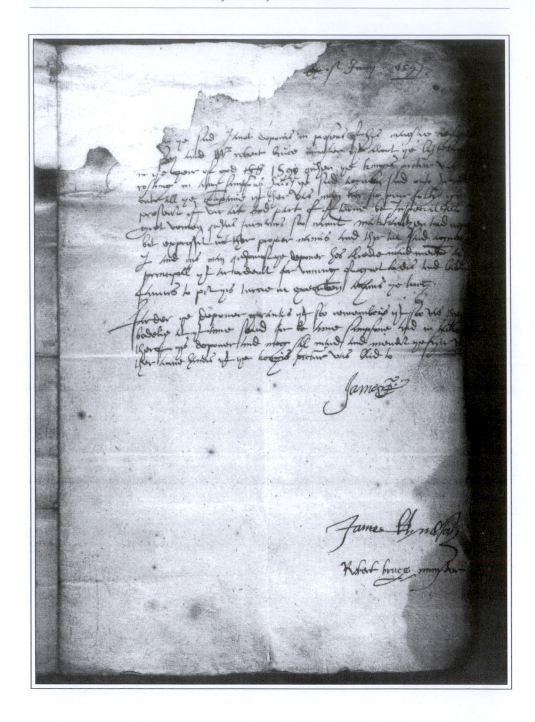

Plate 16   Manuscript page of JC 26/2/11 (document 14) recording the deposition of Janet Kennedy incriminating Euphame MacCalzean and Barbara Napier. It was taken in June 1591 before the king, James Lindsay and Robert Bruce, who all signed it.

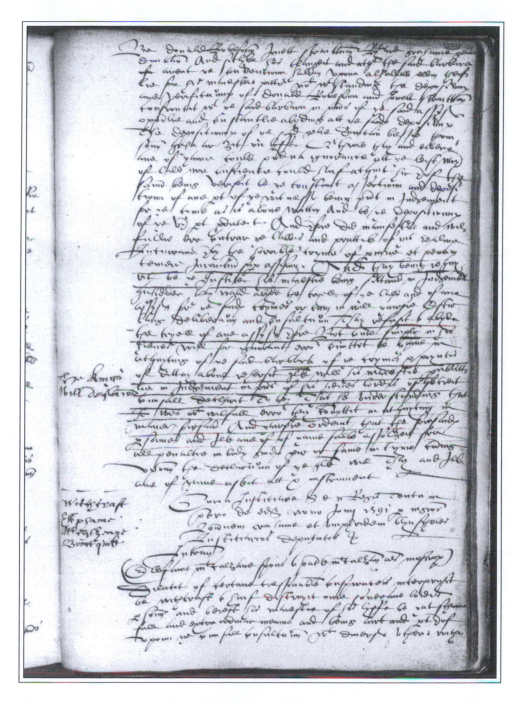

Plate 17   Manuscript page of JC 2/2 (documents 22 and 23) recording the submission to the king on 7 June 1591 of the assizers at Barbara Napier's trial, with the words 'The king's will declared' noted in the margin. The record of Euphame MacCalzean's trial that took place on 9–15 June 1591 immediately follows, with the words 'Witchcraft: Euphame MacCalzean burned quick' noted in the margin.

Plate 18   Late seventeenth-century view of Haddington, the town in East Lothian which was one of the centres of prosecution in the witch hunt.

Part 2

TEXTS

Chapter 7

WITCH HUNTING: EXAMINATIONS, CONFESSIONS AND DEPOSITIONS

Before the trials suspects were detained, interrogations were conducted and depositions taken, and this evidence was recorded and retained for production at trial. Confrontation of the accused with witnesses, that is the bringing of these persons face to face with each other, took place before the trial and could be repeated at it. And witnesses could be confronted with other witnesses. Interrogations were repeated, as in the case of Agnes Sampson.

There were virtually no limits to what constituted admissible evidence at a witchcraft trial. Rumour and reputation were included alongside things allegedly said and done.[1] The investigators were trying to form a plausible story from the fragmentary evidence which they gathered. The legal test was the same as a storytelling test. Is it a convincing story? Do the incidents hang together? Are the characters involved likely to have acted as reported? Are the motivations plausible? Statements and confessions can be understood in terms of the common stock of cultural knowledge that both constitutes them and makes sense of them to interrogators and accused, as well as in terms of the particular circumstances of the person who is compelled to speak.

The examinations and depositions make no mention of torture being used in the process of examination, and from them one would not suspect that torture had been used.[2] But if *News* is at all accurate, Agnes Sampson was tortured after initially refusing to confess: the king and his council 'caused her to be conveyed away to prison, there to receive such torture as hath been lately provided for witches in that country'. A casual postcript by Bowes in a letter of 15 April to Burghley is equally chilling:

> This daye Robert Greyson, one of the three witches to have bene examyned, died, and as it is thought by the extremyty of the tortours applyed to him. He hath confessed litle . . .[3]

Fear of torture seems to have weighed heavily with Ritchie Graham in his decision to inform against Bothwell. When Bothwell was tried in August 1593, 'divers honest men of Edenbroughe . . . deposed that Richard Greyme said to theme that he must eyther accuse the Erle Bothwell falselye, or els endure such tormentes as no man were able to abyde'. Indeed Graham's own brother deponed on that occasion that Ritchie accused Bothwell 'for feare of maymynge with the bootes and other tortures'.[4]

Most of the documents record the examinations and depositions of persons whose names appear in the dittays and *News from Scotland*: Geillis Duncan, Agnes Sampson, Janet Stratton, Donald Robson and Bessie Thomson. No record has survived of any examination of Dr Fian, the first of those tried and executed. At some stage these persons and what they had to say were thought sufficiently important for them to be brought from the area around Prestonpans to Edinburgh to be questioned before members of the privy council, and sometimes before the king himself, who, according to *News*, 'took great delight to be present at their examinations', and whose signature can be seen at the bottom of some documents. The accused were presumably apprehended and examined first in their local areas. The first report we have of the king and his council examining witches in Edinburgh is Bowes's letter of 28 November 1590. If these examinations had started earlier than 28 November it is likely that Bowes would have mentioned them earlier, so perhaps the accused were brought to Edinburgh in late November 1590. Agnes Sampson and Geillis Duncan were both supposedly free to dance at the convention at North Berwick kirk on 31 October 1590. Their apprehension, initial examinations in Haddington or Tranent, and their transfer to Edinburgh must all have happened in November 1590.

Pre-trial examinations and depositions, late 1590 – early 1591

The earliest documents, probably from late November/early December 1590, are examinations of Geillis Duncan and Agnes Sampson (document 1). Both record the execution of a few witches (Kate Graw or Gray, David Steel, Janet Campbell) as having already happened by late 1590. These persons are mentioned in Sampson's dittay as having been at a convention at Garvet church, which Bowes dates 5 November 1589.[5]

In document 1 Sampson confesses to an attempt at *maleficium* against David Seton which involved raising the devil. This, taken together with Duncan's affirmation before her execution in December 1591 that she had slandered some of the accused and 'that she was caused [made to] and persuaded so to do by the two David Setons in Tranent and others',[6] provides confirmation of *News*'s depiction of Seton as the 'discoverer' of the alleged witches. The predictions about the king having boys and then girls may identify some anxiety about the succession. The devil also told Agnes Sampson that the queen should never come home unless the king fetched her. Insofar as there is any hint of political conspiracy in these early depositions it is in the plotting to stay the queen's homecoming and sending a letter about it. This incident is mentioned in Fian's dittay in December. A model for this story could have been provided by the news from Denmark in July 1590 that five or six witches had been apprehended in Copenhagen, 'upon suspicion that by their witche craft they had staied the Queen of Scottes voiage into Scotland, and sought to have staied likewise the King's retorne'.[7] Bowes also reported to Burghley the arraignment of some witches in Edinburgh who had made and melted a wax image of the 'yong laird of Wardhouse', but did not mention Scottish witches conspiring against the king nor a wax image of James. If there had been any thought of conspiracy against the king involving a wax image in July 1590, Bowes would have mentioned it. Yet the wax image of the king, according to later depositions, was already displayed at a convention on 31 July 1590. The chronology of witchcraft events that emerges from these documents is constructed retrospectively as the process of examination and deposition goes on, and is, in most respects, imaginary.

In a letter of 7 December Bowes reported to Burghley that the king by his 'own special travell [effort]' had drawn Agnes Sampson to confess. The examinations in which this took place, on 4–5 December 1590, are reported in document 2. This examination is very important, for within it, between the earlier and later items, we can trace the way a cunning woman is turned into a witch by the process of legal interrogation, and how Agnes Sampson's witchcraft is fashioned into its more or less final form. She was interrogated about the attempt to heal Lady Edmiston, a story that has clearly been told before, and the king pointed out contradictions in this story. Under pressure from the king 'to confess the truth' she is recorded by the document as confessing to three features of classic European witchcraft: calling on the devil, the pact at first meeting, and a witches' meeting. These features were already there in Sampson's confessions in document 1 but in a more diffuse, less elaborated form. This document records these narratives virtually word for word as they appear in Sampson's dittay, although without all the details and names of attenders in the description of the North Berwick convention in the dittay (item 50). The next day Sampson's confession brought *maleficium* and convention together in the story of the meeting at Foulstruther to destroy David Seton in almost exactly the words of the first part of item 49 of her dittay, which then goes on to give other details.

Some time in January 1591 Agnes Sampson was examined before the master of work (document 4). The effect of this examination is to connect Agnes Sampson explicitly with Barbara Napier and also to hint at her association with Euphame MacCalzean. This is the first record we have of the two Edinburgh women being implicated in witchcraft accusation.

The next document in chronological order is probably document 5. It records the testimony of ?Bessie Thomson, Donald Robson and Janet Stratton about the supposed convention in a field at Acheson's Haven (31 July 1590), first mentioned here and already the site of treason. The wax image in the first examination is identified as the king's image by Donald Robson, who claimed that it was handled at the convention by more than twenty people, including Barbara Napier and Euphame MacCalzean. Not only were these women incriminated but so was Bothwell. Bowes's shrewd comment in November 1590 that 'some of good qualities are like to be blotted by the dealinges of the wickett sorte'[8] proved to be accurate, as the Edinburgh women are directly implicated in magical treason against the king, and Bothwell is represented as funding that enterprise.

Document 6 also contains depositions by Geillis Duncan, Janet Stratton and Donald Robson. It must be one or both of these sets of depositions (documents 5 and 6) that are referred to in the charges against Napier listed in the trial of her jurors on 7 June 1591, and which Robson, Stratton, Graham and Duncan affirmed again in Napier's presence on that day. It is very likely that documents 5 and 6 were records of a series of depositions made quite close together in time, i.e. the end of January 1591. Since document 5 is the more incriminating about Napier, it may be that it is this set of depositions which was being referred to on 7 June 1591, as was document 7, a brief deposition by Janet Stratton. It is also likely that what the king had in mind when he called the lords of session in to pronounce on whether *socii criminis* (associates in the crime) might testify in certain actions[9] is the validity of these very depositions, and the validity of the deponers' affirming them in court.

Witchcraft and treason: depositions, May – June 1591

After document 7 (30 January 1591) there is a gap in time in the extant material until 4 and 5 May 1591 when we find Janet Stratton, Geillis Duncan, Donald Robson and Bessie Thomson deponing yet again: Stratton in Holyroodhouse and the others the next day in the nether tolbooth in Edinburgh.

Between the end of January and May many things had happened and we know that accused witches were still being examined during this period. Some of 'the worst sort of witches' escaped to England and David Seton was to be sent in search of them.[10] The king was particularly anxious that one of these witches should be returned to Scotland and there are several references to her in Bowes's letters in February. She was apprehended in England, imprisoned in Berwick and returned to Scotland.[11] Although she is not named, it is likely that she was '[Janet] Kennedy the witch of Reydon, lately in England' mentioned by Bowes on 14 June, two of whose depositions in June before the king (documents 13, 14) have survived. On 23 February, when he reported Agnes Sampson's confession, Bowes said that some witches (including 'Grey Meal') had been burned in Haddington and that '[t]here are moe then fourtie apprehendit and under triall and examinatioun instantlie [at the moment]'.[12] Robert Grierson died on 15 April, it was thought because of torture, so examinations were still going on then.[13]

In April there was an intensificaton of the attempt to implicate Bothwell in treasonable witchcraft. On 15 April 1591 Bowes reported the king's saying that as a result of Ritchie Graham's examination before the council, the charges against Bothwell are 'come to a greater matter'. Graham had said that Bothwell had urged him to devise the king's end. The means were the ones familiar from the depositions and dittays: a wax image, toad venom, and a part of a calf's head. Bothwell was also accused by Geillis Duncan and others, who also implicated Bowes in the plot.[14] Bothwell was called to answer charges before the council on 16 April and was confronted with Graham and his accusations.[15]

But, according to Melville, the main source of accusation against Bothwell was Agnes Sampson:

> Specially ane renowned midwyf callit Anny Sampsoun, affirmed that sche, in company with nyn uthers witches, being convenit in the nycht besyd Prestounpannes, the devell ther maister being present standing in the midis of them; ther a body of wax schaipen and maid be the said Anny Sampsoun, wrappit within a lynnyng claith, was first delyverit to the devell; quhilk efter he had pronuncit his werde [word], delyverit the said pictour to Anny Sampsoun, and sche to hir nyxt marrow, and sa every ane round about, saying, this is K. James the sext, ordonit to be consumed at the instance of a noble man Francis Erle Bodowell.[16]

Agnes Sampson had of course been executed at the end of January and could not contest this ascription of information to her. Similarly the late Agnes Sampson is the agent and protagonist of the story in Janet Stratton's deposition on 4 May. In that deposition convention and treasonable magic are thoroughly integrated with each other, and that treasonable magic is performed at the express command of Bothwell.

The other depositions, at least one taken next day (document 9), confirmed Janet Stratton's story, particularly about the Acheson's Haven convention.

A few days later and the accusation of treason came yet closer to Euphame MacCalzean. On 7 May both MacCalzean and her servant Bessie Nisbet were examined at Holyroodhouse. There are two features common to the process of incrimination of both Bothwell and the Edinburgh women: the interrogation of their servants, and allegations about sending letters. The latter, ironically, we may recall, was a technique used to incriminate James's own mother, Mary queen of Scots. MacCalzean was questioned about sending letters to people imprisoned in the tolbooth, including her servant (and sometime nurse) Janet Drummond. She alternately admitted and denied sending, writing or composing various letters. Janet Drummond appears in MacCalzean's dittay as 'your old agent', which represents her as a go-between and messenger: taking charms to bewitch Marie Sandelands and prevent her marriage (item 14, 15), taking messages to and from Agnes Sampson (item 16), and taking the alleged wax image of MacCalzean's father-in-law to Agnes Sampson to have it enchanted (item 19). The last incident, in which the image was in a box hidden inside a goose, is alluded to at the end of the examination in document 12.

The last depositions we have before the trial of Euphame MacCalzean are those of Janet Kennedy, probably early in June 1591. The examiners were a formidable group: on one occasion the king, the duke of Lennox and two important ministers of the kirk, on another day the king and two ministers. In document 13 Janet Kennedy deponed about her first meeting with the devil about thirty years before. Kennedy said she saw 'a [?man] beside the said Agnes, of mean stature, about 30 years of age as appeared to the deponer, and with little hair on his face, and being but whey lean faced'. This must be meant to suggest Bothwell, who in 1591 was twenty-eight. This is the unique moment in the records when it is insinuated that Bothwell actually attended a convention. This deposition represents him as eager to have the *maleficium* effected on the king: he wanted to take the image prematurely out of Agnes Sampson's hand, and later at her house urged her to make the fire hotter to melt the image. In document 14 Janet Kennedy reiterated the story about the roasting of the king's image around Lammas 1590. Agnes Sampson is again ventriloquised to incriminate MacCalzean and Napier by name, although rather coyly, and Bothwell by implication.

Agnes Sampson is a constant presence in all these documents. But she is no longer the woman who prescribed eggs in vinegar and iris for sick folk, or rubbed whisky on a laird's son who was ill.[17] She is now being represented as the confidante and equal of great lords and ladies, and a 'principal' in a conspiracy with national consequences. The stakes have been raised quite considerably by June 1591. At this moment in time, if Kennedy's depositions can be dated before Bowes's letter of 14 June, Bothwell was in prison. Euphame MacCalzean's trial had probably started, but she may not have been convicted yet (12 June), and had not been sentenced, as this did not happen until 15 June. Barbara Napier was being detained under surveillance to see if she was pregnant. What one guesses from Bowes's letters is a growing expectation that Bothwell would be tried for consulting witches to destroy the king, and this would be a knock-on effect of the conviction of Barbara Napier and Euphame MacCalzean. Bothwell was not actually tried on this charge until August 1593, as he escaped from Edinburgh Castle on 21 June 1591, four days before Euphame MacCalzean's execution.

On 19 June 1591 Robert, Lord Seton, took a deposition from Janet Stratton, who was imprisoned at Seton Palace, before a notary public. Stratton and Robson (who was imprisoned in Tranent) now repudiated their May depositions that Agnes Sampson had said that the wax image of the king had been commissioned by Bothwell. Stratton added that she had never seen Bothwell.

Depositions after Euphame MacCalzean's death, June – December 1591

After Euphame MacCalzean's execution on 25 June, there was clearly an attempt to exonerate her. The depositions of Janet Stratton and Donald Robson had repeatedly incriminated her, probably from late January 1591 onwards, as attending conventions, handling the wax image of the king, and having commissioned it in some way. At her trial Euphame MacCalzean was confronted with the testimony of Robson and Janet Stratton that she was at the conventions at both Acheson's Haven and North Berwick kirk and that she had handled the king's image. On 4 July Robson deponed (document 16) that he had had never known MacCalzean before he saw her in the tolbooth in Edinburgh and denied not only that he had seen her at the conventions at Acheson's Haven and North Berwick but also his own presence there. On the same day at Seton Palace Janet Stratton made a similar statement (document 17). These attempts may not have been with the intention of simply clearing MacCalzean's good name. Her conviction had entailed the loss of her estates: exoneration of the crime of witchcraft improved the chances of her heirs recovering them. Some of these estates, forfeit through her conviction, were eventually returned by act of parliament on 5 June 1592.

The process of the gradual unravelling of the story of witchcraft and treason that had been previously constructed continued on 4 December 1591. A deposition on that day (document 18) returns us to Geillis Duncan and David Seton, with whom the story of witchcraft began, according to *News from Scotland*. Almost exactly a year after she had deponed about a meeting in North Berwick kirk, Geillis Duncan and Bessie Thomson, who were about to be executed on the castle hill in Edinburgh, denied that they knew Barbara Napier and Euphame MacCalzean, and Duncan blamed the two David Setons in Tranent and others. Unlike the depositions of Stratton and Robson on 4 July, this was a very public declaration 'in presence of the people there convened'. Presumably this confession did nothing to stay her own execution. And it returns us, after the allegations of treason and conspiracy, to a small town and its local quarrels.

Notes

[1] Smith 1972: xlvii, notes that rumour and '"the notoriety of her (the panel's) guiltiness" are about as much as the prosecutor could hope for by way of evidence in the absence of a confession'. These are likely to have been features of many of the (mostly lost) witchcraft trials of 1590–7 in local jurisdictions. The evidence presented in the justiciary court trials in Edinburgh seems to be more detailed and specific but it often depends on a similar base of rumour and reputation.

[2] Compare how the notary of an inquisitorial court records such details, Tedeschi 1993: 89.

[3] *CSPS* x 502.

[4] *Border Papers* 1894–6: i 488.

[5] *CSPS* x 464.

[6] Document 18.

[7] *CSPS* x 365.

[8] *CSPS* x 425.

[9] *CSPS* x 522.

[10] *CSPS* x 457.

[11] *CSPS* x 460, 463, 471, 487.

[12] *CSPS* x 467.

[13] *CSPS* x 502.

[14] *CSPS* x 501–2.

[15] *CSPS* x 504–5.

[16] Melville 1827: 395.

[17] See document 2.

Document 1

Examinations and Confessions of
Geillis Duncan and Agnes Sampson

?before December 1590

The fragmentary notes at the top of the page indicate particular questions the examiners had in mind to ask the examinates. The 'ring' mentioned in these notes is presumably the one in Agnes Sampson's dittay, item 35, which she supposedly enchanted for Barbara Napier to gain the favour of Lady Angus.

At the start Geillis Duncan seems to be confessing to a meeting, in the middle of the firth, between the Scottish witches and a witch from Copenhagen ('Coppenhown'). There were rumours current that the storms that troubled the voyages of James and Anne from Denmark to Scotland were caused by witches working in both Denmark and Scotland (Larner 1984: 11). If we believe *News from Scotland*'s account of Geillis Duncan's confession incriminating Agnes Sampson, then these examinations may be among the earliest that are extant, that is before December 1590. They would seem to precede the more ordered interrogations and responses in document 2, in which Sampson is represented as breaking down and confessing to the king and giving a fuller story. These record a rather random series of events and details, and the meeting at North Berwick kirk does not yet seem very important or prominent. Although there is no break in the document, the examination of Agnes Sampson takes over from that of Geillis Duncan at the words, 'Agnes confesses she got some silver, and gave twenty shillings to "Grey Meal"'. Because of the recurrence of many of the items here in Agnes Sampson's dittay, we can be sure that it is her examination which the rest of the document records.

Sampson has clearly been imprisoned in Haddington tolbooth, but has at some point been brought to Edinburgh, and in this examination is responding to a series of questions. The fragmentary notes specify some of the things which she was to be asked, and she 'confesses' in response to questions about her meetings with the devil.

★

to be speered[†] concerning [   ]
concerning them that wer[e]
concerning the ring
memorandum to speer concerning [   ] dall[   ]

Gillie confesses that in the midst of the firth they met with the [   ] of Coppenhown,[†] where after they had gotten her name they commoned[†] togethe[r]. She[†] has given out[†] all the tokens[†][1] of the said woman, the name of the place [   ] fra Bessie Thomson confesses that the Irish[2] tailor and his wife had most commo[   ] her of any and that they understood her well, and she them.

She takes on her conscience[†] that she knew nothing of the intention of their gan[   ] there but only to obey him[†] that commanded her.

The last was at North Berwick. She rode to the town end and past her gan[   ] put in the horse, then she gaid[†] to the kirk. There were there sundry clad with taffetas.[†][3] There was no conjuration nor sealing[†] amongst themselves but so mickle as[†] every one answered him when he spake to them. She danced henmost[†] in the rank and 'Grey Meal'[†] with her, but she gaid first in over the kirk stile.

She confesses that 'Grey Meal' was received in service of the devil eft[†] about [?the hills of Skuggill?], where she was not sat by.
Balnaird]
A [?wachep?] of Duddingston brought her a mutch[†] of the laird of Balnaird to whom she confessed that he was witched and very sore handled.[†]

She confesses,[4] and 'Grey Meal' in like manner, that when the devil had them to the ship he promised that none of them should be seen. He promised to them gear enough[†] and said they should all perish; but he disappointed them of the gear.

[†] **speered** asked, questioned
[†] **Coppenhown** Copenhagen
[†] **commoned** talked
[†] **She** i.e. Geillis Duncan
[†] **given out** reported
[†] **tokens** distinguishing marks
[†] **She ... conscience** she gives her word
[†] **him** i.e. the devil?
[†] **gaid** went
[†] **with taffetas** in taffeta gowns
[†] **sealing** sealing of the pact?
[†] **so mickle as** inasmuch as

[†] **henmost** furthest back
[†] **Grey Meal** John Gordon, nicknamed 'Grey Meal' (the dirty sweepings from a mill, the meal used for feeding poultry), supposedly kept the door at the convention at North Berwick. Bowes reports that he had been burned at Haddington by 23 February 1591 (*CSPS* x 467).
[†] **eft** afterwards
[†] **mutch** cap
[†] **sore handled** grievously afflicted
[†] **gear enough** sufficient possessions

Agnes confesses she got some silver, and gave twenty shillings[5] to 'Grey Meal'.

She confesses that being in Haddington tolbooth there came down a fire from the high house to the lower house and a long black thing at the end of it.

She confesses that i[t] was the devil, but spake not.

She confesses that a sickness being taken of man be laid on some living creature, either man or beast, that cometh first over that which is laid in their way and she willing to lay that sickness on a dog, it lighted on one William Douglas.

She confesses the delivery of the bill out of her own hand.

She confesses that the devil told her she should be tane, but it should not be for seven year and able[†] not in her lifetime: he promised to save her from that.

She confesses that the wife of Payston sat betwixt 'Grey Meal' and her.
Grierson and Fian]
She confesses that Robert Grierson gaid in first in the boat.
He sat in the fore end[†] and John Fian beside [   ].
Grierson and Fian]
Item, in the kirk of North Berwick they were in like manner together, they being moved[†] at the naming of Robert.
The bill, Grierson, Fian]
The devil comma[   ] them all that was his servants to hold their tongues:[6] Fian, Grierson, 'Grey Meal', Gillie Duncan, Bessie Thomson, Irish Marion, George Mott's wife, Anny Sampson, Christian Lud, the goodwife of Spilmersford, then in George Mott's house. Robert Grierson drank to Agnes Sampson. The clerk had the first vote who made the convention.

She confesses that they were all crabbed[†] that Robin Grierson had gotten all at the wrack of the ship and the rest nothing.

She confesses the bill[†] was to raise the storm for staying of the queen's coming home.

She confesses that whenever sho called upon 'Eloa' he appeared[7] incontinent.[†]

She confesses that she consulted with the devil for the relief of Robert Cass: the devil refused to grant that to her. She answered, 'I man[†] have it'. Then said he, 'It shall light upon thyself'. She, thinking to relieve herself suddenly

---

† **able** perhaps
† **fore end** front part of the boat
† **moved** roused to anger
† **crabbed** cross

† **bill** letter
† **incontinent** immediately
† **man** must

again, received it.[†] She took the sickness off him by her prayer, and would have laid it on a dog, but it alighted[8] on Alexander Douglas who died in thirty days.

Agnes confesses that she was on large law head[†]

[   ] he was named [Rob]ert Grierson. They were all angry w[   ]
[   ] she alighted before she came to the kirk
[   ] were[9] all angry when Robert Grierson was
[   ] that named him. He lifted up his gown and every one kissed his arse. The men were turned nine times about and the women six times.
[   ] Sh[e] was in the ship where the uncouth[†] women were where the Irish tailor [   ] them and that she gave to 'Grey Meal' twenty shillings. She confesses that Ritchie Graham was [   ] and says 'Shame fall him'.[†] They shipped in[†] at North Berwick in a boat like a chimney[10] or a [   ] Some women rowed with oars. She drank to[†] Graham in white wine and he to them.

[S]he confesses that the devil brought the wine out of the ship's bottom and gave it out of his hand to them and that he remained there after they came out and raised the storm immediately.

She confesses that within this two year they were in a ship with an uncouth woman.

Saturday before noon

She[†] confesses that at every convention the first thing he demands is if they have kept promise to him.

She confesses that article[†] of David Seton, and that which was like the glass was glass indeed mixed with pieces of cords and other things to gar it work which the devil gave to her.[†]

She confesses that at (   ) there was a cord hauled at the devil's command[11] which she pulled not but she cried 'Haul! Hola!'[12] And the end of it was heavy and the devil came up at the end of it and speered if they were all good servants. There were there at the hauling[13] Geillis Duncan, Bessie Thomson and 'Grey Meal'.

She confesses that they made their consultation there to know how they

---

[†] **She … received it** since the devil refused to relieve Robert Cass's sickness, Agnes Sampson took the sickness upon herself, hoping that she might be able to relieve herself of the sickness
[†] **large law head** presumably the large conical hill that is North Berwick law
[†] **uncouth** unknown

[†] **Shame fall him** may disgrace fall on him
[†] **shipped in** took ship?
[†] **drank to** toasted
[†] **She** i.e. Agnes Sampson
[†] **article** point (of accusation)
[†] **to gar … to her** to make efficacious the things which the devil gave her

might wrack David Seton[14] which alighted on the hind's cattle.

She confesses that she was out of Scotland oft enough† on the sea. When they were once in their boat they slipped away so speedily that there was no stay.† Their assignations† were all given between five and six at even.

She confesses that the devil told her of the Michaelmas storm and that it would do mickle scathe† both by sea and land.

She confesses that the devil said the ministers would destroy the king and all Scotland, and if he would use his counsel† he should destroy them.

She confesses the delivering of the bill to Gillie Duncan by the clerk.

She confesses that the devil said it should be hard to[15] the king† to come home and that the queen should never come except the king fetched her. She enquired whether the king would have lads or lasses. He† answered that he should have lads and then lasses.

She and Gillie Duncan, Bessie Thomson and Irish Marion, 'Grey Meal', met[16] at Ormiston wood betwixt the wood and the halls of Foulstruther pertaining to† David Seton. The tryst was warned by the devil† who came to her that day after noon. They drew at† a cord and cried 'Haul! Haul!' 'What should I haul?' 'Haul up our master'. And with that he fetched up his head and the earth troubled.† Then Gillie Duncan speered, 'Will we get the thing that we crave?' He said 'Yea', and passed forward.† That was at Ormiston bridge. The first that should gang over the glasses that were laid on the bridge should take the sickness.

The Sprite appeared six times to her. The first was in a mill when she gave herself to him. He bad let alone her moaning.† If she would be his servant she should not want. Before she knew what spirit it was she consented.† [17] She received the mark at that time. She knew not that he had marked her while† the second time that he appeared and then he told† he had marked her. The second time was beside Bara[18] a ten weeks after the first, being warned by himself the night before in a man's likeness saying 'Be at sic a part the morrow† and I shall tell you what ye shall do'. There was there Kate

---

† **oft enough** quite often
† **stay** delay
† **assignations** arrangements about meetings
† **mickle scathe** great damage
† **if he would use his counsel** 'if the king would take his own counsel' seems more likely than 'if the king would take devil's counsel'
† **hard to the king** difficult for the king
† **He** i.e. the devil
† **pertaining to** belonging to
† **The tryst … the devil** the devil gave advance notice of the meeting

† **drew at** pulled
† **troubled** shook
† **passed forward** went away
† **He bad … her moaning** he told her to stop her lamenting. In Agnes Sampson's dittay we learn that her husband had recently died.
† **consented** came to an agreement (with the devil)
† **while** until
† **told** said
† **Be … the morrow** be at such and such a place tomorrow

Graw, Davie Steel, which were both burned sensine, and herself. For the third he desired them to be true to him. He speered at[†] her if she had found anything sore that first night he had been at her. She said that she had a sore[†] above her knee. He said he had given her that and it should be heal belive.[†] She says it was ever war and war[†] while he spake to her. The third meeting was betwixt Cousland and Carberry at a dike side,[†] where he appeared like a man clad in black. This was two years after.[19] The fourth time was coming out the gate[†] from Dalkeith was to learn[†] her to meet beside the 'Pans[†] the next day where he met them in form of a hay ruck where they be[???]d in and gaid o'er the sea. Before she came there were sundry embarked. There were there sundry with taffetas. Of the whole she knew four before rehearsed.[†]

taffetas]

They were eight and forty hours on the sea in the boat which flew like a swallow. She came to a ship side. Sundry gaid in but she remained in the boat. There was wine given to them in a great cup and they drank about. Being in the ship he was like a man. They landed in that same part they shipped in, but the devil vanished away before they landed. This was in summer.[20] The fifth time was about this time twelvemonth was,[†] going till[†] Haddington to warn her to [   ] next day betwixt the 'Pans and North Berwick to pass on the sea to the ship [   ] that gaid in over.

[†] **speered at** asked	[†] **learn** instruct
[†] **a sore** a sore place	[†] **the 'Pans** Prestonpans
[†] **heal belive** quickly healed	[†] **before rehearsed** already mentioned
[†] **war and war** worse and worse	[†] **twelvemonth was** a year ago
[†] **dike side** side of a wall	[†] **till** to
[†] **gate** road	

Document 2

Examination and Confession of Agnes Sampson

4–5 December 1590

This is a series of three leaves, with writing in a very neat hand on all sides. At various points the letter 'S' appears in the margin. We have assumed this is the abbreviation for *scribe*, *scriptum* or *scripta*, that is, these passages were to be copied to form the substance of the accusation in Sampson's dittay.

In June 1591 King James told Barbara Napier's jurors that he had been occupied for three-quarters of a year 'siftyng out' the witches (*CSPS* x 524). This puts his examinations of the witches back as far as November 1590. The examinations and confessions of Agnes Sampson in this document are among the earliest extant documents recording part of that process, and they were taken on the mornings and afternoons of Friday 4 and Saturday 5 December 1590, about six weeks before her trial and execution at the end of January 1591. It is reasonable to assume that these examinations took place at Holyroodhouse, as *News* records examinations of Agnes Sampson before the king there.

She was examined on 'sundry articles laid to her charge'. The first few items (1-6) are concerned with her healings and advice given about sickness; in items 5-7 we hear of her prayer for the first time. Item 10 shows her as a typical cunning woman diagnosing *maleficium*. Many of these items (e.g. healing Lady Kilbaberton, the laird of Redhill's son and so on) later formed part of her dittay. The king then intervenes decisively. This account describes him noting inconsistencies and contradictions in Sampson's testimony about the incident involving the healing of Lady Edmiston, then charging Sampson 'straitly to confess the truth, which she did as after followeth'. Bowes wrote to Burghley on 7 December 1590 that the king by his 'owne special travell' had drawn Agnes Sampson to confess (*CSPS* x 430), and the dates of these examinations show that he was reporting the news of the immediately preceding days. In June 1591 the king told Barbara Napier's jurors that 'whatsoever hath bene gotten from them hath bene done by me my selfe' (*CSPS* x 524).

It is in this document that we see a cunning woman turned into a witch. Sampson first denied healing some persons, but admitted prescribing some 'natural' remedies such as eggs, vinegar, iris and wine (items 1–5). She denied receiving any of the sick people's clothes, as presumably the suspicion was she professed diagnosis and perhaps cure from these clothes. She admitted combining remedies and her prayer

(5–7), but only admitted reluctantly to healing by her prayer alone. Sampson was clearly aware of the implications of admitting to having performed a cure which could not be classed as natural. At least this is the sense of the item, as this edition punctuates the manuscript, which reads:

> She grants that she healed Laird Parkie's lass, who had the power of her side tane from her, by her prayer only. This she granted with difficulty

This deposition is seminal, as its contents were to form the basis of what is reported in Sampson's dittay and also 'Certane notes of Agnes Samsone her confession' which Robert Bowes sent to Burghley on 23 February 1591. The dittay reproduces some material in this document almost word for word, particularly the story of the black dog in the well, and the much-repeated account of the convention in North Berwick kirk.

The turning point is the story about the dog. It is first told in the extant documents here, but it has been told before during the process of examination, as the king alludes to contradictions in details of a previous version. It is only after the king has charged Sampson to confess that we are given the version which will appear again with little change in Sampson's dittay. It is the story of dealings with and invocation of the devil. After a full account of the incident with the dog, Sampson then produces an account of her first meeting with the devil, his appearances, conventions, the attempted magical destruction of David Seton, and other matters. All these will be found in her dittay.

There are also some things in this document that we do not find again in later ones: names of clients and details of techniques (eggs in vinegar, fleur-de-lis in white wine, whiskey) of some healings in the early items; the devil's appearance sometimes as a foal or stag.

We also find some traces of leading questions in this document. 'She denies that after he [the devil in the shape of a dog] had appeared she put him away again with any sacrifice' looks like an attempt by Sampson's examiners to construct witchcraft as a species of ceremonial idolatry in which sacrifice was offered to the devil. One interesting passage concerns the king's issue and his relations with the kirk:

> She confesses that the devil said to her the king should hardly come home, but that the queen should never come except he fetched her with him. She enquired of him if the king should have any bairns. He answered that he should have first lads and then lasses. He said also to her that the ministers would destroy the king and all Scotland, but if he would use his counsel he should destroy them.

There is nothing about either Barbara Napier or Euphame MacCalzean in this document as we have it.

On the first side, after the first four lines, only the numbers in the margin have been cropped off the manuscript so the sense is not broken.

★

[   ] one

[   ] on Friday

[   ]gnes being demanded of sundry articles laid to her charge, some things [   ] is well done, some she denied straitly[†] as followeth.

[   ]ded if she had healed George Newton's wife, she denied that ever she had.

[   ] her being inquired whether she had sent her counsel,[†] she said she knew not.

[   ] She granted[†] her counsel given to John Duncan's wife: to take an egg steeped[†] in vinegar [   ] for her disease. She denied first[†] that she knew how the egg should be used, and thereafter confessed.

[   ] She denied the sending of any of her sons, daughters or god-daughters[†][1] to any patient [   ] or that they had any knowledge in her craft.[†]

[   ] She denied the receiving of any clothes of any person and in special[†] out of Edinburgh or fra James Pulwart's wife.

5   She confesses that she healed the lady of Kilbaberton with the fleur-de-lis[†] steeped in white wine a-night, and that she said a prayer in the meantime which she rehearsed[†] in presence of the examinators.[†]

6   She confesses that she learned her skill and her prayer from her father who told her that if her prayer stopped the patient would die; if it stopped not he would live.

7   She confesses that she healed the laird of Redhall's son with rubbing aquavite[†] on him and saying of her prayer.

8   She denies that meeting John Downie coming out of Clerkintown she should have tane him by the little finger, and saying some words to him, he healed.[†]

9   She grants that she healed Laird Parkie's lass, who had the power of her side tane from her, by her prayer only. This she granted with difficulty.[†]

10   She confesses that Robin Dickson was bewitched by pickils[†] of wheat in his doublet and that she told him thereof and counselled him not to wear that doublet again but that[†] he had tane out the pickils of wheat before. She grants that he mended not while[†] she had told him and that she knows when one is witched, but would not tell by what manner.

11   She confesses that on Hallow Even she healed (   ) the sheriff's

---

[†] **straitly** precisely
[†] **counsel** advice
[†] **granted** admitted
[†] **steeped** soaked
[†] **She denied first** at first she denied
[†] **god-daughters** daughters-in-law
[†] **craft** particular skill
[†] **in special** particularly
[†] **fleur-de-lis** iris or lily

[†] **rehearsed** recited
[†] **examinators** examiners
[†] **aquavite** whiskey
[†] **healed** was healed
[†] **This ... difficulty** but she admitted this unwillingly
[†] **pickils** grains
[†] **but that** unless
[†] **while** until

wife with her prayer only, who had gotten an evil blast betwixt the chamber and the hall.

12   She confesses that Alison Ker[2] dwelling in Cunningham being witched by Katrine Gray was healed by her prayer.

13   She denies that she knew anything of the boat that perished betwixt the Burntisland and Leith but that she heard mean[†] made for it.

14   She denies that ever Gillie Duncan was in her company or that she knew her.

[   ]

prophecy S]

She confesses that one is w[   ]er prayer if it sto[   ]
is bewitched. If it stop the second time there is no reme[   ].

bona S]

She confesses that (   ) desiring her to [   ] 'No, no—ye believe not that I can help yow. If ye belie[   ] that she healed her after that.

She denies Mr John Kelly's attestation concerning (   ) [   ].

Mala]

She confesses that at Patrick Edmiston's house of Newtown on a s[   ] in a fair moonlight night, being in the garden with his three daughters [   ] saw a black dog which made them all to fall for fliedness;[†] what should ha[   ] she could not tell.

This article[†] being insisted upon by the king's Majesty and these contrarieties gathered upon her words,[†] to wit that they fell all together at the sight of the dog and that she was sent for after they had seen the dog and had been affrayed[†] for[†] him; secondly that the Lady Littledean[3] only saw the dog and therefore she said that they saw the dog come out of the well[† 4] altogether; thirdly that they slew the dog and thereafter the dog passed over the dyke from them; fourthly that they fell altogether and that they fell all sundry. These contrarieties being gathered,[†] his Majesty charged[†] straitly[†] to confess the truth, which she did as after followeth.

---

† **mean** arrangements
† **fliedness** fright, alarm
† **article** point
† **contrarieties … words** contradictions accumulated in what she had said
† **affrayed** frightened
† **for** by

† **well** the MS has 'wall', an alternative word form of 'well'
† **These contrarieties being gathered** these contradictions being collected together
† **charged** i.e. charged her
† **straitly** severely

Her confession to the king's Majesty

She confesseth that she was sent for that day in the morning to heal the lady. She told to the gentlewomen that she should tell them that night whether the lady would heal or not, and appointed them to be in the garden after supper.

Mala S]

Betwixt five and six at even she passed to the garden herself to devise upon[†] her prayer, at what[†] time she charged the devil, calling him 'Eloa' to come and speak to her; who came in over the dyke in likeness of a [ ] dog and came so near to her that she was affrayed and charged[†] him on the law he lived on to come no nearer, but to answer her. She demanded whether the lady would live or not. He said her days were gone. Then he demanded of[†] the gentlewomen her daughters where they were.[5] She said to him that the gentlewomen were to be there. He answered that one of them should be in peril and that he should have one of them. She answered it should not be so, and so departed[†] from her howling. Fra[6] this time while[†] after supper he remained in the well. When the gentlewomen came i[n] the dog came out of the well and appeared to the lady of (   ) whereat she was afraid. In the meantime another of the said gentlewomen, lady of Tersonie, ran to the well, being forced and drawn by the devil who would have drowned her,[7] and had drowned her were not the said Agnes and the other[†] of the gentlewomen gat a grip of her, and with all their force drew her aback again, which made them all afraid. The dog passed away thereafter, over the dyke with a howl. Then she said to the gentlewomen that she could not help the lady in respect that her prayer stopped, and that she was sorry for it.

First put all that appertaining together. Mala. Her first entress in her art]

Being demanded[†] how she began to serve the devil, she confessed that after the death of her husband the devil appeared to her in likeness of a man who commanded her [ ]nowledge him as her master and to renounce Christ; whereunto she granted. [   ] moved by her poverty and his promises that she should be made rich and her bairns [ ] that he should give her power to be avenged on her enemies. And after that [ ]ppointed time and place for their next meeting. He marked her above the [ ]ch she believed had been a hurt which she had received from one of her bairns [ ] was in the bed with her (for she had one in every side of her) which hurt was not [ ] for a half year. At the second time which he appeared he commanded her to call him 'Eloa' which she pronounces 'Hola'.

[†] **devise upon** consider
[†] **what** which
[†] **charged** commanded
[†] **demanded of** asked about

[†] **departed** i.e. he departed
[†] **while** until
[†] **other** rest
[†] **demanded** asked

She confesses that had not been the occasion[†] present which forced her, she would never have left him, and that when she was tane first she had vowed not confess anything, and was that same day resolved never to confess, were not[†] his Majesty's speeches that had moved her, whereof she praised God that had wrought a repentance in her and a sense and feeling[†] of her sins.

Her confession after noon

[Ma]la]
Item, she confesses that the devil appears whiles like a foal or a stag,[†] whiles[†] like a dog, whiles like a turs[†] or ruck of hay and siclike[†] other forms, always black.

She denies that after he had appeared she put him away[†] again with any sacrifice, but charged him on the law that he lived on to pass away.
S]
She confesses that by foreknowledge of the devil she told Patrick Porteous that he would live eleven year.
S]
She confesses that she was at the convention of Bara where Meg Steel, Kate Gray and Janet Campbell was with her, and another who is dead sensine, being altogether five in number. They convened by east the kirk[†] at the burn side. Janet Campbell was burned thereafter.[8]
S]
Two years thereafter she was at the convention betwixt Cousland and Carberry where they were three, whereof Janet[9] Stratton in Payston was one. She quarrelled[†] her master there that in respect she had never gotten good of him she would renounce him. She grants[†] she renounced him not, but boasted[†] to renounce him. He promised to her that nothing should go against her. What he promised to every one of the rest she could not tell, for spake to every one severally.[†] She tarried not long at that time with him. He commanded them to be true servants and so departed.

---

† **occasion** opportunity
† **were not** were it not
† **feeling** apprehension
† **stag** in 1597 Andro Man confessed that he supposedly saw the devil, whom he called Cristsonday, 'cum out of the snaw in liknes of a staig' (Murray 1921: 45)
† **whiles … whiles** at one time … at another time
† **turs** bundle

† **siclike** suchlike, similar
† **put him away** dismissed him
† **by east the kirk** east of the kirk
† **quarrelled** reproached
† **grants** admits
† **boasted** threatened
† **for spake to every one severally** for the devil spoke individually to everybody

Mala S]

She confesses that she command[   ] 'Grey Meal' being in the [   ] hind's house to renounce his God and to serve a better mas[   ] want. She gave him a drink of milk there and sence[   ].

Convention]

She confesses that the devil in man's likeness met her going out in the fie[   ] five and six at even, being her alone,[†] and commanded her to [   ] next night.

S]

She passed there on horse back convoyed[†] by [   ] Coupar and lighted at the kirk yard or a little befor[   ] hours at even. They danced in langis[†] the kirk yard. Gilli[   ] them on the trump, John Fian led all the rest. Agnes Sampson and h[   ] followed next besides these. There were there Kate Gray, George Mott's wife, Robe[   ]. They were in all above an hundred persons, whereof there were six men and all the rest women. The women made first their homage and next the men. The men were turned nine times widdershins[†] about and the women six times. John Fian blew up the doors and blew [   ] in the lights which were like mickle[†] black candles sticking round[†] about the pulpit. The devil start up himself in the pulpit like a mickle black man and called every man by his name and everyone answered him, 'Here, master!'. Robert Grierson being named, they ran all hirdy-girdy[†] and were angry, for it was promised that he should be called 'Robert the Comptroller'. The first thing he[†] demanded was if they had all kept promise and been good servants and what they had done since the last time they had convened. At his command they opened up three graves, two within and one without[†] the kirk, and took of the joints of their fingers, toes and noses and parted them amongst them. The said Agnes got for her part a winding-sheet and two joints which she tint negligently.[†] The devil commanded them to keep the joints upon them while[†] they were dry and then to make a powder of them to do evil withall. Then he commanded them to keep his commandments, which was to do all the evil they could. Before they departed they kissed all his arse.[†] [10] He had on him a gown and a hat which were both black; and they that were assembled part[†] stood and part sat. John Fian was ever nearest to the devil at his left elbow: 'Grey Meal' kept the door.

[†] **being her alone** when she was alone
[†] **convoyed** attended
[†] **in langis** in and along
[†] **widdershins** anti-clockwise
[†] **mickle** large
[†] **sticking round** set up around
[†] **hirdy-girdy** in uproar

[†] **he** i.e. the devil
[†] **without** outside
[†] **tint negligently** she took care of negligently, i.e. inadvertently lost
[†] **while** until
[†] **they kissed all his arse** they all kissed his arse
[†] **part** some of them

Her confession on Saturday afternoon,
the 5 of December

Mala]
S]
She confesses that the goodwife of Spilmersford, 'Grey Meal', Geillis Duncan, Bessie Thomson, Janet Stratton and herself with certain others, to the number of nine convened at Foulstruther, and there had their consultation how they might wrack[†] David Seton and his goods.

Convention]
And first, Gilles Duncan, Bessie Thomson and 'Grey Meal' hauled a cord at the bridge and she cried 'Haul! Hola!' The end of it was very heavy. [   ] had drawn [the dev]il came up at the end of it and speered if thay had all [   ]ants. Then they demanded him what way thay might wrack David Seton. [   ] he gave them some pieces of glass[11] mixed with pieces of cords and some [   ]mong them which he commanded them to saw[†] in the moor as they did, but [   ]ghted on the hind's goods.

[C]onfesses that she had been oft enough[†] out of Scotland on the sea in their riddles[†] [   ] they were once in, they made no stay but slid speedily away and remained some [   ]es forty-eight hours, sometimes longer, sometimes shorter, upon ships or uncouth[†] coasts.
S]
She confesses that the devil foretold her of the Michaelmas storm and that great scathe[†] would be done both by sea and land.

She confesses there was a bill[†] written by John Fian and delivered to Gillie Duncan to bear to Leith to Janet Fairlie. And confesseth the drowning of the boat, in all points conform[†] to the said Gillie Duncan's deposition.
S]
She confesses that the devil said to her the king should hardly come home,[†] but that the queen should never come except he fetched her with him. She enquired of him if the king should have any bairns. He answered that he should have first lads and then lasses. He said also to her that the ministers would destroy the king and all Scotland, but if he would use his[†] counsel he should destroy them.

[†] **wrack** destroy
[†] **saw** scatter
[†] **oft enough** quite often
[†] **riddles** sieves
[†] **uncouth** unknown
[†] **scathe** harm

[†] **bill** document, letter
[†] **conform** corresponding
[†] **should hardly come home** should come home with difficulty
[†] **his** the pronoun is ambiguous, meaning either the devil's or the king's own counsel

SJ

She confesses that she was in the ship that perished at North Berwick called *The Grace of God*. They shipped[†] all in at North Berwick in a boat like a chimney to the number of twenty persons. Some women rowed with oars. The devil passed before them like a rick of hay. The most part of them went in over the ship: some remained in the boat. The devil brought out from the bottom of the ship wine and other cheer[†] and gave them; whereof they gave a part out over the ship's side to them that was in the boat. They saw none of the mariners[12] nor yet saw the mariners them.[†] When they departed from the ship the devil remained himself under the ship's bottom. And immediately after they landed, the evil wind (as they call it) blew and the storm rose[13] whereby the ship perished. She gave to 'Grey Meal' twenty shillings, being in the ship, as she says for his good onwaiting[†] on her at that time, which he confessed.[14]

SJ

She confesses in like manner that the devil advertised[†] her to gang to a ship where there was an uncouth woman whose tokens[†] she confesseth conform to 'Grey Meal' his deposition. The Irish tailor and his wife were principals. Being [   ]

for he was one of the principals and that he ha[   ].

[†] **shipped all** all boarded ship
[†] **cheer** entertainment, especially food and drink
[†] **nor yet … them** neither did the mariners see them

[†] **onwaiting** attendance
[†] **advertised** directed
[†] **tokens** distinguishing marks

Document 3

Deposition of Geillis Duncan

5 December 1590 and 15 January 1591

This leaf is written on both sides. One side begins with an examination of Geillis Duncan in which she is confronted with the testimony of Bessie Thomson. The top of the page is fragmentary, and what is legible is:

[   ] Duncan on Saturday
[   ]5 of December confronted
with [Be?]ssie Thomson

The first part of this side, dated on a Saturday in December (1590), is written in the same neat hand that wrote the examination and confession of Agnes Sampson in document 2. The last third of this page, dated 15 January (1591), is in the same hand that wrote document 1, the examinations of Geillis Duncan and Agnes Sampson. This Saturday in December can only be 5 December, that is the same day as the second day of the examination of Agnes Sampson 4–5 December, recorded in document 2. The first section is an examination of Geillis Duncan, who has been confronted with the testimony of Bessie Thomson against her. It is concerned with supposed incidents at sea, which are also reported in Agnes Sampson's dittay, items 35 and 36. The next section, an examination of Geillis Duncan dated 15 January (1591), is about the writing and delivering of letters preparatory to raising the storm in September 1589 to hinder Queen Anne's homecoming to Scotland, by 'baptising' a cat in the chimney crook and throwing it into the sea. Both this confession and Agnes Sampson's dittay describe clandestine meetings and fear of discovery (Agnes Sampson's dittay, item 50). The deposition on 15 January also seems to be that of Geillis Duncan.

The other side of the leaf continues in the same second hand. Although the top of the second side is fragmentary, the sense runs on: we are still hearing about what Agnes Sampson said to David Nimil's wife and Sampson's dealings with her. In the section beginning 'Gillie Duncan and Agnes Samson being confronted with Jane[t?] Fairlie . . .', it is difficult to know who is saying what.

★

[   ] Duncan on Saturday
[   ]5 of December confronted
with [Be?]ssie Thomson

[   ]s that when they passed to the ship to the uncouth[†] women that she
[   ]homson were commanded to remain in the there boats.[†] Robert Grierson
[   ] the boats to the ship side while[†] they should come out again. Agnes [   ]
gave her a drink of white wine as it were out of a window[1] in over the [   ]d
and would not suffer her to come in.

[C]onfesses that John Fian their clerk made a letter at (   ) (   ) house
and Agnes Sampson delivered the said letter to her to be had to Leith to the
token[†] that Agnes offered her a drink of wine which she refused and took a
drink of ale.

Agnes Sampson]
The said Agnes confesses the token but denies that she was the deliverer of
the letter.

S]
The said Gillie, as she was commanded, she delivered the letter at Leith in
Janet Fairlie's house to the said Janet, the two Linkups, the two Stobies.[2]
The bill being delivered, the said Gillie would have been away but Janet
followed her to the bridge to have brought her again[†] but Gillie gave her on
the mouth[†] and came her way. After the which time she immediatel[y] fell
sick and remained sick a quarter of a year.

Janet Campbell]
Within eight days after the said bill Agnes Sampson, John Fian, Gillie Duncan
and Meg Din baptised a cat in the Webster's house in manner following.
First two of them held one[†] a finger in the one side of the [?chim]ney crook
and another held another finger in the other side, the two nebs[†] of the
fingers meeting together into the crook. Then they put the cat thrice through
the links of the crook and passed it thrice under the chimney. Thereafter at
Begie Tod's house they knit to the four feet of four joints of men. Which
being done, the said Janet fetched it to Leith and about midnight she and
the four above named come to the pier-head, and saying these words, 'See
that there be no deceit among us', they cast the cat in the sea so far as they
might, which swam over and came back again.

[†] **uncouth** unknown
[†] **in the there boats** there in the boats
[†] **while** until
[†] **to the token** by the password
[†] **to have brought her again** to have accompanied
her back

[†] **gave her on the mouth** hit her on the mouth?
kissed her on the mouth?
[†] **held one** each held
[†] **nebs** tips

The 15 of January

Immediately after the death of the earl of Angus on Hansel Monday[†] was a year,[†] about two after noon, Agnes Sampson came out of Lady Pogie's house together with the said lady, David Nimil's wife of Dalkeith called Katrina Hamilton.

Agnes Sampson prophecy]

They passed to the king's ford of Dalkeith Water and sent Geillis Duncan up the brae[†] to gather a broad-leaved[3] grass and to sit there while they had done. She looked back and saw a black man with them whom she saw[4] wading[5] out of the well. She speered at[†] Agnes what he was. She answered, 'It was not a man, it was but the waf[†] of my cloak'. Immediately after they came in to David Nimil's back cellar[†] where they drank wine and ale and dang the hussie[†] out of the house and put the said Geillis fra them[6] a little space. Then Agnes Sampson said to David Nimil's wife 'Ye are ganging[†] to lay two hundred marks or title on land to James Douglas the laird of (   )
gang your way if ye swi[   ]
shall never have bairn to be [   ]
it is of truth that within a [   ]r his only s[   ].

Item, the said Agnes and David Nimil's wife [   ]
flowers and other herbs and gave to a [   ]
David Nimil's wife and to part with his a[   ]
thereafter the said George fell in love with her was [   ]
by her in her own house to the wrack[†] of the said G[   ]
the said David's wife said to Geillis when Agnes Sampson [   ] well days are gone of ought else her but good.[† 7]

Agnes transported]

Gillie Duncan depones that Agnes Sampson said 'Now the king is going to f[?etch] his wife but I shall be there before them'.

Gillie Duncan and Agnes Sampson being confronted with Jane[t] Fairlie they constantly[†] affirmed the one the sending of the bill, the oth[?er][†] the

---

[†] **Hansel Monday** the first Monday of the New Year when gifts were given

[†] **after ... a year** a year after the death of the earl of Angus, on Hansel Monday

[†] **brae** hill-side

[†] **speered at** asked

[†] **waf** flapping

[†] **back cellar** back room

[†] **dang the hussie** drove the housewife

[†] **ganging** going

[†] **wrack** destruction

[†] **well ... good** the meaning of this sentence, part of which is missing, is not clear. Nimil's wife seems to be bewailing the passing of the good days.

[†] **constantly** steadfastly

[†] **the one ... the oth[?er]** i.e. Gillie Duncan and Agnes Sampson

delivering of it to Janet. She constantly denies it, as in like manne[?r] that ever any of the Linkups were in her house or she in theirs. She denies in like manner that when Mr Thomas Ballenden brought her out of Leith, she hearing of the Linkups that she should have said that she was not a witch, which notwithstanding is of truth.

She depones that Janet Campbell of Carrie was at the baptising of the cat and at the convention of North Berwick. She was niknemus[†] 'Maiden'. She strave[†] with Janet Fairlie which of them should cast the cat in the sea.

She depones that the said Janet Fairlie was at Michaelmas last in the kirk of North Berwick with the rest of the Stobies and Linkups.

[†] **nicknemus** nicknamed   [†] **strave** argued

Document 4

Examination of Agnes Sampson

January 1591

This is an examination of Agnes Sampson and took place in January 1591, before the master of work, the official in charge of the king's buildings. It took place before 27 January, the date of Agnes Sampson's trial. She was executed on 28 January.

The document is fragmentary at the top left corner. The items confessed and denied are bracketed together in the margin. These fall into three: in the first group Sampson confesses to items of conjuration and those implying pact, such as the mark; in the second she denies items concerning convention; in the third she confesses to an association with Barbara Napier, who is represented as seeking Agnes's advice and magical help, thus laying Napier open to accusation under the 1563 act of consulting with witches and sorcerers. The last confession insinuates a similar relationship with Euphame MacCalzean. Much of the information extracted here will later appear in Agnes Sampson's dittay.

Sampson is now denying things she had earlier confessed to, such as the convention at Foulstruther to destroy David Seton. Most interesting is the item, 'She denies the convention of North Berwick: she confesses this again', where we may suspect torture may have been used to change her denial. Some items which have been established in some detail before (the first appearance of the devil, the mark) are noted briefly at the beginning. What this document is intent on are connections with Barbara Napier, who has not featured in previous examinations and depositions. There is one explicit brief allusion to helping Euphame MacCalzean, and two implicit ones in the references to the wax image of John Moscrop and to Janet Drummond (Mac-Calzean's servant).

The reverse has a deletion mark through it and is in the same hand that wrote at right angles to the main text in document 7. The formality of the language may suggest that it is a draft of the accusation against Agnes Sampson, for this material is the basis for what will become the penultimate items, 51 and 52, in Agnes Sampson's dittay, which deal with the magical aid she gave Barbara Napier: to harm the man called Archie and to gain the favour of Jean Lyons, then Lady Angus. These items in Agnes Sampson's dittay enable us to make guesses as to the contents of the lacunae.

★

[　]January before the master of work
[　]John Gedde
Agnes Sampson

[Conf]irms the article of raising of the devil in form of a black dog at
[d]eath of the old Lady Edmiston.[†][1]
[　] confesseth the first appearing of the devil.
[S]he confesseth the mark.[†]
The first warning of the meeting at Bara, he[†] being in visible form.
The second meeting at Carberry.
The third was about the conjuring of the picture of wax concerning Mr
John Moscrop.[†]
She confesses the sending of Janet Drummond to her[†] to consult concerning
Pumpherston.[†]
She denies Foulstruther.[†]
She denies the sending of the bill and that she was in George Mott's house.[†]
She denies the sailing on the sea.
She denies the convention of North Berwick: she confesses this again.[†][2]

She confesses thrice meeting with Barbara Napier, the first time at Dalkeith
where they had no conference[†] except only that she[†] speered what was good
for my Lady Angus who had an infirmity[†] of vomiting.[†] The next time the
said Agnes being in Cameron, the said Barbara sent her maiden[†] to tell her[†]
that she would[†] come and speak with her, which she did immediately. The

---

[†] **raising ... Lady Edmiston** the full story is given in Agnes Sampson's dittay, item 38.

[†] **the mark** i.e. the devil's mark

[†] **he** i.e. the devil

[†] **Mr John Moscrop** item 41 of Agnes Sampson's dittay reports that she was convicted of making a wax image of John Moscrop, Euphame Mac-Calzean's father-in-law, at MacCalzean's request

[†] **to her** that is, Sampson confesses that Janet Drummond was sent to her by Euphame Mac-Calzean

[†] **Pumpherston** MacCalzean was accused of trying to impede the marriage of the laird of Pumpher-ston and also of trying to gain his love by magic, for which she used Janet Drummond, her servant and former nurse, to carry charms, and also as her go-between with Agnes Sampson. See MacCalzean's dittay, items 12–17.

[†] **Foulstruther** i.e. the convention at Foulstruther where nine witches plotted the destruction of David Seton. See Sampson's dittay, item 49.

[†] **She denies ... George Mott's house** the 'bill' was a letter summoning witches to raise a storm to prevent Queen Anne's homecoming. Suppos-edly, John Fian wrote the letter in George Mott's house in Prestonpans and Agnes Sampson delivered it. See Sampson's dittay, item 40.

[†] **she confesses this again** having denied attend-ance at the North Berwick convention, she then confesses it again

[†] **conference** talk

[†] **she** i.e. Barbara Napier

[†] **infirmity** illness

[†] **except only ... of vomitting** the first item of Barbara Napier's dittay accused her for 'seeking of consultation from Annie Sampson, a witch, for the help of Dame Jean Lyon, Lady Angus, to keep her from vomiting when she was in breeding of bairn'

[†] **maiden** female servant

[†] **her** i.e. Agnes Sampson

[†] **she would** i.e. Barbara Napier wished that Agnes would come and speak with her

first purpose[†] was concerning her husband who was then in the west country[†] and prayed[†] her to send him home again whole[3] and fair[†] and to keep him from scathe[†] because she feared some unfriends.[†] Agnes speered whom she feared. She answered there was one Archie fra whose scathe she would have him kept.[†] Her answer was she should do the best she could, and promised to have a picture of wax ready against[†] the next meeting which she should take and put under their bed feet[†] whom she feared. The picture was made the third or fourth day after she promised. For her reward she got alsmickle[†] linen cloth as to make a courchie.[†] She[4] furnished wax herself. This meeting was in an old barn or suchlike[5] house upon a loch stray.[†][6]

She confesses that at the third meeting at Cameron she required of[†] Agnes how she might obtain my Lady Angus's favour to get her gear[†] again which she had [ ] her hands. The said Agnes said to her 'Lend me that ring which ye have on your finger and I shall do well enough, and shall give you it again within a fourteen days.'[†] She said her prayer upon[†] the ring and delivered it again.

She confesses the inputting[†] of the moulds[†] under the bed feet of Euphame MacCalzean.

Sampson & [ ]

Ye are accused that after long familiar[ ] with Barba[ ]
Bridgend and other places, and that the said Barbara ha[ ]
Archie had done her wrong and asked your counsel [ ]
Ye answered, 'The help that I can make, I will'. And [ ]
the said Barbara at the next meeting brought un[ ] some yellow wax
in alsmickle new linen cloth[7] which she gave you to [ ]
picture ye kept two or three days and [ ]
end of the dovecot[8] of Craigmillar in the devil's [ ]
power to the said picture, that as it should melt a[ ]

[†] **purpose** discussion
[†] **west country** the west of Scotland
[†] **and prayed** and Barbara beseeched her
[†] **whole and fair** uninjured in body and appearance
[†] **scathe** harm
[†] **unfriends** enemies
[†] **kept** protected
[†] **against** by
[†] **under their bed feet** under the foot of the bed

[†] **alsmickle** as much, enough
[†] **courchie** kerchief
[†] **upon a loch stray** by the side of a little stream running into a loch?
[†] **required of** questioned
[†] **gear** possessions
[†] **within a fourteen days** within a fortnight
[†] **upon** over
[†] **inputting** putting
[†] **moulds** graveyard earth

so should that man whose picture it was consume [   ]
while[†] he were utterly destroyed. And so ye deliv[   ]
unto her again who said unto you 'Take tent[†] y[   ]
to stay this purpose'.

Item, ye are accused and indited that ye enchanted a l[   ] ring with a stone
in it to the said Barbara to the end that she might procure [   ] Jean Lyon's
favour and love, then Lady Angus, and gave the sa[   ] ring again to her to
be used to the effect and sic other ends which are to be revealed in their
own time.

Document 5

Depositions of ?Bessie Thomson, Janet Stratton and Donald Robson, and Confrontation of Barbara Napier and Euphame MacCalzean by the Depositions of Robson, Stratton and Ritchie Graham

date uncertain

These confessions and examinations are not dated, or the date is missing. Since Barbara Napier and Euphame MacCalzean were confronted with testimony against them, we have assumed that they come after document 4 in which Agnes Sampson confessed meeting Barbara Napier and Napier's consultation of her. The fragmentary heading 'The [　] council' suggests that these examinations were conducted before members of the king's council.

The name of the person who confesses first is missing. The second is Donald Robson, the third Janet Stratton. The subject of the first confession must be one of the women who were alleged to have attended a convention at Foulstruther and there consulted together about the destruction of David Seton. Since this confession mentions both Agnes Sampson and Gillie Duncan, it can be neither of them. The other women who are named in Sampson's dittay as being at the Foulstruther convention are the goodwife of Spilmersford (Meg Begtoun), Bessie Thomson, and 'Agnes' i.e. Janet Stratton. Barbara Napier and Euphame MacCalzean are then confronted, that is brought face to face, with various witnesses (Gillie Duncan, Donald Robson, Janet Stratton) who testify against them, but both Napier and MacCalzean deny the accusations and refuse to confess.

Barbara Napier is confronted with Janet Stratton and Donald Robson, whose confessions have named her as being present at the Acheson's Haven convention and who now repeat their accusations face to face with Napier. Ritchie Graham affirms that he composed a conjuration which Napier wrote down; and Graham's servant, John Fairlie, claims that she sent gifts and tokens to Ritchie Graham through him. Graham was sufficiently educated to string together some garbled but ominously suggestive Latin which may have the general sense of wishing uncleanness and perhaps syphilis on the king: 'Hominum aratum regnum valui kethi imundum prosita munda metanas dium sipilus'. After this Barbara Napier briefly denies all these accusations.

Euphame MacCalzean is also confronted with Robson, Duncan and Stratton, who implicate her in the conventions at Acheson's Haven and North Berwick, and of handling the magical image of King James. She too denies these accusations.

The confessions and examinations are mainly concerned with the supposed convention at Acheson's Haven on Lammas Eve (31 July) 1590, where a wax image of King James was produced and handled (see the king's letter to Barbara Napier's assize, and MacCalzean's dittay, item 9). Clearly, there is an attempt here to implicate Barbara Napier and MacCalzean in these meetings. The first confession also mentions the *maleficium* attempted against David Seton which instead alighted on his daughter.

Bothwell appears explicitly as promising money and food to Agnes Sampson, and implicitly in Euphame MacCalzean's cryptic promise that in James's place, 'The realm will not want a king'.

The [   ] council

Confesses that she rec[?eived pie]ces of glass at Foulstruther beside Ormiston Bridge fra Gillie Duncan and spread [?the]m upon the ground against[†] David Seton, which lighted upon the lass.[†]

She confesses the picture of wax[†] at Acheson's Haven delivered to Agnes Sampson, which was wambled[†] in a white clout or a piece white paper[†] of the length of an arm, and that it gaid about[†] fra hand to hand and fra her to Gillie Duncan. Every one said a word or two, having it in their hand. The devil appeared like a quoyle[†] of hay at this convention.

Donald Robson

Confesses there were more nor[†] twenty at the convention at Acheson's Haven that handled the picture. Agnes Sampson brought the picture to the field; she delivered it to Barbara Napier. Fra Barbara it was given to Euphame MacCalzean; fra Euphame to Meg Begtoun of Spilmersford. It passed through eight or nine women. At last it came to Robin Grierson; fra him to the devil. They spake all 'James the Sixth' amongst them handling the picture.[†] The devil was like a man. Agnes Sampson said that there would be both gold and silver and victual gotten fra my Lord Bothwell. There were

---

[†] **against** i.e. with hostility against
[†] **lighted upon the lass** i.e. alighted upon David Seton's daughter
[†] **picture of wax** wax image
[†] **wambled** rolled
[†] **piece white paper** a piece of white paper

[†] **gaid about** went around
[†] **quoyle** bundle
[†] **nor** than
[†] **They spake all … the picture** they all said 'James the Sixth' to each other as they handled the image

there besides[†] the foresaid, Catharine[1] Wallace and Janet Stratton, Charles Wat in Garvet, who offered to deliver the picture back to the thief[†] again to cummer[†] the king. The said deponer[†] was once in his[†] house. He depones in like manner that there was four hoods of velvet and four or five taftas[†] amongst them. There were women of Leith and of the 'Pans there. He delivered the picture to Geillis Duncan[2] and fra her to Janet Stratton and received it from Catharine Wallace. They convened in the gloaming[†] and did their turn[†] in the night.

Janet Stratton

She confesses there were three score at this convention.
She confesses there were thirteen that she knew: Agnes Sampson, Barbara Napier, Euphame MacCalzean, Robert Grierson, Donald Robson, herself, Geillis Duncan, Catharine Wallace, George Mott's wife, Bessie Thomson. She confesses 'James the Sixth' was named there in handling of the picture and that Agnes Sampson should have received gold, silver and wheat.

Barbara Napier

Donald.
Janet Stratton]
The said Donald and Janet Stratton being confronted[†] with Barbara, depones as above that she[†] received the picture from Agnes Sampson at Acheson's Haven.
Richard Graham]
Being confronted with Richard Graham he affirms that he dited[†] and she wrote these words following: 'Hominum aratum regnum valui kethi imundum prosita munda metanas dium sipilus',[†] being together in the yard, and her

---

[†] **besides** in addition to
[†] **the thief** i.e. the devil?
[†] **cummer** trouble, distress
[†] **deponer** deponent, i.e. Donald Robson
[†] **his** presumably Charles Wat's
[†] **four hoods ... five taftas** velvet hoods and taffeta gowns, metonymic descriptions for women of high social standing
[†] **gloaming** evening twilight
[†] **turn** business

[†] **being confronted** i.e. Barbara Napier is confronted by Robson and Stratton
[†] **she** i.e. Barbara Napier
[†] **dited** composed
[†] *Hominum ... sipilus* This passage, in what must be Latin, is contracted in the MS and can be made to produce no certain sense, not least because it is unclear what are imperatives and what neuter plural nouns. It seems to be something about a ploughed kingdom and cleanliness and uncleanliness.

daughter Bessie Car and a son[†] of hers with her. This was a conjuration that should have been cast into that liquor which was conspired[3] against the king. It should have been cutted and cast in and was delivered by Marion Loch to Agnes Sampson.[4] He depones that she wrote to him a writing eighteen year since and subscrived[†] it 'I Barbarie' and no more.[†] He avows in like manner she wrote him an obligation[†] of four score pounds subscrived 'I Bar.' and that she showed him a letter sent to her from the laird of (　　　　) and within [　] [?hea]rt drawn through with a dart.[†]

John Fairlie]

Item, that she sent to Richard [?a gold]en ring to Fintry by one John Fairlie. These foresaid and sundry other tokens[†] avowed by him are denied by her. The said John Fairlie is confronted with Barbara who avows the receiving of the foresaid ring about Yule was a year,[†] together with forty shillings in testons[†] and half mark piece with an ell of linen and pair of gloves and certain leaves,[†] and that s[he] bade him tell his master that her son was very sick and desired him to he[?al] him. She denies all this constantly.[†]

Euphame MacCalzean

Donald Robson]

Being confronted with Donald Robson, he affirms to have seen her at the kirk of North Berwick and at the new haven called Acheson's Haven where she had the pict[ure] of wax in her hand, which she[†] denies constantly.

Gillie Duncan.

Janet Stratton]

Being confronted with Gillie Duncan she[†] affirms to have seen her at North Berwick kirk. Being confronted in like manner with Janet Stratton she[†] depones to have seen her at North Berwick together with Agnes Sampson and Barbara Napier, and that she was at the boat drowning where she received

---

[†] **daughter … son** i.e. Napier's daughter and son?
[†] **subscrived** signed
[†] **no more** nothing else
[†] **obligation** bond, promissory note
[†] **dart** arrow
[†] **tokens** signs
[†] **Yule was a year** last Yule

[†] **testons** silver coins of the reign of Mary queen of Scots of the value of four shillings Scots
[†] **leaves** leaves of paper?
[†] **constantly** steadfastly
[†] **she** i.e. MacCalzean
[†] **she** i.e. Duncan
[†] **she** i.e. Stratton

great riches. The said Janet received fifteen shillings. Donald affirms that being at North Berwick they demanded amongst them 'Who is yon[†] that seeks the picture?' It was answered by them every one to another, 'It is Euphame MacCalzean'. It was speered[†] where would they get a king again. Euphame answered, 'The realm will not want a king'.

[†] **yon** that person over there   [†] **speered** asked

Document 6

Confessions and Depositions of Geillis Duncan, Janet Stratton and Donald Robson

?29 January 1591

This is a sheet folded into two leaves. One hand has written the first three sides; another hand has written at right angles on f. 1^v and f. 2^r. The latter seem to be rough notes about Bessie Nisbet (Euphame MacCalzean's servant, see document 11) and various other matters, and is very difficult to decipher.

These confessions and depositions concern the supposed meeting at Acheson's Haven, and clearly form a stage in the building of an account that finds its fullest form in the king's letter to the assize which acquitted Barbara Napier. The king's letter echoes this material closely. For example, Janet Stratton's deposition of an exchange with the devil ("'Master, we have a turn ado and we would fain be at it if we could, and therefore help us to it". He answered, "I shall do it, but it will be long because it will be thwarted"') occurs almost *verbatim* in the king's letter.

Geillis Duncan's deposition is partly concerned with Robert Bowes, the English ambassador, and there seems at one point to have been an attempt to implicate him in a conspiracy with Bothwell and the 'wives of Edinburgh'. He is mentioned again in the notes about Janet Stratton. In one letter to Burghley, Bowes says that he himself had been implicated by a shameless and drunken woman, whom this document suggests must have been Geillis Duncan:

> And yet in the discription of my person they have so farre erred as the King and the examiners sufficientlie condempned the tale, notwithstanding that this rogish woman perswaided that the Inglish ambassadour, being a litle black and fatt man with black haire, and soone after the King's departure into Denmark—as I am informed— had bene with them in a celler and given them gold to hange up and charme a tode for the hurte of the King in his life, and to hinder the issue to come of his bodie. (*CSPS* x 462)

This letter was dated 23 February 1590 (i.e. 1591), so these depositions were taken before that date. If this supposition is correct then the only possible date for Donald Robson's deposition is 29 January 1591. In another letter to Burghley (15 April

1591), Bowes reveals that the king 'said that Jely Dunkyn and others confessed at first that Bothwell had dealt with them, but afterwards denied it and accused him [Bowes]' (*CSPS* x 502). This 'bill' read in Napier's cellar must be the letter whose inscription, reception and consequences are described in Agnes Sampson's dittay, item 40. It was sent with the intention of getting witches at Prestonpans and Leith to raise winds to hinder the queen's homecoming to Scotland (September 1589, 'in the beginning of harvest' as Duncan deponed). Duncan claimed that Barbara Napier received the letter and sent for Euphame MacCalzean. Duncan also identifies Bothwell as the 'mover' of the manufacture of the king's image. Donald Robson told the story of Robert Grierson's criticism of the devil at North Berwick kirk and his importuning of the devil for the king's image.

The confession of Donald Robson (whom we discover here was more than sixty years old) contributed details to the final fully elaborated description of the North Berwick convention in the dittay against Barbara Napier's jurors. For example, 'He confesses that the devil had a black gown and a skull bonnet, evil-favoured, on his head. He confesses that Euphame MacCalzean required Grierson to speer at the devil for the picture, naming the king's picture which should have been roasted. She cried out that they might hear that were beside.' According to the dittay against Napier's assizers, the devil was 'clad in a black tatty gown, and an evil-favoured skull-bonnet on his head' and at the convention 'the said Robert found great fault with the devil, and cried out that all which was beside might hear, because His Highness' picture was not given them as was promised'.

[1]591

[Gillie] Duncan confesses that she was at Acheson's Haven, where there were eight or ten[1] principals and about thirty inferiors assembled. The six[2] were Euphame MacCalzean, Barbara Napier, Agnes Sampson, John Fian, Robert Grierson, George Mott's wife, Bessie Thomson, the wife of Saltoun Mill, Gillie Duncan, Janet Stratton, Donald Robson,[3] where Agnes Sampson proponed[†] the matter to lay the dropped toad with strong wash[†] in the king's way for his destruction. They named his Majesty's name in Latin.

Janet Stratton depones in this matter

'Master, we have a turn ado and we would fain be at it if we could, and therefore help us to it'. He answered, 'I shall do it, but it will be long because it will be thwarted',[4] and thereafter there was one directed[†] to seek one of his Majesty's linen clothes to do the turn withall.

[†] **proponed** put forward for consideration   [†] **directed** instructed
[†] **strong wash** stale urine, used for bleaching
clothes

Gillie Duncan depones that it is not a year since she saw Master Bowes in Haddington, riding through the gate by the cross. This was a little while before he heaved[†][5] the Lord Bothwell's bairn. She depones that she kenned him never[6] but in Edinburgh,[†] and that she saw him not in Barbara Napier's house, but heard his words there in the cellar where Euphame MacCalzean was, and Barbara, Agnes Sampson and John Fian, where the bill[†] was read which she brought from Agnes Sampson out of George Mott's house. This was in the beginning of harvest. She delivered the bill to Barbara Napier in her own hall, none being present but her servants and bairns. Immediately Barbara directed her servant to Euphame to come to her, which she did in the gloaming.[†] There were certain other wives of Edinburgh with them, and amongst others one named Ranking who should have cast the droppings of the toad down before the king.

Janet Stratton depones that the Earl Bothwell should have been the mover[†] to have the picture, and was named there. She depones that the devil appeared first like a turs of hay.[†]

Janet depones that she neither saw John Cockburn nor heard him, but Bessie Thomson depones conform[†] to the foresaid.

Gillie Duncan affirms of now[†] that the king's life w[ ]ed by Bar[ ]e N[ ] Euphame MacCalzean. Besides there were Marion Ranking, and one Nevin, Annie Sampson and Meggie Thomson. They met all first in the high house[†] and from tha[ ] gaid to the lower house[†] to the cellar and sat down to eat and drink where they had roasted fowls and sweetmeat.[†] Agnes Sampson caused Barbara give her meat. She confesses she was in the hall but not in the cellar.

[ ]he 29 of [ ]e 1591 in presence of the council

Donald Robson, of the age of three score and more, confesses that he saw Robert Grierson beside the pulpit at North Berwick kirk where he found

---

[†] **heaved** stood sponsor to: to heave is 'to lift a child from the font as sponsor' (*DOST sv* 'heve'). On 8 March 1590 Richard Douglas wrote to Archibald Douglas of the particularly magnificent banquet Bothwell held after his daughter's baptism 'by reason of the honour done to him by her majestie [i.e. Elizabeth I], by her ambassador being a witness therunto' (*CSPS* x 247).
[†] **kenned … Edinburgh** she only knew him in Edinburgh

[†] **bill** letter
[†] **gloaming** twilight
[†] **mover** instigator
[†] **turs of hay** bundle of hay
[†] **conform** corresponding
[†] **of now** at the present time
[†] **in the high house** on the top storey of the house
[†] **lower house** bottom of the house
[†] **sweetmeat** confectionery

faul[t] with the devil because the king's picture was not made; who promised it should be the next meeting.

He confesses that Grierson was in the boat[7] where he was headsman.[†]

He confesses that the devil had a black gown and a skull bonnet, evil-favoured, on his head.

He confesses that Euphame MacCalzean required[†] Greirson to speer at the devil for the picture, naming the king's picture which should have been roasted. She cried out that they might hear that were beside. He depones that he heard never of the picture but that time. He confessed voluntarily of the picture at the first time, not being demanded of any person.

He confesses that John Cockburn commanded him to work the destruction upon David Seton's goods, and promised him fifty pound for the doing of it. He commanded him to gang to Agnes Sampson to seek her help. He depones that he told John Cockburn that he was a witch.

Bessie Nisbet[8]

Janet Adamson, wedwife, dwells in this side of Janet Folart's two closes. She is com[????] to have lying in woods about two hundred marks worth in and specially[†] a [?brave] book [???] value to [???] covered with goldsmiths' work which was [?????] four [?????] book as some of her jewels.

Janet Stratton repeated before his Majesty,
the lord chancellor, Crawford, Morton.

Of the toad dripping etc. by Lord Bothwell who hecht[†] silver, gold and victual to Agnes Sampson for doing of it.

And the picture was first spoken of by R. Grierson.

I was never in sea but [?thereby] that the boat drowned and they took me with them and, as I shall answer to God, Barbara Napier was there and heard never word of the English ambassador, and let them that will speak it, speak, and trow her not that said it.[†]

Grierson thinks he will not be [?kenned] for sic a man and the devil possessed him, and ye may well ken that he could not lease the garden and [?fessin?] it about his craig and I have no more to say but of the wasted words as I [???????????????????].

Donald said it was true that he said of the picture: Effie said 'Grierson speak it to the devil' and he had denied nothing that he spake to his g[   ].

---

† **headsman** leader
† **required** instructed
† **specially** particularly

† **hecht** promised
† **trow ... said it** don't believe the woman who said it

servant to Martha

Bessie Nesbit was sent to my Lady Angus by Euphame MacCalzean to declare that if any trusty friends were sent to Barbara to promise kindness to her, that she would confess freely some things that may favour for her, and well done by her and her husband, otherwise would be as ready to do her evil.

the said Bessie Nisbet[9]

Document 7

Deposition of Janet Stratton

?30 January 1591

This is a single leaf written only on one side, and covering only a quarter of the page. It is a deposition by Janet Stratton, taken the penultimate day of [January?] 1591. If this is the date, then the deposition was taken two days after the execution of Agnes Sampson on 28 January.

Euphame MacCalzean was eventually 'indicted for being at the convention held at the new haven called the Fiery Hills at Lammas lastwas'. For the connections between Agnes Sampson, Barbara Napier and Lady Jean Lyons, sometime wife of the earl of Angus, see Agnes Sampson's dittay, item 52, Barbara Napier's dittay, items 1 and 2, and the king's letter. Stratton implied that the meeting at the Fiery Hills was to bring about the death by image magic of Archibald, earl of Angus, at the instigation of his then wife, Jean Lyons, and that Barbara Napier had acted as go-between. On 8 May 1591 Napier was acquitted of consulting Agnes Sampson for making the earl's image.

the penult of [   ]e 1591[1]

Janet Stratton depones that about three year since† Agnes Sampson, Barbara Napier and Euphame MacCalzean being at the Fiery Hills, Agnes Sampson raised the devil and said to him she had something ado† concerning a lord. Where they received a picture. Agnes Sampson received the same and delivered it to Barbara, and she delivered it to Euphame, and Euphame rendered† the same to her again. The picture should have been roasted

---

† **since** ago
† **ado** to do

† **rendered** returned

during the space of a quarter of a year and upon the roasting of it they should have said this word, 'Master' thrice at every time.

She affirms that the earl of Angus' last wife called Lyon sent Barbara to Agnes Sampson for that effect[†] because of an eindling[†] betwixt her goodman[†] and her.

[†] **for that effect** with that purpose
[†] **eindling** jealousy
[†] **goodman** husband

Document 8

Deposition of Janet Stratton

4 May 1591

This is a deposition of Janet Stratton, taken at Holyroodhouse in the presence of the king, the duke of Lennox and others, on 4 May 1591. The presence of Chancellor Maitland, Bothwell's enemy, may explain in part the highly incriminating statements made about Bothwell in this deposition.

This is a single sheet folded in two. The first leaf is written on both sides in a neat and tidy scribal hand in well-formed sentences, which are neatly punctuated. Then f. 2^r is blank, and on f. 2^v there are some notes.

The boat drowning in September 1589 is represented as the occasion when Agnes Sampson mentioned cryptically that 'a gentleman' had commissioned her to destroy a man and that she had to go to Edinburgh. Then a month before the Lammas meeting in 1590 at Acheson's Haven (Fiery Hills) we are given a picture of the dripping of the toad and the mixing of the 'wash' in Agnes Sampson's house. This mixture 'was sent to Edinburgh to the women who should use it there'. Janet Stratton deponed that at Prestonpans eighty people were convened, including Barbara Napier and Euphame MacCalzean.

The story in Janet Stratton's deposition of 4 May is strikingly 'literary'. It is economically told, and tightly organised in its narrative, with three meetings providing a beginning, middle and end: on the sea in September 1589, Acheson's Haven at Lammas 1590, and North Berwick. Threes are a feature of the story: Agnes Sampson's three fingers stirring the mixture, the triple invocation of 'My master'. Agnes Sampson is given a brief but powerful speech to the devil, which is rhetorically artful and elegant in its appositions ('James Stewart, prince of Scotland'), balanced clauses ('that he has promised and should give us'), apostrophe ('Master Mahoun'), *synonymia* ('this turn wrought and done'), and its tendency to isocolon (the repetition of phrases of equal length and corresponding structure). It is also a speech in which the devil is addressed as 'Master Mahoun', a name he has in the poetry of Dunbar and Montgomerie.

> Take there the picture of James Stewart, prince of Scotland. And I ask of you, Master Mahoun, that I may have this turn wrought and done, to wrack him for my Lord Bothwell's sake and for the gold and silver that he has promised and should give us, with victual to me and my bairns.

This artful elegance of expression, together with suggestions of elite ideology evidenced by such phrases as 'Anne Sampson incalled the enemy', makes one more than usually suspicious that this deposition has been contaminated, or indeed shaped, by the interests of the examiners. It implies that the treasonable plot against the king was of long standing: it was talked of a year and a half before, furthered the previous July and taken yet further at the North Berwick convention on 31 October 1590. It was supposedly planned by a large, organised group in the pay of Francis, earl of Bothwell.

★

> At Holyroodhouse the fourth day of May,
> the year of God 1591[1]
> in presence of the king's Majesty, and
> of the duke's grace of Lennox,[†] my lord
> chancellor,[†] master clerk secretary, the
> depute captain of Edinburgh Castle, laird of Carmichael,[2]
> Mr Almonssar advocate clerk of Edinburgh.

Janet Stratton re-examined declares that at their coming off[†] the sea the time of the drowning of the boat[†] which was in September 1589, Anne Sampson showed[†] them that a gentleman had burdened her with a turn[†] and for which purpose she behoved[†] to have a toad to wrack[†] a man and spoke no more speech[†] at that time, but said she behoved to pass[†] to Edinburgh.

In this matter was[†] no other thing done while[†] about a month or thereby[†] before the meeting at the Fiery Hills of Prestonpans which was upon Lammas Eve that last was. Anne Sampson got the toad and dripped the same above the fire in her house, and after she had gotten the same dripping[†] in a latten[†] dish, she caused this deponer[†] get the mixture or wash[3] for her part,[†] who brought the same to Anne Sampson's house, where the same was mixed

---

[†] **the duke's grace of Lennox** i.e. his grace, the duke of Lennox

[†] **chancellor** Sir John Maitland (?1545–1595), lord chancellor of Scotland from 1587, an enemy of Bothwell and an instigator of the charges against him of having had recourse to witches

[†] **coming off** i.e. landing after their sea journey

[†] **drowning of the boat** the wreck of the boat sailing from Burntisland to Leith on 7 September 1589, mentioned in *News*

[†] **showed** announced to

[†] **burdened her with a turn** given her a job to do

[†] **she behoved** it was necessary for her

[†] **wrack** destroy

[†] **spoke no more speech** said no more

[†] **pass** go

[†] **was** there was

[†] **while** until

[†] **thereby** thereabouts

[†] **dripping** i.e. the drops from the toad

[†] **latten** yellow brass

[†] **deponer** deponent

[†] **for her part** i.e. this was Janet Stratton's particular task

together and heated[4] on the fire, Anne Sampson stirring the same with her three fingers. At which time there was present the said Anne Samp-son, this deponer, Katie Wallace, wife to James Sparrow of the mill[5] of Saltoun and Meg Begtoun.

This dripping of the toad mixed, as said is, was also black as pitch[6] and was sent to Edinburgh to the women who should use it there. At the mixing of it Anne Sampson incalled the enemy[†] saying 'My master' three times.

Thereafter upon Lammas Even that last was, Anne Sampson advertised[†] this deponer and trysted her[†] to meet at Kingsburn[7] and they two, and with them Donald and Anne Dunlop, came to the convention to Prestonpans, where there was convened before them[†] Barbara Napier, Effie MacCalzean, Meg Begtoun, Bessie Thomson, Gellie Duncan, Robert Grierson and Margaret Acheson, wife to George Mott, and sundry others to the number of sixty or thereby. But it was only these special persons that stood in a ring and had the picture after mentioned in their hands.

The purpose of their convening[†] at that time was to conjure or enchant a picture of wax which Anne Sampson brought with her and showed to them that were with her by the gate. Like as[†] she showed the same to all the laif of[†] the company at her coming to the 'Pans, and every one of them had it in their hands that time about[†] and spake certain words upon the same,[†] standing in a burgh,[†] and it passed widdershins about;[†] Anne Samson having the said picture first in her left hand which she, at the devil's bidding[8] delivered to Barbara Napier. Barbara Napier delivered it to Effie Mac-Calzean. The said Effie delivered it to Katie Wallace and she delivered the same to Meg Begtoun, and she to Donald Robson, and he to Bessy Thomson and she to Gillie Duncan and she to this same deponer, Jennie Stratton, who delivered the same to Anne Dunlop, and she to Robert Grierson and he to Margaret Acheson (George Mott's wife) and she again to the said Anne Sampson, who delivered in[†] the devil's hands, whom Anne Sampson

---

[†] **incalled the enemy** invoked the devil; 'incall' is usually used in relation to God or the saints. The expression 'incalled the enemy' is an example of elite thought and expression, both in 'incalled' and the notion of the devil as the enemy of God.
[†] **advertised** informed
[†] **trysted her** arranged a meeting with her
[†] **convened before them** already met before they got there

[†] **convening** meeting
[†] **Like as** in the same way
[†] **the laif of** the rest of
[†] **about** in turn
[†] **upon the same** i.e. they spoke magic words over the image
[†] **burgh** enclosed space
[†] **passed widdershins about** it was passed around anti-clockwise
[†] **who delivered in** who delivered it into

had raised, and he was there standing in likeness[†] of a black priest,[†] with black clothes like a hair mantle.

Item, declares that Anne Sampson said to the devil 'Take there the picture of James Stewart, prince of Scotland. And I ask of you, Master Mahoun,[†] that I may have this turn wrought and done, to wrack[†] him for my Lord Bothwell's sake and for the gold and silver that he[†] has promised and should give us, with victual to me and my bairns'.

Item, declares that Anne Sampson showed to the devil that she had done that which was directed anent[†] the dripping of the toad, and could not be the thing that she did it for, and he answered that he could not do till(?) it.

Item, declares that[†] was yellow, and wound in a cloth and was little less nor[†] half an ell[†] long. And declares that they was at home again by four hours in the morning and met not at any convention thereafter while[†] upon All Hallow Even in the kirk of North Berwick, to crave[†] the said picture again.

Depositions

Depositions of
Janet Stratton,
Donald,[†] Gillie Duncan
and Bessie Thomson[†]

Janet Stratton and Richard Graham's depositions.

[†] **in likeness** in the shape of
[†] **priest** usually used, especially after the Reformation, of a Roman catholic cleric
[†] **Mahoun** Mahoun, deriving from Mohammed, was a name for the devil, and is particularly common in the poetry of Dunbar. It is also to be found in Montgomerie's *Flyting*, 429 (Simpson 1995: 15).
[†] **wrack** destroy
[†] **he** i.e. Bothwell
[†] **anent** concerning

[†] **that** the image
[†] **nor** than
[†] **half an ell** an ell is a measure, usually of cloth. The Scottish ell was 37.2 inches, so half an ell was about 18 inches.
[†] **while** until
[†] **crave** ask for
[†] **Donald** i.e. Donald Robson
[†] **Depositions ... Thomson** this must refer to the next set of depositions, document 9.

Document 9

Examinations of Geillis Duncan, Donald Robson and Bessie Thomson

5 May 1591

This is in the same hand as document 8 and is another sheet folded into two leaves, the first leaf written on both sides. This is dated 5 May 1590 (i.e. 1591), the day after the previous examination. The focus of these examinations is the wax image of the king and its commissioning by Bothwell. On the verso of f. 2 James has been practising his signature.

Geillis Duncan claimed to be unable to remember some things, but 'she remembers well that she heard my Lord Bothwell spoken of'. Donald Robson had a patriotic concern for his country, for when 'Anne Sampson spake to him of the destruction of, the king, this deponer said to her "Alas, what will come [become] of Scotland then?"'. Bothwell is again incriminated as providing funds for the 'turn'. Some shrewd political comment is put into the mouth of Robert Grierson, who like Agnes Sampson was also dead by this time: 'Rob Grierson answered and said that it would be long or [a long time before] the gold came out of England'. Both James and Bothwell asked for and sometimes received money from Elizabeth in England, but the supply was often sporadic.

Gillie Duncan, re-examinate, declares that she was present at the convention in Prestonpans and agrees with Jennie Stratton anent the number and names of the special persons that were present thereat, and that she got the said thing or picture in the cloth delivered in her hands, and gave the same out of her hand to Jenny Stratton. And that she heard the king named, but not with his own name, as she remembers, but was called 'goodman' or sic another word. And the words that ilk one of them spake she cannot remember upon. But she remembers well that she heard my lord Bothwell spoken of. And that the thing was done for gold and silver and victual to help Anne Sampson and her bairns.

Donald Robson, re-examinate, declares and grants[†] that he was at the convention in Prestonpans and came to it in company of Anne Sampson and Jennie Stratton. And that Anne Sampson told them of the picture and errand for which it was to be used, by the gate to the 'Pans and told it openly[†] at her coming there. And by the gate where Anne Sampson spake to him of the destruction of the king, this deponer said to her 'Alas, what will come[†] of Scotland then?' To whom she answered, 'Ye have mickle to care for.[†] Ye will not want, but get enough so long as ye live'. And as to the number of the persons present at the said convention and their standing in a burgh and giving of the said picture of wax out of ilk one of their hands to other[†] is conform to[†] Jennie Stratton and Gillie Duncan,[1] but denies[†] that he saw the devil[2] there. The words, he said, were spoken in Latin and he cannot repeat them again at this time.

Item, declares that the thing was sought to be done for my Lord Bothwell, and Anne Samson prepared and promised the gear, for the gold would be shortly gotten out of England and she should give to the others their part thereof, and she would get victual to the help of her and her bairns. And Rob Grierson answered and said that it would be long or[†] the gold came out of England.

[?????]   At Edinburgh in the nether tolbooth
upon Wednesday the fifth day of
May, the year of god 1590[†]
years, in presence of the king's Majesty and
of the persons of the council that
were present the day preceding,[†] together
with Sir James Melville of Halhill.

Bessy Thomson, re-examinate, grants and confesses that she was present at the new haven in Prestonpans the time of the convention there about the conjuring of the picture of wax, and heard the words but understood them not, nor presently[†] remembers not on them. She cannot tell who delivered the picture in[†] her hands, but she remembers well that she delivered the

---

[†] **grants** admits
[†] **openly** without concealment
[†] **come** become
[†] **mickle to care for** many to care for; presumably his family
[†] **ilk one … to other** each one giving it into the hands of another

[†] **conform to** corroborated by
[†] **denies** he denies
[†] **long or** a long time before
[†] **1590** *sic*, but this must be an error for 1591
[†] **the day preceding** i.e. 4 May, see document 8
[†] **presently** at the moment
[†] **in** into

same in Gillie Duncan's hand. She grants that she was present at the raising of the dead corpses in the kirk and kirk-yard of North Berwick. She said she cannot tell if the devil was present at the convention of the new haven or not or whether she saw[3] him. And thereafter said that he was there in a cloud like a [???] truss.

[????]

Jam　　　James R

James R

Document 10

The Substance of a Letter from Ritchie
Graham to the King

---

date uncertain

This is a single leaf, written on one side in a large clear hand. Richard Graham has been complaining of his treatment. Graham, fearing to die at the hands of the law or of Bothwell, had asked to live in prison or in banishment and promised to reveal all he knew about Bothwell (*CSPS* x 561). Graham had clearly made some sort of deal (Bothwell would later say with some of the king's council) to testify or confess in certain ways. At Bothwell's trial on August 1593 it emerged that

> Greyme did never accuse Bothwell in any thing till such tyme as he had a warrant under the councelles handes . . . that if he wold speake simply and trewly what he knewe, his life should be preserved, and he should lyve in Sterling castle, where he should feare no mans mallice and have good allowance. After which warrant, then in all depositions ever after he toucht Bothwell. (*Border Papers* i 487)

In a letter to Maitland in mid-June 1591, which ends with some instructions about imprisoned witches, James told him 'garre see that richie grahme want not his ordinaire allowance [see to it that Richie Graham does not lack his ordinary allowance]' (BL Additional MS 23,341 f. 41). Order was eventually given for Graham's execution on 24 February 1592 (*CSPS* x 649).

★

The tenor[†] of the bill sent by Richard
Graham to the master of work[†]
to give to the king's Majesty.

In the first part of this bill he mened[†] his hard handling in the tolbooth and
want of entertainment in meat and cloth,[†] against condition made to him.[†]

He declared that condition was made that he should be warded[†] in the
castle of Stirling[1] and entertained, himself and a servant, honestly for his
surety[†] against his jailers.[2]

He desired, seeing that he had kept condition to[†] them in saying that which
he was desired or promised, that they would keep condition to him in warding
and entertainment in cloth and meat, as is above written.

This bill was publicly read at the master's household table before the master
of work, presently the same to the king's Majesty.[†]

William Shaw,
master of work
[?Durhame] of authority.

[†] **tenor** substance
[†] **master of work** 'an official who superintends
    building operations' (*OED*)
[†] **mened** complained of
[†] **want of … cloth** lack of provision made for him
    in the way of food and clothes

[†] **against … to him** contrary to the agreement
    made with
[†] **warded** imprisoned
[†] **surety** safety
[†] **kept condition to** kept the bargain with
[†] **presently the same** i.e. the letter was then read
    to the king

Document 11

Examination of Euphame MacCalzean's Servant, Bessie Nisbet

7 May 1591

This is an examination, at Holyroodhouse on 7 May 1591, of Euphame MacCalzean's servant Bessie Nesbit, and then Margaret Weston, about the attempted delivery of a letter sent by MacCalzean concealed in a loaf of bread to Kate Muirhead or Jennie Stewart, who must have been in prison, presumably in the tolbooth.

At Holyroodhouse the 7th day of May 1591

Bessie Nesbit, servant to Effie MacCalzean, grants[†] that her mistress yesterday gave her a loaf[1] in her napkin willing to get the same convoyed[†] to Kate Muirhead or Jennie Stewart, which loaf or mainschot[†] the deponer delivered to Margaret Weston, servant to James Nesbit, javelor.[†]

Margaret Weston,[2] servant to James Nesbit, javelor, being examined says that Bessie Nesbit, servant to Effie MacCalzean, came till yesterday about ten hours before noon,[†] and gave her a loaf and a napkin[†] about the same[†] with many knots, and bade give[†] the same to Katie Muirhead or Jennie

---

† **grants** admits
† **willing … convoyed** giving her orders to get it carried
† **mainschot** a roll of the finest wheaten bread
† **javelor** jailer

† **ten hours before noon** i.e. 10.00 in the morning
† **napkin** table-napkin
† **about the same** wrapped around the loaf
† **bade give** commanded her to give

Stewart. This she showed to her master, and at the appearing of the napkin[†] the loaf fell in two and the writing[†] fell down, and (   ) Tailor[3] that was present cried 'Treason!'

Euphame MacCalzean grants she wrote two or three letters, but undelivered.[†] She was consulting with her woman. Grants she wrote the writing. Bade read it to Jennie Drummond and bring it again, and to the skipper more nor[†] twenty days syne.

[†] **at the ... napkin** when the napkin came into sight
[†] **writing** letter

[†] **but undelivered** but they were not delivered
[†] **nor** than

Document 12

Examination of Euphame MacCalzean

7 May 1591

This is a sheet folded in two, written on one side. Euphame MacCalzean has now been imprisoned and is being questioned about letters. This follows on from the examination of her servant Bessie Nesbit in document 11 about letters, and is taken at Holyroodhouse on the same day, 7 May.

At Holyroodhouse, the seventh of May 1591

Euphame MacCalzean, inquired[†] if she has written anything syne she entered in prison, grants[†] twice to her husband, once to the present fourteen days syne; to none in the town except it be for debts.[†] Inquired if she has written to any in the tolbooths, denies and specially to Janet Drummond denies.[†] Denies that she has written to Katie Muirhead or that she sent any letter in a loaf to her. The letter being shown to her she thinks it is her handwriting.[1] Grants that she sent meat[†] to them that are in the tolbooth twice or thrice in a week[2] —they cry so miserably.[†] She will not affirm that it is her handwriting. She thinks it is her handwriting rather nor not her handwriting.[†] Grants both the letters been seen by her, that both are her handwriting and says that she has written five or six times to this effect.[†] Grants that she put it not

---

[†] **inquired** asked
[†] **grants** admits
[†] **except ... debts** except about debts
[†] **Inquired ... denies** asked if she has written to anyone in the tolbooths she denies that she has, and she particularly denies having written to Janet Drummond

[†] **meat** food
[†] **cry so miserably** they call out so pitifully
[†] **She thinks ... handwriting** she thinks it is her handwriting (on balance) rather than that it isn't
[†] **to this effect** to this end

in a loaf. She sent not the letter out. Howbeit[†] she wrote not all the circum-stances[†] she wrote the effect[†] of it. Jennie Drummond took the goose and the buist[†] and gold and silver fra Margaret Fraser to Anne Sampson.[3] Denies that she sent this or any other letter to Janet Muirhead.

Euphame MacCalzean

Euphame MacCalzean's depositions

[†] **Howbeit** although
[†] **circumstances** details
[†] **effect** substance
[†] **buist** box. See MacCalzean's dittay, item 19, where she was accused of attempting to kill her father-in-law, John Moscrop, by a wax image which had been delivered in a box hidden inside a goose to Sampson.

Document 13

Deposition of Janet Kennedy

?June 1591

This is a single sheet of paper, folded to make two leaves. One one side is written '[   ] wife of Reddon's depositions. Janet Kennedy's depositions to his majesty', and on the other is Kennedy's deposition.

This is a witchcraft examination conducted in the presence of King James, the duke of Lennox and the ministers David Lindsay and James Gilstone. Janet Kennedy is presumably the woman mentioned by Bowes in a letter of 14 June 1591:

> This trial of Mackallean is thought to touch Bothwell narrowly, and Kennedy the witch of Reydon, lately in England, has secretly told the King sundry matters against the earl agreeing with Graham, his chief accuser. (*CSPS* x 531–2)

This might date this deposition in June 1591. The earlier part of the examination recounts the first meeting of a witch with the devil who masqueraded as a palmer(?) with a book. It is a traditional story of the devil appearing first in a holy shape, an 'old [pa?]lmer clad in white', then promising a good life if Kennedy kept his commands. Agnes Sampson is again represented as the most important witch. An interesting detail in Kennedy's deposition is her claim that she went to conventions in spirit, and her spirit was drawn out of her by Sampson. On to these familiar narratives (of a first meeting, compact with the devil, and attendance at meetings) is added the political material. Barbara Napier is incriminated by implication, as Agnes Sampson had an image of the earl of Angus. On 8 May Napier had been accused, but acquitted, of consulting Agnes Sampson about an image of the earl of Angus. But this story of the earl of Angus's image seems a preparation for an analogous but more serious story of a 'turn' with an image, for the deposition moves on quickly to the manufacture of the king's image before the convention at Lammas 1590. Another wax image, that of King James, was shown by Agnes Sampson to Janet Kennedy.

★

[   ]day in presence of the [   ]
[   ]ke of Lennox and James Gilstone minister
[   ] Mr David Lindsay.[†]

[   ] she depones that about thirty years or thereby,[†] about the [   ] in the day there came till[†] her house a man like an old [?pa]lmer[†] clad in white, who after divers speeches had with her showed forth[†] a book he had in his hand and caused her to swear upon that that she should take her[†] to the judgement of God and forsake the foul thief[†] and all his works,[†] to keep her from temptation; and yet the deponer[†] confesses that while[†] after that time she never knew what temptation meant. As it appeared by his next resorting unto her, at which time he more plainly discovered[†] himself unto her, desiring her to keep his commands, and promised her that in so doing she should purchase[†] a good life unto herself.

Whereby the deponer grants[†] that now she perceives it was an evil spirit appeared unto her in that likeness.[†] For after that, Agnes Sampson sent word unto her by one called Brown,[1] her daughter, desiring her to come unto her, and upon her refusal she threatened[†] her in Agnes Sampson's name and said that the said Agnes [????] she refused to come unto her self would compel whether she would or not the pith[†] of her body to come unto her, as after it fell or sorted out.[†]

For at divers times fra that time forth the said Agnes would by her enchantments, when this deponer was lying in her bed in the night, draw forth her spirit, as it appeared[†] to her, and make it to be transported to the convention to assist at their deeds.[†] And among the rest the deponer remembers of[†] two principal turns[†] she saw done at the convention.

[†] **David Lindsay** (1531?–1613), the king's chaplain who had married James and Anne at Uppsala and, together with Robert Bruce, had crowned her in the abbey kirk in May 1590
[†] **thereby** thereabouts
[†] **till** to
[†] **[pa?]lmer** a pilgrim who had been to the holy land and who was distinguished by carrying a palm leaf
[†] **showed forth** displayed
[†] **take her** deliver herself up
[†] **the foul thief** i.e. the devil
[†] **forsake … his works** ironically, on his first visit, the disguised devil asks Kennedy to 'renounce the devil and all his works', in the formula of the invitation to a child's godparents at baptism

[†] **deponer** deponent
[†] **while** until
[†] **discovered** revealed
[†] **purchase** acquire
[†] **grants** agrees
[†] **likeness** shape
[†] **threatened** commanded
[†] **pith** strength of spirit. Agnes Sampson threatened to compel Janet's spirit to come to her, if she would not come to her in body.
[†] **sorted out** so happened
[†] **appeared** seemed
[†] **deeds** doings
[†] **remembers of** remembers
[†] **turns** acts

The first was that about a three or four year syne. She saw Agnes Sampson, who a summer night betwixt the Midsummer and Lammas had a long small[†] picture of wax in her hand, black hued, which was devised[†] for the earl of Angus' destruction and put in a [????] or basin full of water and made to grow weak and so to melt away, and this was done in the fields, but in what place she knows not because it was in the night.

The next turn s[ ]
upon the fields in a p[ ]
showed unto this deponer a[ ] great [ ]
a picture of yellow wax shorter than the other[†] w[ ]
linen cloth where the other was bare, which [ ]
King James as the said Agnes reported, being [ ]
put him down thereby by great lords and ladies for [ ]
their favour and kindness. Which putting down said Agnes [ ]
make them all [?upon] were there. And at this time stood a[ ]
beside the said Agnes, of mean[†] stature, about thirty years of age as appeared to the deponer, and with little hair on his face, and being but whey[2] lean faced,[†] and he would have had the picture out of the said Agnes' hand, but she would not give it while she had done [ ]ting with it. For within a month thereafter, about the Lammas, in a fair summer night with starlight, the same company convened again in a little landward house[†] [?????] the moor which appeared to be Agnes Sampson's house, where the deponer saw the said Agnes take the king's picture out of the cloth, and laying down the cloth beside the fire made for the purpose, lay the picture again to have made it fried[†3] by the fire as the custom is, but it would not. Whereupon the man whom of the deponer before spake[†] desired the said Agnes to make the fire bolder,[†] but all that could not help. Whereupon Agnes Sampson said that all was in vain they assayed against the king for nothing of their craft could do at him.[†]

Further the deponer affirms that the king needs to be feared of nothing under God,[†] for she saw by experience at that time all that the devil might do against the king and yet took no effect.[†]

[†] **long small** long and slender
[†] **devised** planned
[†] **the other** i.e. the 'long small picture of wax' devised for the destruction of the earl of Angus
[†] **mean** middling
[†] **whey lean faced** with a pale, lean face
[†] **landward house** house in the country
[†] **fried** tortured by heat
[†] **whom of ... spake** about whom the deponent

spoke earlier
[†] **bolder** fiercer, hotter
[†] **all ... at him** everything they attempted against the king was pointless, as no magic of theirs could affect him
[†] **nothing under God** nothing in the world
[†] **saw ... no effect** saw through her experiences everything the devil might do against the king, and yet none of it had any effect

James R

Lennox

J Sandilands
David Lindsay,
minister of Leith

James Gilstone, minister
of Great [?????]

Document 14

Another Deposition of Janet Kennedy

?June 1591

This is one sheet folded into two leaves. On the verso of f. 2 is written 'The wyfe of reddennis despositionis'.

[   ] of June: 1591

[   ] the said Janet depones in presence of his Majesty, Mr David [Lind?]say and Mr Robert Bruce, minister,[†] that about the last Lammas in the year of God 1590[1] when the king's picture was [   ] roasting in Anny Sampson's house, that the said Agnes said unto her and unto all the company that there was more[† 2] nor[†] sic poor folks then present that was art and part[†] of that turn, but in special[†] two great women whose surnames she named 'MacCalzean' and 'Napier', but expressed not their proper names. 'And these two,' said Agnes, 'I and this man', whom of[†] the deponer has already made mention, 'are the principal that are ordained for winning of great lords' and ladies' favours to put this turn in execution against the king'.

---

† **Robert Bruce, minister** (1554–1631), minister in Edinburgh who was appointed extrordinary privy councillor during James's absence in Norway and Denmark. He had annointed Anne queen in May 1590.
† **was more** the MS seems to read 'vas man', where

'man' may be a mistake for 'mair'
† **nor** than
† **art and part** in the capacity of an accessory or accomplice
† **in special** particularly
† **whom of** of whom

Further, the deponer grants that she remembers that she was there bodily[†] at that time, send for by Annie Sampson and, in [?????] there this deponer and Meg Steel made and mended[†] the fire w[   ] their own hands that the king's picture was laid to.

James R

James Lindsay

Robert Bruce, minister

[†] **bodily** corporeally, as opposed to the times she attended a convention only in spirit; see document 13

[†] **mended** tended

Document 15

Depositions of Janet Stratton and
Donald Robson to a Notary Public

19 June 1591

This is a single leaf with a deposition of Janet Stratton before a notary public, taken at Seton and Tranent on 19 June 1591. Stratton now denies that she knew any evil of Bothwell, or indeed that she had ever seen him. The reverse reads: 'Janet Stratton and Donald / Robson's deniall' and 'Janet Stratton and / Donald's depositions'.

> At Seton and Tranent respective[†] the
> nineteenth day of June, the year of God 1591.[1]

The which day in presence of me, notary public,[2] and witnesses underwritten, compeared[†] the right noble and potent lord Robert, Lord Seton, and past to the personal presence of Janet Stratton, for the time[†] captive within his [   ] pit of Seton for the crime of sorcery alleged committed by her, and earnestly desired her to declare to him her whole knowledge that she had of the earl Bothwell, and if she understood him to have been a consulter with witches, or a practiser of witchcraft, and in special[†] if ever he had dealt with her or any other thereanent.[†]

Whose answer was then to the said noble lord in these terms. 'As I shall answer to God, I never knew the Earl Bothwell but to be a noble man', and

---

† **respective** respectively
† **compeared** put in an appearance

† **for the time** at that time
† **in special** particularly
† **thereanent** with relation to that matter

that he never by[†] her knowledge dealt any manner of way[†] either with her, or with any other to the hurt[†] of any man, or yet that ever she saw him in the face and knew him by[†] another man, except that by report[†] she heard him accounted[†] a noble man.

This I testify to be of truth,[†] by these presents. Subscrived[†] with my hand, day, year and place foresaid, in presence of the said noble lord Robert, Lord Seton, Thomas Seton of Northrig and George Seton his son.

This same deposition was given in presence of David Seton in Tranent, the same day, by Donald (   ),[†] Highland man, who also was detained captive for sorcery.

Alexander Cook notarius ad premissa requisitus

---

† **by** to
† **any manner of way** in any way
† **hurt** harm
† **by** apart from
† **report** rumour

† **accounted** considered
† **of truth** true
† **Subscrived** Signed
† **Donald (   )** presumably Donald Robson

Document 16

Deposition of Donald Robson to Notaries Public

4 July 1591

This is a deposition of Donald Robson taken on 4 July 1591 at about 9.00 a.m, on the same day as Janet Stratton's (document 17). Both were taken by David Ogilvy before Robert Gardiner and Stephen Bannatyne, notaries public: Robson's at David Seton's house in Tranent, Stratton's at Seton Palace. Ogilvy had been one of the prolocutors (spokesmen) for Euphame MacCalzean at her trial and was Patrick MacCalzean's son-in-law. Both documents are written in the same hand and have the signatures of the same notaries.

Both depositions are clearly part of an attempt to exonerate the late ('umwhile') Euphame MacCalzean, who had been burned less than two weeks before, on 25 June 1591. Robson and Stratton retract their earlier claims of familiarity with Euphame MacCalzean and their accusations of witchcraft against her, and they 'also declared what ever [they] had spoken of the said umwhile Euphame, that the same was for fear of [their] life and torment, and by compulsion'.

Apud Tranent, quarto die mensis Julii anno domini millesimo quingentesimo nonagesimo primo, ac regni supremi domini nostri regis anno vigesimo quarto.[†]

The which day in presence of us notaries public and witnesses underwritten an honourable man, Mr David Ogilvy, passed to the personal presence[†] of Donald Robson, being in the house and keeping of David Seton elder in

---

[†] *Apud Tranent … vigesimo quarto* 'At Tranent, 4 July, the year of our Lord 1591, and the twenty-fourth year of the reign of our sovereign lord the king.'

[†] **personal presence** presence

Tranent, and required of him[†] what he knew or understood of umwhile[†] Euphame MacCalzean, sometime spouse to Patrick MacCalzean, touching any manner of witchcraft. Who made special and general[†] declaration of his knowledge towards her thereof, of the which deposition follows in manner underwritten, that is to say the deposition of Donald Robson made in presence of us notaries public and witnesses underwritten upon the fourth day of July, the year of God 1591 years;[1] being inquired by Mr David Ogilvy, son to my Lord Ogilvy, of certain particular points of witchcraft as follows.

In primis, the said Donald Robson being inquired by the said Mr David when and where he knew umwhile Euphame MacCalzean, sometime spouse to Patrick MacCalzean, the said Donald declared, as he should answer to God, that he never knew her but when he saw her in the tolbooth of Edinburgh.

Item, the said Mr David inquired further at the said Donald if he had been at the great convention of witches at the kirk of North Berwick and if he saw the said Euphame there or if he saw her at Acheson's Haven, Broomhill, or any other place or time where the king's Majesty's picture was inquired for by them, who answered and declared as he should answer to God, as said is,[†] that he was never in those places nor at no convention, nor at no place where witchcraft was, neither yet that he never saw the said umwhile Euphame in the same place, nor never knew her to use nor exercise any kind of witchcraft, nor knew nothing of the king's picture; and also declared that what ever he had spoken of the said umwhile Euphame, that the same was for fear of his life and torment,[†] and by compulsion concerning witchcraft. And declared whatever he had spoken of before of the said Euphame concerning witchcraft was false and feigned,[†] as he should answer to God. At once[†] the said Donald declared before the witnesses underwritten that he had *simpliciter*[†] denied all and whatsoever he spake of the said umwhile Euphame concerning witchcraft before her death.

Upon the which requisition[†] and deposition made by the said persons in manner above specified, the said Mr David asked instruments[†] of us notaries public underwritten. This was done in the dwelling house of the said David Seton elder, on the east side of the town of Tranent, as said is, about nine hours before noon or thereby, before these witnesses: the said David Seton

---

[†] **him** i.e. Donald Robson
[†] **umwhile** the late
[†] **special and general** both particular and general
[†] **as said is** as the saying goes
[†] **torment** torture
[†] **feigned** fictitious, invented

[†] **At once** immediately
[†] *simpliciter* unconditionally
[†] **requisition** request, demand
[†] **asked instruments** (Scots law) requested a duly authenticated record of the proceedings

elder, George Weddell, Alexander Bell, James Adamson collier,[†] Ninian Weir, Robert Gairdner, and Steven Bannatyne, notaries underwritten:

> *Robertus Gardnar notarius publicus in premissa requisitus testantibus meis signo et subscriptione manualibus*

> *Ita est Stephanus Bannatyne connotarius publicus in premissis requisitiis manu propria*[†]

[†] **collier** coal miner
[†] ***Robertus ... propria*** 'Robert Gardiner, notary public, witness? to the foregoing, as witnessed by my seal and signature. Similarly, Stephen Bannatyne, connotary public, witnessing to the foregoing with my own hand.'

Document 17

Deposition of Janet Stratton to Notaries Public

<hr>

4 July 1591

This is a deposition of Janet Stratton, taken by David Ogilvy before notaries public at Seton Palace on 4 July 1591. On the reverse, a twentieth-century hand has written in pencil 'Witchcraft against His Majesty. Justiciary Processes 1591. Box 2'. On the reverse of the document written in a contemporary hand is 'Janet Stratton'. This deposition is in the same hand and has the same signatures of the notaries as Donald Robson's deposition at Tranent (document 16). Both these depositions were taken on the same day.

This is clearly part of an attempt to clear the name of Euphame MacCalzean, as is the deposition of Donald Robson.

Apud palacium de Seton quarto die mensis Julii anno domini millesimo quingentesimo nonagesimo primo ac regni supremi domini nostri regis anno vigesimo.[†]

The which day, in presence of us notaries public and witnesses underwritten, an honorable man Mr David Ogilvy, son lawful[†] to my Lord Ogilvy, passed to the personal presence of Janet Stratton, being in prison at my Lord Seton's palace, and required of her what she knew or understood of umwhile Euphame MacCalzean, sometime spouse to Patrick MacCalzean, touching any manner witchcraft,[†] who made special and general declaration of her knowledge toward[†] thereof. Of the which her deposition and declaration follows in manner underwritten.

<hr>

[†] *Apud palacium … vigesimo* 'At Seton Palace, the fourth day of the month of July, the year of our Lord 1591 and the fifteenth year of the reign of our sovereign lord the king.'

[†] **son lawful** legitimate son
[†] **any manner witchcraft** any sort of witchcraft
[†] **toward** with regard to this

The deposition of Janet Stratton made in presence of us notaries public and witnesses underwritten upon the fourth[1] day of July the year of God 1591 years; being inquired[†] by Mr David Ogilvy, son to my Lord Ogilvy, of certain particular heads and points[†] of witchcraft as follows.

In primis, the said Janet Stratton being inquired by the said Mr David when and where she knew umwhile Euphame MacCalzean, sometime spouse to Patrick MacCalzean, the said Janet declared, as she should answer to God, that she never knew the said umwhile Euphame MacCalzean but[†] when she knew her in presence of the king's Majesty.

Item, the said Mr David inquired further at the said Janet if she had been at the great convention of witches at the kirk of North Berwick and if she saw the said umwhile Euphame there, or if she saw the said umwhile Euphame at Acheson's Haven, Broomhills or any other place or time where the king's Majesty's picture was inquired for by them. Who answered and declared, as she should answer to God, as said is,[†] that she was never in those places nor at no convention nor place where witchcraft was, neither yet[†] that she never saw the said umwhile Euphame in the same place nor never knew her to use or exercise any kind of witchcraft, nor knew nothing of the king's Majesty's picture. And also declared whatever she had spoken of the said umwhile Euphame, that the same was for fear of her life and torment,[†] and by compulsion, and declared whatever she had spoken of before of the said umwhile Euphame concerning witchcraft, the same was false and feigned,[†] as she should answer to God. At once[†] the said Janet declared that she had *simpliciter*[†] denied all and whatever she had spoken of the said umwhile Euphame ay concerning witchcraft[†] before her death.

Upon the which requisition[†] and deposition made by the said persons in manner above specified, the said Mr David asked instruments[†] of us notaries public underwritten. This was done at the gate[†] of the prison house of my Lord Seton that is upon[†] the wall of his lordship's palace, wherein the said Janet was for the time,[†] about three hours after noon or thereby; before

---

[†] **inquired** asked
[†] **heads and points** items and matters
[†] **but** other than
[†] **as said is** as the saying is
[†] **neither yet** on no occasion
[†] **for fear … torment** through fear for her life and of being tortured
[†] **feigned** made up
[†] **At once** immediately
[†] *simpliciter* unconditionally

[†] **whatever … concerning witchcraft** whatever she had ever spoken of the late Euphame in relation to witchcraft
[†] **requisition** formal request
[†] **asked instruments** asked for a formal record of the proceedings
[†] **gate** entrance
[†] **upon** near, bordering on
[†] **for the time** at the time

these witnesses: Sir John Seton of Barnes, knight; Mr Walter Ogilvy; Steven Bannatyne, schoolmaster to my Lord Seton's bairns; Mr John Pap, servitor to the said Sir John Seton; Patrick (   ), servitor to the said Patrick MacCalzean.

> *Robertus Gardinar notarius publicus in premissa requisitus testante meis signo et subscriptione manualibus*[†]

> *Ita est Stephanus Bannatyne connatarius publicus in premissa requisitus manu propria*[†]

[†] ***Robertus ... manualibus*** 'Robert Gardiner, notary public, asked about the foregoing, as witnessed by my hand by my seal and signature'

[†] ***Ita ... propria*** 'Similarly, Stephen Bannatyne, connotary public, asked about the foregoing, by my own hand'

Document 18

Denial at the Scene of Execution by Geillis Duncan and Bessie Thomson to Notaries Public[1]

4 December 1591

This is a denial at the place of execution on the castle hill, Edinburgh, on 4 December 1591, by Geillis Duncan and Bessie Thomson, that they ever knew Barbara Napier and Euphame MacCalzean to be witches.

Apud Edinburgh quarto die mensis Decembris, anno domini millesimo quingentesimo nonagesimo primo, regnique supremi domini nostri regis vigesimo quinto anno.[†]

The which day, in presence of us connotaries public and witnesses under-written, compeared[†] personally Patrick MacCalzean, Mr David Ogilvy his son-in-law, and Archibald Douglas, brother to Robert Douglas of Carschogil, passed[†] re[?????] to the personal presence of Geillis Duncan and Bessie Thomson where they were standing to be executed in the castle hill of Edinburgh for certain crimes of witchcraft.

And there the said Patrick, Mr David and Archibald heartily[†] and with effect asked and inquired the said Geillis and Bessie and either of them there, after they had been delivered free,[†] asked and inquired by John Cairns,

---

[†] **Apud ... anno** 'At Edinburgh, 4 December, the year of our Lord 1591, and in the 25th year of our sovereign lord's reign'
[†] **compeared** there appeared

[†] **passed** went
[†] **heartily** earnestly
[†] **delivered free** had their bonds taken off?

reader[†] in Edinburgh, to acknowledge and confess their sins in presence of the people there convened and to show forth and speak the truth. And when they had cried to confess the same now before God, and in presence of the people for relief of their souls and consciences, to wit if ever they had known umwhile Euphame MacCalzean and Barbara Napier to be witches, or ever to use any point[†] of sorcery or witchcraft at any time or in any place of this realm, and specially at North Berwick kirk, Broomhill, against any person or persons, and chiefly against his Majesty's most noble person.

To the which it was answered and declared, first by the said Geillis Duncan, for her part, that as she should answer on her soul and conscience before God, that she never knew the said Barbara, nor the said umwhile Euphame to be any witches or to use any point of sorcery or witchcraft in any of the places foresaid, or in any other part, against his Majesty's most noble person, or any other person or persons, either[†] that yet she knew any vice or crime done by either of them at any time bygone. And being demanded[†] why she had bruited[†] and slandered them of before thereanent,[†] she answered that she was caused[†] and persuaded so to do by the two David Setons in Tranent and others, and that it was but all leasings,[†][2] of the which she craved[†] God forgiveness.

And siclike,[†] the said Bessie Thomson being also inquired and commanded by the said parties anent her knowledge in the premiss,[†] who answered and made her declaration in the like form and manner as the said Geillis did.

Whereupon the said Patrick MacCalzean, Mr David Ogilvy[3] and Archibald Douglas asked instruments, one or more, fra us connotaries public undersubscriving.[†] This was done about three hours after noon or thereby, day, years and place, reign, foresaid. Before these witnesses: James Nicholl, Thomas Fisher, baillies of the said burgh of Edinburgh, John Cairns, James Henryson [?Erdaris] there, William Shaw, master of work to his Majesty, John Clerk, Robert Forrester, Alexander Henryson, Minges Baker, servants of the said burgh, John Leirmont messenger there, and George Bisset, scribe, with others divers.[†]

[†] **reader** a reader in the reformed church, who read lessons and performed some of the other functions of the minister
[†] **point** instance
[†] **either** or
[†] **demanded** questioned
[†] **bruited** spread the rumour
[†] **slandered ... thereanent** slandered them previously concerning this
[†] **caused** made to
[†] **leasings** lies
[†] **craved** begged
[†] **siclike** similarly
[†] **in the premiss** of the foregoing matter
[†] **undersubscriving** signed below
[†] **others divers** many others

*Ita est Adamus Schaw notarius publicus ad premissa et requisitus
testante manu mea propria.
Ita est Jacobus Justice connotarius ad premissa etiam spralitus?
requisitus testante manu mea propria.*[†]

Gellie Duncan
Bessie Brown

[†] **Ita ... mea propria** 'So, Adam Shaw, notary public, witness? to the foregoing, as witnessed by my hand. So, James Justice, connotary ???? to the foregoing, as witnessed by my own hand.'

Textual Notes to Documents 1 to 18

Document 1

[1] SRO document JC 26/2/13
tokens] takinis
[2] Irish] earche
[3] taffetas] taftas
[4] She confesses] *another hand takes over here*
[5] twenty shillings] xx ss
[6] comma[ ] them ... their tongues] comm[ ] / |thaim {to hald} all that was his servants to hald / thair toings|
[7] 'Eloa' he appeared] eloa {sho} he appeared
[8] alighted] lichted
[9] [ ] were] {Jhon fe} [ ] wer
[10] chimney] chimlay
[11] hauled at the devil's command] hailled |at the devils command|
[12] she cried 'Haul! Hola!] sho {g} cryed |haile| hola
[13] hauling] healing
[14] wrack David Seton] wrak the {hynds} David Setoun
[15] She confesses ... hard to] *these two lines are marked with asterisks in the MS*
[16] Irish Marion, 'Grey Meal', met] Erche marioun |gray meill| mett
[17] consented] counnscendit
[18] Bara] barach
[19] The second ... years after] *this section is marked at the end with an X.*
[20] The fourth ... in summer] *this section is marked at the end with an X*

Document 2

[1] SRO document JC 26/2/12
god-daughters] guid daughteris
[2] Ker] Kar
[3] Littledean] littill deane
[4] well] wall
[5] but to answer ... they were] |but to answer hir. Sho / demandit whither the / lady wald live or nocht / he said her dayes were gane / then he demandit of the / gentil wemen her daughters quhair thay wer| *marginal addition; an asterisk in the main text of the manuscript indicates the point of insertion*
[6] howling. Fra] youling {sho chargit him to tell quhidder the Lady wald leive he answered sho sowld die} fra
[7] and appeared ... drowned her] |and appeared to the lady / of (   ) quhair at sho was / affraid in the meane tyme an|uther| of / the said gentill wemen lady of tersonie ran to the wall being / forced and drawin be the / divell quha wald haue drou/ned her| *MS; marginal addition with the place for insertion in the main text of the manuscript marked with an asterisk*
[8] She confesses ... burned thereafter] *this item is scored through with two oblique lines*
[9] Janet] {Agnes} |Jonat|
[10] arse] airs
[11] glass] glaces
[12] mariners] marinellis
[13] rose] raise
[14] which he confessed] quhilk he confessit *MS in another hand*

Document 3

[1] SRO document JC 26/2/3
window] windoc
[2] Stobies] Stobbus
[3] broad-leaved] bred leaft
[4] whom she saw] whom sau
[5] wading] wyding
[6] Gilles fra them] gilles {out at the dur} fra thame
[7] well ... good] weill dayes are gane of ought ell her but gud

Document 4

[1] SRO document JC 26/2/4
Edmiston] Admiston
[2] She denies ... again] *this item is marked with an asterisk in the margin*
[3] whole] heall
[4] courchie. She] curche {and twa half mark peices the ane} sho
[5] suchlike] sic a lyk
[6] loch stray] lok stray
[7] in alsmickle new linen cloth] {of |ÿellow| wax} in |alsmickil| new |lining| claith
[8] dovecot] dowcat

Document 5

[1] SRO document JC 26/2/1
Catharine] {bessie} |catarine|
[2] Geillis Duncan] {Jonat stratoun} Gilleis
duncane
[3] conspired] {castin in} conspyred
[4] and was delivered ... to Agnes Sampson]
|and was delyvered be marion loch to
Agnes Sampson| *in margin*

Document 6

[1] SRO document JC 26/2/19
eight or ten] {sax} |eight or ten|
[2] The six] *although the scribe changed* sax *to*
eight to ten *in the previous sentence, he made*
no change here
[3] the wife of Saltoun Mill ... Donald Robson]
|the wyf of Saltian mill/ gillie duncane
{the w} / Jonat Stratton, donald Robeison
/ *marginal addition with caret in text*
[4] thwarted] thortored
[5] heaved] huive
[6] she kenned him never] she kend never
[7] was in the boat] was in {at the drowning}
the boat
[8] Bessie Nisbet] Bessie {Janet} Nisbet *this*
material is in a different hand and is written
in the bottom quarter of the page, and at right
angles to the main text
[9] *These eleven lines are in the bottom quarter of*
f. 2ʳ, at right angles to Donald Robson's
deposition

Document 7

[1] SRO document JC 26/2/14

Document 8

[1] SRO document JC 26/2/15
1591] m vc four scoir ellevin ÿeiris
[2] capitan ... Carmichael] |capitane of
Edinburgh castell Laird of carmichaell|
[3] mixture or wash] |maister or| washe
[4] heated] hett
[5] mill] mychill
[6] pitch] pik
[7] and trystet ... Kingsburn] |and trystet

{him} hir to meit at kingisburne| *addition*
in margin, with the point of insertion in the
text marked X
[8] at the devil's bidding] |at the devillis
bidding| *marginal addition with caret*
indicating the point of insertion in the main
text

Document 9

[1] SRO document JC 26/2/16
and Gillie / Duncan] and {anne} gely /
{sampsonn} Duncanne
[2] saw the devil] saw {|not|} the devill
[3] was present ... she saw] wes {thair}
|present at the convention of the new
havin| or not {and gif} or quhether she
saw

Document 10

[1] SRO document JC 26/2/17
Stirling] striviling
[2] jailers] Jewilleris

Document 11

[1] SRO document JC 26/2/21
loaf] laif
[2] Margaret Weston] margaret {nysbett}
|westoun|
[3] (   ) Tailor] (   ) talÿeour
MS; it is not clear whether talÿeour *is a*
surname or occupation. We have assumed that
the space was for a forename.

Document 12

[1] SRO document JC 26/2/22
handwriting] handwrite
[2] week] oulk
[3] Anne Sampson] anne {gibson} |samp-
son|

Document 13

[1] SRO document JC 26/2/10
Brown] brunn

² whey] waye
³ fried] frieit

Document 14

¹ SRO document JC 26/2/11
God 1590] god {158} 1590
² was more] vas man

Document 15

¹ SRO document JC 26/2/18
1591] Im Vc forscore ellevin ÿeris
² notary public] notour publict

Document 16

¹ SRO document JC 26/2/23
1591 years] I^m V^c four scoir ellewin ÿeiris

Document 17

¹ SRO document JC 26/2/8
fourth] feird

Document 18

¹ SRO document JC 26/2/20
² leasings] Leisingis
³ Ogilvy] ogillie

Chapter 8

RECORDS OF THE WITCHCRAFT TRIALS: DITTAYS

A dittay (from Old French *ditté*, something written) is the indictment against an accused person. The dittays of four persons accused of witchcraft from December 1590 to June 1591 and tried before the justiciary court in Edinburgh have survived. The four persons are John Fian, alias Cunningham, Agnes Sampson, Barbara Napier and Euphame MacCalzean. In addition, records of Bothwell's trial in August 1593 have also survived.

John Fian and Agnes Sampson were dealt with quickly in December 1590 and January 1591, their trials each taking one day. There is then a gap until Barbara Napier's trial begins on 8 May 1591. The process of trying the two Edinburgh women, Napier and MacCalzean, was more prolonged and difficult, lasting until 15 June 1591.

The trial

A trial was often summarily conducted, although preliminaries could take a long time. John Fian's and Agnes Sampson's trials each took one day, but in Euphame MacCalzean's case the process took longer owing to the objections made by her prolocutors. In the justiciary court the *panel* (the accused person) was tried by an *assize* (jury), before a *justiciar* (judge) or one or more *justice deputes*. In these four dittays, John Graham and Humphrey Blynschelis sat as justice deputes at Fian's trial and for some of Euphame MacCalzean's trial. Graham sat alone as justice depute for the latter stages of MacCalzean's trial. Humphrey Blynschelis sat alone at the trials of Sampson and Napier, but Blynschelis was joined by John Graham when Napier's assize were arraigned for wilful error in acquitting her. In some cases *assessors* were appointed by the privy council and parliament to sit with judges, particularly where either of these bodies had conducted preliminary investigations,[1] as the privy council had in the examinations of these accused persons. In Napier's trial David Carnegie of Colluthie and Sir James Melville of Halhill sat as assessors together with the justice depute. The *pursuer* (prosecutor) in these cases was the *king's advocate*, David McGill, who held that position 1582–96, and is named as pursuer at the beginning of all four dittays. The king's advocate was the representative of the crown: the dittays regularly style David McGill 'advocate to our sovereign lord'. The panel could sometimes be represented by *prolocutors*, especially when the accused was someone of substance.[2] When the charge was disputed, representation was commonly made by one or more advocates as prolocutors. Barbara Napier had five prolocutors and Euphame MacCalzean six; Fian and Sampson presumably had none. Mackenzie said that advocates in criminal cases were called 'prolocutours', but the term seems to have included all those speaking on the behalf of the accused, not just lawyers.[3]

The justiciary court[4]

In the early sixteenth century the courts of parliament, the lords of the privy council, and the justiciars were all held in Edinburgh in the tolbooth, a few feet west of the kirk of St Giles. These courts were also held at times in various buildings in Edinburgh, sometimes in Holyroodhouse. In 1560 the old tolbooth was thought insufficient and too noisy and so a new 'Council House' was to be built. Meanwhile the court sat in the aisle of St Giles and the old tolbooth was adapted as a gaol. The new building was really part of the church and was known as the 'New Tolbooth' or Parliament House. It had two stories with an entrance in the High Street. The justiciary court was held on the ground floor. Here the court sat until 1639 except when the plague drove it out of Edinburgh.

The king's advocate

In sixteenth-century Scotland a crime was still considered as a wrong done to an individual for which compensation was necessary, rather than an offence against the community. The function of king's advocate as public prosecutor emerged in the late sixteenth century, and this signalled a centralising of royal power, and the emergence of the idea of the state's interest in the legal process. An act of 1587 gave the king's advocate the title to pursue slaughters and other 'odious crimes', even though the interested parties in a case might 'be silent' or come to an agreement. Although private prosecution remained the normal way of initiating criminal procedures, after that date we find the king's advocate pursuing some crimes alone, especially crimes affecting the welfare of the state, such as treason. The privy council might command the advocate to prosecute certain crimes affecting public security, for example saying mass.[5] Although the king's advocate is described as acting 'for his highness' interest', his emerging role is that of agent for the state.[6]

Depositions

Depositions produced during pre-trial inquiries and interrogations were in most cases the evidence adduced at trials, which is why we find so much of the wording of dittays to be almost *verbatim* that of depositions. Depositions were equivalent to evidence given on oath before a court. After 1587 all evidence was heard by the assize in the presence of the accused.[7] Depositions were provided to the jury or read aloud to them, and, exceptionally, witnesses were produced formally to adhere to their depositions.[8] This happened in Barbara Napier's trial where Ritchie Graham, Donald Robson and Janet Stratton appeared in the court to affirm their depositions, and Napier was 'confronted' with Robson and Stratton, both 'openly and constantly abiding at [standing by] the said depositions'.

Sentence

Death was the penalty for crimes which 'cannot be repaired [remedied]',[9] such as murder, mutilation, giving refuge to rebels, witchcraft, and sometimes bestiality and incest. Execution for witchcraft was by strangling and then burning.

The Accused

John Fian

Fian's is the first of the dittays and is dated 26 December 1590. It incriminated Robert Grierson,[10] Michael Clark and Agnes Sampson, all of whom Fian said he saw at North Berwick kirk. Fian seems to have had a number of names: John Cunningham, 'Johnne Sibbet, *alias* Cunninghame',[11] and John Fean or Fian (dittays), or Dr Fian (*News*). According to *News* he was master of the school in Prestonpans, and in another source 'scoolemaister at Tranent'.[12] At his execution he supposedly confessed to adultery with thirty-two women.[13] Apart from some later references, we have to rely on Fians's dittay and *News* as the main sources of information. No pre-trial examinations of his have been found, although no systematic search has been made in the Scottish Record Office.[14]

   In a witchcraft prosecution any inferences about the accused's individual voice or sensibility are confined by the evidence of the extant records. These inferences, let alone the general veracity of these records, are problematic for obvious reasons: the impossibility of some events recounted, the effect on the records of processses of questioning, accusation and trial, the various interests of the accusers and examiners. In addition the accused was often *in extremis*, as

Fian was if *News from Scotland* represents accurately his tortures. It is impossible to say where the accused's imagination leaves off and their examiners' begins. Nevertheless, it would also be wrong to suppose that the accused never made any contribution, voluntary or involuntary, to those records, or that the contents of such texts are not in any way inflected by the individual deponent.[15] Comparing Fian's dittay with others, which represent the same events, suggests certain conclusions.

Fian's dittay has a more formal, literary quality than some others, perhaps attributable to his profession as schoolmaster. It is primarily an account of dealings with the devil, and one which seems to give access to subjective responses: reflective, affective and intimate. It suggests a religious imagination and occasionally has almost devotional resonances in its account of his relationship with the devil, as when the devil tells Fian 'he . . . should never let a tear fall from their [his servants'] eyn so long as they served him'.[16] This personal religious sensibility is lacking in Sampson's dittay, although both recount some of the same events.

When the devil first appeared, Fian was in reflective mood, lying in a box bed in Tranent 'musing and pensing', and contemplating revenge.[17] The devil requested adoration and homage, and promised him prosperity and on another occasion happiness. His subsequent relationship with the devil is the most personal and intimate of all the witches. The dittay has scriptural echoes in Satan's promise to his servants that he would raise them up at the latter day gloriously. The account of Fian's being 'carried and transported to many mountains as though through all the world' may echo the Gospels' accounts of the temptation of Christ.[18] The North Berwick convention in Fian's dittay is represented in the particular terms of a religious service: candles, pulpit, the enigmatic text of the devil's sermon, the 'lessons' Satan gives his followers. If a religious imagination is at work in Fian's dittay then it is that of the reformed religion, discernible in its Scriptural echoes, from texts favoured by the reformers (the Gospels, Revelation, Psalms), and in its pulpit, preaching and lessons. According to *News*, Fian was 'but a very young man', and so imaginatively a child of the reformation.

Fian's dittay provides accounts of witchcraft which are closest to those of continental demonologists, particularly in witchcraft as false religious belief. It is also unique among the dittays in its accounts of transvection.[19] Like some continental witches,[20] and Janet Kennedy,[21] Fian travelled in spirit to the meeting while his body lay at home in a trance. He experienced 'great ecstacies and trances, lying by the space of two or three hours dead'. He travelled, 'his sprite taken, [he] suffered himself to be carried and transported to many mountains as though through all the world, according to his own depositions' and 'as if he had been soughing athwart the earth', 'skimming over all the sea without land'. King James remembered these striking phrases and echoed them in *Demonology* II iv and v. By contrast, Agnes Sampson travelled prosaically to the convention on horseback, accompanied by her son-in-law. It is only Fian's dittay which has candles burning blue at the convention, as at continental sabbats.[22] Item 19 of Fian's dittay is a particularly dense collocation of stereotypical accusations against continental witches. Some are typical activities at the sabbat: denying God and religion, giving faith to and adoring the devil, recruiting new converts, and also inhuman and monstrous actions, such as dismembering corpses, especially those of unbaptised babies. The second kind is a list of classic *maleficia*: killing men by sea and land, destroying corn, cattle and goods, and raising tempests and stormy weather. This list is so formulaic that it almost echoes the famous catalogue of witches' crimes by Innocent VIII in his bull *Summis Desiderantes* (1484), which prefaced editions of the *Malleus*.

At his execution John Fian denied witchcraft and confessed only that he had 'abused the people that way'.[23] Bowes wrote to Burghley on 23 February 1591 that 'John Fianne, executed in Edinburgh, at his death denied all he had acknowledged, saying he told those tales by fear of torture and to save his life', and that he denied some particulars, such as participation in the conspiracy to stay queen Anne's voyage to Scotland, 'obstinatlie unto the death'.[24]

Agnes Sampson

Agnes Sampson had a long-established career as a cunning woman and healer, diviner, and, particularly, midwife. Item 19 relates dealings with Isobel Hamilton and James Power 'six or seven years since or thereby' and shows Sampson practising her craft as early as 1585. Early sources describe her as 'Agnes Sampson, grace wyffe [midwife], alias callit, the wyse wyff of Keyth' and 'ane renowned midwyf'.[25] Spottiswoode records her as serious and rather imposing: 'most remarkable, a woman not of the base and ignorant sort of Witches, but, Matron-like, grave and setled in her answers, which were all to some purpose'.[26] Sinclair, writing in the late seventeenth century, says 'that she may seem to have been not so much a white Witch, as an holy Woman'.[27]

The first twenty or so items of her dittay list diagnoses, predictions and healings, the regular repertoire of both early modern English cunning folk and the French *devin*,[28] producing a local reputation for occult power that might eventually turn into an accusation of witchcraft. Items 12–14 attribute her foreknowledge to the devil. The precarious position of healer whose reputation for healing could easily switch to suspicion of *maleficium*, especially if the cunning woman fell out with a client, is illustrated in item 39.

Some of Sampson's diagnoses reveal popular supernaturalism: affliction by elf-shot, and a belief that a woman would not recover if she remained 'upon the ground'. Her predictions were about length of life, illness and its cure, storms and damage. She also protected livestock from disease, and helped in childbirth. Agnes Sampson's clientele came from a wide social range: a servant, a poor woman sent by a cutler's friends, a skipper's wife, the wife of the sheriff of Haddington, and also members of the minor gentry Lady Roslin, Lady

Kilbaberton, the laird of Reidshill's son, Lady Edmiston. The ambit of her practice seems to have been mainly in and around Haddington, but sometimes further afield.

Like other cunning folk she offered counter-magic to those suffering from bewitchment. In summer 1590 she advised Robert Dixon in Bolton, who may have been one of her assizers, to stop wearing a doublet in which a woman whom he had got with child, or her mother, 'had put some wheat or other things'. She cured the sheriff of Haddington's wife, bewitched 'by the witch of Mirrielaws by the blast of evil wind on Halloween', Alison Ker bewitched by Catherine Gray, and Robert Carington's wife bewitched by the late John McGill, a witch who occurs more than once in these documents and whose *maleficia* Agnes Sampson countered several times. One remarkable instance of counter-magic was her curing of the late Robert Kerse in Dalkeith, who had been bewitched by 'a westland warlock' in Dumfries. She took his sickness upon herself and then tried to transfer it to a dog or cat, but it alighted on Alexander Douglas in Dalkeith, who died. Robert Kerse recovered.

The chief item in her repertoire was the perilous business of predicting whether the sick should live or die, sometimes by divination from clothing. In some cases of illness invocation of the devil was required. But Agnes Sampson's main techniques were the use of her 'prayer', which she had learned from her father rather than her mother, as was often the case in English witchcraft. In cases of illness, if she halted in her prayer the diagnosis was poor, if she did not it was good. Her dittay devotes a great deal of attention to this prayer, even giving it in full in item 32. This prayer is always stigmatised in the dittay, either by an opprobrious epithet, 'devilish prayer(s)', or in a doublet where it is coupled with a more or less magical or devilish practice: 'skill and prayer', 'prayer and incantation', 'prayer and devilish charms', 'prayer and conjuration'.

The prayer itself is a vernacular and popular, although impeccably orthodox, version of the Creed: as Sinclair noted it contains 'the main points of Christianity'.[29] It is like many of the pre-reformation vernacular prayers—and charms —that were used by the laity.[30] In its rendering of some credal clauses it is theologically scrupulous, as in these on the Second Person of the Trinity: 'Into his dear son, Christ Jesu, / Into that anaplie lord I trow'. Here the unusual adjective 'anaplie' (single, sole) renders the uniqueness of the Son in the Apostles' Creed ('Filium Eius *unicum*'). The prayer's echoes of the Creed are sometimes very close (for example, 'Was gotten of the Holy Ghost, / Born of the Virgin Mary') and the first seventeen lines faithfully follow the sequence of the Creed, from a belief in one God through to the resurrection of the dead. The prayer's clauses on the Holy Ghost and the church are particularly interesting:

> I trow also in the Holy Ghost;
> In Holy Kirk my hope is most,
> That holy ship where hallowars wins
> To ask forgiveness of my sins.

Again, the sequence suggests the Apostles' Creed ('Credo in Spiritum Sanctum, Sanctam Ecclesiam Catholicam, Sanctorum Communionem'). There is an interesting difference here between the spiritual fellowship (*communionem*) of saints, and an actual ship where the saints dwell. The prayer's attention to the saints ('hallowars') and their intercession is striking—and catholic. The loose syntax of these lines allows the sense that the church, figured as a shipload of saints, has the power to intercede for sinners.[31]

If Fian's religious imagination was that of the reformed religion, Sampson's magical practices are informed by the old religion in which she was brought up. The previously orthodox catholic piety, sentiment and petitions of Agnes Sampson's prayer explain its stigmatisation by her protestant examiners as 'prayer and incantation', and 'devilish'. In Agnes Sampson's long diagnostic prayer we find the intercession of saints; in her shorter 'prayer and conjuration for healing of sick folks' we find an adjuration to sickness 'With all the virtues of the mass'. This second prayer, with its attention on Christ's sufferings on the cross, is like many other early modern charms which incorporate religious imagery. It is particularly like a rhyme 'Medicina pro Morbo Caduco et le Fevr'.[32] When Agnes Sampson charmed the cattle of Richard Spens and James White against disease, she went between them in their byres, stroking them and repeating the 'Ave Maria'.

The dittay changes from item 33 onwards. Although there are still items instancing healing and counter-magic, most describe diabolic witchcraft, convention and conspiracy. These begin with Agnes Sampson's service to the devil, whom she first encountered, like many continental witches, after the death of her husband. If we take the record of a witchcraft accusation to be, in some way, a collusive construction by examiners and examined, then we may see in item 33 a mixture of the domestic and demonological. We may conjecture Sampson's contribution to be the coincidence of the devil's first appearance with her husband's death, the anxiety about poverty and her children's future, and the explanation that the mark might have been caused by her children. The demonological details contributed by her examiners in repeated examinations would be those features constituting Sampson's encounter with the devil as contracting apostate service: the renunciation of Christ, the devil's mark given at a night meeting. Similarly the story of the afflicted Lady Edmiston (item 38), Agnes Sampson's resistance to the devil's plans to have one of Lady Edmiston's daughters, and her part in dragging her back from a well, may have been Sampson's attempt to write herself into this narrative as resisting the devil, like other instances in witchcraft pamphlets.[33]

There is political content in Agnes Sampson's dittay. Item 14, a general predicting of storms, is followed by her foreknowledge (item 15) that Anne of Denmark would never come to Scotland unless the king fetched her. This accusation stands out in a catalogue of otherwise routine accusations of predictions and healings. Item 40 is redolent of conspiracy, a community of 'sisters', consultations, letters and 'bills' and messages which are endemic and significant in the dittays (and more so in the pre-trial material), plots to raise a storm to stay the queen's homecoming, and anxious words exchanged at midnight at the pier-head in Leith: 'See that there be no deceit among us'. There was allegedly subversive cooperation between a group at Leith and one at Prestonpans: 'at their meeting they should make the storm universal throughout the sea'. The means of raising the storm was bizarre and is constructed, particularly here and in *News*, as an irreligious 'baptism' of a cat. Although she was acquitted (item 26) of meeting the witch of Carberry and others at Newton kirk, disinterring corpses and making powders of the bodies, Sampson was found guilty of having attended a number of other conventions: at Garvet, between Cousland and Carberry, and at Foulstruther where David Seton's destruction was planned.

The most extended narrative is that of the North Berwick meeting which also appears in John Fian's dittay. This is the dittay's narrative climax and is succeeded only by two items that incriminate Barbara Napier, and a general formulaic condemnation of Sampson.

It is not until the later items that we hear of the two Edinburgh women who were subsequently drawn into the witch hunt. Items 41–2 accuse Sampson of having made a wax image to destroy MacCalzean's father-in-law. MacCalzean also acquired powders from Sampson to put under her bed to alleviate her labour pains. Later in the dittay there are instances of serious *maleficium*, some incriminating Euphame McCalzean. At Euphame's request, Agnes Sampson made a wax image of her father-in-law, and this *maleficium*, or more strictly sorcery, was heinous as it included conjuration of the devil who in turn 'conjured' the wax image. Sampson's association with Napier is also described in two items: Napier was provided with a wax image of a man called 'Archie', as well as a ring with which to win the favour of Lady Angus. These items record the gradual implication of Napier and MacCalzean in accusations in witchcraft, or of consulting witches, which emerged in the examinations of Sampson in late 1590 and early 1591.

The ideological direction discernable in Sampson's dittay, therefore, is from healing and counter-magic, through instances of *maleficia*, to the diabolic and conspiratorial, and includes latterly the incrimination of the prominent Edinburgh women who are the subjects of the next two dittays.

The witches' conventions in the dittays of Fian and Sampson

North Berwick kirk appeared early in Fian's dittay and later as the location of a meeting of the devil's servants when the devil preached. In Fian's dittay this meeting has some classic features of the sabbat.[34] Witches' conventions recur in Agnes Sampson's dittay, but for Sampson, denial of Christ and the compact seem to have been a private affair (item 33) and did not take place at a meeting as in many continental accounts. The convening to delay the queen's homecoming by a storm seems to have taken place in a house in Prestonpans, as did the 'baptism' of the cat (item 40). Only in item 50, with its special heading 'Convention at the kirk of North Berwick', do we find again some of the classic sabbat features: large numbers, dancing, widdershins movements, acclamation of the devil as master, the devil's enquiries after the witches' doings, the making or distribution of maleficial powders, and the 'shameful kiss'.

However, the meetings, although they have some features of the continental sabbat, avoid some of the more spectacular ones; there is no cannibalism, sexual orgy, sex with the devil, or infanticide.[35] There is eating and drinking at some meetings of the witches, but not of disgusting or tasteless food; and there is dancing, but not the grotesque and joyless prancings described by European demonologists.[36] At this stage of the witch hunt, and in Sampson's dittay, there is no story of magical conspiracy against the king.

Barbara Napier[37]

We know little about Barbara Napier. Her dittay says that she was married to Archibald Douglas, brother of the laird of Carschogill. Calderwood says she was 'spous to Archibald Dowglass of Pergill' and sister to William Naper of Wright's Houses.[38]

Moysie insisted on the previous good reputation of the three women tried: 'Barbara Neapper and Euphane McKallian and Agnes Sampson, wemen of guid reputatioun afoir wer teane as witches',[39] but in other respects they differed, as did the nature of their trials. A close reading of the opening of Napier's dittay shows some of the differences. On 8 May two assessors, David Carnegie and Sir James Melville, presumably appointed by the privy council, sat with the justice depute. Unlike Fian and Sampson, Napier and MacCalzean were sufficiently well-connected to be represented by prolocutors, and Napier had five. Two of them, John Moscrop and John Russell, would also be prolocutors for Euphame MacCalzean. John Moscrop was presumably a relation of Euphame MacCalzean's husband, Patrick Moscrop. There were important people ranged against and for the panel. Even before the trial started representations ('allegiances') were made on Barbara Napier's behalf against the list of accusations, and the challenges lasted until two in the morning.[40] The members of the assize are significant too: it contained the king's porter, the master of his ale cellar, the man in charge of feed for his horses, and the king's coalman, who no doubt were expected to vote for the king's interest, though in the end not all did. It also included David Seton of Foulstruther. Bowes wrote that Napier objected to some of her assizers, 'in whose places others of this towne—where she hath many kynsfolske [sic] an freendes of good credyt—were receyvd [appointed]', and also noted that no judgement was given on 9 May.[41]

The accusations against Napier were also different in kind from those against Sampson. Bowes wrote to Burghley the day after (9 May 1591) that Napier had been arraigned for practising the destruction of the king at Bothwell's instigation, and also for the death of the earl of Angus, and for consulting witches. She was charged not with witchcraft but consulting with witches. This was an offence under the 1563 act, as the second item points out ('and so for contravening of the act of parliament in consulting with her and seeking of her help, being a witch'), and punishable by death, although no one ever had been executed for the offence.

> Barbara Naper was convicted onlie of consulting with Richard Graham and Agnes Sampsone. That she consulted for the death of the king or the Erle of Angus she denied. In respect of the Act of Parliament against naiked consultatioun was not putt in executioun, it was thought hard to execute her.[42]

The assize on 8 May 1591 convicted Napier for consulting Agnes Sampson on various matters, and of consulting Ritchie Graham to help her son. It acquitted her on three counts including two serious charges: consulting Sampson about making a wax image to destroy Archibald Douglas, earl of Angus, and of being at the North Berwick convention. However, North Berwick kirk had not yet become the site of treason against the king at this point in the dittays.

Although Napier had been convicted of consultation of witches, by 10 May no sentence had been passed. On that day a letter from the king arrived at the justiciary court asking why not, and reiterating the points of dittay upon which Napier had been convicted. It was the king's will that the legal sentence be passed against Napier and that she be strangled and burned at the castle hill. Napier's dittay again repeats the charges, and the sentence of death was passed. Napier claimed that she was with child and there was a stay of execution. The dittay seems to suggest that this claim was made in court after sentence was passed, although Calderwood has it take place at the eleventh hour, just before execution:

> When the staike was sett in the Castell Hill, with barrells, coales, heather, and powder, and the people were looking for present executioun, her freinds alledged she was with child, wherupon the executioun was delayed, till that alledgance was tryed.[43]

The assize of error

Four weeks later, on 7 June, David McGill proceeded against twelve of the assize who had acquitted Napier. The three members of the original assize not listed, and whom we may assume were willing to convict Napier, were George Boig, the keeper of the king's ale cellar, John Seton, the king's coalman, and David Seton.

It is important to differentiate the proceedings on 10 May and 7 June. On 10 May James wrote asking why sentence had not been passed, since Napier had been convicted of consulting witches. On 7 June, twelve members of the assize were accused of having come to the wrong verdict on the three counts on which they acquitted Napier, the most important being attendance at the North Berwick convention.

James summoned twelve of the assizers to the tolbooth on 7 June 1591 and addressed them. Robert Bowes wrote to Burghley, giving a full account of the king's address.[44] At first they asked to be represented by John Russell, one of Napier's prolocutors, but under pressure from James they yielded themselves to the king's will. This was a wise move as James said at the end of his address that he would otherwise have inferred a wilful ignorance from their resistance, 'which must have bene sharply punished'. The king admitted that his appearance at the tolbooth was unusual for it had not been the custom for kings in Scotland to sit in person in criminal trials (James had only done it twice), and an assize of error was unusual in itself. James argued (disingenuously?) that although for the king to sit in a case touching men's lives would be a 'note of rigour [sign of the severe application of the law]', an assize of error could only result in a penalty by which men lost their goods. The particular reason that had prompted him had been that assizes often failed to condemn the guilty, and particularly that verdicts were affected by considerations of kin and friendship: men were 'more for freendes then for justice'. Secondly, witchcraft was grown very common and it was an odious crime which necessitated special criminal procedure.[45]

Partly because of the unusualness of these legal proceedings, this incident has been seen not only as significant in the witch hunt of 1590–1, but also in the history of Scottish law in the late sixteenth century, and indeed in the growth of the king's authority in the 1590s.[46] It was clearly the opinion of many, including the king himself, that Napier had escaped the rigour of the law through the agency of kin and friends,[47] relationships which often thwarted the administration of justice in sixteenth-century Scotland. James hinted at a network of support for Napier: 'I see the pride of these witches and their freendes', and he would return to the supporters of witches in more general terms in *Demonology* I vii, where he complained of those who 'consult, enquire, entertain, and oversee' magicians.

In this speech James was already voicing views about witchcraft and law which would be expressed later in *Demonology* (III vi). Witches are odious to the laws of God and man, and it is the special duty of the prince or magistrate to pursue them. In both speech and treatise James alludes to the same biblical verse (Proverbs 17.26) which regards freeing the guilty to be as great a crime as condemning the innocent. God will not allow the innocent to be slandered of witchcraft. Since witchcraft is a matter of treason, the evidence of children, women and notorious persons ought to be allowed. In this James reveals that like many writers on witchcraft he considered witchcraft a *crimen exceptum*,[48] in which unusual legal procedures might be required. A few days before, James had consulted the lords of session and others about who might act as witnesses in legal actions of *lesae majestatis* and heresy. The king pressed the clearly reluctant lords of session, 'Whereupon it [was] resolved and registred that women, infantes, infamous persones and *socii criminis* may be receyved in the accions mencioned'. Bowes reported that this would not be extended to witchcraft.[49] However, the evidence of 'infamous persons' (e.g. Janet Stratton, Geillis Duncan and Ritchie Graham) was certainly heard against both Napier and MacCalzean. Indeed in a later trial, that of Isobel Young in the justiciary court in Edinburgh in 1629, the prosecution made the point that the evidence of women and *socii criminis* was allowable in cases of witchcraft, and cited the case of Euphame MacCalzean as precedent:

> Likeas this is the constant practicqz in this Justice Court, and has the warrand of a statute of Session in anno 1591 as was practised upon Euphan McAllian in her trial that same year 1591.[50]

It is in the dittay against the assizers that the accusation against Napier is carried forward and elaborated. It details a set of allegations against Napier which have not previously appeared in this or other dittays, implicating Napier in treason against the king. In the sequence of dittays it is here that the witches' conventions are first represented as sites of treasonable activity: Barbara Napier is accused that 'she gave her presence in the most devilish and treasonable convention held by her and her complices'.

The witches' convention in the assizers' dittays

The dittay against the assizers gives detailed accounts of two different conventions. When the king was encountering Huntly's rebel forces at the Brig of Dee in April 1589, Napier allegedly consulted Ritchie Graham. She had heard a rumour that the king would be harmed and Graham told her that she, Euphame MacCalzean and Donald Robson 'should be three of the doers' of this harm. Secondly it was alleged that she attended a witches' convention at Acheson's Haven, the harbour of Prestonpans. This is the dittays' first mention of this as opposed to the North Berwick convention. It was held a few months after the king's return from Denmark, on Lammas Eve, that is 31 July 1590. The devil was present and Napier and MacCalzean were two of the nine 'principals' who sat nearest him, an important word which also has the legal sense of the actual perpetrators of a crime, as opposed to mere accomplices. At that meeting Sampson proposed the destruction of the king. A wax image was to be given to Napier and MacCalzean to be roasted. Meanwhile the devil gave instructions to harm the king by liquor dripped from a toad and laid in his way, so that, in the ominous and insinuating words of the dittay, 'another might have ruled in his Majesty's place, and the ward might have gone to the devil'. 'Another' here could only mean Bothwell.

The second convention is the notorious meeting on All Hallows Eve 1590 in North Berwick kirk. This account recapitulates very closely the form of words in Sampson's dittay; we hear again of the dance in the kirkyard accompanied by Geillis Duncan on her trump and led by 'John Fian, miselled [disguised]'. But this time Barbara Napier dances too, in first place after Fian, and MacCalzean is among the crowd, whose names are otherwise very much the same as in Sampson's dittay. The devil again gets nimbly into the pulpit, but now we get a much fuller description:

> And the devil start up [sprang up] in the pulpit, like a mickle black man, with a black beard sticking out like a goat's beard, and a high-ribbed nose falling down sharp like the beak of a hawk, with a long rumple, clad in a black tatty gown, and an evil-favoured skull-bonnet on his head. And having a black book in his hand, called on every one of them, desiring them all to be good servants to him and he should be a good master to them, and they should have enough and never want for.

This is an interesting mixture whose basis is the traditional manifestation of the devil as a black man, or a man dressed in black, as in the dittays of Fian and Sampson. In addition the devil is a monstrosity (he was 'grim' in Fian's dittay) composed of various animal characteristics. He seems like the hybrid monster in Reginald Scot's famous description, or that described by Melville,[51] or the little clawed monster in the pulpit in the engraving in *News*. His accessories are now those of a Calvinist minister: black gown, skull-bonnet and book. The increased elaboration here includes a parody of godly attendance and instruction at the kirk: secular conspiracy goes hand in hand with a parody of godly practices.

There are other new features in this description. Robert Grierson, egged on by MacCalzean, berates the devil for not providing the king's image as promised. The devil assures Napier and MacCalzean that the image will be given to them 'right soon'. The narrative then returns to the formulae of the earlier dittays which are like the standard programme of the sabbat, but the devil again offends his followers when he fails to call them by their witches' nicknames.

In the dittay against the jurors the material for the description of the convention must have come from Donald Robson, Janet Stratton, Geillis Duncan and Bessie Thomson. It specifically names these people, and they were present to verify their testimonies to Napier's assize. Indeed, we have some of the pre-trial examinations and depositions on which this account was based. It is in fact a revised version of events which has been rewritten for this dittay. The familiarity with the devil, the willingness even to berate him, came from the popular supernaturalism of the examinates. The North Berwick convention is an astonishingly democratic meeting presided over by a devil who can be criticised. He is unlike the terrifying monster and tyrant of many continental accounts, who is worshipped by his followers whom he often punishes autocratically. We may even see this moment as an image of political argument and challenge. It is difficult to see what the examiners would have gained from such a construction of the devil, and the rather burlesque events in this account and Sampson's dittay where, in a Bakhtinian tumult, the angry witches run 'hirdy-girdy'. The devil berated in North Berwick kirk for late delivery of an image is not the super-subtle and supremely powerful enemy of God of the demonologists. He is, at least in part, the devil of popular belief,[52] ballads and stories, of many proverbs and popular woodcuts,[53] who has close, chatty relationships with clowns in early modern drama.[54] Bessie Dunlop, burned for witchcraft in 1576, was on familiar and domestic terms with the devil as Thom Reid.[55] As Jim Sharpe observes, a popular view of the devil is still something that requires research.[56]

The narrative of conspiracy aganst the king stretches back to April 1589, before James's marriage to Anne. It relates persistent magical plotting against the king, and its origins coincide with that moment just 'before the common bell rang for fear the earl Bothwell should have entered in Edinburgh'. The 'turn', and the various ways the conspirators try to accomplish it, now becomes the focus of attention. The story is one of conspiracy tenaciously fostered, but which must always fail: even the devil is not encouraging about the prospects of success, and the king's enchanted image is always promised, always deferred. There is a reticence about pronouncing the king's name, at least in English, as if in the dittays there is reluctance to represent the royal presence. In the dittays, as opposed to the depositions, the king's image never properly appears. At the Acheson's Haven convention Agnes Sampson is appointed to make the image, which she does and gives to the devil, but at the North Berwick meeting it is the devil's failure to provide the enchanted image which causes protest. If it *were* produced then Napier and MacCalzean would melt it: their function is to be 'the doers of it'; Agnes Sampson and the devil would provide the means, Napier and MacCalzean would perform the act.

After the reiteration of all this material, with 'his Majesty sitting in judgement' in the tolbooth on 7 June, Barbara Napier's jurors submitted to the king's will and were acquitted of wilful error. We hear little more of Barbara Napier. According to early accounts she escaped execution. Hume wrote that 'afterward no body insisting in the pursuit of her, she was set at libertie'.[57] We know that Napier was still alive, and presumably detained, in June 1591. James was still in pursuit of her and was monitoring Napier's claim that she was pregnant. He wrote to Maitland:[58] 'Trye by the medicinairis aithis gif Barbara Nepair be with bairne or not. Tak na delaying ansour. Gif ye finde scho be not, to the fyre with her presesentlie [sic], and cause bouell [disembowel] her publiclie.'[59] She was executed in Haddington, along with five others, in 1591.[60]

Euphame MacCalzean

We know a little more about Euphame MacCalzean than the other accused: she was the only daughter and heiress of Thomas MacCalzean (d. ?1581), an advocate and senator of the College of Justice.[61] By the husband, Patrick Moscrop, whom she was accused of attempting to murder, she had three daughters and at least two sons, one of whom called Thomas (items 2, 18) died young. Recent research has shown that MacCalzean was related by marriage to David Seton, for her husband's sister Katherine was David Seton's wife.[62] Patrick and Euphame MacCalzean are mentioned twice in the register of the privy council, once on 31 January 1586 when they appealed against the provost and baillies of Edinburgh lodging persons with the plague on their land, and again on 28 March 1589 when Patrick MacCalzean was cautioned to pay some money.[63] Euphame MacCalzean was a prosperous Edinburgh woman, with a number of servants and a nurse, unlike the popular stereotype of the witch as an old, poor woman on the margins of society. Pitcairn supposes that she was catholic and a partisan of Bothwell's, though he gives no evidence for either assertion.[64] Both Napier and MacCalzean were supposedly the links between Bothwell and the witches. Ritchie Graham had confessed 'that the Erle Bodowell had knawlege of him be Effie Mackalloun and Barbery Naper, Edenbrough wemen'.[65]

The heading of MacCalzean's dittay clearly formulates the charge of treasonable witchcraft against the sovereign: 'Dilated of certain treasonable conspiracies, enterprised by witchcraft, to have destroyed our sovereign lord's person and bereft His Majesty of his life'. Some of MacCalzean's prolocutors were lawyers even more formidable than Napier's. Unsurprisingly, in view of her father, MacCalzean had supporters from the legal profession, and her husband, Patrick Moscrop, was the son of the advocate John Moscrop.[66] Not only was she represented by some of Napier's prolocutors, but apparently by John Skene as well. Can this be the eminent jurist who from 1589 was jointly king's advocate with David McGill, and the author of a number of important works on Scots law, one of which, the *Regiam Majestatem*, was printed in 1597, the same year as *Demonology*?[67] This is curious as he had accompanied James to Denmark and according to the *Dictionary of National Biography* was zealous in his persecution of witches.

In the dittays of the three accused women we see three different constructions of women as witches. In Sampson we see a healer and prognosticator, whose power is then revealed to come from the devil: a cunning woman transformed into a witch. Barbara Napier is represented as an apparently 'honest-like' woman who nevertheless consulted with witches and attended their meetings. Euphame MacCalzean is represented in two ways which are interconnected: a maleficent witch and an undutiful, rebellious wife.

MacCalzean was accused of witchcraft, the first instance being over ten years earlier in April 1577. Surprisingly there is more attention in this dittay than in any other to ordinary *maleficium*. A number of the points of dittay against MacCalzean describe witchcraft in terms of *maleficium* to cause disease or death (e.g. items 1, 8, 9, 10, 11, 17), or consulting with witches to bring these about (items 3, 4, 5, 13, 19, 20). MacCalzean's *maleficium* is found in association with its long-time companion *veneficium* (poisoning or witchcraft), for she was accused of poisoning various people, or of practices where witchcraft and poisoning overlapped (eg items 5, 6, 13). There were many precedents in classical literature for the association of magic and poisoning, and the word *venefica* could mean either 'poisoner' or 'witch'. There was also intense philological discussion by both exegetes and demonologists of the exact meaning of *mecasapha*, one of the Hebrew words for 'witch' in the bible, which occurs, among other places, in the notorious prohibition against allowing witches to live in Exodus 22.18.[68] Poison was often the means a woman in the early modern period used to murder her husband,[69] and poisoning and witchcraft go together in some Scottish witchcraft cases.[70]

One of the accusations against MacCalzean was attempting to murder her husband through witchcraft. Only close reading reveals that this attempt did not succeed, for the dittay's insistence on the consultation for 'poisoning' Patrick Moscrop implies the attempt was successful. Patrick Moscrop was still alive in 1592 to pay 5,000 merks to regain MacCalzean's estates for their daughters.[71] MacCalzean is also represented as a rebellious and undutiful wife, a shrew who even in the first year of her marriage drove her husband abroad with her 'undutiful behaviour and impatience' (item 5). Her dittay represents her as a certain female stereotype associated with witchcraft in the early modern period: the rebellious and quarrelsome woman, the bad wife, the scold and shrew.[72] And female magic and unruliness are connected in this dittay by another gender-related aspect of witchcraft, as MacCalzean is reported to have made love charms, consulted witches about present and future husbands, impeded marriages, and practised witchcraft to acquire or dispose of partners. Love magic and trafficking with witches in love matters were seen as female practices: in classical literature in the stereotype of witch bawds such as Ovid's Dipsas and de Rojas' Celestina,[73] and perhaps also in reality in early modern Europe.[74] Love potions and poisons often go together in discussions of magical *philtra*; and both the scold and the witch dealing in love magic are urban stereotypes.[75] MacCalzean and Napier were both city women, unlike the rural cunning woman Agnes Sampson.

MacCalzean's murder of her husband's kin is implicitly unnatural (item 9), as are using her daughter to allure a lover (item 12), and killing children (items 17, 22). She is also represented as malicious and vengeful (items 8, 10), two characteristics of witches which supposedly prompted their evil deeds, as James remarks in *Demonology* II ii–iii. She is also unnatural in avoiding by magical means the penalty that God imposed on Eve's daughters, the 'natural and kindly pain' of childbirth (item 18).[76]

There is far more intrigue in MacCalzean's dittay: consultations, messages, sending servants on missions, plotting, magical objects hidden in a goose, or a child's apron, or an old black cap. Some aspects of the construction of MacCalzean as a woman immersed in the heady atmosphere of witchcraft, intrigue, marital scandal and sexual scheming (and disease), and high politics, is similar to the construction of that other wife, witch and murderess in the even more spectacular case of Frances Howard, countess of Essex.[77]

It is easier to see what MacCalzean's examiners and judges intended than to see what she was. It is in the narrative of her dittay that treason and witchcraft are most successfully combined, for the story of conspiracy against the king is retold by analogy in the story of a witch who tries to kill her husband. In the homologies of the early modern period the king was to his subjects or realm, as the husband was to his wife.[78] James deployed these analogies in *The Trew Law of Free Monarchies* and *Basilikon Doron*, and in his first address to the English parliament.[79] A wife's disobedience to her husband, or even her shrewish behaviour, let alone her attempt to murder him, was a rebellious or treasonable act.[80] With this analogy in mind, similar motifs emerge in the stories of MacCalzean's plotting against her husband and conspiring against the king. Both are treasonable attempts to kill which fail. MacCalzean's inquiry after 'witty or skilfull women' who could make her husband love her, or failing that let her dominate him (item 4), is like Bothwell's alleged attempt first to win the king's favour by magic, or if that failed to destroy him by it.[81] The phrase 'cut him away' is used of both Patrick Moscrop (item 5) and of the king. MacCalzean attempted not just to dispose of her lord, but to replace him with another man. She was accused of consulting a witch 'whereby ye might get another goodman' (item 3), just as the intention of touching the king with magical poison was 'that another might have ruled in His Majesty's place'. Her poisoning activities are like those attempted against the king, especially to infect the victim's clothes or linen, or to touch him with a poisonous mixture. Like Patrick Moscrop (item 5), the king too exposed himself to the perils of the seas, and there are attempts to kill both men after a return from a sea voyage (item 6). There are other similar details in both narratives, such as the incessant sending of secret messages. The crimes with which MacCalzean was charged represent in miniature those that the entire group of witches is supposed to have committed against the king

As in Sampson's and Napier's dittays, the convention comes at the end. It achieved its fullest elaboration in Napier's dittay and there was no need to repeat the details in this dittay. However, MacCalzean was charged with attending four conventions: North Berwick, Acheson's Haven (first called Fiery Hills), an earlier one at Broomhills, at which a storm was raised to stay the queen's homecoming, and also a convention which caused the destruction of a boat travelling between Leith and Kinghorn.

MacCalzean's suporters pleaded and argued for her from 9 to 11 June, until on 12 June she was convicted of ten items. Arnot said that she was found guilty by a jury of landed gentleman of note.[82] The assize did not convict her of attempting to kill her husband, but she was convicted on counts of witchcraft and consultation with witches, of murdering her husband's nephew, and two counts of treasonable attendance at conventions. Bowes wrote to Burghley on 14 June that MacCalzean was convicted on nine counts.[83] On 15 June the court pronounced a uniquely terrible sentence of death—she was to be burned alive—and forfeiture of her estates. Bowes reported on 19 June that she attempted the same ploy as Barbara Napier, pleading pregnancy to gain a stay of execution. Bowes wrote cryptically about MacCalzean as she approached execution.

> It is looked [expected] that in respect of her presente condicion shee will reforme her selfe, and disclose the truth in her knowledge: but the sownd of the prayses gyven by many—wishing the end of her lyfe to be rather with the danger of her owne soule then to the perill of their freendes to be accused by her—doth so prevayle with her as there is litle hope of any change in her.[84]

One can only surmise, as Bowes wrote, that she could still have been a danger to Bothwell. As Bowes wrote on 14 June, MacCalzean's trial was thought to touch Bothwell closely.[85] The sentence against MacCalzean was carried out on 24 June 1591.[86] This was three days after Bothwell broke out of prison and escaped.

The estates, forfeit through her conviction, were eventually returned by act of parliament on 5 June 1592, as James was 'tuichit [touched] in honour and conscience', and determined that her posterity should not suffer.[87] But the estates of Cliftonhall were retained by the king's favourite Sir James Sandelandis to whom James had given them.

Conclusion

Some general conclusions are possible about the events represented and the stories implied in these four dittays. There are differences between the two earlier (December 1590–January 1591) and the two later dittays (May–June 1591). Some of the changes are fairly obvious. We move from the country to the town. Fian's doings were located in and around Tranent and Prestonpans; Agnes Sampson had quite a wide 'practice' in East Lothian. With Napier and MacCalzean, the location shifts to Edinburgh and the Canongate. The geography imagined in MacCalzean's dittay is urban, with servants and messages moving around a small area of the town. There is also a change in class. The protagonists of the first two dittays are a country schoolmaster and a cunning woman; whereas the protagonists of the last two are prosperous Edinburgh women, one of whom comes from an important legal family, who have contacts with nobles, Lady Angus and the earl of Bothwell. And in the dittays of Napier and MacCalzean we move nearer and nearer to the court and the king, and into the world of national politics with the Brig of Dee, the raid of Dumfries, and the earl of Bothwell.

The stories in the dittays of May and June become more precise and specific, accounts more coherent and detailed. The time scheme when various meetings and assignations supposedly took place is clearer in the later accounts, and witchcraft becomes more ominous. Apart from meetings with the devil, Fian and Agnes Sampson seem culpable of little more to the modern reader than sexual transgression and trivial magic. Apart from one attempt at *maleficium*, Agnes Sampson is guilty of no more than prognostication and healing. Euphame MacCalzean emerges from these records as the most fully fledged witch. It is in the proceedings against Napier's jurors that the convention at North Berwick appears in its most fully elaborated and detailed form. It is not even dated in Fian's and Sampson's dittays and it is not until the dittays of Napier and MacCalzean that it becomes the setting for the attempt to kill the king by image-magic. What we can witness as we read through the dittays from December 1590 to June 1591 is the retelling of a story of witchcraft until that story becomes convincing and coherent as a narrative of treason.

Bothwell's trial for witchcraft finally took place on 10 August 1593. A lengthy account of the trial itself was sent to Burghley by Carey, who had succeeded Bowes as ambassador, and can be found in *Border Papers* ii 486–9. After the indictment against Bothwell was read, David MacGill delivered in court Ritchie Graham's depositions, which were the main source of the accusations against Bothwell that were recorded in the dittay against him. Document 26 is a draft of the indictment. Document 24 looks like a record of Ritchie Graham's depositions which formed the basis of the accusation against Bothwell. Document 25 is a list of Bothwell's assizers.

Bothwell's trial took place at a time when Bothwell was politically in the ascendant and James was at a low political ebb (see section on Bothwell in Chapter 1). The documents' relative narrative and circumstancial incoherence reflect the failure of the authorities convincingly to represent Bothwell as having played a part in the stories of the North Berwick witches.

Notes

[1] Smith 1972: xxvi.

[2] Smith 1972: xxiii.

[3] Smith 1972: xxiv.

[4] Most of the following information is taken from Dickinson 1958.

[5] Smith 1958a: 37–40; Smith 1958b: 432–5; Smith 1972: v.

[6] For an interrogation of the part played by witch hunting in state-building in Scotland see Levack 1996.

[7] Smith 1958b: 438.

[8] Smith 1972: xiv.

[9] Smith 1972: lix, quoting Mackenzie.

[10] Robert Grierson is mentioned by name in *News*.

[11] Calderwood 1842–9: v 115.

[12] *Historie of James the Sext* 1825: 241.

[13] Calderwood 1842–9: v 116.

[14] See Larner 1981: 36; Larner 1984: 27.

[15] For some discussions of and approaches to this important issue, see Ginzburg 1983; Ginzburg 1990: 1–16, 156–64; Roper 1994: 202–6; Gibson 1997; Gaskill 1998.

[16] For God wiping away tears, see Psal. 116.8, Isa. 25.8, Ezek. 24.16, Rev. 7.17 and 21.4; and for the promise of resurrection, John 6.39–40, 44, 54, and also Job 19.25–6.

[17] On revenge as motive see Gaskill 1996.

[18] Luke 4.5. These Gospel accounts of Christ's temptation (Matthew 4.1–11; Luke 4.1–13) were often cited in discussions of the devil's power to carry witches to their meetings.

[19] Demonologists regularly discussed transvection, often debating whether the witches only experienced it in a trance, or whether they were physically transported through the air to their meetings. Most, even the sceptical Wier, were reluctant to deny the possibility of physical transvection, partly because of Christ's transportation by the devil to the temple in Jerusalem or the angelic transportation in the Apocrypha of Habakkuk to Babylon. For some European discussions, see Bodin 1580: II v ff. 89ᵛ–94; Boguet 1929: xvii, 46–51; Daneau 1575: sigs F7, G7ᵛ–8ᵛ, H5. James himself discussed transvection in *Demonology* II iii. For English discussions: Scot 1886: V vi; Cotta 1616: 38–40; Holland 1590: E3ᵛ–4; Cooper 1617: 257. See also Clark 1997: passim.

[20] See Zika 1989–90: 38–40.

[21] See document 13.

[22] See, for example, Boguet 1929: 55–6.

[23] Calderwood 1842–9: v 116.

[24] *CSPS* x 463, 467.

[25] *Historie of James the Sext* 1825: 241; Melville 1827: 395; Calderwood 1842–9: v 115.

[26] Spottiswoode 1668: 383. Arnot's description, 'a grave matron-like woman, of a rank and comprehension above the vulgar' (1785: 349), is presumably merely rewording Spottiswoode.

[27] Sinclair 1871: 22.

[28] Briggs 1989: 21–31.

[29] Sinclair 1871: 22.

[30] Duffy 1992: 53–87, 209–98.

[31] For the sources of the image of the *navicella*, the ship of the church, see Kirschbaum 1968–76: iv 62–7.

[32] Duffy 1992: 286–7; see generally Duffy 1992: 266–98, and Gray 1974.

[33] Compare the stories in Elizabeth Bennet's examination of her initial spiritual and physical resistance to her familiars Sucking and Lierd in W. W., *A True and just Recorde* (1582) (Rosen 1991: 122–4).

[34] For some early modern European accounts and discussions of the sabbat see Remy 1930: I xiv–xxiii 47–73; Guazzo 1988; Boguet 1929; Bodin 1580; and for some recent accounts and discussions Robbins 1959: 414–24; McGowan 1977; Ginzburg 1990; Ginzburg 1993; Muchembled 1993; Rowland 1993; Clark 1997.

[35] Protestant authors generally seem to have been less interested in the sabbat and in the sexual activities of witches than catholic ones; see Clark 1997: 528–9. However, accounts of the sabbat may be found in Daneau 1575: F6ᵛ–G3 and Cooper 1617: 88–127, 258–9; see also Holland 1590: E2ᵛ–Fᵛ. The North Berwick convention is one of the closest approximations to the sabbat in early modern Britain.

[36] Remy 1930: I xvii 60–1.

[37] For a useful account account of the proceedings against Barbara Napier and her jurors see Stafford 1953: 107–111.

[38] Calderwood 1842–9: v 115, 128.

[39] Moysie 1830: 85.

[40] *CSPS* x 514.

[41] *CSPS* x 514.

[42] Calderwood 1842–9: v 129.

[43] Calderwood 1842–9: v 128.

[44] *CSPS* x 521–5.

[45] *CSPS* x 525, 523.

[46] Willock 1966: 240–2; Williamson 1979: 48–63.

[47] Williamson 1979: 48–9; Calderwood 1842–9: v 128.

[48] See Larner 1984: 35–67.

[49] *CSPS* x 522.

[50] Larner 1981: 180.

[51] Melville 1827: 395–6.

[52] However, 'popular culture' and its sources are both notoriously problematic; see Scribner 1989.

[53] See, for example, Scribner 1987: 277–99.

[54] See, for example, the conversation between Miles and a devil in Greene's *Friar Bacon and Friar Bungay*, scene xv, and the affectionate relationship of Cuddy Banks with the devil-dog Tom in Dekker, Ford and Rowley's *The Witch of Edmonton*.

[55] Pitcairn 1833: I iii 49–58.

[56] Sharpe 1996: 253.

[57] Hume 1644: 32.

[58] This letter is wrongly dated by *CSPS* as April 1591, and vaguely by Akrigg 1984: 112 as 'Spring'. Wormald 2000: 168n notes that M. Lee Jnr 1959: 231n dates it correctly as 14–19 June.

[59] BL Additional MS 23, 341, ff. 40ᵛ–41, punctuation added. This letter may also be found in Akrigg 1984: 112–15.

[60] Yeoman forthcoming.

[61] For Thomas MacCalzean see Pitcairn 1833: I iii 247–8; Brunton and Haig 1832: 149–51.

[62] Yeoman forthcoming.

[63] *RPCS* iv 45, 370.

[64] Pitcairn 1833: I iii 249.

[65] Melville 1827: 397.

[66] Wormald 2000: 167.

[67] On John Skene see *DNB*; Omond 1883: i 60–7.

[68] See, for example, Scot 1886: V ix 62; Gifford 1587: C2ᵛ–C3; Holland 1590: B3ᵛ–B4.

[69] Dolan 1994: 30.

[70] Smith 1972: xxxviii.

[71] Pitcairn 1833: I iii 248.

[72] For rebellious and shrewish women see Davis 1975; for stereotypes of disorderly and other sorts of women in relation to witchcraft see Larner 1981: 89–102; Larner 1984: 84–8; Wiesner 1993: 218–

38; Brauner 1995. Underdown 1985: 119–21, 127 connects witchcraft, scolding and dominant women.

[73] Baroja 1965: 33, 40, 101–2.

[74] See Burghartz 1988: 68; Roberts 1996.

[75] Baroja 1965: 102; Underdown 1985: 123; Scot 1886: VI vi–vii; Roberts 1996: 67.

[76] See Genesis 3.16.

[77] On this see Lindley 1993.

[78] For the legal relationship of husband and wife in Scotland see Paton 1958: 69–115.

[79] See Goldberg 1986.

[80] See also Underdown 1985: 116–19.

[81] Documents 24 and 26.

[82] Arnot 1785: 350.

[83] *CSPS* x 530.

[84] *CSPS* x 531.

[85] See Janet Kennedy's depositions to the king about the wax image of him, and about Barbara Napier and Euphame MacCalzean, some time in June 1591, documents 13 and 14.

[86] Pitcairn 1833: I iii 248.

[87] Pitcairn 1833: I iii 248.

Document 19

The Trial of John Fian

26 December 1590

Curia justiciarie supremi domini nostri regis, tenta 26° Decembris 1590 per magistros Joannem Graham et Umphridem Blynschelis.[††]

Convict[†] *of divers points of witchcraft and burned.]*[1]
John Fian,[†] alias Cunningham, last dwelling in Preston.
Convicted of divers points of witchcraft contained in the dittay.[†]
Compeared[†] the same Mr David McGill[†] of Cranstoun Riddel, advocate[†] to our sovereign lord, as pursuer,[†] and produced a dittay against the said John Fian.

[†] *Curia ... Umphridem Blynschelis* 'The justiciary court of our sovereign lord the king, held on 26 December 1590, by Masters John Graham and Humphrey Blynschelis'. *P* adds 'Justiciaros Deputatos' (justice deputes) after Blynschelis.

[†] **Blynschelis** this name is a variation of Blindsell, a surname derived 'from the occupation of seeling or covering the eyes of falcons used in hawking' (Black 1962: 83)

[†] **Convict** convicted

[†] **Fian** variously spelled in the dittays and *News*, often as Fean. Calderwood gives yet another form, 'Johne Sibbet, *alias* Cunninghame' (Calderwood 1842–9: v 115).

[†] **dittay** statement of charges against an accused person, indictment

[†] **Compeared** put in an appearance, especially in a court of justice

[†] **David McGill** king's advocate from June 1582 until his death in 1596 (Omond 1883: i 42–68)

[†] **advocate** the king's advocate, chief law-officer of the crown and its representative in civil litigation and treason trials

[†] **pursuer** prosecutor

Assisa [†]

John Wilson in Edinburgh	Thomas Craig there
Richard Newtoun in Tranent	John Colville there
William Strathearn there[†]	James Watson there
Patrick Halyeort there	John Jakit[2] there
James Milton there	Thomas Wright there

Robert Seton there
Robert Thriske, merchant, burgess[†] of Edinburgh
John Donaldson, merchant there
Robert Smith, merchant there

Which persons of assize being chosen, sworn and admitted[†] upon the said John Fian's assize, he being accused by dittay of the said crimes, they removed themselves altogether forth of court to the assize house, where they chose the said James Watson chancellor.[†] And have reasoned upon[†] the points[3] of the said dittay and resolved[†] therewith, re-entered again in the said court where they, by the mouth of the said chancellor,[†] found, pronounced and delivered the said John Fian, alias Cunningham, to be filed[†] and convict.

(1)   First,[†] that when the devil appeared and came to him when he was lying in his bed in Tranent in Thomas Trumbill's chamber, musing and pensing[†4] how he might be revenged[†] of the said Thomas, who had offended him in not spargeing[†] of his chamber as he had promised, his face being toward the wall, the devil appeared to him with[†] white raiment, where he[†] spake to him in these terms, or ever he[†] spake to him, 'Will ye be my servant and adore me and my servants? And ye shall never want'.[†] And also that he

---

[†] **Assisa** (Latin) assize, jury
[†] **there** i.e. as above, in Tranent
[†] **burgess** citizen, freeman of burgh, and therefore member of the assize
[†] **admitted** accepted
[†] **chancellor** foreman of the jury
[†] **reasoned upon** discussed
[†] **resolved** came to a decision
[†] **by the mouth ... chancellor** the said chancellor acting as spokesman for the group
[†] **filed** found the charges justified and the accused guilty
[†] **(1) First** the points in Fian's dittay are summarised in Sinclair's seventeenth-century history of Scottish witchcraft, *Satan's Invisible World Discovered* (Sinclair 1871: 27–8)
[†] **musing and pensing** reflecting and giving thought to; pensing from 'pensant' (French),

thinking, cogitating (*P*); see James on the devil finding a good time first to approach witches 'lying pansing in their bed' (*Demonology* II ii)
[†] **revenged** revenge is often cited by demonologists as a reason for people becoming witches (e.g. Boguet 1929: 22)
[†] **spargeing** casting with lime; white-washing or cleansing (*P*)
[†] **with** in
[†] **he** i.e. the devil (*P*)
[†] **or ever he** before he (i.e. Fian)
[†] **And ... want** a regular first promise from the devil to prospective servants was 'that they will never lack for anything' (Boguet 1929: 22); 'For such of them as are in great misery and poverty, he allures to follow him by promising unto them great riches and worldly commodity' (*Demonology* II ii)

should be revenged of his enemies, like as[†] the said devil persuaded him to burn Thomas Trumbill's house, in respect, he[†] said, he[†] had not kept promise. (2)   Item, filed for suffering of himself to be marked by the devil with a rod[†] the second night that he appeared to him in white araiment, as said is,[†] in his bed, and for feigning of himself to lie sick in the said Thomas Trumbill's chamber, where he was strucken[†] in great ecstasies and trances,[†] lying by the space of two or three hours dead, his sprite taken,[†] and suffered himself to be carried and transported to many mountains as though through all the world, according to his own depositions.[†]
(3)   Item, filed, according to his own confession, for the abusing of his body with Margaret Spens, widow in (   ), promising to have married her. But at Satan's command he stayed, who said to him if he married her he should tyne[†] him and mickle riches.[†]
(4)   Item,[†] filed for the suffering of himself to be carried to North Berwick kirk[†] (he being lying in a closed bed[†] in Prestonpans), as if he had been soughing athwart the earth,[†][5] where Satan commanded him to make him homage with the rest of his servants; where he thought he saw the light of a

---

[†] **like as** for instance
[†] **he** i.e. the devil
[†] **he** presumably Trumbill, who had failed in his promise to whitewash the chamber
[†] **marked ... rod** the devil regularly marked his European followers, but the use of a rod is unusual. The rod figures again in Fian's report of the devil appearing to him in prison in *News*.
[†] **as said is** as has been said
[†] **strucken** struck
[†] **ecstasies and trances** some continental witches were observed in a trance when they thought they travelled to the sabbat. Demonologists debated whether transportation to witches' meetings was actually physical or only in a dream or vision. Bodin has a chapter 'De l'ecstace, ou ravissement des Sorciers' (Bodin 1580: II v ff. 89ᵛ–94), and Boguet debates whether witches may go to the sabbat in spirit only, while their bodies remain home in bed, but concludes that they do not (Boguet 1929: xvii, 46–51).
[†] **his sprite taken** his spirit caught up
[†] **ecstasies ... depositions** compare, 'And some saith that their bodies lying still as in an ecstasy, their spirits will be ravished out of their bodies and carried to such places' (*Demonology* II iv)
[†] **tyne** lose, forfeit
[†] **But ... riches** if Fian married Margaret Spens, he (Fian) would lose both him (i.e. the devil's favour) and great riches. The devil sometimes expressed an aversion to marriage by his servants: 'I prithee, Faustus, talk not of a wife'

(Marlowe 1993: A–text, II i 146–7).
[†] **(4) Item** this is the first description, later elaborated and expanded in the dittays, of the supposed convention in North Berwick kirk. See also Sir James Melville's description (Melville 1827: 395–6).
[†] **North Berwick kirk** several demonological works say that witches met in churches (Nider in *Malleorum quorundam maleficarum*, Frankfurt 1582: 714–15; Cooper 1617: 90), and Danish witches supposedly renounced God in churches (Ankarloo and Henningsen 1993: 358–9); James also writes that the devil 'may the more vively counterfeit and scorn God, he oft-times makes his slaves to convene in these very places which are destinate and ordained for the convening of the servants of God (I mean by churches)' (*Demonology* II iii)
[†] **closed bed** a box bed
[†] **soughing athwart the earth** rushing with a whistling sound over the earth; 'This suggests the idea of skimming along the surface of the earth with the swiftest flight. "Souchand" also denotes a rushing sound, like that of an arrow whizzing through the air' (*P*). 'Another way [of the transport of witches] is somewhat more strange, and yet is it possible to be true: which is by being carried by the force of the Spirit which is their conductor, either above the earth or above the sea swiftly to the place where they are to meet' (*Demonology* II iv).

candle standing in the midst of his servants, which appeared blue low;[†] and Satan stood as in a pulpit, making a sermon of doubtsome[†] speeches, saying 'Many comes to the fair and buys not all wares';[†] and desired him not to fear, though he was grim,[†] for he had many servants who should never want and should ail nothing so long as their hair was on,[6] and should never let a tear fall from their eyn so long as they served him.[†] And gave their lessons[†] and commands to him as follows: 'Spare not to do evil[†] and to eat, drink and be blithe,[†] taking rest and ease', for he should raise them up at the latter day gloriously.[†]

(5) Item, filed for the being in company with Satan at his conventions,[†] where he saw Robert Grierson,[†] Michael Clark, Annie Sampson, with sundry others; where he and all the rest kissed him behind, and some his arse;[†] and

---

[†] **blue low** 'an inevitable consequence of the presence of the "foul fiend"' (*P*). At the sabbat witches offered Satan in homage candles which burned with a blue flame (Boguet 1929: 55–6).

[†] **doubtsome** ambiguous, dark

[†] **Many ... wares** This enigmatic and proverb-like statement seems to have been the 'text' of the devil's sermon. Calderwood's account gives it in a different form: 'Sindrie of the witches confessed they had sindrie times companie with the devill, at the kirk of Northberwick, where he appeared to them in the likenesse of a man with a redde cappe, and a rumpe at his taill, [and] made a harangue in maner of a sermoun to them; his text, "Manie goe to the mercat, but all buy not"' (Calderwood 1842–9: v 115–16). The devil may be echoing 'For manie are called, but fewe chosen' (Matthew 22.14), which is the climax of the parable of the wedding feast at which the king ordered that the guest without the wedding garment be cast into outer darkness where there was weeping and gnashing of teeth.

[†] **grim*** fierce

[†] **should never ... served him** *P* notes the superstition that witches could not weep, as does Roughead (1936: 158). But here surely the devil promised his servants that they would not sorrow, echoing God's promises, e.g. 'God shal wipe away all teares from their eyes' (Revelation 7.17); and see also Psalms 116.8; Isaiah 25.8; Ezekiel 24.16; Revelation 21.4.

[†] **lessons** piece of formal teaching; the devil gave instructions for evil at the sabbat

[†] **Spare not to do evil** at the sabbat the devil 'urges them to do all the harm that they can' (Boguet 1929: 60)

[†] **blithe** happy

[†] **for he ... gloriously** whatever the devil meant here, he is using the language of the bible when it promises resurrection. The devil here makes the same promises to his servants as Jesus, 'I wil raise him up at the last day' (John 6.44; see also John 6.39–40, 54). At the meetings of continental witches the devil often often promised happiness in this life and the next: 'Et le Diable luy promit une ioye, & felicité eternelle' (Bodin 1580: II iv f. 84).

[†] **conventions** assemblies; 'convention' is regularly used in the documents for the witches' meeting. It also means 'covenant', 'compact', so also invokes the notion of 'pact'.

[†] **Robert Grierson** 'Robert Grierson, skipper' was one of the witches accused by Geillis Duncan (see *News*). He was dead by 15 April 1590, for in a postcript to a letter of this date Bowes says 'This daye Robert Greyson, one of the three witches to have bene examyned, died, and as it is thought by the extremyty of the tortours applyed to him. He hath confessed litle, and yet it is said by the rest he was pryvy to all their accions' (*CSPS* x 502).

[†] **kissed ... arse** see *News*. The 'shameful kiss' (*osculum infame*) was a regular gesture of homage at the sabbat (Bodin 1580: II iv f. 83; Boguet 1929: 56; Guazzo 1988: 25; Cooper 1617: 90). As early as 1303 a bishop of Coventry was accused at Rome of a number of crimes, including offering homage to the devil and kissing his behind (Murray 1921: 127). The phrase 'and some his arse' might suggest that only *some* of the convention specifically kissed the devil's arse, although all kissed him 'behind'.

at the same time for the bewitching and possessing of William Hutson in Windygoul with an evil sprite.[†]

(6)   Item, filed for suffering himself to be carried to the sea with Satan. And at the first he was skimming[7] over all the sea without land,[†] in a boat accompanied with the persons above written and being of the foreknowledge of the leak that struck up in the queen's ship, as the devil foretold him.

(7)   Item, filed for the raising of winds at the king's passing to Denmark and for the sending of a letter to Marion Linkup[†][8] in Leith to that effect, bidding her to meet him and the rest on the sea within five days; where Satan delivered a cat out of his hand to Robert Grierson giving the word to 'Cast the same in the sea! Hola!' And thereafter being mounted[†] in a ship and drank ilk one to others,[†] where Satan said 'Ye shall sink the ship', like as they thought they did.

(8)   Item, filed for assembling himself with Satan at the king's returning from Denmark, where Satan promised to raise a mist and cast[†] the king's Majesty in England. And for performing thereof, he took a thing like to a football which appeared to the said John like a wisp,[†] and cast the same in the sea, which caused a vapour and a reek[†] to rise.

(9)   Item, filed for being in company with Satan in the kirk of North Berwick, where he appeared to him in the form of a black man[†] within the pulpit thereof; and after his out-coming of the kirk pointed[†] the graves and stood above them which were opened in three sundry parts, two within and one without,[†] which the women dismembered the dead corpses[†] and bodies being therein with their gulleis;[†] and incontinent[†] was transported without words.

[†]   **bewitching ... sprite** presumably the young man described in *News* who 'once in twenty-four hours he fell into a lunacy'

[†]   **without land** out of sight of the land

[†]   **Linkup** 'In the trial of Agnes Sympson, 1590, the name is misprinted Lenchop and as Linkup in the trial of Dr Feane' (Black 1962: 438)

[†]   **mounted** seated

[†]   **drank ilk one to others** drank healths to one another

[†]   **cast** wreck

[†]   **wisp** 'of straw' conjectured *P*; 'a wreath of any kind'

[†]   **reek** cloud of mist

[†]   **black man** the devil often appeared as a black man, or a man dressed in black (for instances see Murray 1921: 33–43). Françoise Secretain gave herself to the devil who had appeared as 'a

big black man' and Boguet says that if the devil appears as a man it is always as a black man (Boguet 1929: 5, 20); 'Et quelquefois le Diable se monstroit en guise d'homme fort noir & hideux' (Bodin 1580: f. 85).

[†]   **pointed** indicated

[†]   **two within and one without** explained by the fuller version in Agnes Sampson's dittay item (50), 'two within and one without the kirk', i.e. two inside and one outside the kirk building

[†]   **dismembered the dead corpses** robbing tombs, dismembering the bodies of the dead and using parts of them for witchcraft are the activities of some witches in classical literature, and especially of Lucan's Erictho (Lucan, *Pharsalia* VI 515–68)

[†]   **gulleis*** 'large clasp-knives' (*P*)

[†]   **incontinent** immediately

(10)   Item, filed for opening of locks,[†] and specially a lock in David Seton's younger[†] in Tranent; and siclike[†] for the opening of the said David's foregate,[†] the key thereof being lying upon the board[†] at the supper. As also filed for the opening of a lock by his sorcery in David Seton's mother's, by blowing[†] in a woman's hand, himself sitting at the fire-side.

(11)   Item, filed for the being coming forth of Patrick Humphrey's son's house in the mill undernight[†] from his supper, and passing to Tranent on horseback and a man with him; by his devilish craft raised up four candles[†] upon the horse's two lugs,[†] and another candle upon the staff which the man had in his hand, and gave such light as if it had been daylight. Like as[†] the said candles returned with the said man while[†] his homecoming, and caused him fall dead at his entress[†] within the house.

(12)   Item, filed for the witching[†] and possessing of William Hutson with an evil sprite, which continued with him twenty-six weeks; like as the said sprite departed and left him how soon[†] the said John was taken and apprehended.

(13)   Item, filed for being in company with Annie Sampson, Robert Grierson, Kate Gray and others upon Hallowmass Even. They embarked in a boat beside Robert Grierson's house in the 'Pans[†] and sailed over the sea to a tryst[†] they had with another witch; where they entered within a ship and drank good wine[†] and ale therein: and thereafter causing the said ship and boat to perish with the persons being therein and then returning home.

(14)   Item, filed for the using by way of witchcraft of modevart[†] [9] feet upon him in his purse, given to him by Satan for this cause: that so long as he had them upon him he should never want silver.[†]

(15)   Item, filed for being in North Berwick kirk at a convention with Satan and other witches, where Satan made a devilish sermon, where the said John sat upon the left side of the pulpit nearest him. And the sermon being

---

[†] **opening of locks** a talent attributed to some magicians; some conjuring books promise to instruct magicians 'to open locks' (BL Royal MS, XVII A XLII, f. 6). A magical opening of locks may also be imagined in the cauldron scene in *Macbeth*: 'Open, locks, whoever knocks' (Shakespeare 1988: *Macbeth* IV i 63).

[†] **David Seton's younger** at the house of the younger David Seton

[†] **siclike** similarly

[†] **foregate** front gate

[†] **board** table

[†] **blowing** ? by blowing through the curled fingers and thumb of the woman's hand

[†] **undernight** during the night

[†] **four candles** this explains the woodcut in the quartos of *News* of a man riding a horse with flaming brands on it. This story is not included in *News* itself.

[†] **lugs** ears

[†] **Like as** in the same way

[†] **while** until

[†] **entress** entrance

[†] **witching** bewitching (*P*)

[†] **how soon** as soon as

[†] **the 'Pans** i.e. Prestonpans

[†] **tryst** appointment to meet

[†] **drank good wine** continental witches enter cellars and drink all the wine (see Ginzburg 1990: 73)

[†] **modevart** mole

[†] **silver** money

ended, he came down and took the said John by the hand and led him widdershins[†] about. And thereafter caused him kiss his arse.

(16)   Item, filed for the chasing of a cat in Tranent, in the which chase he was carried high above the ground with great swiftness (and as lightly as the cat herself) over a higher dyke, nor he was able to lay his hand to the head of. And being inquired to what effects he chased the same, answered that in a convention held at Broomhill[10] Satan commanded all that were present to take cats; like as he for obedience to Satan chased the said cat purposely to be cassin[†] in the sea to raise winds for destruction of ships and boats.

(17)   Item, filed that forasmuch as by his art of witchcraft, magic and sorcery he gave himself[†] to declare to any man how long they should live and what should be their end, if they would tell you the day of their birth, like as he foretold the same to Marion Weddell, that her son should not live fifteen days, which came to pass as he spake.

(18)   Filed for declaring of the like to Alexander Bovis' wife in Edinburgh, and saying her son should be short while in her,[†] aucht as[†] he died within a short space thereafter.

(19)   Item, filed for the receiving of their directions[†] and commandments from Satan: first to deny God and all true religion;[†] secondly to give his faith to the devil and adoring him; thirdly he said to the devil that he[†] should persuade as many as he could to his[†] society; fourthly[11] he dismembered the bodies of the dead corpses and specially of bairns unbaptized;[†] fifthly he destroyed men by sea[12] and land, with[†] corns, cattle and goods, and raised tempest and stormy weather, with[13] the devil himself blowing in the air, etc.

(20)   Item, filed for a common notorious witch and enchanter.[†]

[†]   **widdershins** anti-clockwise; contrary to the course of the sun (*P*)

[†]   **cassin** cast, thrown

[†]   **gave himself** 'professed, gave out' (*P*)

[†]   **short while in her** i.e. a short time in her womb

[†]   **aucht as** and just so

[†]   **directions** instructions

[†]   **to deny … religion** denial of religion as a condition of service to the devil is already recorded in the Dominican Johann Nider's *Formicarius*, finished *c*. 1435 (*Malleorum quorundam Maleficarum* 1582: II 716). The *Malleus* and a host of later demonological treatises report similar stories, particularly of oaths taken at continental sabbats.

[†]   **he** i.e. Fian

[†]   **his** i.e. the devil's

[†]   **bairns unbaptized** Scot notes that among charges made against witches by continental demonologists is that they sacrifice 'children to the divell before baptisme' and also boil unbaptised infants (Scot 1886: II ix 25–6)

[†]   **with** as well as

[†]   **enchanter** John Fian's dittay is followed in *P* by a reprint of *News*

Document 20

The Trial of Agnes Sampson

27 January 1591

Witchcraft: Agnes Sampson][1]

Curia Justiciarie supremi domini nostri regis, tenta in pretorio de Edinburgh 27 Januarii 1590 [i.e. 1591] *per magistrum Umphridem Blynschelis justiciarium deputatum.*[†]

Intrant[†]

Convict and burned]
Agnes Sampson in Nether Keith.
Dilated[†] of the particular points of witchcraft contained in dittay.
Pursuer:[†] Mr David McGill of Cranstoun Riddel, advocate to our sovereign lord.

Assisa

John Spens in Saltoun	Robert Dixon in Bolton
William Bartram in Carfrae	William Stenhouse in Barns
Edmund Bartram in Hopes[2]	William Peris in Haddington
David Robeson in Broadwoodside[†]	Mathew Young there
William White in Colstoun Mill[†]	James Ritchieson
	Alexander Young there

Chancellor]

[†] **Curia ... deputatum** 'The justiciary court of our sovereign lord, the king, held in the court of Edinburgh, 27 January 1590 [i.e. 1591], by master Humphrey Blynschelis, justice depute.'
[†] *Intrant* they (i.e. the parties) enter
[†] **dilated** accused, charged

[†] **Pursuer** prosecutor
[†] **Broadwoodside** 'Broadwood syid' appears on the map of Lothian by Hondius 1636
[†] **Colstoun Mill** Colstounmill is marked on the map of Lothian by Blaeu 1654

> Robert Byres there
> Robert Kyle there
> William Strathearn in Tranent
> Gilbert Edington in Haddington
> Bernard Brown there
> Robert Bagbie there

Which persons of assize being chosen, sworn and admitted,[†] after accusation of the said Agnes by dittay, who removed themselves altogether forth of court to the assize house where after choosing of the said William White chancellor, they reasoned and voted upon the points of the said dittay. And being thoroughly resolved therewith, re-entered again in judgement, where they by the mouth of the said chancellor found, pronounced and declared the said Agnes.

Here follows the articles of her dittay whereof she was convict by, in number 53.][†]

(1)   To be filed and convict of foreknowledge and telling by her witchcraft that William Markeston, servant to Thomas Watson in Inveresk, was but a dead man.

(2)   Item, filed and convict that William Blake's son's sark[†] being sent to her, she by her witchcraft declared that the sickness that he had was an elf-shot.[†]

(3)   Item, filed and convict for using of witchcraft in healing of John Thomson in Dirleton who remained cripple notwithstanding thereof.

(4)   Item, filed and convict for telling by her witchcraft that Many Nicolson, goodman in North Berwick, being sick, she should lay her life for his,[3] who notwithstanding died thereof.

(5)   Item, filed and convict for showing by her witchcraft to a poor woman who was sent to her by the friends of David Lyndsay, cutler[4] in Dalkeith, who had lain thirty weeks sick and had not spoken three days before the said poor woman came to her, that if he lived over Wednesday[†] that he would not die of the malady; who mended of[†] the same according to her declaration.

[†]   **admitted** accepted
[†]   **Here follows ... in number 53** Robert Bowes enclosed a long note of the confession of Agnes Sampson in a letter to Burghley, 23 February 1590. It says that of 'the 102 articles of her dittay sche confessit 58' (*CSPS* x 467)
[†]   **sark** shirt
[†]   **elf-shot** disease produced by agency of evil spirits; shot at by elves. Sinclair has different details of this item, as he mentions Agnes Sampson's skill in diseases and 'that the sickness of William Black was an Elf-Shot' (Sinclair 1871: 22).
[†]   **over Wednesday** through Wednesday
[†]   **mended of** recovered from

(6)   Item, filed and convict that forasmuch as John Peiny being in Preston, being at[5] a certain time very sick she, by her incantation and prayer, made him to convalesce of his sickness.

(7)   Item, filed for using of her prayer and incantation to have healed (   ) Haliburton, goodman of Inchcarne, being then in sickness, and declaring that no chirurgeonry[†] and no physic could help him, who deceased as she told the same.

(8)   Item, filed for coming to Bessie Aikenhead, spouse to Thomas Vans in Haddington, and using her[†] prayer and devilish charms for recovering of her health to her.

(9)   Item, filed that she being sent for to the Lady Roslin who was sick, she knew by her devilish prayer that the said lady was not able to recover, and therefore she would not come to her.

(10)   Item, filed and convict that she being brought to John Young's wife, skipper[6] at Barfoot,[7] at Pasch last was,[†] that was sick for the time. The said Agnes' counsel being sought anent[†] her health, she declared and answered that she would never be well so long as she remained upon the ground,[†] where she was for the time; but desired[†] that she should be transported of[†] the said ground, and she would either die or mend; who being transported at[8] her command shortly thereafter departed this life.

(11)   Item, filed that she had foreknowledge by her witchcraft of diseased persons if they would live or not, or who was witched[†] persons;[†] to wit, that if she stopped once in her prayer the sick person was bewitched, and if the prayer stopped twice the diseased person would die.

(12)   Item, filed and convict that she foreknew of the devil,[†] and told Patrick Porteous, that he would live but eleven years.

(13)   Item, filed that she was made foreknown of the devil of the last Michaelmas storm and that there would be great scathe[†] both by sea and land.

(14)   Item, filed that she was made foreknown by the Sprite[†] that the queen's Majesty would never come in this country except the king fetched her.

(15)   Item, filed and convict that she learned her skill and prayer from her father, who told her that when she was suited to[†] any sick person and that if

---

[†] **chirurgeonry** treatment of diseases and injuries
[†] **her** i.e. Agnes Sampson's
[†] **Pasch last was** last Easter
[†] **anent** concerning
[†] **ground** land, property, residence (*P*)
[†] **desired** i.e. Agnes Sampson desired
[†] **of** from
[†] **witched** bewitched (*P*)
[†] **Item ... witched persons** 'Item, sche confessit that sche knew quhen anie was bewitchit be the

smel of their linning clothis or the sueit therein, and be luiking on them' (*CSPS* x 465)
[†] **she foreknew of the devil** she obtained foreknowledge from the devil
[†] **scathe** damage, especially injury supposed proceeding from witchcraft
[†] **Sprite** 'term used to designate Satan, as it was dangerous to use his name rashly' (*P*)
[†] **suited to** asked to attend; made suit to (*P*)

she stopped in her prayer she would not pass[†] to the sick person, and if she stopped not she would pass and the person diseased would live.

(16)   Item, filed and convict that she by her devilish prayer told that James Kirkcaldy's wife, burgess of Haddington, would convalesce[9] of her sickness.

(17)   Item, filed for healing of John Ker[†] of (   ), being sick in all men's judgement to the death, who lay in Alexander Fairley's house in Long-niddry, and that by her prayers and incantations.

(18)   Item, for healing of John Duncan in Musselburgh of his sickness by her devilish prayers.

(19)   Item, for the foretelling of Isobel Hamilton's death, spouse to James Power, and telling that she could not amend her except the devil was raised. And her goodman[†] being a sparing[†] man and would not wear expense,[†] she would not raise him and told that she was bewitched; and this was done six or seven years since[†] or thereby.

(20)   Item, convict for the curing of the goodwife of Cameron[†] who gaid[†] upon stilts[†] after her birth,[†] and that by witchcraft.

(21)   Item, convict for healing of the laird of Reidshill's[†][10] son by witchcraft, whom the chirurgeons had given over.[†]

(22)   Item, filed and convict of the curing of Robert Dixon in Bolton[11] in summer last was,[†] who was suspect by the woman he got the bairn with, or her mother, who had put some wheat or other things in his doublet, and caused him to leave off the said doublet.

(23)   Item, for the curing of John Cockburn the sheriff of Haddington's wife, who was witched by the witch of Mirrielaws by the blast of evil wind on Halloween.

(24)   Item, filed and convict of curing by her witchcraft, incantation and saying of devilish prayers, of Alison Ker, spouse to John Reston, of a sickness contracted by her by the mean of Catherine Gray, a witch, with the which sickness she was diseased by the space of three years preceding that the said Agnes cured her.

(25)   Item, filed and convict of the using of her devilish art of witchcraft in curing of (   ), spouse to Robert Carrington in Traprain, who was bewitched by umwhile[†] John McGill, desiring the said Robert to pass and take the said John McGill, and give him fair words and desire him to pass to

---

[†] **pass** go
[†] **John Ker** in *News* Agnes Sampson confesses that she had tried to obtain some of the king's linen on which to work *maleficium* with magical toad-venom 'which she practised to obtain by means of one John Kers'
[†] **goodman** husband
[†] **sparing** frugal, economical
[†] **wear expense** bear the expense
[†] **since** ago

[†] **Cameron** 'Kamron' is between Edinburgh and Craigmillar on Blaeu 1654
[†] **gaid** went
[†] **stilts** crutches
[†] **after her birth** after giving birth
[†] **Reidshill's** 'Reidshill' appears on Blaeu 1654
[†] **given over** given up on
[†] **summer last was** last summer
[†] **umwhile** the late

his sick wife, and if he gaid with fairness,[†] good it was. But if he would not, desired him to cause a young man go to him and inquire who gart[†] him do it, and to cause him come to his wife. And if he refused to come, to bring him against his will; who being brought in her presence, she was twice in twenty-four hours extreme wood[†] and out of her wit.

Nota: acquit[†] of this]

(26) Item, acquit[12] of her devilish practices and namely[†] of her passing to Newton[13] kirk undernight with the witch of Carberry and others, and there taking up[†] the buried people and jointing of them,[†] whereof she made enchanted powder[†] for witchcraft.

(27) Item, filed[14] for coming to Robert Bailey in the 'Pans'[†] son[†] in summer last, who was very sick for the time, and only gripping[†] him and speaking some words of charming went her way, and the child was cured and made hail[†] of his sickness.

(28) Item, convict for healing of John Hamilton in Samuelston, who being troubled with a sickness in his feet, he come to you and ye sent him hail of the said sickness upon the morn after his coming.

(29) Item, filed and convict for coming to James Liberton's wife in Over Liberton who was sick, using of her devilish prayers for her health, and said when she passed away if she came not again shortly she would depart away.[†] She not returning, the said James's wife departed within three days.

(30) Item, filed and convict for healing of the Lady Kilbaberton by her devilish prayers, who was diseased of a heavy[†] disease.

(31) Item, and filed and convict at for curing of umwhile Robert Kerse in Dalkeith who was heavily tormented with witchcraft and disease laid on him by a westland warlock[†] when he was in Dumfries, which sickness she took upon herself and kept the same with great groanings and torment while[†] the morn, at[15] which time there was a great din heard in the house. Which sickness she cast off herself in the close,[†] to the effect a cat or dog might[16] have gotten the same. And notwithstanding, the same was laid upon

---

[†] **gaid with fairness** went with fair words
[†] **gart** caused, made
[†] **wood** mad
[†] **acquit** acquitted
[†] **namely** especially
[†] **taking up** disinterring
[†] **jointing** taking away the joints for preparing charms, see items 42 and 50 of this dittay (*P*)
[†] **enchanted powder** at continental sabbats witches received powders with which to do harm (see Bodin 1580: II iv ff. 86ᵛ–88)
[†] **the 'Pans** Prestonpans (*P*)
[†] **Robert Bailey in the 'Pans' son** i.e. the son of

Robert Bailey of Prestonpans
[†] **gripping** touching, taking hold
[†] **hail** in good health, sound in body
[†] **and said ... depart away** Agnes Sampson said when she (Agnes) went away, that if she (Agnes) did not come again shortly, James Liberton's wife would die
[†] **heavy** serious
[†] **westland warlock** a warlock from the west of Scotland
[†] **while** until
[†] **close** courtyard, passage

Alexander Douglas in Dalkeith, who dwined[†] and died[17] therewith, and the said umwhile Robert Kerse was made hail.[†]

(32)   Item, convict for the foretelling by her devilish prayer to umwhile Patrick Hepburn in Bangly's[18] wife that her husband being sick would die because her prayer stopped, and therefore refused to pass and visit him. Which prayer was rehearsed[†] by her in manner following:

Agnes Sampson's prayer to her patients, for life or death.][†]

> I trow[†] in almighty God that wrought[†]
> Both heaven and earth and all of nought;
> Into his dear son, Christ Jesu,
> Into that anaplie[19] lord I trow;
> Was gotten of the Holy Ghost,
> Born of the Virgin Mary,
> Stoppit[†][20] to heaven that all well then[†][21]
> And sits at his Father's right hand.
> He bade us come and there to doom[†]
> Both quick and dead, as he thought convene.[22]
> I trow also in the Holy Ghost;
> In Holy Kirk my hope is most,
> That holy ship where hallowars wins[†]
> To ask forgiveness of my sins;
> And syne[†] to rise in flesh and bone
> The life that never more has gane.[†]
> Thou sayest Lord—loved mocht ye be!—
> That formed and made mankind of me,
> Thou cost me[†] on the holy cross
> And lent me body, soul and voice,
> And ordained me to heaven's bliss.
> Wherefore I thank thee, Lord, of this.

[†] **dwined** wasted, pined

[†] **which sickness ... made hail** see Sinclair (1871: 22): 'Her taking the sick Parties pains and sickness upon her self for a time, and then translating them to a third Person'. For witches' transference of sickness to other humans or animals in the Franche-Comté in the late sixteenth century, see Boguet 1929: 108–10.

[†] **rehearsed** recited

[†] **Agnes ... death** a doggerel version of the Apostles' Creed 'perhaps one of the monkish rhymes before the period of the Reformation, which Anny had got by heart' (*P*). Pitcairn prints the rhyming couplets together in one long line. Sinclair (1871: 23) quotes another two short

rhyming prayers that Agnes Sampson is supposed to have taught to people.

[†] **trow** believe (*P*)

[†] **wrought** made

[†] **stoppit** ascended, rendering the Creed's *et ascendit in coelum*

[†] **all well then** ?so that all was then well, i.e. after Christ's ascension into heaven.

[†] **doom** judgement

[†] **That ... wins** that holy ship where the saints dwell

[†] **syne** afterwards

[†] **never more has gane** has no end

[†] **cost me** made an exchange for me

And all your hallowaris loved be
To pray to them to pray to me
And keep me from that felon fee[†]
And from the sin that soul would slay.
Thou, Lord, for thy bitter passion
To keep me from sin and worldly shame
And endless damnation
Grant me the joy never will be gane[†]
Sweet Jesus Christus. Amen.

(33)   Item, filed and convict that the first time she began to serve the devil was after the death of her husband, and that he appeared to her in likeness of a man, who commanded her to acknowledge him as her master and to renounce Christ. Whereunto she granted,[†] being moved by poverty and his promises that she and her bairns should be made rich, and should give her power to be revenged of her enemies. And after that he appointed time and place for their night meeting. And that time, in sign that she was become his servant, he marked her in the right knee, which mark she believed to have been a hurt received by her from one of her bairns that was lying in the bed with her; which hurt was not hail for half a year.

(34)   Item, filed and convict that the devil appeared to her in likeness of a dog, at whom she sought her hail responses[†]. And when she put him away she charged him to depart 'on the law he lives on',[†] who with those words is conjured[†] and passes away.[†]

(35)   Item, filed and convict for sailing with certain her complices[†] out of North Berwick in a boat like a chimney (the devil passing before them like a rick[23] of hay) to a ship called *The Grace of God*, in the which she entered, and the devil caused her drink wine and gave her other good cheer,[†] whereof she and her company gave a part to them that was in the flott boat.[†] And at her being there she saw not the mariners, neither they saw her. And when they came away the devil raised an evil wind, he being under the ship, and

---

[†] **felon fee** terrible inheritance, i.e. original sin
[†] **never will be gane** never will be gone, i.e. will never have an end
[†] **granted** agreed, consented
[†] **her hail responses** all her responses
[†] **on the law he lives on** by the law he lives by
[†] **conjured** magically adjured; this use of a formulaic charge to depart is like the formal 'licence to depart' given in manuscript conjuring books by magicians to conjured spirits when they have temporarily finished with their services
[†] **Item ... away** compare Sincair's account (1871: 24)
[†] **complices** accomplices
[†] **cheer** entertainment, especially food and drink
[†] **flott boat** ship's long-boat

caused the ship perish. And she delivered twenty shilling to 'Grey Meal',[†] who was with her in the said ship, for his on-waiting.[†]

(36)   Item, filed upon her own confession, that she by art of witchcraft sailed to a ship where there was an uncouth[†] woman, and the Irish[†] tailor and his wife was principals[†] there, and that Richard Graham was another of the principals who had wrought mickle mischief.

(37)   Item, filed and convict for coming to Alison Inglis, David Robson's wife, then being sick, who chased her away and would not suffer her[24] to use her witchcraft to the healing of his wife, because she was bruited[†] to be a witch, and having met with the said David Robson's servant she said to him if his master had not spoken the words he spake, his wife had been a hail woman and ganging[†] on her own feet.

(38)   Item, filed and convict that when she was sent for to heal the old Lady Edmiston when she lay sick, before the said Agnes departed, she told to the gentlewomen that she should tell them that night whether the lady would hail[†] or not, and appointed them to be in the garden after supper, betwix five and six at even. She passed to the garden to devise upon[†] her prayer, at[25] what time[†] she charged the devil, calling him 'Eloa',[†][26] to come and speak to her. Who came in over the dyke[†] in likeness of a dog, and came so near to her that she was effrayed[†] and charged him on the law that he lived on to come no nearer, but to answer her. And she demanded whether the lady would live or not. He said her days were gone. Then he demanded if the gentlewomen her daughters, where they were; and she said that the gentlewomen said that they were to be there. He answered, one of them should be in peril and that he should have one of them. She answered, it should not be so, and so departed[†] from her howling. From this time, while after supper, he remained in the well.[†][27] When the gentlewomen come in,

---

[†]   **Grey Meal** his real name, John Gordon, is given in Barbara Napier's dittay and by Calderwood (Calderwood 1842–9: v 116). His nickname 'Grey Meal' means the dirty sweepings from a mill, the meal used for feeding poultry. He was 'one of the warlocks who "kepit the dur" at the grand convention at North Berwick' (*P*); and according to Melville, 'ane auld sely pure plowman' (Melville 1827: 396). Bowes reports that he had been burned at Haddington by 23 February 1591 (*CSPS* x 467).

[†]   **on-waiting** attendance (*P*)

[†]   **uncouth** unknown

[†]   **Irish** either (1) Irish or (2) Highland

[†]   **principals** leaders; probably also in the legal sense of the actual perpetrators of a crime, as opposed to merely accomplices

[†]   **bruited** rumoured; reported (*P*)

[†]   **ganging** going

[†]   **hail** heal

[†]   **devise upon** think out

[†]   **at what time** at which time

[†]   **Eloa** that this reading is to be preferred to 'Elva' (*P* and Sinclair 1871: 24) is confirmed by Agnes Sampson's confession to King James: 'At the second time which he appeared he commanded her to call him "Eloa" which she pronounces "Hola"' (document 2)

[†]   **dyke** wall

[†]   **effrayed** frightened

[†]   **so departed** i.e. so he departed

[†]   **well** a well, draw-well, in which the devil remains until after supper and in which, a moment later, he will try to drown one of the gentlewomen

the dog came out of the well and appeared to them, whereat they were effrayed. In the meantime one of the said gentlewomen, the Lady Torsenye, ran to the well, being forced and drawn by the devil, who would have drowned her, were not the said Agnes and the rest of the gentlewomen got[†] a grip of her, and with all her[†] forces drew her aback again, which made them all effrayed. The dog passed away thereafter with a howl. Then she said to the gentlewomen that she could not help the lady in respect that her prayer stopped, and that she was sorry for it. Moreover, after that, she and one of her sisters carried her dead[†] to a chamber where she remained frenetic[†] three or four days, and cripple a quarter of a year until she used her devilish enchantments to conjure the Sprite again. And she abade with her the time that she lay, and when she could not bide longer herself she sent her son to bide with her. And when either of them was present, she was well enough, but when they both left her she was as evil[†] as she was of before.

(39)   Item, convict for that she having done pleasure[†] to the goodwife of Galashiels, for the which she[†] did not satisfy[†] her so soon as the said Agnes desired it, and therefore she said to the said goodwife that she should repent it. And within few hours thereafter the said goodwife took a woodness[†] and her tongue shot out of her head and swallowed like a pot.[†] Wherefore she sent to her the thing that she desired, and prayed her to come to her. And she bade the servant go away home, for the goodwife was well.

(40)   Item, filed and convict of the delivery of a letter which John Fian, clerk, made[†] in George Mott's[28] back house[†] in the 'Pans, accompanied with the goodwife of the house, Gelie Duncan, Bessie Robson, Jockie 'Grey Meal', Janet Gaw,[†] Irish Marion, the webster's[29] wife of Seton,[†] Robert Grierson, the goodwife of Spilmersford Mill called Meg Begtoun, James Sparrow's wife called Kate Wallace, who convened there for raising of storm to stay the queen's homecoming to Scotland. After consultation whether Gelie Duncan or Bessie Thomson was meetest to send the letter with, and concluded[†] to send the said Gelie, which letter was sent to Marion Linkup[30] in Leith. The

---

[†] **were not … get** had not … got

[†] **her** possibly just Agnes Sampson here. The manuscript's 'hir' could be singular or plural, i.e. 'their' or 'her'.

[†] **dead** in a swoon (*P*)

[†] **frenetic** deranged

[†] **evil** unwell

[†] **having done pleasure** having done a good turn or favour

[†] **she** i.e. the goodwife of Galashiels

[†] **satisfy** pay

[†] **woodness** madness (*P*)

[†] **swallowed like a pot** she made a gulping noise like something cooking in a pot

[†] **a letter which John Fian, clerk, made** 'Jhone Feane … confessit … that he wrote ane letter at one convention and send it to Leith for raising ane storm there … to stay the Quene of Scotland to come in Scotland' (*CSPS* x 467)

[†] **George Mott's back house** at the rear of George Mott's house; see *News*: 'George Mott's wife dwelling in Saltpans'

[†] **Gaw** is an alternative form of the surname 'Gall', which was also pronounced 'Gaw'

[†] **webster's wife of Seton** the wife of the cloth-weaver of Seton

[†] **concluded** decided

effect[†] whereof is this: 'Marion Linkup, ye shall warn the rest of the sisters to raise the wind, this day at eleven hours, to stay the queen's coming in Scotland', like as they that were convened at the 'Pans should do for their part by east,[†31] and to meet them that were in the 'Pans, and at their meeting they should make the storm universal throughout the sea. And within eight days after the said bill was delivered, the said Agnes Sampson, Janet Campbell, John Fian, Gelie Duncan and Meg Din[32] baptized a cat in the webster's house[†] in manner following. First, two of them held a finger in the one side of the chimney crook,[†] and another held another finger in the other side, the two nebs[†] of the fingers meeting together. Then they put the cat thrice through the links of the crook[†] and passed it thrice under the chimney. Thereafter at Begie Todd's house they knit[†] to the four feet of the cat four joints of men.[†] Which being done the said Janet fetched it to Leith, and about midnight she and the two Linkups[33] and two wives called Stobie came to the pier-head and saying these words, 'See that there be no deceit among us', and they cast the cat in the sea so far as they might, which swam over and came again. And they that were in the 'Pans cast in another cat in the sea. At eleven hours after which by their ensorcery[†34] and enchantment, the boat perished betwix Leith and Kinghorn,[†] which thing the devil did and went before with a staff[†] in his hand.

(41)   Item, filed and convict for making of a picture of wax to the similitude[†] of Mr John Moscrop, father-in-law to Euphame MacCalzean at the said Euphame's desire, for the destruction of the said Mr John, and passed with the said picture to a brae[†] above a water on the lands of Keith, and raised the Sprite who conjured the picture to serve for the destruction of the said Mr John,[†] and delivered the same to Janet Drummond,[†] servitor[†] to the

---

[†] **effect** gist

[†] **by east** to the eastward (*P*)

[†] **webster's house** the cloth-weaver's house; although it is difficult to tell if 'webster' is the surname or the occupation, since the former was derived from the latter

[†] **chimney-crook** an iron hook in a kitchen chimney on which pots are hung over the fire

[†] **nebs*** tips

[†] **thrice through the links of the crook** three times past the chain of the pot-hook

[†] **knit** tied

[†] **Thereafter ... joints of men** in 1608 the Longniddry witches went to the house of Beigis Todd and there a cat was passed through Beigis Todd's crook (Pitcairn 1833: I iii 452–3)

[†] **ensorcery** sorcery; *DOST* and *OED* record neither 'insorcery' nor 'ensorcery', but *OED* gives 'ensorcell', 'to enchant'

[†] **the boat perished betwix Leith and Kinghorn** this is presumably the boat described in *News* that perished coming from Burntisland to Leith in a storm in early September 1589

[†] **staff** the devil held a white wand when he appeared to John Fian in prison (*News*)

[†] **to the similitude** in the likeness of

[†] **brae** steep bank

[†] **Item ... Mr John** 'Item, sche [i.e. Agnes Sampson] confessit that upon ane complent of ane woman of the frowardnes of her father-in-law and her earnest desyre to be quite of him, sche made ane picture of wax and raisit ane spirit at ane wattersyde beside ane breire bush, desyrit him to inchant it to serve for his destructioun' (*CSPS* x 465)

[†] **Janet Drummond** 'a Hieland wife' (Calderwood 1842–9: v 115)

[†] **servitor** servant

said Euphame, and bade her put the same under her godfather's[†][35] bed-head or bed-feet, and this she did four years syne, before the said Euphame was delivered of her last birth.

(42)   Item, filed and convict for putting of moulds[†][36] or powder, made of men's joints and members in Newton kirk, under Euphame MacCalzean's bed ten days before her birth,[†] which moulds she conjured with her prayers for staying[†] and slaking of grinding the time of her birth.[†]

(43)   Item, convict of the taking off the pain and sickness of the Lady Hermiston the night of her delivery of her birth.

(44)   Item, filed of using of a prayer and conjuration when she healed sick folks, whereof the tenor[†] follows:

Agnes Sampson's prayer and conjuration for healing of sick folks.]

All kinds of ills[37] that ever may be,
In Christ's name I conjure thee.
I conjure thee, both more and less,
With all the virtues of the mass;[38]
And right so by the nails sore[39]
That nailed Jesus[40] and no more;
And right so by the same[†] blood
That reeked[†][41] over the ruthfull rood.[†]
Forth of the flesh and of the bone[42]
And in the earth and in the stone,[†]
I conjure thee in God's name.[†]

(45)   Item, filed and convict for the charming of George Dixon's horse and cattle from dying, whereof there died thirteen kine, oxen and horses by the evil mean of John McGill. And she having received a stone[†] of cheese and half a stone of butter from the said George's wife, there died none thereafter.

(46)   Item, filed and convict for the charming of the kine and oxen of Richard Spens, farmer,[†][43] for the time at[44] Hermiston, and James White in

---

[†]   **godfather's** father-in-law's
[†]   **moulds** graveyard earth, remains of corpses
[†]   **birth** i.e. birth of her child
[†]   **staying** stopping
[†]   **slaking of grinding the time of her birth** rendering less acute the grinding pains of her labour; 'grinding' is 'in midwifery, the distinctive epithet of the pain in the first stage of labour' (*OED*)
[†]   **tenor** substance
[†]   **same** the original 'samin' preserves the metre lost in the modernisation to 'same'

[†]   **reeked** steamed
[†]   **That ... rood** that flowed over the piteous cross
[†]   **Forth ... in the stone** the ills are conjured out of the body and into the earth
[†]   **All kinds ... God's name** unless he is just giving comparable examples ('as these two prayers the Black and White Pater Noster in Meeter'), Sinclair seems to credit Agnes Sampson with another two prayers which he gives in full (1871: 22–3)
[†]   **stone** fourteen pounds in weight
[†]   **farmer** tenant farmer

Gosford, by going up between two and two of them in their byres, stroking of their backs and wombs,[†] and saying *Ave Maria* oft over.

(47)   Item, filed for being at the convention where Meg Steel, Kate Gray[† 45] and Janet Campbell was with her, and another dead sensine,[†] being altogether five in number, which was at the kirk of Garvet by east burn side.[†]

(48)   Item, for being at the convention betwix Cousland and Carberry,[†] where there was Agnes Stratton[†] together with the witch of Carberry and herself, where she quarrelled her master[†] the devil, and that in respect she had never gotten good of him, and said she would renounce him, but did it not. And he promised to her at that time that nothing should go against her.

(49)   Item, filed and convict that she with the goodwife of Spilmersford,[†] Geillis Duncan, Bessie Thomson, 'Grey Meal', Agnes Stratton, with certain others to the number of nine, convened at Foulstruther,[†] and there had there consultations how they might wrack[†] David Seton and his goods. And first Geillis Duncan, Bessie Thomson and 'Grey Meal' hauled a cord at the brig and the said Agnes Sampson cried, 'Haul! Hola!'.[†] The end of it was very heavy and when they had drawn, the devil came up at the end of it and speered[†] if they had been all good servants. Then they demanded him what way they might wrack David Seton and his goods. He gave to them clear[†] things, as it were some pieces of glass,[†] brayed[†] and mixed with some pieces of cords, and some other things among them, and bade lay a thread langis[†] the moor, and commanded to saw[†] the pieces of glass langis the moor, so that whatsoever came over first should perish suddenly. But the said David being stayed to come[†] that day, as they thought he should have done, the

---

[†] **wombs** bellies

[†] **Meg Steel, Kate Gray** the emendation here from the unlikely name 'Meg Stillcart Gray' of the MS is made on the authority of document 2, where Agnes Sampson confesses to a convention 'quhair Meg steill, Kat Gray and Jonat Campbell was with her'

[†] **another dead sensine** another person, since dead

[†] **convention ... east burn side** this meeting is dated 5 November 1589 by Bowes (*CSPS* x 464)

[†] **convention betwix Cousland and Carberry** this convention is dated 'thre in November' by Bowes (*CSPS* x 464)

[†] **Agnes Stratton** probably an error for Janet Stratton. An item in the confession of Agnes Sampson (document 2) mentions '{Agnes} |Jonat| Stratton'

[†] **quarrelled* her master** reproached her master

[†] **the goodwife of Spilsmerford** 'the goodwife of Spilmersford Mill called Meg Begtoun' (see item 40)

[†] **convened at Foulstruther** at 'Foulesutherw Mure' on 'nyne in November' 1589 according to Bowes (*CSPS* x 464)

[†] **wrack** destroy

[†] **Hola!** 'And being ask'd what words she used when she called the spirit, she said her word was "Holla, Master"' (Spottiswoode 1668: 383)

[†] **speered** asked

[†] **clear** bright

[†] **He gave ... glass** 'The devill gave them glistering things as thei had bene peces of stampit glass' (*CSPS* x 464)

[†] **brayed** ground small

[†] **langis** along

[†] **saw** cast

[†] **stayed to come** detained from coming

wrack lighted in[†] the hind's goods and his daughter, who ever since has been heavily vexed with terrible visions and apparitions, and her body tormented with an evil sprite, wherewith she has been possessed most pitifully.[†] Whereof she was the chief instrument, receiving good deed[†] from James Porteous and Richard Crummy to the end foresaid, and directed Bessie Thomson and Anny Stratton to the place of Foulstruther to crave a lock[†] salt over the door head,[†] which if they had gotten the wrackment had lighted on David Seton and his goods. And because the salt was refused, the wrackment lighted upon the hind's bairn[† 46] and his goods.

Convention at the kirk of North Berwick]

(50)   Item, filed and convict forasmuch as she confessed before his Majesty[†] that the devil in man's likeness met her going out in the fields from her own house at Keith betwix five and six at even, being her allane[†] and commanded her to be at North Berwick kirk the next night. And she passed there on horseback,[†] convoyed[†] by her godson[†] called John Couper, and lighted at the kirk-yard, or a little before she came to it, about eleven hours at even. They danced[†] along the kirk-yard. Gelie Duncan played to them on a trump;[†] John Fian, misselled,[†] led all the rest. The said Agnes and her daughter followed next. Besides, there was Kate Gray, George Mott's wife, Robert Grierson, Catherine Duncan, Bessie Wright, Isobel Gillour,[47] John Ramsay's wife, Annie Richardson, Janet Gaw, Nicoll Murray's wife tailor,[†] Christian

---

[†] **lighted in** alighted on

[†] **who ever since ... most pitifully** 'And the hynds daughter hes bene vexit with strange and terribill apparitions, as namlie of ane man callit Jhone and ane woman callit Bessie quhom sche saw and herd bot none els. Thei scratch and nip her, and pullis her with violence from the hands of them that holds her' (*CSPS* x 464–5)

[†] **good deed** benefit

[†] **lock** small quantity

[†] **door head*** threshold

[†] **bairn** i.e. Seton's daughter, who suffered visions and torment by a spirit

[†] **confessed before his Majesty** a letter of 7 December 1590 from ambassador Bowes to Burghley records that the king 'by his owne especiall travell' drew Agnes Sampson to confess (*CSPS* x 430)

[†] **being her allane** she being unaccompanied; the devil may reveal himself to witches 'upon their walking solitary in the fields' (*Demonology* II ii)

[†] **on horseback** demonologists acknowledged that conveyance to the witches' meeting need not always be supernatural (see Boguet 1929: 45–6)

[†] **convoyed** accompanied

[†] **godson** son-in-law

[†] **danced** continental demonologists describe the witches' dance at the sabbat, but that is far more grotesque than this dance in the kirk church-yard: back to back (Bodin 1580: II iii f. 82[v]); grotesque and confused (Boguet 1929: 52, 56–7); fatiguing and laboursome (Guazzo 1929: 37–8). Bodin discussed the witches' dance and said that it caused madness in men and abortions in women (Bodin 1580: II iii ff. 88–9).

[†] **trump** there were pipes at the continental sabbat for the dancing, and the devil sometimes played the flute (Boguet 1929: 56)

[†] **misselled** muffled, disguised; 'though why he should have been so does not appear' (Roughead 1936: 160); 'they dance, at their assemblies, back to back, and are now for the most part masked' (Boguet 1929: 52, 56). In his *Masque of Queenes* Jonson notes that at witches' meetings sometimes 'they are vizarded and masked' (Jonson 1969: 81.37–8).

[†] **Nicoll Murray's wife tailor** the wife of Nicoll Murray, the tailor

Carrington alias 'Licked',[48] Maisie Aichesoun, Marion Paterson, Alexander Whitelaw, Marion Nicolson, Marion Baillie, Janet Nicolson, John 'Grey Meal', Isobel Lauder, Helen White, Margaret Thomson, Marion Shiel, Helen Lauder, Archie Henillis wife, Duncan Buchanan, Marion Congilton, Bessie Gullen,[49] Bessie Brown the smith's wife, Thomas Burnhill and his wife, Gilbert McGill, John McGill, Catherine McGill, with the rest of their complices, above[†] a hundred persons, whereof there was six men and all the rest women. The women made first their homage and next the men. The men were turned nine times widdershins about, and the women six times. John Fian blew up the doors[†] and blew in the lights, which were like mickle black candles[†] sticking round about the pulpit. The devil start up[†] himself in the pulpit, like a mickle black man and called every man by his name, and every one answered, 'Here, master!' Robert Grierson being named,[†] they ran all hirdy-girdy[†] and were angry for it was promised that he should be called 'Robert the Comptroller'[†] alias 'Rob the Rower'[†] for exprem-ing[†] of his name. The first thing he[†] demanded was if they kept all promise and been good servants, and what they had done since the last time they had convened at his command.[†] They opened up the graves, two within and one without the kirk, and took of the joints[†] of their fingers, toes and nose, and parted them among them, and the said Agnes Sampson got for her part a

---

[†] **'Licked'** presumably because 'it hath lately been found that the devil doth generally mark them with a privy mark, by reason the witches have confessed themselves that the devil doth lick them with his tongue in some privy part of their body before he doth receive them to be his servants' (*News*)

[†] **Bessie Gullen** this does seem to be the reading of the ms here, although she appears as 'Bessie Cowan' in the dittay against Barbara Napier's jurors. The surname may be a version of 'Gullen' or 'Gullane', a place-name in the parish of Dirleton, East Lothian (Black 1962: 332). The preceding surname is also a place-name in East Lothian.

[†] **above** more than

[†] **blew up the doors** Stafford conjectured 'apparently preliminary ceremonies' (Stafford 1953: 99); but Danish witches blew in through the keyholes of churches and renounced God; 'the feature of blowing through the keyhole must have been part of a popular belief, but it is impossible to discover how it made its way into the witch mythology' (Ankarloo and Henningsen 1993: 358)

[†] **mickle black candles** witches offered the devil black candles at the sabbat (Guazzo 1929: 35; Daneau 1575: sig E[v])

[†] **start up** sprang up

[†] **being named** i.e. referred to by his real name

[†] **hirdy-girdy** in uproar; *DOST* cites this passage as its instance of 'hirdiegirdie'*

[†] **Comptroller** the keeper of a counter-roll serving to check a treasurer's accounts; a household officer having control of expenditure

[†] **Rower** Margaret Murray glossed this as meaning one who 'kept the rows or rolls' (Murray 1921: 85), i.e. 'treasurer', although *OED* does not give this sense. However, in the light of Grierson's other title here, 'Robert the Comptroller', this may be a better sense than 'oarsman'.

[†] **expreming** expressing in words, stating

[†] **he** i.e. the devil

[†] **The first thing ... his command** compare Boguet's account of the sabbat, 'they render to Satan an account of what they have done since the last assembly; and those are most welcome ... who have done the most mischief and wickedness' (Boguet 1929: 59)

[†] **joints*** section; *DOST* conject

winding sheet and two joints, which she tint negligently.[†] The devil commanded them to keep the joints upon them while they were dry, and then to make a powder[†] of them to do evil withall. Then he commanded them to keep his commandments, which were to do all the evil they could. Before they departed they kissed his arse. He had on him a gown and a hat[†] which were both black; and they that were assembled, part stood and part sat. John Fian was ever nearest to the devil at his left elbow; 'Grey Meal' kept the door.[†]

(51)   Item, filed and convict that when homeliness[†] was contracted betwix her and Barbara Napier in Dalkeith, Cameron, Bridgend and such places, the said Barbara lamented unto her that a man called Archie[†] had done her great wrong, and asked her counsel how to be avenged of him. Whose answer was that she should make the help she could. And after question[† 50] betwix them, the said Agnes prepared a bonny small picture of yellow wax which she enchanted and conjured under the name of 'Archie' at the east end of the dovecot of Craigmillar[†] in the devil's name, and gave power to the said picture, that as it should melt away before the fire, so should that man whose picture it was consume and pine away, while[†] he were utterly consumed. And so delivered the said picture unto the said Barbara, who said unto her, 'Take good tent[†] that nothing be wrought to stay the purpose'.

(52)   Item, filed and convict that she enchanted by her sorcery a little ring with a stone in it to the said Barbara Napier, which ring she received from the said Barbara, that she might[51] allure Dame Jean Lyon's heart (then Lady Angus)[†] to love and favour her. Which ring she sent again with her daughter within ten days thereafter to the said Barbara, to be used to the effect foresaid.

(53)   Item, for a common notorious witch, and user of sorceries and enchantments, with the invocation of the devil, her master, abusing the poor

---

[†] **she tint negligently** she took care of negligently, carelessly, i.e. inadvertently lost

[†] **powder** at the continental sabbat witches received powders and potions with which to do subsequent harm (Ginzburg 1990: 1). At the sabbat the devil gave witches a powder or ointment with which to waste the fruits of the earth and kill men and beasts (Boguet 1929: 60, 66–9).

[†] **gown and a hat** 'gown, and an Coat' (Sinclair 1871: 26)

[†] **kept the door** Calderwood reports that 'Grey Meal' tried to avoid the kiss: 'Johne Gordoun, *alias* Graymeale stood behind the doore, to eshew, yitt it behoved him also to kisse at last' (1842–9: v 116)

[†] **homeliness** familiarity, intimacy

[†] **a man called Archie** presumably 'the goodman of Cowhill's brother called Archie' mentioned in Barbara Napier's dittay

[†] **question** discussion

[†] **Craigmillar** there was a castle at Craigmillar and it was there that James spent time waiting for Anne's arrival and where he finally resolved to go and fetch her

[†] **while** until

[†] **Take good tent** take good care

[†] **Dame Jean Lyon ... then Lady Angus** Dame Jean Lyon, Lady Angus, was the eldest daughter of Patrick, 9th Lord Glamis. Her second husband, Archibald, earl of Angus, died in 1588 and the death was ascribed to witchcraft.

simple people therewith,[†] drawing them from the leaning to the mercy of God and to believe in the support of the devil.

Sentence contra Agnes Sampson, convict of witchcraft, to be burned in the castle hill etc.]

For the which cause, the said Agnes was ordained by the justice pronounced by the mouth of James Shiel, dempster,[†] to be taken to the castle of Edinburgh and there bound to a stake and worried[†] while she was dead, and thereafter her body to be burned in ashes[†] and all her moveable goods[†] to be escheat[†] and inbrought[†] to our sovereign lord's use etc.

[†] **abusing ... therewith** echoing the 1563 act which describes magical practitioners as 'abusand the pepill' and 'abusaris'

[†] **dempster** court officer who pronounced sentence as directed by the clerk or judge

[†] **worried** strangled

[†] **burned in ashes** 'Sampsoun wes brunt, and died weill' (Moysie 1830: 85); 'Sche deit maist penitentlie for her sinnis, and abusing of the simple people renuncet the devil, quhom sche oftentymes callit "Fals deceuer of God's pepill":

and had hir only refuge to God's mercie in Christ Jesus, in quhom alane sche was assurit to be saif, as that theif quha hang at his right hand' (*CSPS* x 467)

[†] **moveable goods** property other than heritage (land and houses)

[†] **escheat** forfeited; in the case of treason escheat of all property was incurred

[†] **inbrought** confiscated; 'escheat and inbrought' is a legal formula; see *DOST sv* inbrocht

Document 21

The Trial of Barbara Napier

8–10 May 1591

THE TRIAL OF BARBARA NAPIER:
8 May 1591

Witchcraft: Barbara Napier.
Convict.

Nota the parts hereof by themselves[1] *at length]*[††]

Curia Justiciarie supremi domini nostri Regis in pretorio de Edinburgh ottavo Maii 1591 per magistrum Umphridem Blynschelis justiciarum deputatum et assessores[†] *magistrum David Carnegie de Colluthie*[†] *et dominum Jacobum Melvile de Halhill.*[††]

Intrant

[†] **at length** fully

[†] **Nota … at length** the addressee and sense of this marginal instruction, not transcribed by Pitcairn, are not clear. The MS reads 'Nota the partes heirof be the selff att lenth'.

[†] *assessores* assessors sitting as advisers to the judge. This is the only occasion in the dittays of these witchcraft trials when assessors are mentioned as sitting with the judge, and is an indication of the particular significance of Barbara Napier's trial. David Carnegie and Sir James Melville were important men.

[†] *David Carnegie de Colluthie* (1575–1658), later Sir David Carnegie of Kinnaird, Lord Carnegie and earl of Southesk, titles conferred on him by King James after his accession to the English throne. He was to escort Queen Anne to Eng-

land after James's accession in 1603.

[†] *Jacobum Melvile de Halhill* Sir James Melville of Halhill (1535–1617) had been privy councillor to Mary queen of Scots and was present at James's baptism. He was a diplomat whose counsel the king constantly sought and he had been recently knighted on the king's return from Denmark. His *Memoirs* are an important source for political and historical events in late sixteenth-century Scotland where the witches are mentioned (Melville 1827: 395–7).

[†] *Curia justiciarie … de Halhill* 'The justiciary court of our sovereign lord the king, in the court of Edinburgh, 8 May 1591, by master Humphrey Blynschelis, justice depute, and assessors master David Carnegie of Colluthie and Sir James Melville of Halhill.'

Barbara Napier, spouse to Archibald Douglas, burgess of Edinburgh. Dilated of sundry points of witchcraft contained in dittay given against her by Mr David McGill of Cranstoun Riddel, advocate to our sovereign lord.

Pursuer: Mr David McGill, advocate.[2]

Prolocutors for the panel:[†]
Mr John Russell
Mr John Moscrop
William Napier, burgess of Edinburgh
Alexander Napier ⎫
Andrew Napier   ⎭ burgessses

The justice, after proponing[†] of diverse allegiances[†] by the panel against the dittay and answers made thereto at length (contained in the minutes book), ordained[3] the said Barbara to be put to the trial of an assize for the crimes contained in dittay.

Assisa

John Boig,[4] master porter[†] to
 his Majesty
George Boig, master of the ale
 cellar
Walter Bell at the Mill of Dean

Hector Clawie, burgess of the
 Canongate
James Galbraith averiman[†]
 to his Majesty

Patrick Sandilands tailor, burgess of
 Edinburgh
Mr Archibald Wilkis, burgess of
 the Canongate
Andrew Cuthbertson, burgess of
 Edinburgh
Robert Cunningham, burgess there

William Harper, burgess there

David Seton in Foulstruther
William Justice, merchant burgess of Edinburgh
John Seton, coalman[5] to his Majesty
John Mowbray, merchant burgess
David Fairley, merchant burgess

[†] **Prolocutors for the panel** spokesmen for the accused
[†] **proponing** setting forth
[†] **allegiances** allegations of right or title advanced in a court of law; clearly representations were

made to the court on Napier's behalf by her prolocutors
[†] **porter** doorkeeper
[†] **averiman** man in charge of provender for horses

Which persons of assize, being chosen, sworn and admitted, after accusation of the said Barbara by dittay of the crimes therein contained, and diverse allegiances proponed against the dittay and answers made thereto, removed out of court to the council house of Edinburgh where, after choosing of the said Robert Cunningham chancellor, they reasoned and voted upon the whole points of dittay, and being thoroughly resolved therewith re-entered again within the said court. And there by the mouth of the said chancellor found, pronounced and declared the said Barbara Napier

(1)   To be filed, culpable and convict of the seeking of consultation from Annie Sampson, a witch, for the help of Dame Jean Lyon, Lady Angus, to keep her from vomiting when she was in breeding[†] of bairn.

(2)   Item, for the consulting with the said Annie Sampson for causing of the said Dame Jean Lyon, Lady Angus, to love her and to give her the gear[†] owing her again, and giving of a ring for this purpose to the said Annie while she had sent her a courchie[†] of linen; and so for contravening of the act of parliament[†] in consulting with her and seeking of her help, being a witch.

(3)   Item, for the consulting with the said Annie Sampson anent the help of her husband Archibald Douglas, when he was in the westland[†] at the raid of Dumfries; her husband being for the time under feud with[†] the house of Cowhill.

(4)   Item, for consulting with Ritchie Graham, a necromancer and abuser[†] of the people, in seeking of help at him to her son, and gratifying[†] him therefore with three ells of bombesie[†] and five quarters of brown.[†] This was done in John Ramsay's house outwith[†] the west port of Edinburgh, incontrare[†] the tenor[†] of the act of parliament made thereanent.[†] At the which time she inquired at the said Ritchie Graham if the king would come home or not.

(5)   Item, for the haunting[†] and consulting with a witch and necromancer against the tenor of the act of parliament made thereanent.

[†] **in breeding** i.e. pregnant
[†] **gear** goods
[†] **courchie** kerchief, a sort of head-gear then worn (P)
[†] **contravening ... parliament** Barbara Napier is repeatedly accused under the part of the 1563 act which made it illegal to 'seik ony help, response or consultatioun' from witches and sorcerers, and made such consultation punishable by death
[†] **westland** west of Scotland
[†] **under feud with** at enmity with

[†] **abuser** like item 53 of Agnes Sampson's dittay, echoing the 1563 act. Graham is often described using this formula.
[†] **gratifying** rewarding
[†] **bombesie*** bombasine
[†] **brown** i.e. brown cloth
[†] **outwith** beyond
[†] **incontrare** contrary to
[†] **tenor** terms
[†] **thereanent** concerning the matter already mentioned, i.e. consulting with sorcerers
[†] **haunting** frequenting the society (P)

(6)   And acquit the said Barbara of consulting with the said Ritchie for a stolen doublet[6] of umwhile George Ker's, her husband.[†]
Acquit]

(7)   Item, for consulting with Annie Sampson anent the making of umwhile Archibald, earl of Angus's picture to his destruction.[†]
Acquit]

(8)   Item, for being at the convention of North Berwick, and the whole heads[†] of the dittay, except the heads whereof she was convict.
Acquit]

BARBARA NAPIER'S TRIAL CONTINUED:
10 May 1591

Curia justiciarie supremi domini nostri Regis, tenta in pretorio de Edinburgh decimo Maii 1591, per magistrum umphridem blynschelis justiciarium deputatum[†][7]

Barbara Napier indicted:[8] *Doom pronounced against her.]*

Intrant

Barbara Napier.

The which day a letter produced subscribed[†] by the king's Majesty and his highness' chancellor[†] for pronouncing of the doom underwritten against the said Barbara, of the which precept[†] the tenor follows:

[†] **consulting ... husband** presumably Napier is accused of consulting with Ritchie Graham about the whereabouts of stolen goods

[†] **Item ... to his destruction** Archibald Douglas, 8th earl of Angus (1555–1588), a zealous presbyterian who was a friend of Sir Philip Sidney. He had troubled relations with King James, intrigued with the English court and was part of the Gowrie conspiracy. He died at the age of thirty-three. 'His death was ascribed to witchcraft: and one *Barbary Nepair* in Edinburgh (wife to *Archibald Douglas*, of the house of Cashogle) was apprehended on suspition, but I know not whether shee was convicted of it or not: onely it was reported that she was found guiltie, and that the execution was deferred, because she was with childe, but afterward, no body insisting in the pursuit of her, she was set at libertie. *Anna Simson*, a famous witch, is reported to have confessed at her death, that a picture of waxe was brought to her, having *A. D.* written on it, which (as they said to her) did signifie *Archibald Davidson*, and (shee not thinking of the Earle of Angus, whose name was *Archbald Douglas*, and might have beene called *Davidson*, because his father's name was *David*) did consecrate or execrate it, after her forme, which (she said) if she had knowne to have represented him, she would not have done it for all the world' (Hume 1644: 432).

[†] **heads** items

[†] *Curia justiciarie ... justiciarium deputatum* 'The justiciary court of our sovereign lord the king, held in the court of Edinburgh, 10 May 1591, by master Humphrey Blynschelis, justice depute.'

[†] **subscribed** signed

[†] **his highness' chancellor** Sir John Maitland

[†] **precept** written instruction

Justice,[9] Justice clerk and your deputes, we greet you well. Forasmuch as Barbara Napier, spouse to Archibald Douglas, burgess of Edinburgh, was convict in a court of justiciary held in our tolbooth of Edinburgh the eighth day of May instant,[†] for the seeking of consultation from Annie Sampson, a witch,[10] for the help of Dame Jean Lyons, Lady Angus, to keep her from vomiting when she was in breeding of bairn, and for the consulting with the said Agnes for causing of the said Dame Jean Lyons, Lady Angus, to love her and to give her the gear owing[11] her, and giving a ring to the said Annie, which she had sent her a courchie of linen and suchlike for the consultation with the said Annie anent the help of her husband when he was in the westland at the raid of Dumfries, he being under feud for the time with the house of Cowhill; and for the consulting with Ritchie Graham, a necromancer and abuser of the people, in seeking of help of him to her son, gratifying[†] him therefore in John Ramsay's house at the west port of Edinburgh. And inquiring of him at the same time if the king would come home or not, and for consulting and haunting[†] with witches and necromancers, express against the acts of parliament made thereanent.

Whereupon[†] no doom[†] is pronounced against her as yet. Our will is herefore,[†] and we charge you that incontinent[†] after the sight hereof, ye pronounce the doom against her for the said crimes, according to the laws of our realm and acts of parliament; that is to say, that she shall be tane[†] to the castle hill of the burgh[†] of Edinburgh and there bound to a stake beside the fire and worried[†] thereat while she be dead. And thereafter her body burned in the said fire and all her moveable goods escheated to our use as convict of the said crimes; as ye will answer to us upon your office and obedience. Whereanent[†] these presents[†] shall serve you as sufficient warrant. Subscribed with our hand at Holyroodhouse the tenth day of May 1591. *Sic subscribitur James Rex, Joannes cancellarius.*[†]

Whereupon immediately thereafter the said justice depute adjudged[†] by the mouth and declaration of William Gray, dempster of the said court, who pronounced by doom.

[†] **instant** this current month
[†] **gratifying** rewarding
[†] **haunting** frequenting the society
[†] **Whereupon** upon which
[†] **doom** sentence; Barbara Napier was convicted on the first five items in the dittay, which all describe consulting with witches. This was punishable by death under the 1563 act, and the king's letter demands to know why sentence has not been passed.

[†] **herefore** therefore
[†] **incontinent** immediately
[†] **tane** taken
[†] **burgh** town
[†] **worried** strangled
[†] **Whereanent** concerning which
[†] **these presents** this document
[†] *Sic subscribitur ... cancellarius* 'Signed James Rex, J[ohn Maitland], chancellor'
[†] **adjudged** sentenced judicially

Repetition of the articles of her conviction.]
That forasmuch as the said Barbara was culpable, filed and convict by the said assize for the seeking consultation from Annie Sampson, a witch, for the help of Dame Jean Lyon, Lady Angus, to keep her from vomiting when she was in breeding of bairn. Item, for consulting with the said Annie at the Cameron for causing of the said Dame Jean Lyon, Lady Angus, to love her and to give her her gear again when she was addicted[†] to her, and giving of a little ring to the said Annie at that time off her finger, for the purpose; while the said Barbara had sent her a courchie of linen, contravening thereby the act of parliament in seeking of help from her, being a witch.

Item, for consulting with the said Annie Sampson anent the help of her husband, Archibald Douglas, who was in the west country at the raid of Dumfries under feud with the goodman of Cowhill's brother called Archie. And that for the slaughter of the goodman of Cowhill, committed by her goodman's brother, which consultation was likewise at the Cameron for the time. And likewise for the consulting with Ritchie Graham, a necromancer and abuser of the people, in seeking of help of him to her son in the dwelling house of John Ramsay outwith[†] the west port, and gratifying of him therefore incontrare[†] the tenor of the acts of parliament made thereanent. And likewise for haunting and consulting with a witch and necromancer, express against the tenor of the said acts of parliament, as at more length is contained in the dittay made thereupon.

Sentence contra Barbara Napier: to be burned in the castle hill of Edinburgh; moveables escheat.][†]
That therefore the said Barbara shall be tane to the castle hill of the burgh of Edinburgh, and there bound to a stake beside the fire and worried thereat while she be dead. And thereafter her body burned in the said fire and all her moveable goods escheat to our sovereign lord's use, as convict of the said crimes.
After pronouncing of the which doom, the said Barbara declared that she was with bairn,[†] and therefore alleged that no execution of the said doom could be used against her while she was delivered[12] of her birth, and thereupon asked instruments.[†]

[†] **addicted** indebted
[†] **outwith** beyond
[†] **incontrare** against
[†] **moveables escheat** moveable goods, that is personal belongings, confiscated
[†] **with bairn** a woman sentenced to execution used sometimes 'to plead her belly', i.e. claim she was with child, as pregnant women could not be executed until they were delivered. Compare

Calderwood's account: 'When the staike was sett in the Castell Hill, with barrells, coales, heather, and powder, and the people were looking for present executioun, her freinds alledged she was with child, wherupon the executioun was delayed, till that alledgeance was tryed' (Calderwood 1842–9: v 128)

[†] **asked instruments** (Scots law) requested a duly authenticated record of the proceedings

Document 22

The Trial of Barbara Napier's Assizers for Wilful Error

7 June 1591

Curia Justiciarie supremi domini nostri Regis, tenta in pretorio de Edinburgh septimo die mensis Junii 1591; magistros Joannem Graham et Umphridem Blynschelis Justiciarios deputatos.[†]

Intrant

For error: lord advocate against twelve of the assizers who clanged[†] *Barbara Napier of the articles of treason and witchcraft underwritten, mentioned in her dittay:]*[†]

Voluntate][†][1]

John Mowbray, merchant and burgess of Edinburgh
David Fairley,[2] merchant, burgess there
Robert Cunningham, burgess there
Andrew Cuthbertson, burgess there
Patrick Sandilands, tailor, burgess there
William[3] Justice, merchant, burgess there

[†] ***Curia justiciarie ... justiciarios deputatos*** 'The justiciary court of our sovereign lord the king, held in the court of Edinburgh, 7 June 1591; masters John Graham and Humphrey Blynschelis, justice deputes.'

[†] **clanged** acquitted

[†] **For error ... dittay:** 'In the meane tyme, these that were upon her assise were summouned to underly the law upon Moonday, the seventh of June, for wilfull errour, in cleanging her in treasoun against the king's persoun. The jurie men came in the king's will' (Calderwood 1842–9: v 128)

[†] ***Voluntate*** i.e. they will come 'in the king's will [*voluntate*]'

William Harper, merchant, burgess there
Mr Archibald Wilkie, burgess of the Canongate
Walter[4] Bell at the Mill of the Dean
Hector Clavie,[5] burgess there
John Boig, master porter to his Majesty
James Galbraith, averiman to his Majesty[†]

Dilated of manifest and wilfull error, committed by them in acquitting of Barbara Napier, spouse to Archibald Douglas, brother to the laird of Carschoggill, of the points of treason and witchcraft underwritten.

Pursuer: Mr David McGill of Cranstoun Riddel, advocate to our sovereign lord for his Highness' interest.

The same day the persons on panel[†] be dilated and accused by dittay contained in our sovereign lord's letters, purchased[†] at the instance of the advocate against them, and produced by him in judgement, whereof the tenor follows:

James, by the grace of God &c. That where Barbara Napier, spouse to Archibald Douglas, was upon the eighth day of May 1591 years, accused in a court of justiciary held in the tolbooth of Edinburgh, for seeking help, response and consultation at Richard Graham, notorious and known necromancer, a common abuser of the people, both against the will and ordinance of God and acts of parliament and law of the country. And specially forasmuch as during our sovereign lord's being at the Brig of Dee[†] before the common bell[†] rang for fear the Earl Bothwell should have entered in Edinburgh, she declared to the said Richard that she heard a woman say that our sovereign lord would get scathe[†] by a toad or gangrell,[†] and desired of him what he thought thereof, and that he would show to her his opinion thereof the morn.[†] Who[†] consulted with the Sprite[†] thereanent and received by his response that his Majesty would be troubled by convention[†] of women,

---

[†] **John Mowbray ... averiman to his Majesty**
Bowes enclosed a note of the king's oration in the tolbooth on 7 June 1591 to Burghley and in it gave a list of names of the assize: 'Archibald Wilky of Cannygate, Chauncellour or foreman; David Fernely, burgess of Edenburgh; Robert Cunyngham, Hector Clevy, James Justice, Patricke Sandilandes, John Mowbery, James Fergeson, *ibidem*; John Bell of Belles myll; John Bog, George Bog, David Seaton, John Seaton, James Carbright [Galbraith]' (*CSPS* x 522)
[†] **on panel** accused

[†] **purchased** obtained
[†] **Brig of Dee** military encounter between the catholic earls Huntly and Errol and King James at the Brig of Dee, April 1589
[†] **common bell** the bells in all the towns and villages
[†] **would get scathe** would be harmed
[†] **gangrell*** toad
[†] **the morn** the next day
[†] **Who** i.e. Ritchie Graham
[†] **Sprite** the devil (*P*)
[†] **convention** an assembly, meeting

through the dropping[†] of a toad. And also Richard, laughing upon her, declared there at that same time that she, Effie MacCalzean and Donald Robson[†] should be three of the doers of it. Which when she heard she shook her head, which was affirmed by the said Richard Graham in her and the said persons' presence.

And siclike[†] the said Barbara was accused that she gave her presence[†] in the most devilish and treasonable convention held by her and her complices in the devil's name upon Lammas Even[†] last, at the new haven called Acheson's Haven,[†] betwix Musselburgh and Prestonpans, since his Majesty's come forth of Denmark; where was assembled nine principals: to wit, Agnes Sampson, Janet Stratton, Euphame MacCalzean, herself, John Fian, Robert Grierson, George Mott's wife in Preston, Margaret Thomson in Stirling and Donald Robson. Which nine persons the devil, who was with them in likeness of a black man, thought most meet[†] to do the turn for the which they were convened. And therefore he set them nine nearest to himself in a company;[†] and they, together with the wife of Saltoun Mill and the rest of the inferiors, to the number of thirty persons standing scarce the length of a board[†] from the foresaid nine persons, in another company. Agnes Sampson proponed the destruction of his Highness' person, saying to the devil 'We have a turn ado,[†] and we would fain[†] be at it, if we could; and therefore help us to it'. The devil answered he should do what he could, but it would be long to because it would be thwarted.[†6] And he promised to her and them a picture[†] of wax and ordained her and them to hang, roast and drop a toad,[†] and to lay the drops of the toad mixed with strong wash,[†] an adder skin, the thing in the forehead of a new-foaled foal,[†] in his Highness' way, where his Majesty

---

[†] **dropping** dripping
[†] **Donald Robson** is this 'Donald the Man, the gleed ['gleyit', squint-eyed] Hieland witche' (Calderwood 1842–9: v 129)?
[†] **siclike** similarly
[†] **gave her presence** attended
[†] **Lammas Even** 31 July, the evening before Lammas, 1 August
[†] **new haven called Acheson's Haven** the harbour of Prestonpans, now called Morrison's Haven, but still called new haven or Acheson's Haven at the beginning of the eighteenth century (Carlisle 1813: ii *sv* Preston Pans). Acheson's Haven is the name shown on Blaeu's map 1654.
[†] **meet** suitable
[†] **company** group
[†] **board** table
[†] **turn ado** job to be done
[†] **fain** gladly
[†] **thwarted** frustrated (*P*)
[†] **picture** image
[†] **drop a toad** allow the liquid to drop from a dead toad
[†] **strong wash** stale urine (*P*), used for bleaching clothes
[†] **thing ... foal** there were three possible interpretations of the Greek word *hippomanes* ('horse-madness') found in classical literature. One was a growth in a new-born foal's forehead (Pliny, *Natural History* VIII lxvi; Lucan, *Pharsalia* VI 454–8). It was credited with magical properties but was usually used in love magic: 'There is in the Frogges side, a bone caled *Apocynon*, and in the heade of a young Colte, a bounch named *Hippomanes*, both so effectuall, for the obteining of love, that who so getteth either of them, shall winne any that are willyng' (Lyly 1902: ii 115). On the *hippomanes* see Forbes 1935. Ritchie Graham confessed to knowledge of details of *maleficia* against the king: the making of a wax image, 'one tode to be enchanted and hanged up, and a peece of the head of a yonge calfe newly calfed to be taken' (*CSPS* x 501–2).

would gang in-owre or out-owre,[†] or in any passage where it might drop upon his Highness' head or his body, for his Highness' destruction, that another might have ruled in his Majesty's place,[†] and the ward[†] might have gone to the devil. At the which convention his Highness' name was pronounced in Latin, and Agnes Sampson was appointed to make the picture and to give it to the devil to be enchanted. Which she made indeed and gave it to him, and he promised to give it to the said Barbara, and to Effie MacCalzean at the next meeting to be roasted.[†] Margaret Thomson was appointed to drop the toad.[†] There was one appointed[†] to seek some of his Highness' linen cloths to do the turn with. And Gelie Duncan upon the fifteenth day of December last was, in the said Barbara's face[†] and Effie MacCalzean, avowed on them both at the first sight she saw her after her coming to the abbey[†] and before she had spoken three perfect speeches afore her, affirmed that Agnes Sampson met with her and the said Effie in the said Barbara's own house, and the said Gelie Duncan and Bessie Thomson being there also, together with John Fian who said to Gelie that he would go west to his father and eiked[†] further that there was a toad hanging by the heels three nights, and dropped betwix three oyster shells and nine stones sotten[†] three nights. At what time no man looked[†] or suspected to have heard any such thing, as the particular depositions of the said Donald Robson and Janet Stratton, who constantly abaid at the same,[†] which was repeated by the advocate. The depositions of Gelie Duncan and Richard Graham, every one for their own parts and circumstances being confronted together,[†] manifested and made plain.

And, siclike the said Barbara was accused that she gave her bodily presence upon Allhallow Even lastwas, 1590 years, to the frequent[†] convention held at the kirk of North Berwick, where she danced endlong[†] the kirkyard, and Gelie Duncan played on a trump.[†] John Fian, miselled,[†] led the ring; Agnes

---

[†] **gang in-owre or out-owre** go backwards or forwards

[†] **another … place** this must be an insinuating allusion to Bothwell

[†] **ward** glossed as 'warld' by *P*; perhaps used in literal sense of rule, government

[†] **picture … roasted** the most famous precedent for this attempt on a Scottish king's life by roasting a wax image is the witches of Forres and their melting before the fire a wax image of King Duff (Sinclair 1871: 101). The story is given in the 1587 edition of Holinshed's *Chronicles* (Bullough 1957–75: vii 479–80).

[†] **drop the toad** cause the toad to drip

[†] **one appointed** 'one John Kers, … attendant in

his Majesty's chamber' according to *News*

[†] **in … face** in the presence of the said Barbara

[†] **abbey** ?the abbey of Holyrood

[†] **eiked** said in addition

[†] **sotten** (past participle of 'seethe') cooked or steeped in liquid

[†] **looked** anticipated

[†] **abaid at the same** stood by their statements

[†] **confronted together** brought face to face with each other

[†] **frequent** well-attended

[†] **endlong** along the length of

[†] **trump** Jew's harp. Calderwood (1842–9: v 116) reports the devil played the trump.

[†] **miselled** disguised, muffled, masked (*P*)

Sampson and her daughters and all the rest following the said Barbara, to the number of seven score of persons. Of the which number was Effie MacCalzean, Katherine Gray, Margaret Aitcheson, Donald Robson, Robert Grierson, Katherine Wallace, Meg Begtoun, Janet Campbell, Janet Logan, John Gordon *alias* 'Grey Meal', the porter's wife of Seton, Janet Stratton, Bessie Thomson, Catherine Duncan, Bessie Wright, Isobel Gyllour,[7] John Ramsay's wife, Annie Ritcheson, Janet Gall, Nicoll Murray's wife tailor, Christian Carrington *alias* 'Licked', Masie Aitcheson, Marie Paterson, Alexander Whitelaw, Marion Nicolson, Marion Baillie, Janet Nicolson, Isobel Lauder, Helen White, Margaret Thomson, Marion Shaw, Helen Lauder, Malie Geddie, Duncan Buchanan, Marion Congilton, Bessie Cowan, Bessie Brown, the smith's wife, Thomas Brownhill and his wife, Gilbert McGill, John and Katherine McGill, with divers others to the number above written. At the which place and time the women made first their homage and were turned six times widdershins about. John Fian blew up the kirk doors and blew in the lights, which were like mickle black candles held in an old man's hand[†] round about the pulpit. And the devil start up[†] in the pulpit, like a mickle black man, with a black beard sticking out like a goat's beard, and a high-ribbed nose falling[†] down sharp like the beak of a hawk, with a long rumple,[†] clad in a black tatty[†] gown, and an evil-favoured skull-bonnet[†] on his head.[†] And having[8] a black book in his hand, called on every one of them, desiring them all to be good servants to him and he should be a good master to them, and they should have enough and never want for.[†] Robert Grierson and John Fian stood[9] on his left hand, and the said Robert found great fault with the devil, and cried out that all which was beside might hear,[†] because his Highness' picture was not given them as was promised: the said Effie MacCalzean remembering and bidding the said Robert Grierson to speer[†] for the picture, meaning his Majesty's picture, which

---

[†] **in an old man's hand** compare Jonson, *Masque of Queenes* 'in her hand a torch made of a dead man's arm' (Jonson 1969: 83.88–9)

[†] **start up** sprang up

[†] **falling** ?sloping

[†] **rumple** rump, tail

[†] **tatty** ragged

[†] **evil-favoured skull-bonnet** an ill-favoured or ugly sort of skull-cap (*P*). Calderwood reports the devil 'in the likenesse of a man with a redde cappe, and a rumpe at his taill' (Calderwood 1842–9: v 116).

[†] **And the devil ... head** Sir James Meville interviewed some of the participants at the alleged North Berwick meeting. The devil appeared in the pulpit 'cled in a blak gown, with a blak hat upon his head ... having lyk leicht candelis rond about him'. He was 'cauld lyk yce; his body was hard lyk yrn, as they thocht that handled him; his faice was terrible, his noise lyk the bek of ane egle, gret bournyng eyn; his handis and legis wer herry, with clawes upon his handis, and feit lyk the griffon, and spak with a how [hollow] voice' (Melville 1827: 395–6).

[†] **never want for** 'These that had beene bussie in their craft, he said were his beloved, and promised that sould want nothing they needed' (Calderwood 1842–9: v 116)

[†] **that all ... might hear** so that all those who were close by might hear

[†] **speer** ask

should have been roasted. Robert Grierson said these words: 'Where is the thing ye promised?', meaning the picture of wax devised for roasting and undoing of his Highness' person, which Agnes Sampson gave to him. And Robert cried to have the turn done,[†] yet his Highness' name was not named, while they that were women named him, craving in plain terms his Highness' picture. But he answered, it should be gotten the next meeting, and that he would hold the next assembly for that cause the sooner: it was not ready at that time. Robert Grierson answered, 'Ye promised twice, and beguiled us', and four honest-like women[†] were very earnest and instant[†] to have it. And the said Barbara and Effie MacCalzean got then a promise of the devil that his Highness' picture should be gotten to them two, and that right soon. And this matter of his Highness' picture was the cause of that assembly, in token whereof the devil commanded the said Barbara and all her company to keep his commandments, which were to do all the evil they could. Also there was then three dead corpses tane up and jointed: the nails and joints were parted[†] among them. The devil commanded them to keep the joints upon them while the same dried, and then[10] to make powder thereof to do evil with. After the which, their homage being made as the fashion is in kissing of the devil's arse, they parted for that time without any more done. Except that Effie MacCalzean, Robert Grierson and the said Barbara happened to be named[†] there, which offended all the company, and that they should not have been named with their own names, but[11] Grierson to have been called 'Rob the Rower', Effie to be called 'Can' and the said Barbara to be called 'Naip'.[†] And true this is and proven by Donald Robson, Janet Stratton, Gelie Duncan and Bessie Thomson, who are yet on life.[†] Which being put to the knowledge of an inquest, they[†] notwithstanding, upon the ninth day of the month and year of God foresaid, clanged and acquit by favour and partial means the said Barbara Napier.

That forasmuch as during his Majesty's being at the Brig of Dee the day before the common bell rang for fear the earl Bothwell should have entered in Edinburgh, she declared to the said Richard Graham that she heard a

---

[†] **have the turn done** have the job done
[†] **honest-like women** women of respectable appearance, well-dressed women, perhaps implying that there were prosperous women like Barbara Napier and Effie MacCalzean there; compare the woodcut in *News*, where the women are shown as well-dressed
[†] **instant** insistent
[†] **parted** divided up
[†] **named** i.e. called by their real names
[†] **'Rob the Rower ... Naip'** Scottish witches seem sometimes to have taken nicknames related to their real ones, see the deposition of Annabil Stewart in 1677 that 'the new name the devil gave her, was *Annippy*' (Sinclair 1871: 10). On the continent witches supposedly renounced their baptism, were rebaptised in the devil's name and were given a new name (Boguet 1929: 24–5) and 'this is the reason why witches usually have two names' (Bodin 1580: f. 80ᵛ).
[†] **on life** alive
[†] **they** i.e. the assize

woman say that the king would get scathe by a toad or gangrell,[†] desired of him what he thought thereof and that he would show to her his opinion thereof the morn.[†] Who consulted with the Sprite thereanent, who received by his response that his Majesty would be troubled by convention of women through dropping of a toad and also Richard, laughing upon her, declared to her at the same time that she, Barbara Napier, Effie MacCalzean and Donald Robson should be three of the doers of it; which when she heard she shook her head, which was affirmed by the said Richard Graham in her and the assize presence.[†]

And siclike has clanged the said Barbara of the convention held by her and her complices upon Lammas Even at the new haven called Acheson's Haven, for dropping of a toad and consulting for a picture concerning our person.[†] The same being verified to the assize in the said Barbara's presence by Donald Robson, Janet Stratton, Richard Graham, Gelie Duncan. And siclike has clanged and acquit the said Barbara anent the convention held upon Allhallow Even chiefly for his Majesty's picture, notwithstanding the depositions and verifications of Donald Robson and Janet Stratton, confronted with the said Barbara in presence of the said assize, openly and constantly abiding at[†] the said depositions. The depositions of the said Gelie Duncan, Bessie Thomson who are yet on life where through they and every one of them could pretend no ignorance at the least, neither of law nor conscience, could have acquit her thereof, the same being verified by the constant assertion and deposition of one part of the witnesses being present in judgement for the time as is above written, and by the depositions of the other part produced.

And therefore did manifestly and wilfully err contrar the laws and practic[†] of the realm, incurring thereby the horrible crime of perjury *et penam temere jurantium super assisam*.[†]

And they being required by the justice, his Majesty being sitting in judgement,[†] whether they would abide the trial of the law and of an assize

---

[†] **gangrell** as *P* notes, here the evidence is recapitulated

[†] **the morn** the next day

[†] **her ... presence** i.e. in her presence and that of the assize. Ritchie Graham has been brought to the trial to affirm his testimony.

[†] **our person** i.e. the king

[†] **abiding at** standing by

[†] **practic** normal practice

[†] **et penam ... assissam** the punishment of those who heedlessly conspire when serving on an assize

[†] **sitting in judgement** in court; this indicates the unusual presence of the king himself in the court room. As James admitted in his oration to the assize at the tolbooth on 7 June 1591, 'it hath not bene the custome that the Kings of this realme my forebeers should sit in persone upon cryminall causes, neither have I my selfe done it save onely twise' (*CSPS* x 523).

for the said crimes, or come in will[†] therefore, after long deliberation and consultation they refused to abide the trial of an assize therefore, but came *simpliciter*[†] in his Highness' will for ignorant error committed by them in acquitting of the said Barbara of the crimes and points of dittay above rehearsed.

The king's will declared]

Which will his Majesty publicly in judgement in presence of his Highness' lords of secret council[†] declared to be, that he understanding that it was not wilful error they committed in acquitting in manner foresaid. And therefore ordained that the foresaid persons and each one of them shall be assoiled[†] from all penalty in body, goods, gear or fame[†] [12] in time coming. Upon the declaration of the which will they, and each one of them, asked act and instrument.

[†] **come in will** submit themselves to the king's will; 'to come in will' is now an obsolete Scottish expression (*OED* 'will' *sb.* 17b)

[†] *simpliciter* (Latin) unconditionally [legal]

[†] **lords of secret council** privy councillors

[†] **assoiled** acquitted, declared free

[†] **goods, gear or fame** goods, possessions or reputation

Document 23

The Trial of Euphame MacCalzean

9–15 June 1591

THE TRIAL OF EUPHAME MACCALZEAN
9 June 1591

Witchcraft: Euphame MacCalzean burned quick.][†]

Curia Justiciarie supremi domini nostri regis, tenta in pretorio de Edinburgh nono Junij 1591 per magistros Joannem Graham et Umphridem Blynscheles Justiciarios deputatos etc.[†]

Intrant

Euphame MacCalzean, spouse to Patrick MacCalzean alias Moscrop.
Dilated of certain treasonable conspiracies, enterprised[†] by witchcraft, to have destroyed our sovereign lord's person and bereft his Majesty of his life, by that shameful and extraordinary means, and being art and part[†] thereof upon the counsel and consultation with divers other witches of her society and divers other crimes of witchcraft committed by her, at length specified in the dittay made thereupon.
Pursuer: Mr David McGill of Cranstoun Riddel, advocate to our sovereign lord.[1]

[†] **quick** alive
[†] ***Curis justiciarie ... deputatos &c*** 'The justiciary court of our sovereign lord the king, held in the court of Edinburgh, 9 June 1591, by masters John Graham and Humphrey Blynschelis,

justice deputes etc.'
[†] **enterprised** attempted
[†] **being art and part** in the capacity of an accessory or accomplice (legal)

Prolocutors for the panel:[†]
Mr John Moscrop
Mr David Ogilvy
Robert Ker, in Duddingston
Henry Nisbett, burgesss of Edinburgh
Mr John Russell
Mr John Skene

Compeared the said Mr David McGill, advocate, and produced a dittay made at length against the said Euphame and contracted in these heads[†] underwritten, to be put to the knowledge of an assize, whereof the tenor follows:

Euphame MacCalzean, her dittay.]

1 Article]

(1)   Euphame MacCalzean, ye are indicted and accused for art and part of the bewitching of Michael Marjoribanks by striking of him by witchcraft with an extraordinary disease, by taking of the power and hability[†] of his right side, arm and leg from him by yourself and your complices by your mean,[†] committed in April 1577.

(2)   Item, indicted for consulting with Catherine Campbell an Irish woman, known to be a notorious witch, and entertaining her in your own house and Barbara Tour's house, seeking help of her to your bairns, specially to help your son, Thomas, by your art, to whom ye sent his sark to that effect with Helen Inglis, your servant, and two thirty shilling pieces[2] for her help.

(3)   Item, for consulting with the said Catherine anent the bewitching and slaughter of Patrick Moscrop, your husband, whereby ye might get another goodman,[†] and consulting with her whom ye should marry.

(4)   Item, indicted of art and part of the trafficking[†] with Agnes Somervall, spouse to Gilbert Anderson in Dunferm-line, a common trafficker[†] with witches, inquiring of her if she knew any witty[†] or skilful women in the country that will either cause your husband love you or else get your will of him. To whom ye gave two fair clean sarks of your husband's to be carried over the water[†] to be enchanted by them. At the same time your husband fell in sickness. Which sarks she took with her to that effect and brought home again, by her enchanted. And thereby seeking help, response and consultation of witches to the destruction of your spouse by witchcraft.

[†]   **Prolocutors for the panel** spokesmen for the accused

[†]   **contracted in these heads** brought together under these main headings. 'This is stated to be only an abstract of the dittay and contractit in thir heidis' (*P*).

[†]   **hability** use

[†]   **mean** agency

[†]   **goodman** husband

[†]   **trafficking** dealing

[†]   **common trafficker** one who habitually deals with

[†]   **witty** wise

[†]   **over the water** i.e. over the Firth of Forth

(5)   Item, indicted of art and part of the poisoning of the said Patrick Moscrop, your husband, upon deadly malice contracted against him the first year of your marriage, by giving of him[3] of poison, and cast the rest thereof in the closet,[†] whereby his face, neck, hands and whole body brake out in red spots; which poison was expelled by his youth. And seeing the same took no effect as ye devised, ye still continued in your undutiful behaviour and impatience to see him on life[†] whom ye pressed[†] by all means possible to cut away.[†] The said Patrick, being wearied of his life by the daily trouble he had in your company, was compelled for safety of his life to expone[†] himself to the seas and to pass to France in your default,[†] like as ye to be quit[†] of him spared not in all parts to seek a hundred crowns for his furniture[†] away, and spared not speak that your goodman was passing to France and bade the fiend go with him.

(6)   Item, indicted and accused that increasing in your devilish consultation with witches to the wrack and destruction of the said Patrick, your husband, and after he had returned out of France, ye still invying[†] his health and seeking to destroy him by witchcraft foresaid, ye sent your said husband's doublet with Josias Couper, your servant, early in the morning to Catherine Campbell, the witch-wife dwelling in the Canongate. Which doublet the said witch sprinkled with blood and enchanted it with other sorceries, and rendered it again to the said Josias, your servant, which he brought home afore his master's rising. After the which, your husband contracted a heavy[†] disease and pined therein many months, which was no natural sickness, as was testifed and declared by the chirurgeons. Like as[†] the said consultation was revealed thereafter by the said Josias, your servant, for the discharge of his conscience;[†] and he for that cause passed off[†] the country to Danzig.[4]

(7)   Item, indicted that to make you[5] perfect and well-skilled in the said art of witchcraft, ye[6] caused another witch who dwelled in Saint Ninian's Row inaugurate[†7] you in the said craft with the girth of a great beaker,[†8] turning the same oft over your head and neck and oftimes round about your head. Which was revealed by Marion Love, daughter to Catherine Lyell younger, to the said Catherine her mother.

---

† **closet** privy
† **impatience ... on life** impatience at seeing him alive
† **pressed** endeavoured
† **cut away** remove
† **expone** expose
† **in your default** because of your wrongdoing, misbehaviour
† **quit** free
† **furniture** 'his outfit and furnishing for his voyage' (P)

† **invying** being vexed at
† **heavy** serious
† **Like as** in the same way
† **for ... conscience** for the easing of his conscience
† **passed off** left
† **inaugurate** formally instal; 'inaugurate' is a verb generally used of a monarch or minister, so its use here implies a parody of a political or religious ceremony
† **girth of a great beaker** ?the rim of a large vessel

(8)   Item, ye are indicted that ye, having conceived a deadly malice against the said Catherine and Walter Scott, her spouse, for declaration of your inauguring foresaid, seen and perceived by the said Marion Love, ye by your art of sorcery and witchcraft bewitched her and her husband in their bodies, goods and gear; and so for art and part of bewitching of the said Catherine Lyell and Walter Scott in their bodies, goods and gear, to their great scathe, hurt and heirship.[†]

(9)   Item, indicted of bewitching, by your art of sorcery, of umwhile John Houston, son to William Houston, your husband's sister son, being a young man of seventeen years of age, by the which witchcraft he died. And so for art and part of the cruel slaughter and murder of him, only for revealing of your undutiful behaviour to your husband, he being familiar in your house, as the tokens[†] contained in the said dittay at more length verifies.

(10)   Item, indicted that ye having conceived a deadly malice against Janet Cockburn, daughter to John Cockburn, maltman[†] in Haddington, for the down-bringing[†] of your purse, belt, glass and clothes out of the chamber; and having laid down the same upon the board,[†] your husband took up your said purse and would have opened it, but opened it not; for the which ye said to the said Janet, 'Well maiden, have ye letten[†] this be done? Ye shall repent it from your heart'. Catherine Carruthers, alias called Irish Janet, and ye laid in her way and passage such enchanted moulds and powder that in short space thereafter there came a swarf[†] over her heart and such a flaffing[†] in her breast as it had been some quick thing peching[†] and panting, heaving up her body; wherewith she is diseased half an hour every time. She takes it[†] oft in the night and oft in the day, continuing sometimes half a day, having more strength nor[†] her accustomed manner in time of her health. And so for laying of moulds and powder by witchcraft and inchantment in the said Janet Cockburn's gait,[†] by the which she conceived a sickness and was mickle troubled therewith, and is yet, by your art of witchcraft.

(11)   Item, for the cruel slaughter and destruction of umwhile Euphame Punfray by witchcraft.

(12)   Item, for alluring by your devilish witchcraft, enchantment and incantation, of Joseph Douglas of Pumpherston[9] to love you, under colour[†] and cloak[†] of[10] marriage with your daughter, and for the destruction of your

---

[†] **heirship** harm
[†] **tokens** indications
[†] **maltman** dealer in malt
[†] **down-bringing** bringing downstairs
[†] **board** table (*P*)
[†] **letten** let
[†] **swarf** swooning (*P*)
[†] **flaffing*** fluttering

[†] **some quick thing peching** some living thing puffing
[†] **she takes it** she is affected by it
[†] **nor** than
[†] **gait** path
[†] **colour** pretence
[†] **cloak** disguise

husband. In token whereof ye gave him a craig chain,[†] two belt chains, a ring, an emirent[†] and others your jewels.[†]

(13)   Item, indicted for the consulting with Janet Cunningham in the Canongate, also called 'Lady Bothwell', an old indicted witch of the finest champ,[†] eighteen years syne or thereby,[†] for to have poisoned Joseph Douglas of Pumpherston, and that by a potion of composed[†] water which ye sent John Tweddall your servant for to be brought up to Barbara Tour's house in a chopin stoup,[†] which was received by him and delivered to the said Barbara.

(14)   Item, indicted and accused for sending with Janet Drummond, your servant, with certain witchcraft of deliberate mind[†] to have bewitched Marie Sandelands, a maiden at that time under promise of marriage to Joseph Douglas of Pumpherston, she being then in the Braidshaw, and to dissuade her first from the said promise of marriage of the said Joseph because he had given his promise and faith to another gentlewoman, and that he had the glengor[†] himself.

(15)   Item, indicted that by your art of witchcraft ye travailed[†] to stay and impede the marriage of the laird of Pumpherston with Marie Sandelands, and to that effect directed Janet Drummond, sometime your nurse, with some of your charms and enchantments to offend[†] the person of the said Marie, whereby the said marriage might have been stayed.

(16)   Item, indicted of the seeking help, consultation and response from Annie Sampson as a witch and known to be a notorious witch, for recovering of your jewels and emirents again from the laird of Pumpherston and that by frequent sending of Janet Drummond, your sometime nurse, to the said Annie to that effect above seven times. And in the one of the times she raised the Sprite by voice and not bodily,[†] who declared that the same should be delivered to the said Janet Drummond, their messenger, sent to seek the response.

(17)   Item, indicted of the bewitching of two of the laird of Pumpherston's bairns (his eldest son and daughter) to the death.

(18)   Item, indicted of consulting and seeking help at the said Annie Sampson, a notorious witch, for relief of your pain in the time of the birth

---

[†]   **craig chain** neck chain (*P*)
[†]   **emirent** emerald; *P*'s reading and gloss have been adopted, as the context for this instance and the other two instances of the word make it probable. However, the word in the MS looks like 'emdent' in all three cases.
[†]   **others your jewels** other of your jewels
[†]   **champ*** style
[†]   **eighteen years ... thereby** eighteen years ago, or thereabouts; i.e. about 1573
[†]   **composed** compounded from various substances?

[†]   **a chopin stoup** a drinking-vessel containing a Scottish half-pint, which is roughly equivalent to an English quart; *DOST* cites this passage as its illustration of 'chopene'*
[†]   **with deliberate mind** with a deliberate intention
[†]   **glengor** venereal disease; '*Lues venerea*' P
[†]   **travailed** laboured
[†]   **offend** injure
[†]   **by voice ... bodily** i.e. the devil was audible but not visible

of your two sons, and receiving from her to that effect a bored stone,[†] to be laid under the bolster put under your head, enchanted moulds and powder put in a piece paper[†] to be used and rolled[† 11] in your hair; and at the time of your drowse[† 12] your goodman's sark to be presently tane of him and laid wambled[† 13] under your bed-feet. The which being practised by you, as ye had received the same from the said Annie and information of the use thereof, your sickness was cast off you unnaturally in the birth of your first son upon a dog which ran away and was never seen again. And in the birth of your last son the same practice foresaid was used, and your natural and kindly[†] pain unnaturally cast of you upon the wanton[†] cat in the house, which likewise was never seen thereafter.

(19)   Item, indicted for art and part of the consulting with the said Annie Sampson for the destroying of Mr John Moscrop, your father-in-law, by witchcraft, about four years syne or thereby. And to this effect, sending with Janet Drummond, your servant, a picture of wax sent in a buist[†] enclosed within a goose to the said Annie, and a serviette[†] with beef wambled about the goose; which picture the said Annie gave to the devil to be enchanted. And the same, being enchanted by him, was sent home again to you with the said Janet Drummond for doing of the turn, as the said Annie declared that it should serve.

(20)   Item, indicted for your devilish consultation with Agnes Sampson, partly by yourself and partly by the trafficking of your old agent Janet Drummond, how to be revenged upon Mr John McGill's wife. And resolution being tane with Agnes Sampson, a notorious witch, she sent you some witchcraft and enchantments with the said Janet Drummond, which ye cast in at Mr John McGill's window, which was a bairn's apron and half-cloth[†] with something bound therein. And this matter being revealed by others your servants,[†] caused the said Janet Drummond to deny the same when it was laid to her charge, like as she has confessed that she was daily and nightly troubled with terrible spectacles and visions, as she visibly in a chamber floor of yours at two after noon saw a naked man stand[14] in the midst of the said chamber with a white sheet about him, as also Janet Aitcheson your servant, being sent at twelve hours at even to draw a drink, saw likewise a naked man behind her with a sark, the sleeves of the sark upon his legs and the tail about his head,[†] which terrified her. Which vision's

---

[†] **bored stone** 'Bored stone, probably a Fairy-stone,—a stone having a natural hole formed by the action of water, &c' (*P*)

[†] **piece paper** piece of paper

[†] **rolled** rolled up

[†] **drowse** fainting-fit; birth-pangs or throes (*P*)

[†] **wambled** rolled up; folded up (*P*)

[†] **kindly** natural

[†] **wanton** frisky, skittish

[†] **buist** small box; box chest (*P*)

[†] **serviette** table napkin

[†] **bairn's apron and half-cloth** a child's apron or pinafore, and neckcloth

[†] **others your servants** by your other servants

[†] **the sleeves ... his head** i.e. he is wearing the shirt upside-down

man[†] have proceeded of your devilish art of witchcraft. As also the said Janet Aitcheson was troubled with urchins,[†][15] which witchcraft foresaid was cast in again at the said Mr John McGill's window and being found and opened out kithed[†] to be a picture of clay in portrait[†][16] of Elizabeth Home, spouse to the said Mr John, sewed in a winding sheet, about the which was an old black mutch[†] wambled, therein inclosed five clues[†] of sundry colours of worset,[†] as of black, red, orange, yellow and blue, which sorceries Agnes Sampson confessed ye made yourself, as also the said Agnes Sampson confessed that Janet Drummond brought to her the same old mutch which she enchanted. Like as also the said Janet Drummond has confessed the carrying thereof to the said Agnes.

(21)   Item, for making of a picture of flour and clay for bewitching of Elizabeth Home, spouse to Mr John McGill, and causing cast the same in at the said Mr John's kitchen window for that effect.

(22)   Item, indicted for art and part of the slaughter and destruction by your devilish craft of witchcraft and enchantment of Lilias MacCalzean, daughter to Mr Henry MacCalzean, a bairn of six year old, and that by rubbing of her face with your napkin[†] upon a Sunday afternoon, when she fell upon the calsay[†] at your close head[†] thereby.

(23)   Item, indicted and accused of the conventicle[†] had at North Berwick kirk twenty days before Michaelmas 1590 and there inquiring for the king's picture, given by Annie Sampson to the devil to be enchanted for the treasonable destruction of the king.

Treason]

(24)   Item, indicted for being at the convention held at the new haven called the Fiery Hills[17] at Lammas lastwas to the effect immediately above written.

Treason]

(25)   Item, indicted and accused for a convention held by you and other notorious witches, your associates, at the Broomhills which ye and they took the sea, Robert Grierson being your admiral and masterman,[†] passed over the sea in riddles[†] to a ship where ye entered with the devil your master therein, where after ye had eaten and drunken, ye cast over a black dog that

---

[†] **vision's man** i.e. visionary man

[†] **urchins** goblins; 'Urchions, hedgehogs ... perhaps the term is used for imps of the devil' (*P*); compare 'Urchins / Shall forth at vast of night, that they may work / All exercise on thee' (Shakespeare 1988: *The Tempest* I ii 328–30)

[†] **kithed** was revealed

[†] **a picture of clay in portrait** i.e. a clay image portraying Elizabeth Home

[†] **mutch** cap; *DOST* records this passage as an illustration of 'much'*

[†] **clues** balls of thread

[†] **worset** worsted yarn

[†] **napkin** pocket handkerchief?

[†] **calsay** stretch of paving

[†] **close head** end of the passageway opening on to the street

[†] **conventicle** meeting, often of a clandestine or illegal kind

[†] **masterman** leader

[†] **riddles** flat-bottomed sieves

skipped[†] under the ship, and thereby ye hewing[†] the devil your master therein, who drowned the ship by tumbling,[†] whereby the queen was put back by storm.

(26)   Item, indicted for consulting with the said Annie Sampson, Robert Grierson and divers other witches for the treasonable staying of the queen's homecoming by storm and wind, and raising of storm to that effect, or else to have drowned her Majesty and her company by conjuring of cats and casting of them in the sea at Leith and the back of Robert Grierson's house. *To stay the queen's homecoming].*

(27)   Item, indicted for art and part of the destruction of a boat betwix Leith and Kinghorn and threescore of persons therein, by your convention, by other witches, and by your and their witchcraft, as is notorious.[†]

(28)   Item, for a common witch.

The which day, the said dittay being read to the said Euphame in judgement, as it was produced at length by the advocate and drawn summarily in heads, as is above mentioned, after divers objections made against the same by her and her prolocutors and divers protestations made in her name and answers made thereto by the advocate,[†] the justice found by interlocutor[†] that the said heads should be put to the knowledge of an assize; and the assize being chosen that she might propone[†] her defences to the said assize.

Assisa

James Johnston of Elphinstone	Alexander Fairley of Braid
( ) Anstruther younger of that ilk	( ) Graham of Knockdolian
Mr William Leslie of Cunlie	David Preston of Craigmillar
John Logan, portioner[†] of Couston	( ) Balfour of Bandon
James Inglis, merchant, burgess of Edinburgh	David Balfour of Bello

James Elphinstone in Bogie
Clemmett Kincaid of the Coitts
George Mowtray of Seafield

[†] **skipped** slipped
[†] **hewing** an alternative forming of 'howing', a call to incite sailors or horses to action
[†] **tumbling** rolling about
[†] **Item ... as is notorious** for the sinking of this ship in early September 1589, see *News*
[†] **after ... advocate** 'no notice is preserved in the Record, of the long pleadings which occupied

the whole of this and the two following. Neither has any record been kept of the evidence adduced' (*P*).
[†] **interlocutor** judgement made in the course of a suit
[†] **propone** set out
[†] **portioner** joint heir

John Drummond of Slipperfield
James Somervall of Humbie

The justice deputes by reason of divers objections made by the panel against the points of dittay above written to the assize, and answers made thereto by the advocate, and that they continued while seven hours at even,[†] continued the matter to the morn in the same form, sort[18] and effect, and[19] it was then and caused incarcerate[†] the said Euphame and warn the assize to be present the morn at eight hours in the morning, each person under the pain of a hundred pounds.

EUPHAME MACCALZEAN'S TRIAL CONTINUED:
10 June 1591

Cura Justiciarie supremi domini nostri regis, tenta in pretorio de Edinburgh decimo Junii 1591 per magistrum Joannem Graham.[†]

10 Junii][20]

Partibus et assisa comparentibus ut supra.[†] The justice, by reason yet of the objections made by the panel against the points of dittay and the depositions of sundry persons made for verification thereof and answers made thereto, they having continued while seven hours at even, continued the said matter in same form, sort and effect as is now, and imprisoned the said Euphame while the morn, and warned the persons of assize to compear[†] the morn, ilk[†] person under the pain of a hundred pounds.

EUPHAME MACCALZEAN'S TRIAL CONTINUED:
11 June 1591

Curia justiciarie supremi domini nostri regis tenta in pretorio superiori de Edinburgh xi° Junii 1591 per magistrum Joannem Graham, justicarium deputatum.[†]

Intrant

[†] **while seven hours at even** until seven o'clock in the evening
[†] **caused incarcerate** imprisoned
[†] *Curia justiciarie ... Graham* 'The justiciary court of our sovereign lord the king, held in the court of Edinburgh, 10 June 1591, by master John Graham.'
[†] *Partibus ... supra* (Latin) the parties and the

assize being present, as above
[†] **compear** put in an appearance
[†] **ilk** each
[†] *Curia ... justiciarium deputatum* 'The justiciary court of our sovereign lord the king held in the superior court of Edinburgh, 11 June, by master John Graham, justice depute.'

Euphame MacCalzean]
(Euphame MacCalzean spouse to Patrick Moscrop).
Dilated of certain crimes of witchcraft and treason, specially contained in
the dittay above written.

Pursuer: Mr David McGill of Cranstoun Riddel, advocate to our sovereign
lord.

Prolocutors for the panel:
      Mr John Moscrop
      Mr David Ogilvie
      Robert Ker, burgess of Edinburgh
      Henry Nisbett, burgess there
      Mr John Russell
      Mr John Skene

Assisa

James Johnston of Elphinstone	Alexander Fairley of Braid
( ) Anstruther, younger of that ilk	( ) Graham of Knockdolian
Mr William Leslie of Cunlie	David Prestoun of Craigmillar
John Logan, portioner of Couston	( ) Balfour of Bandon
James Inglis, merchant, burgess of Edinburgh	David Balfour of Bello

      James Elphinstone in Bogie
      Clemmett Kincaid of the Coitts
      George Mowtray of Seafield
      John Drummond of Slipperfield
      James Somervall of Humbie

The same day, after proponing of the whole objections by the panel against
the dittay and verifications thereof, and answers made thereto by the
advocate, the persons[21] being chosen, sworn and admitted, they removed
altogether forth of court to the council house where they remained all that
night. And after the choosing of James Johnston of Elphinstone chancellor
of the said assize, they voted and reasoned upon the points of the said
dittay and continued pronouncing of their deliverance[†] while the morn.

[†] **continued pronouncing of their deliverance**
adjourned announcing their judgement; the
phrase is composed of legal technicalities

EUPHAME MACCALZEAN'S TRIAL CONTINUED:
12 June 1591

Curia Justiciarie tenta 12 Junii 1591 per magistrum Joannem Graham.[†]

Intrant

Euphame MacCalzean her articles of convicted being ten in number.]
(Euphame MacCalzean)
The which day the persons of assize, after long deliberation and continuance in the council-house upon the reasoning and voting upon the points of the said Euphame MacCalzean's dittay,[†] being thoroughly advised therewith,[†] re-entered again in court. And there by the mouth of the said James Johnston of Elphinstone, chancellor, found, pronounced and declared the same Euphame:

(1)   To be filed, culpable and convict of consulting with Catherine Campbell, an Irish woman with a falling nose,[†] dwelling for a long space in the Canongate head, a notorious witch, and entertaining the said Catherine in her own house and in the house of Barbara Tours, the relict[†] of umwhile James Harlaw seeking help of her to her bairns, specially to Thomas her son whom she sent his sark with Helen Inglis her servant.
(2)   Item, of the bewitching by her art of sorcery of John Houston, son to William Houston, her husband's sister son, a young man of seventeen years of age, whereby he died; and so for art and part of the slaughter of the said umwhile John by the said art.
(3)   Item, of the consulting with Janet Cunningham in the Canongate head, alias called 'Lady Bothwell', an old indicted witch of the finest champ, eighteen years syne or thereby, for poisoning of Joseph Douglas of Pumpherston and that by a potion of composed water, which she sent her servant John Tweddall for to be brought up to Barbara Tour's house in a chopin stoup, which was received by him and delivered to the said Barbara.
(4)   Item, of the seeking help, consultation and response from Annie Sampson, known a notorious witch, for recovering of her jewels and emirent again from the laird of Pumpherston and that by the frequent sending of Janet Drummond, sometime her nurse, to the said Annie to that effect above seven times.

[†]   *Curia justiciarie ... Graham* 'The justiciary court held 12 June 1591 by master John Graham.'
[†]   **long deliberation ... dittay** 'The procurators pleaded so subtillie for her, that the assise could not be resolved before the 13th of June' (Calderwood 1842–9: v 128)

[†]   **being thoroughly advised therewith** having carefully reflected on it
[†]   **a falling nose** ?a sharp nose
[†]   **relict** widow

(5)   Item, for consulting with Annie Sampson, a witch, for getting of moulds from her to be used by the said Euphame in relief of her pain in her birth of her two sons.

(6)   Item, of art and part of the consulting with Annie Sampson for destroying of Mr John Moscrop, her father-in-law by witchcraft about four years syne or thereby. And to that effect sending with Janet Drummond, her servant, a picture of wax sent in a buist enclosed within a goose to the said Annie, and a serviette with beef wambled about the goose. Which picture the said Annie gave to the devil to be enchanted, and the same being enchanted by him was sent home again to her with the said Janet Drummond for doing of the turn, as the said Annie declared to the said Janet that it should serve thereto.

(7)   Item, found her culpable of making of a picture of flour and clay for bewitching of Marie Home, spouse to Mr John McGill, and causing cast the same[†] in at Mr John McGill's kitchen window to that effect.

(8)   Item, culpable for the treasonable conventicle had by her, Annie Sampson, John Fian and divers others at North Berwick kirk, twenty days before Michaelmas 1590. And there inquiring for the king's picture, given by the said Annie Sampson to the devil to be enchanted by him for the treasonable destruction of the king.

For destruction of the king.]

(9) Item, convict of the treasonable convention held by her and them at the new haven called Acheson's Haven at Lammas last was 1590 to the treasonable effect immediately above written, viz. in seeking of a picture to the treasonable destruction of the king.

Idem][†]

(10)   Item, convict of common witchcraft and sorcery, and using of the said witchcraft against sundry his Highness' lieges.

And also acquit the said Euphame of the whole remaining points contained in her dittay foresaid, whereof she was accused.

[†] **causing cast the same** causing the same to be   [†] **Idem** (Latin) the same, i.e. 'For destruction of
cast   the king'

EUPHAME MACCALZEAN'S TRIAL CONTINUED:
15 June 1591

Curia justiciarie supremi domini nostri regis tenta xv[to] Junii 1591 per magistrum Joannem Graham justicarium deputatum[†]

Doom of forfeiture[† 22] *pronounced against Euphame MacCalzean]*
The which day Euphame MacCalzean, spouse to Patrick Moscrop, alias MacCalzean, being presented on panel as she that was convict of before by a condign assize[†] in a court of justiciary held in the said tolbooth of Edinburgh the twelfth day of June instant, for the consulting with Catherine Campbell, an Irish woman with a falling nose, dwelling for a long space in the Canongate head, a notorious witch, and entertaining of the said Catherine in her own house and in the house of Barbara Tours, the relict of umwhile James Harlaw writer,[†] seeking help of her to her bairns, specially to Thomas, her son, to whom she sent his sark with Helen Inglis, her servant.

Item, likewise for her bewitching, by her art of sorcery, of umwhile John Houston, son to William Houston, and her husband's sister son, a young man of seventeen years of age, whereby he died, and so for art and part of the slaughter of the said umwhile John by the said art.

Item, for consulting with Janet Cunningham in the Canongate, alias called 'Lady Bothwell', a old indicted witch of the finest champ, eighteen years syne or thereby, for poisoning of Joseph Douglas of Pumpherston, and that by a potion of composed water, which she sent her servant John Tweddall for, to be brought up to Barbara Tour's house in a chopin stoup, which was received by him and delivered to the said Barbara.

Item, for seeking help, consultation and response from Annie Sampson, known a notorious witch, for recovering of her jewels and emirent from the laird of Pumpherston, and that by the frequent sending of Janet Drummond, sometime her nurse, to the said Annie to that effect above seven times.

Item, for the consulting with the said Annie Sampson, a witch, for getting of moulds from her to be used by the said Euphame in relief of her pain the time of the birth of her two sons.

Item, for art and part of the consulting with the said Annie Sampson for the destroying of Mr John Moscrop, her father-in-law, by witchcraft about four years syne or thereby and to that effect sending with Janet Drummond her servant a picture of wax sent in a buist enclosed in a goose to the said

---

[†] ***Curia justicariae ... deputatum*** 'The justiciary court of our sovereign lord the king, held 15 June 1591 by master John Graham, justice depute.'

[†] **doom of forfeiture** sentence of confiscation of lands

[†] **condign assize** an assize suitable to the case or parties concerned

[†] **writer** attorney, law-clerk

Annie, and a serviette with beef wambled about the goose; which picture the said Annie gave to the devil to be enchanted, and the same being enchanted by him was sent home again to the said Euphame with the said Janet Drummond for doing of the turn, as the said Annie declared to the said Janet that it should serve thereto.

Item, for making of a picture of flour and clay for bewitching of Marie Home, spouse to Mr John McGill, and causing cast the same in at the said Mr John's kitchen window to that effect.

Item, for the treasonable conventicle held by her, Annie Sampson, John Fian and divers others at North Berwick kirk twenty days before Michaelmas, the year of God 1590 years, and there inquiring for the king's picture given by the said Annie Sampson to the devil to be enchanted by him for the treasonable destruction of the king.

Item, for the treasonable convention held by her and them at the new haven called Acheson's Haven at Lammas last was, the year of God 1590 years, to the treasonable effect immediately above written, viz. in seeking a picture to the treasonable destruction of the king.

Sentence against Euphame MacCalzean: To be burned quick and forfeit.

Item, of common witchcraft and sorcery and using of the said witchcraft against sundry of his Highness' lieges.

For the which crimes the said justice depute ordained the said Euphame by the mouth of William Gray, dempster, as culpable and guilty thereof, to be taken to the castle hill of Edinburgh and there bound to a stake and burned in ashes, quick[†] to the death and all and sundry her lands, heritages,[†] tacks,[†] steadings,[†], rooms,[†] possessions, corns, cattle, goods and gear to be forfeited and escheat to our sovereign lord's use.

[†] **quick** alive. 'This was the severest sentence ever pronounced by the Court, even in the most atrocious cases. In ordinary instances of Witchcraft, the culprit was previously strangled at the stake, before being burnt' (*P*). But Calderwood, on the other hand, says that she was strangled: 'She was wirried and burnt to ashes upon the 25th of June. She tooke it on her conscience that she was innocent of all the crymes layed to her charge' (Calderwood 1842–9: v 128).

[†] **heritages** property
[†] **tacks** farms
[†] **steadings** buildings
[†] **rooms** pieces of ground

Document 24

Document Recording Evidence Against
the Earl of Bothwell

date unknown

Document 24 consists of two sheets attached together, one of which is written only on one side. On f. 1ʳ is written 'Richard Graham / warlock and / others / August 1593 / Witches /', and on another (very faintly) 'dittay upon the earl Bothwell'.

This is written in the same hand as document 26 and records accusations against Bothwell. From the nature of this text, its contents, and the account of the trial given by Carey in *Border Papers* ii 486, which said that Graham's depositions were brought into the court at Bothwell's trial, we may conjecture that these sheets are a copy of part of Graham's depositions against Bothwell. Its reference to 'the said dittay' indicates that it is not part of Bothwell's dittay itself. Graham seems to be the source of most of the information it contains. The similarity of some of the contents in documents 24 and 26 confirms Carey's observation on Graham's depositions, that the indictment itself was 'drawn out of them'.

★

And to the [   ]
ber in summer before [   ]
Angus your good[   ]
ye being in Mr John [   ]
chamber in the head of [   ]
by you by your servan[   ] [   ]
Richard forth of John [   ]
the back of the town wall [   ]

---

† **high chamber** upper room

up to the said high chamber[†] in Mr [　]
which time ye named to him the decla[　]
cit how ye might cut away[†] the king [　]
receipt[†][1] in the first part of the said dittay [　]
And further, the said Ninian Chirnesyde [　]
came to Thomas Lawson's house in the West [　]
the said Richard was for the time, and br[　]
town to Sir James Newton's house where[　]
from your place[†] of Crichton and spake with him [　]
sic James [?Drymmie] your servant being [?east one of where?]
At the which time ye remember the said Richard offered to you a remedy to
cause the king love you, made of a herb, to be put in your mouth or to be
borne upon you when ye should come to the king, which was delivered to
the said Ninian Chirnesyde. Which[†] then likewise[†] at your command
delivered to the said Richard four angel-nobles.[†]

And siclike[†] to the token[†] that ye are guilty of the said conspiracy, ye remember
at another time thereafter when the said Richard came to you the second
time to Crichton where ye sent a servant of the said Ninian Chirnesyde's to
the Monklands for the said Richard, who[†] gat[†] him in John Wood's house in
the Monkland, who convoyed[†] him to you to Crichton where he dined with
you in the place. And thereafter ye conferred with him in Sir James Newton's
house for performance[†] of the said purpose.[†] And after, the said Richard
came back fra you again to the Westhouse where he remained that night.
The said Ninian Chirnesyde came to him the morn thereafter and showed
him that ye had sent away his direction[†] to a woman whose name ye knew
not. And if she thought his counsel good that ye would reward the said
Richard the better. When[†] the said Richard passed therefore home to his
house in the [?Ryÿares?] in the Monkland.

And also to the token that ye are guilty the said consulting, ye remember ye
sent the said Ninian Chirnesyde's boy for the said Richard to Sandy
Johnston's house called [?Coiss] for the war, and bad the boy desire him to
come to a know[†] beside the Westhouse and meet you. And then ye sent the

---

[†] **cut away** remove
[†] **receipt** received
[†] **place** palace
[†] **Which** i.e. Ninian Chirnesyde
[†] **likewise** in like manner
[†] **angel-nobles** English coins first struck in 1465
    bearing the figure of the archangel Michael
[†] **siclike** in the same manner
[†] **to the token** as evidence

[†] **who** i.e. Ninian Chirnesyde's servant
[†] **gat** found
[†] **convoyed** accompanied
[†] **performance** carrying out
[†] **purpose** objective
[†] **direction** instruction
[†] **When** at that time
[†] **know** knoll, hillock

boy again to the said know with a tablet as a token[†] to the said Richard to come to a glen under the college kirk[†] of Crichton and there to meet with you. Which he did, and ye met him there and devised upon[†] the purpose foresaid.

And further ye remember ye bade the said Richard inquire of the Sprite[†] what should become of you, what death ye should die, and if ye should be in favour of the prince. Who[†] raised the Sprite, which declared to him that ye should be in danger of your life by your prince and that ye should be murdered; and that the Sprite said likewise that ye should be slain.

[　] ye consulted with the said umwhile
[　]is foresaid ye about [?Martinmas]
[　] Hallowmas send one Nesbet
[　]ne Chirnesyde to the said Richard
[　] Stone's house of Castlecary and
[　]ly because there was to commission
[　] And in case he happened to be [?taken]
[　] of you but rather of Master Bowes
[　]wes was like Bothwell and ye sent a bill[†]
[　] desiring the said Richard to come east quickly to
[　] as after ye sent three several bills to the said
[　] The first before the taking of the witches, the
[　] after some witches were taken, and the third betwixt Hallowmas and [?Martinmas] foresaid. The first writing of[†] Kelso desiring the said Richard to come to Edinburgh. The other two were written of Edinburgh desiring him to come ane[†] to Lithgow[† 2] and the other to Kirkliston[3] where the said Ninian should meet with him. And all subscrived[†] by your writ who (　　　　). The effect[†] of the which letters was reproving[†] the said Richard that he was failing in doing of your turns, for if ye had not appointed to him[†] ye had gotten others to do the same, and desiring the said Richard to come to you. Who stayed to come[†] fearing, because your malicious enterprise took no effect as you desired, that ye should have slain him.

[†] **token** sign
[†] **college kirk** collegiate church
[†] **devised upon** made plans for
[†] **the Sprite** the devil
[†] **Who** i.e. Richard Graham
[†] **bill** letter, document
[†] **of** from
[†] **ane** alone

[†] **Lithgow** i.e. Linlithgow
[†] **subscrived** signed
[†] **effect** substance
[†] **the effect ... reproving** the purport of these letters was to chide
[†] **appointed to him** selected him for the job
[†] **stayed to come** delayed from coming

As also the said Ninian Chirnesyde was directed[†] by you to the said Richard, after he[†] was apprehended and detained captive in the justice clerk's house in the Canongate and sent for John Graham, servant to the justice clerk and desired him to speak the said Richard anent[†] the writing sent by the said Ninian to him, and to keep the matter secret; and to declare that the same was written to him for the help of the said Ninian's mother who was sick. Like as[†] he should declare the same, whereby their declarations might gang together;[†] and sent a forty shilling piece with the said John to the said Richard. And there the said Ninian came to my lord justice clerk's woman's house where the said Richard was, and drunk a pint of wine with him and desired him to keep all things secret. Where he gave him another forty shilling piece.

Which all[†] was done by your direction,[†] which ye cannot deny, and was clearly and constantly allowed[†] and confessed by the said umwhile Richard before his decease.

[†] **directed** sent
[†] **he** i.e. Richard Graham
[†] **anent** concerning
[†] **Like as** similarly
[†] **their declarations ... together** their statements might agree

[†] **Which all** all of which
[†] **direction** instructions
[†] **clearly and constantly allowed** plainly and steadfastly admitted

Document 25

List of the Earl of Bothwell's Assizers

10 August 1593

This is a full list of the thirty-eight noblemen and lairds from whom Bothwell's actual assizers were selected. The men who formed the assize, whose names may be found in *CSPS* xi 144, have 'qt' opposite their names. David McGill was yet again the pursuer.

The names of the assize against Francis earl Bothwell[1]

qt	P	The earl of Atholl	P		The laird of Dalmahoy
qt	P	The earl of Montrose	P		The laird of Skirling
qt	P	The lord Livingstone			
qt	P	The lord Seton			
qt	per	The lord Forbes			
qt	P	The lord Innermeath			
	P	The lord Ochiltree			
		The lord Borthwick			
		The lord Semple			
qt	P	The master of Gray			
qt	P	The master of Somerville			
qt	per	The lord Struther			
qt	P	The laird of Buchanan			
	P	The laird of [???????]			
qt	P	The laird of Inverleith			
		The laird of Blachan			
qt	P	The laird of Caldwell			
qt	P	The laird of Reidhall			
qt	P	The laird of Bass			

			The laird of Wachton	
	P	X	The laird of Hermiston	
	P		The laird of Greenhead	
qt	P		The laird of Roslin	
qt	P		The laird of Ferniherst	
	P		The laird of Teaigchall	
	P		The laird of Lethenty	
	P		The laird of Restalrig	
	P		The laird of East Nisbit	
	P		The laird of Traquair	
	P		The laird of Polmain	*Assisa*
	P		The laird of Sirmton	Mr David MacGill
	P		{deletion}	
	P		The laird of Danrod	
	P		The laird of Dowhill	
	P		The laird Kinnear	
	P		The laird of Airth	

Document 26

The Trial of the Earl of Bothwell

10 August 1593

These are two leaves, fragmentary at the top of the pages and written on both sides in the same hand, which is also the hand of document 24. They contain a draft of the dittay presented to the justiciary court of Edinburgh, 10 August 1593, that acquitted Bothwell of an accusation of trying to kill the king by witchcraft. The chancellor, Montrose, has subscribed his name to the record. Richard Graham, who provided the main evidence for the accusation against Bothwell, was executed in February 1592. This document is dated 10 August 1591, which must be an error for 1593.

★

Francis earl [   ]
foreknowledge [   ]
conspiracy w[   ]
some and others [   ]
sovereign lord his [   ]
truction of his high[   ]
of his life by the [   ]
ry witchcraft and d[   ]
set down and agreed upon b[   ]
Richard Graham, umwhile Agnes Samps[   ]
witches their associates in their devi[   ]
turally and unthankfully[†] against yo[   ]
prince to whom not only by bl[   ]
benefits ye were so highly obliged[1] [   ]
have consulted, devised and attempted at [   ]

[†] **unthankfully** ungratefully

your coming out of France and other part bey[   ]
the year of God 1582 years[2] and specia[   ]
years of God 1587, 1588, 1589, 1590 and [   ]
years monthly at the least divers months of the said years within divers
parts of this country and in special within the town of Edinburgh in Mr
John Provand's house in a high chamber[†] thereof. Where, ye having
directed your servant Ninian Chirnesyde to bring the said Richard to
you, ye met there with the said umwhile Richard Graham, a notorious
witch and sorcerer. And there had your conference, device[†] and consultation with him anent the conspiracy foresaid, and declared to him that
ye were surely[†] informed by a man of science[†] in Italy or Almaine[† 3] that
your prince should cause execute you[†] and that ye feared your life should
be taken by him. And therefore ye desired to understand of the said
Richard if it was of truth,[†] for ye would rather procure[†] the taking of the
prince's life or[†] the prince took yours. And to this effect[†] desired the
said Richard to be resolved[†] with his devilish sprite thereanent, which
the said umwhile Richard at your desire granted[†] to do. Who being
resolved with the sprite declared that the king's Majesty would do you
no harm. Like as the said Richard, after he left you in Mr John Provand's
house, having passed[†] to the Westhouse to Thomas Lawson's house there,
where he remained certain days. Ye sent your servant Ninian Chirnesyde
to the Westhouse for him, desiring him to meet you in Crichton. Who
convoyed[†] the said umwhile Richard to Sir James Newton's house in
Crichton where ye met with him and conferred anent the purpose
foresaid, for cutting away of[†] his Highness' life by witchcraft and enchantments, in respect ye feared your life should be taken by him. Where the
said umwhile Richard as yet[†] declared to you that he could not find[†] by
the sprite that ye should be troubled or in danger anyways[†] by the prince.

Nevertheless, ye not satisfied[†] nor content to desist and leave your
malicious enterprise against his Majesty's most noble person, ye therefore
sent for the said umwhile Richard to the Monklands, to John Wood's
house, desiring him to come and speak with you in Crichton where he

---

[†] **high chamber** upper room	[†] **to this effect** to this end
[†] **device** plan	[†] **resolved** satisfied, confirmed
[†] **surely** with certainty	[†] **granted** agreed
[†] **a man of science** a man skilled in the science of magic	[†] **passed** gone
	[†] **convoyed** accompanied
[†] **Almaine** Germany	[†] **cutting away of** ending
[†] **cause execute you** cause you to be executed	[†] **as yet** up to this time
[†] **of truth** true	[†] **find** ascertain
[†] **procure** contrive	[†] **anyways** in any way
[†] **or** before	[†] **ye not satisfied** you not being satisfied

[　] you in the hall of your place

[　] after denied to the said Sir

[　] ye declared to him that ye

[　] favour and that no remedy[4] which

[　] purpose would take effect. And

[　]yet to you not showing the said

[　]ing for there was a wife[†] who [????]

[　] the king were cut not away his

[　] not fail to cause cut you away,[†] which woman

[　] to have been Anny Sampson. Like as[†] the said Anny

[　]son declared the same secretly to the said umwhile Richard

[　]me the time she was kept in the abbey of Holyroodhouse

[　] therefore ye inquired of the said umwhile Richard what way ye should go to work to cut away the king's Majesty's most noble person and bereave his Highness of his life.[†] Who, being advised with the sprite[†] which he raised in the Westhouse before he came to you to Crichton, declared to you that there was sundry means to perform that matter: to wit, by an enchanted picture[†] of wax, or with dropping[†] of a poisoned toad, mixed with strong wash[†] with the flesh of the forehead of a new-foaled foal and the skin of an adder.[†] At the which time ye answered to the said Richard that ye would speak with the said wife and other wise women, and if their counsel agreed with his that ye should reward him the better. Like as thereafter ye sent the said Ninian Chirnesyde's boy for the said Richard, he being in Sandy Johnston's house called [?Cois] for the [?war] beside the halyards, desiring him to meet you at the know[†] beside the Westhouse and to lie[†] at the said know while[†] ye came to him. Which know was at the burn side[†] under[†] the shepherd's house of Crichton, betwixt the said shepherd's house and the place of Crichton. Where the said umwhile Richard came, and he being lying[†] there ye sent the boy for him to meet you in a glen under the place of Crichton where ye met with the said umwhile Richard. And in your conference[†] showed him that ye had sent his counsel to a wife and bade her send the same to the rest of her sisters to be advised with.[†] And promised if the same took any effect to reward him honestly.[†] And then ye inquired of

---

[†] **wife** woman

[†] **to cause ... away** to cause you to be removed

[†] **Like as** similarly

[†] **bereave ... his life** take away his Highness's life

[†] **advised with the sprite** counselled by the devil

[†] **picture** image

[†] **dropping** dripping

[†] **strong wash** stale urine (used for bleaching clothes)

[†] **strong wash ... adder** see notes on this list, p. 255

[†] **know** knoll

[†] **lie** stay

[†] **while** until

[†] **the burn side** by the side of the stream

[†] **under** below

[†] **lying** lodging

[†] **conference** talk

[†] **advised with** cognizant of

[†] **honestly** appropriately

the said Richard if he knew any women to be trusty and meet[†] for the execution of the said purpose. Who gave no answer to you at the first time, but delayed for a certain space while he raised the sprite by his devilish incantations, prayer and invocations under the said shepherd's house by making of a triangle [???]. Where having inquired of the sprite, at your command, what persons were most meet to execute and perform the conspiracy foresaid, the sprite answered that Euphame MacCalzean, Barbara Napier, Robert Grierson, Anny Sampson, John Fian, Maggie Thomson in Stirling,[5] Janet Stratton, George Mott's wife in Preston, and Irish[†] Donald, which persons the said sprite nominated[†] to him as meetest for the purpose foresaid. And in the raising of the sprite, he conjured him[†] that he should not trouble[†] the air, the water or the earth. And then proponed[†] likewise to the said sprite how our sovereign lord the king's Majesty might be gotten cutted[†] way [   ]
thing in the [   ]
master an[   ]
wax should be m[   ]
said should be [   ]
enterprise and work [   ]
the said Richard aft[   ]
you, and that ye desired him [   ]
his counsel and that ye should [   ]
picture of wax was made by Anny S[   ]
wife called Janet Stratton [   ]
to the said umwhile Richard and likewise [   ]
Sampson granted to him[†] that she made [   ]
at your command. Which picture was d[   ]
to be conjured and that there would come behind h[   ]
tell more nor[†] she did. And the said compos[   ]
poison with the mixtures foresaid was made by the said Mag[   ]
Thomson and certain others to be cast in the gate[†] where the king's Majesty should have come in and out, and should have touched his Highness' person only and a servant called John Kers[†] whom she envied.[† 6]

And thereafter, ye continuing and proceding further in your undutiful and malicious enterprise against his Highness' most noble person, ye sent the

---

[†] **trusty and meet** trustworthy and suitable
[†] **Irish** Highland
[†] **nominated** mentioned by name
[†] **conjured** made him swear
[†] **trouble** disturb
[†] **proponed** proposed
[†] **gotten cutted** made away with

[†] **granted to him** admitted to him
[†] **nor** than
[†] **gate** way
[†] **John Kers** the name appears in *News from Scotland*
[†] **whom she envied** against whom she had a grudge

said Ninian Chirnesyde's boy for the said Richard to the said Sandy Johnston's house called [Cois] for the war beside the halyards to come and meet
you in Haddington where he came with the boy and could get no lodging
while[†] the said Ninian Chirnesyde placed him[†] in one John Burtrun's house
where he remained by[†] the space of eight days. And met with you within
four days after his coming in a new house in Haddington where there was
none dwelling, and there ye renewed your former conference[†] with the
said Richard. And declared to him ye was not able to purchase[†] the king's
favour for any thing he could give you,[†] and that the said Richard beguiled[†]
you or else had no knowledge. And that there was a wife[†] who showed you
alsmickle[†] as the man of Italy or Almaine: that except ye cutted the king
away the king would cut you away. Where likewise ye declared to him that
his last counsel[†] anent the dropping of the toad, and composition of the
poison with the mixtures foresaid for cutting away of his Majesty's most
noble person and life, was used and wrought nought.[†] And that the picture
of wax was given to the enemy[†] to have been conjured but was not gotten
again. Which was known also to the said umwhile Richard Graham who
said to you at that time that Robert Grierson reproved[†] the dev[il] in the
pulpit of North Berwick at their convention in the kirk thereof for the long
holding[†] of the king's picture, which the devil promised should be delivered
at the next meeting. To whom the said Robert Grierson answered 'Ye
promised twice and have[7] beguiled us'. And therefore ye desired
[　　]sall what ye should do
[　　] said wicked enterprise who
[　　]tion of the mixtures foresaid
[　　] make a new picture of wax
[　　]is foresaid for performing of the said
[　　] renewed betwixt you and the said [?con]
[　　] other times and places since your
[　　] out of France in the eighty second[8] year[†] of God and
[　　] riding betwixt Crichton and [?????]ton with the said
[　　] Richard, as also in Kelso and divers other parts of
[　　] country and with divers other persons, where ye consulted
[　　] the said umwhile Richard and enticed[9] with him[†] to follow forth the

---

[†] **while** until
[†] **placed him** found him accommodation
[†] **by** for
[†] **conference** talk
[†] **purchase** procure
[†] **for any ... give you** i.e. Bothwell had failed to get the king's favour as a result of any charm given him by Graham
[†] **beguiled** deceived

[†] **wife** woman
[†] **showed you alsmickle** revealed to you as much
[†] **counsel** advice
[†] **wrought nought** had no effect
[†] **the enemy** i.e. the devil
[†] **reproved** rebuked
[†] **long holding** retention for a long time
[†] **eighty second year** i.e. 1582
[†] **enticed with him** enticed him

said devilish and unnatural purpose, and to help the persons foresaid to cut away his Highness' most noble person and bereave him of his life by the means above specified. Who at your desire promised to do the same by all means he could.

And siclike ye consulted with the said umwhile Richard Graham and remaining witches foresaid,—at the least the said witches consulted among themselves at your desire during the time the king's Majesty was forth[†] of the country in Norway and Denmark, how his Highness might be halden forth[†] of the country and never suffered to return home again. As also before his Highness' departing the said persons consulted at your desire intent[†] he departed of the country how he might be halden[†] of the same and not suffered to return.

Which hail premiss[†] was done and put into practice by the said Richard Graham, Annie Sampson and other persons above specified of[†] the foreknowledge, counsel and device[†] of you and the said umwhile Richard, like as the same was granted, confessed and deponed by the said umwhile Richard, Annie Sampson and divers others of the said persons at divers times before their decease, in presence of his Majesty and council and in presence of sic other persons as were appointed for their trial. In the which confessions they continued[†] to the hour of their death, being executed to the death for the said crimes.

And so ye are guilty of the treasonable and unnatural consulting and devising[†] with the said umwhile Richard Graham and other notorious witches and sorcerers for destroying and cutting off of his Majesty's most noble person and bereaving him of his life. Wherein ye at the least the said persons be your special desire and command did their exact diligence[†] to have performed the said wicked purpose. Whereof by the mighty providence of God he had not been miraculously preserved.[†]

[†] **forth** out
[†] **halden forth** kept out
[†] **intent** with the intention that if
[†] **halden** kept out
[†] **hail premiss** all the foregoing
[†] **of** with
[†] **device** plan, scheme

[†] **continued** persisted
[†] **devising** plotting
[†] **did their exact diligence** they precisely endeavoured
[†] **Whereof ... preserved** i.e. if it had not been for God's mighty providence, he would not have been miraculously preserved

Decimo Augusti 1593 in curia justiciarie tenta
in praetorio de Edinburgh.[†]

The assize in a vote acquits the earl Bothwell of the whole dittay above written, and that touching the destruction of his Majesty's person by witchcraft as is particularly above deduced.[†][10] In witness whereof the chancellor has subscribed these presents.[†]

Montrose

[†] ***Decimo ... de Edinburgh*** 'The 10 August 1593 in the justiciary court held in the court of Edinburgh.'

[†] **deduced** prosecuted
[†] **these presents** presumably the members of the assize

Textual Notes to Documents 19 to 26

Document 19

1   SRO document JC 2/2 ff. 195–6
    Convict ... burned] *in margin*
2   Jakit] Hakit *P*
3   upon the points] upointis; (upoun the)
    points *P*
4   musing and pensing] mwsand and
    pensand
5   soughing athwart the earth] souchand
    athoirt the eird
6   on] onn; one *P*
7   skimming] skumand *MS, P*
8   Lookup] Linkup
9   modevart] modewart *P*
10 Broomhill] brumhallis; Brumhoillis *P*
11 fourthly] ferdlie
12 sea] sie; fie *P*
13 with] and; as *P*

Document 20

1   SRO document JC 2/2 ff. 201–6
    Witchcraft: Agnes Sampson] *in margin*
2   Hopes] hoipis
3   his] hers; his *conj. P*
4   cutler] cuitler; tinkler *P*
5   at] att; one *P*
6   skipper] schipard
7   Barfoot] bairfute
8   at] att; one *P*
9   would convalesce] wald {die} convales
10 Reidshill's] reidhallis
11 Bolton] bowtoun
12 Item, acquit] Item {convict} acquit
13 Newton] Natoun
14 Item, filed] Item {acquit} fylit
15 at] att; one *P*
16 might] nycht; mycht *P*
17 died] deitt; departit *P*
18 Bangly's] banglais
19 anaplie] aullholie *CSPS* x 465
20 Stoppit] stepped *CSPS* x 465
21 all well then] all weill thann; all went then
    CSPS x 465
22 convene] quhome *CSPS* x 466
23 rick] ruk *MS, P*
24 her] ẙow; ẙow (hir) *P*
25 at] att; one *P*

26 Eloa] Elva *P*
27 well] wall *MS, P*
28 Mott's] mutis
29 webster's] wobsteris
30 Lookup] Lenchop
31 by east] beeist
32 Din] Dyn; Dunn *P*
33 Lookups] Linkhop
34 ensorcery] insorcerie *MS, P*
35 godfather's] guid faderis
36 moulds] mwildis
37 ills] illis; evils *CSPS* x 466
38 mass] mess
39 sore] sa
40 nailed Jesus] naillit Jesus; nailit dere Jesus
    CSPS x 466
41 reeked] raikit; reikit *P*
42 bone] bane; vane *CSPS* x 466
43 farmer] fermorer *MS, P*
44 at] in *P*
45 Meg Steel, Kate Gray] meg stillcart gray
46 bairn] barne
47 Gillour] Gylour
48 'Licked'] Likit; Lukit *P*
49 Bessie Gullen] bessie {congiltoun} gwlenn
50 question] quttiounn; puttioune *P*
51 that she might] sche mycht sche mycht;
    that sche mycht *conject. P*

Document 21

1   SRO document JC 2/2 ff. 213–14
    themselves] the self
2   advocate] advocatt; Advocat to our
    soverane lord for his hienes interes *P*
3   made thereto ... ordained] maid thairto
    att lenth contenit in the minuitis buik
    ordanit; maid thairto, ordanit *P*
4   Boig] Brig *P*
5   coalman] coilman; Crilman *P*
6   doublet] dowlet; dowblet *P*
7   *justiciarium deputatum*] *Just*
8   indicted] indyet
9   Justice] Rex. Justice *P*
10 a witch] *rest of this paragraph omitted by P*
11 owing] auchtand
12 while she was delivered] quhill sho was
    delyver

Document 22

Continuation of document 21.

[1] *Voluntate*] *in margin*
[2] Fairley] fairlie; Fernely *CSPS* x 522
[3] William] *MS, P;* James *CSPS* x 522
[4] Walter] John *CSPS* x 522
[5] Clavie] Clevy *CSPS* x 522
[6] thwarted] thoirterit
[7] Gyllour] Gylloun *P*
[8] head. And having] heid & haifand; heid; haifand *P*
[9] Fian stood] Fien stuid; Fien (they) stuid *P*
[10] then] thay; than *P*
[11] but] Robert *P*
[12] goods, gear or fame] guidis geir or fame; guidis or same *P*

Document 23

[1] SRO document JC 2/2 ff. 221–6.
sovereign lord] soverane lord; soverane lord (for his hienes interest) *P*
[2] two thirty shilling pieces] twa xxx s pecis
[3] giving of him] gewing of him : gewing to him *P*
[4] Danzig] danskin
[5] you] hir; hir (ÿow) *P*
[6] ye] sche; sche (ye) *P*
[7] inaugurate] in augwrat
[8] girth of a great beaker] girth of ane grit bikar*
[9] Pumpherston] Punphrastounn
[10] of] and; and (of) *P*
[11] rolled] rowit
[12] drowse] drowis*
[13] wambled] woumplit *MS, P*
[14] at two ... stand] att twa eftir none ane naikit man att twa aftir none stand; at twa after none, saw ane naikit man stand *P*
[15] urchins] hurchiounis

[16] a picture of clay in portrait] ane pictour of clay {and} in {ane} portrat; ane pictour of clay and ane portrat *P*
[17] Fiery Hills] fyrie hoillis; Fayrie-hoillis *P*
[18] sort] sorte; force *P*
[19] and] as *P*
[20] 10 Junii] 11 Junii
[21] the persons] The {ass} persounes; the above persounes *P*
[22] forfeiture] forfaltour

Document 24

[1] SRO document JC 26/2/5
receipt] reseit
[2] Lithgow] Lytgw
[3] Kirkliston] Kirklisounn

Document 25

[1] SRO document JC 26/2/7

Document 26

[1] SRO document JC 26/2/6
obliged] obleist
[2] 1582 years] Im Vc Lxxxij ÿeiris
[3] Almaine] almanÿie
[4] remedy] remeid
[5] Stirling] striveling
[6] envied] Invyit
[7] have] hes
[8] 82nd] lxxxii
[9] enticed] intiscit
[10] and that ... deduced] |and that tuiching the destructioun of / his maiesties person be witchcraft as is particularlie / deduceit| *in margin in MS; a caret in the main text indicates where it is to be added*

Chapter 9

WITCH HUNT PROPAGANDA:
News from Scotland

––––––

News from Scotland is the first work printed in Scotland or England which is solely about Scottish witchcraft, and there were none in the early seventeenth century. There is an account of the trial and execution of some witches at Irvine in 1618, but this seems to have existed only in manuscript until it was printed about 1855.[1] The flow of material about witchcraft in Scotland came in the late seventeenth century when the period of the major witch hunts was over.[2] Although there is some truth in Larner's claim that *News* 'is a classic sixteenth-century English pamphlet',[3] it is far more colourful, sensational and violent than sixteenth-century English pamphlets printed after the apprehension and arraignment of witches.[4]

Of all the texts generated by the North Berwick witch trials, *News from Scotland* is the most propagandistic. *Demonology*, although suffused with a particular ideology involving theology, demonology, witchcraft and magistracy, disguises this by its rhetorical strategies, especially the apparent openness of its dialogue form. *Demonology* was written when the North Berwick witch hunt was abating, but *News from Scotland* was written in the midst of the ongoing witch hunt. From this position in time and events it registers even more directly than *Demonology* the authorities' struggle to contain, define, and interpret to their advantage the disparate events and persons of the witch hunt begun in late 1590.

The historical circumstances of *News*'s production—the fact that it was written to serve urgent political ends and published so quickly, probably in late 1591— are sharply registered in its language and form. The sections that follow read *News* using the techniques of literary analysis in order to suggest how it selects and shapes 'historical' material from the early months of the witch hunt, and to what ends. What is 'historical' and what 'imaginary' is, of course, always problematical. What sorts of material make up the text? Who is writing, and what are the writer's (or writers') intentions? What is at stake in the way the stories are told? How does it work to persuade? What is its ideology?

The authorship of *News*

The 'authorship' of *News* is problematic in two main ways. Firstly, no author's name appears in the first quartos. Secondly, it may be more appropriate to speak of more than one author in the case of some late sixteenth- and early seventeenth-century English pamphlets that give an account of a witchcraft case or trial. These pamphlets were often put together by a publisher from various legal documents: informations, examinations, and records of trials.[5] Although the word 'publisher' is not used until the eighteenth century in the modern sense of someone whose business it is to issue or produce books for another, it seems the only term to use of the person who acquired a text, paid for copies of it to be manufactured and then sold them. This person may on occasion have been the printer, at other times the bookseller.[6] 'Publisher' is used in this discussion of *News* for the person who provided the printer with the text, in the knowledge that in some cases these persons were one and the same. In the case of witchcraft pamphlets we may suppose the publisher to have written the prefaces often found before the main body of the pamphlet, and also to have been the editor of various legal materials that he acquired in several ways and which reported the career, examination and trial of witches. One of the earliest sixteenth-century witchcraft pamphlets, *The Examination of John Walsh* (1566), is a clear and simple example of this process. The latter part of the pamphlet is a lightly edited version of the record of Walsh's examination before an ecclesiastical court in Exeter,[7] while the self-confessed address of 'The Printer to the Christian Reader' is a few pages of anti-papist rant against 'fat belly Moonkes, flattering Friers, and idle lusty Priests', and stories of necromantic popes, pieced together from various sources.

News is a more complicated case. The writer of its preface may well be the publisher. He is concerned to make public the 'true' version of events, as opposed to false versions currently circulating. In his address to the reader he twice uses both the words 'published' and 'publish' of his activities; and although he may just mean that he is making the story generally known,[8] it is more likely that he means he is issuing the book for sale,[9] thus identifying himself as a publisher.

It is difficult to go much further in identifying this person, but, if we follow the arguments of Blayney, one of the booksellers of *News* is more likely than the printer to have written the preface to the reader. Of the three versions of the original quarto of *News*, the second and revised edition of Pollard and Redgrave, *Short-title Catalogue of English Books 1475–1640* (1986), gives William Wright as the bookseller of two editions printed respectively by E. Allde? and T. Scarlet. The third was printed for Thomas Nelson with no printer named. In 1591–2 William Allde, who probably printed one of the editions of *News* for Wright, printed a variety of works: among them news from abroad, a handwriting manual, sermons by Henry Smith, some works by Robert Greene, and a few plays, including a newly corrected version of Kyd's *The Spanish Tragedy* and *Arden of Faversham*. Thomas Scarlet, who printed the other editions for Wright, was also very active in 1591–2.[10] The years 1590–2 saw many books printed for both William Wright and Thomas Nelson.[11] Wright specialised in ballads, broadsides, newsbooks and ephemeral literature, so *News from Scotland* was exactly the sort of work which he sold. Thomas Nelson too was known to sell ballads.[12]

If the publisher did write the preface, then the rest of the pamphlet is a narrative of witchcraft shaped in particular ways and to particular ends, and is not merely a lightly edited version of legal materials. This part of *News*, headed 'A true discourse of the apprehension of sundry witches lately taken in Scotland . . .' and beginning 'God, by his omnipotent power . . .', is a narrative to demonstrate God's providential care of King James, 'the greatest enemy [the devil] hath in the world', and is told by a self-conscious authorial voice. The only candidate for the authorship of *News* was named in Sir James Melville's *Memoirs*, probably written in the early seventeenth century, but not printed until 1683. This is James Carmichael (1543?–1628), minister of Haddington,[13] on the strength of Melville's comment on the witches of Lothian, that their activities 'wald hardly get credit be the posterite; wherof Mester James Carmichell minister of Haddingtoun has ther history and haill depositions'.[14] The implication is that Carmichael has the authoritative sources to allow him to write an authoritative account. Melville's involvement in witchcraft examinations and in Napier's trial makes it likely his comment is accurate.

There is circumstantial evidence supporting the assumption that Carmichael was the author. He became a national figure in 1584 when he fled to England along with other anti-episcopalian ministers following the execution of the earl of Gowrie, leader of the Ruthven Raid in which King James was captured in a protestant *coup*. Carmichael was exiled until 1588, during which time he earned part of his living in Cheapside engaged in literary activity, including writing a Latin grammar for schoolboys. The London literary connections Carmichael made then would have been useful in arranging the publication of *News*. Other political contacts provided him with reasons for taking an interest in the 1590–2 witch hunt. Along with other Scots exiles he met English statesmen including Bowes who was to become English ambassador to Scotland; and he corresponded with the earl of Angus who was an ardent supporter of the presbyterians. It was the same earl of Angus whose death in 1588 would eventually be charged to the witchcraft of Barbara Napier who is named in *News*.

Carmichael became a leading figure in church and political affairs. He was called on several times during his career to exercise his intellectual skills in particular tasks. The editor of his proverbs in Scots describes him as a 'talented, scholarly and highly educated man . . . [with an] intimate knowledge of the classics', and with 'a talent for public business'.[15] He was minister of Haddington in 1570–84 and again from 1588. He was also master of its grammar school until 1576. By 1578 he was prominent in church affairs, when he was chosen as one of the drafters of the *Second Book of Discipline* (1578). In the 1590s, at the request of the kirk's general assembly, he compiled a record of all assembly acts. In 1592 he was appointed to attend a weekly council at Edinburgh regarding the practices of papists and those who favoured them. In 1608 the privy council asked the Haddington presbytery to release him for two months so that he might proof-read the Scots translation of Sir John Skene's edition of *Regiam Majestatem* (1609).[16]

Carmichael may well provide a link between local witchcraft cases in East Lothian and the 'discovery' of conventions of witches plotting against the king's life. Agnes Sampson was first brought before a church court in Haddington in September 1589 when Carmichael could well have been involved, though she was not then sent to trial. Before the witch hunt began in late 1590 Carmichael had been involved in court affairs as the writer of an account of the coronation of Queen Anne in May 1590. On 31 May 1590 Bowes enclosed an account of the coronation 'set forth by Mr James Carmichael' in a letter to Burghley.[17] An account survives that may well be Carmichael's, 'The forme and maner of the quenis majesties coronatioun at the kirk of Holyrudhous, 17 May 1590'.[18] It is not known why Carmichael might have written this account, but the fact that it was handed to Bowes who sent it to Burghley as an official summary suggests authorisation by James, especially since aspects of the coronation ceremony devised by the king met clerical opposition. James would have seen the advantage of a leading cleric providing the official view of events. If Carmichael did write of the coronation, it perhaps prompted James to ask him for an account of the witch trials that also touched him closely.

The clearest evidence for Carmichael's involvement in the witch trials comes from years later. On 27 March 1615, Carmichael wrote from Haddington to King James. For writing 'ane pairt of the commoun grammar'[19] and attending 'fyftein monethes upoun the examinationes of divers witches' he had been given an allowance, which apparently had not been paid. The letter asked James to renew 'the former precept'.[20] The letter confirms Carmichael's sustained, officially supported involvement in witchcraft examinations. If Carmichael's involvement began with the first cases in autumn 1590 then it would have lasted until the end of 1591. Further evidence of his active involvement in witch trials comes in Patrick Adamson's manuscript history of Scotland, where we read that 'the king himselfe and Mr. James Carmichaell Minister was much exerceised all this season [1591] in Dalkeith in tryall of witchcraft and witches'.[21] John Ferguson hoped that Carmichael was not the author of *News*, 'for there could hardly be a worse brand on one's reputation and memory than the penning of it'.[22] Recent biographers of Carmichael seem to agree with Ferguson; they disregard Carmichael's probable authorship of this pamphlet.[23]

The making of the text

Melville's brief comment suggests something about the source of Carmichael's account. In using the word 'depositions' Melville is saying that Carmichael had access to the written records of the pre-trial examinations and depositions.[24] In which case, the raw material of much of *News* would have been the pre-trial examinations, not the dittays. This hypothesis is supported by the use in *News* of the words 'examined', 'examination' and 'deposition'. We also know from Carmichael's 1615 letter that he was present at the witches' examinations.

The title-page of the quartos claim that they were 'Published according to the Scottish copy'. 'Copy' could mean a number of things at this time: a manuscript transcript, a printed account, an original text, a manuscript or printed matter prepared for printing. 'According to the Scottish copy' could mean that there was a previous edition of *News* printed in Scotland, just as the 1603 quarto of the *Demonology* printed in England for William Aspley and W. Cotton says on its title page that it is 'Printed . . . according to the copie printed at Edinburgh'. However, no such previous edition of *News* is extant, nor is there any reference to one. We have suggested that the substance of *News* is Carmichael's shaping of the depositions towards an implied panegyric of James. It was Carmichael's account that was the 'Scottish copy', and we do not have to suppose a lost Scottish edition. Indeed Larner thought it probable that *News* was written directly for an English reading public. However, a Scottish edition may well have been planned. Early on in the proceedings against the witches on 28 November 1590, Bowes told Burghley that the 'the full trialls of their [the witches'] causes are intended to be hereafter published'.[25] In a later letter, 23 February 1591, Bowes wrote that the king will have the witches's examinations printed soon after they are ended.[26]

If the publisher gave Carmichael's account to the printer as 'copy', he may well have made some minor changes to make it suitable for English readers. The title itself may be the publisher's since it implicitly addresses an English readership, offering it recent events from a foreign country. As Larner notes, the orthography of *News* is English,[27] and only rarely does the quarto retain a Scottish spelling, as in the report of the witches' reel: '*Gif* [our italics] ye will not goe before . . .'. There are instances of partial anglicisation and hence of the Scottish origins of some words or phrases: for example, 'deputy bailiff' for 'baillie depute'. The English writer has inserted explanatory phrases for the English reader. Lothian is described as 'a principal shire or part of Scotland, where the king's Majesty useth to make his chiefest residence'; the 'fore-crag' is glossed as 'forepart of her throat'; and the 'turkas' is noted as being a word 'in Scottish . . . which in England we call a pair of pincers'. In the word 'we' the English reviser explicitly identifies with the pamphlet's English readers. An English point of view is also signalled in scattered phrases, such as torture having been provided 'in that country', and Fian's execution as 'according to the law of that land'. The Scots surname MacCalzean defeated attempts to anglicise it for it appears in Q as 'Meealrean' and in the manuscript as 'Meealreane'.

The depositions come from a third writer, the scribe who transcribed the accused's words into legally acceptable language. Paragraphs beginning with 'Item' indicate legal records as their source. And behind the legal discourse lie the words spoken by the accused themselves. Although mediated first through a legal document then through a sensational pamphlet, the accused's words do lie somewhere behind the language of *News*.

News therefore is a composite text that combines and processes words from a number of speakers and writers: the accused, the scribes, James Carmichael, the English publisher. In addition it contains four woodcuts, two of which were commissioned by the publisher, and two of which came from the printer's stock. Its production was subject to ideological and market forces, with the Scottish writer having to satisfy James's wish for self-justification, and the English publisher having to satisfy rapidly the market for sensational pamphlets.

Date

All the quartos of *News* are undated, but Pantzer suggests ?1592 as a date for them. There is little external evidence for dating the pamphlet, with no Stationers' Register entry, so we have to fall back mainly on whatever evidence *News* offers. And if we accept the argument that *News* is an English publisher's edition of Carmichael's 'Scottish copy', then this complicates the question of the pamphlet's date, as the printed text could well have been issued some time later than the composition of Carmichael's account.

In the address to the reader the author says that he has published *News* to counteract manifold untruths in circulation about the witches, one of which was that the witches were discovered by a pedlar travelling to Tranent who 'was conveyed at midnight from Scotland to Bordeaux in France'. Rosen compared this story with that of Richard Burt, as recounted in G. B.'s *A Most Wicked Work of a Wretched Witch* (1592), with his aerial transport to Harrow;[28] but this seems too slight a similarity for necessarily dating *News* later than 1592.

News reports the execution of Dr Fian 'in the end of January last past, 1591', although it may have been a few weeks earlier. It does not specifically report the execution of Agnes Sampson, which was 28 January 1591, although she may be thought to be included in a general list of witches of whom *News* repeatedly tells us that some have been executed, while others remain in prison. The wording of these passages is close to a proclamation of 25 June 1591 denouncing Bothwell's part in a conspiracy that had been 'confessit be sum of the same kynd alreddy execute to the deid and sum utheris yit on lyve reddy to be execute for the same cryme',[29] and so may indicate a date at about this time.

Various possibilities fit this scenario of some witches executed, others detained in prison. Agnes Sampson, and possibly Dr Fian, were executed in late January

1591. Bowes's letter of 23 February 1591 records that a number of executions had taken place in Edinburgh and Haddington.[30] Euphame MacCalzean was not executed until June 1591 and Ritchie Graham not until February 1592. *News* also says that Barbara Napier and Euphame McCalzean have been 'apprehended'. A letter of James to Chancellor Maitland in April 1591 suggests that both Napier and MacCalzean were in custody at that time.[31] The witches 'detained in prison' may refer, but not certainly, to the detention of Barbara Napier and Euphame MacCalzean. We hear very little of either in *News* and certainly do not learn of their fate from it. They are mentioned in only one paragraph, which ends with one of the pamphlet's statements that some witches remain to be dealt with:

> The said Geillis Duncan also caused Euphame MacCalzean to be apprehended, who conspired and performed the death of her godfather . . . She also caused to be apprehended one Barbara Napier for be-witching to death Archibald, last earl of Angus . . .

This might suggest a time of writing before May–June 1591 when Barbara Napier and Euphame MacCalzean were tried, and the latter executed on 25 June 1591.

However, in *News* Agnes Sampson is 'conveyed away to prison, there to receive such torture as hath been lately provided for witches in that country'. On 26 October 1591 the privy council issued a commission for the discovery of witchcraft with power of examination and putting to torture.[32] But Agnes Sampson could not have been tortured under the terms of this commission as her trial and execution took place at the end of January 1591. The writer of *News* may be here conflating the general practice of examination accompanied by torture with the particular provisions made by the privy council in October 1591. If he knows of the privy council commission, then this would mean that the date of the writing of the pamphlet could not be before late 1591.

Finally, the title-page of *News* tells us of 'Doctor Fian, a notable sorcerer, who was burned at Edinburgh in January last, 1591'. This suggests that the printer prepared this title page before the end of 1591. This date accords with the little external evidence we have. Bowes's letter of 23 February 1591 still anticipates the printing of the witches' examinations. Towards the end of the Preface to *Demonology* James tells his readers:

> And who likes to be curious in these things, he may read, if he will hear of their practices, Bodinus' *Démonomanie* (collected with greater diligence than written with judgement), together with their confessions, that have been at this time apprehended.

'Their' confessions are those of the North Berwick witches, and in the Folger MS the sentence runs on 'quhilkis all are to be set furthe in print'. These words are crossed through in the manuscript, apparently by James himself, and do not appear in the 1597 quarto of *Demonology*.[33] They apparently anticipate the publication of *News* and suggest an early date for the writing of *Demonology*. All this evidence suggests late 1591 as the date for the issue of *News from Scotland* in print in London, and some time between February and June of that year for the composition of Carmichael's account. This would accord with the speed with which some English witchcraft pamphlets were printed.[34]

News as fiction and history

The pamphlet was published anonymously without the authority conveyed by a named author; its authority derives from its anonymity and its source in the documentary record of the court cases. Although the writer, presumed to be Carmichael, derived a good deal of narrative coherence from his material, points of incoherence and discontinuity in his stories are apparent. These show the resistance of the 'historical' material to being shaped to a single point of view. A 'news' pamphlet has to retell events as convincing stories for their moral to shine through. Analysing how *News* turns history into narrative throws into relief the pamphlet's ideology.

Fact and fiction in a popular pamphlet are not clearly distinguishable; and indeed the downright impossible appeared in early modern records as fact. When Natalie Zemon Davis investigated the mercy pleas presented to sixteenth-century French law courts she found that they contained fictional elements that should not be seen as perjury, but rather as contributions to creating a convincing story. Far from undermining the supplicants' cases, these fictional elements helped to convince the court: 'fiction did not necessarily lend falsity to an account; it might well bring verisimilitude or a moral truth'.[35] Davis was investigating court records that are more like the depositions produced for the Scottish court than the pamphlet crafted for English readers. But *News* too can be seen to be reshaping its historical elements, and fictionalising them in order to achieve its particular ideological ends.

The story of Geillis Duncan and David Seton

The pamphlet's first story about Geillis Duncan is brief but incoherent. It starts like a ballad or folk tale: 'Within the town of Tranent in the kingdom of Scotland there dwelleth one David Seton', but the evidence for identifying Duncan as a witch is weak. She falls under suspicion because she started to practise healing skills 'upon a sudden', and 'in short space' performed 'matters most miraculous'. The explanation of Duncan's being merely a traditional cunning woman is disregarded by those in authority; instead, a diabolic explanation moves the story (by means of torture) to its conclusion in Duncan's confession that 'all her doings' had been in response to the devil, and that 'she did them by witchcraft'. The disjointed account only makes sense if the notion that the devil entices women to act for him is assumed from the start. Historical events are reduced to a narrative that is meant to show the reality of witchcraft and the power of the magistrate to discover it. Duncan's confession, which supposedly affirms the discovered truth, can be seen as the victim's helpless accession to the idea violently imposed on her. Nevertheless, this story of discovery is important as the only account in the surviving texts of an origin for the witch hunt of 1590–2.[36]

Duncan is a girl whose behaviour men in authority cannot comprehend. If witch hunts arise from conditions of social stress, then *News* may offer clues to the social stresses that set off this witch hunt. Duncan's nocturnal absences are minor infringements of the rules for household servants, and her healing power is familiarly that of the wise woman, but her behaviour is seen as bewildering ('in great admiration and wondered thereat'), fearful ('in great suspicion'), and alien ('extraordinary and unlawful'). Seton's patriarchal household is disturbed by the maidservant who should be subordinated by gender and class; and Seton is also a baillie depute responsible for imposing the king's law in the district. Duncan's transgression and power seem to threaten wider patriarchal power, and the hostile questioning searches for the source of that power. Seton and the rest find the 'enemy's mark' that confirms Duncan as the witch they have already decided she is. We may see Duncan's insubordination as a manifestation at a domestic, local level of rebellion against patriarchal authority. The stresses caused by continuing political disorder in 1590—social, ideological, psychological—appear to be repeated in a tiny domestic incident. Transferred to a maidservant-witch, rebellion becomes identifiable and punishable.

The pamphlet's revelation that 'innumerable others' are witches in the area confirms the truth of the story. Indeed the account rapidly places the witches in the legal process: they are 'taken', 'detained in prison', and subject to the king's 'will and pleasure'. The veracity of Duncan's story is then confirmed by the historical events of the 'discovery', trial and execution of other witches. Duncan herself was not executed until December 1591.[37]

Agnes Sampson

The account of Agnes Sampson concentrates on her confessions of the witches meeting the devil and plotting against the king's life, already given a narrative shape in the pre-trial processes. But there is no narrative conclusion to the Sampson story; instead it ends with her voicing Christian orthodoxy—that the king would not have survived the plots 'if his faith had not prevailed above their intentions'. The ending of Sampson's execution, which took place at the end of January 1591, is not mentioned. Laura Levine describes the pamphlet's structure as a series of stories depicting escalating violence stemming from the increasing threat that each witch's unknowability presents to the authorities' sense of reality.[38] Seen in this way, Sampson's last words represent her rejection of the diabolic and her return to orthodoxy. The pamphlet only uses as much of the stories of real people as it needs to achieve its aim of demonstrating the real and ongoing threat presented by witches to royal power, a threat that is spiritual, theological and political.

The gentlewoman and the heifer

The account of John Fian, like that of Sampson, combines narrative framing with what we suppose, on the evidence of his dittay, to be passages edited from his examinations, although these have not survived. Like Sampson he is apprehended, imprisoned, tortured, and brought before the king to confess. Narrative is mixed with material from the legal record. Included in the account of Fian's confession is his attempt to use love magic on a gentlewoman. This story is particularly difficult to interpret in relation to the historicity or fictionality of *News*. Is it an account of real events, or entirely fictional, or a mixture of both? What is its origin? It may be Carmichael adapting a story in Apuleius' *The Golden Ass*,[39] in order to bolster his material on Fian, which consists of accusations of his being register to the devil at the witches' meetings and of causing the possession of a gentleman. Or it may be a story told by the educated Fian to his interrogators in order to provide a confession by talking of minor love magic. It is even possible that the story was added by the London publisher keen to make the pamphlet more sensational. However, a sentence in the middle of the story suggests Carmichael's religious response.[40] The story is made to yield a protestant moral of God's direct, personal intervention in the world in a way that counteracts the witches' belief in the personal intervention of the devil. The discovery of Fian's sorcery is taken as a sign from God 'to declare that he was heavily offended with his [Fian's] wicked intent', and that God 'did . . . work by the gentlewoman's means' to thwart Fian's 'intents'.

Despite this moralising comment, the story of the gentlewoman and the heifer belongs to the genre of fiction. It is like a fabliau in its sexual scheming, magic, and comic conclusion in which a plotter's amatory schemes recoil on him. The fabliau reversal is the popular correlative of the providence of a protestant God who intervenes in the world. One puzzling detail confirms its fictionality: the fact that Fian is instantly suspected of attempting love magic because the gentlewoman's mother 'was a witch of herself'.[41] The mother's witchcraft, casually mentioned, suggests a fictional world where magic and witchcraft are commonplace and unremarkable. A reader may momentarily forget that the question of whether a woman is a witch is precisely what is at issue in the witch-hunt. It is only after extreme torture that Agnes Sampson confesses 'those persons aforesaid to be notorious witches'. Yet in this story magic and witchcraft are the stock-in-trade of ordinary people in a folk-tale world of quick-wittedness, trickery and popular justice. The heifer, worked upon by magic and counter-magic, falling in love with Fian and 'leaping and dancing upon him', is the comic, retributive justice of a fabliau.

The comic conclusion, however, is wrenched to yield a moral about diabolism. Just as Duncan's tormentors believed her to be a witch, so 'all men' imagined that Fian 'did work by the devil', so that he became known 'among the people of Scotland' who 'secretly nominated [him] for a notable conjurer'. This flourish is then followed by Fian's being tortured to make him confess. The moral story provides the connecting link between fiction and history.

The account of Dr Fian does not yield a conclusion displaying poetic justice like the story of the gentlewoman. His story ends in his execution, which the writer sees as manifesting 'the due execution of justice' as well as 'a terror to all' who might try to deal with witchcraft. But this ending is less conclusive than that of the story of the gentlewoman and the heifer. Indeed by finally rejecting his confession Fian overturns the demands of his interrogators, and ultimately the king, that he confess to being a witch.

Truth and falsehood in *News*

News is composed from legal depositions, fictional stories, woodcuts, theological and moral generalisation, sensational scenes. It aims to establish the truth of the witches' conspiracy, the devil's personal involvement, and the king's response to treason, and to assert a notion of kingship that flows from these. These truths are established by setting them against various falsehoods.

The publisher's address insists on the truth of what *News* recounts. It repeatedly contrasts the 'manifold untruths' that are circulating about the witches and 'the true discourse' that he has published. 'Truly', 'truth', 'more truth', 'truly published', 'verity', 'so true' describe the pamphlet; 'untruths', 'miraculous and incredible', 'false' describe the rumours about the witches. Readers are those with 'honest minds who are desirous to be informed of the verity and truth of their confessions', though with the assurance that truth is 'more strange than the common report'. Since truth and strangeness go together, the 'gentle reader' can enjoy the pamphlet's violent and sexual stories with a clear conscience.

The publisher's address is conventional: it whets the appetite for what follows, and authorises the book's questionable pleasures. Nevertheless the distinction between truth and falsehood is important for *News*, as it is for *Demonology* and indeed for official justice. That distinction is confounded in one of the woodcuts where images of 'true' events are combined with the 'false' event of the pedlar being transported to Bordeaux. The mixing of 'true' and 'false' images, like the incoherent narratives, permits readers to disregard questions of truth that are ostensibly at issue, and instead enjoy a world of undifferentiated supernatural wonders. The woodcut's mixing of true and fanciful images may result from speedy production processes, and the woodcut maker's receiving information about what images to produce without having the text to hand. Readers are enticed by strangeness and 'wonderful matters' even as they are invited to seek the truth.

In the main body of the text, which this edition assigns to Carmichael, truth is claimed on the basis of the depositions of the accused. Repeatedly the writer points to his judicial sources, and the depositions acquire increased authority by having been taken in King James's presence. The witches' magical power is set against the king's investigations; and as the examinations, underwritten by the royal presence, reveal and punish wrongdoing, so the power of the king, operating through the law, is proved to be greater than the magic of the witches. It is the truth-discovering royal examiner who is shown to have supernatural power.

The writer's implied presence at the centre of events also guarantees truth. He is able to report how the king reacted with 'great admiration' when he witnessed the man whom Fian bewitched; and even what the king thought when Fian retracted his confession. And he recounts the conversation between Agnes Sampson and the king in which Sampson tells James what was said between Anne and himself on their wedding night. This story exists nowhere else in the records, and it seems unlikely that anyone would risk inventing it. The story itself hinges on questions of truth and falsehood. A scene of extraordinary intimacy is evoked between Sampson and James in which power relations are momentarily inverted. Sampson challenges James's dismissal of her and other accused as 'extreme liars' by claiming to know the wedding night conversation. This claim gives her momentary control of the scene as she takes 'his Majesty a little aside' and tells him the conversation; and this compels him into 'acknowledging her words to be most true' and to give 'more credit to the rest which is before declared'. At this moment Sampson is the one who discovers and attests the truth, taking for herself the powers that are supposed to lie with the king. Sampson's moment of dominance is costly for as she compels the king to accept her 'supernatural' knowledge as the truth she defines herself as a witch. It was common belief, and a commonplace joke in Elizabethan plays, that anyone in possession of secret or intimate knowledge about someone else must be a witch:

> . . . this drudge or diviner laid claim to me, called me Dromio, swore I was assured to her, told me what privy marks I had about me—as the mark of my shoulder, the mole in my neck, the great wart on my left arm—that I, amazed, ran from her as a witch.[42]

In the pamphlet the incident is meant to provide the best possible proof (because it concerns the king) of the threat of witches' magic. But the meaning of the scene is ambiguous for it shows truth running in two directions. Truth is meant to be the preserve, ultimately, of the sovereign who can discover and judge it; but here truth, and the power to discover it, lies with a witch.

The body in *News*

In *News* the search for incontrovertible proof of the reality of witchcraft extends beyond the criminal record, or even the king's presence at the examinations. The interrogators search for proof of the accused's guilt in the devil's mark on their bodies. Geillis Duncan's accusers try to force a confession by torture, but finding her resistant they 'suspecting that she had been marked by the devil (as commonly witches are) made diligent search about her, and found the enemy's mark to be in her fore-crag'. The satanic sign on Duncan's throat gives Seton and his associates supposedly irrefutable, physical proof of adherence to the devil. A mark is found on Duncan's and Sampson's bodies in *News*, which on the *female* body is a sign of her spiritual transformation. The men 'made diligent search about' Duncan, but the torture of Sampson is more violent and sexualised, culminating in the devil's mark being 'found on her privities', after which 'she immediately confessed whatsoever was demanded of her'. But on Fian's body, though it is 'narrowly searched . . . it could not in any wise be found'. The fears that Fian generates are not sexual, at least as reported in *News*; rather they stem from his acting as the devil's clerk at the conventions. The extreme violence directed against him suggests the rage of his accusers at a man perverting his patriarchal power as a schoolmaster, and shifting allegiance to the devil's oppositional patriarchy.[43] The mark historicises the devil, showing him entering history at real times and places and engaging with real women and men.

Violence

Only in the text of *News from Scotland* does violence appear so extensively and graphically. No sign of the torture of the accused appears in the judicial documents; and indeed such documents in Scotland and England could not record torture, for they record simply words spoken under examination, not the violent means that compelled those words nor the questions asked. *News* uniquely provides a glimpse of the official violence that was in fact ever present, and frequently activated. Official versions of this witch hunt not only omit the violence of torture from the record, they locate all violence on the side of the witches: theirs are the plots to kill individuals and destroy the commonwealth, and their witchcraft prompts the violence necessary to uncover it. In *News* violence is represented as a spectacle that 'discovers' witchcraft.

   News is the chief source for details of the tortures endured by the North Berwick witches, though an account book of 1592 records payment to a jailor 'for careing the buitts [carrying the boots] to the abbay, castell and Dalyell at sindry tymes'.[44] *News* mentions the pilliwinks, a kind of thumbscrew, the turkas, a pair of pincers to pull out the fingernails, and the boots, a wooden case encircling the leg from the ankle to the knee into which wedges were driven with a heavy hammer between the casing and the leg. The use of torture was generally informal and illegal, and physical cruelty was regularly inflicted on witchcraft suspects in local areas, of which Mackenzie complained in the seventeenth century.[45] The statement that 'when it came to witchcraft . . . torture in all but name, and frequently in name also, was applied to all victims',[46] is as true of 1590s cases as of seventeenth-century ones.

The use of torture in the case of Agnes Sampson is different. Sampson, accused by Geillis Duncan, was taken to Holyroodhouse and examined by the king and his council, and the torture she suffered was presumably at their express command, motivated in part by fear of conspiracy and treason.

Dr Fian's torments were the most terrible, with the boots being used on him. The boots seem to have been used in Scotland especially in cases of extreme gravity, such as treason and witchcraft,[47] two crimes which merged in the North Berwick cases. Fian's tortures seem to have been expressly at the king's orders, for after the boots and the discovery of pins in his tongue he was 'immediately . . . brought before the king, his confession was taken, and his own hand willingly set thereunto'. After his escape, recapture and subsequent denial of his first signed confession, Fian 'was commanded' to be subjected to the turkas and boots again, which made his legs unserviceable for the rest of his short life.[48] Remarkably, he died refusing to affirm his first confession, protesting that 'what he had done and said before was only done and said for fear of pains which he had endured'. And of his confession of attendance at conventions, and conspiracy to wreck the queen's journey to Scotland, we learn from Bowes's letter to Burghley of 23 February 1591 that 'all he denyit obstinatlie unto the death'.[49]

The devil and the convention

The pamphlet's most sensational news is the appearance of the devil at a witches' convention, in which the devil instructs the witches to direct their arts against the newly wed James and Anne. Drawn largely from Agnes Sampson's depositions, these passages present a particularly difficult problem. Does the pamphlet reflect what the writer found in the examinations, which are probably the collusive fantasies of interrogators and interrogated? Or are these passages the invention of the writer of the pamphlet? The issue is further complicated if we suppose that Carmichael was present at the questioning of the accused, and also wrote the pamphlet that claims to report their answers.

The devil's relations with the women are represented in the devil's mark. Details, again found only in *News*, of how the devil 'doth lick them with his tongue in some privy part of their body' emphasise the women's aberrant sexuality, especially in Agnes Sampson's mark found 'upon her privities'. Female sexuality is given more prominence here than in the depositions or dittays, an indication possibly of Carmichael's knowledge of demonological lore. The pamphlet ignores the men reported in the depositions and dittays as present at North Berwick, except for John Fian, and depicts an almost exclusively female gathering. Although the writer adds that the witches confessed that the devil 'would carnally use them', no such confession is in the dittays. *News* foregrounds female sexuality as alien, and potentially subversive; and ignores male sexuality.

It has no concept of sodomy that would represent men's sexual attachment to the devil as politically subversive. Although intimate, private sexual activity is imagined between an individual woman and the devil, the witches at the communal gathering at North Berwick are, as Robin Briggs has observed, 'rather well behaved'[50] despite there being two hundred of them 'making merry and drinking by the way'. There is no sexual orgy for the women at the sabbat to enjoy, and in sex with the devil there is 'little pleasure' because his penis is cold. The devil's demand that those at the sabbat kiss his naked buttocks is sexual, but not for his or their pleasure; rather it is a religious punishment, 'a penance', and a parodic sign of feudal allegiance.

The devil is represented in *News* as a feudal superior and a protestant minister in ways that mimic and parody those social roles. The devil is one 'whom [the witches] served' and to whom they have 'privately sworn' loyalty, and whose buttocks they have to kiss as a 'sign of duty to him'. His having sex with the women is subsumed into political subordination as he claims a *droit de seigneur*: 'when the devil did receive them for his servants, and . . . they had vowed themselves unto him, then he would carnally use them'. Like a feudal superior, he receives 'their oaths for their good and true service towards him', and questions Fian if he will continue 'his faithful service according to his first oath'. To Fian it is specifically as a secular office holder that the devil appears 'with a white wand in his hand' symbolising his power, finally withdrawn when it is broken. The devil also imitates protestant ministers. He takes his place in the pulpit of North Berwitck kirk as the proceedings begin, and according to the title page 'preached' to the witches, the quintessential protestant practice. We might detect in the account of his sermons as 'ungodly exhortations' that included inveighing against the king of Scotland a parody of a minister's typically impassioned denunciation of sin and the ungodly. When the devil appears to Fian in prison he is 'apparelled all in black', suggesting the Genevan gown of the Calvinist cleric.[51]

Performance in *News*

A remarkable feature of *News* is the accused's performance of some of their diabolic actions before the king and members of his privy council. Carmichael may have had this in mind, as well as the king's interrogating the accused, when he wrote of the king daring to 'hazard himself in the presence of such notorious witches'. And yet, as they are described in *News*, these performances seem anything but hazardous: the king sends for Geillis Duncan to play on the Jews' trump as she did for the dance at North Berwick kirk and takes 'great delight' in it; and John Fian brings to the king the gentleman he has possessed and the man falls into 'a madness . . . to the great admiration of his Majesty and others then present'. The account of Agnes Sampson's telling James about the wedding night conversation is also a kind of performance in the two figures moving 'a little aside' in the presence of onlookers to share private speech. Compare, for example, stage directions in Renaissance plays, such as 'They stand aside', when Hermione and Polixenes converse privately in Shakespeare's *The Winter's Tale*.[52]

The witches are not simply threatening: they are also entertaining and fascinating for the king and council. But more importantly, their performances are convincing ones: Duncan plays the same dance that she played as the revellers entered the kirk; and Fian's possessed gentleman screeches, bends and capers 'so that all the gentlemen in the chamber were not able to hold him, until they called in more help, who together bound him hand and foot'. Stephen Greenblatt asserted of repeat performances of supernatural occurrences, '[p]erformance kills belief',[53] but the repeatability of these actions before the king and council does not make them less authentic, rather it confirms their reality. James requests the performance of what has supposedly happened as a way of testing the truth of those claims. Performance overcomes scepticism and confirms belief.

Levine sees these moments in *News* as 'a means of authenticating testimony', as performances that are understood 'not as representations, but (oddly) as pieces of historical evidence',[54] and she relates them to the larger question of the threat posed by witches' magic to 'the philosophical underpinnings of reality as the examiners construct it'.[55] This, she argues, is part of the general fear in the culture of early modern Scotland and England of theatrical representation's power to undermine by its signs the things those signs represent. In its search for the 'reality' of witchcraft, then, the court takes Duncan's and Fian's performances not as fictional imitations of real actions but as actual repetitions of the actions themselves. In this sense the court refuses theatre's distinction of imitation and real, and insists that performances prove the reality of witches' magic. James was able in other contexts to see a king's power as itself 'performed', but the author of *News*, and perhaps James himself, were concerned to show witches' power as real, and hence the countervailing magic of the king also as real.

Years later in another country James and Anne were to see in an actual theatrical performance witches depicted as harmless and unreal when Ben Jonson presented his *Masque of Queens* at Whitehall in February 1609. There the witches appear in an antimasque of grotesque dancing and futile spells, only to be dispelled by the proper, real power of the queens led by Queen Anne herself. The action of this masque hovers, as all masques do, on the borderline between the real and the fictional, as the legitimate power in Anne and James's real presences supposedly replaces the witches' *maleficia*. But the sophisticated spectator is meant to recognise the blend of playful and real action. For the reader of *News* no such sophisticated response is permitted: we are led to recognise two opposing real powers of malevolence and legitimacy. But as in Jonson's masque the moments of performance before the king recounted in *News* function as antimasque, symbolising the disorderliness and evil that the king's good power will subdue and replace. When James hears the servant girl make the same twanging on her Jew's harp that accompanied the communal singing and dancing as the crowd entered the kirk to meet the devil, he encounters an image of disorder: lower-class, discordant, disordered. Similarly, the possessed man displays grotesque, disordered physical strength that is literally subdued by the courtiers who 'bound him hand and foot'. The writer of *News* anticipates the structure of Jonson's masques by recounting face-to-face encounters between the observing, understanding king and disordered, ultimately futile evil. Carmichael sets up an ideological opposition between witches and king that is resolved in favour of the king's legitimate magic.

Political witchcraft

By the time *News* was written in 1591 Bothwell was suspected of having consulted with witches about the king, and yet no mention of Bothwell is made in *News*. This significant absence highlights the pamphlet's political tactics which avoid confronting in print the real political challenge of the earl and his protestant supporters. Instead the devil appears as an alternative enemy whose opposition provides an inverted image of the king's own position and power. *News* is the first draft of a theory of Scottish kingship that would be repeated, refined and developed in *Demonology*, *Basilikon Doron* and *The Trew Law of Free Monarchies*. The devil's followers, unlike Bothwell's, were weak and disposable. Bothwell was the symbol of opposition to James at least in southern Scotland. But the argument of *News* avoids him, and the tangled network of support and complicity at court around him, and focuses instead on the devil in whom confrontation is simple and absolute.

The political scene in *News* is reduced to the figure of the king, with his consort and courtiers barely appearing. Opposed to the king is the devil, whose followers have abandoned their proper allegiance to James and transferred their loyalties to him. The pamphlet's political aim is to consolidate James's position as king by having the devil declare that the king was the greatest enemy he had in the world, thus signifying that James was crucially implicated in the natural and supernatural scheme of things as the mighty opposite to Satan, as Satan himself had testified to actual women. A mystical kingship is being fashioned as the reader is asked to consider how James managed to avoid the 'great danger to his person and the general state of the land' by facing the witches personally. The pamphlet's final peroration, with its dense concentration of biblical allusions, aligns the king with God and against the diabolic attachment of the witches: 'he is the Lord's anointed, and they but vessels of God's wrath; he is a true Christian and trusteth in God, they worse than infidels'. In this sharply simplified scheme of things, James's alignment with God dispenses with God's ministers, even though ministers took James's escape from witchcraft as a sign of God's favour to him. Mr James Melville gave the kirk's official version:

In the yeir 1590, the King, accompanied with his Quein, cam hame the first of May, to the grait joy and contentment of all the countrey. Divers practesies of witchcraft and devilrie was against him, as he was certified of therefter, bot the mercifull and mightie hand of God watched ower him, and preserved him at the ernest prayers of his fathfull servands the ministers, whom then he acknawlagit to be his maist fathfull freinds.[56]

As Stuart Clark observes, James 'used the privilege of inviolability to set public magistrates like himself decisively apart from ordinary men and their concerns'.[57]

Notes

[1] *Trial, Confession and Execution of Isobel Inch . . . at Irvine, Anno 1618* (?1855); see Ferguson 1899: 96.

[2] Larner 1981: 32.

[3] Larner 1981: 31.

[4] A number of these sixteenth-century English witchcraft pamphlets are reprinted in Rosen 1969. See also Gibson 1997.

[5] See Leuschner 1995: 1–29; Gibson 1997.

[6] See Blayney 1997: especially 389–92.

[7] Devon Record Office, Chanter MS 855B, ff. 310–12.

[8] *OED v.* 1, 2.

[9] *OED v.* 4

[10] STC 1991: iii 2, 150.

[11] STC 1991: iii 191, 123.

[12] McKerrow 1910: 303–4, 198.

[13] On Carmichael see Cameron 1993: 139; Scott 1866–71: i 311–12; Carmichael 1957: 31–42.

[14] Melville 1827: 396.

[15] Carmichael 1957: 29–30, 41.

[16] Carmichael 1957: 29–41.

[17] *CSPS* x 307.

[18] This is printed in *Papers Relative to the Marriage* 1828: 49–56. The editor notes there that 'This paper has long been preserved in the repositories of the Mar family. The then countess of Mar acted a conspicuous part in the ceremony', x.

[19] This was the *Grammaticae Latinae, de etymologia liber secundus* (Cambridge 1587) which Carmichael had dedicated to James. See also *RPCS* v 92.

[20] BL Additional MS 19 402, f. 120.

[21] Quoted in Carmichael 1957: 36; from Dr Patrick Adamson, 'History of Scotland', Edinburgh University Library, MS. La. III 203. The editor of Carmichael 1957, M. L. Anderson, comments in the sentence immediately following Adamson's quotation, 'Carmichael's own story of this enquiry and trial would have been worth reading'.

[22] Ferguson 1899: 47.

[23] See Carmichael 1957: 36.

[24] See *OED* 'deposition' *sb.* 5; *DOST* 'deposition'.

[25] *CSPS* x 425.

[26] *CSPS* x 463.

[27] Larner 1981: 31.

[28] Rosen 1969: 191.

[29] *RPCS* iv 644.

[30] *CSPS* x 467.

[31] *CSPS* x 510.

[32] *RPCS* iv 680.

[33] Dunlap 1975: 43.

[34] John Walsh was examined for witchcraft and sorcery before the bishop of Exeter on 20 August 1566, and *The Examination of John Walsh* was printed on 23 December 1566. Elizabeth Sawyer was executed for witchcraft at Tyburn on 19 April 1621, and Henry Goodcole's *The Wonderfull Discoverie of Elizabeth Sawyer* was printed the same year. Pamphlets about cases in Windsor in 1579, Chelmsford in 1579, and St Osyth in 1582 all came out in the same year as the cases were tried. Fastest of all was *The Examination and Confession of Certaine Wytches at Chensforde*, which was printed in August 1566, less than a month after

the examinations and confessions were taken. See Rosen 1991: 72–82, 83–157; Ewen 1933: 144–6, 149–52, 155–64.

35 Davis 1988: 3–4.

36 For a discussion of this episode see Normand 1997: 107–11.

37 See document 18.

38 See Levine 1994: 120–33, especially 120–1.

39 A sorceress in love with a handsome young man orders her servant to gather cuttings of his hair from the barber's floor for her to work love magic on. But the servant has to drop the hair she has gathered when the barber sees her theft, and, afraid to fail in her assignment, takes hair from goatskins instead. Her mistress's magic brings the goatskins to life whereupon the servant's lover 'kills' the animated goatskins. The servant and her lover make love, but the mistress remains disappointed. See Apuleius 1935: 123–9.

40 'But God, who knoweth the secrets of all hearts and revealeth all wicked and ungodly practices . . . did so work by the gentlewoman's own means that in the end the same was discovered.'

41 Compare Levine 1994: 129–32.

42 Shakespeare 1988: *The Comedy of Errors*, III ii 145–9.

43 A schoolmaster's importance for his local community is indicated by Alexander Home's induction to Prestonpans grammar school in 1606: 'having been presented master of the school of the Pans, the whole parishioners, on 8th July, being asked how they approved of him as schoolmaster, they, in token of their approbation, took him by the hand, faithfully promising to concur for the furtherance of the work yet to be done, and keep the schoolmaster and scholars skaithless; finally, it was thought meet that the whole visitors and parishioners present should enter the school, and there hear him teach'; Grant 1876: 238.

44 See *DOST* bute *n.* 2. The quotation presumably refers to Holyrood Abbey and Edinburgh Castle.

45 Mackenzie 1678: 86–7.

46 Smith 1972: xvii.

47 Melville 1905: 237.

48 Some of these instruments of torture are discussed and illustrated in Melville 1905: 225–48.

49 *CSPS* x 467.

50 Briggs 1996a: 54.

51 Kirk 1980: 26, notes that in Scotland 'the black teaching gown—the so-called Geneva gown—replaced the white surplice and cope, which continued to be worn during divine service in England'.

52 Shakespeare 1988: *The Winter's Tale*, I ii 110 SD.

53 Greenblatt 1988: 109.

54 Levine 1994: 133.

55 Levine 1994: 121.

56 Melville 1829: 187.

57 Clark 1997: 576.

Document 27

News from Scotland

published ?late 1591

News from Scotland,

declaring the damnable life and death of Doctor[†] Fian,[1] a notable
sorcerer, who was burned at Edinburgh in January last, 1591.

Which doctor was register[†] to the devil that sundry times preached
at North Berwick kirk to a number of notorious witches.

With the true examinations[†] of the said doctor and witches
as they uttered them in the presence of the Scottish king.

Discovering how they pretended[†] to bewitch and drown his
Majesty in the sea coming from Denmark, with such
other wonderful matters as the like hath not
been heard at any time.

Published according to the Scottish copy.[†]

[†] **Doctor** an honorary title given to a schoolmaster or an assistant master
[†] **register** registrar, clerk, keeper of records
[†] **examinations** statements made by the accused
when examined

[†] **pretended** attempted
[†] **Scottish copy** 'copy' can mean a number of
things: a manuscript transcript, a printed
account, or any material prepared for printing

To the Reader.

The manifold untruths which are spread abroad concerning the detestable actions and apprehension of those witches, whereof this history following truly entreateth,[†] hath caused me to publish the same in print.[†] And the rather for that[†] sundry written copies[†] are lately dispersed thereof, containing: that the said witches were first discovered by means of a poor pedlar travelling to the town of Tranent, and that by a wonderful manner he was in a moment conveyed at midnight from Scotland to Bordeaux[2] in France (being places of no small distance between[3]) into a merchant's cellar there; and after, being sent from Bordeaux into Scotland by certain Scottish merchants to the king's Majesty, that he discovered[†] those witches and was the cause of their apprehension; with a number of matters miraculous and incredible, all which, in truth, are most false.[†]

Nevertheless, to satisfy a number of honest minds who are desirous to be informed of the verity and truth of their confessions, which for certainty[†] is more stranger than the common report runneth[†] and yet with more truth, I have undertaken to publish this short treatise which declareth the true discourse[†] of all that hath happened, and as well what was pretended by those wicked and detestable witches against the king's Majesty, as also by what means they wrought the same.[†]

All which examinations, gentle reader, I have here truly published, as they were taken and uttered in the presence of the king's Majesty, praying thee to accept it for verity, the same being so true as cannot be reproved.[†]

A true discourse[†]
of the apprehension of sundry
witches lately taken in Scotland,[4] whereof
some are executed and some are
yet imprisoned.

With a particular recital[†] of their examinations,
taken in the presence of the king's Majesty.

[†] **entreateth** treats
[†] **in print** a letter to Burghley from Robert Bowes on 23 July 1590 says that the 'the full trialls of their [i.e. the witches'] causes are intended to be hereafter published', *CSPS* x 425
[†] **And the rather for that** and all the more because
[†] **copies** these may have been either manuscript or printed accounts
[†] **discovered** revealed
[†] **that the said ... most false** other stories of aerial transportation were being told in 1592 in G B's *A Most Wicked Worke of a Wretched Witch* (Rosen 1991: 191) and in *The English Faust Book* (Jones 1994)
[†] **for certainty** as far as the facts go
[†] **than the common report runneth** than rumour has it
[†] **discourse** succession of events
[†] **they wrought the same** they did those things they attempted
[†] **reproved** rejected
[†] **discourse** narrative
[†] **recital** account

God, by his omnipotent power, hath at all times and daily doth take such care and is so vigilant for the weal[†] and preservation of his own, that thereby he disappointeth the wicked practices and evil intents[†] of all such as, by any means whatsoever, seek indirectly to conspire anything contrary to his holy will. Yea, and by the same power he hath lately overthrown and hindered the intentions and wicked dealings of a great number of ungodly creatures, no better than devils, who, suffering themselves to be allured[5] and enticed by the devil whom they served, and unto whom they were privately[†] sworn, entered into the detestable art of witchcraft, which they studied and practised so long time that in the end they had seduced by their sorcery a number of others to be as bad as themselves, dwelling in the bounds of Lothian,[6] which is a principal shire or part of Scotland, where the king's Majesty useth[7] to make his chiefest residence or abode. And to the end[†] that their detestable wickedness, which they privily had pretended against the king's Majesty, the commonweal of that country with the nobility and subjects of the same, should come to light, God of his unspeakable[†] goodness did reveal and lay it open in very strange sort,[†] thereby to make known unto the world that their actions were contrary to the law of God and the natural affection which we ought generally[†] to bear one to another. The manner of the revealing whereof was as followeth.

Within the town of Tranent in the kingdom of Scotland there dwelleth one David Seton,[8] who, being deputy bailiff[†] in the said town, had a maidservant called[9] Geillis Duncan, who used secretly to be absent[10] and to lie[11] forth of[†] her master's house every other night. This Geillis Duncan took in hand[†] to help all such as were troubled or grieved with any kind of sickness or infirmity, and in short space did perform many matters most miraculous. Which things, forasmuch as she began to do them upon a sudden, having never done the like before, made her master and others to be in great admiration,[†] and wondered thereat. By means whereof[†] the said David Seton had his maid in some great suspicion that she did not[12] those things by natural and lawful ways, but rather supposed it to be done by some extraordinary and unlawful means.[13]

Whereupon her master began to grow very inquisitive, and examined her which way and by what means she was able to perform matters of so great

---

[†] **weal** welfare
[†] **intents** designs
[†] **privately** secretly
[†] **And to the end** and with the purpose
[†] **unspeakable** inexpressible
[†] **in very strange sort** in a very strange way
[†] **generally** as a whole, collectively
[†] **deputy bailiff** i.e. 'baillie depute', a magistrate;

in Scotland a baillie is a town magistrate and 'depute' after an office means 'appointed' not 'substitute'; see *DOST sv.* baillie 3
[†] **to lie forth of** to stay overnight away from
[†] **took in hand** undertook
[†] **admiration** astonishment
[†] **By means whereof** in consequence of this

importance; whereat[†] she gave him no answer. Nevertheless, her master,[†] to the intent that[†] he might the better try[†] and find out[14] the truth of the same, did with the help of others torment her[†] with the torture of the pilliwinks[†] upon her fingers, which is a grievous[†] torture, and binding or wrinching[†] her head with a cord or rope, which is a most cruel[†] torment also, yet would she not confess anything. Whereupon they, suspecting that she had been marked by the devil (as commonly witches are),[†] made diligent search about her, and found the enemy's[†] mark to be in her fore-crag,[†] or forepart of her throat; which being found, she confessed that all her doings was done by the wicked allurements and enticements of the devil, and that she did them by witchcraft.

After this her confession, she was committed to prison where she continued for a season;[†] where immediately she accused these persons following to be notorious witches, and caused them forthwith to be apprehended one after another: viz. Agnes Sampson the eldest witch of them all, dwelling in Haddington, Agnes Tompson[†] of Edinburgh, Doctor Fian, alias John Cunningham, master of the school at Saltpans[†] in Lothian,[15] of whose life and strange acts you shall hear more largely in the end of this discourse. These were by the said Geillis Duncan accused, as also George Mott's[16] wife dwelling in Saltpans,[17] Robert Grierson, skipper,[18] and Janet Bandilands,[† 19] with the

---

[†] **whereat** to which

[†] **her master** Mackenzie noted that a witch's accusers were likely to be 'Masters, or Neighbours' (Mackenzie 1678: 87)

[†] **to the intent** in order that

[†] **try** extract

[†] **did ... torment her** local gentlemen and magistrates seem to have taken it upon themselves to extract information from suspected witches, but Seton's examination with torture of Geillis Duncan was strictly illegal

[†] **pilliwinks** also called 'pilniewinks', and 'thumbikins' in Scotland, an instrument of torture like the thumbscrew; George F. Black tried them out and testified to their 'terrible agony' (Black 1938: 16); for illustrations of pilliwinks and discussion of their use, see Melville 1905 and Brook 1891

[†] **grievous** severe

[†] **wrinching** tightening and twisting

[†] **cruel** very painful; here and elsewhere in the pamphlet 'cruel' and 'grievous' do not signify any disapproval of the tortures, but merely indicate a degree of severity

[†] **marked by ... witches are** it was a belief in continental Europe and in Scotland that witches were marked, usually in a hidden or secret place, or sealed by the devil as his own, and as a sign of their compact with him. The site of the mark

was often believed to remain insensible to pain. See Bodin 1580: ff. 79ᵛ–80; Boguet 1929: 128–30; Daneau 1575: F4ᵛ–5; Robbins 1959: 135–7.

[†] **enemy's** the devil is often referred to in early modern Scotland as the 'enemy of God'

[†] **fore-crag** front of the neck; used more commonly in Scotland than England

[†] **season** period of time

[†] **Agnes Tompson** the extant dittays and depositions contain no record of an Agnes Tompson among the names of the witches, although they mention a Bessie Thomson and Margaret Thomson. Bessie Thomson's name occurs in both dittays and depositions frequently, often after that of Geillis Duncan. The name 'Agnes Tompson' here is likely to be an error because later in *News* information ascribed to her is actually provided in the dittays by Agnes Sampson.

[†] **Saltpans** i.e. Prestonpans, where salt was produced from sea water

[†] **Janet Bandilands** this is the only witch in this group whose name does not occur in the dittays. Neither 'Bandilandis' (*D*) nor 'Blandilandis' (*G*) seems a common Scottish surname. Sandilands is the name of one of the jurors in Barbara Napier's trial and Euphame MacCalzean was accused of having bewitched Marie Sandelands, and 'Bandilands' may be an error for this.

porter's[20] wife of Seton, the smith at the Brig halls,[†][21] with innumerable others in those parts,[22] and dwelling in those bounds aforesaid; of whom some are already executed, the rest remain in prison to receive the doom of judgement at the king's Majesty's will and pleasure.

The said Geillis Duncan also caused Euphame MacCalzean[23] to be apprehended, who conspired and performed the death of her godfather,[†] and who used her art upon a gentleman being one of the lords and justices of the session,[†] for bearing good will to her daughter. She[†] also caused to be apprehended one Barbara Napier for bewitching to death Archibald, last earl of Angus,[†] who languished to death by witchcraft and yet the same was not suspected, but that he died of so strange a disease as the physician[24] knew not how to cure or remedy the same. But of all other the said witches,[†] these two last before recited[†] were reputed for as civil, honest women as any that dwelled within the city of Edinburgh, before they were apprehended. Many other[25] besides were taken dwelling in Leith who are detained in prison until his Majesty's further will and pleasure be known, of whose wicked doings you shall particularly hear, which was as followeth.

This aforesaid Agnes Sampson, which was the elder[†] witch, was taken and brought to Holyroodhouse[26] before the king's Majesty and sundry other of the nobility of Scotland, where she was straitly[†] examined; but all the persuasions which the king's Majesty used to her with the rest of his council might not provoke or induce her to confess anything, but stood[†] stiffly[†] in the denial of all that was laid to her charge. Whereupon they caused her to be conveyed away to prison, there to receive such torture as hath been lately provided for witches in that country.

And forasmuch as by due examination of witchcraft and witches in Scotland it hath lately been found that the devil doth generally mark them with a privy mark,[27] by reason the witches have confessed themselves that the devil doth lick them with his tongue in some privy part of their body before he doth receive them to be his servants; which mark commonly is given them

---

[†] **Brig halls** 'covered market in Edinburgh' (Rosen 1991: 193)

[†] **godfather** i.e. father-in-law. McCalzean was accused and convicted as being 'art and part of the consulting with the said Annie Sampson for the destroying of Mr John Moscrop, your father-in-law' (document 23); compare also document 20 for the conviction of Agnes Sampson for making the image

[†] **lords and justices of the session** since 1532 the court of session had been the supreme civil tribunal in Scotland; its judges were styled lords of session

[†] **She** i.e. Geillis Duncan

[†] **Archibald ... Angus** at her trial Barbara Napier was acquitted by the assize of consulting with Agnes Sampson for making an image to destroy Archibald, earl of Angus

[†] **But of ... said witches** but among all the other witches mentioned here

[†] **recited** named

[†] **elder** oldest

[†] **straitly** rigorously

[†] **stood** i.e. but she stood

[†] **stiffly** resolutely, stubbornly

under the hair in some part of their body whereby it may not easily be found out or seen,[†] although they be searched. And generally so long as the mark is not seen to those which search them, so long the parties that hath the mark will never confess anything.[†] Therefore by special commandment this Agnes Sampson had all her hair shaven[†] off in each part of her body, and her head thrawn[†] with a rope according to the custom of that country, being a pain most grievous, which she continued[†] almost an hour, during which time she would not confess anything, until the devil's mark was found upon her privities;[†] then she immediately confessed whatsoever was[28] demanded of her,[†] and justifying[†] those persons aforesaid to be notorious witches.

Item,[†] the said Agnes Sampson[29] was after brought again before the king's Majesty and his council, and being examined of the meetings and detestable dealings of those witches, she confessed that upon the night of Allhollon Even last,[†] she was accompanied as well with the persons aforesaid as also with a great many other witches to the number of two hundred; and that all they together went to[30] sea each one in a riddle or sieve,[†] and went in the same very substantially[†] with flagons of wine, making merry and drinking by the way[†] in the same riddles or sieves, to the kirk[31] of North Berwick in

---

[†] **privy mark … or seen** the devil supposedly marked sorcerers and witches in a secret place on their bodies as a sign of his power over them; see Daneau 1575: F4ᵛ–5

[†] **never confess anything** Boguet says witches must be stripped and have all their hair shaved off, to discover any mark on their bodies, or drugs hidden in their hair that produce taciturnity and insensibility from pain when tortured. Unless these are discovered they will never confess (Boguet 1929: 125–6 and article xiv, 216).

[†] **shaven** 'to thintent the judges and such as are set in aucthoritie of life and death, and to enquire of such matters, may the better perceive, let them specially provide, that when any of these shalbe convented before them, to poulle [i.e. poll, crop the hair] and shave them where occasion shall serve, al the body over, least haply the marke may lurke under the heare in any place' (Daneau 1575: sig F5); Scot notes the inquisitorial practice that if witches do not confess 'everie haire in their bodie must be shaven off with a sharpe razor' (Scot 1886: II ii 17)

[†] **thrawn** bound around and twisted

[†] **continued** endured

[†] **privities** private parts, genitals. The witch's mark given by the devil or a mark indicating where the English witch fed her familiar was supposedly frequently found on or near the genitals; Martin Del Rio recommended searching for the mark near the sexual or excretory organs, and Guazzo says that in women the devil's mark is found on the breasts or private parts (Guazzo 1929: 15).

[†] **demanded of her** asked of her

[†] **justifying** confirming

[†] **Item** this word, usually signifying the clause of a document, may be an indication that the author is using material from the examinations of the witches

[†] **Allhollon Even last** All Hallows' Even, i.e. Halloween, 31 October, is the night before All Saints' (All Hallows') Day.

[†] **sieve** a mode of transportation known also to a witch in eighteenth-century Hungary (Klaniczay 1993: 246); wonderful and unnatural transportation to the sabbat is common in continental accounts

[†] **substantially** physically, really

[†] **by the way** as they went; drinking wine in ships is mentioned in the dittays (documents 19 and 20)

Lothian; and that after they had landed, took hands on the land and danced[†] this reel[32] or short dance, singing all with one voice:

> *Commer*[†] *go ye before, commer go ye;*
> *If* [† 33] *ye will not go before, commer let me.*[†]

At which time she confessed that this Geillis Duncan did go before them playing this reel or dance upon a small trump, called a Jew's trump,[† 34] until they entered into the kirk of North Berwick.

These confessions made the king in a wonderful admiration,[†] and sent for the said Geillis Duncan, who upon the like trump did play the said dance before the king's Majesty, who in respect of the strangeness of these matters took great delight to be present at their examinations.

Item, the said Agnes Sampson[35] confessed that the devil being then at North Berwick kirk[36] attending their coming in the habit[†] or likeness of a man, and seeing that they tarried over long, he at their coming enjoined them all to a penance,[† 37] which was that they should kiss his buttocks[†] in sign of duty to him; which being put over the pulpit bare,[† 38] everyone did as he had enjoined them. And having made his ungodly exhortations,[†] wherein he did greatly inveigh against[†] the king of Scotland, he received their oaths for their good and true service towards him, and departed; which done, they returned to sea, and so home again. At which time the witches demanded of the devil why he did bear such hatred to the king, who answered, by reason[†] the king is the greatest enemy he hath in the world. All which their confessions and depositions are still extant upon record.

[†] **danced** dancing, usually of a disordered kind, often back to back, and led by the devil, was one stage in proceedings at the sabbat; compare 'then fal they to dauncing, wherin he leadeth the daunce, or els they hoppe and daunce merely about him, singing most filthy songes made in his prayse' (Daneau 1575: sig F7ᵛ)

[†] **Commer** 'a female gossip or intimate friend' (*DOST*)

[†] **If** the reading of *Q*, 'Gif', is a rare instance of the retention by the pamphlet of the original Scots

[†] **Commer ... let me** only the first line of this distich is reported by Calderwood (Calderwood 1842–9: v 116)

[†] **trump ... Jew's trump** Jew's harp; a simple musical instrument played by being held between the teeth and struck with the finger. The dittays agree with *News* in describing Geillis Duncan playing the trump; in Calderwood's account it is the devil who plays (Calderwood 1842–9: v 116)

[†] **admiration** astonishment

[†] **habit** bodily appearance

[†] **penance** Olaus Magnus reports that those who were late for the devil's service were punished (Ankarloo 1993: 289)

[†] **kiss his buttocks** for the 'shameful kiss' (*osculum infame*) as a regular gesture of homage to the devil at the meetings of witches, see the note on Fian's dittay, item 5 (document 19) and *Demonology* II iii

[†] **bare** i.e. naked. Kissing the devil's bare arse is indicated in an examination of Agnes Sampson: 'He lifted up his gown and every one kissed his arse' (document 1).

[†] **ungodly exhortations** Fian's dittay says that the devil preached in the pulpit in North Berwick kirk (document 19)

[†] **inveigh against** violently denounce

[†] **by reason** because

Item, the said Agnes Sampson confessed before the king's Majesty sundry things which were so miraculous[39] and strange as that his Majesty said they were all extreme liars.[40] Whereat she answered she would not wish his Majesty to suppose her words to be false, but rather to believe them, in that she would discover such matter unto him as his Majesty should not any way doubt of. And thereupon taking his Majesty a little aside, she declared unto him the very words which passed between the king's Majesty and his queen at Upslo[†] in Norway the first night of[41] their marriage,[42] with their answer each to other; whereat the king's Majesty wondered greatly, and swore by the living God that he believed that all the devils in hell could not have discovered the same, acknowledging her words to be most true; and therefore gave the more credit to the rest which is before declared.

Touching this Agnes Sampson,[43] she is the only woman who by the devil's persuasion should have intended[†] and put in execution the king's Majesty's death[44] in this manner. She confessed that she took a black toad and did hang the same up by the heels three days, and collected and gathered the venom as it dropped and fell from it in an oyster shell, and kept the same venom close covered until she should obtain any part or piece of foul[†] linen cloth that had appertained to the king's Majesty,[45] as[†] shirt, handkercher, napkin[†] or any other thing; which she practised[†] to obtain by means of one John Kers,[46] who being attendant[†] in his Majesty's chamber, desired[†] him for old acquaintance between them to help her to one—or a piece of—such a cloth as is aforesaid, which thing the said John Kers[47] denied to help her to, saying he could not help her to it.

And the said Agnes Sampson,[48] by her depositions since her apprehension, saith that if she had obtained any one piece of linen cloth which the king had worn and fouled she had bewitched him to death, and put him to such extraordinary pains as if he had been lying upon sharp thorns and ends of needles.

Moreover, she confessed that at the time when his Majesty was in Denmark, she, being accompanied with the parties before specially named, took a cat and christened it, and afterward bound to each part of that cat the chiefest[49] parts[† 50] of a dead man, and several joints of his body; and that in the night following the said cat was conveyed into the midst of the sea by all these witches sailing in their riddles or sieves, as is aforesaid; and so left the said

---

† **Upslo** i.e. Oslo; having been married by proxy at Kronborg Castle, Denmark, 20 August 1589, James and Anne were married in person at Oslo, 24 November 1589
† **intended** planned
† **foul** used
† **as** such as

† **napkin** pocket handkerchief or neckerchief, rather than table napkin
† **practised** contrived
† **attendant** a servant
† **desired** i.e. she desired
† **the chiefest parts** the biggest bones

cat right before[†] the town of Leith in Scotland. This done, there did arise such a tempest in the sea as a greater hath not been seen;[†] which tempest was the cause of the perishing of a boat or vessel coming over from the town of Burntisland[† 51] to the town of Leith, wherein was sundry jewels and rich gifts which should have been presented to the now queen of Scotland, at her Majesty's coming to Leith.[†]

Again it is confessed,[52] that the said christened cat was the cause that the king's Majesty's ship, at his coming forth of Denmark, had a contrary wind to the rest of his ships then being in his company, which thing was most strange and true, as the king's Majesty acknowledgeth; for when the rest of the ships had a fair and good wind, then was the wind contrary and altogether against his Majesty. And further, the said witch declared that his Majesty had never come safely from the sea, if his faith had not prevailed above[53] their intentions.[†]

Moreover, the said witches being demanded[†] how the devil would use them when he was in their company, they confessed that when the devil did receive them for his servants, and that they had vowed themselves unto him, then he would carnally use them,[†] albeit to their little pleasure, in respect of his cold nature;[†] and would do the like at sundry other times.

As touching the aforesaid Doctor Fian, alias John Cunningham, the examination of his acts since his apprehension declareth the great subtlety of the devil and therefore maketh things to appear the more miraculous. For being apprehended by the accusation of the said Geillis Duncan aforesaid,

---

[†] **right before** (in the sea) directly facing

[†] **Moreover ... had not been seen** the raising of a storm by Agnes Sampson and others to stay the queen's coming, which involved 'christening' a cat and throwing it into the sea, is described in item 40 of Sampson's dittay

[†] **Burntisland** a town on the other side of the Firth of Forth from Leith

[†] **This done ... to Leith** these storms took place in September 1589. In letters of 8 October 1589, William Ashbey dates the loss of the boat as 7 September in a letter to Walsingham and 8 September in a letter to Burghley: 'Madam Kenedie, who was with the late Quene in England, and divers gentlewomen and marchants of Eden-browghe, to the nomber of fourtie that perished, with plate and hangings brought hither for the mariage, which was all lost' (*CSPS* x 165–6). Madam Kennedy was Sir James Melville's sister-in-law: 'The stormes wer also sa gret heir, that ane boit perissit betwen Brunteland and Leith, wherin was a gentilwoman callit Jene Kenete, wha had bene lang in England with the Quen his Maiesteis mother and was sen syn maried

upon my brother the maister houshald [master of the household] to hir Maieste, Sir Andro Melville of Garvok ... the vehement storm drave a schip forceably upon the said boit, and drownit the gentilwoman and all the personnes except twa. This the Scotis witches confessit unto his Maieste to have done' (Melville 1827: 369–70).

[†] **intentions** designs

[†] **demanded** questioned

[†] **carnally use them** sex with the devil in human or animal form is a frequent accusation in continental trials and a feature of the sabbat; Bodin discusses 'Si les sorciers ont copulation avec les Demons' (Bodin 1580: II vii ff. 104–9). Only in *News* are the North Berwick witches reported as confessing to sex with the devil: it is not to be found anywhere in the dittays.

[†] **cold nature** continental witches sometimes reported that sex with the devil was unpleasurable, or was even accompanied by discomfort or pain, and that his penis and sperm were cold (e.g. Boguet 1929: 5, 31; Bodin 1580: II vii f. 105; and for many other references Murray 1921: 176–81)

who confessed he was their register, and that there was not one man suffered to come to the devil's readings[†] but only he, the said doctor was taken
and imprisoned and used with the accustomed pain[†] provided for those
offences, inflicted[54] upon the rest as is aforesaid.

First, by thrawing[†] of his head with a rope, whereat he would confess
nothing. Secondly, he was persuaded by fair means to confess his follies, but
that would prevail as little.[†] Lastly, he was put to the most severe and cruel[†]
pain in the world, called 'the boots';[†] who after he had received three strokes,
being enquired if he would confess his damnable acts and wicked life, his
tongue would not serve him to speak. In respect whereof the rest of the
witches willed[†] to search his tongue, under which was found two pins thrust
up into the head,[†] whereupon the witches did say, 'Now is the charm stinted',[†]
and showed that those charmed pins were the cause he could not confess
anything. Then was he immediately released of the boots, brought before
the king, his confession[†] was taken, and his own hand willingly set thereunto,[†]
which contained as followeth.

First, that at the general meetings of those witches he was always present;
that he was clerk[†] to all those that were in subjection to the devil's service
bearing the name of witches; that alway he did take their oaths for their true
service to the devil, and that he wrote for them such matters as the devil
still[†] pleased to command him.

Item, he confessed that by his witchcraft he did bewitch a gentleman
dwelling near to the Saltpans, where the said doctor kept school, only for
being enamoured of a gentlewoman whom he loved himself. By means of
which his sorcery, witchcraft and devilish practices he caused the said
gentleman that once in twenty-four hours he fell into a lunacy[†] and madness,
and so continued one whole hour together. And for the verity of the same,[†]
he caused the gentleman to be brought before the king's Majesty, which was
upon the 24 day of December last.[†] And being in his Majesty's chamber,

---

[†] **readings** reading aloud of written matter;
especially after 1560 the reading of set prayers
or Scripture; this continues the close parody of
a kirk service, as a 'reader' was an office established in the first Book of Discipline (1560) to
read the Scriptures and set prayers in the
absence of an ordained minister. Although the
office was abolished by the general assembly in
1580, it lingered on.

[†] **pain** torture

[†] **thrawing** binding about and twisting

[†] **that would prevail as little** that had as little
success

[†] **cruel** extreme (rather than 'pitiless')

[†] **the boots** a device in which 'the prisoner's legs
were held in iron tubes, and wedges hammered

in between the flesh and the metal' (Rosen 1991:
198)

[†] **willed** i.e. urged the torturers

[†] **up into the head** up to their heads

[†] **stinted** stopped

[†] **confession** this is not extant

[†] **willingly set thereunto** i.e. he voluntarily signed
the confession

[†] **clerk** secretary, scribe

[†] **still** always

[†] **a lunacy** a fit of insanity

[†] **And for ... the same** and to verify this

[†] **December last** i.e. December 1590. Apparently
Fian brought the lunatic gentleman into the
king's presence two days before his trial on 26
December 1590.

suddenly he[†] gave a great screech[55] and fell into a madness, sometime bending himself, and sometime capering so directly up[†] that his head did touch the ceiling of the chamber, to the great admiration of his Majesty and others then present; so that all the gentlemen in the chamber were not able to hold him,[†] until they called in more help, who together bound him hand and foot, and suffering[†] the said gentleman to lie still until his fury[†] were past, he within an hour came again to himself. When being demanded of[†] the king's Majesty what he saw or did all that while, answered that he had been in a sound sleep.

Item, the said doctor did also confess that he had used means sundry times to obtain his purpose and wicked intent of the same gentlewoman, and, seeing himself disappointed of his intention, he determined[†] by all ways he might to obtain the same, trusting by conjuring, witchcraft and sorcery to obtain it in this manner.[†]

It happened this gentlewoman, being unmarried, had a brother who went to school with the said doctor, and calling his scholar to him,[†] demanded if he did lie[†] with his sister, who answered he did. By means whereof he[†] thought to obtain his purpose, and therefore secretly promised to teach him without stripes,[†] so[†] he would obtain for him three hairs of his sister's privities[†] at such time as he should spy[56] best occasion for it; which the youth promised faithfully to perform,[57] and vowed speedily to put it in practice, taking a piece of conjured paper[†] of his master to lap[†] them in when he had gotten them. And thereupon the boy practised[†] nightly to obtain his master's purpose, especially when his sister was asleep.

But God, who knoweth the secrets of all hearts and revealeth all wicked and ungodly practices, would not suffer the intents of this devilish[58] doctor to come to that purpose[†] which he supposed it would; and therefore to declare that he was heavily offended with his wicked intent, did so work by

---

[†] **he** i.e. the gentleman
[†] **capering so directly up** leaping straight up so high
[†] **were not able to hold him** extraordinary strength was interpreted as a sign of supernatural affliction, particularly of demonic possession
[†] **suffering** leaving
[†] **fury** violent frenzy
[†] **demanded of** questioned by
[†] **determined** decided
[†] **in this manner** there is nothing like the following story in John Fian's dittay. There is a very similar story in Apuleius, *The Golden Ass*.
[†] **calling his scholar to him** i.e. Fian called his scholar to him
[†] **lie** sleep in the same bed

[†] **he** i.e. John Fian
[†] **without stripes** without beating him
[†] **so** if
[†] **privities** private parts; pubic hair is especially appropriate as the object of operation in an act of amatory magic
[†] **conjured paper** enchanted paper. A similar case of a young man using charmed paper was heard before the *parlement* of Paris, in which the man was accused 'that by certaine scroles or papers, and such like charmes, he attempted the honour and chastitie of one whom he loved' (Le Loyer 1586: 294–310).
[†] **lap** wrap
[†] **practised** tried
[†] **come to that purpose** achieve that successful conclusion

the gentlewoman's own means that in the end the same was discovered and brought to light. For she being one night asleep and her brother in bed with her, suddenly cried out to her mother, declaring that her brother would not suffer her to sleep. Whereupon her mother, having a quick capacity,[†] did vehemently suspect Doctor Fian's intention, by reason she was a witch of herself, and therefore presently arose and was very inquisitive of the boy to understand his intent, and the better to know the same did beat him with sundry stripes, whereby he discovered[†] the truth unto her.

The mother, therefore, being well practised in witchcraft, did think it most convenient[†] to meet with[†] the doctor in his own art; and thereupon took the paper from the boy, wherein he should have put the same hairs, and went to a young heifer which never had borne calf nor gone to the bull,[†] and with a pair of shears, clipped off three hairs from the udder of the cow, and wrapped them in the same paper, which she again delivered to the boy, then willing him to give the same to his said master, which he immediately did.

The schoolmaster, so soon as he had received them, thinking them indeed to be the maid's hairs, went straight and wrought his art[†] upon them. But the doctor had no sooner done[59] his intent to them, but presently the heifer or cow whose hairs[60] they were indeed, came unto the door of the church wherein the schoolmaster was,[†] into the which the heifer went, and made towards the schoolmaster, leaping and dancing upon him,[61] and following him forth of the church and to what place so ever he went, to the great admiration of all the townsmen of Saltpans, and many other who did behold the same.

All which although in the beginning he denied and would not confess, yet having felt the pain of the boots (and the charm stinted, as aforesaid) he confessed all the aforesaid to be most true, without producing any witnesses to justify the same;[†] and thereupon before the king's Majesty he subscribed[†] the said confessions with his own hand, which for truth remaineth upon record in Scotland.[†]

The report whereof made all men imagine[†] that he did work it by the devil, without whom it could never have been so sufficiently[†] effected; and thereupon the name of the said Dr Fian (who was but a very young man)

[†] **quick capacity** sharp mind
[†] **discovered** revealed
[†] **convenient** appropriate
[†] **meet with** counter, respond to
[†] **heifer ... to the bull** the magical logic is that the virginal young cow substitutes for the girl
[†] **wrought his art** worked his magic
[†] **door ... schoolmaster was** 'School was taught in the church porch, often extended into a kind

of annexe' (Rosen 1991: 200)
[†] **justify the same** show him to be innocent of the charges
[†] **subscribed** signed
[†] **which for truth ... in Scotland** these are not extant
[†] **imagine** consider
[†] **sufficiently** completely

began to grow so common among the people of Scotland that he was secretly nominated for[†] a notable conjurer.

After that the depositions[62] and examinations of the said Doctor Fian alias Cunningham was taken, as already is declared, with his own hand willingly set thereunto, he was by the master of the prison committed to ward,[†] and appointed to a chamber by himself, where, forsaking his wicked ways, acknowledging his most ungodly life, showing that he had too much followed the allurements and enticements of Satan, and fondly practised his conclusions[†] by conjuring, witchcraft, enchantment, sorcery,[†] and such like, he renounced the devil and all his wicked works, vowed to lead the life of a Christian, and seemed newly converted[63] towards God.

The morrow after, upon conference had with him,[†] he granted[†] that the devil had appeared unto him in the night before,[†] apparelled all in black with a white wand[†] in his hand, and that the devil demanded of him if he would continue his faithful service[64] according to his first oath and promise made to that effect. Whom (as he then said) he utterly renounced to his face, and said unto him in this manner: 'Avoid,[†] Satan, avoid! For I have listened too much unto thee, and by the same thou hast undone[†] me,[†] in respect whereof I utterly forsake thee'. To whom the devil answered, 'That once ere[65] thou die thou shalt be mine'. And with that (as he said) the devil brake the white wand,[†] and immediately vanished forth of his sight.

Thus all the day this Doctor Fian continued very solitary, and seemed to have care of[†] his own soul, and would call upon God, showing himself penitent for his wicked life. Nevertheless, the same night he found such

---

[†] **nominated for** got a name for being

[†] **committed to ward** put in prison

[†] **fondly practised his conclusions** foolishly practised his experiments

[†] **conjuring ... sorcery** although demonologists defined, derived and distinguished these words as technically meaning different practices, it is likely that here they are no more than vague synonyms. See the similarly imprecise catalogue in the *English Faust Book*: 'figures, characters, conjurations, incantations, with many other ceremonies belonging to these infernal arts, as necromancy, charms, soothsaying, witchcraft, enchantment' (Jones 1994: 92, lines 52–5).

[†] **upon conference had with him** after he had been talked with

[†] **granted** admitted

[†] **the devil ... night before** Boguet too allows that the devil may visit witches in prison (Boguet 1929: xlvi 132–6)

[†] **white wand** 'often carried as a mark of office' (Rosen 1991: 200). In the case of Bessie Dunlop, the devil, whom she called Thom Reid, ap-

peared to her with 'ane quhyte wand in his hand' (Pitcairn 1833: I iii 51).

[†] **Avoid** leave me

[†] **undone** ruined

[†] **Avoid ... undone me** this sort of outburst is stereotypically reported of recanting magicians, such as Henry Cornelius Agrippa, who at the point of death supposedly turned on the devil who had served him in the shape of a black dog, crying '*Abi a me perdita bestia, quae me perdidisti*: that is Depart from me thou wicked beast whiche hast destroyed me' (Agrippa 1569: sig *3ᵛ)

[†] **brake the white wand** either a sign of Fian's renunciation of magic, as in Prospero's 'I'll break my staff' (Shakespeare 1988: *The Tempest* V i 54), although in this symbolic gesture magicians usually break their own staffs; or, more probably, the devil's resignation of his authority over Fian, as breaking one's staff symbolised the ending of an office: 'the Earl of Worcester / hath broke his staff, resigned his stewardship' (Shakespeare 1988: *Richard II*, II ii 58–9)

[†] **have care of** be anxious about

means that he stole the key of the prison door and chamber in the which he was, which in the night he opened and fled away to the Saltpans, where he was always[†] resident, and first apprehended. Of whose sudden departure when the king's Majesty had intelligence,[†] he presently[†] commanded diligent inquiry to be made for his apprehension, and for the better effecting thereof he sent public proclamations into all parts of his land to the same effect. By means of whose hot and hardy[†] pursuit he was again taken and brought to prison, and then being called before the king's Highness he was re-examined,[66] as well touching[†] his departure as also touching all that had before happened. But this doctor, notwithstanding that his own confession appeareth remaining in record under his own handwriting, and the same thereunto fixed[†] in the presence of the king's Majesty and sundry of his council, yet did he utterly deny the same.

Whereupon the king's Majesty, perceiving his stubborn wilfulness,[67] conceived and imagined that in the time of his absence he had entered into new conference and league[†] with the devil his master, and that he had been again newly marked, for the which he was narrowly[†] searched, but it could not in any[68] wise be found. Yet for more trial of him to make him confess, he was commanded to have a most strange torment which was done in this manner following. His nails upon all his fingers were riven[†] and pulled off with an instrument called in Scottish a 'turkas', which in England we call a pair of pincers, and under every nail there was thrust in[69] two needles over even[70] up to the heads. At all which torments notwithstanding the doctor never shrunk[†] any whit, neither would he then confess it the sooner for all the tortures inflicted upon him. Then was he with all convenient speed, by commandment, conveyed again to the torment of the boots, wherein he continued a long time and did abide[†] so many blows in them that his legs were crushed and beaten together as small as might be, and the bones and flesh so bruised that the blood and marrow spouted forth in great abundance, whereby they were made unserviceable for ever. And notwithstanding all these grievous pains and cruel torments he would not confess anything; so deeply had the devil entered into his heart, that he utterly denied all that which he had before avouched, and would say nothing thereunto but this: that what he had done and said before was only done and said for fear of pains which he had endured.

[†] **always** permanently
[†] **intelligence** information
[†] **presently** there and then
[†] **hot and hardy** rapid and determined
[†] **touching** concerning
[†] **fixed** sealed

[†] **conference and league** agreement and compact
[†] **narrowly** closely
[†] **riven** tugged out
[†] **shrunk** flinched
[†] **did abide** endured

Upon great consideration therefore taken by the king's Majesty and his council, as well for the due execution of justice upon such detestable malefactors,[71] as also for example sake to remain a terror to all others hereafter that shall attempt to deal in the like wicked and ungodly actions, as[†] witchcraft, sorcery, conjuration[†] and such like, the said Doctor Fian was soon after arraigned, condemned, and adjudged by the law to die, and then to be burned according to the law of that land provided in that behalf.[†] Whereupon he was put into a cart and, being first strangled, he was immediately put into a great fire, being ready provided for that purpose, and there burned in the castle hill of Edinburgh on a Saturday in the end of January last past, 1591.[†] The rest of the witches which are not yet executed remain in prison till further trial, and knowledge of his Majesty's pleasure.[†][72]

This strange discourse[†] before recited[†] may[73] perhaps give some occasion of[†] doubt to such as shall happen to read the same, and thereby conjecture that the king's Majesty would not hazard himself in the presence of such notorious witches lest thereby might have ensued great danger to his person and the general state of the land, which thing in truth might well have been feared. But to answer generally to such, let this suffice: that first, it is well known that the king is the child and servant of God, and they but servants to the devil; he is the lord's anointed,[†] and they but vessels of God's wrath;[†] he is a true Christian and trusteth in God, they worse than infidels,[†] for they

---

[†] **as** such as

[†] **Upon great ... witchcraft, sorcery, conjuration** as the pamphlet describes the sentencing and execution of Fian, it may be echoing the terms of the 1563 act of parliament against 'usaris or abusaris foirsaidis of Witchcraftis Sors-arie or Necromancie'

[†] **in that behalf** for that purpose

[†] **Saturday ... 1591** we have no date for Fian's execution other than a Saturday at 'the end of January' 1591 as given here in *News*. The end of January 1591 was certainly the time of the trial and execution of Agnes Sampson, and this may have influenced the author of *News*. John Fian's dittay is dated 26 December 1590 and one would expect execution normally within a very few days or even the day after, i.e. 27 December 1590. Bowes mentions his execution in a letter of 23 February 1591.

[†] **rest of the witches ... Majesty's pleasure** it is not clear who these witches are. In a note sent to Burghley on 23 February 1591 Bowes records the executions of Agnes Sampson, Dr Fian and other witches as having taken place, and 'moe then fourtie apprehendit and under triall and examinatioun instantlie' (*CSPS* x 467). Donald

Robson, Janet Stratton, Geillis Duncan and Bessie Thomson were still alive at the time of Barbara Napier's trial, 8 May 1591 (document 22).

[†] **discourse** narrative

[†] **recited** told

[†] **occasion of** grounds for

[†] **lord's anointed** the phrase is used of kings in some books of the Old Testament, twice in 1 Samuel 24: 'And he said unto his men, The lord kepe me from doing that thing unto my master the lords Anointed, to lay mine hand upon him: for he is the Anointed of the lord' and 'I will not lay mine hand on my master: for he is the lords Anointed' (Bassandyne: 1 Samuel 7 and 11)

[†] **vessels of God's wrath** 'What and if God wolde, to shewe his wrath, and to make his power knowen, suffer with long patience the vessels of wrath, prepared to destruction?' (Bassandyne: Romans 9.22)

[†] **infidels** literally 'unfaithful'; those who do not believe in Christianity, often applied particularly to Muslims; presumably the witches are worse than infidels as they have knowingly rejected their baptism and Christian faith

only trust in the devil who daily serves them till he have brought them to utter destruction. But hereby it seemeth that his Highness carried a magnanimous[†] and undaunted mind not feared with[†] their enchantments, but resolute in this: that so long as God is with him, he feareth not who is against him.[†] And truly the whole scope[†] of this treatise doth so plainly lay open the wonderful providence of the Almighty,[74] that if he had not been defended by his omnipotency and power, his Highness had never returned alive in his voyage from Denmark; so that there is no doubt that God would as well defend him on the land as on the sea, where they pretended[†] their damnable practice.[75]

FINIS.

[†] **magnanimous** noble and courageous
[†] **feared with** frightened by
[†] **so long ... against him** 'If God be on our side, who can be against us' (Bassandyne: Romans 8.31). The chapter goes on (8.33) 'Who shall lay ony thing to the charge of God's chosen?'. In his description of the witches' supposed conspiracy againt the king, Melville too attributes

James's preservation to his virtue: 'And certanly he is a man of God, and dois na wrang wittingly, bot is inclynit to all godlynes, justice, and vertu, therfore God hes preserved him in the midis of many dangers' (Melville 1827: 396).
[†] **scope** object, end
[†] **they pretended** they (i.e. the witches) attempted

Textual Notes to *News from Scotland*

1. damnable life and death of Doctor Fian] *D, L*; damnable life of Doctor Fian *G, Web, Rox*
2. Bordeaux] Burdeux *Q*
3. no small distance between] *D*; small distance between *G, Web*
4. in Scotland] in Scotland: *Q*; in scotland at Edenborough in January last 1591 *MS*
5. allured] *Q*; inlured *MS*
6. Lothian] Lowthian *D*; Lowthinn *G, Gent Mag*; Lowthen *Webster*
7. useth] *Q*; use *MS*
8. David Seton] David Seaton *Q*
9. maidservant called] maid servant called *D*; maide called *G*
10. to be absent] *D*; to absent *G, Webr*
11. and to lie] *D*; and lie *G*
12. not] *Q*; note *MS*
13. extraordinary and unlawful] *Q*; extra-ordinarye means *MS*
14. and find out] *Q*; and trie out and ffinde *MS*
15. Lothian] Lowthian *Q*
16. Mott's] *Motts Q*; Wats *MS*
17. Saltpans] *D*; Lowthian *G, Web*
18. skipper] *Q*; shipper *MS*
19. Janet Bandilands] Iennit Bandilandis *D*; Iennet Blandilandis *G*; Jannet Blandilandis *Web*; Grnuitt Baueilomis *MS*
20. porter's] porters *D*; potters *G, Gent Mag, Web*
21. Brig halls] Brigge Hallis *Q*; bridge Hallis *MS*
22. those parts] *G, Web*; that parts *D*; that place and parts *MS*
23. MacCalzean] Meealrean *Q*; Meealreane *MS*
24. physician] Phisition *Q*; physicians *Gent Mag*
25. apprehended. Many other] *Q*; apprehended others *MS*
26. Holyroodhouse] Haliriud house *Q*; Halleriude house *MS*
27. privy mark] *Q*; private mark *Gent Mag*
28. confessed whatsoever was] *Q*; confessed was *MS*
29. Agnes Sampson] *Web*; Agnis Tompson *Q*
30. to] *G, Web, MS*; by *D*
31. kirk] Kirke *G*; Kerke *D*; church *MS*
32. reel] reill *Q*; Riddle *MS*
33. If] Gif *Q*
34. playing ... trump,] *Q*; playinge upon a smale trumpe called a Jews trumpe this Ridle ore daunce aforesaid *MS*
35. Agnes Sampson] *Web*; Agnes Samson *MS*; Agnis Tompson *Q*
36. kirk] Kerke *Q*; churche *MS*
37. enjoined them all to a penance] *Q*; put them all to a pennaunce *MS*
38. bare] barre *D*; bar *Gent Mag*; bare *G, Web, MS*
39. Majesty ... miraculous] *Q*; majestie such wonderous things soe meraculous *MS*
40. all extreme liars] *Q*; all lyes *MS*
41. first night of] *Q*; first of *MS*
42. night of their marriage] *D*; night of mariage *G, Web*
43. Agnes Sampson] Agnis Sampsone *MS*; Agnis Tompson *Q*
44. king's Majesty's death] *Q*; kings death *MS*
45. king's Majesty] *Q*; kings majesties bodie *MS*
46. Kers] *Q*; bres *MS*
47. Kers] *Q*; Bres *MS*
48. Agnes Sampson] *MS, Web*; Agnis Tompson *Q*
49. cat the chiefest] *Q*; catt theefeste *MS*
50. parts] *D*; parte *G*
51. Burntsisland] Brunt Iland *Q*; Brante Ilande *MS*
52. it is confessed] *Q*; shee confessed *MS*
53. above] *Q*; agaynst *MS*
54. inflicted] *Q*; afflicted *MS*
55. screech] scritch *Q*; screach *Gent Mag*
56. spy] *Q*; finde *MS*
57. perform] *Q*; doe *MS*
58. devilish] *Q*; wicked *MS*
59. had no sooner done] *Q*; note soe soone done *MS*
60. heifer or cow whose hairs] *Q*; heifere whose haiers *MS*
61. came ... him] *Q*; came into the church where the scoole master was and mad towardes him leaping and dauncinge upon him *MS*
62. depositions] *Q*; dispositions *MS*
63. converted] *D, L, G, Web, Gent Mag*; connected *Harrison, Rosen*

[64] service] *Q*; servante *MS*
[65] once ere] *Q*; once before *MS*
[66] re-examined] *Q*; examinede *MS*
[67] stubborn wilfulness] *Q*; stubborn wicked-
nes and willfullness *MS*
[68] any] *Q*; noe *MS*
[69] in] *Q*; under *MS*

[70] needles over even] *Q*; needles even *MS*
[71] upon ... malefactors] *Q*; upon him and all
other such mallifactors *MS*
[72] pleasure] *Q*; will and pleasure *MS*
[73] may] *Q*; manie *MS*
[74] the Almighty] *Q*; Thallmightie *MS*
[75] practice] *Q*; practisses *MS*

Chapter 10

THEORISING THE WITCH HUNT: JAMES VI'S *Demonology*

The date of *Demonology*

Demonology could in theory have been written any time between 1591 and 1597, and within these limits scholars have favoured either an early date or a late one, arguing that James was motivated by either the examinations and trials of 1590–1 or another outbreak of witchcraft prosecutions in 1597.[1] In this edition an early date is preferred for the following reasons.

A sense of the urgent and the immediate pervades *Demonology*'s preface and the opening exchanges between Philomathes and Epistemon. Although a claim to have written in haste or carelessly is a conventional humanist gesture,[2] the king's pressing desire in his preface 'to dispatch in post' his work and his sense of 'the fearful abounding at this time in this country' of witches may suggest that the work was written hard on the heels of the examination of the witches in 1590–1 in which James took a leading role, or was even begun at a time when the examinations and trials were still proceeding in the first half of 1591. On the other hand it is conventional for writers of demonological treatises to claim that witches are plentiful and increasing at an alarming rate and to claim to have been provoked into writing by the erroneous and 'damnable' opinions of previous and recent writers, in James's case the moderately sceptical works of Johann Weyer and Reginald Scot.[3] These works can hardly have been the immediate cause prompting James to write as the first edition of Weyer was in 1563 and of Scot's *Discoverie* in 1584, suggesting that the immediate stimulus was James's experience of witch prosecutions.[4] Nevertheless, the opening exchanges between *Demonology*'s two speakers indicate more than a conventional

gesture of haste. They indicate a pressing topicality for the discussions: Philomathes refers to 'these strange news, which now only furnishes purpose [provides
the only topic of conversation] to all men at their meeting' and Epistemon
replies that 'so clear and plain confessions in that purpose have never fallen
out in any age or country'.[5] Similarly, at the opening of book II, Philomathes
anticipates that Epistemon will argue from 'the daily practic and confession of
so many' (II i).

James's descriptions in book II of some witchcraft practices have such a close
similarity to and even verbal echoes of details recorded in the dittays of the
trials from the early months of 1591 or of the pre-trial confessions and
depositions of 1590–1, that these too point to a time when the material was
fresh in James's mind. In addition, when James is arguing (II i) that witches
need not be melancholic, but can be rich, worldly-wise, fat and merry, the initials
'E M', 'R G' and 'B N' have been added in the margin of the Folger MS of
Demonology.[6] Whose hand added these initials is uncertain, but Rhodes Dunlap
suggested it was that of James Carmichael.[7] This suggests that James still had
fresh in his mind his dealings ('as may be presently seen by many that have at
this time confessed') with quite particular witches: E[uphame] M[acCalzean],
R[ichard] G[raham] and B[arbara] N[apier]. And towards the end of the Preface
in the 1597 quarto, James tells his readers:

> And who likes to be curious in these things, he may read, if he will hear
> of their practices, Bodinus' *Démonomanie* (collected with greater
> diligence than written with judgement), together with their confessions,
> that have been at this time apprehended.

'Their' confessions were not just those of witches generally at the end of the
sixteenth century, but specifically those of the North Berwick witches. In the
Folger MS the sentence runs on 'quhilkis all are to be set furthe in print',
apparently anticipating the publication of *News from Scotland*. The end of this
sentence is crossed through in the manuscript, apparently by James himself,
and does not appear in the 1597 quarto.[8] If the publication of *News* is to be
dated late 1591, then this would put the date of James's completed and revised
text of *Demonology* in the Folger MS, which is substantially that of the 1597
printed text, earlier in 1591.

The sources of *Demonology*

It would have been surprising if, when writing *Demonology*, James had not drawn
on his own experiences of the examination and trial of witches, just as in France
Boguet, Rémy and de Lancre, when writing their demonologies, drew on theirs.
In all these cases there is a two-way exchange. In examining or prosecuting
witches demonologists are likely to bring certain theoretical presuppositions
and expectations to bear, and these are likely to affect and shape the testimonies
of the accused and the records of those testimonies. Those records, or memories

of them, are in turn fed (along with other materials) into the demonological works which these men write.

James's recollections of passages from the dittays (or from the pre-trial examinations which provided material for them) are sometimes very close. James writes of the devil's first approach to people who will become witches 'either upon their walking solitary in the fields, or else lying pansing [ruminating] in their bed, but always without the company of any other' (II ii). Here he is remembering the devil's first approach to Dr Fian 'when he was lying in his bed in Tranent in Thomas Trumbill's chamber, musing and pensing how he might be revenged of the said Thomas' and how '[Agnes Sampson] confessed before his Majesty that the devil in man's likeness met her going out in the fields from her own house at Keith betwix five and six at even, being her alone'. James's discussion of transvection in spirit to the convention also recalls Fian's dittay. James writes (II iv) that witches are

> carried by the force of the Spirit which is their conductor, either above the earth or above the sea swiftly to the place where they are to meet— which I am persuaded to be likewise possible . . . And some saith that their bodies lying still as in an ecstacy, their spirits will be ravished (II iv).

Fian was accused that

> he was struckin in great ecstacies and trances, lying by the space of two or three hours dead, his sprite taken, and suffered himself to be carried and transported to many mountains as though through all the world, according to his own depositions . . . Item, filed for the suffering of himself to be carried to North Berwick kirk (he being lying in a closed bed in Prestonpans), as if he had been soughand athwart the earth . . . Item, filed for suffering himself to be carried to the sea with Satan. And at the first he was skimming over all the sea without land.

Other recollections of pre-trial and trial materials where the verbal echoes are not so strong are: witches meeting in churches, the devil preaching in the pulpit and the shameful kiss (II iii), exhuming corpses at the convention to make powders, raising storms, causing possession, making wax and clay images and melting them, and transference of diseases and using magical powders to cure.

Clearly, the bible is one of the main sources for James. In *Demonology* it is the prime authority and final court of appeal in an argument. There is an absence of citation of classical instances which are used in many demonologies to supplement the rather meagre number of biblical instances of magic.

As Christina Larner pointed out, it is difficult to trace specific sources of the *Demonology*.[9] This is partly because the typical nature of James's short treatise makes it difficult to say precisely which previous demonological treatises influenced his work, but 'he had read diligently, if not widely, in the Continental lore of the subject'.[10] From the preface we gather that he had read, or at least implied that he had read, the following demonological works: Reginald Scot,

The Discoverie of Witchcraft (London 1584), Johann Weyer, *De Praestigiis Daemonum* (first edition Basle 1563), Jean Bodin, *De la Démonamanie des Sorciers* (Paris 1580), the part of Andreas Gerardus Hyperius, *Lieux Communs de la Religion Chrestienne* (Geneva 1568) dealing with the abilities of devils, and the *Admonitio de Superstitionibus Magicis Vitandis* (Copenhagen 1575) of Niels Hemmingsen. He also mentions a book giving practical instructions for the invocation of spirits, the *Liber Quartus* of pseudo-Agrippa of Nettesheim. If he read this last work he may have read also Agrippa's *De Occulta Philosophia Libri Tres* (Cologne 1533) with which the *Liber Quartus* was often bound, as it is in the Paris edition of 1575 and its reprints.[11] It is sometimes suggested that Hemmingsen's *Admonitio* particularly affected *Demonology*, largely because James met Hemmingsen in the winter of 1589–90. Some passages in both treatises have a general similarity, but since the points in these passages are rather commonplace in many demonologies (e.g. the rise of magic in Persia, the illicit nature of recourse to magic in cases of affliction or illness caused by magic) it is difficult to be certain. Recent commentators have doubted whether James and Hemmingsen even discussed demonological matters at their meeting.[12]

None of the demonological works mentioned by James is listed as being in his library, which did contain other works by their authors: Bodin's *République* handsomely bound, some theological works by Niels Hemmingsen, and Agrippa's *De Vanitate*.[13] Pierre Boaistuau, *Les Histoires Prodigieuses*, which James mentions in passing as 'the book of the histories prodigious,' was also in the young king's library.[14]

Despite his stigmatisation of Reginald Scot's 'damnable opinions', evidence suggests James drew on Scot for information, and all the authorities mentioned in the preface to *Demonology* are cited in Scot. Scot was an important agent of transmission of demonological information to British readers from continental works such as Bodin's *Démomomanie* and the *Malleus Maleficarum*, two works which he cites in translation at some length. It seems likely that James drew on Scot's discussion of the witch of Endor in I i, as did Holland. James could have found descriptions of conjurations and magic circles (I v) in both Agrippa and Scot. Passages about pretended demonic hierarchies and the demons assigned to the four points of the compass (I vi) sound very like Scot, although Scot himself got his list, and the four demonic kings of the compass points, from the *Pseudomonarchia Daemonum* in later editions of Weyer's *De Praestigiis*.[15]

The form, nature and purpose of *Demonology*

Demonology and demonologies

The eighty-one pages in the 1597 quarto of *Demonology* make it a very modest volume compared with the treatises of Johann Weyer, Jean Bodin (just over 500 pages in the 1580 edition) or Reginald Scot, let alone the 1,000 pages in three volumes of the Jesuit Martin del Rio's *Disquisitionum Magicarum Libri Sex*

(Louvain 1599, 1600). However, it covers many of the same questions as these more extensive works, although less copiously, less elaborately and with fewer marginal citations. It is closest in size and kind to three other dialogues on witchcraft: *De Veneficis, quos olim Sortilegos, Dialogus* (Geneva 1574), an octavo of 127 pages by the Calvinist minister, philologist and professor of theology Lambert Daneau (1530–95), which was translated into English as *A Dialogue of Witches* (1575); Henry Holland's *A Treatise against Witchcraft* (Cambridge 1590); and the puritan George Gifford's *A Dialogue concerning Witches and Witchcraftes* (1593). Daneau's treatise, like James's and Henry Holland's, is a two-handed dialogue and anticipates some of the tactics of *Demonology*. Its dialogue is between an authoritative teacher, Theophilus, and his 'feed', Anthony, a sceptical, inquiring and intelligent pupil, although he modestly pleads 'the slownesse of my understandyng'.[16] Anthony gives Theophilus the right prompts, objects with the right intelligent doubt to be overcome, and gets patted on the head when he comes up with the right response.[17] The dialogues of both Daneau and King James appeal to the prime authority of Scripture for argument, example and proof, both have philological interests, and both stress the reliance people must have on God in the face of afflictions caused by witchcraft.

Demonology is 'neither original nor profound' as a demonological treatise,[18] but its lack of these qualities makes it typical. Notestein, however, thought that it was as able a work of its kind as anything in English up to the time of Joseph Glanville in 1668.[19] Its uniqueness lies in its being the only demonology by a Renaissance monarch. It makes a series of discursive moves in ways that are standard, even commonplace, in demonological treatises of the sixteenth and early seventeenth ceturies. It discusses a series of familiar topics. Can magicians really command devils? Why and within what limits does God permit the devil through his human agents to do harm? It asks standard questions and offers standard answers: How does the the devil bring about apparent miracles or wonders? 'Because he excelleth in nature, in swiftnes of motion, and in knowledge.'[20] It offers simple exegeses of the usual biblical passages such as the evocation of Samuel by the witch of Endor (1 Samuel 28) and the wonders (not miracles) performed by Pharaoh's magicians in contest with Moses and Aaron (Exodus 7 and 8). In addition, and in spite of the king's liking 'to speak scholastically' (Preface), it discusses these familiar *topoi* with comparative brevity and simplicity.

Many of the points James makes are the often iterated commonplaces of most demonological writings: God's omnipotence and the necessity of his permission for the devil to act as his instrument or even executioner ('as God's hangman'). Consequently, in one sense the devil's powers are severely limited and not even supernatural. He cannot through his own abilities see the future (I i), and his power lies in deception, pretence and tricks which make him seem more powerful than he is. His apparent miracles are only false wonders in imitation of God's real ones. All magical practices have effect not through any independent power innate in their practitioners or independently accessed by them through words or ceremonies, but by pact, either tacit or express, with the devil. Tacit pact is implicit in those who attempt magical operation of any kind; express pact is when practitioners knowingly make a formal agreement with the devil to serve him. A distinction between magic and witchcraft is one only in appearance. Both witches and magicians have no real agency in their practices: magicians only seem to command devils, witches only serve them (I iii). There is no power in magical operations in themselves to command spirits; it is yet another of the devil's tricks to make us think so. Nevertheless there is such a thing as witchcraft: it is an act of disobedience and of religious or moral apostasy (I ii).

The subjects of the three books of *Demonology* are respectively magic, witchcraft, and the nature and operations of spirits. Although all three were often treated together within one demonological treatise, apparitions and spirits could also be the subject of a separate work, and there are a number of sixteenth- and seventeenth-century treatises devoted exclusively to spirits and apparitions.[21]

Aims and genre

In the preface James declares two aims typical of many demonological treatises: to convert doubters to a belief in witches and to urge the punishment of witches.[22] The treatise has therefore both 'pastoral' and juridical interests. The first aim aligns James with theologians and pastors; the second with inquisitors, lawyers and judges. As a king he saw himself as both instructing and judging. 'It is patently clear, for instance both from *Newes from Scotland* and from his speech to the jurors of Barbara Napier, that James wished to play the part of the people's teacher and patriarch.'[23] On 7 June 1591, when he addressed those jurors, James spoke of the necessity of rightly instructing sceptics: 'As for them who thinke these witchcraftes to be but fantacyes, I remmyt them to be catechised and instructed in these most evident poyntes'.[24] As Clark has observed, nearly all protestant demonological treatises were written by pastors or those in a position to influence the training of protestant ministry.[25] The king was intent, like the protestant pastors Hemmingsen, Hyperius, Danaeus and Gifford, on inculcating a right protestant belief about witchcraft. This stressed the grave spiritual errors and dangers in a misunderstanding of the true nature of witchcraft, and also in illicit dealings with witches themselves, such as seeking their help in cases of illness or *maleficia*. The Scottish witchcraft act of 1563, unlike the English witchcraft act of the same year, had legislated against consulters of witches. As an observer and intended victim of witchcraft, and also as a magistrate who had investigated, intervened in, and urged the prosecution of witches, James was concerned with the proper treatment, examination and punishment of witches. *Demonology*, like many other demonologies, reserves this topic to the work's end and treats it most fully in its final pages.

Demonology's aim to instil right belief in a lay audience is characteristic of the homiletic nature of protestant treatises.[26] James chose the vernacular and the dialogue 'to make this treatise the more pleasant and facile', just as Gifford used the 'Dialogue, to make the fitter for the capacity of the simpler sort'.[27] James's dialogue, however, is not as accommodating as Gifford's. Gifford would never have used the scholastic and logical terms, or displayed the etymological derivations from Greek, and the Latin tags, that James does. The headnote to the first chapter of *Demonology*, which was an interlinear addition made by James himself to the Folger MS, promises that Epistemon and Philomathes will 'reason the matter' dialectically. If James had in mind the generality of the literate laity as one audience, he had his fellow demonologists as another. The former were likely to associate themselves with Philomathes, the latter with Epistemon.

The dialogue

The dialogue was a popular form in the fifteenth and sixteenth centuries in Europe.[28] This was due partly to a humanist desire to imitate the models of admired classical authors such as Cicero, Lucian, and Plato who in his dialogues, according to Sidney, 'feigneth many honest burgesses of Athens to speak of such matters, that, if they had been set on the rack, they would never have confessed them'.[29] The dialogues of Cicero, Erasmus and also Lucian were texts used in schools, indeed W. Kempe in *The Education of Children* had written in the sixteenth century of children of eight, that 'Dialogs are most easie for their capacitie'.[30]

The dialogue was sometimes used for controversial issues, including witchcraft. In *Strix* by the humanist Gianfrancesco Pico della Mirandola, two of the four speakers are Apistius ('unbeliever') and Strix the witch herself.[31] Daneau's *De Veneficis* (Geneva 1574) was translated into English in 1575, and Holland's dialogue (1590) and Gifford's (1593) were contemporary with the North Berwick witch prosecutions. Henry Holland's brother Robert wrote a Welsh dialogue on witchcraft, *Tudor and Gronow* (c.1595).[32] The dialogue was still being used for discussions of witchcraft in 1718, the date of *A Historical Essay concerning Witchcraft* by Bishop Francis Hutchinson, 'the man who gave the *coup de grâce* to the witch delusion in England'.[33] This took the form of a dialogue about witchcraft between a clergyman, a Scottish lawyer and an English juryman.

Demonology's dialogue form scarcely masks its didactic and catechistic strategy, and the catechism itself, the most popular form of instruction about matters of faith, was itself a form of dialogue. *Demonology*, like Daneau's *Dialogue*, is a 'closed' dialogue in which a master expounds answers in response to a pupil's questions. Its catechistic strategy is plainly revealed in the holograph fragment of I i–iii in MS Bodley 165, where the speech prefixes of the two speakers are not even the transparently-named Philomathes ('lover of knowledge') and Epistemon ('knowledgeable'), but simpy 'Q[uestion]' and 'A[nswer]'. Epistemon sometimes takes a schoolmasterly sharp tone with Philomathes: 'I see if you had taken good tent to the nature of that word hereby I named it, ye would not have been in this doubt nor mistaken me so far as ye have done' (I v), or a schoolmasterly jocular one: 'I think ye take me to be a witch myself, or at least would fain swear yourself prentice to that craft' (I v).

Authority, argument and proof

Witchcraft and scripture

The title of a late seventeenth-century English treatise on witchcraft testifies not only to a persisting belief in witchcraft, but also to the arguments and authorities regularly called on to support such a belief. J. Brinley's *A Discourse proving by Scripture and Reason and the best Authors, Ancient and Modern, that there are Witches* (1686) invokes three areas of proof: scripture, reason, and ancient and modern authorities. These were the usual bases of argument in demonologies, and indeed many other sorts of treatise, and were those, for example, that King James used when he wrote *The Trew Law of Free Monarchies* (1598).[34] In the English translation of Daneau's *Dialogue*, Theophilus displays the sort of argument and proof from written authority deployed in witchcraft treatises, and the customary privileging of the prime authority of scripture:

> There are three only meanes and places ['places' renders somewhat imprecisely the Latin text's *loci* (grounds of proof)] to prove any thing, yea although it seeme altogether incredible, which three thinges be these: Aucthoritie of men, experience of the thing, & reason founded upon upright judgement of mynd, which places wil all confirme our opinion, not one only, although one were sufficient. And first as touching authoritie, there are playne and evident testimonies to be gathered out of holy scriptures, and also of other aucthours, most evidently confirming that there are such kindes of witches in the world, which we cal divelish sorcerers.[35]

The preface to Hemmingsen's *Admonitio*, which James had read, is full of exhortations 'to lift our eyes to the light of God's word',[36] and numerous English treatises about witchcraft testify to the bible's being both the foundation and touchstone of their arguments.[37] When Epistemon cites Jeremiah in *Demonology* I iv to declare predictive astrology illicit, he calls the scriptures 'an infallible ground to all true Christians', for 'it was, above all, the bible on which authors relied for support—often to the exclusion of all other authorities'.[38] The opening chapters of all three books of *Demonology* cite biblical passages when establishing the subjects of these books. The primacy of scripture is asserted in the argument to *Demonology* I i ('Proven by the Scripture that these unlawful arts *in genere* have been and may be put in practice'), re-asserted in the argument to II i when James turns more particularly to witchcraft ('Proved by the Scripture that such a thing can be'), and in III i, 'we are certified by the scriptures' of the apparitions of spirits by Isaiah and Jeremiah.

The Old Testament contains brief condemnations of divination and magical practices, including the sentence of death pronounced on witches in Exodus.[39] More substantial biblical passages were read from patristic times as providing instances of magic or showing the power of the devil: Job's affliction, with God's permission, by Satan; Saul's consultation of the witch of Endor; the contest of Moses and Aaron with Pharaoh's magicians; Simon Magus; the girl with the spirit of python exorcised by Paul.[40] All these are cited by James, many at the end of I i, and come in the wake of *Demonology*'s discussion of the witch of Endor. The citations of these passages accumulate evidence from scripture and reinforce its prime authority.

The initial discussion of 1 Samuel 28 implicitly establishes scripture as the most important authority and also the touchstone for other arguments and authorities. In its course other biblical citations are used to support, elucidate or expand the argument. The verses alluded to are those found again and again in demonological discussion, such as Satan's ability to transform himself into an angel of light (2 Corinthians 11.14) and the lying wonders which will accompany Antichrist (2 Thessalonians 2.11–12). Book I, which opens with one exegetical debate, ends with another, as Epistemon corrects Philomathes' interpretation of Acts 7.22, 'And Moses was learned in all the wisdome of the Egyptians'. Philomathes had taken this to mean that Moses was skilled in magic,[41] and was entertaining the possibility that magic might in some instances be lawful. As in the discussion of the witch of Endor, the argument comprises a network of inter-meshing biblical texts.

After brief exchanges between Philomathes and Epistemon, discussion turns immediately to exegesis of the bible's most extended narrative of the practice of magic. 1 Samuel 28 tells of King Saul's visit to the witch of Endor, and Philomathes shrewdly anticipates Epistemon's use of this:

> EPISTEMON . . . that witchcraft and witches have been and are, the former part is clearly proved by the Scriptures, and the last by daily experience and confessions.

> PHILOMATHES I know ye will allege me Saul's pythoness . . .

This incident was one of the most discussed biblical instances of witchcraft; 'of Samuels apparition . . . now adayes there is greate contention and reasoning', as Lavater observed,[42] and it appears regularly in demonological discussions.[43] Although it was virtually impossible to write a demonological treatise without addressing 1 Samuel 28, the story must have had a particular interest for James. Old Testament kings, including Saul, were often invoked as types or patterns by early modern monarchs or their supporters.[44] 1 Samuel 28 also provided a narrative of a beleagured king's dealings with witchcraft. James was both a king and a demonologist who had recent dealings and conversations with witches, indeed who arguably in conversation with Agnes Sampson had 'consulted' her.

He listened to her revelations about conversations on his wedding night, and in one of her pre-trial examinations Sampson had passed on the devil's prediction about offspring and also the devil's advice on dealing with the ministers.[45] In addition, Francis, earl of Bothwell, an alternative and would-be king, was regularly accused in 1591–3 of dealings with witches very like Saul's, including attempts to know his political future.

In the discussion of 1 Samuel 28 Philomathes and Epistemon eventually agree that Samuel was not raised. This was the usual understanding of this passage as 'all Christians of whatsoever religion agrees upon that', as Epistemon (inaccurately) asserts. There were three traditional explanations of 1 Samuel 28 which all assumed it reported a supernatural incident: Samuel was really raised by the witch's magic, Samuel or a demon appeared at God's command, 'Samuel' was an impersonating demon. In their discussion Philomathes and Epistemon are largely personifications of a familiar dialectic about this incident and reach the usual conclusion: something was raised at Endor but 'the ghost of Samuel' was an impersonating demon, an opinion shared even by the sceptical Weyer.[46] However, Philomathes is given a rather unusual argument: that it was all a trick perpetrated by the woman of Endor, and no spirit of any kind was raised. This unusual explanation is that given by Reginald Scot,[47] who does not accept the majority opinion of the devil impersonating Samuel. Although James railed against Scot's opinions, and although *Demonology* comes to the usual orthodox conclusion about the witch of Endor, there is good reason to suppose that James is drawing on Scot's exposition of 1 Samuel 28 in the *Discoverie*. Henry Holland gave his interlocutor Mysodaemon some of Scot's arguments about 1 Samuel 28, so that the orthodox Theophilus could knock them down.[48] Similarly Philomathes is set up with Scot's explanation so that Epistemon can counter it with orthodox exposition. Scot and James's Philomathes assume that the woman was a trickster, and emphasise Saul's extreme physical and mental state (Scot describes him as 'straught of mind'). But it is the orthodox Epistemon who says, like Scot, that the woman used preparatory 'conjurations' and that Saul was in another room ('in another chamber', 'in hir closet'[49]) when the apparition was conjured up.[50] We have found the latter supposition, which the biblical text does not support,[51] nowhere else.[52]

In some ways James's appropriation of part of Scot's treatment of the witch of Endor would not be unusual. Demonologists regularly discussed standard subjects (transformation, transvection, sexual relations with demons), discussed the same notable biblical examples, and repeated, rewrote and discussed passages from earlier demonologists. If James based his discussion of 1 Samuel 28 on Scot, then giving Philomathes some of Scot's points is not really surprising, for Philomathes' views are usually there to be corrected or emended. What is more interesting is that some of Scot's information is given to Epistemon. In witchcraft dialogues the author can be often detected through his authoritative and orthodox spokesman, as in the cases of Gifford's Daniel, Holland's Theophilus, and James's Epistemon. In Epistemon's discussion of the witch of

Endor, James borrows the voice of the man whose damnable opinions he criticised in his preface. The Hebrew word used in 1 Samuel 28 of the woman at Endor was usually rendered in Greek as *engastrimythos* (one who speaks from the belly), and in Latin often as *ventriloqua*, as Scot points out.[53] She was literally ventriloquised, by her spirit speaking in her stomach. In his discussion of this important biblical *topos*, at some moments the author of *Demonology* actually allowed the ventriloquism of the orthodox Epistemon by the sceptical Scot.

Etymology and taxonomy

The exact meaning of biblical words for magic and its practitioners, and their translation in classical and vernacular languages, became an important issue in demonological writing. *Demonology* I iii and II ii display etymologies and taxonomies characteristic of many Renaissance demonologies that regularly examined meanings and etymologies, or false etymologies, of words for magical practices and practitioners, and also categorised the magic arts and kinds of divination. Weyer examined the words for magical practitioners in the Old Testament, as had Daneau;[54] and Bodin took up and countered Weyer's philological arguments in his 'Refutation des opinions de Jean Wier' in *Démonomanie*.[55] Many of the books of Scot's *Discoverie* (VI–VII, IX–XIII, XV) take as their point of departure the interpretation of the eight different Hebrew words for magicians and diviners in the bible, a method found in other demonologies.[56]

To distinguish between magic and witchcraft, and between different sorts of magical practice, as James does in books I and II of *Demonology*, had long been traditional. There are philological and taxonomic discussions of magic in classical and medieval works. There were taxonomies of divination and magic arts in Cicero, *De Divinatione Deorum*, and Varro, whose classification of divination by the four elements became a commonplace, and is mentioned by James (I iv). Medieval taxonomies of magic include the important section *De magis* in the *Etymologies* (VIII ix) of the encyclopaedist Isidore of Seville, which considers the possible origins of magic, mentions classical and biblical instances, and considers different kinds of divination and magic. Isidore's discussion was followed by those of many medieval writers.[57] In a tradition of fanciful and also false etymologies some discussions followed Isidore, who for example explained *divini* (diviners) as deriving from *quasi deo pleni* (full of the god, i.e. inspired).[58] *Malleus Maleficarum* notoriously used a false etymology to demonstrate women's superstitious practices arising from weak faith: '"Woman [*foemina*]" comes from "faith [*fe*]" and "less [*minus*]", because she always has and keeps less faith'.[59]

James gives a very Isidorean etymology, *incubus . . . ab incubando*, in III iii. He also gives a derivation of *necromanteia* which already had a place in the discussion of the magic arts in Isidore's *Etymologies*. James's description of necromancy as this 'black and unlawful science' bears traces of the old false etymology for *nigromantia* and the medieval English 'nigromancy' and 'negromancy' as a 'black art'. Thomas Ady protested in 1656 against interpretation of single words and against James's discussion of 'necromancy' in particular: 'what Logician doth not know that it is not a legal manner of arguing, but most absurd to draw a Conclusion from the bare signification of words, or from what words may signifie?'[60] The etymology of the word 'magic' and its Persian origins had been discussed by Pliny,[61] and is found in many demonologies, such as Hemmingsen's *Admonitio*. Hemmingsen discussed the word right at the beginning of his treatise and offered an explanation very like James's:

> Those whom the Greeks called 'wise men [*sophos*]' the Persians called 'magicians [*magos*]'; hence the Greek '*sophia*' and the Persian '*magia*' for 'wisdom [*sapientia*]', particularly for the superior understanding of nature and observation of the movements of the heavenly bodies and the effects they have on things here below.[62]

James turns to etymology again when he considers the derivation of 'sorcery' in II ii.

Such discussions were given a new impetus by Renaissance enthusiasm for the philology, exegesis, editing and translation of both classical and biblical texts. Philological discussions in Renaissance demonologies had a place within concerns with the exact signification of words fostered by both Renaissance humanism and the protestant reformation. In demonological treatises, as elsewhere in the sixteenth and seventeenth centuries, the significations of words were sharply contested, never more so than when the text was that of the bible. James cites some of the biblical passages containing these contested words as historical authority for the existence of magic and witchcraft: Exodus 22.18 and 1 Samuel 28.7, which contain the Hebrew *mechassepha* and *b'lt 'wb*, rendered respectively by the Greek Septuagint as *pharmakous* and *gunaika engastrimython*, by the Vulgate as *maleficos* and *mulierem habentem pythonem*, and by the Geneva bible as 'witch' and 'a woman having a familiar spirit'. The exact signification of the noun in Exodus 22.18, which the Bassandyne bible gives as 'Thou shalt not suffre a witche to live', was literally a matter of life and death. As Filmer put it, 'The Point in Question is briefly this: whether such a Witch as is condemend by the Lawes, and Statutes of this Land, be one and the same with the Witch forbidden by the Law of Moses'.[63] Philomathes is again made the mouthpiece of comparatively 'advanced' and sceptical views when, at the beginning of book II, he says of some scriptural passages, 'it is thought by some that these places speak of magicians and necromancers only, and not of witches'. Philomathes' view is a very moderate scepticism. Weyer and Scot suggested that the words might signify a whole variety of less sinister persons: poisoner, fraud, ventriloquist. Here, as was the case with the discussion of the witch of Endor, Philomathes' 'role is . . . that of a surrogate Weyer or Scot',[64] that of sceptic.

Dual classification and contrariety: antithesis, inversion and parody

Demonology's thought, taxonomy and rhetoric are marked by a series of contrarieties. Stuart Clark has identified contrariety and dual classification as characteristic of Renaissance demonological writing about witchcraft, and indeed James's *Demonology* is cited as a typical example in the first section of his authoritative study of demonological thought.[65] Contrariety was important as both an idea and a characteristic of the tropes in demonological treatises.

In *Demonology* these contrarieties are especially noticeable in the first two books, which form a pair. These are concerned respectively with the binary pairing of magic practised by a male, learned magician, and witchcraft practised by a socially inferior, female witch. In book I dual classification determines the preliminary taxonomy of magical arts and the book's discussion of magic: two sorts of magical practitioners, each with two names (magicians and necromancers; witches and sorcerers); two sorts of motivations for magicians and witches, with witches' motivation further divided into revenge and poverty (I ii); two sorts of people who fall to magic, learned and unlearned; and two areas excite their interest, judicial astrology and natural properties (I ii–iii). The argument of I vi exemplifies James's tendency to think in binaries: 'The devil's contract with magicians. The division thereof in two parts.'

Book II insists on witchcraft as the very opposite of God's revealed religion and a godly society, both of which the devil and witches nevertheless ape and mimic in their practices. The witch is, in Larner's words, 'an enemy of God and of the godly society'.[66] The antitheses are most elaborate in II iii and v, a series of 'contrarieties' in which the devil is seen to ape God and the Christian religion, and tries to thwart the propagation of the kingdom of Christ. The strongest statement in *Demonology* of the devil as 'the very contrary opposite to God' is in the last chapter of this book (II vii).

Constructing witchcraft and the devil in terms of contrariety is common in demonological thought. But James's participation in the questioning and prosecution of the East Lothian witches, and indeed his oblique part in producing texts representing them (depositions, dittays, *News from Scotland*), may have made him particularly attentive to certain demonological commonplaces or *topoi*. Contrariety is a feature of the texts produced by the legal process (the dittays), and *News from Scotland*, which were written before *Demonology*. The dittays detail the parody of a kirk service and of godly behaviour in the meetings in North Berwick kirk, and many passages in *Demonology* book II echo the dittays. In *News* can be found the opposition between the witches and the devil on the one hand, and on the other the godly king, 'the greatest enemy he hath in the world', which is particularly clear in the series of *antitheta* in the pamphlet's peroration:

> the king is the child and servant of God, and they but servants to the devil; he is the lord's anointed, and they but vessels of God's wrath; he is a true Christian and trusteth in God, they worse than infidels.

The texts produced about the witches in 1590–1, prior to *Demonology*, both represent the devil and the witches as disorderly and yet also represent their activities as mimicking the orderly and the godly. If the construction of witchcraft as inversion and misrule was a habit of thought of many writers of demonologies, these ideas must have been especially prominent in the mind of a royal demonologist whose office as king was the epitome of orderly control.[67] Much of the discussion of witchcraft as mimicry and parody in *Demonology* is a theorisation of motifs already present in the legal records and in *News from Scotland*.

In book I there first appears a crucial theme of the devil as an imitator of God, to be developed more fully in book II. The devil as 'God's ape [*simia Dei*]', often repeated in demonological works, is at least as early as Tertullian, in the second century AD.[68]. Hemmingsen gives an extended account of the activities of the devil as *simia Dei*: just as God has his word, sacraments and spirit, so also the devil has his, in his attempt to set up false worship in place of true.[69] Like continental demonologists, both catholic and protestant, James sees witchcraft as a species of idolatry: 'the devil (as God's ape) counterfeits in his servants this service and form of adoration that God prescribed and made his servants to practise' (II iii). Witchcraft (like catholicism in some protestant polemic) renews the false practices of pagan religions: oracles, false religious ceremonies, divination and omens, visions and dreams. If the magican's career imitates the processes of education, then the witch's parodies the godly Christian life. 'Convention', the word regularly used for the witches' meetings in the dittays and *Demonology*, was also used for formal political and ecclesiatical meetings.[70] Epistemon shows Philomathes a series of antitheses: the witches' mark apes the seal of baptism; where the minister offers godly instruction, the devil instructs in mischief. In 1629 Richard Bernard would offer an elaborate and systematic set of twenty-nine points of similar comparisons on opposite pages at the end of *A Guide to Grand-Jury Men* entitled respectively 'Behold what the Lord hath done' and 'Behold what Satan hath done'. These include assemblies, sabbaths, a covenant, marks and worship, so that 'in these few things . . . Satan observeth the Lords doings and sayings and therein strives to bee like him'.[71]

The devil's ways are the opposite of God's, but they also imitate them: both the godly and witches meet in churches and the devil too has his sacraments. The devil was God's absolute opposite, yet terrifyingly sometimes his skilled impersonator, thus enormously complicating the good Christian's already difficult task of distinguishing true from false. This is a particular case of the Renaissance's anxiety, acute in the first book of Spenser's *Faerie Queene* and Shakespeare's *Macbeth*, about instances where evil is really the exact opposite of good but imitates it in apparent likenesses. Some diabolic imitations are readily apparent and follow a principle of simple inversion of religious doctrine and practice, with the practices of witchcraft as opposite in effect and intention to those of orthodox religion. More dangerous and insidious are those instances where the devil does not obviously 'ape' but 'dissimules' (the word is James's, II iii), as in his temporary encouragement of purity, but only as a prelude to the far more heinous sin of divination, or his 'feigning' of God when he pretends to be a just revenger. This leads to one of his boldest moves, and one several times described in the dittays, his feigning of the godly minister, preaching in the pulpit.

Protestant parodies

At European sabbats witches supposedly did things upside down and backwards, and at their meetings travestied the doctrines and rites of the church, desecrating the cross, renouncing their baptism, and adoring the devil rather than God. The lawyer Henri Boguet recounted a travesty of the mass that represented witchcraft as anti-religious and specifically anti-catholic, in its minutely rigorous inversions of catholic vestment, ritual and ceremonial.[72] The language of inversion and parody was shared by both catholic and protestant demonologists, but although there was little disagreement between them on some fundamental demonological matters, there were still 'differences of accent' and emphases in both their thought and representations.[73]

The *Demonology* of the protestant King James, like the dittays of the witches' trials, represents witches' 'conventions' as parodies of kirk practices. James's notion of witchcraft as an anti-religion is particularly protestant in that the minister, preaching, religious instruction and the 'convening' of the godly are the objects of imitation and parody. One of the most striking images from the Scottish witchcraft texts produced in the 1590s is a mockery of the protestant minister preaching in the pulpit. James says in *Demonology*,

> But further, witches oft-times confess not only his [the devil's] convening in the church with them, but his occupying of the pulpit, yea, their form of adoration to be the kissing of his hinder parts.

The author of *News*, perhaps James Carmichael, uniquely added the irreverent detail that the devil's 'buttocks [were] . . . put over the pulpit bare', suggesting a further parody, of the afflatus of godly teaching from the pulpit. James's treatment in *Demonology* of the 'shameful kiss' is a revealing example of the way in which he differently accents a feature of the sabbat commonly reported by continental demonologists. In the dittays kissing the devil's arse is part of the regular procedure at the convention, usually before the 'congregation's' departure, but its nature and function remain largely unexplained, except once it is called a gesture of homage: 'their homage being made as the fashion is in kissing of the devil's arse'.[74] In *News* it is a 'penance' for being late, or again a 'sign of duty'. In *Demonology* James provides a new and ingenious interpretation: in it the devil mocks that moment in Exodus 33 where Moses sees 'the hinder parts of God'. This interpretation reveals a very protestant parodic economy, and attention to a scriptural moment in the progress of God's covenant with Israel. A protestant spiritual understanding of scripture, which clearly distinguishes literal and spiritual significations, is made material, fleshly and gross. James points out that in Exodus 33 'the hinder parts of God . . . is spoken but *anthropopatheian* [by way of personification]'. The devil's literalness goes against protestant spiritual understanding, especially that of scripture. Arguably the devil's (wilful mis-)understanding is like that of catholics as seen by Reformation protestants, painfully literal-minded and 'carnal'.[75] It seems in many protestant demonological treatises that the devil's prime aim is to draw mankind into exactly this sort of theological confusion and 'superstition', in which the material and spiritual become confused.[76] A construction of diabolic or magical practices as 'carnal' mimickings of religious thought and practice, as those are properly understood in spiritual and specifically protestant terms, can be seen elsewhere in *Demonology*.

The description of witches' practices in *Demonology* book II clearly draws on the supposed practices of the East Lothian witches: making wax and clay images, curing and transferring diseases, and jointing corpses to make magical powders. James's argument that magical substances and practices of themselves have no efficacy is standard, and his determination to show magical practices as apings of religion is that of other protestant demonologists, such as Hemmingsen and Daneau. More particularly, his liking for the *simia Dei* idea has him represent magical practices as apings of a very protestant notion of the sacraments. Protestant demonologists regularly say that witches' practices ape the remaining two sacraments of the protestant church, the eucharist and baptism, and also a protestant understanding of those sacraments. James, Hemmingsen and Daneau say that the instruments which seem to produce magical effects, such as words, magical diagrams, characters, wax images, ointments, are not only imitations of God's sacraments, but that in a subtle ploy Satan is deceptively parodying a protestant *idea* of a sacrament, which was defined famously, in the words of the Catechism, as 'an outward and visible sign of an inward and spiritual grace given unto us, ordained by Christ himself, as a means whereby we receive the same, and a pledge to assure us thereof'. Daneau describes magical figures in almost exactly these same terms of signs and pledges made to men: they are 'pleadges and tokens onely of Satan's promises unto them'. Daneau says (and Hemmingsen agrees)[77] that the devil continues to ape God in that the visible instruments of *maleficia*, the wax images and powders, are not in themselves efficacious, but actually have the same relation to supernatural operation as the elements (bread and wine, water) in a protestant understanding of the sacraments which they imitate. Magical instruments were Satan's apings of the sacraments, with two aims: to bring the real sacraments into contempt by imitation, and to confuse and seduce people, especially the simpler sort, into misbelief and 'superstition', by muddling them about the real nature of a sacrament and how it operates.[78] For the devil attempts to collapse the careful protestant system of sacramental signifieds into their signifiers, in order to deceive and destroy men, for he 'turneth the force and effect of the thinges which are signified, unto the signes which doo signifie them'.[79]

In James's exposition of *maleficium* (II v) the proper understanding of the relationship of words and materials to the operation of *maleficium* is the same as a protestant understanding of the operation of the sacrament which it apes. The material elements in the case of either a charm (powders, images) or a sacrament (bread, water) have no supernatural efficacy in themselves or through the operation of any human agent on them. In protestant sacraments heavenly effects are in no way dependent on their 'earthly' elements. James's exposition is complicated by his analogy with a miracle in which Jesus opened the eyes of a blind man by applying a mixture of clay and spittle to his eyes (John 9.1–7). The important theological point is that this real miracle (as opposed to a false magical wonder), which by definition suspends or transcends usual natural laws and properties, depended not at all on the apparent material agent (here, clay), or any miraculous change in it. To admit anything else would allow the possibility of *the* miraculous transformation of the eucharistic elements and hence 'the little transubstantiate god in the papists' mass' (II iv).

Nor would a false miracle of healing by the devil 'really' depend at all on any material agents or forms of words used during the effecting of the wonder. The difference in the devil's false wonder would be that the devil would actually be using natural, although sometimes wonderful properties, manipulated with unique and experienced skill and rapidity, to bring about an effect.

Demonology book I

Book I involves taxonomies of arts and sciences and of forbidden arts; and the difference between magic, the main subject of book I, and witchcraft, the subject of book II, is announced in I ii. Although James says that the less learned may come to magic through the devil's rudiments (simple charms, superstitious practices, divination), it is the learned magician who preoccupies him in book I. Magic tempts the 'restless minds' of learned and dissatisfied men, moved by curiosity and a Faustian desire for knowledge, who are at risk when the pursuit of apparently lawful sciences, or of those on the margins of natural and occult enquiries, shades into magic (I iv). Despite James's etymological attempt to keep them distinct, the line is not always clear between astronomy, lawful uses of astrology, judicial astrology ('the devil's school') and divination. It is easy to slide 'upon the slippery and uncertain scale of curiosity' from the 'perilous' *study* of ceremonial magic to the *practice* of conjuration, from the tacit pact involved in any magical practice, to express and formal contract with the devil.

James allows a distinction between magic and witchcraft in difference of motivation, learning, class and practice, but disallows any in kind: both are equally damnable and the practitioners of both operate with diabolic assistance. So James allows only a strictly limited truth to the popular distinction between magician and witch: that the former commands the devil and the latter serves him. He wishes to refute the popular distinction of magician and witch, which conceived of the former as less culpable than the latter.

James writes of magic as a quasi-educational process with its rudiments, school and scholars. If magicians are, at least in part, scholars and gentlemen, witches are peasants and tradesmen. Book I is predominantly a male world: male teachers, princes, magicians, scholars, even legions of spirits which are commanded by 'princes, dukes and kings' (I vi). Magicians may be the companions to princes and are their equals in education, pretence to power and status. Some anxiety in this first book comes from the insidious closeness of some magicians to the great who patronise, protect and consult them:

> Upon custom we see that diverse Christian princes and magistrates, severe punishers of witches, will not only oversee [overlook] magicians to live within their dominions, but even sometimes delight to see them prove some of their practics. (I vi)

Although this, and a complaint that magistrates don't prosecute magicians with sufficient vigour, are familiar points in demonologies, James may be thinking particularly of Bothwell's patronage of Ritchie Graham. And in England John Dee was still receiving the continuous although cautious patronage of Elizabeth I, who visited him in Mortlake in 1580 and again with the Polish prince Albert Laski, Sir Philip Sidney and other gentlemen in 1583.[80]

In spite of Epistemon's full answer to Philomathes' enquiries about magical practices, circles and conjurations (I v), we needn't assume any deep knowledge of these on James's part. Even a cursory reading of Scot, Weyer and Agrippa would have provided the details he gives which seem to come mainly from demonologies, with the odd detail recalled from the practices of the Lothian witches. James says that the devil appears as an animal, such as a dog, or only manifests himself as a voice, to the 'baser sort' of magician. Agnes Sampson confessed in James's presence that the devil appeared as a dog when she was consulted by Lady Edmiston,[81] and according to her dittay, Sampson had once raised the devil 'by voice and not bodily'. James's description of a magician's career and abilities (a spirit attendant as a servant, foretelling of great events, the production of banquets and airy impressions of armies and castles, I vi) sounds like those in contemporary romances and plays:

> . . . yea, he will make his scholars to creep in credit with princes by foretelling them many great things part true, part false, . . . And he will also make them to please princes by fair banquets and dainty dishes carried in short space fra the farthest part of the world. (I vi)

Book I's analysis of a magician's career, with its origins in the thirst of great minds for knowledge, through conjuration and a pact in blood, to the eventual discovery by magicians that 'their knowledge, for all that they presume thereof, is nothing increased except in knowing evil, and the horrors of hell for punishment thereof', is remarkably like that of Marlowe's *Dr Faustus*. The Faust story, with its roots in early saints' lives, was popular in Europe in the sixteenth century and provided an influential narrative of a magician's career. In book I magic is often represented as a tragic fall of knowledge and scholarship.

Book II

Book II turns from magic to witchcraft, from the male world of magicians, books and romance, to the female world of witches, their maleficial practices and conventions, details of which can be paralleled in the trial accounts. It is in this book that the demonological commonplace 'The more women the more witches', as Henry Holland puts it,[82] is very briefly raised (II v). The subject of women and witchcraft has been discussed more in the twentieth century than it was in the sixteenth.[83] James offers familiar arguments of the greater frailty of the female sex and the devil's familiarity with it since his deception of Eve. He deals with the point without the lengthy misogyny in the *Malleus Maleficarum*. James espouses the same sort of 'soft' conventional anti-feminism as Weyer and Scot,[84] one that emphasises the mental and physical weakness of women and their credulity, rather than their malice, untrustworthiness, or sexual depravity. From casual asides ('such kind of charms as commonly daft wives use', I iv; 'little trifling turns that women have ado with', II v) James shows no high respect for the sex in *Demonology*, but neither is he aggressively misogynistic. Philomathes' brisk request 'Return now where ye left', after the one brief exchange on the subject, suggests that the connection between women and witchcraft was not a pressing concern of the king's.

In II i Philomathes tries to pre-empt the discussion with some of Weyer's and Scot's sceptical ploys: that magic and witchcraft are different and the bible condemns only the former; that witchcraft is explained by physiological theories of the imagination, disturbed humours, and particularly melancholy. Book II then settles down to an account of witchcraft. It draws less on Daneau's 'aucthoritie' than book I and far more on the king's recent 'experience of the thing' as its argument relies on 'the daily practic and confession of so many' (II i). As shown above, it echoes material in the pre-trial examinations and in the dittays. Epistemon's statement about the socially superior sort of witch (II ii) may well recall James's suspicions, and indeed particular pursuit, of the prosperous Edinburgh women Barbara Napier and Euphame MacCalzean.

> Such as though rich, yet burn in a desperate desire of revenge, he allures them by promises to get their turn satisfied to their heart's contentment. (II ii)

The word 'turn' is used by the dittays exclusively for a maleficial attempt to kill: four times of the witches' plots to kill James himself, and three times of MacCalzean's plot to kill her father-in-law by image magic. The king's recent experiences are used initially either to rebut Philomathes' straw-man objections or to provide particular illustration. So Philomathes' excuse that witches are simple, solitary and melancholic is immediately answered by James's memories of prosperous, gregarious and 'merry' folk who were witches (II i).

To match a typical magician's career in book I, we have a witch's career outlined in II ii, starting with the first meeting with the devil and going on to the instruction of the marked witch in how to do evil. James has a very clear idea of the process of the 'initiating' (Philomathes' word, II iii) of a witch, familiar from continental accounts. But in addition, in 'her confession to the king's Majesty' on 4 December 1590,[85] Agnes Sampson described a course of events like the one given by James here, which subsequently formed item 33 of her dittay. This comprised the first solitary meeting with the devil and his promises to help, the second meeting and entering into the devil's service, renunciation of baptism and receiving the devil's mark. At the next meeting the devil appears to fulfil his promises of obtaining wealth or revenge for the witches.

James's discussion of the curing and transferring of diseases (II v) exhibits a concern of many demonologists, and particularly protestant writers,[86] about the problem of maleficial illness and how one ought to respond. It posed a series of pressing theoretical and practical problems for an afflicted laity and their pastors. Can a witch cause disease, and remove it? If a witch removes diseases mustn't she be a good witch? May we employ witchcraft to alleviate or cure diseases? How can the use of magic to alleviate or cure disease be bad? The cold comfort James offers is a protestant assertion of God's providence and his use of the devil as his hangman. God uses affliction to destroy the wicked, but also to test and discipline the elect. Prayer and amendment of life are recommended and magic may never be used to cure disease. Like Hemmingsen,[87] James says that this may cure the body, but only at the expense of the soul's perdition.

The penultimate chapter treats a common topic in demonologies: whether witches have power over their examiners and judges. Again, this must particularly have interested the king who had spent months examining the Lothian witches and who told Barbara Napier's jurors in June 1591 that 'whatsoever hath bene gotten from them hath bene done by me my selfe'.[88] James says confidently that if the magistrate is diligent in examination and punishment, then God will not 'permit their master to trouble or hinder so good a work' (II vi). The peroration of *News* raised a similar question but stilled fears for James's safety by asserting God's protection and support.

James's distinction between private and official action against witches may reflect the frequency with which private persons did take action in sixteenth-century Scotland.[89] He is insistent that the witches' power is reduced when she is legally apprehended by 'the lawful magistrate'—an opinion common to demonologists such as Bodin and Rémy,[90] and perhaps also a popular one. James's experiences again inform the section about the devil visiting his servants in prison: this is supposedly what happened to Dr Fian according to *News*.

The last chapter of book II, about apparitions, provides a bridge to the fuller discussion of spirits in book III. James uses a common protestant trope, that the times of papistry are analogous to pagan times before Christ's incarnation:

both were troubled with false wonders, apparitions, oracles and visions, and magic arts flourished.[91] Christ's coming, which silenced the oracles, had a recent analogue in the establishment of the Gospel by the Reformation and consequently of godly protestant monarchies. Reginald Scot claimed that oracles (i.e. papist false prophecies) ceased in England in the time of Henry VIII and his daughter Elizabeth.[92] James clearly knows the interpretation of Revelation 6.2 as the preaching of the Gospel, and seems to think that apparitions of devils troubling mankind have been superseded by magic and witchcraft. James anticipated Keith Thomas when he wrote that ghosts and spirits appeared in Britain in papist times, but since the Reformation magic and witchcraft have flourished.

Book III

The main subject of book III is the manifestations of troublesome spirits. In it is observable the Reformation's effect on a protestant imagination of history and its understanding of pneumatology, and also the severely limited recourse now available against spirits for ordinary people. Book III is a rag-bag in which James also deals in passing with various miscellaneous topics, for example werewolves and incubi.

In protestant pneumatology all apparitions of spirits could only be illusions or diabolical manifestations: the godly dead were in Abraham's bosom, the damned in hell, and, since miracles were now ceased in the age of the Gospel, angels were hardly ever (if ever) sent on errands to humans. According to James, angels never appear in the shape of the dead, although spirits may temporarily animate dead bodies. As Epistemon had said in II ii, 'all we that are Christians ought assuredly to know that since the coming of Christ in the flesh, and establishing of his church by the apostles, all miracles, visions, prophecies and appearances of angels or good spirits are ceased'.

James's four categories of diabolic manifestation are devils who haunt places, those who haunt people, those who possess people, and those called fairies. All are examples of 'the devil's conversing in [moving about on] the earth' and all these kinds of spirit are really the same. The operations of the first three categories may be the result of maleficial witchcraft, but book III is more concerned with spirits' independent dealings with humanity. The prime authorities for the first category are biblical, such as the brief lists of mysterious creatures inhabiting ruins in Isaiah 13 and Jeremiah 50.9.[93] The troubling of houses by spirits is a sign of their inhabitants' sins, and householders are allowed only the same recourse as victims of *maleficium*: prayer and amendment of life.[94] As Thomas has argued,[95] the same Reformation which constructed a catholic past in which spirits roved, had also deprived people of traditional religious recourses against the depredations of these spirits, leaving them only with the options of endurance, patience and prayer.

Another consequence of the Reformation was that in the sixteenth century demonic possession and exorcism (I iv) increasingly became the subjects of polemic and propaganda.[96] English puritans claimed that power to exorcise was a sign of divine approval, as did catholics, as James notes, 'for confirming of their rotten religion'. James enters into the confessional dispute when he rejects catholic signs of possesion like terror of sacramentals and sacred symbols. The signs he accepts are the biblically evidenced (physical strength), from contemporary observation of physical symptoms (swelling and rigidity of the body, a hollow voice), and traditional (sudden access of new knowledge or proficiency in languages). Even though he allows, with the protestant polemicists, that many possessions are counterfeit, 'it is a curious circumstance that James seemingly recognized the reliablity of . . . Romish exorcisms',[97] since he also allows (as Samuel Harsnett would never have done) that papists may be able to exorcise if they follow Christ's precept to cast out devils in his name, and his recommendation of prayer and fasting (Matthew 17.21). This would seem perilously close to granting efficacy to exorcism *ex opere operato* (proceeding from a power in the act itself), regardless of confessional affiliation.

On fairies James takes a line very like Scot's that, like other apparitions, they were illusions that flourished in papist times. His description of belief in a fairy king and queen and their court seems to record popular Scottish belief, the beliefs of 'sundry simple creatures' as James calls it, like those of Bessie Dunlop.[98]

Among the miscellaneous subjects James deals with is the names given to devils, often dealt with in demonologies near their beginnings.[99] Others are werewolves (III i) and incubi (III iii), which continental writers treat in assocation with the practices of witches or the powers of devils, and are alien to the general run of English and Scottish witch trials. Werewolves are usually treated in continental demonologies as part of the question of transformation, incubi as part of the question whether witches can have sex with demons. Despite Philomathes' proprietary possessive adjective in 'our werewolves', they were not a British phenomenon. Gifford mentions them as delusions the devil inflicts on witches in 'Germany and other countries',[100] and the only English pamphlet describing a case is a translation from German.[101] Epistemon takes the relatively sceptical line that lycanthropia indicates an excess of melancholy. He accepts melancholy as an explanation of werewolves, and men's beliefs that they are beasts (or pitchers), which he would not accept from Philomathes as an explanation for witchcraft.

James allows the existence and operation of *incubi* and *succubi* on the usual understanding that the devil assumes a dead body or steals sperm. His belief that no conception is possible by either of these methods was not universally held. Many demonologists thought demons could transport sperm with sufficient rapidity to cause conception, although technically the father was the man whose sperm was stolen (or who willingly ejaculated if he had consensual sex with a *succubus*). As in book II, the argument here is from natural philosophy. James denies the sceptics' elision of the *incubus* and the oppression of the nightmare.

Book III returns finally to the punishment of witches, a topic raised in II vi, which discussed the conduct of magistrates. Many demonologies devoted their final pages to the practical matters of how to deal legally with witches and the behaviour, particularly in protestant countries, of secular magistrates.[102] In these two concluding chapters we find some of the material which, together with *Demonology*'s general emphasis on contrariness and antithesis, led Clark to see *Demonology* as expressing the king's views of ideal monarchy and political order.[103] Here, James's elision of 'prince, or supreme magistrate' is significant. Epistemon advises the death penalty, and on the same grounds as Perkins: as a punishment for idolatry, not *maleficium*. James extends the punishment to consulters, just as he urged it in the case of Barbara Napier. Epistemon's belief that God will not allow the devil to take the shape of innocent people is unorthodox.

Notes

[1] See Dunlap 1975: 43–4; Craigie 1982: 153; Larner 1981: 31.

[2] More claims that the composition of *Utopia* was 'hurried and impromptu' (More 1964: 3) and Erasmus that the idea of *The Praise of Folly* came to him when he was riding back from Italy (Erasmus 1979: 1). In his dialogue on witchcraft, *Strix*, Gianfrancesco Pico della Mirandola says that he dashed the work off in ten days, prompted by the doings of witches a few months previously (Burke 1977: 35).

[3] Jean Bodin's *De la Démonomanie des Sorciers* (1580) has a large section entitled 'Refutation des opinions de Jean Wier' (ff. 218–52) and Reginald Scot's *Discoverie of Witchcraft* (1584) was provoked in part by 'Sprenger's fables . . . [and] Bodin's bables' (1886: xxv). Filmer's *An Advertisement to the Jury-men of England* (1653), is written largely as a reply to William Perkins, *A Discourse of the Damned Art of Witchcraft* (1610.

[4] Boguet 1929: xxiv; Gifford 1862: 8; Clark 1997: 321–45.

[5] Although other witchcraft dialogues also claim to be prompted by recent events and trials, compare Daneau 1575: sigs B–B2 and Gianfrancesco Pico, *Strix* (Burke 1977: 35).

[6] Folger MS V.a.185: 39. See Dunlap 1975.

[7] Dunlap 1975: 43.

[8] Dunlap 1975: 43.

[9] Larner 1962: 122–3; Larner 1984: 16.

[10] Notestein 1965: 97.

[11] See Roberts 1996; Ferguson 1924.

[12] See Riis 1988: 121; Maxwell-Stuart 1997: 212–13.

[13] Warner 1893: xlii, xlviii, lii.

[14] *Demonology* III i; Warner 1893: li.

[15] For example the edition printed at Basle 1583, columns 913–34. However, this information is also quite commonplace. For example, the four demonic rulers of points of the compass were known about by William of Auvergne (Thorndike 1923–58: ii 343–4) and were raised by the conjuror 'Jonys of Oxford' in 1532 (*Letters and Papers, Foreign and Domestic, of the Reign of Henry VIII*, v 694–5).

[16] Daneau 1575: B3ᵛ.

[17] Daneau 1575: sigs E4ᵛ, F2ᵛ, D2ᵛ–3, I3.

[18] Clark 1977: 156.

[19] Notestein 1965: 100–1.

[20] Holland 1590: sig C2ᵛ.

[21] The Swiss pastor Ludwig Lavater's *De Spectris, Lemuribus et Magnis atque Insolitis Fragoribus* (Geneva 1570) was translated into English as *Of Ghostes and Spirites Walking by Nyght* by Robert Harrison (1572) and book 1 of Pierre Le Loyer's *IIII Livres des Spectres ou Apparitions des Esprits* (Angers 1586) was translated into English by Z.

Jones as *A Treatise of Specters or Straunge Sights* (1605).

22 For views on the examination, trial and punishment of witches, and the conduct and duties of Christian magistrates and judges, see Kramer and Sprenger 1971: 409–567; Boguet 1929: 211–38; Daneau 1575: sig B4ᵛ; Holland 1590: sigs K4ᵛ–L4ᵛ; Perkins 1610 181–215, 246–51. See also Clark 1997: 560–71.

23 Clark 1977: 165.

24 *CSPS* x 524.

25 Clark 1993: 54.

26 Clark 1993: 56.

27 Gifford 1862: v.

28 For recent work on the Renaissance dialogue, much of which is about the Italian dialogue, see Burke 1989; Armstrong 1976; Marsh 1980; Snyder 1989; Jones-Davies 1984, especially Mack, 'The Dialogue in English Education', 189–209; Cox 1992; Deakins 1980.

29 Sidney 1973: 97.13–16.

30 See Mack in Jones-Davies 1984: 189–209; Kempe is cited 197.

31 Gianfrancesco Pico della Mirandola, *Libro detto Strega o delle Illusioni del Demonio* (Bologna 1524). On this dialogue see Burke 1977: 32–52.

32 The text is reprinted in Jones 1956: 161–73; see also Clark and Morgan 1976.

33 Robbins 1959: 253.

34 James VI and I 1994: xvii.

35 Daneau 1575: sig C8.

36 Hemmingsen 1575: sig A3.

37 Daneau 1575: sigs A3–3ᵛ; Gifford 1587: sig B2; Holland 1590: sig A3; Cooper 1617: I ii 25–6.

38 Clark 1993: 57.

39 Exodus 22.18; Leviticus 19.31, 20.6 and 27; Deuteronomy 18.10–12; 2 Kings 23.24; 1 Chronicles 10.13–14; Jeremiah 10.2.

40 1 Samuel 28; Job 1; Exodus 7–8; Acts 8; Acts 16.16–18.

41 Moses already had a reputation as being skilled in magic in Pliny, *Historia Naturalis*, XXX ii, and Celsus regarded him as a wizard, Thorndike 1923–58: i 437. Alchemical works were attributed to him, Thorndike 1923–58: i 195.

42 Lavater 1929: 127.

43 For an account of some patristic exegeses

see Simonetti 1989; Smelik 1977; Leone Allacci, *S P N Eustathii Archiepiscopi Antiocheni, et Martyris, In Hexahemeron Commentarius . . . Leo Allatius . . . Dissertationem de Engastrimytho Syntagmate* (Lugduni 1629); and Benedict Hahn, *Spectrum Endoreum* (Jena 1663). The Italian religious reformer and sometime regius professor of divinity at Oxford, Peter Martyr Vermigli (1500–62), has an extended commentary on 1 Samuel 28, and addresses at length such issues as what it was that the woman of Endor called up, whether the devil can foretell the future, and whether it is licit to consult him, *In Duos Libros Samuelis Propehetae . . . Commentarii Doctissimi* (Tiguri 1570), ff. 155ᵛ–168ᵛ. Johann Weyer discusses the incident in *De Praestigiis* (Weyer 1991: II ix–x 127–33), and Lavater 1929: 127–45. For discussion in English treatises see Coxe 1561: sig B2; Scot 1886: VII i–xiv 108–16; Gifford 1587: sigs Eᵛ–F2; Holland 1590: Cᵛ–C3; Perkins 1608: I iv 23–4, III iii 108–16; Mason 1612: 71–3; Cooper 1617: I viii 150–4.

44 See Clark 1997: 619–33; Williamson 1979: 39–47.

45 See document 2.

46 Weyer 1991: II ix–x.

47 George Gifford may be thinking of Scot when in a discussion of 1 Samuel 28 in his *Discourse* he says that 'sundry vaine and ridiculous cavils are gathered and patched together, to prove that it was neither the Devill nor Samuel, but a meere cousenage by the Witch, or by some companion' (Gifford 1587: sig E3ᵛ).

48 Holland 1590: Cᵛ–C2ᵛ. Holland explicitly gives marginal references to Scot.

49 Scot 1886: VII xii 118. Holland notes this part of Scot's explanation (Holland 1590: sig C2).

50 Scot 1886: VII xi 115.

51 It presumably proceeds from Saul's first asking the woman who it was she saw (1 Samuel 28.13), although Saul then sees Samuel (as Epistemon says), bows before him and talks to him (28.14–20). Scot says that 1 Samuel 28.21, 'Then the woman came out unto Saule', is evidence of the woman having been 'in hir closet' (VII xii 118).

52 The idea is mentioned in Filmer 1653: 20, but James is cited as its source.

53 Scot 1886: V i.

54 Daneau 1575: sigs B7^v–C4.

55 Weyer 1991: II i 93–8; Daneau 1575: sigs B7^v–C4; Bodin 1580: ff. 220–225^v.

56 Daneau 1575: sigs C2–C4; Gifford 1587: sigs B3–C4; Holland 1590: sigs B3^v–D4^v; Filmer 1653: 15–20.

57 Isidore of Seville 1911: VIII ix. This discussion influenced later ones: Rabanus Maurus (*c*. 780–865), *De magicis artibus*, a large section of which is taken almost verbatim from Isidore; Burchard of Worms (d. 1025), *Decretum*; Hugh of St Victor (d.1141), *Didascalion*, VI xv. These discussions by Rabanus Maurus, Burchard of Worms and Hugh of St Victor may be found in Migne, *Patrologia Latina*, 110, 1097–9; 140, 839–40 and 176, 810–2. See also Thorndike 1915; Thorndike 1923–58: ii 13–15; Flint 1991: 50–8; Kieckhefer 1990: 11.

58 Isidore 1911: VIII ix 14.

59 'Dicitur enim Foemina à Fe, et minus: quia semper minorem habet & servat fidem' (Kramer and Sprenger 1971: part 1, q 6, 95).

60 Ady 1656: 148.

61 'Without doubt it [magic] arose in Persia', Pliny, *Historia naturalis*, XXX ii.

62 'Quos Graeci *sophos* hos Persae Magos nominarunt: unde *sophia* Graecis, & Persis Magia, dicta est Sapientia, eaque potissimum quae est naturalium rerum excellens cognitio: & perscrutatio motuum corporum coelestorum: & in effectuum eorundem in hisce rebus inferioribus' (Hemmingsen 1575: sig B). Such a statement is common: compare 'Le mot de Magie est Persique, & signifie, Science des choses divines & naturelles: & Mage, ou Magicien, n'est rien autre chose, que Philosophe' (Bodin 1580: II i f. 51).

63 Filmer 1653: 1.

64 Clark 1977: 167.

65 Clark 1977: especially 173–6; Clark 1980: especially 117; Clark 1997: 31–79.

66 Larner 1981: 5.

67 Clark 1977: 177. See also Clark 1997: 549–59.

68 McGowan 1977: 192.

69 Hemmingsen 1575: sigs B4–6^v

70 See *OED* convention *sb*. 4, 5; and *DOST* convention *n*. 2–4.

71 Bernard 1629: 260–6.

72 'Afin de toucher icy quelque chose de la Messe, qu'ils celebrent au Sabbat, ce que je ne puis ecrire sans horreur: dautant que celuy, qui est commis à faire l'office, est revestu d'une chappe noire sans crois, & apres avoir mis de l'eau dans le calice, il tourne le doz à l'autel, & puis esleve un rond de rave teinte en noir, au lieu del'hostie, & lors tous les Sorciers crient à haute voix 'Maistre aide nous'. Le Diable en mesme temps pisse dans un trou à terre, & fait de l'eau beniste de son urine, de laquelle, qui dit la messe, arrouse tous les assitans avec un asperges noire' (Boguet 1608: XXII, 141).

73 Clark 1993: especially 45–50.

74 Document 22.

75 See Lake 1989.

76 Boguet's explanation of the 'shameful kiss' was that it parodied the kiss given to relics, 1608: 142–3.

77 Hemmingsen 1575: sigs B4^v–5^v has the same view of the sacraments and of the devil's aping them in magical signs and characters, images, bindings and ointments.

78 See Clark 1997: 457–88.

79 Daneau 1575: sigs H8^v–I. 'Praeterea hoc modo simiarum more vera illa Sacramenta quae Deus dedit ecclesiae suae, imitari studet, et in contemptum adducere, pariaque ipse facere videtur posse, denique in ipsa signa rei signatae vim et effectum traducit' (Daneau 1574: 96).

80 Halliwell 1842: 8–9, 20. On Dee and Elizabeth see French 1972: esp 6–9, 33–4, 62–3, 183–90, 196–9.

81 Document 2.

82 Holland 1590: B4^v.

83 For two overviews and full bibliographies see Clark 1997: 106–33; Wiesner 1993: 218–38.

84 Weyer 1991: III vi 181–3; VI xxvi 552–6; VI xxvii 567–76; Scot 1886: I iii 5–6; III ix 41–3; III xi 45–6.

85 Document 2.

86 See Clark 1997: 477–88.

87 Hemmingsen 1575: sig C5.

88 *CSPS* x 524. For a discussion of James's interest in witchcraft in relation to his

ideas about the godly 'magistrate' see Clark 1977.

[89] See Mackenzie 1678: 86–7.

[90] Clark 1971: 166.

[91] Holland 1590: f. 14ᵛ; Perkins 1608: I iv 25; Roberts 1616: 3. See also Lake 1989.

[92] Scot 1886: VIII vi 133.

[93] See note on *ziim* and *iim* in III i.

[94] Holland 1590: sigs Hᵛ–H3ᵛ says the same.

[95] Thomas 1973: 58–132.

[96] On possession and exorcism, see Thomas 1973: 477–92; Walker 1981; Macdonald 1991; Greenblatt 1988: 94–128; Clark 1997: 389–434.

[97] Notestein 1965: 98.

[98] See above, chapter 4. For similarly familiar dealings with fairies in England incorporated into an accusation of witchcraft see *The Examination of John Walsh* (1556), a cunning man from Dorset (Rosen 1991: 64–71).

[99] Weyer 1991: I v 12–14.

[100] Gifford 1862: 94.

[101] *A True Discourse Declaring the damnable Life and Death of One Stubbe Peeter* (1590). On werewolves see Oates 1989.

[102] Clark 1997: 549.

[103] Clark 1977: 156–7.

Document 28

Demonology

The Preface

To the Reader

The fearful abounding[†] at this time[†] in this country[†] of these detestable slaves of the devil, the witches or enchanters, has moved me (beloved reader) to dispatch in post[†] this following treatise of mine. Not in any wise,[†] as I protest, to serve for a show of my learning and engine,[†] but only, moved of conscience,[†] to press[†] thereby so far as I can to resolve the doubting hearts of many, both that such assaults of Satan are most certainly practised, and that the instruments[†] thereof merit most severely to be punished—against the damnable opinions of two principally in our age, whereof the one, called Scot,[†] an Englishman, is not ashamed in public print to deny that there can be such a thing as witchcraft; and so maintains the old error of the Sadducees[†]

[†] **abounding** abundance; demonologists often claim in their prefaces that witches are now plentiful or multiplying 'even as worms in a garden' (Boguet 1929: xxiv); in Gifford's *Dialogue* Samuel claims 'they say there is scarce any towne or village in all this shire, but there is one or two witches at the least in it' (Gifford 1862: 8); see also Daneau 1575: sigs B–B2

[†] **at this time** the evocation here of present urgency indicates that James may have been writing when the prosecution of the witches of East Lothian was still proceeding; compare below 'these strange news, which now only furnishes purpose to all men at their meeting' (p. 357)

[†] **in this country** Scotland

[†] **to dispatch in post** to write quickly. The claim to have written in haste is a conventional humanist gesture.

[†] **in any wise** in any way

[†] **engine** mental ability, ingenuity; wit (*BL*)

[†] **of conscience** by conscience

[†] **press** endeavour (*BL*)

[†] **the instruments** i.e. the witches

[†] **Scot** Reginald Scot (?1538–99), Kentish author of the most sceptical sixteenth-century English treatise on witchcraft, *The Discoverie of Witchcraft* (1584). There is a popular, although dubious, tradition that on his succession to the English throne James had copies of the *Discoverie* burned by the public hangman (see Craigie 1982: 110–12).

[†] **Sadducees** Jewish sect that denied the immortality of the soul, the resurrection of the body, and the existence of angels and spirits

in denying of spirits. The other called Wierus,[†] a German physican, sets out a public apology[†] for all these craftsfolk,[†] whereby, procuring for their impunity,[†] he plainly betrays himself to have been one of that profession. And, for to make this treatise the more pleasant and facile,[†] I have put it in form of a dialogue which I have divided into three books: the first speaking of magic[†] in general and necromancy[†] in special;[†] the second of sorcery,[†] and witchcraft;[†] and the third contains a discourse of all these kinds of spirits and spectres[†] that appear and trouble persons, together with a conclusion of the whole work.

My intention in this labour is only to prove two things, as I have already said: the one, that such devilish arts have been and are;[†] the other, what exact trial and severe punishment they merit. And therefore I reason[†] what kind of things are possible to be performed in these arts, and by what natural causes[†] they may be. Not that I touch every particular thing of the devil's power, for that were infinite, but only, to speak scholastically[†] (since this cannot be spoken in our language), I reason upon *genus*,[†] leaving *species*[†] and *differentia*[†] to be comprehended[†] therein. As, for example, speaking of the power of magicians in the first book and sixth chapter, I say that they can suddenly cause to be brought unto them all kinds of dainty dishes[†] by their familiar spirit,[†] since as a thief he delights to steal, and as a spirit he can subtly and suddenly enough transport the same. Now under this *genus*

[†] **Wierus** Johann Wier or Weyer (*c*.1515–88), Dutch physician, author of *De Praestigiis Daemonum* (Basle 1563), a sceptical treatise on witchcraft

[†] **apology** defence

[†] **craftsfolk** here, people skilled in occult arts

[†] **procuring for their impunity** trying to make them immune from punishment

[†] **facile** easy to understand

[†] **magic** here used generally for the production of marvellous phenomena by occult forces or the assistance of spirits. Taxonomies of magic are features of discussions from Isidore of Seville (*Etymologies*, VIIIB iv) to sixteenth–century demonological treatises of the sort James is writing.

[†] **necromancy** properly, divination by the spirits of the dead (Greek: *nekromanteía*), but more generally any magic ('negromancy' or 'nigromancy') from the medieval Latin *nigromantia*, 'the black art'

[†] **in special** in particular

[†] **sorcery** magic, enchantment. Renaissance treatises liked to derive the word from Latin *sortiarius*, a caster of lots.

[†] **witchcraft** the causing of harm with the assistance of spirits and through an arrangement with

the devil; here distinguished from sorcery and magic

[†] **spectres** apparitions

[†] **have been and are** that there have been and are such (*BL*)

[†] **reason** discuss

[†] **natural causes** reasons in the ordinary course of nature

[†] **scholastically** scholar-like (*BL*); in the manner of scholasticism (the medieval system of theology which used logic to analyse Christian dogma)

[†] *genus* in Aristotelian logic, a large class of things. James says he is speaking in large terms and categories.

[†] *species* a smaller class of things, a sub-class of *genus*

[†] *differentia* that attribute of a thing which distinguishes its *species* from other *species* in the same *genus*

[†] **comprehended** included

[†] **dainty dishes** compare Marlowe 1993 A–text IV. ii where Mephistophiles brings grapes to the Duchess of Vanholt

[†] **familiar spirit** a helpful demon attached to a particular person, often in the form of an animal (e.g. a cat)

may be comprehended all particulars depending thereupon, such as the bringing wine out of a wall (as we have heard oft to have been practised) and such others; which particulars are sufficiently proved by the reasons of the general, and such like. In the second book of witchcraft in special, and fifth chapter, I say and prove by diverse arguments that witches can, by the power of their master,[†] cure or cast on[†] diseases. Now by these same reasons that prove their power by the devil of diseases in general,[†] is as well proved their power in special:[†] as of weakening the nature of some men to make them unable[†] for women, and making it to abound[†] in others more than the ordinary course of nature would permit. And such like in all other particular sicknesses.

But one thing I will pray thee to observe in all these places where I reason upon the devil's power, which is[†] the different ends and scopes that God, as the first cause,[†] and the devil, as his instrument and second cause,[†] shoots at[†] in all these actions of the devil (as God's hangman).[†] For where the devil's intention in them[†] is ever to perish[†] either the soul or the body (or both of them) that he is so permitted to deal with,[†] God, by the contrary, draws ever out of that evil glory to himself, either by the wrack[†] of the wicked in his justice, or by the trial of the patient and amendment of the faithful,[†] being wakened up with that rod of correction.

Having thus declared unto thee, then, my full intention in this treatise thou wilt easily excuse, I doubt not, as well my pretermitting[†] to declare the whole particular rites and secrets of these unlawful arts, as also their infinite and wonderful practices, as being neither of them pertinent to my purpose.

[†] **their master** i.e. the devil, often addressed as 'Master' at witches' meetings; see Agnes Sampson's dittay, document 20; 'The devil start up himself in the pulpit, like a mickle black man and called every man by his name, and every one answered, "Here, master!"'

[†] **cast on** make someone contract. For instances of such curing and casting on of diseases, see Agnes Sampson's dittay, especially item 31.

[†] **their power ... general** their general power over diseases

[†] **power in special** power over particular afflictions

[†] **unable** sexually impotent; for discussions of whether witches can cause impotence see Kramer and Sprenger 1971: part II q1 vi, 260–9; Boguet 1929: 90–1; Guazzo 1988: II iv 91–5; Scot 1886: IV iv 61–2

[†] **making it to abound** greatly increasing sexual potency

[†] **which is** namely

[†] **first cause** the first originator and creator of the world

[†] **instrument and second cause** agent and second cause of a particular effect, after God as the first cause of it

[†] **shoots at** aims at

[†] **God's hangman** the executor of God's justice or punishment; a common way of thinking of the devil: 'the divell is the Lord's executioner' (Gifford 1862: 32)

[†] **in them** i.e. in all these actions

[†] **perish** destroy

[†] **that he ... deal with** i.e. the soul or body which God allows the devil to affect

[†] **wrack** overthrow (*BL*)

[†] **the trial ... of the faithful** a very protestant perception of God's use of the devil to try his elect; compare Gifford, 'For, touching the godly, the Lord doth use Satan to afflict them in their bodies and in their goods, for to trie their faith and patience' (Gifford 1862: 33)

[†] **pretermitting** failing to mention (some aspects of the subject)

The reason whereof is given in the hinder end[†] of the first chapter of the third book. And who likes to be curious[†] in these things, he may read, if he will hear of their practices, Bodinus' *Démonomanie*[†] (collected with greater diligence than written with judgement),[†] together with their confessions, that have been at this time apprehended.[† 1]

If he would know what hath been the opinion of the ancients concerning their power, he shall see it well described by Hyperius[†] and Hemmingius,[†] two late German writers, besides innumerable other neoteric theologues[†] that write largely upon that subject. And if he would know what are the particular rites and curiosities of these black arts (which is both unnecessary and perilous) he will find it in the fourth book of Cornelius Agrippa,[†] and in Wierus, of whom I spoke.

And so wishing my pains in this treatise (beloved reader) to be effectual in arming all them that read the same against these above mentioned errors, and recommending my good will to thy friendly acceptation,[†] I bid thee heartily farewell.

JAMES REX

[†] **hinder end** last part

[†] **curious** unnecessarily inquisitive

[†] **Bodinus'** *Démonomanie* Jean Bodin (1530–96), political philosopher and author of *De la Démonomanie des Sorciers* (Paris 1580), of which there were ten editions before 1604. Book IV gives a detailed discussion of the prosecution of witches; and sixty-five pages are devoted to a refutation of Johan Weyer's *De Praestigiis*.

[†] **(collected with ... judgement)** James implies that Bodin assiduously collects information about magic, but in providing so much detail for the inquisitive he shows lack of judgement

[†] **together ... at this time apprehended** i.e. the confessions of the North Berwick witches. In Folger MS V.a.185 the sentence runs on 'quhilkis all are to be set furthe in print', which must anticipate the publication of *News*. This ending to the sentence is crossed through in the manuscript, apparently by James, and does not appear in the 1597 quarto.

[†] **Hyperius** Andreas Gerardus Hyperius (1511–64), German theologian. James must be thinking of sections of his *Lieux Communs de la Religion Chrestienne; ou Methode de Theologie* (Geneva

1568); bk II, 365–411 discusses the nature and abilities of devils. Part of this section appeared in an English translation, *Commonplaces taken out of A. Hyperius ... Whether the Devils have bene the Shewers of Magicall Artes*, trans. R. V[aux] (1581).

[†] **Hemmingius** Niels Hemmingsen (1513–1600), Danish protestant theologian, professor of Greek, Hebrew and theology, and author of *Admonitio de Superstitionibus Magicis Vitandis* (Copenhagen 1575), in which he held that magic was a diabolic and not a human invention. James met Hemmingsen at his home in Roskilde in the winter of 1589–90.

[†] **neoteric theologues** modern theologians; divines of these late times (*BL*)

[†] **Cornelius Agrippa** Heinrich Cornelius Agrippa of Nettesheim (1486–1535), author of three books on magic, *De Occulta Philosophia* (Cologne 1533). A pseudo-Agrippan fourth book on magic, *Liber Quartus de Occulta Philosophia*, which gives detailed instructions for conjuring, was attributed to him, but his pupil, Johann Weyer, denied Agrippa's authorship in *De Praestigiis*, II v.

[†] **acceptation** acceptance

Demonology,

in form of a dialogue.[†]

FIRST BOOK

ARGUMENT:[†] The exord[†] of the whole. The description of magic in special.

CHAPTER I

ARGUMENT: Proven[†] by the scripture that these unlawful arts *in genere*[†] have been and may be put in practice.

PHILOMATHES[†] and EPISTEMON[†] reason the matter.

PHILOMATHES I am surely very glad to have met with you this day, for I am of opinion that ye can better resolve me of something, whereof I stand in great doubt, nor any other whomwith[†] I could have met.
EPISTEMON In what I can, that ye like to speer at[†] me, I will willingly and freely tell my opinion, and if I prove it not sufficiently I am heartily content that a better reason carry it away[†] then.
P. What think ye of these strange news, which now only furnishes purpose[†] to all men at their meeting—I mean of these witches?
E. Surely they are wonderful.[†] And I think so clear and plain confessions in that purpose[†] have never fallen out[†] in any age or country.
P. No question—if they be true—but thereof the doctors[†] doubts.

[†] **dialogue** a literary form popular in the Renaissance which relates a discussion between two or more persons.
[†] **ARGUMENT** summary of the subject matter (of the first book)
[†] **exord** beginning (from the Latin 'exordium')
[†] **Proven** proved (*BL*)
[†] *in genere* as a group
[†] **PHILOMATHES** 'lover of knowledge' (Greek)
[†] **EPISTEMON** 'knowledgeable' (Greek); the name of Pantagruel's tutor in Rabelais, *Gargantua and Pantagruel*.

[†] **whomwith** with whom
[†] **speer at** put a question to; demand of (*BL*)
[†] **a better reason carry it away** a better argument win the day
[†] **only furnishes purpose** provides the only topic of conversation; affordeth matter of talk (*BL*)
[†] **they are wonderful** the news is astonishing
[†] **in that purpose** in the matter being discussed (i.e. witchcraft)
[†] **fallen out** happened
[†] **the doctors** the learned

E. What part of it doubt ye of?

P. Even of all, for ought I can yet perceive: and namely,[†] that there is such a thing as witchcraft or witches. And I would pray you to resolve me thereof if ye may, for I have reasoned with sundry in that matter and yet could never be satisfied therein.

E. I shall with good will do the best I can, but I think it the difficiler,[†] since ye deny the thing itself in general. For as it is said in the logic schools, *Contra negantem principia non est disputandum*.[†] Always for that part, that witchcraft and witches have been and are, the former part[†] is clearly proved by the scriptures, and the last[†] by daily experience and confessions.

P. I know ye will allege me Saul's pythoness,[†] but that, as appears, will not make much for you.[†]

E. Not only that place, but diverse others. But I marvel why that should not make much for me.

P. The reasons are these. First ye may consider that Saul (1 Samuel 28) being troubled in spirit, and having fasted long before (as the text testifieth), and being come to a woman that was bruited[†] to have such knowledge, and that to inquire so[†] important news—he having so guilty a conscience for his heinous offences, and specially for that same unlawful curiosity and horrible defection[†]—and then the woman crying out upon the sudden in great admiration[†] for the uncouth[†] sight that she alleged to have seen, discovering

---

[†] **namely** especially
[†] **difficiler** more difficult
[†] ***Contra ... disputandum*** one ought not to dispute with someone who denies first principles
[†] **the former part** i.e. that witches 'have been'
[†] **the last** i.e. that witches 'are'
[†] **Saul's pythoness** Saul's consultation of the witch of Endor (1 Samuel 28) was a crucial passage for demonological discussion. Faced with a Philistine army, and having failed to get an answer from God or his prophets, Saul sent for a woman at Endor who had 'a familiar spirite' (Geneva, 1 Samuel 28.6). He consulted her in disguise and requested she raise the dead prophet Samuel, who appeared and prophesied Saul's death. There were three traditional positions on this important passage: that Samuel was really raised by magic, that Samuel or a demon appeared at God's command, that 'Samuel' was an impersonating demon. The last was regarded as most orthodox. See pp. 335–37. Many demonologists, including Scot and James himself, discuss the exact meanings of the words for 'witch' in Hebrew, Greek and Latin scriptures, including the one in this passage. In the Vulgate bible, *pythonissa* occurs in a verse describing Saul's death and transgressions, including consulting 'one that had a familiar spirit [*pythonissam*]' (1 Chronicles 10.13); compare 'The woman of *Endor* is comprised under this word *Ob*; for she is called *Pythonissa*' (Scot 1886: VII viii 111). In 1 Samuel, Saul's request to his servants 'Seeke mee a woman that hath a familiar spirite' (Geneva, 1 Samuel 28.7) is '*quaerite mulierem habentem pythonem*'. *Pytho* (late Latin, 'familiar spirit, demon that possesses a soothsayer') in turn gave rise to *pythonissa*, one of the late Latin words for 'witch' or 'sorceress', and hence to the English word 'pythoness' used from the fourteenth century onwards. The *NRSB* reads: 'Then Saul said to his servants, "Seek out for me a woman who is a medium, so that I may go to her and inquire of her"' (1 Samuel 28.7).
[†] **not make much for you** will not be a telling point in your argument
[†] **bruited** rumoured
[†] **so** such (*BL*)
[†] **defection** falling away from religious faith
[†] **admiration** wonder
[†] **uncouth** strange (*BL*)

him to be the king (though disguised), and denied by him before. It was no wonder, I say, that his senses being thus distracted he could not perceive her feigning of her voice, he being himself in another chamber and seeing nothing. Next, what could be or was raised? The spirit of Samuel? Profane and against all theology! The devil in his likeness? As unapparent,[†] that either God would permit him to come in the shape of his saints[†] (for then could never the prophets in those days have been sure what spirit spake to them in their visions), or then that he could foretell what was to come thereafter. For prophecy proceedeth only of God, and the devil hath no knowledge of things to come.[†]

E. Yet if ye will mark the words of the text, ye will find clearly that Saul saw that apparition. For, giving you[†] that Saul was in another chamber[†] at the making of the circles and conjurations[†] needful for that purpose (as none of that craft will permit any others to behold at that time), yet it is evident by the text that how soon that once[†] that unclean spirit was fully risen, she called in upon Saul. For it is said in the text that 'Saul knew him to be Samuel', which could not have been by the hearing tell[†] only of an old man with a mantle,[†] since there was many more old men dead in Israel nor[†] Samuel, and the common weed[†] of that whole country was mantles. As to the next, that it was not the spirit of Samuel, I grant. In the proving whereof ye need not to insist, since all Christians of whatsoever religion agrees upon that,[†] and none but either mere ignorants or necromancers or witches doubts thereof. And that the devil is permitted at some times to put himself in the likeness of the saints, it is plain in the scriptures, where it is said that 'Satan

---

[†] **unapparent** unlikely

[†] **saints** holy men

[†] **prophecy ... to come** orthodox theological discussions of prophecy insist that only God has real foreknowledge, as James goes on to say, and God may convey this information to his prophets. The devil may come by such information indirectly, or he may make an informed or shrewd guess about the future.

[†] **giving you** granting you

[†] **Saul was in another chamber** 1 Samuel 28 says nothing of this, or that the woman then 'called in upon Saul' to come and see the apparition. However, Reginald Scot, who argues that the woman tricked Saul, says 'she departed from his prescence into hir closet, where doubtles she had her familiar; to wit some lewd craftie preest' (Scot 1886: VII xii 117).

[†] **conjurations** i.e. the magic rituals of drawing circles on the ground and uttering certain words

to make devils appear

[†] **how soon that once** once

[†] **hearing tell** hearing the matter being spoken about

[†] **mantle** short loose cloak without sleeves. James is remembering 'An olde man commeth up lapped in a mantell' (Geneva, 1 Samuel 28.14).

[†] **nor** than

[†] **common weed** usual form of clothing

[†] **all Christians ... that** most demonological discussions of the witch of Endor, catholic or protestant, could not allow the apparition to have been Samuel, as this would have granted magic the power to raise God's dead prophets. The marginal note in the Bassandyne bible on 'Saul knew that it was Samuel' (1 Samuel 18.14) comments 'To his imagination, albeit it was Satan, who to blinde his eyes toke upon him the forme of Samuel, as he can do of an Angel of light'.

can transform himself into an angel of light' (2 Corinthians 11.14).[†1] Neither could that bring any inconvenient[†] with it to the visions of the prophets, since it is most certain that God will not permit him so to deceive his own, but only such as first wilfully deceives themselves by running unto him, whom God then suffers to fall in their own snares, and justly permits them to be illuded[†] with great efficacy of deceit, because they would not believe the truth (as Paul sayeth).[†] And as to the devil's foretelling of things to come, it is true that he knows not all things future, but yet that he knows part,[†] the tragical event of this history[†] declares it (which the wit of woman could never have forespoken). Not that he hath any prescience[†] which is only proper to God,[†] or yet knows anything by looking upon God as in a mirror (as the good angels do)—he being forever debarred from the favourable presence and countenance of his creator—but only by one of these two means: either as being worldly wise, and taught by a continual experience ever since the creation,[†] judges by likelihood of things to come according to the like that hath passed before,[†] and the natural causes in respect of the vicissitude of all things worldly;[†] or else by God's employing of him in a turn,[†] and so foreseen thereof,[†] as appears to have been in this, whereof we find the very like in Michea's prophetic discourse to King Ahab[†] (1 Kings 22). But to prove this my first proposition—that there can be such a thing as witchcraft and witches—there are many more places in the scriptures than this (as I

[†] **Satan can transform ... of light** this verse from Corinthians is regularly quoted in demonological treatises and became proverbial in the sixteenth century (Tilley 1950 D231). Augustine quotes the verse in his discussion of the witch of Endor, *Quaestiones veteris et novi testamenti XXVII* (Migne XXXV: 2233–4).

[†] **inconvenient** unseemly incongruity

[†] **illuded** tricked

[†] **(as Paul sayeth)** see 2 Thessalonians 2.7–12, a passage traditionally interpreted as speaking of the Antichrist, with his 'powers and signs and lying wonders'. James is particularly remembering 'And therefore God shall sende them strong delusion, that they shoulde beleeve lyes, That all they might be damned which beleved not the trueth' (2 Thessalonians. 2.11–12).

[†] **part** in part

[†] **this history** i.e. the story about Saul

[†] **prescience** ability to foretell the future

[†] **only proper to God** exclusively belonging to God

[†] **either ... creation** demonologists often stress the great knowledge and experience of demons, e.g. Boguet 1929: xli–xlii

[†] **either as being ... before** Augustine, *De*

Divinatione Daemonum (written *c.*406–11), a classic formulation and explanation of the devil's apparent divinatory abilities, informed later discussions such as James's here. 'Divination by demons comes about through three causes. They excel in the sharpness of their senses, swiftness of motion, and their long-standing experience of things' (*De Divinatione Daemonum*, cap. III).

[†] **natural causes ... things wordly** the course of nature in the world's changing circumstances

[†] **a turn** a task

[†] **foreseen thereof** as he was previously informed (by God)

[†] **King Ahab** Ahab, king of Israel, was promised by four hundred prophets that he would recapture the town of Ramoth-gilead. Ahab also consulted the prophet Michea, who had never prophesied any good for him. Michea first prophesied success but when pressed revealed that God had sent a lying spirit to the other prophets, and he himself then correctly predicted Ahab's defeat and death. God's deceitful employment here 'of a lying spirit in the mouth of all these thy prophets' (1 Kings 22.23) was the subject of much demonological discussion.

said before). As first, in the law of God it is plainly prohibited (Exodus 22).[†] But certain it is that the law of God speaks nothing in vain, neither doth it lay curses or enjoin punishments upon shadows, condemning that to be ill[†] which is not in essence or being,[†] as we call it. Secondly, it is plain that Pharaoh's wicked wise men imitated a number of Moses' miracles (Exodus 7 and 8)[†] to harden the tyrant's heart thereby. Thirdly, said not Samuel to Saul, 'that disobedience is as the sin of witchcraft'? (1 Samuel 15).[†] To compare to a thing that were not, it were too too absurd. Fourthly, was not Simon Magus[†] a man of that craft (Acts 8)?[†] And fifthly, what was she that had the spirit of python[†] which was exorcised by Paul (Acts 16)?[†] Besides innumerable other places[†] that were irksome to recite.

CHAPTER II

ARGUMENT: What kind of sin the practisers of these unlawful arts commit. The division of these arts, and what are the means that allures any to practise them.

[†] **Exodus 22** 'Thou shalt not suffer a witch to live' (Exodus 22.18), the most famous biblical proscription against witchcraft, which was used by many writers to justify the execution of witches. *NRSB* reads: 'You shall not permit a female sorcerer to live'.

[†] **ill** evil

[†] **which ... being** which does not have a real existence in itself

[†] **Exodus 7 and 8** Pharaoh's magicians imitated Moses' and Aaron's miracles with varying degrees of success (Exodus 7.10–13, 7.22, 8.7, 8.18). Like Aaron they changed their rods into serpents, but Aaron's serpent swallowed those of the magicians (Exodus 7.10–13). Demonological treatises regularly argued that it was only Aaron's rod that was really and miraculously transformed; the magicians' rods were transformed only in appearance, by diabolic agency, by a sleight of hand. For English discussions see Scot 1886: XIII xx–xxi 180–1; Gifford 1587: sigs E–E3; Holland 1590: sigs B4ᵛ–C; Perkins 1610: IV ii 159–65; Mason 1612: 31–2; and also Weyer 1991: II viii 122–6.

[†] **(1 Samuel 15)** *NRSB* reads: 'For rebellion is no less a sin than divination' (1 Samuel 15.23), and both the Geneva and Bishops' bibles have 'For rebellion is as the sinne of witchcraft'

[†] **Simon Magus** yet another instance of biblical magic regularly discussed. In canonical scripture, Simon 'used witchcraft, and bewitched the

people of Samaria' (Acts 8.9), was baptised, but, in the act of simony (named after him), offered St Peter money in exchange for the power of the Holy Ghost (Acts 8.9–24). In the apocryphal *Acts of Peter*, Simon Magus ('the magician') worked wonders with the aid of demons and had a contest of miracles in Rome with St Peter. St Peter's prayer caused him to fall to his death when flying above Rome. The early church fathers Justin Martyr (1 *Apologia* XXVI) and Irenaeus (*Adversus Haereses* I xxiii) identified him as a magician and heretic.

[†] **(Acts 8)** verse 9 in *NRSB* reads, 'Now a certain man named Simon had previously practised magic in the city and amazed the people of Samaria, saying that he was someone great'

[†] **the spirit of python** Acts 16.16–18 tells of 'a certain maide having a spirite of divination' (Acts 16.16; Vulgate: *puellam quandam habentem spiritum pythonem*). The Geneva marginal gloss on Acts 16.16 notes that this spirit 'could gesse, and foredeeme of things, past present and to come: which knowledge in many things God permits to the devill'.

[†] **what was she ... python** 'One day, as we were going to the place of prayer, we met a slave girl who had a spirit of divination and brought her owners a great deal of money by fortune-telling' (*NRSB* Acts 16.16)

[†] **other places** i.e. other places in the bible

P. But I think it very strange that God should permit any mankind (since they bear his own image) to fall in so gross and filthy a defection.

E. Although man in his creation was made to the image of the creator (Genesis 1),[†] yet through his fall, having once lost it, it is but restored again in a part by grace[†] only to the elect.[†] So all the rest, falling away from God, are given over in the hands of the devil—that enemy—to bear his image, and being once so given over the greatest and the grossest impiety is the pleasantest and most delightful unto them.

P. But may it not suffice him to have indirectly the rule,[†] and procure the perdition of so many souls by alluring them to vices, and to the following of their own appetites, suppose he abuse[†] not so many simple souls in making them directly acknowledge him for their master?[†]

E. No surely, for he uses every man, whom of[†] he hath the rule, according to their complexion[†] and knowledge. And so, whom he finds most simple, he plainliest discovers himself unto them. For he being the enemy of man's salvation, uses all the means he can to entrap them so far in his snares as it may be unable to them[†] thereafter (suppose they would)[†] to rid themselves out of the same.

P. Then this sin is a sin against the Holy Ghost.[†]

E. It is in some, but not in all.

P. How that? Are not all these that runs directly to the devil in one category?[2]

E. God forbid, for the sin against the Holy Ghost hath two branches: the one a falling back from the whole service of God, and a refusal of all his precepts; the other is the doing of the first[†] with knowledge, knowing that they do wrong against their own conscience and the testimony of the Holy Spirit, having once had a taste of the sweetness of God's mercies (Hebrews 6).[†] Now, in the first of these two all sorts of necromancers, enchanters or

---

[†] **man ... creator (Genesis 1)** 'Then God said, "Let us make humankind in our image, according to our likeness ..."' (*NRSB* Genesis 1.26)

[†] **by grace** by the unmerited favour of God

[†] **the elect** those chosen by God for salvation

[†] **to have indirectly the rule** to have domination by indirect means

[†] **suppose he abuse** but that also he must abuse (*BL*)

[†] **But ... master?** i.e. Would it not satisfy the devil more to lure many souls indirectly to moral viciousness, rather than fewer souls to acknowledge him directly by practising witchcraft?

[†] **whom of** of whom

[†] **complexion** character

[†] **unable to them** as it shall be impossible to them

[†] **(suppose they would)** even if they so wished

[†] **sin against the Holy Ghost** Jesus characterises the sin against the Holy Ghost as unforgiveable (Matthew 12.31–2, Mark 3.29, Luke 12.10), and so its identity preoccupied theologians. It was variously identified as impenitence, despair or presumption.

[†] **the first** i.e. a lessening in complete service to God

[†] **(Hebrews 6)** 'And have tasted of the good worde of God' (Hebrews 6.5)

witches are comprehended,[†] but in the last, none but such as errs with this knowledge[†] that I have spoken of.

P. Then it appears that there are more sorts nor one that are directly professors[†] of his service. And if so be, I pray you to tell me how many and what are they?

E. There are principally two sorts, where-unto all the parts of that unhappy art are redacted.[†] Whereof the one is called magic or necromancy, the other sorcery or witchcraft.

P. What, I pray you, and how many are the means whereby the devil allures persons in any of these snares?

E. Even by these three passions that are within ourselves: curiosity in great engines;[†] thirst of revenge for some torts deeply apprehended;[†] or greedy appetite of gear,[†] caused through great poverty.[†] As to the first of these, curiosity, it is only the enticement of magicians or necromancers; and the other two are the allurers of the sorcerers or witches, for that old and crafty serpent (being a spirit) he easily spies our affections, and so conforms himself[†] thereto to deceive us to our wrack.[†]

CHAPTER III

ARGUMENT: The significations and etymologies of the words of[†] 'magic' and 'necromancy'. The difference betwixt necromancy and witchcraft. What are the entresses[†] and beginnings that brings any to the knowledge thereof.

P. I would gladly first hear what thing it is that ye call magic or necromancy.

[†] **comprehended** included

[†] **such as errs with this knowledge** those who move away from God in full consciousness of what they are doing

[†] **professors** those who claim knowledge of and allegiance to

[†] **redacted** reduced, brought (*BL*)

[†] **curiosity in great engines** ambition in those with great intelligence, or ambition in great enterprises; curiosity in great wits (*BL*)

[†] **for some torts deeply apprehended** because of some deeply felt wrongs

[†] **of gear** for possessions; gain (*BL*)

[†] **Even ... great poverty** curiosity (Cooper 1617: III ii–vii 329, 339–43), revenge (Potts 1613: sig O3ᵛ; Margaret and Phillip Flower 1619: sig B2ᵛ–3) or poverty (Daneau 1575: sig E2ᵛ; Potts 1613: sig O3ᵛ) are often given as motivations for witchcraft. The devil promised Fian 'that he should be revenged of his enemies' and that he should never want (document 19, item 1).

[†] **conforms himself** adapts himself

[†] **to our wrack** to our destruction

[†] **words of** words

[†] **entresses** entrances, initiations into a subject

E. This word 'magic'[†] in the Persian tongue imports[†] as much as 'to be a contemplator or interpreter of divine and heavenly sciences'. Which being first used amongst the Chaldees,[†] through their ignorance of the true divinity, was esteemed and reputed amongst them as a principal virtue, and therefore was named unjustly with an honourable style. Which name the Greeks imitated, generally importing[†] all these kinds of unlawful arts.[†] And this word 'necromancy' is a Greek word compounded of *nekrôn* and *manteia*, which is to say 'the prophecy by the dead'. This last name is given to this black and unlawful science by the figure synecdoche,[†] because it is a principal part of that art, to serve themselves with dead carcages[†] in their divinations.

P. What difference is there betwixt this art and witchcraft?[3]

E. Surely, the difference vulgar put[†] betwixt them is very merry,[†] and in a manner true—for they say that the witches are servants only, and slaves to the devil, but the necromancers are his masters and commanders.

P. How can that be true, that any men being specially addicted[†] to his service can be his commanders?

E. Yea, they may be, but it is only *secundum quid*.[†] For it is not by any power that they can have over him, but *ex pacto* allanerly[†] whereby he oblices[†] himself in some trifles to them that he may on the other part obtain the fruition[†] of their body and soul, which is the only thing he hunts for.

P. A very inequitable contract forsooth. But I pray you discourse unto me, what is the effect and secrets of that art?

E. That is over-large a field ye give me. Yet I shall do good-will[†] the most summarily that I can,[†] to run through the principal points thereof. As there

---

[†] **'magic'** from Greek *magikós*, pertaining to a *magos*, Persian priest and wiseman, hence 'enchanter'. The nature of the wise men from the east (*magi*) who visited the infant Jesus (Matthew 2.1) exercised early writers; see Thorndike 1923–58: i 372, 396, 443–4, 471–9, 506, 518–19. Compare with James's statement here 'The common opinion is, that this [i.e. magic] is a Persian woorde, whereunto Porphirie and Apulei do assente, and that in their language it signifieth a Priest, a wise man, and a Philosopher' (Agrippa 1569: f. 54ᵛ).

[†] **imports** signifies

[†] **Chaldees** literally, native of Chaldea, but often used, because of the Chaldeans' reputation for soothsaying, to mean those skilled in occult arts and astrology

[†] **importing** meaning

[†] **This word 'magic' ... arts** Hemminsgen's *Admonitio* too notes the Persian origin of the word, its good meaning as the contemplation (*perscrutatio*) of heavenly science, and its Greek equivalents (Hemmingsen 1575: sig B)

[†] **synecdoche** the figure of speech by which the part indicates the whole (or vice versa). Here, divination by the dead is made to stand for all magic.

[†] **carcages** carcasses

[†] **difference vulgar put** difference ordinarily understood

[†] **merry** laughable

[†] **addicted** bound

[†] **only *secundum quid*** in one particular respect only (a term from neo-Aristotelian scholastic philosophy)

[†] ***ex pacto* allanerly** solely because of an agreement (with the devil); 'allanerly' is also a legal term appropriate to the idea of pact

[†] **oblices** obliges; bindeth (*BL*)

[†] **the fruition** the pleasure of possessing, the enjoyment

[†] **do good-will** willingly do

[†] **the most summarily that I can** as briefly as I can

are two sorts of folks that may be enticed to this art (to wit, learned or unlearned), so is there two means which are the first stirrers-up and feeders of their curiosity, thereby to make them to give themselves over to the same. Which two means I call the devil's school and his rudiments.[†] The learned have their curiosity wakened up and fed by that which I call his school: this is the astrology judiciar.[†] For diverse men, having attained to a great perfection in learning and yet remaining over-bare[†] (alas) of the spirit of regeneration[†] and fruits[†] thereof, finding all natural things common,[†] as well to the stupid pedants[†] as unto them, they assay to vindicate unto them a greater name[†] by not only knowing the course of things heavenly, but likewise to climb to the knowledge of things to come thereby. Which, at the first face[†] appearing lawful unto them, in respect the ground[†] thereof seemeth to proceed of natural causes only, they are so allured thereby that, finding their practice to prove true in sundry things, they study to know the cause thereof. And so mounting from degree to degree upon the slippery and uncertain scale[†] of curiosity, they are at last enticed, that where lawful arts or sciences fails to satisfy their restless minds, even to seek to that black and unlawful science of magic. Where, finding at the first that such diverse forms of circles and conjurations rightly joined thereunto[†] will raise such diverse forms of spirits to resolve them of their doubts;[†] and attributing the doing thereof to the power inseparably tied or inherent in the circles, and many words of God[†] confusedly wrapped in,[†] they blindly glory of themselves, as if they had by their quickness of engine[†] made a conquest of Pluto's dominion,[†] and become emperors over the Stygian habitacles.[†] Where in the meantime (miserable wretches) they are become in very deed bondslaves

---

[†] **rudiments** basic elements. James seems to be thinking of magic as a quasi-educational process. Rudiments are the first principles taught in a subject, and 'school' may be used in its medieval sense of a body of teachers and students in a university. In *As You Like It* Orlando reports that Ganymede (the disguised Rosalind) 'hath been tutored in the rudiments / Of many desperate studies by his uncle, / Whom he reports to be a great magician' (Shakespeare 1988: V iv 31–3), and Valdes promises Faustus 'First I'll instruct thee in the rudiments' (Marlowe 1993: A text, I i 163).

[†] **astrology judiciar** judicial astrology, the art of judging the influence of the stars and planets on human affairs

[†] **over-bare** quite destitute

[†] **regeneration** spiritual rebirth

[†] **fruits** effects

[†] **common** ordinary, well-known

[†] **stupid pedants** dull-minded word-mongers (*BL*)

[†] **assay ... name** try to claim for themselves a greater reputation

[†] **at the first face** at first sight

[†] **ground** fundamental principle

[†] **scale** ladder

[†] **rightly joined thereunto** properly combined with them

[†] **resolve them of their doubts** settle their uncertainties; compare Marlowe 1993: A–text, I i 81–2, 'Shall I make spirits fetch me what I please, / Resolve me of all ambiguities'

[†] **words of God** Hebrew, Greek and Latin names of, and synonyms for, God were used in conjuration

[†] **confusedly wrapped in** included in a fragmentary and disordered way

[†] **quickness of engine** quick wits

[†] **Pluto's dominion** the underworld (of which Pluto is the god)

[†] **Stygian habitacles** dwelling places in the underworld (where the river Styx flows); habitations of hell (*BL*)

to their mortal enemy; and their knowledge, for all that they presume thereof, is nothing increased except in knowing evil, and the horrors of hell for punishment thereof, as Adam's was by the eating of the forbidden tree[†] (Genesis 3).

CHAPTER IV

ARGUMENT: The description of the rudiments and school, which are the entresses[†] to the art of magic. And in special[†] the differences betwixt astronomy and astrology. Division of astrology in diverse parts.

P. But I pray you likewise forget not to tell what are the devil's rudiments.
E. His rudiments I call first, in general, all that which is called vulgarly the virtue[†] of word, herb and stone, which is used by unlawful charms without natural causes.[†] As likewise all kind of practics,[†] freits,[†] or other like extraordinary actions which cannot abide the true touch[†] of natural reason.
P. I would have you make that plainer by some particular examples, for your proposition is very general.
E. I mean either by such kind of charms as commonly daft[†] wives use for healing of forspoken goods,[†] for preserving them from evil eyes,[†] by knitting[†] rowan trees (or sundriest[†] kind of herbs) to the hair or tails of the goods, by curing the worm,[†] by stemming[†] of blood, by healing of horse-crooks,[†] by turning of the riddle[†]—or doing of suchlike innumerable things by words, without applying anything meet to the part offended,[†] as mediciners[†] do. Or else by staying[†] married folks to have naturally ado[†] with other, by knitting

---

[†] **as Adam's was ... tree** 'Then the Lord God said, "See, the man has become like one of us, knowing good and evil ... "' (*NRSB* Genesis 3.22)
[†] **entresses** entrances (*BL*)
[†] **in special** particularly
[†] **virtue** power
[†] **which is ... natural causes** brought about by the power of unlawful spells, outside the realm of natural physical laws
[†] **practics** clever, deceitful tricks
[†] **freits** superstitious charms and actions
[†] **abide the true touch** withstand the true test
[†] **daft** foolish
[†] **forspoken goods** bewitched possessions (including animals)
[†] **evil eyes** looks which can inflict injury

[†] **knitting rowan trees** tying branches of rowan
[†] **sundriest** many different
[†] **worm** e.g. tapeworm
[†] **stemming** staunching (*BL*)
[†] **horse-crooks** lameness in horses
[†] **riddle** divination by a pair of shears stuck into a sieve and held by two persons was used for the detection of theft and recovery of lost property; see Thomas 1973: 213–14
[†] **anything ... offended** anything suitable to the injured part
[†] **mediciners** people who practice medicine
[†] **staying** preventing
[†] **to have naturally ado** to have sexual relations; see note on **unable** p. 355

so many knots upon a point[†] at the time of their marriage. And suchlike things which men use so to practise in their merriness.[†] For fra[†] unlearned men (being naturally curious, and lacking the true knowledge of God) find these practices to prove true—as sundry of them will do by the power of the devil for deceiving men, and not by any inherent virtue in these vain words and freits—and being desirous to win a reputation to themselves in suchlike turns, they either (if they be of the shamefaster[†] sort) seek to be learned by some that are experimented[†] in that art, not knowing it to be evil at the first. Or else (being of the grosser[†] sort) run directly to the devil for ambition or desire of gain, and plainly contract[†] with him thereupon.

P. But methinks these means which ye call the school and rudiments of the devil are things lawful, and have been approved for such[†] in all times and ages; as, in special, this science of astrology which is one of the special members[†] of the mathematics.

E. There are two things which the learned have observed from the beginning in the science of the heavenly creatures[†] (the planets, stars and such like). The one is their course and ordinary motions, which for that cause is called *astronomia*, which word is a compound of *nomos* and *asterôn*, that is to say, 'the law of the stars'; and this art, indeed, is one of the members of the mathematics, and not only lawful but most necessary and commendable. The other is called *astrologia*, being compounded of *asterôn* and *logos*, which is to say 'the word and preaching of the stars', which is divided in two parts: the first, by knowing thereby the powers of simples,[†] and sicknesses, the course of the seasons and the weather, being ruled by their influence; which part depending upon the former[†] (although it be not of itself a part of mathematics, yet it is not unlawful, being moderately used) suppose not[†] so necessary and commendable as the former. The second part is to trust so

---

[†] **upon a point** on a length of cord or lace (used to fasten clothing together where buttons would now be used). On '*les noueürs d'esguillettes* [knotting the points]' see Boguet 1608: 182; Cotgrave, *A Dictionarie of the French and English Tongues* (1611), sig Kk6: '*avoir l'esguillete nouée* signifies, to want an erection. This impotencie is supposed to come by the force of certaine words uttered by a charmer, while he ties a knot on the parties cod peece-point', and 'they wil tie a knot upon a point, as our cuntreymen speake, that is to say, they can hinder and binde maryed couples that they shal not pay their due one to the other' (Daneau 1575: E8). For discussions of the magical use of such knotted cords (*ligatures*) to cause impotence, see Boguet 1928: 78, 91; Guazzo 1988: II iv 91–5; and Robbins 1959: *sv ligature* 305–7.

[†] **merriness** fun
[†] **fra** when (*BL*)
[†] **shamefaster** humbler
[†] **experimented** experienced
[†] **grosser** coarser, more ignorant
[†] **contract** enter into a formal agreement
[†] **approved for such** proved as such
[†] **special members** the particular sub-divisions
[†] **heavenly creatures** those things created by God in the heavens. There was also some debate in the Renaissance as to whether the stars were 'animals'.
[†] **simples** plants or herbs (used for medicinal purposes)
[†] **which part ... the former** i.e. this part of astrology is dependent on astronomy, the knowledge of the motions of heavenly bodies
[†] **suppose not** even though not

much to their[†] influences as thereby to foretell what commonweals shall flourish or decay, what persons shall be fortunate or unfortunate, what side shall win in any battle, what man shall obtain victory at singular[†] combat, what way and of what age shall men die, what horse shall win at match-running; and diverse such like incredible things, wherein Cardanus,[†] Cornelius Agrippa and diverse others have more curiously then profitably[†] written at large. Of this root last spoken of spring innumerable branches, such as the knowledge by the nativities,[†] the chiromancy,[†] geomanty,[†] hydromanty,[†] arithmanty,[†]physiognomy,[†] and a thousand others which were much practised and holden in great reverence by the gentiles[†4] of old. And this last part of astrology whereof I have spoken, which is the root of their branches, was called by them *pars fortunae*.[†] This part now is utterly unlawful to be trusted in or practised amongst Christians, as leaning to no ground[†] of natural reason; and it is in this part which I called before the devil's school.

P. But yet many of the learned are of the contrary opinion.

E. I grant, yet I could give my reasons to fortify[†] and maintain my opinion, if to enter into this disputation it would not draw me quite off the ground[†] of our discourse, besides the misspending of the whole day thereupon. One word only I will answer to them, and that in the scriptures (which must be an infallible ground to all true Christians), that in the prophet Jeremiah (Jeremiah 10)[†] it is plainly forbidden to believe or hearken unto them that prophesy and forespeak[†] by the course of the planets and stars.

[†] **their** i.e. the stars'

[†] **singular** single

[†] **Cardanus** Girolamo Cardano (1501–76), Italian astrologer and writer on medicine, mathematics, physics and philosophy. He was arrested by the Inquisition in 1570 for casting the horoscope of Christ. James is probably thinking of parts of his *De Subtilitate* (1550) or *De Rerum Raritate* (1557); see Thorndike 1923–58: v 563–79.

[†] **more curiously then profitably** more elaborately than usefully

[†] **nativities** horoscopes drawn up at birth

[†] **chiromancy** palmistry

[†] **geomanty** either divining by the motions and noise of the earth, or by the shapes made by earth thrown on the ground; or divination by a number of dots placed on paper at random. In a passage much repeated in later taxonomies of magic, the scholiast Servius commenting on *Aeneid* 3.359 reported the Roman scholar Varro (116–27 BC) to have described divination by the four elements. On geomancy and hydromancy and other forms of divination by the four elements, see Agrippa, *De Occulta Philosophia* (Paris 1567) I lvii. *Geomantia di Pietro di Abano* (Venice 1542) gives instructions for divinations by dots, as does Agrippa 1567: II xlviii.

[†] **hydromanty** divining by the actions of water (such as its ebb or flow)

[†] **arithmanty** divining by numbers

[†] **physiognomy** predicting someone's future by the shapes and lines of their face. On chiromancy and physiognomy, see Joannes ab Indagine, *Introductiones ... in Chyromantiam, Physiogniam* (Strassburg 1522), English translation 1558.

[†] **gentiles** pagans

[†] ***pars fortunae*** the grammar of fortune (i.e. the ordered, meaningful signs by which fortune can be read)

[†] **ground** basis

[†] **fortify** strengthen

[†] **ground** subject

[†] **(Jeremiah 10)** 'Thus saith the Lord, Learne not the waye of the heathen, and be not afraide for the signes of heaven, though the heathen be afrayde of such' (Jeremiah 10.2)

[†] **forespeak** foretell

CHAPTER V

ARGUMENT: How far the using of charms is lawful or unlawful. The description of the forms of circles and conjurations, and what causeth the magicians themselves to weary thereof.

P. Well, ye have said far enough in that argument.[†] But how prove ye now that these charms or unnatural practics[†] are unlawful? For so many honest and merry[†] men and women have publicly practised some of them, that I think if ye would accuse them all of witchcraft ye would affirm more nor ye will be believed in.

E. I see if you had taken good tent[†] to the nature of that word hereby[†] I named it, ye would not have been in this doubt nor mistaken me so far as ye have done. For although as none can be scholars in a school and not be subject to the master thereof, so none can study and put in practice (for the study alone and knowledge is more perilous nor offensive,[5] and it is the practice only that makes the greatness of the offence)[†] the circles and art of magic without committing a horrible defection from God. And yet, as they that read and learn their rudiments are not the more subject to any schoolmaster if it please not their parents to put them to the school thereafter, so they who ignorantly prove these practics[†] (which I call the devil's rudiments), unknowing[†] them to be baits casten out by him for trapping such as God will permit to fall in his hands; this kind of folks, I say, no doubt are to be judged the best of,[†] in respect they use no invocation[†] nor help of him (by their knowledge[†] at least) in these turns, and so have never entered themselves in Satan's service. Yet to speak truly for my own part (I speak but for myself), I desire not to make so near riding,[†] for in my opinion our enemy is over-crafty[†] and we over-weak (except the greater grace of God[†]) to assay[†] such hazards wherein he presses[†] to trap us.

P. Ye have reason forsooth, for as the common proverb saith, 'They that sup

---

[†] **in that argument** on that subject
[†] **practics** practices
[†] **merry** good-natured
[†] **taken good tent** paid close attention
[†] **hereby** in that place
[†] **for the study ... offence** James is saying that knowledge of conjuring is very dangerous, but that it is its actual practice which makes it an offence
[†] **prove these practics** try out these tricks
[†] **unknowing** not knowing (*BL*)
[†] **the best of** better (than the other sort)

[†] **invocation** summoning the devil to appear using a magic formula
[†] **by their knowledge** knowingly
[†] **to make so near riding** to ride so closely (to the devil); the sense is that those who try conjuring, even without invoking the devil, are 'sailing close to the wind'
[†] **over-crafty** all too clever
[†] **we over-weak ... grace of God** i.e. we are very weak, unless strengthened by God's grace
[†] **assay** attempt
[†] **presses** strives

kale[†] with the devil have need of long spoons'.[†] But now, I pray you go forward in the describing of this art of magic.

E. Fra[†] they be come once unto this perfection in evil, in having any knowledge (whether learned or unlearned) of this black art, they then begin to be weary of the raising of their master by conjured circles, being both so difficile[†] and perilous, and so cometh plainly to a contract with him wherein is specially contained forms and effects.[†]

P. But I pray you, or ever[†] you go further, discourse me somewhat of their circles and conjurations, and what should be the cause of their wearying thereof. For it should seem that that form[†] should be less fearful yet than the direct haunting and society with that foul and unclean spirit.

E. I think ye take me to be a witch myself, or at least would fain[†] swear yourself prentice to that craft. Always[†] as I may, I shall shortly satisfy you in that kind of conjurations which are contained in such books which I call the devil's school. There are four principal parts: the persons of the conjurers; the action of the conjuration; the words and rites used to that effect; and the spirits that are conjured. Ye must first remember to lay the ground[†] that I told you before, which is that it is no power inherent in the circles, or in the holiness of the names of God blasphemously used, nor in whatsoever rites or ceremonies at that time used, that either can raise any infernal spirit, or yet limitate[†] him perforce[†] within or without these circles.[†] For it is he only, the father of all lies,[†] who having first of all prescribed that form of doing—feigning himself to be commanded and restrained thereby—will be loath to pass the bounds of these injunctions; as well[†] thereby to make them glory in the empiring[†] over him (as I said before), as likewise to make himself so to be trusted in these little things that he may have the sic better commodity[†] thereafter to deceive them in the end with a trick once for all—

[†]   **kale** a kind of cabbage (and hence the broth in which it is a principal ingredient); pottage (*BL*)

[†]   **proverb saith ... spoons** as James says, the proverb was common in the sixteenth century; see Tilley 1950: S771

[†]   **Fra** after (*BL*)

[†]   **difficile** difficult; instructions for conjuration in Renaissance manuscripts testify to a complicated and arduous process. As the magician Pope Alexander VI comments in anticipation of a conjuration, 'Now must I laboure like a collyers horse', Barnabe Barnes, *The Devil's Charter*, ed. J. C. Pogue (Ann Arbor 1977) IV i 1893.

[†]   **wherein ... effects** in which ways of proceeding and results are specifically included

[†]   **or ever** even before

[†]   **form** way of proceeding (i.e. encountering evil spirits by means of circles and conjurations)

[†]   **fain** willingly

[†]   **Always** yet

[†]   **lay the ground** establish the fundamental truth

[†]   **limitate** confine within prescribed boundaries (of the circles)

[†]   **perforce** by force

[†]   **Ye must ... these circles** it was orthodox demonological belief that there was no power to compel spirits to appear inherent in magical words, conjurations, rituals or diagrams, as Marlowe's Mephistophilis explains to Faustus (Marlowe 1993: A–text, I iii 45–55)

[†]   **the father of all lies** 'the devil ... was a murderer from the beginning, and abode not in the truth, because there is no truth in him. When he speaketh a lie, he speaketh of his own: for he is a liar, and the father of it' (John 8.44)

[†]   **as well** in addition

[†]   **empiring** ruling (*BL*)

[†]   **sic better commodity** greater opportunity (*BL*)

I mean the everlasting perdition of their soul and body. Then laying this ground, as I have said, these conjurations must have few or more in number of the persons conjurers[†] (always passing the singular number),[†] according to the quality of the circle, and form of apparition. Two principal things cannot well in that errand be wanted:[†] holy water[†] (whereby the devil mocks the papists),[†] and some present of a living thing unto him.[†] There are likewise certain seasons, days and hours that they observe in this purpose.[†] These things being all ready and prepared, circles are made triangular, quadrangular, round, double or single, according to the form of apparition[†] that they crave. But to speak of the diverse forms of the circles, of the innumerable characters and crosses[†] that are within and without and out-through[†] the same, of the diverse forms of apparitions[†] that that crafty spirit illudes them with, and of all such particulars[†] in that action, I remit it[†] to over many that have busied their heads in describing of the same, as being but curious and altogether unprofitable. And this far only I touch,[†] that when the conjured spirit appears, which will not be while[†] after many circumstances, long prayers and much muttering and murmuring of the conjurers[†] (like a papist priest dispatching a hunting mass),[†] how soon,[†] I say, he appears, if they have missed one iota[†] of all their rite, or if any of their feet once slide over the circle through terror of this fearful apparition, he pays himself at

---

[†] **persons conjurers** the persons who are conjuring

[†] **passing the singular number** more than one; Scot reproduces a conjuration from Weyer instructing 'one must always be with you' (Scot 1886: XV iv 327)

[†] **wanted** lacking

[†] **holy water** the pseudo-Agrippan *Liber Quartus*, against which James warns his readers in his preface, instructs the magician to 'sprinkle the circle with holy water' (Agrippa 1567: 562)

[†] **papists** derogatory term regularly used by protestants at this time for catholics

[†] **living thing** spirits sometimes demanded the sacrifice of a living thing in a circle and would not answer questions without such a sacrifice (see Coxe 1561: sig A9ᵛ)

[†] **There are … this purpose** for magical considerations of hours of the day and night, and days of the week see the *Heptameron* of pseudo-Peter of Abano (Agrippa 1567: *Heptameron, passim*)

[†] **form of apparition** particular appearance of the spirit

[†] **characters and crosses** magical signs and symbols and crosses

[†] **out-through** over the whole area of; throughout (*BL*)

[†] **diverse forms of apparitions** for 'an inventarie of the names, shapes … and effects of divels and spirits' and the extraordoinary forms they took, see Scot 1886: XV ii 314–27. See also the pseudo-Agrippan *Liber Quartus* for forms taken by planetary spirits (Agrippa 1567: 531–5).

[†] **particulars** details

[†] **remit it** leave it for consideration

[†] **touch** mention

[†] **while** until

[†] **which will … the conjurers** spirits were notoriously reluctant and tardy in responding to conjurations: '*Quid tardatis? quid moramini?*' ('What's the hold-up? What's the delay?') as a conjuration in the *Heptameron* impatiently asks them (Agrippa 1567: 566). Conjurations had often to be repeated and intensified, and a *Clavicula Salominis* tells the magician what to say in the case of delays it obviously anticipates, BL Additional MS 36,674, ff. 7–8.

[†] **hunting mass** 'a short mass said in great haste for hunters who were eager to start for the chase' (*OED*)

[†] **how soon** as soon as (*BL*)

[†] **iota** smallest particle

that time in his own hand[†] of that due debt[†] which they ought[†] him, and otherwise would have delayed longer to have paid him: I mean, he carries them with him body and soul. If this be not now a just cause to make them weary of these forms of conjuration, I leave it to you to judge upon, considering the longsomeness of the labour, the precise keeping of days and hours (as I have said), the[6] terribleness of apparition, and the present peril that they stand in, in missing the least circumstance or freit that they ought to observe. And on the other part,[†] the devil is glad to move them[†] to a plain and square dealing with him, as I said before.

CHAPTER VI

ARGUMENT: The devil's contract with the magicians. The division thereof in two parts. What is the difference betwixt God's miracles and the devil's.

P. Indeed, there is cause enough, but rather to leave him at all than to run more plainly to him, if they were wise he dealt with. But go forward now, I pray you, to these turns fra[†] they become once deacons[†] in this craft.

E. From time that they once plainly begin to contract with him, the effect of their contract consists in two things: in forms and effects, as I began to tell already (were it not ye interrupted me), for although the contract be mutual, I speak first of that part wherein the devil oblishes[†] himself to them. By forms,[7] I mean in what shape or fashion[†] he shall come unto them when they call upon him. And by effects, I understand in what special sorts of services he binds himself to be subject unto[†] them. The quality of these forms and effects is less or greater according to the skill and art of the magician. For as to the forms, to some of the baser sort of them he oblishes himself to appear at their calling upon him by such a proper name which he shows unto them, either in likeness of a dog, a cat, an ape, or suchlike other beast, or else to answer by a voice only.[†] The effects are to answer to such demands as concerns curing of diseases, their own particular menagery,[†] or

---

[†] **in his own hand** in person
[†] **due debt** i.e. the person's body and soul, pledged when the contract with the devil, implicit in the magician's practice of magic, was entered into
[†] **ought** owed
[†] **on the other part** on the other side (of the bargain)
[†] **to move them** to persuade
[†] **fra** after (*BL*)
[†] **deacons** master craftsmen (though it usually means the chief officials of a craft or trade)

[†] **oblishes** obliges, puts himself under obligation to; bindeth (*BL*)
[†] **fashion** manner
[†] **to be subject unto** to owe obedience and allegiance to
[†] **voice only** James may be remembering part of Euphame MacCalzean's dittay (document 23, item 16), that she had consulted Agnes Sampson who 'in the one of the times she raised the Sprite by voice and not bodily'
[†] **menagery** management of affairs (*Craigie*); housewifery (*BL*)

such other base things as they require of him. But to the most curious sort, in the forms he will oblish himself to enter in a dead body, and there out of[†] to give such answers of the event[†] of battles, of matters concerning the estate of commonwealths,[†] and such like other great questions.[†] Yea, to some he will be a continual attender in form of a page. He will permit himself to be conjured for the space of so many years either in a tablet[†] or a ring, or such like thing which they may easily carry about with them.[†] He gives them power to sell such wares to others, whereof some will be dearer and some better cheap,[†] according to the lying or true speaking of the spirit that is conjured therein. Not but that in very deed all devils must be liars, but so they abuse the simplicity of these wretches that become their scholars, that they make them believe that at the fall of Lucifer some spirits fell in the air, some in the fire, some in the water, some in the land; in which elements they still remain.[†] Whereupon they build, that such as fell in the fire or in the air, are truer than they who fell in the water or in the land, which is all but mere trattles,[†] and forged by the author of all deceit. For they fell not by weight, as a solid substance, to stick in any one part; but the principal part of their fall, consisting in quality[†]—by the falling from the grace of God wherein they were created—they continued still thereafter, and shall do while the latter day, in wandering through the world as God's hangmen, to execute such turns[†] as he employs them in. And when any of them are not occupied in that, return they must to their prison in hell (as it is plain in the miracle that Christ wrought at Gennezareth) (Matthew 8)[†] therein at the latter day to be all enclosed for ever. And as they deceive their scholars in this, so do they in imprinting in them the opinion that there are so many princes,

---

[†] **there out of** i.e. from out of the dead body

[†] **event** outcome

[†] **the estate of commonwealths** the condition of countries

[†] **he will oblish ... great questions** James may be thinking of Lucan's account of Pompey's consultation of the Thessalian witch Erictho to know the outcome of the battle of Pharsalus and hence the fate of the Roman state. She temporarily reanimates the corpse of a recently dead soldier to answer Pompey's questions (*Pharsalia* VI 413ff).

[†] **tablet** 'An ornament of precious metal or jewellery, flat in form, which was worn about the person' (*Craigie*)

[†] **conjured ... about with them** Scot gives an operation 'to have a spirit inclosed into a christall stone or berill glasse, or into anie other like instrument' (Scot 1886: XV xii 344–6)

[†] **some will ... better cheap** some will be an expensive, some a better bargain

[†] **at the fall ... remain** according to the often-cited

On the Operation of Daemons ascribed to the Byzantine Platonist Michael Psellus (1018–*c*.1078) there were six different kinds of devils; of these, four kinds were associated with the four Aristotelian elements. Scot summarises Psellus' opinions in the 'Discourse of Divels and Spirits' appended to the *Discoverie* (Scot 1886: 414–15). There is an exposition of the fall of spirits into the elements in Greene 1964: ix 57–74.

[†] **trattles** prattle; tales (*BL*)

[†] **quality** the condition (of their previous existence in heaven). The contrast is between thinking of the angels' fall as being a change in their material existence (falling by their own weight), and their spiritual condition (falling from God's grace).

[†] **turns** affairs (*BL*)

[†] **miracle ... Gennezareth** Matthew 8.28–34 recounts how Jesus orders the demons to leave two demoniacs and enter swine which then plunge into the sea to their deaths

dukes and kings amongst them,[†] every one commanding fewer or more legions, and empiring in diverse arts, and quarters of the earth.[†] For though that I will not deny that there be a form of order amongst the angels in heaven,[†] and consequently was amongst them before their fall, yet, either that they brook[†] the same sensine,[†] or that God will permit us to know by damned devils such heavenly mysteries of his which he would not reveal to us neither by scripture nor prophets, I think no Christian will once think it. But, by the contrary, of all such mysteries as he hath closed up with his seal of secrecy, it becometh us to be contented with an humble ignorance, they being things not necessary for our salvation.[†] But to return to the purpose: as these forms wherein Satan oblishes himself to the greatest of the magicians are wonderful curious, so are the effects correspondent unto[†] the same. For he will oblish himself to teach them arts and sciences, which he may easily do being so learned a knave as he is: to carry them news from any part of the world, which the agility of a spirit may easily perform; to reveal to them the secrets of any persons,[†] so being they be once spoken, for the thought none knows but God, except so far as ye may guess[8] by their countenance, as one who is doubtlessly learned enough in the physiognomy; yea, he will make his scholars to creep in credit[†] with princes by foretelling them many great things part true, part false, for if all were false he would tine[†] credit at all hands, but always doubtsome[†] as his oracles were. And he will also make them to please princes by fair banquets and dainty dishes carried in short

---

[†] **them** i.e. the devils

[†] **there are ... of the earth** James is again thinking of the list in Scot (1886: 314–27) which grades devils into kings, dukes, earls, marquesses and so on, and counts up the legions that each commands. Different devils are credited with the ability to teach different arts' (Procell 'teacheth geometrie and all the liberall arts', 322), and some are associated with points of the compass ('quarters of the earth'): '*Amaymom* king of the east, *Gorson* king of the south, *Zimimar* king of the north, *Goap* king and prince of the west may be bound from the third houre till noone, and bound from the ninth houre till evening' (XV iii 327).

[†] **order amongst the angels in heaven** traditionally there were nine orders of angels, ranging from the highest hierarchy of the seraphim down to ordinary angels. The classic statement is in the *Celestial Hierarchies* of (pseudo-) Dionysius (early sixth century AD), who divided the angels into three triads, each containing three orders. This is followed by Aquinas, *Summa*

I[a], q 108. See also Gregory the Great, *XL Homiliarum in Evangelia* Hom. XXXIV (Migne, *PL* 76, 1246–59). There was a tradition that there were correspondingly nine orders of demons: 'There are scholastic theologians who divide evil spirits into nine classifications, as if in opposition to the nine orders of angels' (Agrippa 1567: III xxviii 360).

[†] **brook** enjoy (*BL*)

[†] **that they ... sensine** they possess that same order since

[†] **things not necessary for our salvation** technically, *adiaphora*, things indifferent and doctrinally non-essential

[†] **correspondent unto** corresponding to

[†] **reveal ... the secrets of any persons** compare 'I'll have them read me strange philosophy / And tell the secrets of all foreign kings' (Marlowe 1993: A–text, I ii 88–9)

[†] **creep in credit** inveigle themselves into favour

[†] **tine** lose

[†] **doubtsome** ambiguous

space fra the farthest part of the world.[†] For no man doubts but he is a thief, and his agility (as I spake before) makes him to come such speed.[†] Such-like,[†] he will guard his scholars with fair armies of horsemen and footmen in appearance,[†] castles and forts;[†] which all are but impressions in the air, easily gathered by a spirit drawing so near to that substance himself.[†] As in like manner he will learn[†] them many jugglery tricks at cards, dice and such like, to deceive men's senses thereby; and such innumerable false practics which are proven by over-many in this age, as they who are acquainted with that Italian called Scoto[†] yet living can report. And yet are all these things but deluding of the senses and no ways true in substance; as were the false miracles wrought by king Pharaoh's magicians[†] for counterfeiting Moses.[†] For that is the difference betwixt God's miracles and the devil's: God is a creator—what he makes appear in miracle, it is so in effect.[†] As,[†] Moses' rod being casten down was no doubt turned in a natural serpent. Whereas the devil (as God's ape),[†] counterfeiting that by his magicians, made their wands

---

[†] **please princes ... of the world** Faustus brings the Duchess of Vanholt 'a dish of ripe grapes' from the other side of the world (Marlowe 1993: A text, IV ii), and Greene's Friar Bacon entertains Henry III's guests with a splendid banquet (Greene 1964: ix 244–65). William Tyndale, the biblical translator, was shown at Antwerp 'a notable magician in the place, whose use was at Feasts, or when they used to meet at Supper, to bring to the Table, whatever Wines, or delicious Fruit, the Company would desire' (Sinclair 1871: 154).

[†] **to come such speed** to have such success

[†] **Such-like** in that way

[†] **fair armies ... in appearance** compare 'Like lions shall they guard us when we please, / Like Almaine rutters with their horsemen's staves, / Or Lapland giants, trotting by our sides' (Marlowe 1993: A–text, I i 126–8)

[†] **castles and forts** compare 'Nor / know I how sufficiently to recompense your great deserts / in erecting that enchanted castle in the air' (Marlowe 1993: B–text, IV vi 1–3)

[†] **drawing...himself** being so like air himself. Angels and devils have no material body, but can make use of air (the most immaterial form of matter and so most like the immaterial spirits themselves) in order to create pseudo-bodies which can be perceived by people, and which in the case of devils will be used deceptively to appear as real people.

[†] **learn** teach

[†] **Scoto** Scoto of Mantua, a sixteenth-century Italian entertainer famous for his sleight of

hand, who appeared before Elizabeth I in 1576. Ben Jonson's Volpone disguises himself as Scoto of Mantua (*Volpone*, II ii). For further contemporary allusions see Jonson 1925–52: ix 704.

[†] **King Pharaoh's magicians** Exodus 7.8–12: 'So Moses and Aaron went to Pharaoh and did as the Lord had commanded; Aaron threw down his staff before Pharaoh and his officials, and it became a snake. Then Pharaoh summoned the wise men and the sorcerers; and they also, the magicians of Egypt, did the same by their secret arts. Each one threw down his staff, and they became snakes; but Aaron's staff swallowed up theirs' (*NRSB* Exodus 7.10–12). See above, note on **Exodus 7 and 8** (p. 361).

[†] **for counterfeiting Moses** to counterfeit the miracles done by Moses (*BL*)

[†] **in effect** in physical reality. The traditional theological distinction was that only God, directly or through his prophets and saints, worked miracles above the course of nature (*miracula*); the devil, directly or through his agents, could only produce wonders (*mira*).

[†] **As** for example

[†] **ape** mimic; a commonplace of demonological thought '*le Diable se fait singe en tout du Dieu vivant* [in everything the devil apes the living God]' (Boguet 1608: 141), which drew on the tag '*diabolus simia Dei* [the devil is God's ape]'. It had become proverbial in the sixteenth century (see Tilley 1950: D247) that the devil imitates and parodies God; compare Perkins 1610: II 46–7; Cooper 1617: I iii 48.

to appear so only to men's outward senses, as kithed[†] in effect by their being devoured by the other. For it is no wonder that the devil may delude our senses, since we see by common proof that simple jugglers will make an hundred things seem both to our eyes and ears otherwise than they are. Now as to the magicians' part of the contract, it is in a word that thing which I said before the devil hunts for in all men.

P. Surely ye have said much to me in this art, if all that ye have said be as true as wonderful.

E. For the truth in these actions, it will be easily confirmed to any that please to take pain upon[†] the reading of diverse authentic histories, and the enquiring of daily experiences. As for the truth of their possibility, that they may be, and in what manner, I trust I have alleged nothing whereunto I have not joined such probable reasons as I leave to your discretion to weigh and consider. One word only I omitted concerning the form of making of this contract, which is either written with the magician's own blood, or else being agreed upon in terms,[†] his schoolmaster[9] touches him in some part,[†] though peradventure no mark remain, as it doth with all witches.[†]

CHAPTER VII

ARGUMENT: The reason why the art of magic is unlawful. What punishment they merit. And who may be accounted guilty of that crime.

P. Surely ye have made this art to appear very monstrous and detestable. But what, I pray you, shall be said to such as maintain this art to be lawful, for as evil as[†] you have made it?

E. I say, they savour of the pan themselves,[†] or at least little better. And yet, I would be glad to hear their reasons.

P. There are two principally that ever I heard used, beside that which is founded upon the common proverb that the necromancers command the devil, which ye have already refuted. The one is grounded upon a received[†] custom, the other upon an authority which some think infallible. Upon

---

[†] **kithed** was made manifest
[†] **upon** in (*BL*)
[†] **in terms** on the terms of the contract (between the person and the devil)
[†] **in some part** on some part of his body. James is thinking of the magician as male. Daneau too says that male sorcerers are marked (Daneau 1575: sig F4ᵛ), and John Fian was marked by the devil with a rod.
[†] **as it doth with all witches** a search for the

witches' mark was a regular feature of their examinations in England and Scotland
[†] **as evil as** however evil
[†] **they savour of the pan themselves** literally, they taste of the saucepan in which they were cooked; they betray their origins (*Craigie*). James is implying that those who defend witchcraft share the same devilish origins as those who practise it.
[†] **received** accepted

custom we see that diverse Christian princes and magistrates, severe punishers of witches, will not only oversee† magicians to live within their dominions, but even sometimes delight to see them prove some of their practics. The other reason is that Moses, being brought up (as it is expressly said in the scriptures) 'in all the sciences of the Egyptians',† whereof no doubt this was one of the principals, and he notwithstanding of† this art pleasing God as he did, consequently that art professed by so godly a man could not be unlawful.

E. As to the first of your reasons grounded upon custom, I say an evil custom can never be accepted for a good law; for the over-great ignorance of the word† in some princes and magistrates, and the contempt thereof in others, move them to sin heavily against their office in that point. As to the other reason, which seems to be of greater weight, if it were formed in a syllogism† it behoved† to be in many terms† and full of fallacies (to speak in terms of logic). For first, that that[10] general proposition affirming Moses to be taught in all the sciences of the Egyptians should conclude that he was taught in magic, I see no necessity, for we must understand that the spirit of God there, speaking of sciences, understands† them that are lawful; for, except they be lawful, they are but *abusivè*† called sciences, and are but ignorances indeed: *Nam homo pictus, non est homo.*† Secondly, giving† that he had been taught in it, there is great difference betwixt knowledge and practising of a thing (as I said before). For[11] God knoweth all things, being always good, and of† our sin and our infirmity proceedeth our ignorance. Thirdly, giving that he had both studied and practised the same (which is more nor monstrous to be believed by any Christian) yet we know well enough that before that ever the spirit of God began to call Moses he was fled out of Egypt (being forty years of age) for the slaughter of an Egyptian,† and in his godfather† Jethro's land first called at the fiery bush,† having remained there other† forty years in exile. So that, suppose† he had been the wickedest man in the world before, he then became a changed and regenerate man, and very little of old Moses remained in him. Abraham was an idolater in Ur of

---

† **oversee** overlook
† **Moses ... Egyptians** a reference to Acts 7.22
† **notwithstanding of** in spite of
† **the word** i.e. the word of God
† **syllogism** argument constructed from two sequent propositions from which a third proposition or conclusion can be drawn. 'A discourse in which a certain thing being stated, something other than what is stated follows of necessity from being so' (Aristotle, *Prior Analytics* 24ᵇ 18).
† **behoved** would be necessary
† **terms** propositions in a syllogism
† **understands** means

† *abusivè* by an improper use (Latin)
† *Nam ... homo* 'For a picture of a man is not a real man' (Latin)
† **giving** granted
† **of** out of
† **slaughter of an Egyptian** 'he sawe an Egyptian smiting an Ebrewe, one of his brethren. And he loked rounde about, & when he sawe no man, he slewe the Egyptian, and hid him in the sand' (Exodus 2.11–12)
† **godfather** father-in-law (*BL*)
† **and in ... fiery bush** see Exodus 3
† **other** another, see Acts 7.23, 30
† **suppose** even though

Chaldee[†] before he was called;[†] and Paul, being called Saul,[†] was a most sharp persecutor of the saints of God[†] while[†] that name was changed.

P. What punishment then think ye merit[†] these magicians and necromancers?
E. The like, no doubt, that sorcerers and witches merit. And rather so much greater, as their error proceeds of the greater knowledge, and so draws nearer to the sin against the Holy Ghost. And as I say of them, so say I the like[†] of all such as consult,[†] enquire, entertain,[†] and oversee[†] them; which is seen by the miserable ends of many that ask counsel of them. For the devil hath never better tidings to tell to any than he told to Saul;[†] neither is it lawful to use so unlawful instruments, were it never for so good a purpose,[†] for that axiom in theology is most certain and infallible: *Nunquam faciendum est malum ut bonum inde eveniat*[†] (Acts 3).[†][12]

[†] **Ur of Chaldee** Abraham's birthplace; see Genesis 11.28–31 and Acts 7.2–4

[†] **called** i.e. by God to perform his spiritual and historical tasks as a patriarch. For Abraham's idolatry in Ur before his calling, James must be thinking of 'Your fathers dwelt beyonde the flood in olde time, even Terah the father of Abraham, and the father of Nachor, and served other gods. And I toke your father Abraham from beyonde the flood, & brought him through all the land of Canaan' (Joshua 24.2–3).

[†] **being called Saul** Saul changed his name to Paul after his conversion to Christianity

[†] **the saints of God** the members of the early Christian church (and so specially favoured of God); 'As for Saul, he made havock of the church, entering into every house, and haling men and women committed them to prison' (Acts 7.3)

[†] **while** until

[†] **merit** deserve

[†] **the like** the same thing

[†] **consult** in 1 Chronicles 10.13 Saul is condemned for his transgression 'in that he soght and asked counsel [Vulgate *consuluit*] of a familiar spirit'; and the Bassandyne adds in the margin 'or witche & sorceresse'

[†] **entertain** have dealings with

[†] **oversee** intentionally overlook (the evil that comes from) them

[†] **For the devil ... to Saul** 'Samuel' (i.e. the devil impersonating Samuel) prophesied to Saul both that Israel would be delivered into the hands of the Philistines, and Saul's own imminent death (1 Samuel 28.19)

[†] **were ... purpose** no matter how good the purpose

[†] **Nunquam ... eveniat** you must never do evil so that good may come of it (Latin)

[†] **(Acts 3)** as Craigie notes, there is nothing like this in Acts 3. James must be paraphrasing Romans 3.8 '*Et non facienda mala, ut veniant bona*' (You must not do evil so that good may come of it). This biblical marginal reference was one of the three James failed to supply when annotating the scribal copy in Folger MS V.a.185. This together with James's own changes made to the scribe's version of the quotation in the text of this MS suggest that it was a quotation James was unsure of (see Craigie 1982: 162, 166). Boguet quotes this verse in a similar context of condemning recourse to magic in any circumstances (Boguet 1929: 111–12), as does Robert Holland (Clark and Morgan 1976: 37) and Daneau (Daneau 1575: sig K8).

THE SECOND BOOK OF DEMONOLOGY

ARGUMENT: The description of sorcery and witchcraft in special.

CHAPTER I

ARGUMENT: Proved by the scripture that such a thing can be, and the reasons refuted of all such as would call it but an imagination[†] and melancholic humour.[†]

PHILOMATHES Now, since ye have satisfied me now so fully concerning magic or necromancy, I will pray you to do the like in[†] sorcery or witchcraft. EPISTEMON That field is likewise very large, and although in the mouths and pens of many,[†] yet few know the truth thereof so well as they believe themselves;[†] as I shall, so shortly[†] as I can, make you (God willing) as easily[†] to perceive.

P. But I pray you before ye go further, let me interrupt you here with a short digression, which is that many can scarcely believe that there is such a thing as witchcraft. Whose reasons I will shortly allege[†] unto you, that ye may satisfy me as well in that as ye have done in the rest. For first, whereas the scripture seems to prove witchcraft to be,[†] by diverse examples, and specially by sundry of the same which ye have alleged, it is thought by some that these places speak of magicians and necromancers only, and not of witches. As in special, these wise men of Pharaoh's that counterfeited Moses' miracles were magicians say they, and not witches; as likewise that pythoness that

---

[†] **imagination** fantasy
[†] **melancholy humour** product of a temperamentally gloomy state of mind. A humour in ancient and medieval physiology and psychology was thought to be one of the four body fluids (blood, phlegm, choler, bile) whose balance in the body determined a person's physical and psychological state; melancholy was bile. James is thinking here of the physiologically and psychologically based scepticism of Weyer and Scot.

[†] **in** about
[†] **although in the mouths and pens of many** *BL* adds 'it bee' after 'although'. Compare 'this question now a dayes is very much disputed upon: being almost no sort of men by whom it is not tossed' (Daneau 1575: sig B3ᵛ).
[†] **so ... themselves** as well as they think they do
[†] **shortly** briefly
[†] **as easily** very easily (*BL*)
[†] **allege** cite
[†] **to be** to exist

Saul consulted with; and so was Simon Magus in the New Testament, as that very style[†] imports. Secondly, where ye would oppone[†] the daily practic and confession of so many, that[†] is thought likewise to be but very melancholic imagination of simple raving creatures. Thirdly, if witches had such power of witching of folks to death as they say they have, there had been none left alive long since in the world but they; at least, no good or godly person of whatsoever estate[†] could have escaped their devilry.

E. Your three reasons, as I take, are grounded, the first of them, *negativè*[†] upon the scripture, the second *affirmativè*[†] upon physic,[†] and the third upon the certain[†] proof of experience. As to your first, it is[1] most true indeed that all these wise men of Pharaoh were magicians of art,[†] as likewise it appears well that the pythoness, with whom Saul consulted, was of that same profession, and so was Simon Magus. But ye omitted to speak of the law of God, wherein are all magicians, diviners,[2] enchanters, sorcerers, witches, and whatsoever of that kind that consult with the devil, plainly prohibited, and alike threatened against.[†] And besides that, she who had the spirit of python in the Acts (Acts 16),[†] whose spirit was put to silence by the Apostle, could be no other thing but a very sorcerer or witch, if ye admit the vulgar distinction to be in a manner true, whereof I spake in the beginning of our conference.[†] For that spirit whereby she conquested[†] such gain to her master[†] was not at her raising or commanding as she pleased to appoint,[†] but spake by her tongue, as well publicly as privately. Whereby she seemed to draw nearer to the sort of demoniacs or possessed, if that conjunction[†] betwixt them had not been of her own consent, as it appeared by her not being tormented therewith, and by her conquesting[†] of such gain to her masters, as I have already said. As to your second reason grounded upon physic—in attributing their confessions or apprehensions[†] to a natural melancholic humour—any that pleases physically[†] to consider upon the natural humour

---

[†] **style** title (of 'magus', meaning 'magician')
[†] **oppone** use in your argument against me
[†] **that** i.e. confession
[†] **estate** social position
[†] *negativè* negatively (Latin)
[†] *affirmativè* positively (Latin)
[†] **physic** medicine
[†] **certain** sure
[†] **magicians of art** learned magicians; compare 'words of art' (Marlowe 1993: A-text, I.i.160)
[†] **But ye ... threatened against** James is thinking of one of the comprehensive condemnations in the Old Testament of several categories of practitioners of magic and divination, perhaps Deuteronomy 18.10–12
[†] **she ... in the Acts** '... a slave girl who had a

spirit of divination and brought her owners a great deal of money by fortune-telling' (*NRSB* Acts 16.16)
[†] **vulgar distinction ... conference** 'the difference vulgar' that Epistemon noted in I iii, i.e. the common opinion that witches are the devil's servants and magicians are his commanders
[†] **conquested** acquired; got (*BL*)
[†] **to her master** for her master
[†] **appoint** arrange, settle upon, decide
[†] **conjunction** combination
[†] **conquesting** getting (*BL*)
[†] **apprehensions** perceptions; conceits, those things which they conceive and persuade themselves (*BL*)
[†] **physically** medically

of melancholy, according to all the physicians that ever writ thereupon, they shall find that that will be over-short a cloak to cover their knavery with.[†] For as the humour of melancholy in the self[†] is black, heavy and terrene,[†] so are the symptoms thereof in any persons that are subject thereunto: leanness, paleness, desire of solitude, and, if they come to the highest degree thereof,[†] mere folly[†] and mania.[†] Whereas, by the contrary, a great number of them that ever have been convict[†] or confessors of witchcraft—as may be presently seen by many that have at this time confessed—they are, by the contrary I say, some of them rich and worldly-wise,[†] some of them fat or corpulent[†] in their bodies, and most part of them[†] altogether given over to the pleasures of the flesh,[†] continual haunting of company, and all kind of merriness,[†] both lawful and unlawful, which are things directly contrary to the symptoms of melancholy, whereof I spake. And further, experience daily proves how loath they are to confess without torture, which witnesseth their guiltiness; where, by the contrary, the melancholics never spare to bewray[†] themselves by their continual discourses, feeding thereby their humour[†] in that which they think no crime. As to your third reason, it scarcely merits an answer. For if the devil their master were not bridled,[†] as the scriptures teacheth us, suppose[†] there were no men nor women to be his instruments, he could find ways enough without any help of others to wrack all mankind—whereunto he employs his whole study,[†] and 'goeth about like a roaring lion' (as Peter saith)[†] to that effect. But the limits of his power were set down before the foundations of the world were laid, which he hath not power in the least jot to transgress.[†] But beside all this, there is over great a certainty

---

[†] **over-short ... knavery with** inadequate explanation to conceal their crafty dealing

[†] **in the self** in itself (*BL*)

[†] **terrene** earthy: earth is the heaviest of the four elements (fire, air, water, earth) of which the world is made up according to ancient Greek philosophy

[†] **highest degree thereof** most intense state of melancholy

[†] **mere folly** complete foolishness

[†] **mania** acute mental derangement

[†] **convict** convicted

[†] **rich and worldy-wise** by these words, in the margin of Folger MS V.a.185: 39, the initials 'E M' [Euphame MacCalzean?] have been written (see Dunlap 1975: 41)

[†] **fat and corpulent** margin of Folger MS V.a.185: 39: 'R G [Ritchie Graham?]'

[†] **most part of them** most of them

[†] **given ... the flesh** margin of Folger MS V.a.185: 39: 'B N [Barbara Napier?]'

[†] **merriness** fun

[†] **spare to bewray** refrain from revealing

[†] **feeding thereby their humour** in that way

increasing their (melancholy) state of mind

[†] **bridled** restrained

[†] **suppose** though (*BL*)

[†] **study** effort

[†] **as Peter saith** 'Be sober and watch: for your adversarie the devill as a roaring lyon walketh about, seking whom he may devoure' (1 Peter 5.8). This verse, expressing the determination, predatoriness and savagery of the devil, was a favourite with demonologists: 'for Satan is like a roaring Lyon, who alwayes runneth about seking whom he may devoure' (Daneau 1575: sig D8ᵛ).

[†] **For if the devil ... transgress** a very protestant assertion of God's omnipotent providence which limits and controls the devil's power. Compare Gifford, 'The high providence of God Almightie and soveraigne rule over all, is set forth unto us in Scriptures ... all the divels in hell are so chained up and brideled by this high providence that they cannot plucke the wing from one poore little wrenne, without speciall leave given them' (Gifford 1862: iii–iv).

to prove that they are,[†] by the daily experience of the harms that they do, both to men and whatsoever thing men possess, whom God will permit them to be the instruments,[†] so to trouble or visit, as in my discourse of that art ye shall hear clearly proved.

CHAPTER II

ARGUMENT: The etymology and signification of that word of 'sorcery'; the first entresses and prenticeship[†] of them that give themselves to that craft.

P. Come on then, I pray you, and return where ye left.

E. This word of 'sorcery' is a Latin word which is taken from 'casting of the lot', and therefore he that useth it is called *sortiarius à sorte*.[†] As to the word of 'witchcraft', it is nothing but a proper name given in our language. The cause wherefore they were called *sortiarii*, proceeded of their practics,[†] seeming to come of[†] lot or chance: such as the turning of the riddle;[†] the knowing of the form of prayers, or such like tokens, if a person deceased would live or die.[†] And in general, that name was given then for using of such charms and freits as that craft teacheth them. Many points of their craft and practics are common betwixt the magicians and them, for they serve both one master, although in diverse fashions. And as I divided the necromancers into two parts, learned and unlearned, so must I divide[3] them in other two,[†] rich and of better accompt,[†] poor and of baser degree. These two degrees now of persons that practise this craft answer to the passions[†] in them, which I told you before the devil used as means to entice them to his service. For such of them as are in great misery and poverty, he allures to follow him by promising unto them great riches and worldly commodity.[†]

[†] **that they are** that they (witches) exist
[†] **whom God ... instruments** whom God will permit to be the instruments (of harm). Demonologists, both catholic and protestant, stressed again and again that it was only with God's permission that the devil, through his agents the witches, was allowed to harm mankind. It is with this point that the *Malleus Maleficarum* opens: 'The first part of *The Hammer of Witches*, which contains the three things which come together in witchcraft: the devil, a witch, and God's permission' (Kramer and Sprenger 1971: part I, q 1) and returns to in part I, q 12. James stresses the necessary permission of God many times in book II.
[†] **prenticeship** apprenticeship
[†] **is called *sortiarius à sorte*** the name 'sorcerer' (*sortiarius*) comes from the word for lot (*sors*, ablative *sorte*). For a similar philological discussion of *sortiarius* see Daneau 1575: sigs B7[v]–8.
[†] **practics** practices
[†] **of** from
[†] **turning of the riddle** see note on **riddle**, p. 366.
[†] **knowing ... would live or die** James may be thinking of Agnes Sampson's diagnostic prayers 'to her patients, for life or death'. See Agnes Sampson's dittay, document 20 *passim* and especially item 32.
[†] **in other two** into another two categories
[†] **of better accompt** of greater social importance
[†] **passions** desires
[†] **commodity** advantage

Such as though rich, yet burn in a desperate desire of revenge, he allures them by promises to get their turn[†] satisfied to their heart's contentment. It is to be noted now that that old and crafty enemy of ours assails none, though touched with any of these two extremities, except[†] he first find an entress ready for him, either by the great ignorance of the person he deals with joined with an evil life, or else by their carelessness and contempt of God. And finding them in an utter despair for one of these two former causes that I have spoken of, he prepares the way by feeding them craftily in their humour,[†] and filling them further and further with despair while he finds the time proper to discover himself unto them. At which time, either upon their walking solitary in the fields, or else lying pansing[† 4] in their bed,[†] but always without the company of any other, he either by a voice or in likeness of a man inquires of them what troubles them; and promiseth them a sudden and certain way of remedy, upon condition, on the other part,[†] that they follow his advice, and do such things as he will require of them. The minds being prepared beforehand, as I have already spoken, they easily agreed unto that demand of his; and syne set another tryst[†] where they may meet again. At which time, before he proceed any further with them, he first persuades them to addict[†] themselves to his service; which being easily obtained, he then discovers what he is unto them, makes them to renounce their God and baptism[†]directly, and gives them his mark[†] upon some secret place of their body. Which remains sore unhealed[†] while his next meeting with them, and thereafter ever insensible,[†] howsoever it be nipped or pricked by any (as is daily proved),[†] to give them a proof thereby that as in that doing he could hurt and heal them, so all their ill- and well-doing thereafter must depend upon him. And besides that, the intolerable dolour[†] that they

---

[†] **turn** desire (*BL*)

[†] **except** unless

[†] **feeding ... humour** cunningly encouraging them in their state of mind

[†] **pansing** thinking (compare French 'penser' to think)

[†] **At which time ... bed** James is remembering the alleged encounters between the devil and Agnes Sampson and John Fian respectively: 'she confessed before his Majesty that the devil in man's likeness met her going out in the fields from her own house at Keith betwix five and six at even, being her allane' (document 20), and 'the devil appeared and came to him when he was lying in his bed in Tranent in Thomas Trumbill's chamber, musing and pensing how he might be revenged of the said Thomas' (document 19)

[†] **on the other part** on the other side (of the contract)

[†] **syne set another tryst** after that arrange another meeting

[†] **addict** commit, 'to attach oneself to another as a disciple or adherent' (*Craigie*)

[†] **renounce God and baptism** the explicit and formal renunciation of God and baptism, usually at the sabbat, was a classic feature of continental witchcraft; see Boguet 1929: IX 24–6

[†] **mark** for the devil's mark see *News*, p.316

[†] **sore unhealed** painfully unhealed

[†] **ever insensible** permanently without feeling

[†] **as is daily proved** i.e. by the practice in witch interrogations of 'pricking', that is piercing or probing a suspect's body, including the genitals, to discover the part that the devil has caused to feel no pain

[†] **dolour** physical pain

feel in that place where he hath marked them serves to waken[†] them, and not to let them rest while their next meeting again; fearing lest otherwise they might either forget him, being as new prentices, and not well enough founded[†] yet in that fiendly folly, or else remembering of that horrible promise they made him at their last meeting, they might scunner[†] at the same, and press to call it back.[†] At their third meeting, he makes a show to be careful to perform his promises, either by teaching them ways how to get themselves revenge, if they be of that sort, or else by teaching them lessons, how by most vile and unlawful means they may obtain gain and worldly commodities, if they be of the other sort.

CHAPTER III

ARGUMENT: The witches' actions divided in[5] two parts: the actions proper to[†] their own persons; their actions toward others. The form of their conventions,[†] and adoring of[†] their master.

P. Ye have said now enough of their initiating in[†] that order. It rests[†] then that ye discourse upon their practices, fra they be passed prentices,[†] for I would fain hear what is possible to them to perform in very deed.[†]
E. [6] Although they serve a common master with the necromancers (as I have before said), yet serve they him in another form. For as the means are diverse which allure them to these unlawful arts of serving of the[7] devil, so by diverse ways use they their practices answering to these means which first the devil used as instruments in them,[†] though all tending to one end: to wit, the enlarging of Satan's tyranny, and crossing[†] of the propagation of the kingdom of Christ so far as lieth in the possibility,[†] either of the one or other sort, or of the devil their master. For where the magicians, as allured by curiosity, in the most part of their practices seek principally the satisfying of the same, and to win to themselves a popular honour and estimation, these witches, on the other part, being enticed either for the desire of revenge or of worldly riches, their whole practices are either to hurt men and their goods, or what

---

[†] **waken** keep them from sleeping
[†] **founded** established
[†] **scunner** feel disgust
[†] **press to call it back** strive to revoke (the promise)
[†] **proper to** pertaining to
[†] **conventions** meetings (*BL*); the word regularly used in the dittays for the witches' meetings
[†] **adoring of** worshipping
[†] **initiating in** being admitted into (*BL*)
[†] **rests** remains

[†] **fra they be passed prentices** after they have passed the stage of being apprentices
[†] **in very deed** in actual deeds
[†] **so by diverse ... in them** so they perform magical practices in different ways corresponding to those methods of enticement which the devil first used as ways to prompt them (to witchcraft)
[†] **crossing** impeding
[†] **possibility** capacity

they possess, for satisfying of their cruel minds in the former, or else by the wrack in whatsoever sort[†] of any whom God will permit them to have power of,[†] to satisfy their greedy desire in the last point.[†] In two parts their actions may be divided: the actions of their own persons, and the actions proceeding from them towards any other. And this division, being well understood, will easily resolve you[†] what is possible to them to do. For although all that they confess is no lie upon their part, yet doubtlessly, in my opinion, a part of it is not indeed according as they take it to be:[†] and in this I mean, by the actions of their own persons. For as I said before speaking of magic, that the devil illudes[†] the senses of these scholars of his in many things, so say I the like of these witches.

P. Then I pray you, first to speak of that part of their own persons, and syne[†] ye may come next to their actions towards others.

E. To the effect that[†] they may perform such services of their false master as he employs them in, the devil (as God's ape) counterfeits in his servants this service and form of adoration[†] that God prescribed and made his servants to practise. For as the servants of God publicly use to convene for serving of him, so makes he[†] them in great numbers to convene (though publicly they dare not) for his service. As none convenes to[†] the adoration of worshipping of God except they be marked with his seal—the sacrament of baptism—so none serves Satan and convenes to the adoring of him that are not marked with that mark whereof I already spake. As the minister sent by God teacheth plainly at the time of their public conventions how to serve him in spirit and truth, so that unclean spirit in his own person teacheth his disciples at the time of their convening how to work all kind of mischief. And craves compt[†] of all their horrible and detestable preceedings past, for advancement of his service. Yea, that he may the more vively[†] counterfeit and scorn God, he oft-times makes his slaves to convene in these very places which are destinate[†] and ordained for the convening of the servants of God (I mean by churches).[†] But[8] this far,[†] which I have yet said,[†] I not only take it to be true in their opinions but even so to be indeed.[†] For the form that he used in

---

[†] **wrack in whatsoever sort** destruction in whatever way possible

[†] **permit them to have power of** allow (the witches) to have power over

[†] **the last point** i.e. the desire for worldly riches

[†] **resolve you** let you decide

[†] **as they take it to be** how they understand it to be

[†] **illudes** deceives

[†] **syne** next

[†] **To the effect that** in order that

[†] **counterfeits ... adoration** falsely imitates in his servants this worship and style of adoration

[†] **he** i.e. the devil

[†] **to** for

[†] **craves compt** demands an account

[†] **the more vively** in a more lifelike way; lively (*BL*)

[†] **destinate** appointed (*BL*)

[†] **I mean by churches** by which I mean churches. Nider records that witches met in church on Sunday before the consecration of holy water and there the new disciple renounced God, his faith and baptism (*Formicarius*, Frankfurt 1582: 718)

[†] **this far** this much

[†] **yet said** just said

[†] **indeed** in reality

counterfeiting God among the gentiles makes me so to think: as God spake by his oracles,[†] spake he not so by his? As God has as well bloody sacrifices, as others without blood,[†] had he not the like? As God had churches sanctified to his service with altars, priests, sacrifices, ceremonies and prayer, had he not the like polluted to his service? As God gave responses[†] by urim and thummim,[†] gave he not his responses by the entrails of beasts, by the singing of fowls, and by their actions in the air? As God by visions, dreams, and ecstasies revealed what was to come and what was his will unto his servants, used he[†] not the like means to forewarn his slaves of things to come? Yea, even as God loved cleanness, hated vice and impurity, and appointed punishments therefore, used he not the like—though falsely, I grant, and but in eschewing the less inconvenient, to draw them upon a greater?[†] Yet dissimuled[†] he not, I say, so far as to appoint his priests to keep their bodies clean and undefiled before their asking responses of him? And fained he not God[†] to be a protector of every virtue, and a just revenger of the contrary? This reason then moves me, that as he is that same devil, and as crafty now as he was then, so will he not spare as pertly in these actions[†] that I have spoken of, concerning the witches' persons. But further, witches oft-times confess not only his convening in the church with them, but his occupying of the pulpit, yea, their form of adoration to be the kissing of his hinder parts;[†] which, though it seem ridiculous, yet may it likewise be true, seeing

---

[†] **oracles** declarations or messages delivered by divine inspiration, including sacred scriptures (*OED*)

[†] **bloody sacrifices ... without blood** for blood sacrifices and other sacrifices prescribed in the Old Testament see, for example, Leviticus 3.1–17, 7.11–38, 10.12–15, 22.17–25

[†] **responses** answers (*BL*)

[†] **urim and thummim** urim ('lights') and thummim ('perfection') were probably a form of lot used to ascertain the will of God (see Numbers 27.21), and in the story of Saul and the witch of Endor, God refused to answer Saul's enquiries about the forthcoming battle with the Philistines through the media of dreams, urim and the prophets (1 Samuel 28.6). They are included in the description of the making of Aaron's vestments (Exodus 28.30) and were worn thereafter on the Jewish High Priest's breastplate.

[†] **he** i.e. the devil

[†] **but in eschewing ... greater** getting them to draw back from the lesser danger only to encourage them to a greater one; i.e. the devil encourages purity and chastity as a necessary preparation before divination (and certain sorts of magic). Thus his servants avoid the lesser dangers of impurity and unchastity only to be drawn on to the more heinous dangers of divination.

[†] **dissimuled** dissembled

[†] **And feigned he not God** and didn't he (the devil) imitate God

[†] **so will he ... in these actions** so he will not restrain himself from behaving as boldly in these actions

[†] **hinder parts** parts of the body situated behind i.e. buttocks and anus. For accounts of the devil preaching in the pulpit of North Berwick kirk and the witches kissing his arse see dittays, document 20 and *News*, p. 319.

we read that in Calicut[†] he, appearing in form of a goat buck,[†] hath publicly that unhonest homage[†] done unto him by every one of the people. So ambitious is he and greedy of honour (which procured his fall) that he will even imitate God in that part, where it is said that Moses could see but 'the hinder parts of God, for the brightness of his glory'.[†] And yet that speech is spoken but *anthropopatheian*.[†]

CHAPTER IV

ARGUMENT: What are the ways possible whereby the witches may transport themselves to places far distant,[†] and what are impossible and mere illusions of Satan; and the reasons thereof.

P. But what way say they, or think ye, it possible that they can come to these unlawful conventions?

E. There is the thing which I esteem their senses to be deluded in, and though they lie not in confessing of it because they think it to be true, yet not to be so in substance or effect.[†] For they say that by diverse means they may convene, either to the adoring of their master or to the putting in

[†] **Calicut** Calicut on the Malibar coast (Craigie 1982). Satan is 'worshipped under the most terrible and monstrous forme that ever we see him drawne and painted in any place' in 'Calycut', a city of the Indians, Edward Fenton, *Certaine Secrete wonders of Nature* (1569), ff. 2ᵛ–3ᵛ. Ben Jonson in a note to 'And saddle your goat', part of a line in his *Masque of Queenes*, notices 'His Majesty also remembers the story of the devil's appearance to those of Calicut, in that form *Demonology* II iii' (Jonson 1969: 528).

[†] **goat buck** one of the forms most often taken by the devil when he presided at the sabbat; 'sometimes he talketh with them in shape of a man, sometimes like a most filthy buck goate [*hirci turpissimi forma*, Daneau 1574: 69]' (Daneau 1575: sig F7ᵛ); Guazzo also says that very often the devil takes the form of a goat at the convention and repeats a story from Florimond de Raemond, *L'Antéchrist* (Lyons 1597) of witches kissing a goat under the tail (Guazzo 1988: 47). Guillaume Edeline, condemned as a sorcerer in 1453, confessed that he had several times been transported to the meetings of sorcerers, renounced God 'and adored the devil in the form of a billy-goat [*en figure de bouc*], kissing him on the anus' (Bodin 1580: f. 81).

[†] **unhonest homage** discreditable sign of allegiance

[†] **brightness of his glory** in Exodus 33 Moses asked to see the glory of God, but was told that no man can see the face of God and live. However, God promised to pass by Moses and to show him his 'back parts': 'And while my glorie passeth by, I wil put thee in a cleft of the rocke, & wil cover thee with mine hand whiles I passe by. After I wil take away my hand, and thou shalt se my backe partes: but my face shal not be sene' (Exodus 33.22–23). The Bassandyne Bible glosses 'backe partes' (Vulgate *posteriora*) as 'So muche of my glorie as in this mortal life thou art able to se'.

[†] ***anthropopatheian*** BL has meticulously added in the margin in Greek *kat'* thus giving the more grammatical and explicable phrase *kat'anthropópátheian* which means something like 'as if he were human', i.e. the bible at this point is accommodating the divine to human sense by speaking as if God had a body

[†] **What are ... far distant** how witches got to their meetings and whether aerial transvection, the means supposedly reported by many witches in Europe, was possible is regularly discussed by demonologists; see Kramer and Sprenger 1971: part II q 1 chap 3; Boguet 1929: XV–XVII; Daneau 1575: sigs G8–H5ᵛ

[†] **in substance or effect** in reality or in fact

practice any service of his committed unto their charge.[†] One way is natural—which is natural riding,[†] going or sailing,[†] at what hour their master comes and advertises them[†]—and this way may be easily believed. Another way is somewhat more strange, and yet is it[†][9] possible to be true: which is by being carried by the force of the Spirit[†] which is their conductor,[†] either above the earth or above the sea swiftly to the place where they are to meet; which I am persuaded to be likewise possible, in respect that as Habakkuk was carried by the angel in that form to the den where Daniel lay.[†] So think I the devil will be ready to imitate God as well in that as in other things, which is much more possible to him to do (being a spirit) than to a mighty wind (being but a natural meteor)[†] to transport from one place to another a solid body, as is commonly and daily seen in practice. But in this violent form they cannot be carried but a short bounds,[†] agreeing with the space that they may retain their breath,[†] for if it were longer their breath could not remain unextinguished, their body being carried in such a violent and forcible manner. As by example, if one fall off a small height his life is but in peril according to the hard or soft lighting,[†] but if one fall from a high and stay[†] rock his breath will be forcibly banished from the body before he can win to[†] the earth, as is oft seen by experience. And in this transporting they say themselves that they are invisible to any other except amongst themselves, which may also be possible in my opinion. For if the devil may form what kind of impressions he pleases in the air, as I have said before speaking of magic, why may he not far easilier[†] thicken and obscure so the air that is next about them,[†] by contracting it straight together,[†] that the beams of any other man's eyes cannot pierce through the same to see them? But the third way of their coming to their conventions is that wherein I think them

---

[†] **charge** responsibility

[†] **natural riding** according to Agnes Sampson's dittay '[the devil] commanded her to be at North Berwick kirk the next night. And she passed there on horseback, convoyed by her godson'

[†] **sailing** on All Hallows' Eve John Fian, Agnes Sampson, Robert Grierson and others 'embarked in a boat beside Robert Grierson's house in the 'Pans and sailed over the sea to a tryst they had with another witch' (John Fian's dittay, item 13)

[†] **advertises them** informs them

[†] **is it** it is

[†] **Spirit** i.e. the devil

[†] **conductor** means of conveyance

[†] **den where Daniel lay** the angelic transportation of Habakkuk from Judea to Babylon where Daniel lay in the lion's den (Apocrypha, Bel and the Dragon verses 33–9; Vulgate Daniel 14.32–8) was often cited in discussions of transvection:

see Kramer and Sprenger 1971: part II q 1 chap 3; Weyer 1991: III xii; Bodin 1580: f. 89; Scot 1888: V vii; Cotta 1616: 38–40

[†] **natural meteor** natural atmospheric phenomenon

[†] **short bounds** limited distance

[†] **agreeing ... breath** corresponding only to the distance over which they are still able to breathe. This belief seems peculiar to James.

[†] **lighting** landing

[†] **stay** steep

[†] **win to** reach

[†] **easilier** more easily

[†] **next about them** immediately surrounding their bodies

[†] **contracting it straight together** condensing it tightly together. The devil can make the air around someone's body denser so that person can be carried along invisible inside this cocoon of air.

deluded: for some of them saith that being transformed in the likeness of a little beast or fowl they will come and pierce through whatsoever house or church,[†] though all ordinary passages be closed, by whatsoever open[†] the air may enter in at. And some saith that their bodies lying still as in an ecstasy,[†] their spirits will be ravished[†] out of their bodies and carried to such places.[†] And for verifying thereof, will give evident tokens,[†] as well by witnesses that have seen their body lying senseless in the meantime, as by naming persons whomwith they met, and giving tokens what purpose[†] was amongst them, whom otherways[†] they could not have known. For this form of journeying they affirm to use most when they are transported from one country to another.

P. Surely I long to hear your own opinion of this, for they are like old wives' trattles[†] about the fire.

E.[10] The reasons that move me to think that these are mere illusions are these. First, for them that are transformed in likeness of beasts or fowls can[†] enter through so narrow passages. Although I may easily believe that the devil could by his workmanship upon the air make them appear to be in such forms, either to themselves or to others, yet how he can contract a solid body within so little room,[†] I think it is directly contrary to itself.[†] For to be made so little and yet not diminished,[†] to be so straightly drawn together[†] and yet feel no pain, I think it is so contrary to the quality of a natural body,[†] and so like to the little transubstantiate god[†] in the papists' mass, that I can never believe it. So to have a quantity[† 11] is so proper to a solid body that, as all philosophers conclude, it cannot be any more without one than a spirit can have one. For when Peter 'came out of the prison, and the doors all locked' (Acts 12)[†] it was not by any contracting of his body in so

---

[†] **for some ... or church** James may be thinking of such stories as Scot's mentions of the magician Stafus (Scot 1886: V i 73; XII v 178) who could 'transforme himselfe into a mouse, and runne into everie little hole'. The story is in Kramer and Sprenger 1971: part II q 1 chap xv, and comes from Nider's *Formicarius*.

[†] **open** opening

[†] **ecstasy** trance

[†] **ravished** carried away

[†] **And some saith ... places** John Fian deponed that 'he was strucken in great ecstasies and trances, lying by the space of two or three hours dead, his sprite taken, and suffered himself to be carried and transported to many mountains as though through all the world, according to his own depositions' (document 19)

[†] **evident tokens** clear signs of proof

[†] **what purpose** what talk (*BL*)

[†] **otherways** otherwise

[†] **trattles** chatter; tales (*BL*)

[†] **can** are supposed to be able to

[†] **so little room** such a small space

[†] **contrary to itself** self-contradictory

[†] **diminished** made less (than the body it was). If a body with a certain size is shrunk to a smaller size, then it is illogical, James argues, to think that it is the same, and not somehow less than what it was.

[†] **straightly drawn together** tightly squeezed together

[†] **quality of a natural body** characteristics of an actual body

[†] **transubstantiate god** the god which is changed from one substance (bread and wine) into another substance (body and blood of Christ) in the catholic mass. The 'little ... god' refers to the communion wafer.

[†] **quantity** certain size

[†] **Peter ... locked (Acts 12)** Peter, even though he was in chains, was delivered from prison in Jerusalem by an angel (Acts 12.5–10)

little room but by the giving place of the door, though unespied by the jailers. And yet there is no comparison, when this is done, betwixt the power of God and of the devil. As to their form of ecstasy and spiritual transporting, it is certain that the soul's going out of the body is the only definition[†] of natural death, and who are once dead, God forbid we should think that it should lie in the power of all the devils in hell to restore them to their life again; although he can put his own spirit in a dead body, which the necromancers commonly practise, as ye have heard. For that is the office[†] properly belonging to God. And besides that, the soul once parting from the body cannot wander any longer in the world, but to the own[†] resting place must it go immediately, abiding the conjunction of[†] the body again at the latter day.[†] And what Christ or the prophets did miraculously in this case,[†] it cannot in no Christian man's opinion be made common with the devil. As for any tokens that they give for proving of this, it is very possible to the devil's craft to persuade them to these means. For he being a spirit, may he not so ravish their thoughts and dull their senses that their body, lying as dead, he may object to[†] their spirits as it were in a dream, and (as the poets write of Morpheus)[†] represent such forms of persons, of places and other circumstances as he pleases to illude them with? Yea, that he may deceive them with the greater efficacy, may he not at that same instant, by fellow angels[†] of his, illude such other persons so in that same fashion, whom-with[†] he makes them to believe that they met, that all their reports and tokens, though severally[†] examined, may every one agree with another. And that whatsoever actions either in hurting men or beasts, or whatsoever other thing that they falsely imagine at that time to have done, may by himself or his marrows[†] at that same time be done indeed; so as if they would give for a token at their being ravished at the death of such a person within so short space thereafter, whom they believe to have poisoned or witched at that instant, might he not at that same hour have smitten that same person by the permission of God to the farther deceiving of them, and to move others

---

[†] **only definition** uniquely the definition

[†] **office** function. Only God has the power to put a soul into a body (at birth) and remove it (at death).

[†] **own** proper

[†] **abiding the conjunction of** waiting for the joining up with

[†] **latter day** Day of Judgement

[†] **And what Christ ... in this case** James distinguishes the devil's temporary animation of a dead body from the truly miraculous restorations to life by the prophets and Christ himself, e.g. Elijah's raising to life of the widow's son (1 Kings 17.17–24) and Jesus's raising of Lazarus (John 11.1–44)

[†] **object to** present himself to the sight of

[†] **Morpheus** the god of dreams; James may well be thinking of the much-imitated passage in Ovid where Morpheus takes the shape of Alcyone's husband, Ceyx, to break the news of Ceyx's death to her in a dream (*Metamorphoses* XI 633–77)

[†] **angels** i.e. evil spirits; so called because all devils were originally angels in heaven who accompanied Satan when he fell from heaven

[†] **whom-with** with whom

[†] **severally** separately

[†] **marrows** associates

to believe them? And this is surely the likeliest way, and most according to reason which my judgement can find out in this and whatsoever other unnatural points of their confession. And by these means shall we sail surely betwixt Charybdis and Scylla,[†] in eschewing[†] the not believing of them altogether on the one part, lest that draw us to the error that there is no witches, and on the other part in believing of it, make us to eschew the falling into innumerable absurdities, both monstruously against all theology divine and philosophy human.

CHAPTER V

ARGUMENT: Witches' actions towards others. Why there are more women of that craft nor men. What things are possible to them to effectuate[†] by the power of their master; the reasons thereof. What is the surest remedy of the harms done by them.

P. Forsooth, your opinion in this seems to carry most reason with it, and since ye have ended then the actions belonging properly to their own persons, say forward now to[†] their actions used towards others.

E. In their actions used towards others three things ought to be considered: first, the manner of their consulting thereupon;[†] next, their part as instruments;[†] and last, their master's part, who puts the same in execution.[†] As to their consultations thereupon, they use them oftest in the churches[†] where they convene for adoring; at what time their master, enquiring at them[†] what they would be at,[†] every one of them propones[†] unto him what wicked turn[†] they would have done, either for obtaining of riches or for revenging them upon any whom they have malice at. Who, granting their demand as no doubt willingly he will (since it is to do evil), he teacheth

---

[†] **Charybdis and Scylla** the story of Scylla and Charybdis had long since been allegorised to mean the dangers and hence the necessary avoidance of two extremes. It was proverbial in the sixteenth century (Tilley 1950: S169). James claims that his explanation of experiences of transvection avoids the two extremes of absolute scepticism and excessive credulity. Daneau also uses the proverb of Scylla and Charybdis to express extremes of wrong belief about witchcraft (Daneau 1575: sig B7).

[†] **eschewing** avoiding

[†] **to them to effectuate** for them to bring about

[†] **say forward now to** now go on to speak about

[†] **manner ... thereupon** way in which they take

advice on that matter (of actions directed at others)

[†] **their part as instruments** their function as the persons who perform the actions

[†] **in execution** into actual effect. The devil has the power to do the evil; the witches act subordinately as his agents.

[†] **churches** for witches' meeting in churches see document 19, John Fian's dittay, and document 20, Agnes Sampson's dittay, and *News*, p. 319

[†] **at them** of them

[†] **would be at** would like to do

[†] **propones** proposes

[†] **wicked turn** ill turn, mischief (*BL*)

them the means whereby they may do the same. As for little trifling turns[†] that women have ado with,[†] he causeth them to joint[†] dead corpses and to make powders thereof,[†] mixing such other things there amongst as he gives unto them.

P. But before ye go further permit me, I pray you, to interrupt you one word, which ye have put me in memory of, by speaking of women. What can be the cause that there are twenty women given to that craft where there is one man?

E. The reason is easy, for as that sex is frailer then man is,[†] so is it easier to be entrapped in these gross snares of the devil, as was over-well proved to be true by the serpent's deceiving of Eva at the beginning, which makes him the homelier[†] with that sex sensine.

P. Return now where ye left.

E. To some others at these times he teacheth how to make pictures of wax[†] or clay,[†] that by the roasting thereof the persons that they bear the name of may be continually melted or dried away by continual sickness. To some he

---

[†] **trifling turns** insignificant matters

[†] **have ado with** are concerned with. Given the context here (the use of powders for women's 'trifling turns') James is probably remembering that Agnes Sampson was convicted of 'putting of moulds or powder, made of men's joints and members in Newton kirk, under Euphame Mac-Calzean's bed ten days before her birth, which moulds she conjured with her prayers for staying and slaking of grinding the time of her birth' (document 20, item 42).

[†] **joint** divide at the joints

[†] **make powders thereof** the jointing of corpses and making of maleficial powder from them is frequently an accusation in the dittays, e.g. Agnes Sampson was 'acquit of her devilish practices and namely of her passing to Newton kirk undernight with the witch of Carberry and others, and there taking up the buried people and jointing of them, whereof she made enchanted powder for witchcraft' (document 20, item 26). At the convention in North Berwick kirk 'they opened up the graves, two within and one without the kirk, and took of the joints of their fingers, toes and nose, and parted them among them ... The devil commanded them to keep the joints upon them while they were dry, and then to make a powder of them to do evil withall' (item 50).

[†] **frailer than man is** a centuries-old belief, deriving from Aristotelian and Christian tradition, that women were by nature physically and morally weaker than men and therefore less able to resist temptation. The greater vulnerability of women to the devil was a commonplace in demonological treatises, and is stated, among others, by Hemmingsen: 'And this is the reason why he uses women more often than men. Women, like Eve, are more easily seduced by Satan' (Hemmingsen 1575: sig C3ᵛ).

[†] **homelier** more intimate

[†] **pictures of wax** wax images. Agnes Sampson was accused of making a 'picture of wax to the similitude of Mr John Moscrop, father-in-law to Euphame MacCalzean at the said Euphame's desire' for his destruction (document 20, item 41) and also 'a bonny small picture of yellow wax which she enchanted and conjured under the name of "Archie"' for Barbara Napier which was to be melted' (item 51). The North Berwick witches' most famous wax image was that intended for the destruction of James himself. 'Robert Grierson said these words: "Where is the thing ye promised?" meaning the picture of wax devised for roasting and undoing of his Highness' person, which Agnes Sampson gave to him' (document 22, Barbara Napier's dittay).

[†] **clay** Euphame MacCalzean was accused of having practised witchcraft against John McGill's wife: 'a picture of clay in portrait of Elizabeth Home, spouse to the said Mr John, sewed in a winding sheet' was cast in at John McGill's window (document 23, item 20)

gives such stones or powders† as will help to cure or cast on† diseases. And to some he teacheth kinds of uncouth† poisons which mediciners understand not (for he is far cunninger than man in the knowledge of all the occult proprieties† of nature). Not that any of these means which he teacheth them (except the poisons which are composed of things natural) can of themselves help anything to these turns that they are employed in. But only being God's ape as well in that as in all other things, even as God by his sacraments, which are earthly of themselves, works a heavenly effect though no ways by any cooperation in them;† and as Christ, by clay and spittle wrought together,† 'opened the eyes of the blind man' (John 9),† suppose† there was no virtue† in that which he outwardly applied; so the devil will have his outward means to be shows,† as it were, of his doing, which hath no part of cooperation in his turns with him,† 12 how far that ever† the ignorants be abused in the

---

† **powders** after witches had made a covenant with the devil, he gave them powders to work harm with; compare 'then geveth he pouders, rootes & poysons unto them' (Daneau 1575: sig F6). In many continental accounts these were distributed at the sabbat, see Bodin 1580: II iii ff. 85, 87.

† **cast on** cause, or perhaps here transfer, as the close similarity of details suggests that James is thinking here of the accusation against Euphame MacCalzean that she consulted Agnes Sampson at the time of the births of her two sons, when Agnes gave her 'to that effect a bored stone, to be laid under the bolster put under your head, enchanted moulds and powder put in a piece paper to be used and rolled in your hair ... The which being practised by you ... your sickness was cast off you unnaturally in the birth of your first son upon a dog which ran away and was never seen again' (document 23, item 18)

† **uncouth** strange

† **occult propieties** secret properties

† **no ways ... in them** in no respect by any

contribution made by the elements themselves (bread and wine, water) which are the material components of the sacraments

† **wrought together** worked together

† **'opened ... man' (John 9)** in John 9.1–7 Jesus cures the blindness of a man blind from birth; 'he spate on the grounde, & made claye of the spettle, and anointed the eyes of the blinde with the clay' (John 9.6)

† **suppose** although

† **virtue** power

† **shows** signs

† **outward means ... turns** i.e. the means (the devil uses) don't play any real part in bringing about the things that he does. The distinction, in Christ's miracles and the sacraments, between the ordinary, worldly things involved and the heavenly power actually brought into play, is mimicked by the devil (the difference between the ordinary things used and the evil effects claimed) in order to make the powers he claims seem like God's.

† **how far that ever** however far

contrary.[†] And as to the effects of these two former parts (to wit, the consultations and the outward means), they are so wonderful as I dare not allege any of them[†] without joining a sufficient reason of the possibility thereof. For, leaving[†] all the small trifles among wives, and to speak of the principal points of their craft—for the common trifles thereof they can do without converting[†] well enough by themselves—these principal points I say are these: they can make men or women to love or hate other, which may be very possible to the devil to effectuate,[†] seeing[13] he being a subtle spirit knows well enough how to persuade the corrupted affection of them whom God will permit him so to deal with; they can lay the sickness of one upon another, which likewise is very possible unto him, for since by God's permission he laid sickness upon Job[†] why may he not far easilier lay it upon any other, for as an old practician[†] he knows well enough what humour domines[†] most in any of us, and as a spirit he can subtly waken up[†] the same, making it peccant or to abound[†] as he thinks meet[†] for troubling of us, when God will so permit him. And for the taking off of it, no doubt he will be glad to relieve[14] such[†] of present pain as he may think by these means to

---

[†] **even as God ... contrary** God by his sacraments, which in themselves are material, brings about a heavenly effect although not through any contribution made by the physical components of the sacrament. Christ opened the eyes of the blind man by applying a mixture of clay and spit, although there was no power in the mixture itself which he applied in his external actions. Just so the devil too will have external instruments to be signs, as it were, of his activity, although the instruments make no contribution to his mischievous operations with them, however much ignorant people are deceived by the opposite opinion.

The Catechism in the Book of Common Prayer defines a sacrament as 'an outward and visible sign of an inward and spiritual grace given unto us, ordained by Christ himself, as a means whereby we receive the same, and a pledge to assure us thereof'. The devil continues to ape God in that the visible instruments of *maleficia*, e.g. wax images and powders, are not in themselves efficacious, but in reality have the same relation to supernatural operation as the elements (bread and wine, water) in the sacraments which they imitate. Hemmingsen has the same view of the sacraments and of the devil's aping them in magical signs and characters, images, bindings and ointments (Hemmingsen 1575: sigs B4ᵛ–5ᵛ). Daneau also thought that magical instruments such as figures or characters had no efficacy in themselves but were Satan's apings of the sacraments, and that in this way the devil 'turneth the force & effect of the thinges which are signified, unto the signes which doo signifie them' (Daneau 1575: sig H8ᵛ–I).

[†] **allege any of them** quote any of them (as evidence)

[†] **leaving** leaving aside (in this discussion)

[†] **without converting** without undergoing 'conversion' to service to the devil

[†] **effectuate** bring to pass (*BL*)

[†] **laid sickness upon Job** Satan's affliction of Job with God's permission was one of the most important biblical narratives of the devil's affliction of mankind with disease and loss, and was much discussed in demonological works. As Scot noted, 'These witchmongers, for lacke of better arguments, doo manie times object Job ... although there be never a word in that storie which either maketh for them, or against me' (Scot 1886: V viii 84).

[†] **practician** practitioner, doctor

[†] **domines** dominates

[†] **waken up** wake up (i.e. make the dominant humour more active)

[†] **peccant or to abound** defective or excessive. James is making the common medical assumption that health depends on the right quantity of each humour and a balance between them, and that ill health comes about when there is a defect or excess in a humour or an imbalance among the humours.

[†] **meet** suitable

[†] **such** i.e. anyone suffering disease

persuade to be catched in his everlasting snares and fetters. They can bewitch and take the life of men or women by roasting of the pictures, as I spake of before, which likewise is very possible to[†] their master to perform. For although (as I said before) that instrument of wax have no virtue in that turn doing,[†] yet may he not very well—even by that same measure that his conjured[†] slaves melt that wax of the fire—may he not, I say, at these same times subtly as a spirit so weaken and scatter the spirits of life[†] of the patient as may make him, on the one part for[†] faintness to sweat out the humour of his body, and, on the other part, for the not-concurrence of these spirits which cause his digestion,[†] so debilitate his stomach that his humour radical[†] continually[15] sweating out, on the one part, and no good new suck[†] being put in the place thereof for lack of digestion, on the other, he at last shall vanish away, even as his picture will do at the fire. And that knavish and cunning workman, by troubling him only at some times, makes a proportion so near[†] betwixt the working of the one and the other[†] that both shall end, as it were, at one time. They can raise storms and tempests in the air either upon sea or land, though not universally,[†] but in such a particular place and prescribed bounds as God will permit them so to trouble. Which likewise is very easy to be discerned from any other natural tempests that are meteors, in respect of the sudden and violent raising thereof, together with the short enduring of the same. And this is likewise very possible to their master to do, he having such affinity with the air as being a spirit, and having such power of the forming and moving thereof, as ye have heard me already declare. For in the scripture that style of 'the prince of the air' (Ephesians 2)[†] is given unto him. They can make folks to become frantic or maniac, which likewise is very possible to their master to do, since they are but natural sicknesses, and so he may lay on these kinds as well as any others. They can make spirits either to follow and trouble persons, or haunt certain houses and affray[†] oftentimes the inhabitants, as hath been known to be done by our witches at this time. And likewise they can make some to be possessed

---

† **to** for
† **in that turn doing** in performing that task (of causing harm)
† **conjured** sworn
† **spirits** the plural 'spirits' is used twice in this sentence in its physiological sense: 'highly-refined substances or fluids ... formerly supposed to permeate the blood and chief organs of the body' (*OED*)
† **for** because of
† **for the ... digestion** because of these spirits not acting together to produce his digestion
† **humour radical** the moisture which is naturally present in the body and is a necessary condition for life

† **suck** sustenance; juice (*BL*)
† **a proportion so near** so close a relationship
† **betwixt ... the other** i.e. the illness and the melting of the wax image; it is the devil's intention, by making the illness end as the wax image finally melts away, to induce belief in the power of the magical practice itself
† **universally** in all places
† **'the prince of the air'** Ephesians 2.2 reads 'the prince that ruleth in the aire' and a marginal note adds 'meaning Satan'. Daneau too quotes this verse, in an argument about aerial transvection (Daneau 1575: sig H2ᵛ).
† **affray** terrify

with spirits, and so to become very demoniacs.[†] And this last sort is very possible likewise to the devil their master to do since he may easily send his own angels to trouble in what form he pleases any whom God will permit him so to use.

P. But will God permit these wicked instruments, by the power of the devil their master, to trouble by any of these means any that believe in him?

E. No doubt, for there are three kinds of folks whom God will permit so to be tempted or troubled: the wicked for their horrible sins, to punish them in the like measure; the godly that are sleeping in any great sins or infirmities and weakness in faith, to waken them up the faster by such an uncouth form;[†] and even some of the best, that their patience may be tried before the world, as Job's was.[†] For why may not God use any kind of extraordinary punishment when it pleases him, as well as the ordinary rods[†] of sickness or other adversities?

P. Who then may be free from these devilish practices?

E. No man ought to presume so far as to promise any impunity to himself, for God hath before all beginnings preordinated[†] as well the particular sorts of plagues as of[†] benefits for every man, which in the own time[†] he ordains them to be visited with. And yet ought we not to be the more afraid for that[†] of any thing that the devil and his wicked instruments can do against us, for we daily fight against the devil in a hundred other ways. And therefore as a valiant captain[16] affrays no more being at the combat,[†] nor stays from his purpose for the rummishing[†] shot of a cannon[†] nor the small clack of a pistolet,[†] suppose[†] he be not certain what may light upon him, even so ought we boldly to go forward in fighting against the devil without any greater terror for[†] these his rarest weapons,[†] nor for the ordinary whereof we have daily the proof.

P. Is it not lawful then by the help of some other witch to cure the disease that is casten by that craft?

[†] **demoniacs** persons whose bodies are inhabited by evil spirits. John Fian was accused of 'the witching and possessing of William Hutson with an evil sprite, which continued with him twenty-six weeks' (document 19, item 12).

[†] **uncouth form** strange kind (of event)

[†] **three kinds ... Job was** protestant demonologists usually ascribe three functions to affliction by witchcraft: the punishment of the wicked, the correction of temporary spiritual laxness, the testing of the faithful. Job was the exemplar of the last function. 'First, God that is most just, by that meanes doth punish the sins of his children ... Wherefore these are justly by God punished, besides that by this kinde of crosse and affliction, God tryeth the patience of his chosen' (Daneau 1575: sigs F3–3ᵛ).

[†] **rods** chastisements

[†] **preordinated** determined beforehand, pre-ordained

[†] **as of** as

[†] **in the own time** in due time (*BL*)

[†] **for that** for that reason

[†] **affrays ... combat** is no more afraid because he is in a battle

[†] **rummishing** roaring (*BL*)

[†] **stays ... cannon** hesitates in his purpose because of the roaring shot of a cannon

[†] **clack of a pistolet** sharp report of a small pistol

[†] **suppose** even though

[†] **for** because of

[†] **rarest weapons** weapons seldom encountered, or choicest weapons

E. No ways lawful,[†] for I gave you the reason thereof in that axiom of theology which was the last words I spake of magic.[†]

P. How then may these diseases be lawfully cured?

E. Only by earnest prayer to God, by amendment of their lives,[†] and by sharp pursuing, every one according to his calling,[†] of these instruments of Satan, whose punishment to the death will be a salutary sacrifice for the patient. And this is not only the lawful way, but likewise the most sure, for by the devil's means 'can never the devil be casten out' (Mark 3),[†] as Christ saith. And when such a cure[†] is used it may well serve for a short time, but at the last it will doubtlessly tend to the utter perdition of the patient both in body and soul.

CHAPTER VI

ARGUMENT: What sort of folks are least or most subject to receive harm by witchcraft. What power they have to harm the magistrate,[†] and upon what respects[†] they have any power in prison; and to what end may or will the devil appear to them therein. Upon what respects the devil appears in sundry[†] shapes to sundry of them at any time.

P. But who dare take upon him to punish them[†] if no man can be sure to be free from their unnatural invasions?[†]

E. We ought not the more of that restrain from virtue that the way whereby we climb thereunto be straight and perilous.[†] But besides that, as there is no

---

[†] **No ways lawful** like Hemmingsen (1575: sigs D–D6ᵛ), Gifford (1862: 45–61), Daneau (1575: K6–8ᵛ) and many other protestant writers, James is adamant that the aid of witchcraft may never be sought to alleviate or cure the effects of a disease caused by witchcraft

[†] **axiom ... magic** Epistemon refers Philomathes to the axiom quoted at the very end of book I, 'You must never do evil so that good may come of it'

[†] **earnest prayer ... lives** Epistemon's first two answers are standard protestant homily; compare Hemmingsen 1575: D6ᵛ–8

[†] **according to his calling** according to his profession

[†] **'can never ... out'** Mark 3.22–30 gives one of the Gospel accounts (compare Matthew 9.34, 12.22–31; Luke 11.14–23) of the exchange between Jesus and the scribes who accuse him of casting out devils through the power of Beelz-

ebub, the prince of devils (Mark 3.22). Jesus asks how Satan can drive out Satan (3.23), for a kingdom or house divided against itself cannot stand.

[†] **cure** i.e. using witchcraft to cure witchcraft

[†] **magistrate** ruler of a nation or community; or any member of the government, or officer charged with administering the laws

[†] **respects** considerations

[†] **sundry** various

[†] **who dare ... them** who would dare take upon himself (the task) of punishing them

[†] **invasions** assaults

[†] **We ought not ... perilous** we ought not to refrain from virtuous action because the way by which we climb to it is narrow and dangerous. Compare 'Because the gate is streicte, & the way narowe that leadeth unto life, & fewe there be that finde it' (Matthew 7.14).

kind of persons so subject to receive harm of them as these that are of infirm and weak faith (which is the best buckler[†] against such invasions), so have they so small power over none as over[†] such as zealously and earnestly pursues them without sparing for[†] any worldly respect.

P. Then they are like the pest[†] which smites these sickerest[†] that fly it farthest[†] and apprehend deepliest the peril thereof.[†]

E. It is even so with them, for neither is it able to them[†] to use any false cure upon a patient, except the patient first believe in their power, and so hazard the tinsel[†] of his own soul. Nor yet can they have less power to hurt any nor such as condemn most their doings, so being[†] it comes of faith and not of any vain arrogancy in themselves.

P. But what is their power against the magistrate?

E. Less or greater according as he deals with them. For if he be slothful towards them, God is very able to make them instruments to waken and punish his sloth. But if he be the contrary, he, according to the just law of God and allowable law of all nations, will be diligent in examining and punishing of them. God will not permit their master to trouble or hinder so good a work.[†]

P. But fra they be once in hands and firmance,[†] have they any further power in their craft?[†]

E. That is according to the form of their detention. If they be but apprehended and detained by any private person upon other private respects, their power no doubt either in escaping or in doing hurt is no less nor ever it was before. But if, on the other part, their apprehending and detention be by the lawful magistrate upon the just respects[†] of their guiltiness

---

[†] **buckler** small round shield. Compare 'For this cause take unto you the whole armour of God ... Above all, take the shield of faith, wherewith ye may quench all the fyrie dartes of the wicked' (Ephesians 6.13, 16).

[†] **so have ... as over** i.e. so they have the least power over

[†] **sparing for** showing restraint on account of

[†] **pest** bubonic plague

[†] **sickerest** most surely

[†] **fly it farthest** flee furthest from it

[†] **apprehend ...thereof** have the deepest concern for its danger

[†] **is it able to them** are they able

[†] **hazard the tinsel** risk the loss

[†] **so being** so long as

[†] **But if ... good a work** Boguet agrees that officers of justice are immune from witches' harms and that God will not allow witches power over the persons of judges (Boguet 1929: 116)

[†] **but fra ... firmance** but from the time when they are in detention and imprisonment

[†] **But fra ... craft** Daneau's Anthony asks Theophilus the same question and is answered 'If I shall saye what I thinke, I wyll aunswere, that they can, if so bee they have any conference with theyr maister Satan. But if you aske mee what the common people think thereof: surely, that they can not'. Theophilus goes on to say that neither the judge's authority nor detention prevents further *maleficium*, as this depends only on 'conference' with Satan, but since his access to witches is made difficult by surveillance in prison, witches cause less harm after their detention (Daneau 1575: I8–K). Popular belief may have been simpler, 'Sir, I have heard, that witches apprehended under hands of lawfull authority, does loose their power' (Heywood and Brome, *The Late Lancashire Witches*), and 'Hypocrite Witches, hence *avaunt*, / Who though in prison yet inchant!' (Andrew Marvell, 'Upon Appleton House', lines 205–6).

[†] **just respects** proper consideration

in that craft, their power is then no greater than before than ever[†] they meddled with their master. For where God begins justly to strike by his lawful lieutenants[†] it is not in the devil's power to defraud or bereave[†] him of the office or effect of his powerful and revenging sceptre.

P. But will never their master come to visit them, fra they be once apprehended and put in firmance?[†]

E. That is according to the estate[†] that these miserable wretches are in. For if they be obstinate in still denying he will not spare, when he finds time to speak with them, either if he find them in any comfort, to fill them more and more with the vain hope of some manner of relief; or else, if he find them in a deep despair, by all means to augment the same and to persuade them by some extraordinary means to put themselves down,[†] which very commonly they do. But if they be penitent and confess, God will not permit him to trouble them any more with his presence and allurements.

P. It is not good using his counsel,[†] I see then. But I would earnestly know, when he appears to them in prison, what forms uses he then to take?

E. Diverse forms, even as he uses to do at other times unto them. For as I told you, speaking of magic, he appears to that kind of craftsmen ordinarily in a form according as they agree upon it amongst themselves; or, if they be but prentices, according to the quality of their circles or conjurations. Yet to these capped[†] creatures he appears as he pleases, and as he finds meetest[†] for their humours. For even at their public conventions he appears to diverse of them in diverse forms, as we have found by the difference of their confessions in that point. For he, deluding them with vain impressions in the air, makes himself to seem more terrible to the grosser[†] sort that they may thereby be moved to fear and reverence him the more; and less monstrous and uncouthlike[†] again to the craftier sort, lest otherwise they might sture and scunner at[†] his ugliness.

P. How can he then be felt, as they confess they have done him, if his body be but of air?

[†] **no greater than before than ever** no greater than before the time when

[†] **lieutenants** deputies (any magistrates lawfully established to carry out God's will)

[†] **bereave** deprive

[†] **But will ... in firmance** The devil, dressed in black with a white wand in his hand, visted John Fian in prison and 'demanded of him if he would continue his faithful service according to his first oath and promise made to that effect' (*News* p.325)

[†] **estate** spiritual condition

[†] **put themselves down** commit suicide; make themselves away (*BL*)

[†] **using his counsel** taking his (the devil's) advice

[†] **capped** foolish. '*DOST* quotes this passage to illustrate the meaning "peevish, ill-humoured", but the Latin rendering of 1619, *coram his ineptis arbitrariam sumit personam* suggests rather its meaning here is really "silly"' (*Craigie*).

[†] **meetest** most suitable

[†] **grosser** simpler

[†] **uncouthlike** strange (*BL*)

[†] **sture and scunner at** be in ill humour with and shrink back through fear

E. I hear little of that amongst their confessions, yet may he make himself palpable[†] either by assuming[†] any dead body and using the ministry thereof,[†] or else by deluding as well their sense of feeling as seeing. Which is not impossible to[†] him to do since all our senses (as we are so weak and even by ordinary sicknesses)[†] will be oftentimes deluded.

P. But I would speer one word further yet concerning his appearing to them in prison, which is this: may any other that chances to be present at that time in the prison see him as well as they?

E. Sometimes they will and sometimes not, as it pleases God.

CHAPTER VII

ARGUMENT: Two forms of the devil's visible conversing in[†] the earth, with the reasons wherefore the one of them was commonest in the time of papistry,[†] and the other sensine. Those that deny the power of the devil deny the power of God, and are guilty of the error of the Sadducees.[†]

P. Hath the devil then power to appear to any other, except to such as are his sworn disciples, especially since all oracles and suchlike kinds of illusions were taken away and abolished by the coming of Christ?[†]

E. Although it be true indeed that the brightness of the gospel at his coming scaled[†] the clouds of all these gross errors in the gentilism,[†] yet that these abusing spirits cease not sensine at some times to appear, daily experience teaches us. Indeed, this difference is to be marked betwixt the forms of Satan's conversing visibly in the world. For of two different forms thereof,

---

[†] **palpable** touchable

[†] **assuming** putting on (i.e. entering and animating a dead body and making it appear alive again)

[†] **the ministry thereof** the active operation of it (i.e. using the body's powers)

[†] **to** for

[†] **as we are ... sicknesses** i.e. as our senses are weakened even by ordinary illnesses

[†] **conversing in** being in people's company on

[†] **the time of papistry** the times of the Christian era under the domination of the Roman church and before the protestant reformation

[†] **Sadducees** see note on p. 353

[†] **especially since ... of Christ** there was a long-standing Christian tradition that pagan oracles, through which devils spoke in their guise as pagan gods, were silenced at either the Nativity or Crucifixion. This was founded in part on Plutarch, *The Obsolescence of Oracles*, 419 B-D, where the Egyptian sailor Thamus heard the cry

'Great Pan is dead' in the reign of the emperor Tiberius, which cry was interpreted as either proclaiming the death of Christ (Gk *pan*, 'all') or the overthrow of Satan. The story is mentioned, among many others, by Lavater 1929: 94–6. There are allusions to the cessation of oracles by Spenser, *Shepheardes Calender*, EK's gloss on May, 54, and by Milton, 'Ode on the Morning of Christ's Nativity' 173–80 and *Paradise Regained*, I 455–64 (see Patrides 1982). Protestant writers were fond of the analogy James draws here between the cessation of lying, diabolical oracles at Christ's coming, and the cessation of papist illusions and deceit at the protestant restoration of the truth of the gospel; see Scot 1886: VIII i–vi.

[†] **scaled** purified

[†] **gentilism** paganism (i.e. those who lived according to one of the old religions, or no religion at all)

the one of them by the spreading of the evangel[†] and conquest of the white horse[†] (in the sixth chapter of the Revelation), is much hindered and become rarer[17] there through.[†] This his appearing to any Christians, troubling of them outwardly or possessing of them constrainedly.[†] The other of them is become commoner and more used sensine: I mean, by their unlawful arts, whereupon[†] our whole purpose[†] hath been. This we find by experience in this isle[†] to be true. For as we know, more ghosts and spirits were seen nor tongue can tell in the time of blind papistry in these countries where now, by the contrary, a man shall scarcely all his time hear once of such things. And yet were these unlawful arts far rarer at that time, and never were so much heard of nor so rife as they are now.

P. What should be the cause of that?

E. The diverse nature of our sins procures at[†] the justice of God diverse sorts of punishments answering thereunto. And therefore, as in the time of papistry, our fathers erring grossly and through ignorance, that mist of errors overshadowed[†] the devil to walk the more familiarly amongst them. And as it were by bairnly[†] and affraying[†] terrors to mock and accuse their bairnly errors. By the contrary, we now being sound of religion, and in our life rebelling to our profession,[†] God justly by that sin of rebellion (as Samuel calleth it)[†] accuseth our life so willfully fighting against our profession.

P. Since ye are entered now to speak of the appearing of spirits, I would be glad to hear your opinion in that matter. For many deny that any such spirits can appear in these days, as I have said.

E. Doubtlessly, who denieth the power of the devil would likewise deny the power of God, if they could for shame. For since the devil is the very contrary opposite to God, there is no better way to know God than by the contrary. As, by the one's power (though a creature)[†] to admire the power of the great creator; by the falsehood of the one to consider the truth of the other; and by the injustice of the one to consider the justice of the other; and by the cruelty of the one to consider the mercifulness of the other; and so forth in

---

[†] **evangel** the gospel, the story of Christ's life and teachings as recorded in the first four books of the New Testament

[†] **conquest of the white horse** 'Therefore I beheld, and lo, there was a white horse, and he that sat on him, had a bowe, and a crowne was given unto him, and he went forth conquering that he might overcome' (Revelation 6.2). In two marginal glosses on this verse the Bassandyne bible says that 'the white horse signifieth innocencie, victorie, & felicitie which shulde come by the preaching of the Gospel' and that 'he that rideth on the white horse, is Christ'.

[†] **there through** through that

[†] **constrainedly** by force

[†] **whereupon** on which topic

[†] **purpose** conversation

[†] **this isle** Britain

[†] **at** from

[†] **overshadowed** protected by being hidden from view (*Craigie*)

[†] **bairnly** childish

[†] **affraying** frightening

[†] **rebelling to our profession** opposing the religious faith we have declared our belief in

[†] **as Samuel calleth it** 'For rebellion is as the sinne of witchcraft' (1 Samuel 15.23)

[†] **creature** a being created by God

all the rest of the essence[†] of God and qualities[†] of the devil. But I fear indeed there be over-many Sadducees in this world that deny all kinds of spirits; for convicting of whose error there is cause enough, if there were no more, that God would permit at some times spirits visibly to kithe.[†]

[†] **essence** inherent nature
[†] **qualities** attributes

[†] **kithe** to show themselves

THE THIRD BOOK OF DEMONOLOGY

ARGUMENT: The description of all these kinds of spirits that trouble men or women. The conclusion of the whole dialogue.

CHAPTER I

ARGUMENT: The division of spirits in four principal kinds.[†] The description of the first kind of them, called *spectra*[†] *et umbrae mortuorum*.[†] What is the best way to be free of their trouble.[†]

PHILOMATHES I pray you, now then go forward in telling what ye think fabulous[†] or may be trowed[†] in that case.
EPISTEMON That kind of the devil's conversing in[†] the earth may be divided in four different kinds, whereby he affrayeth and troubleth[†] the bodies of men. For of the abusing of the soul I have spoken already.[†] The first is where spirits trouble some houses or solitary places; the second, where spirits follow upon certain persons and at diverse[†] hours trouble them; the third, when they enter within them and possess them; the fourth is these kind of spirits that are called vulgarly the fairy.[†] Of the three former kinds ye heard already

---

[†] **four principal kinds** James goes on to list these: spirits who obsess houses and solitary places, those who obsess people, those who possess demoniacs, and fairies

[†] *spectra spectrum* literally means 'form', 'image', and so 'apparition'. '*Spectrum* amongst the Latines doth signifie a shape or forme of some thing presenting it self unto our sight .... The divines take it to be a substance without a body, which being hearde or seene, maketh men afrayde' (Lavater 1929: 1). Le Loyer gives substantially the same definition (Le Loyer 1586: 1).

[†] *umbrae mortuorum* literally 'shadows of the dead'. 'Servius writeth, that *Umbrae* were called *Larvae*: and they called dead mens souls by the name of *Umbrae*' (Lavater 1929: 4).

[†] **of their trouble** of being troubled by them

[†] **fabulous** fictitious

[†] **trowed** believed in (because true)

[†] **conversing in** moving about on

[†] **affrayeth and troubleth** terrifies and harms

[†] **For of ... already** at various points in the first two books James has treated the abuse and deception of mankind by the devil, his seduction of men's souls into error, and his deluding men and women into becoming magicians and witches. He now turns to cataloguing various kinds of spirits and how they may trouble people's bodies.

[†] **diverse** various

[†] **the fairy** supernatural beings supposed to use their magical powers for good or evil over people's affairs. Le Loyer includes fairies among spectres and apparitions: 'the Nymphes of the auncients, which are those whome wee at this day doe call *Fées*, and the Italians *Fate*, in English the *Fayries*' (Le Loyer 1586: 17).

how they may artificially be made[†] by witchcraft to trouble folk. Now it rests[†] to speak of their natural coming,[†] as it were, and not raised by witchcraft. But generally I must forewarn you of one thing before I enter in this purpose: that is that although in my discoursing of them I divide them in diverse kinds ye must notwithstanding thereof note my phrase of speaking in that.[†] For doubtlessly they are in effect but[†] all one kind of spirits, who for abusing the more of mankind[†] take on three sundry shapes and use diverse forms of outward actions, as if some were of nature better than other. Now I return to my purpose. As to the first kind of these spirits that were called by the ancients by diverse names according as[†] their actions were; for if they were spirits that haunted some houses by appearing in diverse and horrible forms and making great din, they were called *lemures*[†] or *spectra*. If they appeared in likeness of any defunct[†] to some friends of his, they were called *umbrae mortuorum*. And so innumerable styles[†] they got according to their actions, as I have said already; as we see by experience, how many styles they have given them[†] in our language in the like manner. Of the appearing of these spirits we are certified[†] by the scriptures where the prophet Isaiah, 13 and 34 cap.,[†] threatening the destruction of Babel and Edom (Isaiah 13, Jeremiah 50),[†1] declares that it shall not only be wracked,[†] but shall become so great a

---

[†] **artificially be made** compelled by (magic) art
[†] **rests** remains
[†] **their natural coming** appearing as a result of their own behaviour and of their own volition
[†] **phrase of speaking in that** particular way of speaking about that
[†] **but** just
[†] **for abusing the more of mankind** in order to deceive mankind more
[†] **according as** corresponding to what
[†] *lemures* the spirits of the dead in Roman religion; 'Some men cal the ghosts of al dead things by the name of *Lemures*' (Lavater 1929: 3); '*Lemures* ... are reckoned amongst the *Larvae* or hurtfull Spirites, and are indeed Divels, which doe appeare in the night, in the form of divers

Beastes: but most commonly in the shape and figure of dead men' (Le Loyer 1586: f. 7ᵛ)
[†] **defunct** deceased person; dead body (*BL*)
[†] **styles** titles
[†] **them** to them
[†] **certified** made certain
[†] **Isaiah 13 and 34 cap.** i.e. Isaiah chapters 13 and 34
[†] **Babel and Edom** the biblical references make it quite clear that the reading of the corrected quarto is to be preferred over 'Jerusalem'. Both Isaiah and Jeremiah also prophesy the desolation of Jerusalem and this probably occasioned the mix-up between the cities.
[†] **wracked** destroyed

solitude[†] as it shall be the habitacle of howlets,[†] and of *ziim* and *iim*,[†] which are the proper Hebrew names for these spirits. The cause why they haunt solitary places, it is by reason that they may affray and brangle the more[†] the faith of such as them alone[†] haunt such places. For our nature is such as in companies we are not so soon moved to any such kind of fear as being solitary, which the devil, knowing well enough, he will not therefore assail us but when we are weak. And besides that, God will not permit him so to dishonour the societies and companies of Christians as, in public times and places, to walk visibly amongst them. On the other part,[†] when he troubles certain houses that are dwelt in, it is a sure token either of gross ignorance or of some gross and slanderous sins amongst the inhabitants thereof, which God by that extraordinary rod[†] punishes.

P. But by what way or passage can these spirits enter in these houses, seeing they allege that they will enter, door and window being steeked?[†]

E. They will choose the passage for their entress according to the form[†] that they are in at that time. For if they have assumed a dead body, whereinto they lodge themselves, they can easily enough open without din any door

---

[†] **solitude** desert (*BL*)

[†] **habitacles of howlets** habitat of owls

[†] **ziim and iim** *ziim* and *iim* (together with *ohiim* in Isaiah 13.21–22) are words occurring in Isaiah 13.21–22, 34.14 and Jeremiah 50.39 in the Bassandyne and Geneva versions of the bible. The precise meaning of the Hebrew words *siyyim* and *'iyyim* in these verses is uncertain, as it was in the Renaissance; see, for example, the variety of interpretations in Wolfgang Musculus, *In Esaiam Prophetam Commentarii Locupletissimi* (Basle 1570: 272–5, 469–72). Jean Calvin commented, 'I cannot well tell how this word *Ziim* should be translated, in regard the opinions of the expositours are so divers' (Calvin, *A Commentarie upon the prophecie of Isaiah* 1609: 151, on Isaiah 13.21). All three Old Testament passages describe the destruction and desolation of cities: Babylon (Isaiah 13, Jeremiah 50) and Edom (Isaiah 34) which will subsequently be inhabited only by wild creatures or spirits of various sorts, depending on the translation of *siyyim* and *'iyyim*. In Isaiah 24.14, *siyyim* is rendered by the Vulgate as *daemonia* (demons), by the Bishops' bible as 'straunge visures [sights]' and by the *NEB* as 'marmots [a kind of rodent]'. For *'iyyim* the Vulgate gives *onocentauris* (ass-centaurs); '*Onocentaurus* is a beaste of a straunge fashion, whiche is reported to be lyke a man in the upper parte, and downwarde lyke an asse' (Lavater 1929: 7), the Bishops' bible 'monsterous beastes'

and *NEB* 'jackals'. The marginal note in the Bassandyne and Geneva bibles comments on *ziim* in Isaiah 13.21: 'which were either wilde beastes, or foules, or wicked spirits, whereby Satan deluded men, as by the fairies, goblins and suche like fantasies'. Calvin comments on Isaiah 34.14–15, 'Some affirme that these beasts are Fayries, others Hobgoblins; others satyres' (Calvin, *A Commentarie upon the prophecie of Isaiah* 1609: 346). James must be thinking primarily of Isaiah 34.14 where the ruins of Edom are inhabited by *ziim*, *iim* and owls: 'There shal mete also Ziim and Iim, & the Satyre shal crye to his fellowe, & the scriche owle shal rest there, and shal finde for her selfe a quiet dwelling' (Geneva). The 'scriche owle' in this verse, which gave James his 'habitacle of howlets', presents further problems of translation: the original Hebrew word is *lîlît* (night-hag) which the Vulgate gives as *lamia* (a sort of female demon). These biblical verses, describing the strange and possibly demonic inhabitants of desolated cities, were often cited as authorities in catalogues, taxonomies and discussions of spirits.

[†] **brangle the more** shake more

[†] **them alone** those who alone

[†] **On the other part** on the other hand

[†] **extraordinary rod** unusual punishment

[†] **steeked** shut

[†] **form** mode of existence

or window and enter in thereat. And if they enter as a spirit only, any place where the air may come in at is large enough an entry for them. For, as I said before, a spirit can occupy no quantity.[†]

P. And will God then permit these wicked spirits to trouble the rest[†] of a dead body before the resurrection thereof?[†] Or if he will so, I think it should be of the reprobate[†] only.

E. What more is the rest troubled of a dead body:[†] when the devil carries it out of the grave to serve his turn for a space, nor[†] when the witches take it up and joint it,[†] or when as swine worts up[†] the graves? The rest of them that the scripture speaks of is not meaned[†] by a local remaining continually in one place,[†] but by their resting from their travails[†] and miseries of this world, while[†] their latter conjunction again with the soul at that time,[†] to receive full glory in both. And, that the devil may use as well the ministry of the bodies of the faithful in these cases as of the unfaithful, there is no inconvenient;[†] for his haunting with their bodies after they are dead can no-ways defile them, in respect of the soul's absence. And for any dishonour it can be unto them, by what reason can it be greater then the hanging, heading[†] or many such shameful deaths that good men will suffer? For there is nothing in the bodies of the faithful more worthy of honour, or freer from corruption by nature, nor[†] in these of the unfaithful while time[†] they be purged and glorified in the latter day, as is daily seen by the vile diseases and corruptions that the bodies of the faithful are subject unto, as ye will see clearly proved when I speak of the possessed and demoniacs.

P. Yet there are sundry that affirm to have haunted such places where these spirits are alleged to be, and could never hear nor see anything.

E. I think well,[†] for that is only reserved to[†] the secret knowledge of God, whom he will permit to see such things and whom not.

[†] **quantity** physical space
[†] **rest** repose
[†] **resurrection thereof** Christians believe that the bodies of the dead will be reconstituted at the Day of Judgement and then, joined once more to the soul, be assigned to their eternal location of heaven or hell
[†] **reprobate** those lost in sin and rejected by God
[†] **What more ... body** which disturbs more the rest of a dead body
[†] **nor** or
[†] **joint it** the North Berwick witches are repeatedly accused in the dittays of taking up dead bodies out of their graves and 'jointing', i.e. dismembering, them
[†] **worts up** roots up
[†] **meaned** signified

[†] **by a ... one place** by remaining continuously in one particular geographical place
[†] **travails** labours; James is thinking of the Apocalypse, to which he often alludes: '... Blessed are the dead which hereafter dye in the Lord. Even so saith the Spirit: for they rest from their labours' (Revelation 14.13)
[†] **while** until
[†] **while their ... time** until their bodies' final joining up again with the soul at that time (the Day of Judgement)
[†] **inconvenient** difficulty
[†] **heading** beheading
[†] **nor** than
[†] **while time** until the time when
[†] **I think well** so I believe
[†] **only reserved to** the sole prerogative of

P. But where these spirits haunt and trouble any houses, what is the best way to banish them?

E. By two means may only the remeid[†] of such things be procured. The one is ardent prayer to God, both of these persons that are troubled with them and of that church whereof they are; the other is the purging of themselves by amendment of life[†] from such sins as have procured[†] that extraordinary plague.

P. But what mean then these kind of spirits when they appear in the shadow of[†] a person newly dead, or to die,[†] to his friends?

E. When they appear upon that occasion they are called wraiths[†] in our language. Amongst the gentiles the devil used that much to make them believe that it was some good spirit that appeared to them then, either to forewarn them of the death of their friend, or else to discover unto them the will of the defunct, or what was the way of his slaughter,[†] as is written in the book of the histories prodigious.[†] And this way he easily deceived the gentiles because they know not God. And to that same effect is it that he now appears in that manner to some ignorant Christians. For he dare not so illude any that knoweth that neither can the spirit of the defunct return to his friend or yet an angel use such forms.

P. And are not our werewolves[†] one sort of these spirits also, that haunt and trouble some houses or dwelling places?

E. There hath indeed been an old opinion of such like things; for by the Greeks they were called *lykanthropoi* which signifieth 'men-wolves'.[†] But to

---

[†] **remeid** remedy

[†] **ardent prayer ... amendment of life** individual and congregational prayer and amendment of life were standard protestant remedies for obsession of houses by spirits (see Lavater 1929: 193-5; Holland 1590: iv sigs H[v]–3[v])

[†] **procured** brought about

[†] **in the shadow of** as the ghost of

[†] **or to die** or about to die

[†] **wraiths** spectral appearance of someone just dead, or about to die

[†] **way of his slaughter** way in which he was murdered

[†] **histories prodigious** although James could be thinking generally of books recounting wonders and marvels, it is more likely that he has in mind specifically the *Histoires Prodigieuses les Plus Memorables qui ayent esté observées* of Pierre Boaistuau, Sieur de Launay (1520–66), first edition Paris 1560 with many subsequent editions in the sixteenth century. There was a copy in James's library (Warner 1891: li). It was translated into English by Edward Fenton as *Certaine Secrete wonders of Nature* (1569). The work contains accounts of wonders, portents and monsters, and James has in mind the many stories of apparitions in chapter 26, 'Visions prodigieuses, avec plusieurs histoires memorables des Spectres, Fantosmes, figures & illusions qui apparoissent de nuict, de jour, en veillant & en dormant' (Paris 1560: ff. 105–22[v]).

[†] **werewolves** people who change from being a human to a wolf; 'Les Alemans les appellent *Wer Wölf*, & les François loups garous, ... Les Grecs les appelloyent Lycanthropes' (Bodin 1580: II vi f. 98)

[†] *lykanthropoi* **which signifieth 'men-wolves'** 'men-wolves' literally translates the Greek *lykanthropoi* (wolf-men). For classical stories of men transformed into wolves see Ovid's tale of Lycaon whom Jupiter transformed into a wolf for killing a hostage and offering him to the god (*Metamorphoses* I 221–43). For Renaissance discussions of werewolves see Weyer 1991: III x 193–4; IV xxiii 342–4; VI xiii 511–18; Scot 1886; Bodin 1580: II vi ff. 94[v]–104; V i 71–4; Boguet 1929: xlvii 136–55.

tell you simply my opinion in this, if any such thing hath been I take it to have proceeded but of a natural superabundance of melancholy.[†] Which, as we read that it hath made some think themselves pitchers,[†] and some horses, and some one kind of beast or other, so suppose I that it hath so vitiate[†] the imagination and memory of some as, *per lucida intervalla*,[†] it hath so highly occupied them that they have thought themselves very wolves indeed at these times. And so have counterfeited their actions—in going on their hands and feet, pressing[†] to devour women and bairns, fighting and snatching with all the town dogs, and in using such like other brutish actions—and so to become beasts by a strong apprehension,[†] as Nebucad-netzar[†] was seven years (Daniel 4). But as to their having and hiding of their hard and scaly sloughs,[†2] I take that to be but eked[†] by uncertain report, the author of all lies.

CHAPTER II

ARGUMENT: The description of the next two kinds of spirits, whereof the one follows outwardly, the other possesses inwardly the persons that they

---

[†] **but of ... melancholy** only from a natural excess in the body of the melancholy humour. James, like many others (Weyer 1991: IV xxiii 343; Le Loyer 1586: x f. 100ᵛ: Perkins 1610: I iv 24) attributes men's convictions that they are changed into wolves to excessive melancholy. In Webster's play *The Duchess of Malfi* (V ii 1–21) a doctor attributes Ferdinand's lycanthropia to an overflowing of melancholy humour.

[†] **think themselves pitchers** think they are pitchers (a large earthenware jug); a story often cited in discussions of melancholy imaginings, which included lycanthropia (e.g. Lavater 1929: ii 11; Le Loyer 1586: x f. 99ᵛ)

[†] **vitiate** abused (*BL*)

[†] ***per lucida intervalla*** (Latin) in lucid intervals, when the delusions have gone; 'A period of temporary sanity between attacks of lunacy' (*OED sv* 'lucid')

[†] **pressing** endeavouring

[†] **strong apprehension** mentally, through a powerful conviction

[†] ***Nebucad-netzar*** In Daniel 4 Daniel interprets King Nebucadnezzar's troubling dream of a tree being cut down to mean that he would be driven out and live with beasts for seven years; '... and he was driven from men, and did eat grasse as the oxen, & his bodie was wet with the dewe of heaven, till his heeres were growen as egles feathers, and his nails lyke birds clawes' (Bassan-

dyne, Daniel 4.30). He was eventually restored to reason and his kingdom. Demonologists debated whether this meant that Nebuchadnezzar was physically transformed into an animal and if this could be evidence for the possibility of other transformations into animals, such as witches of themselves or others. The objections were that Daniel 4.33 seemed to say that the king only ate 'as oxen' and that anyway even real physical transformation would be a miracle performed by God and not reproduceable by the devil. The Geneva and Bassandyne bibles, in a marginal note on 4.22, say 'Not that his shape or forme was changed into a beast, but that he was either striken mad and so avoided mans companie, or was cast out for his tyrannie and so wandered among the beasts and ate hearbes and grasse'. Although some writers (Kramer and Sprenger 1971: part II, q 1, cap 8; Bodin 1580: II vi f. 101) cite Nebucadnezzar as evidence of transformation, at least in appearance even if not substantially, most (e.g. Weyer 1991: IV i 284; IV iv xxii 341–2; Boguet 1929: xlvii 143, 145; Scot 1886: V i 73; V vi 81; Danaeus 1575: sigs F–F2ᵛ: Le Loyer 1586: xii f. 127–130ᵛ; Perkins 1610: I iv 33–4) agree with James that it was 'a strong apprehension' not a physical transformation.

[†] **scaly sloughs** hard outer skin; hairy hides (*BL*)

[†] **eked** added

trouble.† That since all prophecies and visions are now ceased,† all spirits that appear in these forms are evil.

P. Come forward now to† the rest of these kinds of spirits.

E. As to the next two kinds, that is either these that outwardly trouble and follow some persons, or else inwardly possess them, I will conjoin them in one because as well the causes are alike in the persons that they are permitted to trouble, as also the ways whereby they may be remedied and cured.

P. What kind of persons are they that use to be so troubled?

E. Two kinds in special: either such as, being guilty of grievous offences, God punishes by that horrible kind of scourge; or else, being persons of the best nature peradventure† that ye shall find in all the country about them, God permits them to be troubled in that sort† for the trial of their patience and wakening up of their zeal;† for admonishing† of the beholders not to trust over much in themselves, since they are made of no better stuff, and peradventure blotted with no smaller sins (as Christ said, speaking of them upon whom the tower of Siloam†³ fell† (Luke 13). And for giving likewise to the spectators† matter† to praise God that they, meriting no better, are yet spared from being corrected in that fearful form.†

P. These are good reasons for the part of God, which apparently move him so to permit the devil to trouble such persons. But since the devil hath ever a contrary respect† in all the actions that God employs him in, which is, I pray you, the end and mark he shoots at in this turn?

E. It is to obtain one of two things thereby if he may. The one is the tinsel† of their life, by inducing them to such perilous places at such time as he either

---

† **whereof ... that they trouble** James draws the classic and commonplace distinction between obsession (i.e. chronic outward troubling; from Latin *obsedere*, literally 'to beseige'), and possession (inward inhabiting) by spirits

† **prophecies and visions are now ceased** it was a protestant belief that by and large supernatural events such as visions, miracles and prophecies occurred only in the time of Christ, the Apostles and the Primitive Church. Later apparent occurrences were likely to be diabolic or fraudulent.

† **Come forward now to** come to the point of considering now

† **peradventure** perhaps

† **in that sort** in that way

† **Either ... zeal** like affliction caused by witchcraft (see *Demonology* II v), possession is either a punishment of the ungodly or a spiritual trial of and a spur to the righteous

† **admonishing** warning

† **Siloam** this, the form in the corrected quarto of 1597, is that in the Bassandyne bible: 'the toure in Siloam' (Luke 13.4). James presumably originally recalled the form 'Sylo' from his memory of the Vulgate, *'turris in Syloe'*.

† **as Christ ... fell** In Luke 13.1–5, Jesus exhorted those who attributed the misfortune of others to greater sin to repent themselves: 'Or think you that those eightene, upon whome the toure in Siloam fel, and slew them, were sinners above all men that dwel in Jerusalem?' (Luke 13.4). The spectacle of the possession of others is a timely warning against spiritual self-satisfaction.

† **spectators** beholders (*BL*) (of the possessed person)

† **matter** reason

† **fearful form** frightening way

† **contrary respect** opposed intention

† **tinsel** loss

follows or possesses them, which may procure the same. And, such like[†] so far as God will permit him, by tormenting them to weaken their body and cast them in incurable diseases. The other thing that he presses[†] to obtain by troubling of them is the tinsel of their soul, by enticing them to mistrust and blaspheme God, either for the intolerableness of their torments (as he assayed to have done with Job) (Job 1)[†] or else for his promising unto them to leave the troubling of them in case they would so do,[†] as is known by experience at this same time by the confession of a young one[†] that was so troubled.

P. Since ye have spoken now of both these kinds of spirits, comprehending them in one, I must now go back again in speering some questions of every one of these kinds in special. And first, for these that follow certain persons, ye know that there are two sorts of them: one sort that troubles and torments the persons that they haunt with; another sort that are serviceable unto them[†] in all kind of their necessaries,[†] and omit never to forewarn them of any sudden peril that they are to be in. And so in this case I would understand whether both these sorts be but wicked and damned spirits, or if the last sort be rather angels (as should appear by their actions) sent by God to assist such as he specially favours. For it is written in the scriptures that 'God sends legions of angels to guard and watch over his elect' (Genesis 32; I Kings 6; Psalms 34).[†]

E. I know well enough where fra[†] that error which ye allege hath proceeded, for it was the ignorant gentiles that were the fountain[†] thereof. Who, for that[†] they knew not God, they forged in their own imaginations every man

---

[†] **such like** similarly
[†] **presses** labours (*BL*)
[†] **Job** see note on *Demonology* II v
[†] **to mistrust ... so do** i.e. the possessed might either mistrust and blaspheme God spontaneously because their sufferings are intolerable, or they might agree with the devil to mistrust and blaspheme God in exchange for the devil's ceasing to torment them
[†] **a young one** James is clearly thinking of a particular case, although which is not clear. John Fian was accused of possessing William Hutson of Windygoul (dittay, items 5 and 12), who was presumably 'the gentleman dwelling near to the Saltpans' bewitched by Fian in *News* who screeched and capered before the king on 24 December 1590. A number of witches attempted to destroy David Seton but the curse alighted instead on his daughter, 'who ever since has been heavily vexed with terrible visions and apparitions, and her body tormented with an evil sprite, wherewith she has been possessed most pitifully' (Agnes Sampson's dittay, item 49). The

confession of 'a young one' might indicate the latter.
[†] **serviceable unto them** willing to do tasks for them
[†] **in all ... necessaries** for all sorts of material things they require
[†] **Genesis 32 ... Psalms 34** James is thinking of 'Now Jaakob went forthe on his journey & the Angels of God met him' (Genesis 32.1), and perhaps Jacob's wrestling with the angel in the same chapter (Genesis 32.24–32); the cherubim near the oracle of God in Solomon's temple (1 Kings 6.23–29); 'The Angel of the Lord pitcheth rounde about them that feare him, and delivereth them' (Psalms 34.7), upon which verse the Bassandyne bible notes in the margin 'Thogh Gods power be sufficient to governe us, yet for mans infirmitie he appointeth his Angels to watch over us'.
[†] **where fra** from where
[†] **fountain** source
[†] **for that** because

to be still accompanied with two spirits, whereof they called the one *genius bonus*, the other *genius malus*.[†] The Greeks called them *eudaimona* and *kakodaimona*[†] whereof the former they said persuaded him to all the good he did, the other enticed him to all the evil. But praised be God, we that are Christians, and walk not amongst the Cimmerian[†] conjectures of man, know well enough that it is the good spirit of God only who is the fountain of all goodness, that persuades us to the thinking or doing of any good, and that it is our corrupted flesh[†] and Satan that enticeth us to the contrary. And yet the devil, for confirming in the heads of ignorant Christians that error first maintained among the gentiles, he, whiles[†] among the first kind of spirits that I speak of, appeared in time of papistry and blindness and haunted diverse houses without doing any evil, but doing as it were necessary turns up and down the house. And this spirit they called brownie[†] in our language, who appeared like a rough man.[†] Yea, some were so blinded as to believe that their house was all the sonsier,[†] as they called it, that such spirits resorted[†] there.

P. But since the devil's intention in all his actions is ever to do evil, what evil was there in that form of doing since their actions outwardly were good?

E. Was it not evil enough to deceive simple ignorants[†] in making them to take him for an angel of light,[†] and so to account of[†] God's enemy as of[†] their particular friend? Where, by the contrary, all we that are Christians ought assuredly to know that since the coming of Christ in the flesh, and establishing of his church by the apostles,[†] all miracles, visions, prophecies

---

[†] ***genius bonus*** ... ***genius malus*** good spirit, the other evil spirit (Latin)

[†] ***eudaimona*** and ***kakodaimona*** the Greek participle *eudaimon* means 'fortunate' or 'happy', but there is no such noun meaning 'good genius' in Greek. In Greek *kakodaimon* as an adjective means 'possessed by an evil genius' and as a noun 'evil genius'. This word passed into English and is used from the late fourteenth century onwards, for example by Nashe in *Terrors of the Night*, and in Shakespeare's *Richard III* in Queen Margaret's reference to Richard: 'Hie thee to hell for shame, and leave this world, / Thou cacodemon; there thy kingdom is' (Shakespeare 1988: I iii 143–4). Compare 'Les anciens Grecs & Latins remarquent, qu'il y avoit de bons & de mauvais esprits, & appelloient les uns *eudaimonas*, les autres *kakodaimonas*' (Bodin 1580: I iii f. 14).

[†] **Cimmerian** dark and blind (*BL*); the Cimmerians were a mythical people supposed to live in

mist, cloud and perpetual darkness, and who never saw the sun (*Odyssey* XI 14–19)

[†] **corrupted flesh** Christian belief that the human body became a source of evil as a result of Adam and Eve's eating the forbidden fruit in the Garden of Eden

[†] **whiles** sometimes

[†] **brownie** a benevolent spirit or goblin

[†] **rough man** hairy man, the woodwose or shaggy wild man of the woods

[†] **sonsier** luckier

[†] **resorted** came

[†] **ignorants** ignorant people (*BL*)

[†] **angel of light** another allusion to 2 Corinthians 11.14; compare *Demonology* I i

[†] **to account of** to consider

[†] **as of** as if he were

[†] **apostles** the men who followed Christ and spread his teaching after his death in order to form the Christian church

and appearances of angels or good spirits are ceased,[†] which served only for the first sowing of faith, and planting[†] of the church. Where now, the church being established, and the white horse[†] (whereof I spake before) having made his conquest, the law and prophets[†] are thought sufficient to serve us or make us inexcusable,[†] as Christ saith in his parable of Lazarus and the rich man (Luke 16).[†]

CHAPTER III

ARGUMENT: The description of a particular sort of that kind of following spirits, called *incubi* and *succubi*.[†] And what is the reason wherefore these kinds of spirits haunt most the northern and barbarous parts of the world.

P. The next question that I would speer is likewise concerning this first of these two kinds of spirits that ye have conjoined, and it is this. Ye know how it is commonly written and reported that amongst the rest of the sorts of spirits that follow certain persons there is one more monstrous nor all the rest, in respect, as it is alleged, they converse naturally[†] with them whom they trouble and haunt with. And therefore, I would know in two things

---

[†] **since the coming of Christ ... are ceased** it was a protestant tenet, commonplace enough for Shakespeare to allude to it twice, that 'miracles are ceased' (Shakespeare 1988: *Henry V*, I i 68; *All's Well*, II iii 1). Miracles, prophecies and other supernatural interventions in human affairs ceased after the time of the Apostles or the Primitive Church (see Walker 1983). Later apparent occurrences were therefore held likely to be the result of papistry, either through deliberate fraud or because popery allowed the flourishing of superstition or demonic operation (see Lavater 1929: *passim*; Scot 1886: VIII i–vi 125–34).

[†] **planting** first establishing

[†] **white horse** of the Apocalypse; see *Demonology* II vii and note

[†] **law and prophets** a phrase commonly used metonymically for the old dispensation of the time under the law of Moses before Christ, on the authority of Christ himself in Luke 16.16, as James notes

[†] **to serve us or make us inexcusable** to preserve or save us, or render us inexcusable before God; compare 'Therefore thou art inexcusable, o man whoever thou art that judgest' (Romans 2.1)

[†] **the law and the prophets ... (Luke 16)** in Luke 16, in between the parables of the unjust steward, and Lazarus and the rich man, the mocking and covetous Pharisees are told by Jesus 'The Law and the Propehetes endured until John; and since that tyme the kingdome of God is preached, and every man preasseth into it' (Luke 16.16)

[†] **incubi** and **succubi** demons which supposedly had sex with humans in male form (*incubi*) and female form (*succubi*), either by compacting a body of air or animating a dead body. Augustine considered the question of whether spiritual beings might have intercourse with humans (*De Civitate Dei* XV xxiii) and Aquinas explained how. Many continental demonologists held such intercourse to be possible (Kramer and Sprenger 1971: part II q 1 chap 4; Bodin 1580: II vii ff. 104–9; Boguet 1929: xi–xiii 29–40; Guazzo 1988: xi 30–3; Le Loyer 1586: xii f. 126ᵛ), although Weyer of course thinks it imaginary (Weyer 1991: III xix–xxx 231–58). Scot ridicules the idea at some length (Scot 1886: IV i–xii 58–70). See also the entries in Robbins' *Encyclopaedia sv* 'incubus' and 'succubus' (Robbins 1959: 254–9, 490–2).

[†] **converse naturally** have sexual intercourse in the usual way

your opinion herein: first, if such a thing can be; and next, if it be, whether there be a difference of sexes† amongst these spirits or not.

E. That abominable kind of the devil's abusing of men or women was called of old *incubi* and *succubi*, according to the difference of the sexes that they conversed with. By two means this great kind of abuse might possibly be performed: the one, when the devil only as a spirit, and stealing out the sperm of a dead body,† abuses them that way, they not graithly† seeing any shape or feeling anything but that which he so conveys in that part.† As we read of a monastery of nuns which were burnt for their being that way abused. The other mean is when he borrows a dead body and so visibly and, as it seems unto them, naturally as a man converses with† them. But it is to be noted that, in whatsoever way he useth it, that sperm seems intolerably cold† to the person abused. For, if he steal out the nature of a quick person,† it cannot be so quickly carried but it will both tine† the strength and heat by the way, which it could never have had for lack of agitation,† which in the time of procreation is the procurer and wakener-up of these two natural qualities. And if he, occupying the dead body as his lodging, expel the same out thereof in the due time, it must likewise be cold by the participation† with the qualities of the dead body whereout of† it comes. And, whereas ye inquire if these spirits be divided in sexes or not, I think the rules of philosophy may easily resolve a man of the contrary, for it is a sure principle of that art that nothing can be divided in sexes except such living bodies as must have a natural seed to gener† by. But we know spirits hath no seed proper to themselves, nor yet can they gender† one with another.

P. How is it then that they say sundry monsters have been gotten by that way?

E. These tales are nothing but *aniles fabulae*,† for that they have no nature of their own I have showed you already. And that the cold nature of a dead body can work nothing in generation, it is more nor plain, as being already

---

† **difference of sexes** distinction between male and female

† **stealing out ... body** stealing the sperm out of a dead body; Cooper 1617: I vi 120–3 thinks this possible

† **graithly** distinctly

† **that which ... part** i.e. the sperm which he passes to the afflicted woman through his penis

† **converses with** has sex with

† **sperm seems intolerably cold** continental witches who supposedly claimed to have had sex with devils often reported that their semen was cold (e.g. Boguet 1929: xii 31; Guazzo 1988: xi 31). The North Berwick witches complained too of the devil's 'cold nature [i.e. his penis or sperm]' (*News*).

† **nature of a quick person** semen of a living man

† **tine** lose

† **agitation** it was believed that the vigorous movements of the body during sexual intercourse caused the semen to heat

† **participation** sharing

† **whereout of** out of which (*BL*)

† **gener** engender (*BL*); beget offspring

† **gender** produce offspring

† *aniles fabulae* old wives' tales (*BL*); a Latin tag derived from Horace, who writes of a neighbour rattling off old wives' tales, 'garrit anilis / ... fabellas' (*Satires* II vi 77–8)

dead of itself as well as the rest of the body is, wanting the natural heat and such other natural operation as is necessary for working that effect.[†] And in case such a thing were possible (which were allutterly[†] against all the rules of nature), it would breed no monster but only such a natural offspring as would have comed[†] betwixt that man or woman and that other abused person, in case they both being alive had had a do with other.[†] For the devil's part therein is but the naked carrying or expelling of that substance; and so it could not participate with no quality of the same.[†] Indeed, it is possible to the craft[†] of the devil to make a woman's belly to swell after he hath that way abused her, which he may do either by stirring up her own humour, or by herbs, as we see beggars daily do. And when the time of her delivery should come to make her thole great dolours,[†] like unto that natural course,[†] and then subtly to slip in the midwife's hands stalks,[†] stones or some monstrous bairn brought from some other place. But this is more reported and guessed at by others nor believed by me.

P. But what is the cause that this kind of abuse is thought to be most common in such wild parts of the world, as Lapland[†] and Finland or in our north isles of Orkney and Shetland?[4]

E. Because where the devil finds greatest ignorance and barbarity there assails he grossliest,[†] as I gave you the reason wherefore[†] there was more witches of womenkind nor men.

P. Can any be so unhappy as to give their willing consent to the devil's vile abusing of them in this form?[5]

E. Yea, some of the witches have confessed that he hath persuaded them to give their willing consent thereunto, that he may thereby have them feltered the sickerer[†] in his snares. But as to[†] the other compelled sort is to be pitied and prayed for, so is this most highly to be punished and detested.

P. Is not[6] the thing which we call the mare,[†] which takes folks sleeping in their beds, a kind of these spirits whereof ye are speaking?

[†] **working that effect** i.e. being able to inseminate a woman's body

[†] **allutterly** entirely

[†] **comed** come

[†] **had a do with other** had sexual intercourse with each other

[†] **no quality of the same** any real condition of the sexual intercourse with any quality of the semen

[†] **to the craft** by the cunning

[†] **thole great dolours** suffer great physical pain

[†] **natural course** natural process (of childbirth). The devil causes the woman's pain to imitate real birth-pangs.

[†] **stalks** stalks (of cabbages etc.)

[†] **Lapland** had a reputation as a place of witches

and devils in the sixteenth and seventeenth centuries. See Shakespeare, *The Comedy of Errors*: 'And Lapland sorcerers inhabit here' (Shakespeare 1988: IV iii 11). The reputation of Lapland and other northern lands for witchcraft (see Roberts 1616: 20–1) probably owes much to Olaus Magnus, *Historia de Gentibus Septentrionalibus*.

[†] **grossliest** most plainly

[†] **wherefore** why

[†] **feltered the sickerer** entangled all the more securely

[†] **as to** just as

[†] **mare** nightmare; goblin which produces a nightmare by sitting on the chest of the sleeper

E. No, that is but a natural sickness which the mediciners hath given that name of *incubus* unto *ab incubando*.[†] Because it, being a thick phlegm[†] falling into our breast[†] upon the heart while we are sleeping, intercludes so our vital spirits,[†] and takes all power from us, as makes us think that there were some unnatural burden or spirit lying upon us and holding us down.

CHAPTER IV

ARGUMENT: The description of the demoniacs and possessed. By what reason the papists may have power to cure them.[†]

P. Well, I have told you now all my doubts, and ye have satisfied me therein concerning the first of these two kinds of spirits that ye have conjoined. Now I am to enquire only two things at you[†] concerning the last kind: I mean the demoniacs. The first is, whereby[†] shall these possessed folks be discerned[†] fra them that are troubled with a natural frenzy or manie.[†] The next is, how can it be that they can be remedied by the papists' church, whom we counting as heretics, it should appear that one devil should not cast out another, for then would 'his kingdom be divided in itself', as Christ said (Matthew 12, Mark 3).[†]

E. As to your first question, there are diverse symptoms whereby[†] that heavy trouble may be discerned from a natural sickness, and specially three, omitting the diverse vain[†] signs that the papists attribute unto it, such as the raging at holy water, their fleeing aback from the cross, their not abiding the hearing of God named, and innumerable suchlike vain things[†] that were

---

[†] ***ab incubando*** from the Latin 'lying upon'. This etymology is an ancient one and is given by James in a formula typical of Isidore of Seville, who explains the etymological derivation of the spirit *incubus* as '*Incubi* comes from 'weighing down upon', that is from 'debauching' [*Unde et incubi dicuntur ab incumbendo, hoc est stuprando*]' (*Etymologies* VIII xi 103).

[†] **phlegm** one of the four humours, the one which was cold and moist

[†] **breast** chest

[†] **intercludes so our vital spirits** blocks our vital spirits (which sustain life by flowing from the heart into the body through the arteries)

[†] **the papists may have power to cure them** after the Reformation the Roman church claimed even more vigorously that its power to exorcise supported its claim to be the true church; see Thomas 1973: 477–92; Walker 1981

[†] **at you** from you

[†] **whereby** in what way

[†] **discerned** distinguished

[†] **manie** mania, acute mental derangement

[†] **'his kingdom ... Mark 3)** In Matthew 12.22–28 Jesus heals one possessed with a demon that made him blind and dumb. The Pharisees claim that Jesus cast out devils through Beelzebub, the prince of devils, and Jesus replies 'Every kingdome devided against it self, shalbe brought to naught ... So if Satan cast out Satan, he is devided against him selfe: how shall then his kingdome endure?' (Matthew 12.25–26). The same exchange is reported in Mark 3.22–27.

[†] **whereby** by which

[†] **vain** meaningless

[†] **vain things** catholic exorcistic handbooks listed fear of the sign of the cross and holy water as symptoms of possession; see Walker 1981: 11–13

alike fashious and feckless[†] to recite. But to come to these three symptoms then whereof I spake. I account the one of them to be the incredible strength of the possessed creature, which will far exceed the strength of six of the wightest and woodest[†] of any other men that are not so troubled. The next is the bowdening up[†] so far of the patient's breast and belly, with such an unnatural, sturring,[†] vehement agitation within them, and such an irony hardness of his sinews so stiffly bended out that it were not possible to prick out,[†] as it were, the skin of any other person so far. So mightily works the devil in all the members and senses of his body, he being locally[†] within the same, suppose of his soul and affections thereof[†] he have no more power than of any other man's. The last is the speaking of sundry languages,[†] which the patient is known by them that were acquaint with him never to have learned, and that with an uncouth and hollow voice, and all the time of his speaking a greater motion being in his breast then in his mouth. But fra this last symptom are excepted[†] such as are altogether in the time of their possessing bereft of all their senses, being possessed with a dumb and blind spirit (whereof Christ relieved one in the 12 of Matthew).[†] And as to your next demand, it is first to be doubted if the papists, or any not professing the only true religion, can relieve any of that trouble. And next, in case they can, upon what respects[†] it is possible unto them. As to the former, upon two reasons it is grounded: first, that it is known so many of them to be counterfeit, which wile the clergy invents for confirming of their rotten religion.[†] The next is that by experience we find that few who are possessed indeed[†] are fully cured by them, but rather the devil is content to release[†]

[†] **fashious and feckless** annoying and pointless. Catholic exorcistic handbooks listed some of the signs of possession as trembling and horror at the sound of holy words, sacraments (especially confession and the Eucharist), and the names of saints (Girolamo Menghi, *Flagellum Daemonum*, Bologna 1580: 3)

[†] **wightest and woodest** strongest and craziest. The strength of demoniacs was one of their distinguishing features. The Gadarene demoniac was so strong that even though 'he was bound with chaines, and kept in fetters ... he brake the bandes' (Luke 8.29). James was thinking of the gentleman supposedly possessed and brought into his presence by Fian, who in his fit had such great strength 'that all the gentlemen in the chamber were not able to hold him, until they called in more help, who together bound him hand and foot' (*News*)

[†] **bowdening up** swelling up
[†] **sturring** disturbing
[†] **prick out** distend
[†] **locally** in that place (*Craigie*)

[†] **suppose ... thereof** though over his soul and its passions

[†] **speaking of sundry languages** a sudden and expert knowledge of languages was a sign of possession that both catholics and protestants acknowledged; see Walker 1981: 11–13. Compare, 'Why 'tis the devil. ... He's a rare linguist' (Webster, *The White Devil*, V iii 102–5).

[†] **excepted** exempted

[†] **dumb and blind ... the 12 of Matthew** this is the man 'possessed with a devil, bothe blind & domme' (Matthew 12.22) who occasioned Jesus' exchange with the Pharisees which James mentioned earlier in this chapter

[†] **respects** conditions

[†] **confirming of their rotten religion** for the protestant propaganda war in late sixteenth-century England conducted by Samuel Harsnett and John Deacon and John Walker against fraudulent catholic dispossessions, see Thomas 1973: 477–92; Brownlow 1993: 49–66

[†] **possessed indeed** genuinely possessed
[†] **is content to release** is happy to cease

the bodily hurting of them for a short space, thereby to obtain the perpetual hurt of the souls of so many that by these false miracles may be induced or confirmed in the profession of that erroneous religion (even as I told you before that he doth in the false cures, or casting off, of diseases by witches). As to the other part of the argument—in case[†] they can—which rather, with reverence of[†] the learned thinking otherways, I am induced to believe by reason of the faithful report that men sound of religion[†] have made according to their sight thereof, I think if so be,[†] I say these may be the respects whereupon the papists may have that power. Christ gave a commission[†] and power to his apostles to cast out devils, which they according thereunto put in execution.[†] The rules he had them observe in that action were fasting and prayer,[†] and the action itself to be done in his name. This power of theirs proceeded not then of any virtue in them, but only in him who directed them, as was clearly proved by Judas his having as great power in that commission as any of the rest. It is easy then to be understand[†] that the casting out of devils (Matthew 7)[†] is by the virtue[†] of fasting and prayer, and incalling[†] of the name of God, suppose[†] many imperfections be in the person that is the instrument, as Christ himself teacheth us of the power that false prophets shall have to cast out devils.[†] It is no wonder then, these respects[†] of this action being considered, that it may be possible to the papists, though erring in sundry points of religion, to accomplish this if they use the right form prescribed by Christ herein. For what the worse is that action that they err in other things, more than their baptism is the worse that they err in the other sacrament, and have eked many vain freits[†] to the baptism itself?[†]

[†] **in case** in the event that

[†] **with reverence of** with due respect for

[†] **sound of religion** with sound religious beliefs

[†] **if so be** if this be indeed the case (that catholics can cast out devils).

[†] **gave a commission** 'And he called his twelve disciples unto him, and gave them power against uncleane spirits, to cast them out' (Matthew 10.1)

[†] **according thereunto put in execution** put into practice according to what Christ said

[†] **fasting and prayer** in Matthew 17.14–21, when Jesus' disciples fail to cast out a devil, they are told 'How be it this kinde goeth not out, but by prayer and fasting' (Matthew 17.21). This verse was cited as authority by certain puritan exorcists for their practices (Thomas 1973: 479–87).

[†] **understand** understood (*BL*)

[†] **(Matthew 7)** Craigie takes this to be a reference to Matthew 7.22–23, where the workers of iniquity claim to have cast out devils in Christ's name, but since the allusion is particularly to casting out devils by prayer and fasting, the marginal reference may be an error for Matthew 17

[†] **by the virtue** by the power

[†] **incalling** invocation

[†] **suppose** even though

[†] **as Christ himself ... devils** Christ warned his disciples, 'For there shal arise false Christs & false prophetes, and shal shew great signes and wonders, so that, if it were possible, they shulde deceive the verie elect' (Matthew 24.24)

[†] **respects** aspects

[†] **eked many vain freits** added many futile superstitions. James is thinking of the catholic church's retention of such features in baptism as *insufflatio* (the priest ritually breathing in the face of the child), anointing with chrism, and an exorcistic formula adjuring the devil to depart. These ancillary rituals were dropped from protestant Prayer Books; see Thomas 1973: 36–7, 54–6, 478.

[†] **For what ... baptism itself?** Is their error in that action any worse because they err in other things, any more than their baptism is worse because they err in the other sacrament (i.e. the eucharist), and indeed have added many vain superstitions to baptism itself?.

P. Surely it is no little wonder that God should permit the bodies of any of the faithful to be so dishonoured as to be a dwelling place to that unclean spirit.

E. There is it which[†] I told right now would prove and strengthen my argument of the devil's entering in the dead bodies of the faithful. For if he is permitted to enter in their living bodies even when they are joined with the soul, how much more will God permit him to enter in their dead carrions,[†] which is no more man, but the filthy and corruptible case[†] of man. For as Christ saith (Mark 7), 'It is not any thing that enters within man that defiles him, but only that which proceeds and cometh out of him'.[†]

CHAPTER V

ARGUMENT: The description of the fourth kind of spirits called the fairy. What is possible therein,[†] and what is but illusions. How far this dialogue entreats of[†] all these things, and to what end.

P. Now, I pray you, come on to that fourth kind of spirits.

E. That fourth kind of spirits, which by the gentiles was called Diana and her wandering court,[†] and amongst us was called the fairy (as I told you) or 'our good neighbours', was one of the sorts of illusions that was rifest in the time of papistry. For although it was holden[†] odious to prophesy by the devil, yet whom[†] this kind of spirits carried away, and informed,[†] they were thought to be sonsiest[†] and of best life. To speak of the many vain trattles founded upon that illusion—how there was a king and queen of fairy, of such a jolly court and train[†] as they had; how they had a teind[†] and duty, as

---

[†]   **There is it which** there is something else in what

[†]   **carrions** corpses

[†]   **case** container (i.e. body)

[†]   **It is not ... out of him** a paraphrase of 'There is nothing without a man, that can defile him, when it entereth into him: but the things which proceed out of him, are they which defile the man' (Mark 7.15)

[†]   **is possible therein** is real in that matter

[†]   **entreats of** deals with

[†]   **Diana and her wandering court** this is an allusion to a text much quoted and discussed by demonologists, which seemed to provide evidence of night-flying witches. It referred to 'women who believe and claim that they ride at night on certain beasts, with Diana goddess of the pagans and a great multitude of women [*mulieres ... credunt se et profitentur nocturnis horis cum Diana paganorum dea et innumera multitudine*

mulierum equitare super quasdam bestias]'. It was known as part of the canon *Episcopi*, so called from its opening words, '*Episcopi episcoporumque ministri*' and was believed to come from the fourth-century Council of Ancyra, but was probably much later. The earliest text is that given in the early tenth century by Regino of Prüm, *De Ecclesiasticis Disciplinis* (Latin text Migne CXXXII, 352). See Cohn 1975: 210–19 and Kieckhefer 1976: 38–40.

[†]   **holden** considered

[†]   **whom** those whom

[†]   **informed** entered into

[†]   **sonsiest** luckiest; holiest (*BL*)

[†]   **king and queen ... train** for Scottish fairy belief, especially about a fairy court, in the sixteenth century, see the trial of Bessie Dunlop in 1576 (Pitcairn 1833: I ii 49–58)

[†]   **teind** a tithe, a tenth

it were, of all goods;[†] how they naturally rode and went, ate and drank, and did all other actions like natural men and women—I think it liker[†] Virgil's *Campi Elysii*[†] nor anything that ought to be believed by Christians; except in general that, as I spake sundry times before, the devil illuded[†] the senses of sundry simple creatures in making them believe that they saw and heard such things as were nothing so indeed.

P. But how can it be then that sundry witches have gone to death with that confession, that they have been transported with the fairy to such a hill which, opening, they went in, and there saw a fair queen, who being now lighter[†] gave them a stone that had sundry virtues, which at sundry times hath been produced in judgement?

E. I say that,[†] even as I said before of that imaginar[†] ravishing of the spirit forth of the body. For may not the devil object to their fantasy,[†] their senses being dulled and, as it were, asleep, such hills and houses within them, such glistering[†] courts and trains,[†] and whatsoever suchlike wherewith he pleaseth to delude them. And in the meantime, their bodies being senseless, to convey in their hand any stone, or suchlike thing, which he makes them to imagine to have received in such a place.

P. But what say ye to their foretelling the death of sundry persons whom they allege to have seen in these places? That is a soothdream[†] (as they say), since they see it waking.

E. I think that either they have not been sharply enough examined[†] that gave so blunt a reason for their prophecy. Or otherways, I think it likewise as possible that the devil may prophesy to them when he deceives their imaginations in that sort[†] (as well as when he plainly speaks unto them at other times for their prophesying), is but by a kind of vision, as it were, wherein he commonly counterfeits God among the ethnics,[†] as I told you before.

P. I would know now whether these kinds of spirits may only appear to witches, or if they may also appear to any other.

[†] **had a teind ... goods** levied tax (of one tenth) and duty, as it were, on all possessions

[†] **liker** more like

[†] ***Campi Elysii*** the Elysian fields, the abode of the blessed according to Virgil, *Aeneid* V 735, and *Georgics* I 38, where the phrase *Elysios ... campos* is used

[†] **illuded** deluded

[†] **being now lighter** being now delivered of a child

[†] **say that** say about that

[†] **imaginar** imaginary

[†] **object to their fantasy** present to their imagination

[†] **glistering** glistening

[†] **trains** attendants and servants (in royal or noble courts)

[†] **soothdream** dream that correctly foretells the future; true dream (*BL*)

[†] **sharply enough examined** severely enough interrogated

[†] **in that sort** in that way

[†] **ethnics** pagans (i.e. people not subscribing to one of the main religions of the world)

E. They may do to both: to the innocent sort, either to affray[†] them, or to seem to be a better sort of folks nor unclean spirits are; and to the witches, to be a colour of safety[†] for them that ignorant magistrates may not punish them for it, as I told even now. But as the one sort, for being perforce troubled with them ought to be pitied, so ought the other sort (who may be discerned by their taking upon them[†] to prophesy by them), that sort, I say, ought as severely to be punished as any other witches, and rather the more that[†] they go dissemblingly to work.

P. And what makes the spirits have so different names from others?

E. Even the knavery of that same devil, who as he illudes[†] the necromancers with innumerable feigned names for him and his angels, as in special[†] making Satan,[†] Beelzebub,[†] and Lucifer[†] to be three sundry[†] spirits, where we find the two former but diverse names[†] given to the prince of all the rebelling angels by the scripture. As by Christ, the prince of all the devils is called Beelzebub in that place which I alleged[†] against the power of any heretics to cast out devils. By John in the Revelation[†] the old tempter is called Satan, 'the Prince of all the evil angels'. And the last, to wit Lucifer, is but by allegory taken from the day star[†] (so named in diverse places of the scriptures)[†] because of his excellency (I mean the prince of them) in his creation before his fall. Even so, I say he deceives the witches by attributing to himself diverse names, as if every diverse shape that he transforms himself in were a diverse kind of spirit.

[†] **affray** terrify

[†] **be a colour of safety** to provide a pretence of safety

[†] **taking upon them** assuming the right for themselves

[†] **that** because

[†] **illudes** deludes

[†] **in special** in particular

[†] **Satan** *satan* is a Hebrew common noun, meaning 'adversary' or 'plotter', which the Greek Septuagint rendered as *diabolos*: 'Satan in Latin means "adversary" or "transgressor"' (Isidore of Seville, *Etymologies* VIII xi 19). It became a proper name of the devil. It is first used in the bible in 1 Chronicles 21.1, 'And Satan stode up against Israel, and provoked David to number Israel', used extensively in the book of Job and also in the New Testament.

[†] **Beelzebub** another popular name for the devil, indeed for the 'prince of devils', as James observes, on the authority of the New Testament (e.g. Matthew 12.24, 27; Mark 3.22; Luke 11.14–19). It comes from the Hebrew word meaning 'fly-lord'; compare 'Baal-zebub the god of Ekron' (2 Kings 1.2).

[†] **Lucifer** *lucifer* (Latin 'light-bringing) is an epithet for the planet Venus as the morning-star, and is so used in the Vulgate. It is used at Isaiah 14.12 to taunt a fallen king of Babylon; 'How art thou fallen from heaven, o Lucifer, sonne of the morning [*quomodo cecidisti de caelo lucifer qui mane oriebaris*]' and this verse was interpreted by early church fathers such as Origen and Justin to refer to the devil, traditionally the brightest of the angels before his fall.

[†] **sundry** different

[†] **but diverse names** (to be) only different names

[†] **alleged** quoted

[†] **John in the Revelation** 'And the great dragon, that olde serpent, called the devill and Satan, was cast out, who deceiveth all the world' (Revelation 12.9)

[†] **day star** morning star, the name given to the planet Venus when it appears like a bright star in the sky before sunrise

[†] **diverse places of the scriptures** the Vulgate text of the bible uses *lucifer* of a variety of phenomena in the skies; see Job 11.17, 38.32; Psalms 109.3

P. But I have heard many more strange tales of this fairy nor ye have yet told me.

E. As well I do in that as I did in all the rest of my discourse. For because the ground[†] of this conference of ours proceeded of your speering at me[†] at our meeting if there was such a thing as witches or spirits, and if they had any power, I therefore have framed my whole discourse only to prove that such things are and may be, by such number of examples as I show to be possible by reason. And keeps me from dipping any further[†] in playing the part of a dictionary to tell whatever I have read or heard in that purpose, which both would exceed faith,[†] and rather would seem to teach such unlawful arts nor to disallow and condemn them, as it is the duty of all Christians to do.

CHAPTER VI

ARGUMENT: Of the trial and punishment of witches. What sort of accusation ought to be admitted[†] against them. What is the cause of the increasing so far of their number in this age.

P. Then, to make an end of our conference since I see it draws late, what form of punishment think ye merit[†] these magicians and witches? For I see that ye account them to be all alike guilty?

E. They ought to be put to death according to the law of God,[†] the civil and imperial law,[†] and the municipal law[†] of all Christian nations.

P. But what kind of death, I pray you?

E. It is commonly used[†] by fire, but that is an indifferent[†] thing to be used in every country according to the law or custom thereof.

P. But ought no sex, age nor rank to be exempted?

E. None at all, being so used by the lawful magistrate, for it is the highest point of idolatry,[†] wherein no exception is admitted by the law of God.

P. Then bairns may not be spared?

[†] **ground** basis
[†] **proceeded of your speering at me** started by your asking me
[†] **And keeps ... any further** and that (my framing this argument about the existence of witches and spirits) prevents me from lowering myself any further
[†] **exceed faith** go beyond credit (*BL*)
[†] **admitted** allowed
[†] **merit** deserve
[†] **law of God** the Old Testament prohibits magic

and witchcraft at Deuteronomy 18.10–12 and famously punishes its practitioners with death at Exodus 22.18
[†] **imperial law** laws of the Roman empire
[†] **municipal law** laws of particular local communities (in this case Scotland)
[†] **used** done, put into effect
[†] **indifferent** unimportant, subject to acceptable variation
[†] **highest point of idolatry** most extreme form of false worship

E. Yea, not a hair the less of my conclusion,[†] for they are not that[†] capable of reason as to practise[†] such things. And for any being in company and not revealing thereof,[†] their less and ignorant age will no doubt excuse them.

P. I see ye condemn them all that are of the counsel[†] of such crafts.

E. No doubt, for as I said speaking of magic, the consulters, trusters in, overseers,[†] entertainers,[†] or stirrers-up of these craftsfolks are equally guilty with themselves that are the practisers.

P. Whether may the prince then, or supreme magistrate, spare or oversee any that are guilty of that craft[7] upon some great respects known to him?

E. The prince or magistrate, for further trial's cause,[†] may continue[†] the punishing of them such a certain space[†] as he thinks convenient. But in the end to spare the life and not to strike when God bids strike, and so severely punish in so odious a fault and treason against God, it is not only unlawful but doubtless no less sin in that magistrate nor it was in Saul's sparing of Agag. And so comparable to the sin of witchcraft itself as Samuel alleged at that time (1 Samuel 15).[†]

P. Surely then, I think, since this crime ought to be so severely punished,[8] judges ought to beware to condemn any but such as they are sure are guilty, neither should the clattering report of a carling[†] serve in so weighty a case.

E. Judges ought indeed to beware whom they condemn, for it is as great a crime (as Solomon saith) (Proverbs 17), 'To condemn the innocent, as to let the guilty escape free'.[†] Neither ought the report of any one infamous person be admitted for a sufficient proof, which can stand of no law.[†]

P. And what may a number, then, of guilty persons' confessions work against one that is accused?

E. The assize must serve for interpreter of our law in that respect. But in my opinion, since in a matter of treason against the prince, bairns or wives or

---

[†] **Yea, not a hair ... conclusion** Yes, they may be spared, without weakening my conclusion a jot

[†] **that** so (*BL*)

[†] **as to practise** as to be able to practise

[†] **in company ... thereof** in the company of witches and not revealing it

[†] **of the counsel** have knowledge; know something of the doings

[†] **overseers** those who disregard and condone witchcraft

[†] **entertainers** those who tolerate witches, or those who retain them in their households

[†] **for further trial's cause** for the sake of further testing (them)

[†] **continue** postpone. This seems to have James's practice with Ritchie Graham, as he wrote to Maitland at the end of April 1591, 'garr see that

Richie Grahme want not his ordinaire allouaince quhill I take farther ordoure with him' (*CSPS* x 510).

[†] **certain space** certain time

[†] **Saul's sparing ... (1 Samuel 15)** in 1 Samuel 15 Saul initially spared Agag, king of the Amalekites, against God's command through the prophet Samuel, who rebuked him, 'For rebellion is as the sin of witchcraft, and stubborness is as iniquity and idolatry' (1 Samuel 15.23)

[†] **clattering report of a carling** loud-mouthed, meaningless evidence of an old woman

[†] **(as Solomon saith) ... escape free'** Proverbs 17.26

[†] **stand of no law** cannot stand up as evidence under any legal rule

never so defamed persons may of our law† serve for sufficient witnesses and proofs, I think surely that by a far greater reason such witnesses may be sufficient in matters of high treason against God; for who but witches can be proves,† and so witnesses, of the doings of witches?

P. Indeed, I trow they will be loath to put any honest man upon their counsel.† But what if they accuse folk to have been present at their imaginar conventions in the spirit,† when their bodies lie senseless, as ye⁹ have said?

E. I think they are not a hair the less guilty, for the devil durst never have borrowed their shadow or similitude to that turn† if their consent had not been at it. And the consent in these turns is death of the law.†

P. Then Samuel was a witch,† for the devil resembled his shape† and played his person in giving response to Saul.

E. Samuel was dead as well† before that, and so none could slander him with meddling in that unlawful art. For the cause why, as I take it, that God will not permit Satan to use the shapes or similitudes of any innocent persons at such unlawful times, is that God will not permit that any innocent persons shall be slandered with that vile defection,† for then the devil would find ways anew† to calumniate† the best. And this we have in proof by them that are carried with the fairy, who never see the shadows of any in that court but of them that thereafter are tried to have been brethren and sisters of that craft. And this was likewise proved by the confession of a young lass troubled with spirits laid on her by witchcraft, that although she saw the shapes of diverse men and women troubling her, and naming the persons whom these shadows represent, yet never one of them is found to be innocent, but all clearly tried to be most guilty,† and the most part of them confessing the same. And besides that, I think it hath been seldom heard tell of that any-whom persons† guilty of that crime accused, as having known them to their marrows† by eye-sight and not by hearsay, but such as were so accused of

---

† **of our law** under the terms of our law. It was a common argument that since witchcraft was such an exceptional crime (*crimen exceptum*) in both its gravity and in the difficulty of establishing guilt, it was sometimes appropriate to suspend normal legal procedures in dealing with it; see Larner 1984: 35–67.

† **proves** those who provide proof

† **put any ... counsel** make any honest man part of their shared confidence

† **imaginar conventions in the spirit** their spirits to have been present at imaginary meetings

† **shadow or similitude to that turn** outward appearance or likeness for that purpose

† **is death of the law** means a sentence of death

under the law

† **Samuel was a witch** referring once again to the story of Samuel and the witch of Endor

† **resembled his shape** made a resemblance of his physical form

† **as well** long (*BL*)

† **defection** apostasy; falling away (*BL*)

† **ways anew** plenty of ways

† **calumniate** slander

† **clearly ... guilty** clearly, once tried, are proved to be most guilty

† **heard tell ... persons** reported that any persons at all

† **having ... marrows** having been known to their associates

witchcraft, could not be clearly tried upon them,[†] were at the least publicly
known to be of a very evil life and reputation; so jealous[†] is God, I say, of the
fame[†] of them that are innocent in such causes.[†] And besides that, there are
two other good helps that may be used for their trial: the one is the finding
of their mark,[†] and the trying the insensibleness[†] thereof. The other is their
fleeting[†] on the water for, as in a secret murder, if the dead carcass be at any
time thereafter handled by the murderer, it will gush out of blood,[†] as if the
blood were crying to the heaven for revenge of the murderer,[†] God having
appointed that secret supernatural sign for trial of that secret unnatural
crime. So it appears that God hath appointed, for a supernatural sign of the
monstrous impiety of the witches, that the water shall refuse to receive them
in her bosom[†] that have shaken off them the sacred water of baptism, and
wilfully refused the benefit thereof. No not so much as their eyes are able to
shed tears (threaten and torture them as ye please) while first they repent
(God not permitting them to dissemble their obstinacy in so horrible a crime)
albeit the womenkind[†] especially be able otherways to shed tears at every
light occasion[†] when they will, yea, although it were dissemblingly like the
crocodiles.[†]

P. Well, we have made this conference to last as long as leisure would permit.
And to conclude then, since I am to take my leave of you, I pray God to
purge this country of these devilish practices, for they were never so rife in
these parts as they are now.

E. I pray God that so be too.[†] But the causes are over-manifest[†] that make
them to be so rife. For the great wickedness of the people, on the one part,

---

[†] **clearly tried upon them** could not be convicted
     with certainty
[†] **jealous** vigilant in guarding, careful, watchful
[†] **fame** reputation
[†] **causes** legal cases
[†] **mark** mark made by the devil on their bodies
[†] **insensibleness** lack of feeling
[†] **fleeting** floating
[†] **if the dead ... of blood** persons suspected of
     murder were sometimes made to touch the
     victim's corpse: a flow of blood would testify to
     their guilt, as it does when Richard, Duke of
     Gloucester, approaches the corpse of Henry VI
     (Shakespeare 1988: *Richard III* I ii 55–6). See
     also Thomas 1973: 261–2.
[†] **blood crying ... the murderer** God tells the first
     murderer, Cain 'What hast thou done? the voice
     of thy brother's blood crieth unto me from the
     ground' (AV Genesis 4.10). 'Blood will have
     blood' was a proverbial expression in the six-
     teenth century (Tilley 1950: B458).

[†] **the water ... bosom** the water will refuse to allow
     the witch to sink. For examples of women being
     swum as witches see Thomas 1973: 146, 261,
     539, 619, 636, 658 and Rosen 1991: 331–43.
     See also the entry *sv* 'swimming' in Robbins
     1959: 492–4.
[†] **womenkind** women in general
[†] **light occasion** trivial reason
[†] **like the crocodiles** crocodiles were said to weep
     either to trick the unwary into approaching
     them and being eaten, or to show sorrow at
     having eaten them; in either case their tears were
     hypocritical. The expression is already prover-
     bial in the sixteenth century (Tilley 1950: C831);
     see also 'If that the earth could teem with
     woman's tears, / Each drop she falls would prove
     a crocodile' (Shakespeare 1988: *Othello* IV i 245–
     6).
[†] **that so be too** that that (the country's being
     purged of witches) may be so indeed
[†] **over-manifest** all too obvious

procures this horrible defection† whereby God justly punisheth sin by a greater iniquity. And on the other part, the consummation of the world,† and our deliverance† drawing near, makes Satan to rage the more in his instruments† (Revelation 12), knowing his kingdom to be so near an end.† And so farewell for this time.

FINIS.

---

† **procures this horrible defection** brings about this horrible abandonment of faith
† **consummation of the world** completion of the history of the world in the Day of Judgement
† **deliverance** release (from worldly life)
† **rage ... instruments** act more violently through the means he has chosen (including the witches)
† **knowing ... near an end** 'Wo to the inhabitants of the earth, and of the sea: for the devil is come downe unto you which hathe great wrath knowing that he hathe but a short time' (Revelation 12.12). Many demonologists write in the context of an apocalyptic imagination and claim that the prevalence of witches is the work of a raging devil who knows that the end of the world is near, as the verse in the Apocalypse states.

Textual Notes to *Demonology*

Preface

[1] apprehended] *Q2, Craigie*; apprehened *Q1*

First Book

[1] 2 Corinthians] 2. Cor. *Q, Craigie*; 1 Cor. *F*
[2] category?] Categorie? *Q2, F, Craigie*; Categorie. *Q1*
[3] witchcraft?] Witch-craft? *Q2, F, Craigie*; Witch-craft. *Q1*
[4] gentiles] Gentiles *Q2, Craigie*; Gentiles *F*; Gentles *Q1*
[5] for the study alone ... nor offensive] for the studie alone, ... is more perilous nor offensiue *Craigie*; for studie the alone, ... is more perilous nor offensiue *Q1*; for studie the alone, ... is more perillous nor offensiue *Q2 (Aspley), F*; for the study alone, ... is not perillous nor offensiue *Q2 (Hatfield)*
[6] the] *Q2 (Hatfield), F, Craigie*; The *Q1, Q2 (Aspley)*
[7] them. By forms] them. By formes *Craigie*; them) by formes *Q*; them) By formes *F*
[8] ye may guess] yee may ghesse *Q1, Q2 (Aspley), Craigie*; hee may ghesse *Q2 (Hatfield)*
[9] in terms, his schoolmaster] in termes his schole-master *sic. read* (in termes) his schole-master *Craigie*; in termes his schole-master *Q1*; (in termes his schole-master) *Q2, F*
[10] that that] *Q1, Craigie*; that the *Q2 (Hatfield)*
[11] before). For God] *Q2, Craigie*; before) For God *Q1*; before: For God *F*
[12] Acts 3] Actes 3. *F*; Act. 3. *Craigie*; Ast 3. *Q1*; Act 3. *Q2 (Aspley)*; Act. 3. *Q2 (Hatfield)*

Second Book

[1] it is] *Q2, F, Craigie*; it it *Q1*
[2] diviners] Diuiners *Craigie, F*; Diuines *Q*
[3] divide] diuide *Q2 (Hatfield), Craigie*; denie *Q1, Q2 (Aspley)*; deny *F*
[4] pansing] *Q1, Q2 (Aspley), Craigie*; pausing *Q2 (Hatfield)*

[5] in] *Q, Craigie*; into *F*
[6] EPISTEMON] [EPI] *Craigie*; there is no speech prefix for EPISTEMON *here in Q or F*;
[7] serving of the] *Q, Craigie*; seruing the *F*
[8] churches). But] Churches.) But *Q2 (Hatfield)*, Craigie; Churches) But *Q1, Q2 (Aspley), F*
[9] is it] *Q1, Q2 (Aspley), Craigie*; it is *Q2 (Hatfield)*
[10] EPISTEMON] EPI. *Craigie*; there is no speech prefix here for EPISTEMON *in Q or F*
[11] a quantity] a quantity, *Q2 (Hatfield)*; a quantitie, *Q2 (Aspley), F, Craigie*; 1 aquantitie, *Q1*
[12] his turns with him,] his turnes with him *Q, F, Craigie*
[13] effectuate, seeing] *Q2, F*; effectuat, seing *Q1, Craigie*
[14] relieve] *Q2, F, Craigie*; relive *Q1*
[15] radical continually] radicall continually, *Q1, Q2, F*; radicall, continually *Craigie*
[16] captain] Captaine *Q2, Craigie*; Captaine, *Q1*; captaine *F*
[17] rarer] *Q1, Q2 (Hatfield), Craigie*; rather *Q2 (Aspley), F*

Third Book

[1] Babel and Edom] *Babell* and *Edom*: *Q1 (corrected)*; IERVSALEM: *Q1 (uncorrected), Craigie*; Ierusalem: *Q2*; Ierusalem, *F*
[2] scaly sloughs] schellie sloughes *Q1 (corrected)*; schellie sluiches *Q1 (uncorrected), Q2, Craigie*; schelly sluiches *F*
[3] Siloam] Siloam *Q1 (corrected)*; Sylo *Q1 (uncorrected), Q2, F, Craigie*
[4] Shetland?] Schet-land? *Q2, F, Craigie*; Schet-land. *Q1*
[5] form?] forme? *Q2, F, Craigie*; forme. *Q1*
[6] Is not] *Q2 (Hatfield)*; It is not *Q1, Q2 (Aspley), Craigie*; Is it not *F*
[7] craft] craft, *Q2, F, Craigie*; craft? *Q1*
[8] punished,] *Q2, F*; punished. *Q1, Craigie*
[9] ye] *Q1, Q2 (Aspley), F*; yee *Q2 (Hatfield)*; yet *Craigie*

Appendix

Privy Council Orders Relating to the Legal Processes of Witchcraft Trials 1591–7

Privy council commission of 26 October 1591 (*RPCS* iv 680)

Commission for discovery of witches, with power of examination and putting to the torture.

Forsamekle as the Kingis Majestie, with advise of the Lordis of his Secreit Counsale, hes gevin and grantit, and be thir presentis gevis and grantis, his Hienes full power and commissioun, expres bidding and charge, to his trusty and weilbelovitt counsallouris Sir Johnne Cokburne of Ormestoun, justice clerk, Maister David McKgill of Nesbitt, advocate, as alsua to Mr Robert Bruce and Johnne Dunkiesoun, ministeris, Williame Litill, provest of Edinburgh, and Johnne Arnot, burges thairof, or ony three of thame conjunctlie, all and sindrie personis,—alsweill thame quhilkis are alreddy convict, or utheris quhilkis ar detenit captive and hes confessit, and sum that hes not confessit, as alswa all sic utheris as ar dilaitit, or that heireftir salbe accused and dilaited, off committing, using and practizing of witchecraft, sorcherie, inchantment, and uthiris divilish divysis, to the dishonour of God, sklender of his worde, perelling of thair awne saullis, abuseing of the commun people and grite contempt of God, his Majestie, his authoritie and lawis,—to call and convene befoir the saidis commissionaris, or ony three of thame conjunctlie as said is, als oft as neid beis, and thame to try, inquire and examinat, thair depositionis to putt in write, and the same to reporte to his Hienes and his Counsale, to the effect thai may be putt to the knawlege of ane assyis, and justice ministerit as effeiris, or sic uthir ordour takin with thame as to his Majestie and his said Counsall salbe thocht maist meit and convenient,—the personis wilfull or refusand to declair the veritie to putt to tortour, or sic uthir punishement to use and caus be usit as may move thame to utter the treuth, and generallie all and sindrie utheris thingis to do and use that heirin is requisite to be done; ferme and stable haldand and for to hald all and quhatsumevir thingis the saidis commissionaris, or ony three of thame conjunctlie as said is, sall lauchfullie do heirin.

Privy council order permitting standing commissions to be issued in localities, 8 June 1592 (RPCS iv 753–4)

Act appointing Royal Commissioners to assist the Commissioners of the General Assembly.

In respect that the General Assembly of the Kirk has directed commissioners, in 'certane boundis limitat to thame, to travell and tak ordour in all thingis that may serve to the glorie of God and advancement of his trew religioun,—and in speciall to plant kirkis and ministeris quhair thai laik, with prisbitereis quhair thay may be convenientlie had; to tak diligent inquisitioun of papistis, jesuitis, and all sic as trafficquis and travellis in ony thing contrair the trew religioun publictlie professit be his Majestie and liegis of this realme, and ather putt ordour to thame, or uthirwayes, giff thai may nocht, to adjornay thame and charge thame to compeir befoir his Majestie and Secrete Counsale, that thai may be punist according to the lawis maid aganis sic personis; to see how the kirkis that ar decayit may be rapairit; to tak inquisitioun of the present estate of every particulair kirk, in quhais handis it is, and of the rent thairof present and of auld, and of all thingis that may sufficientlie informe the commissionaris depute be his Majestie; to tak ordour anent the particulair locall assignatioun of everie minister of his stipend, and quhatsumevir uther thing is directit in commissioun to the commissionaris of the Generall Assembly,'—his Majesty, 'willing that the saidis commissionaris directit be the Generall Assembley sall not be dissobeyit, be avise of his Prevey Counsale, ordanis commissionis to be past undir his Hienes signett and subscriptioun of the Clerk of the Prevey Counsale contening a blank for names of noblemen, baronis, gentilmen, and magistratis of burrowis to be insert thairin at the chois and discretioun of the saidis commissionaris of the Generall Assembley, makand thame his Hienes justiceis and commissionaris in that parte to the effect undirwrittin, gevand, grantand and committand to thame full pouer, charge and authoritie to assist the saidis commissionaris of the Generall Assembley in executioun of the commissioun thairof grantit to thame in all the heidis and articlis thairof abonespecifeit, and to see that they be nocht dissobeyit; as alswa with pouer to thame to inquire the names suspectit and dilaitit of witchecraft, or seikand responssis or help of thame, and of all strang vagaboundis and idill beggaris, to examinat thame and committ thame to prisone, irnis or stokkis, and to caus prisonis, irnis and stokkis be maid to that effect at all placeis neidfull; to move the puir and impotent to be providit for within thair awne parrochynnis; to assist the commissioner or commissioneris of the General Assembley, and the prisbbitereis, quhair thay ar wele constitute, in thair proceding to deprivatioun of all personis non-resident or unworthie that hes bene providit in title to beneficeis of cure undir prelaceis sen his Hienes coronatioun, according to the Actis of Parliament maid thairenent; and to that effect to call befoir thame be thair awne preceptis all personis neidfull to be callit, summound, inquirit, examinat upoun the heidis, pointis and articlis foirsaidis or ony of thame, or to apprehend and putt in prisone sic as salbe thocht meit in the commoun prisone of the heid burgh of the shire or nixt burgh and place convenient'; court or courts to the effect abovespecified to hold assizes, to summon, choose and cause be sworn, and generally to do all other things necessary to the execution of the premisses. The said commissions shall endure till 1st November next, and farther till the said commissioners be altered or discharged.

Privy council order revoking standing commissions, and establishing privy council control of prosecutions, 12 August 1597 (RPCS v 409–10)

Discharge of commissions of justiciary against witches.

Forsamekle as the Kingis Majestie hes gevin and grantit commissionis to sindrie noblemen, baronis, schireffis, stewartis, baillies, provestis and baillies of burrowis and townis, and uthiris particulair personis, for apprehensioun, tryale and punishement of quhatsumevir personis, dwelling, hanting and resorting within the boundis of their landis, heritage and jurisdictionis, dilaitit or suspect gilty of witchecraft, sorcerie, inchantment, or sic devilishe practizeis, quhairwith the haill land is defyllit; and albeit in that his Majesteis maist eirnist purpois his Heynes intendis to perseveir till that maist odious and abhominable cryme be tryit and punisheit with all extremitie; yit, undirstanding, be the complaint of divers his Heynes lieges, that grite dangeir may enswe to honnest and famous personis gif commissionis grantit to particulair men, beiring particulairis aganis thame, or to ony nowmer of commissionaris conjunctlie and severalie (quhilk in effect gevis pouer to ane or tua or thame to proceid), sall stand and be authorized; thairfoir necessair it is that the saidis commisionis be haillelie revoikit, annullit, and in all tyme cuming dischargeit, lyke as his Majestie be thir presentis revokis, annulis and simpliciter dischargeis the same, haill exercise, jurisdiction and executioun thairof; declairing notwithstanding that, gif ony of the saidis commissionaris or uthiris his Heynes liegis, of gude rank for zeale of justice and haitrent of the said detestable cryme, desyirs commissionis and pouer to be given to thame of new to the effect foirsaid, the same salbe grantit to thame and sum baronis and ministeris unsuspect, to the noumer of three or foure conjunctlie at the fewest. And, considering heirwithall that the consultaris with the saidis wicked and divilishe abusaris, and sutearis of helth and responssis frome thame, ar na lesse gilty, be the lawis of God and man, then thay actuall witcheis and wicked personis, and meritis with thame indifferent and equall punishement, for the better purgeing of the land of that abhominable cryme, procureing the wraith of God without condigne punishement: thairfoir, ordanis letters to be direct to mak publicatioun heirof be oppin proclamatioun at the mercat croceis of the heid burrowis of this realme and uthiris placeis neidfull, quhairthrouch nane pretend ignorance of the same, and to command and charge all and sindrie noblemen, baronis, shereffis, stewartis, baillies, provestis and baillies of burrowis and townis, and utheris personis quhatsumevir, cled with commissioun obtenit particularlie in maner foirsaid, that thay on nawayes tak upoun hand to proceid forder be vertew thairof, certifeing thame that dois in the contrair, and ather proceidis thairby to the executioun of personis to the deid or melling with thair guidis or geir, that the samin salbe slauchteris upoun foirthocht felloun and spuilye respective; and, forder, to command and charge all personis haveing lauchfull pouer and commissioun to proceid in the saidis materis, or that sall obtene ony in tyme cuming for apprehensioun and punishement of witcheis within their awne boundis and jurisdictionis, to extract amd mak ane note of samekle of thair depositionis as concernis or may onywayes concerne the consultaris with the same witcheis or abusaris, and to bring and reporte the same to his Majestie withink xv dayis eftir the samin sall cum to thair knaulege, that ordour may be takin for tryale and punishment of the saidis consultaris, according to the lawis of this realme and thair deserving: certifeing thame that failyeis to mak the said dew advertisment that not onlie thay sall tyne and amit that pairt of the saidis witcheis guidis and geir that micht pertene to thame be vertew of the saidis commissionis, bot lykwayes salbe realie punist in thair personis and guidis, with all rigour, in example of utheris.

BIBLIOGRAPHY

———

In the case of books published before 1800 only place of publication and date are given; and unless otherwise indicated the place of publication is London.

Acts of the General Assemblies (1840) *Acts and Proceedings of the General Assemblies of the Kirk of Scotland, 1560–1618*, ed. T. Thomson, 3 vols, vol.2, 1578–92, Edinburgh: Bannatyne Club.

Acts of the Parliaments (1814) *The Acts of the Parliaments of Scotland 1424–1567*, vol. 2, ed. Thomas Thomson *et al.*, 12 vols, 1814–75, Edinburgh: Record Commission.

Ady, Thomas (1656) *A Candle in the Dark, or a Treatise Concerning the Nature of Witches and Witchcraft.*

Agrippa, Henricus Cornelius Agrippa ab Nettesheim (1567) *De Occulta Philosophia Libri III*, Paris.

—— (1569) *Vanitie and uncertaintie of artes and sciences*, trans. James Sanford.

Akrigg, G. P. V. (1975) 'The Literary Achievement of King James I', *University of Toronto Quarterly* 44: 115–29.

—— (ed.) (1984) *Letters of King James VI and I*, Berkeley and London: University of California Press.

Amussen, Susan Dwyer (1988) *An Ordered Society: Gender and Class in Early Modern England*, Oxford: Basil Blackwell.

Anglo, Sydney (ed.) (1977) *The Damned Art: Essays in the Literature of Witchcraft*, London, Henley and Boston: Routledge and Kegan Paul.

Ankarloo, Bengt (1993) 'Sweden: The Mass Burnings (1668–76)', in Bengt Ankarloo and Gustav Henningsen (eds), *Early Modern European Witchcraft: Centres and Peripheries*, Oxford: Clarendon, 285–317.

Ankarloo, Bengt and Henningsen, Gustav (eds) (1993) *Early Modern European Witchcraft: Centres and Peripheries*, Oxford: Clarendon Press.

Apted, M. R. and Robertson W. N. (1974–5) 'Four "Drolleries" from the Painted Ceiling formerly at Prestongrange, East Lothian', *Proceedings of the Society of Antiquaries of Scotland* 106: 158–60.

Apuleius, Lucius (1935) *The Golden Ass, Being the Metamorphoses of Lucius Apuleius* (Loeb Classical Library), trans. W. Adlington (1566), rev. S. Gaselee, London: William Heinemann; New York: G. P. Putnam's Sons.

Armstrong, C. J. R. (1976) 'The Dialectical Road to Truth: The Dialogue', in Peter Sharratt (ed.), *French Renaissance Studies 1540–70: Humanism and the Encyclopaedia*, Edinburgh: Edinburgh University Press.

Arnot, Hugo (1785) *A Collection and Abridgement of Celebrated Criminal Trials in Scotland, from AD 1536 to 1784*, Edinburgh: William Smellie.

Bale, John (1574) *The Pageant of Popes, Contayninge the Lyves of All the Bishops of Rome*.

Baroja, Julio Caro (1965) *The World of the Witches*, trans. O. N. V. Glendinning, Chicago and London: University of Chicago Press.

Barry, J., Hester, M. and Roberts, G. (eds) (1996) *Witchcraft in Early Modern Europe: Studies in Culture and Belief* (Past and Present Publications), Cambridge: Cambridge University Press.

Bath, Michael (1993) 'Applied Emblematics in Scotland: Painted Ceilings 1550–1650', *Emblematica: an Interdisciplinary Journal for Emblem Studies* 7: 1–52.

Bernard, Richard (1629) *A Guide to Grand-Jury Men*, 2nd edn.

Bingham, C. (1968) *The Making of a King: The Early Years of James VI and I*, London: Collins.

Birrel, Robert (1798) *Diary*, in J. G. Dalyell (ed.), *Fragments of Scotish* [sic] *History*, Edinburgh: Constable.

Black, George F. (1938) *A Calendar of Cases of Witchcraft in Scotland 1510–1727*, New York: New York Public Library; reprinted Arno Press Inc., 1971.

—— (1962) *The Surnames of Scotland: Their Origin, Meaning and History*, New York: New York Public Library; reprint of 1946 edition.

Blayney, Peter W. M. (1997) 'The Publication of Playbooks', in John D. Cox and David Scott Kastan (eds), *A New History of Early English Drama*, New York: Columbia University Press, 383–422.

Bodin, Jean (1580) *De la Demonomanie des Sorciers*, Paris.

Boguet, Henri (1608) *Discours des Sorciers*, 3rd edn, Lyon.

—— (1929) *An Examen of Witches* [*Discours des Sorciers*], trans. E. Allen Ashwin, ed. Montague Summers, London: John Rodker.

Booke of the Universall Kirk (1839) *The Booke of the Universall Kirk of Scotland*, ed. A. Peterkin, Edinburgh: Edinburgh Printing and Publishing Co.

Border Papers (1894–6) *The Border Papers: Calendar of Letters and Papers Relating to the Affairs of the Borders of England and Scotland*, ed. Joseph Bain, 2 vols, Edinburgh: H. M. General Register House.

Brauner, Sigrid (1995) *Fearless Wives and Frightened Shrews: The Construction of the Witch in Early Modern Germany*, Amherst: University of Massachusetts Press.

Briggs, Robin (1989) *Communities of Belief: Cultural and Social Tensions in Early Modern France*, Oxford: Clarendon Press.

—— (1996a) *Witches and Neighbours: The Social and Cultural Context of European Witchcraft*, London: HarperCollins.

—— (1996b) '"Many Reasons Why": Witchcraft and the Problem of Multiple Explanation', in J. Barry, M. Hester and G. Roberts (eds), *Witchcraft in Early Modern Europe: Studies in Culture and Belief*, Cambridge: Cambridge University Press, 49–63.

Brook, Alexander J. S. (1891) 'Notice of a Pair of Thumbikins', *Proceedings of the Society of Antiquaries of Scotland* 25: 463–71.

Brown, Keith M. (1986) *Bloodfeud in Scotland 1573–1625: Violence, Justice and Politics in an Early Modern Society*, Edinburgh: John Donald.

—— (1987) 'The Price of Friendship: The "Well Affected" and English Economic Clientage in Scotland Before 1603', in Roger A. Mason (ed.), *Scotland and England 1286–1815*, Edinburgh: John Donald, 139–62.

—— (1991) 'The Nobility of Jacobean Scotland 1567–1625', in Jenny Wormald (ed.), *Scotland Revisited*, London: Collins and Brown, 61–72.

Brown, P. Hume (ed.) (1891) *Early Travellers in Scotland*, Edinburgh: David Douglas.

Brownlow, F. W. (1993) *Shakespeare, Harsnett and the Devils of Denham*, London and Toronto: University of Delaware Press.

Bruce, Robert (1591) *Sermons Preached in the Kirk of Edinburgh*, Edinburgh.

Brunton, George and Haig, David (1832) *An Historical Account of the Senators of the College of Justice from its Institution in MDXXXII*, Edinburgh: Thomas Clark.

Bullough, Geoffrey (1957–75) *Narrative and Dramatic Sources of Shakespeare*, 8 vols, London: Routledge and Kegan Paul; New York: Columbia University Press.

Burghartz, Susanna (1988) 'The Equation of Women and Witches: A Case Study of Witchcraft Trials in Lucerne and Lausanne in the Fifteenth and Sixteenth Centuries', in Richard J. Evans (ed.), *The German Underworld: Deviants and Outcasts in German History*, London and New York: Routledge, 57–74.

Burke, Peter (1977) 'Witchcraft and Magic in Renaissance Italy: Gianfrancesco Pico and his *Strix*', in S. Anglo (ed.), *The Damned Art: Essays in the Literature of Witchcraft*, London, Henley and Boston: Routledge and Kegan Paul, 32–52.

—— (1978) *Popular Culture in Early Modern Europe*, London, Temple Smith.

—— (1982) 'A Question of Acculturation?', in *Scienze, Credenze Occulte, Livelli Di Cultura*, Florence: Leo S. Olschki, 197–204.

—— (1989) 'The Renaissance Dialogue', *Renaissance Studies* 3: 1–12.

Burrell, S. A. (1958) 'The Covenant Idea as a Revolutionary Symbol: Scotland, 1596–1637', *Church History* 27: 338–50.

Calderwood, David (1842–9) *The History of the Kirk of Scotland*, ed. Thomas Thomson, 8 vols, Edinburgh: Wodrow Society.

Cameron, Nigel M. de S. (ed.) (1993) *Dictionary of Scottish Church History and Theology*, Edinburgh: T. and T. Clark.

Carlisle, Nicholas (1813) *A Topographical Dictionary of Scotland, and of the Islands in the British Seas*, 2 vols, London: G. and W. Nicol.

Carmichael, James (1587) *Grammaticae Latinae, de Etymologia, Liber Secundus*, Cambridge.

—— (1618) *Rudimenta Grammatices, in Gratiam Juventutis Scoticae Conscripta*, Edinburgh.

—— (1957) *The James Carmichaell [sic] Collection of Proverbs in Scots*, ed. M. L. Anderson, Edinburgh: Edinburgh University Press.

Carte Monialium (1847) *Carte Monialium De Northberwic, Prioratus Cisterciensis B. Marie De Northberwic, Munimenta Vetusta Que Supersunt*, Edinburgh: Bannatyne Club.

Chambers, R. (1859) *Domestic Annals of Scotland from the Reformation to the Revolution*, 2 vols, 2nd edn, Edinburgh and London: W. and R. Chambers.

Clark, Stuart (1977) 'King James's *Daemonologie*: Witchcraft and Kingship', in S. Anglo (ed.), *The Damned Art: Essays in the Literature of Witchcraft*, London, Henley and Boston: Routledge and Kegan Paul, 156–81.

—— (1980) 'Inversion, Misrule and the Meaning of Witchcraft', *Past and Present* 87: 98–127.

—— (1993) 'Protestant Demonology: Sin, Superstition, and Society (c.1520–c.1630)', in Bengt Ankarloo and Gustav Henningsen (eds), *Early Modern European Witchcraft: Centres and Peripheries*, Oxford: Clarendon Press, 45–81.

—— (1997) *Thinking with Demons: The Idea of Witchcraft in Early Modern Europe*, Oxford: Clarendon Press.

Clark, Stuart and Morgan, P. T. J. (1976) 'Religion and Magic in Elizabethan Wales: Robert Holland's Dialogue on Witchcraft', *Journal of Ecclesiastical History* 27: 31–46.

Cobbett, W. and Howell, T. B. *et al.* (eds) (1809–26) *A Complete Collection of State Trials*, 33 vols, London: R. Bagshaw, Longman and Co.

Cohn, Norman (1975) *Europe's Inner Demons*, London: Chatto.

Cooper, J. (1902) 'Four Scottish Coronations Since the Reformation', *Transactions of the Aberdeen Ecclesiological Society*, Aberdeen.

Cooper, Thomas (1617) *The Mystery of Witch-craft. Discovering the Truth, Nature, Occasions, Growth and Power thereof.*

Cotta, John (1616) *The Triall of Witch-craft, Shewing the True and Right Methode of the Discouery*, London.

Coulton, G. G. (1933) *Scottish Abbeys and Social Life*, Cambridge: Cambridge University Press.

Cowan, Edward J. (1983) 'The Darker Vision of the Scottish Renaissance: The Devil and Francis Stewart', in Ian B. Cowan and Duncan Shaw (eds), *The Renaissance and Reformation in Scotland: Essays in Honour of Gordon Donaldson*, Edinburgh: Scottish Academic Press, 125–40.

Cowan, Ian B. (ed.) (1960) *Blast and Counterblast: Contemporary Writings on the Scottish Reformation*, Edinburgh: Saltire Society.

—— (1978) *Regional Aspects of the Scottish Reformation*, London: Historical Association.

—— (1982) *The Scottish Reformation: Church and Society in Sixteenth Century Scotland*, London: Weidenfeld and Nicolson.

Cowan, Ian B. and Easson, David E. (1976) *Medieval Religious Houses, Scotland*, 2nd edn, London and New York: Longman.

Cowan, Ian B. and Shaw, Duncan (eds) (1983) *The Renaissance and Reformation in Scotland: Essays in Honour of Gordon Donaldson*, Edinburgh: Scottish Academic Press.

Cox, Virginia (ed.) (1992) *Renaissance Dialogue: Literary Dialogue in its Social and Political Contexts, Castiglione to Galileo*, Cambridge: Cambridge University Press.

Coxe, Francis (1561) *A Short Treatise Declaringe the Detestable Wickednesse, of Magicall Sciences.*

Craigie, James (ed.) (1982) James VI, *Minor Prose Works: 'Daemonologie', 'The True Lawe of Free Monarchies', 'A Counterblaste to Tobacco', 'A Declaration of Sports'*, Edinburgh: Scottish Text Society.

CSD (1985) *A Concise Scots Dictionary*, ed. Mairi Robinson, Aberdeen: Aberdeen University Press.

CSPS x (1936) *Calendar of the State Papers Relating to Scotland and Mary Queen of Scots, 1547–1603*, ed. W. K. Boyd and H. W. Meikle, vol. 10, 1589–1593, Edinburgh: H. M. Stationery Office.

CSPS xi (1936) *Calendar of the State Papers Relating to Scotland and Mary Queen of Scots, 1547–1603*, ed. Annie I. Cameron, vol. 11, 1593–1595, Edinburgh: H. M. Stationery Office.

Dalyell, John Graham (1834) *The Darker Superstitions of Scotland Illustrated from History and Practice*, Edinburgh: Waugh and Innes.

Daneau, Lambert (1574) *De Veneficis, Quos Olim Sortilegos, Nunc Autem Vulgo Sortiarios Vocant*, Geneva.

—— (1575) *A Dialogue of Witches, in Foretime Named Lot-tellers, and Now Commonly Called Sorcerers*.

Davis, N. Z. (1975) *Society and Culture in Early Modern France*, London: Duckworth.

—— (1988) *Fiction in the Archives: Pardon Tales and their Tellers in Sixteenth-century France*, Cambridge: Polity Press.

Deakins, Roger (1980) 'The Tudor Prose Dialogue: Genre and Anti-Genre', *Studies in English Literature* 20: 5–23.

DeRicci, Seymour (1935) *Census of Medieval and Renaissance Manuscripts in the United States and Canada*, 3 vols, New York: H. W. Wilson Co.

Dickinson, W. Croft (1958) 'The High Court of Justiciary', in G. C. H. Paton (ed.), *An Introduction to Scottish Legal History*, (Stair Society vol. 20) Edinburgh: Stair Society, 408–12.

Dickson, R. and Edmond, J. P. (1890) *Annals of Scottish Printing, From the Introduction of the Art in 1507 to the Beginning of the Seventeenth Century*, Cambridge: Macmillan and Bowes.

DNB (1885–) *Dictionary of National Biography*, ed. Leslie Stephen and Sidney Lee, 63 vols, London: Smith Elder and Co.

Dolan, Frances E. (1994) *Dangerous Familiars: Representations of Domestic Crime in England, 1550–1700*, Ithaca and London: Cornell University Press.

Dömötör, Tekla (1980) 'The Cunning Folk in English and Hungarian Witch Trials', in Venetia J. Newall (ed.), *Folklore Studies in the Twentieth Century*, Woodbridge: Brewer, 183–87.

Donaldson, Gordon (1952) 'The Cistercian Priory of St Mary, Haddington', *Transactions of the East Lothian Antiquarian and Field Naturalists' Society* 5: 2–24.

—— (1960a) 'Scottish Presbyterian Exiles in England, 1584–8', *Records of the Scottish Church History Society* 14: 67–80.

—— (1960b) *The Scottish Reformation*, Cambridge: Cambridge University Press.

—— (1965) *Scotland: James V to James VII*, Edinburgh and London: Oliver and Boyd.

—— (1976) 'The Legal Profession in Scottish Society in the Sixteenth and Seventeenth Centuries', *Juridical Review* n.s. 21: 1–19.

—— (1983) *All the Queen's Men: Power and Politics in Mary Stewart's Scotland*, London: Batsford.

Donaldson, Gordon and Morpeth, Robert S. (1973) *Who's Who in Scottish History*, Oxford: Basil Blackwell.

DOST (1931–90) *Dictionary of the Older Scottish Tongue*, ed. W. A. Craigie, A. J. Aitken *et al.*, vols 1–7, Chicago: University of Chicago Press; Oxford: Oxford University Press.

Duffy, Eamon (1992) *The Stripping of the Altars: Traditional Religion in England c.1400–c.1580*, New Haven and London: Yale University Press.

Dunlap, Rhodes (1975) 'King James and Some Witches: The Date and Text of the *Daemonologie*', *Philological Quarterly* 54: 40–6.

Durkan, J. (1962) 'Care of the Poor: Pre-Reformation Hospitals', in David McRoberts (ed.), *Essays on the Scottish Reformation, 1513–1625*, Glasgow: Burns, 116–29.

Dwyer, John, Mason, R. A., and Murdoch, A. (eds) (1982) *New Perspectives on the Politics and Culture of Early Modern Scotland*, Edinburgh: John Donald.

Early Maps of Scotland (1973–83) *The Early Maps of Scotland to 1850*, ed. D. G. Moir, 3rd edn, 2 vols, Edinburgh: Royal Scottish Geographical Society.

Early Views (1919) *The Early Views and Maps of Edinburgh 1544–1852*, Edinburgh: Royal Scottish Geographical Society.

Easson, D. E. (1940–1) 'The Nunneries of Medieval Scotland', *Scottish Ecclesiological Society Transactions* 13: 22–38.

—— (1948) 'The Collegiate Churches of East Lothian', *Transactions of the East Lothian Antiquarian and Field Naturalists' Society* 4: 11–18.

Edgar, J. (1893) *History of Early Scottish Education* Edinburgh: J. Thin.

English Faust Book (1994) *The English Faust Book: A Critical Edition based on the Text of 1592*, ed. John Henry Jones, Cambridge: Cambridge University Press.

Erasmus, Desiderius (1979) *The Praise of Folly*, trans. Clarence H. Miller, New Haven and London: Yale University Press.

Ewen, C. L'Estrange (ed.) (1929) *Witch Hunting and Witch Trials*, London: Kegan Paul, Trench, Trubner; repr. London: Muller, 1971.

—— (1933) *Witchcraft and Demomaniam*, London: Heath Cranton.

Exchequer Rolls (1903) *The Exchequer Rolls of Scotland*, ed. George P. McNeill, 23 vols, Edinburgh, 1878–1908, vol. 22, AD 1589–1594, Edinburgh: H. M. General Register House.

Ferguson, John (1899) 'Bibliographical Notes on the Witchcraft Literature of Scotland', *Publications of the Edinburgh Bibliographical Society*, 3: 37–119.

—— (1924) *Bibliographical Notes on the Treatises De Occulta Philosophia and De Incertitudine et Vanitate Scientiarum of Cornelius Agrippa*, Edinburgh: reprinted from the Publications of the Edinburgh Bibliographical Society.

Ferrier, Walter M. (1980) *The North Berwick Story*, North Berwick: Royal Burgh of North Berwick Community Council.

Filmer, Robert (1653) *An Advertisement to the Jury-men of England, Touching Witches*.

First Book of Discipline (1972) *The First Book of Discipline*, ed. James K. Cameron, Edinburgh: Saint Andrew Press.

Fleming, D. H. (1910) *The Reformation in Scotland: Causes, Characteristics, Consequences*, London: Hodder and Stoughton.

Flint, Valerie (1991) *The Rise of Magic in Early Medieval Europe*, Oxford: Clarendon Press.

Flower, Margaret (1619) *The Wonderful Discoverie of the Witchcrafts of Margaret and Phillippa Flower, Daughters of Joan Flower*.

Folena, Lucia (1989) 'Figures of Violence: Philologists, Witches, and Stalinistas', in Nancy Armstrong and Leonard Tennenhouse (eds), *The Violence of Representation: Literature and the History of Violence*, London: Routledge, 219–38.

Forbes, Thomas R. (1935) 'The Social History of the Caul', *Yale Journal of Biology and Medicine* 25: 503–5.

Foucault, Michel (1979) *Discipline and Punish: The Birth of the Prison*, trans. Alan Sheridan, Harmondsworth: Penguin.

French, Peter (1972) *John Dee: The World of an Elizabethan Magus*, London, Boston, Melbourne and Henley: Routledge and Kegan Paul.

Garrett, C. (1977) 'Witches and Cunning Folk in the Old Regime', in Jacques Beauroy *et al.* (eds), *Popular Culture in France from the Old Regime to the Twentieth Century*: *The Wolf and the Lamb*, Saratoga, California: Anma Libri, 53–64.

Gaskill, M. (1996) 'Witchcraft in Early Modern Kent: Stereotypes and the Background to Accusations', in J. Barry, M. Hester and G. Roberts (eds), *Witchcraft in Early Modern Europe: Studies in Culture and Belief*, Cambridge: Cambridge University Press, 257–87.

—— (1998) 'Reporting Murder: Fiction in the Archives in Early Modern England', *Social History* 23: 1–30.

Gatrell, V. A. C., Lenman, Bruce, and Parker, Geoffrey (eds) (1980) *Crime and the Law: The Social History of Crime in Western Europe since 1500*, London: Europa.

Gibson, Marion (1999) *Reading Witchcraft: Stories of Early English Witches*, London: Routledge.

Gifford, George (1587) *A Discourse of the Subtill Practises of Devilles by Witches and Sorcerers*.

—— (1842) *A Dialogue Concerning Witches and Witchcrafts*, London: Percy Society, vol. 8.

Ginzburg, Carlo (1983) *The Night Battles: Witchcraft and Agrarian Cults in the Sixteenth and Seventeenth Centuries*, trans. John and Anne Tedeschi, London, Melbourne and Henley: Routledge and Kegan Paul.

—— (1984) 'The Witches' Sabbat: Popular Cult or Inquisitorial Stereotype?', in Steven L. Kaplan (ed.), *Understanding Popular Culture: Europe from the Middle Ages to the Nineteenth Century*, Berlin, New York and Amsterdam: Mouton Publishers, 39–51.

—— (1990) *Myths, Emblems, Clues*, trans. John and Anne Tedeschi, London, Sydney, Auckland, Johannesburg: Hutchinson Radius.

—— (1993) 'Deciphering the Sabbath', in Bengt Ankarloo and Gustav Henningsen (eds), *Early Modern European Witchcraft: Centres and Peripheries*, Oxford: Clarendon Press, 121–37.

Goldberg, Jonathan (1986) 'Fatherly Authority: The Politics of Stuart Family Images', in Margaret W. Ferguson, Maureen Quilligan and Nancy J. Vickers (eds), *Rewriting the Renaissance: The Discourses of Sexual Difference in Early Modern Europe*, Chicago and London: Chicago University Press, 3–32.

Gougaud, L. (O. S. B.) (1914) 'La Danse dans les Eglises', *Revue d'Histoire Ecclesiastique* 15: 5–22, 229–45.

Gouldesbrough, Peter (compiler) (1985) *Formulary of Old Scots Legal Documents*, Edinburgh: Stair Society.

Grant, I. F. (1930) *The Social and Economic Development of Scotland Before 1603*, Edinburgh: Oliver and Boyd.

Grant, James (1876) *History of the Burgh and Parish Schools of Scotland*, London and Glasgow: Collins.

Gray, Douglas (1974) 'Notes on Some Middle English Charms', in *Chaucer and Middle English Studies: in Honour of Rossell Hope Robbins*, London: George Allan and Unwin, 56–71.

Green, Charles E. (1907) *East Lothian*, Edinburgh and London: William Green and Sons.

Greenblatt, Stephen (ed.) (1988) *Representing the English Renaissance*, Berkeley, Los Angeles and London: University of California Press.

Greene, Robert (1964) *Friar Bacon and Friar Bungay*, ed. D. Seltzer (Regents Renaissance Drama Series), London: Edward Arnold.

Gregory, Annabel (1991) 'Witchcraft, Politics and "Good Neighbourhood"', *Past and Present* 133: 31–66.

Guazzo, F. M. (1929) *Compendium Maleficarum*, ed. M. Summers, trans. E. A. Ashwin, London: John Rodker.

—— (1988) *Compendium Maleficarum*, ed. Montague Summers, trans. E. Allen Ashwin, New York: Dover Books; London: Constable.

Halliwell, J. O. (ed.) (1842) *The Private Diary of Dr John Dee*, London: Camden Society, no. 19.

Hemmingsen, Niels (1575) *Admonitio de Superstitionibus Magicis Vitandis*, Copenhagen.

Henningsen, Gustav (1982) 'Witchcraft in Denmark', *Folklore* 93: 131–7.

—— (1993) '"The Ladies from Outside": An Archaic Pattern of the Witches' Sabbath', in Bengt Ankarloo and Gustav Henningsen (eds), *Early Modern European Witchcraft: Centres and Peripheries*, Oxford: Clarendon, 191–215.

Hirst, Paul and Woolley, Penny (1982) *Social Relations and Human Attributes*, London: Tavistock.

Historie of James the Sext (1825) *The Historie and Life of King James the Sext, Being an Account of the Affairs of Scotland from the Year 1566 to the Year 1596*, ed. Thomas Thomson, Edinburgh: Bannatyne Club.

Holland, Henry (1590) *A Treatise Against Witchcraft; or A Dialogue Wherein the Greatest Doubts Concerning that Sinne, Are Briefly Answered*, Cambridge.

Holmes, Clive (1984) 'Popular Culture: Witches, Magistrates and Divines in Early Modern England', in Steven L. Kaplan (ed.), *Understanding Popular Culture: Europe from the Middle Ages to the Nineteenth Century*, Berlin, New York and Amsterdam: Mouton Publishers, 85–111.

—— (1993) 'Women: Witnesses and Witches', *Past and Present* 140: 45–78.

Hopkins, Matthew (1647) *The Discovery of Witches*.

Horsley, Richard A. (1979a) 'Who Were the Witches? The Social Roles of the Accused in the European Witch Trials', *Journal of Interdisciplinary History* 9: 689–715.

—— (1979b) 'Further Reflections on Witchcraft and European Folk Religion', *History of Religions* 19: 71–95.

Houston, R. A. (1989) 'Women in the Economy and Society', in R. A. Houston and I. D. Whyte (eds), *Scottish Society 1500–1800*, Cambridge: Cambridge University Press, 118–47.

Houston, R. A. and Whyte, I. D. (eds) (1989) *Scottish Society 1500–1800*, Cambridge: Cambridge University Press.

Hume, David (1797) *Commentaries on the Law of Scotland, Respecting the Description and Punishment of Crimes*, 2 vols, Edinburgh.

Hume, David, of Godscroft (1644) *The History of the Houses of Douglas and Angus*, Edinburgh: E. Tyler.

Hutton, Ronald (1995) 'The English Reformation and the Evidence of Folklore', *Past and Present* 148: 89–116.

Inch, Isobel (1855) *Trial, Confession, and Execution of Isobel Inch, John Stewart, Margaret Barclay and Isobel Crawford, for Witchcraft at Irvine, Anno 1618*, Ardrossan and Saltcoats: A. Guthrie.

Isidore of Seville (1911) *Isidori Hispalensis Episcopi Etymologiarum Sive Originum Libri XX*, 2 vols, Oxford: Oxford Library.

James VI and I (1597) *Daemonologie, in forme of a dialogue, diuided into three bookes*, Edinburgh.

—— (1902) *Lusus Regius, Being Poems and Other Pieces by King James the First*, ed. Robert S. Rait, London: Constable.

—— (1911) *New Poems*, ed. Allan F. Westcott, New York: Colombia University Press.

—— (1918) *The Political Works of James I*, vol. 1, ed. C. H. McIlwain, Cambridge, Mass.: Harvard University Press; London: Oxford University Press.

—— (1955–8) *The Poems* (Scottish Text Society), ed. James Craigie, 2 vols, Edinburgh and London: William Blackwood.

—— (1994) *Political Writings*, ed. Johann P. Sommerville, Cambridge: Cambridge University Press.

Johansen, Jens Christian V. (1993) 'Denmark: The Sociology of Accusations', in Bengt Ankarloo and Gustav Henningsen (eds), *Early Modern European Witchcraft: Centres and Peripheries*, Oxford: Clarendon, 339–65.

Jones, John Henry (1994) *The English Faust Book: A Critical Edition*, Cambridge: Cambridge University Press.

Jones, Thomas (1956) *Rhyddiath Gymraeg, 1547–1618*, Cardiff.

Jones–Davies, M. T. (ed.) (1984) *Le Dialogue au Temps de la Renaissance*, Paris: Jean Touzot.

Jonson, Ben (1925–52) *Ben Jonson*, ed. C. H. Herford, Percy and Evelyn Simpson, 11 vols, Oxford: Clarendon Press.

—— (1969) *The Complete Masques* (The Yale Ben Jonson), ed. Stephen Orgel, New Haven and London: Yale University Press.

The Joyfull Receiving (1590) *The Joyfull Receiving of James the Sixt of that Name King of Scotland, and Queene Anne his Wife, into the Townes of Lyeth and Edenborough the First Daie of May last part, 1590. Together with the Triumphs Shewed before the Coronation of the said Scottish Queene*, London.

Kaplan, Steven L. (ed.) (1984) *Understanding Popular Culture: Europe from the Middle Ages to the Nineteenth Century*, Berlin, New York and Amsterdam: Mouton Publishers.

Kieckhefer, Richard (1976) *European Witch Trials: Their Foundations in Popular and Learned Culture, 1300–1500*, London and Henley: Routledge and Kegan Paul.

—— (1990) *Magic in the Middle Ages*, Cambridge: Cambridge University Press.

Kirk, James (ed.) (1977) *The Records of the Synod of Lothian and Tweeddale, 1589–1596, 1640–1649*, Edinburgh: Stair Society.

—— (1980) '"The Polities of the Best Reformed Kirks": Scottish Achievements and English Aspirations in Church Government after the Reformation', *Scottish Historical Review* 59: 22–53.

—— (1983) 'Royal and Lay Patronage in the Jacobean Kirk 1572–1600', in Norman MacDougall (ed.), *Church, Politics and Society: Scotland 1408–1929*, Edinburgh: John Donald.

—— (1989) *Patterns of Reform: Continuity and Change in the Reformation Kirk*, Edinburgh: T. and T. Clark.

—— (ed.) (1995) *The Books of Assumption of the Thirds of Benefices: Scottish Ecclesiastical Rentals at the Reformation* (Records of Social and Economic History, n.s. 21), Oxford: Published for the British Academy by Oxford University Press.

Kirschbaum, Engelbert (1968–76) *Lexikon der Christlichen Ikonographie*, 8 vols, Freiburg: Herder.

Kittredge, G. L. (1912) *English Witchcraft and James the First* (Studies in the History of Religions), New York: Macmillan.
—— (1929) *Witchcraft in Old and New England*, Cambridge, Mass.: Harvard University Press.
Klaniczay, Gabor (1993) 'Hungary: The Accusations and the Universe of Popular Magic', in Bengt Ankarloo and Gustav Henningsen (eds), *Early Modern European Witchcraft: Centres and Peripheries*, Oxford: Clarendon, 219–55.
Kramer, Heinrich and Sprenger, James (1971) *Malleus Maleficarum*, trans. Montague Summers, London: Arrow.
Lake, Peter (1989) 'Anti-Popery: The Structure of a Prejudice', in Richard Cust and Ann Hughes (eds) *Conflict in Early Stuart England*, Harlow: Longman, 72–106.
Langbein, John H. (1977) *Torture and the Law of Proof: Europe and England in the Ancien Régime*, Chicago and London: University of Chicago Press.
Larner, Christina (neé Ross) (1962) 'Scottish Demonology in the Sixteenth and Seventeenth Centuries and its Theological Background', Ph.D. thesis, University of Edinburgh.
—— (1973) 'James VI and I and Witchcraft', in A. G. R. Smith (ed.), *The Reign of James VI and I*, London and Basingstoke: Macmillan, 74–90.
—— (1975) 'Anne of Denmark, Queen of Scotland: a Demonological Dowry?', *Glasgow University Gazette* June 1975: 1–2.
—— (1981) *Enemies of God: The Witch-hunt in Scotland* London: Chatto and Windus.
—— (1984) *Witchcraft and Religion: The Politics of Popular Belief*, ed. Alan Macfarlane, Oxford: Basil Blackwell.
Larner, C., and Lee, C. H. and McLachlan, Hugh V. (1977) *A Source-book of Scottish Witchcraft*, Glasgow: University of Glasgow, Department of Sociology.
Latham, Jacqueline (1975) '*The Tempest* and King James's *Daemonologie*', *Shakespeare Survey* 28: 117–23.
Lavater , Ludwig (1929) *Of Ghostes and Spirites Walking by Nyght* [1572], ed. J. Dover Wilson and M. Yardley, Oxford: Oxford University Press.
Law, T. G. (1893) *Documents Illustrating Catholic Policy in the Reign of James VI*, Edinburgh: Scottish History Society, vol. 15.
Lee Jr., Maurice (1959) *John Maitland of Thirlestane and the Foundation of the Stewart Despotism in Scotland*, Princeton: Princeton University Press.
—— (1974) 'James VI and the Revival of Episcopacy in Scotland: 1596–1600', *Church History* 43: 50–64.
—— (1980) *Government by Pen: Scotland under James VI and I*, Urbana: University of Illinois Press.
—— (1983) 'King James's Popish Chancellor', in Ian B. Cowan and Duncan Shaw (eds), *The Renaissance and Reformation in Scotland: Essays in Honour of Gordon Donaldson*, Edinburgh: Scottish Academic Press, 170–82.
—— (1990) *Great Britain's Solomon: James VI and I in his Three Kingdoms*, Urbana: University of Illinois Press.
Legge, F. (1891) 'Witchcraft in Scotland', *The Scottish Review* 18: 257–88.
Le Loyer, Pierre (1586) *Quatre Livres des Spectres ou Apparitions et Visions d'Esprits, Anges et Demons*, Angers.
Leith, William Forbes (ed.) (1885) *Narratives of Scottish Catholics under Mary Stuart and James VI*, Edinburgh: William Paterson.
Leneman, Leah (ed.) (1988) *Perspectives in Scottish Social History: Essays in Honour of*

Rosalind Mitchison, Aberdeen: Aberdeen University Press.

Lenman, Bruce (1984) 'The Limits of Godly Discipline in the Early Modern Period with Particular Reference to England and Scotland', in Kaspar von Greyerz (ed.), *Religion and Society in Early Modern Europe 1500–1800*, London: German Historical Institute, and George Allen and Unwin, 124–45.

Letters and Papers, Foreign and Domestic, of the Reign of Henry VIII, ed. J. S. Brewer *et al.*, 21 vols, London: Longman and Co., 1862–1932.

Letters to King James the Sixth (1835) *Letters to King James the Sixth*, Edinburgh: Maitland Club.

Leuschner, Kristin (1995) *Creating the 'Known True Story': Sixteenth- and Seventeenth-Century Murder and Witchcraft Pamphlets and Plays*, Ann Arbor: UMI Dissertation Services.

Levack, Brian P. (ed.) (1992) *Witchcraft in Scotland*, vol. 7 of *Articles on Witchcraft, Magic and Demonology*, New York and London: Garland Publishing.

—— (1995) *The Witch-hunt in Early Modern Europe*, 2nd edn, London and New York: Longman.

—— (1996) 'State-building and Witch Hunting in Early Modern Europe', in J. Barry, M. Hester, G. Roberts (eds), *Witchcraft in Early Modern Europe: Studies in Culture and Belief*, Cambridge: Cambridge University Press, 96–115.

Levine, Laura (1994) *Men in Women's Clothing: Antitheatricality and Effeminization, 1579–1642*, Cambridge: Cambridge University Press.

Liisberg, Bering (1909) *Vesten for So og Osten for Hav: Trolddom i Kobenhavn og i Edinburgh 1590*, Copenhagen: A. Christiansens Forlag.

Lindley, David (1993) *The Trials of Frances Howard: Fact and Fiction at the Court of King James*, London and New York: Routledge.

Loomie, Albert J. (1970–1) 'King James I's Catholic Consort', *Huntington Library Quarterly* 34: 303–16.

Lottes, Günther (1984) 'Popular Culture and the Early Modern State in 16th Century Germany', in S. Kaplan (ed.), *Understanding Popular Culture: Europe from the Middle Ages to the Nineteenth Century*, Berlin, New York and Amsterdam: Mouton Publishers, 147–88.

Louden, David and Whitfield, William (1891) *East Lothian Studies*, Haddington: John Hutchison; Edinburgh: J. Menzies.

Lowell, A. L. (1897–98) 'The Judicial Use of Torture', *Harvard Law Review* 11: 220–33; 290–300.

Lowther, C. (1894) *Our Journall into Scotland, Anno Domini 1629*, Edinburgh: David Douglas.

Lyall, F. (1980) *Of Presbyters and Kings: Church and State in the Law of Scotland*, Aberdeen: Aberdeen University Press.

Lyly, John (1902) *The Complete Works of John Lyly*, ed. R. Warwick Bond, 3 vols, Oxford: Clarendon Press.

Lynch, Michael (1981) *Edinburgh and the Reformation*, Edinburgh: John Donald.

—— (1983) 'From Privy Kirk to Burgh Church: An Alternative View of the Process of Protestantisation', in Norman MacDougall (ed.), *Church, Politics and Society: Scotland 1408–1929*, Edinburgh: John Donald, 85–96.

—— (1985) 'Calvinism in Scotland, 1559–1638', in M. Prestwich (ed.), *International Calvinism 1541–1715*, Oxford: Clarendon, 225–55.

—— (1987) 'The Reformation in Edinburgh: The Growth and Growing Pains of

Urban Protestantism', in Jim Obelkevich, Lyndal Roper, Raphael Samuel (eds), *Disciplines of Faith: Studies in Religion, Politics and Patriarchy* (History Workshop Series), London and New York: Routledge, 283–94.

Lythe, S. G. E. (1960) *The Economy of Scotland in its European Setting 1550–1625*, Edinburgh: Oliver and Boyd.

—— (1973) 'The Economy of Scotland under James VI and I', in A. G. R. Smith (ed.), *The Reign of James VI and I*, London: Macmillan, 57–73.

McClure, J. Derrick (1990) '"O Phoenix Escossois": James VI as Poet', in A. Gardner-Medwin and J. H. Williams (eds), *A Day Estivall: Essays on the Music, Poetry and History of Scotland and England*, Aberdeen: Aberdeen University Press, 96–111.

MacDonald, Michael (1991) *Witchcraft and Hysteria in Elizabethan London: Edward Jorden and the Mary Glover Case*, London and New York: Tavistock/Routledge.

MacDougall, Norman (ed.) (1983) *Church, Politics and Society: Scotland 1408–1929*, Edinburgh: John Donald.

McGowan, Margaret (1977) 'Pierre de Lancre's *Tableau de L'Inconstance des Mauvais Anges et Demons*: the Sabbat Sensationalised', in S. Anglo (ed.), *The Damned Art: Essays in the Literature of Witchcraft*, London, Henley and Boston: Routledge and Kegan Paul, 182–201.

McKay, Denis (1968) '"The Four Heid Pilgrimages of Scotland"', *Innes Review* 19: 76–7.

Mackenzie, George (1678) *The Laws and Customes of Scotland in Matters Criminal*, Edinburgh.

McKerrow, R. B. (ed.) (1910) *A Dictionary of Printers and Booksellers in England, Scotland and Ireland, and of Foreign Printers of English Books 1557–1640* (Bibliographical Society), London: Blades, Each and Blades.

Mackinlay, James M. (1910–14) *Ancient Church Dedications in Scotland*, 2 vols, Edinburgh: David Douglas.

McNeill, F. Marian (1989) *The Silver Bough*, vol. 1, *Scottish Folk-lore and Folk-belief*, Edinburgh: Canongate Classics.

McNeill, Peter (1884) *Tranent and its Surroundings: Historical, Ecclesiastical, and Traditional*, 2nd edn, Edinburgh and Glasgow: John Menzies; Tranent: Peter McNeill.

McNeill, Peter and Nicholson, Ranald (eds) (1975) *An Historical Atlas of Scotland c.400 – c.1600*, St Andrews: Atlas Committee of the Conference of Scottish Medievalists.

MacPherson, J. M. (1929) *Primitive Beliefs in the North-east of Scotland*, London, New York and Toronto: Longmans, Green and Co.

MacQueen, J. *et al.* (1970) 'The Lothian Witches of 1591 and a Link with Burns', *Scottish Studies* 14: 189–91.

McRoberts, David (ed.) (1962) *Essays on the Scottish Reformation, 1513–1625*, Glasgow: Burns.

Maitland Miscellany (1840) *Miscellany of the Maitland Club Illustrative of the History and Literature of Scotland*, Edinburgh: Maitland Club.

Maitland, Sir Richard (1829) *The History of the House of Seytoun to the Year M.D.LIX.*, with the Continuation by A. Kingston to M.DC.LXXXVII, Glasgow: Maitland Club.

Malleorum Quorundam Maleficarum (1582) *Malleorum Quorundam Maleficarum*, Frankfurt.

Marjoribanks, George (1814) *Annals of Scotland, from the Year 1514 to the year 1591*, ed. J. G. Dalyell, Edinburgh: A. Constable.

Marlowe, Christopher (1993) *Dr Faustus A- and B-Texts (1604, 1616)*, ed. David Bevington and Eric Rasmussen, Manchester and New York: Manchester University Press.

Marsh, David (1980) *The Quattrocento Dialogue: Classical Tradition and Humanist Innovation*, London and Cambridge, Mass.: Harvard University Press.

Marshall, Rosalind K. (1983) *Virgins and Viragos: A History of Women in Scotland from 1080 to 1980*, London: Collins.

Mason, James (1612) *The Anatomie of Sorcerie. Wherein the wicked Impietie of Charmers, Inchanters, and such like, is discovered and confuted*.

Mason, Roger A. (1983) 'Covenant and Commonweal: The Language of Politics in Reformation Scotland', in Norman MacDougall (ed.), *Church, Politics and Society: Scotland 1408–1929*, Edinburgh: John Donald, 97–126.

—— (1982) '*Rex Stoicus*: George Buchanan, James VI and the Scottish Polity', in John Dwyer *et al.* (eds), *New Perspectives on the Politics and Culture of Early Modern Scotland*, Edinburgh: John Donald, 9–33.

Maxwell-Stuart, P. G. (1997) 'The Fear of the King is Death: James VI and the Witches of East Lothian', in W. G. Naphy and P. Roberts (eds), *Fear in Early Modern Society*, Manchester and New York: Manchester University Press, 209–25.

Melville, Mr James (1829) *The Diary of Mr James Melvill, 1556–1601*, Edinburgh: Bannatyne Club.

Melville, Sir James (1827) *Memoirs of his Own Life by Sir James Melville of Halhill*, Edinburgh: Bannatyne Club.

Melville, R. D. (1905) 'The Use and Forms of Judicial Torture in England and Scotland', *Scottish Historical Review* 2: 225–48.

Midelfort, H. C. Erik (1981) 'Madness and the Problems of Psychological History in the Sixteenth Century', *Sixteenth Century Journal* 12: 5–12.

—— (1984) 'Sin, Melancholy, Obsession: Insanity and Culture in 16th Century Germany', in S. Kaplan (ed.), *Understanding Popular Culture: Europe from the Middle Ages to the Nineteenth Century*, Berlin, New York and Amsterdam: Mouton Publishers, 113–45.

Mitchison, Rosalind (1974) 'A Parish and its Poor: Yester in the Second Half of the Seventeenth Century', *Transactions of the East Lothian Antiquarian and Field Naturalists' Society* 14: 15–28.

Moody, David (1986) *Scottish Local History: An Introductory Guide*, London: Batsford.

More, St Thomas (1964) *Utopia*, ed. Edward Surtz S.J., New Haven and London: Yale University Press.

Moysie, David (1830) *Memoirs of the Affairs of Scotland 1577–1603*, ed. James Dennistoun, Edinburgh: Bannatyne Club.

Muchembled, Robert (1982) 'Witchcraft, Popular Culture, and Christianity in the Sixteenth Century with Emphasis upon Flanders and Artois', in Robert Forster and Orest Ranum (eds), *Ritual, Religion and the Sacred*, Baltimore and London: Johns Hopkins University Press, 213–36.

—— (1984) 'Lay Judges and the Acculturation of the Masses (France and the Southern Low Countries, Sixteenth to Eighteenth Centuries)', in Kaspar von Greyerz (ed.), *Religion and Society in Early Modern Europe 1500–1800*, London:

German Historical Institute, and George Allen and Unwin, 56–65.

—— (1993) 'Satanic Myths and Cultural Reality', in Bengt Ankarloo and Gustav Henningsen (eds), *Early Modern European Witchcraft: Centres and Peripheries*, Oxford: Clarendon, 139–60.

Murden, William (1759) *A Collection of State Papers Relating to Affairs in the Reign of Elizabeth from 1571–1596 Transcribed from Original Papers Left by William Cecill, Lord Burghley.*

Murray, George, Apted M. R. and Hodkinson, Ian (1966) 'Prestongrange and its Painted Ceiling', *Transactions of the East Lothian Antiquarian and Field Naturalists' Society* 10: 92–132.

Murray, Margaret (1917–18) 'The "Devil" of North Berwick', *Scottish Historical Review* 15: 310–21.

—— (1921) *The Witch-Cult in Western Europe*, Oxford: Clarendon Press.

NEB (1961–70) *The New English Bible*, London: Oxford University Press; Cambridge University Press.

Normand, Lawrence (1996) '"What passions call you these?": *Edward II* and James VI', in D. Grantley and P. Roberts (eds), *Christopher Marlowe and English Renaissance Culture*, Aldershot: Scolar Press, 172–97.

—— (1997) 'Witches, King James, and *The Masque of Queens*', in Claude J. Summers and Ted-Larry Pebworth (eds), *Representing Women in Renaissance England*, Columbia and London: University of Missouri Press, 107–20.

Notestein, Wallace (1965) *A History of Witchcraft in England from 1558 to 1718*, (1st publ. 1911) New York: Russell and Russell.

NRSB (1989) *The Holy Bible: New Revised Standard Version*, London: Collins.

Oates, Caroline (1989) 'Metamorphosis and Lycanthropy in Franche-Comté, 1521–1643', in M. Feher, R. Naddaff and N. Tazi (eds), *Fragments for a History of the Human Body*, Part 1, New York: Zone, 304–63.

Omond, George T. (1883) *The Lord Advocates of Scotland: From the Close of the Fifteenth Century to the Passing of the Reform Bill*, 2 vols, Edinburgh: David Douglas.

Papers Relative to the Marriage (1828) *Papers Relative to the Marriage of King James the Sixth of Scotland with the Princess Anna of Denmark A.D.MDLXXXIX and the Form and Manner of Her Majesty's Coronation at Holyroodhouse A.D.MDXC*, ed. J. T. G. Craig, Edinburgh: Bannatyne Club.

Parker, Geoffrey (1988) 'The "Kirk by Law Established" and the Origins of "The Taming of Scotland": St Andrews 1559–1600', in Leah Leneman (ed.), *Perspectives in Scottish Social History: Essays in Honour of Rosalind Mitchison*, Aberdeen: Aberdeen University Press, 1–32.

Paton, G. C. H. (ed.) (1958) *An Introduction to Scottish Legal History by Various Authors* (Stair Society, vol. 20), Edinburgh: Stair Society.

Patrides C. A. (1982) '"That Great and Indisputable Miracle": The Cessation of Oracles', in *Premises and Motifs in Renaissance Thought and Literature*, Princeton: Princeton University Press.

Paul, James Balfour (1905) *The Scots Peerage*, 9 vols, 1904–14, vol. 2, Edinburgh: David Douglas.

Perkins, William (1610) *A Discourse of the Damned Art of Witchcraft; so farre forth as it is revealed in the Scriptures*, Cambridge.

Peters, Edward (1978) *The Magician, the Witch and the Law*, Hassocks, Sussex: Harvester.

—— (1985) *Torture*, Oxford: Blackwell.

Pitcairn, Robert (1833) *Ancient Criminal Trials in Scotland 1488–1624*, Vol. 1, Edinburgh, Bannatyne Club.

Potts, Thomas (1613) *The Wonderfull Discoverie of Witches in the Countie of Lancaster. With the Arraignement and Triall*.

Prestwich, Menna (ed.) (1985) *International Calvinism 1541–1715*, Oxford: Clarendon.

Pryde, George Smith (1965) *The Burghs of Scotland: A Critical List*, London, Glasgow and New York: Oxford University Press.

Purkiss, Diane (1996) *The Witch in History: Early Modern and Twentieth-Century Representations*, London and New York: Routledge.

Quaife, G. R. (1987) *Godly Zeal and Furious Rage: The Witch in Early Modern Europe*, London and Sydney: Croom Helm.

Read, Conyers (1925) *Mr Secretary Walsingham and the Policy of Queen Elizabeth*, 3 vols, Oxford: Clarendon.

—— (1960) *Lord Burghley and Queen Elizabeth*, London: Jonathan Cape.

Remy, Nicholas (1930) *Demonolatry*, trans. E. A. Ashwin, ed. M. Summers, London: John Rodker.

Riis, Thomas (1988) *Should Auld Acquaintance Be Forgot ... Scottish-Danish Relations c.1450–1707*, Odense: Odense University Press.

Ritchie, A. E. (1880) *The Churches of Saint Baldred*, Edinburgh: J. Moodie Miller.

Robbins, R. H. (1959) *The Encyclopedia of Witchcraft and Demonology*, London: Peter Nevill.

Roberts, Alexander (1616) *A Treatise of Witchcraft*.

Roberts, Gareth (1996) 'Necromantic Books: Christopher Marlowe, *Dr Faustus* and Agrippa of Nettesheim', in D. Grantley and P. Roberts (eds), *Christopher Marlowe and English Renaissance Culture*, Aldershot: Scolar Press, 148–71.

Roper, Lyndal (1994) *Oedipus and the Devil: Witchcraft, Sexuality and Religion in Early Modern Europe*, London and New York: Routledge.

Rosen, Barbara (ed.) (1969) *Witchcraft* (Stratford-upon-Avon Library 6), London: Edward Arnold.

—— (ed.) (1991) *Witchcraft in England, 1558–1618*, 2nd edn, Amherst: University of Massachusetts Press.

Ross, Anthony (1962) 'Reformation and Repression', in David McRoberts (ed.), *Essays on the Scottish Reformation, 1513–1625*, Glasgow: Burns, 371–414.

Roughead, William (1936) 'The Witches of North Berwick', in *The Riddle of the Ruthvens and Other Studies*, revised edn, Edinburgh and London: Moray Press, 144–66.

Rowland, Robert (1993) '"Fantasticall and Devilishe Persons": European Witch-beliefs in Comparative Perspective', in Bengt Ankarloo and Gustav Henningsen (eds), *Early Modern European Witchcraft: Centres and Peripheries*, Oxford: Clarendon, 161–90.

RPCS iv (1881) *Register of the Privy Council of Scotland*, vol. 4, 1585–92, Edinburgh: H.M. General Register House, 1st series publ. 1877–98.

RPCS v (1882) *Register of the Privy Council of Scotland*, vol. 5, 1592–99, Edinburgh: H.M. General Register House, 1st series publ. 1877–98.

Russell, Jeffrey Burton (1984) *Lucifer: The Devil in the Middle Ages*, Ithaca and London: Cornell University Press.

Sanderson, Margaret H. B. (1970) 'Catholic Recusancy in Scotland in the Sixteenth Century', *Innes Review* 21: 87–107.

—— (1975) 'Roman Catholic Recusancy 1560–1603', in P. McNeill and R. Nicholson (eds), *An Historical Atlas of Scotland c.400–c.1600*, St Andrews: Atlas Committee of the Conference of Scottish Medievalists, 89–90, 204–7.

—— (1982) *Scottish Rural Society in the Sixteenth Century*, Edinburgh: John Donald.

—— (1987) *Mary Stewart's People: Life in Mary Stewart's Scotland*, Edinburgh: Thin.

Scot, Reginald (1886) *The Discoverie of Witchcraft*, ed. Brinsley Nicholson, London: E. Stock.

Scott, Hew (1866–71) *Fasti Ecclesiae Scoticanae*, 3 vols, London.

Scribner, R. W. (1987) *Popular Culture and Popular Movements in Reformation Gemany*, London and Rouceverte: Hambledon Press.

—— (1989) 'Is A History of Popular Culture Possible?', *History of European Ideas* 10: 175–91.

Second Book of Discipline (1980) *The Second Book of Discipline*, ed. James Kirk, Edinburgh: Saint Andrew Press.

Seton, George (1882) *Memoir of Alexander Seton, Earl of Dunfermline*, Edinburgh: Blackwood.

—— (1896) *A History of the Family of Seton During Eight Centuries*, 2 vols, Edinburgh: Constable.

Shakespeare, William (1988) *The Complete Works*, Compact Edition, ed. Stanley Wells and Gary Taylor, Oxford: Clarendon Press.

Sharpe, C.K. (ed.) (1818) *Memorialls; or The Memorable Things that fell out within this Island of Brittain from 1638 to 1684 by the Rev Mr Robert Law*, Edinburgh: Constable.

Sharpe, J. A. (1991) 'Witchcraft and Women in Seventeenth-Century England: Some Northern Evidence', *Continuity and Change* 6: 179–99.

—— (1996) 'The Devil in East Anglia: The Matthew Hopkins Trials Reconsidered', in J. Barry, M. Hester, G. Roberts (eds), *Witchcraft in Early Modern Europe: Studies in Culture and Belief*, Cambridge: Cambridge University Press, 237–54.

Sharpe, Kevin (1994) 'The King's Writ: Royal Authors and Royal Authority in Early Modern England', in K. Sharpe and P. Lake (eds), *Culture and Politics in Early Stuart England* (Problems in Focus), Basingstoke and London: Macmillan, 117–38

Sidney, Sir Philip (1973) *An Apology for Poetry*, ed. Geoffrey Shepherd, Manchester: Manchester University Press.

Simmons, T. F. (ed.) (1879) *The Lay Folks Mass Book* (Early English Text Society 71), London: N. Trübner and Co.

Simonetti, Manlio (1989) *La Maga di Endor*, Florence: Nardini Editore.

Simpson, Anne Turner and Stevenson, Sylvia (1981) *Historic North Berwick: The Archaeological Implications of Development* (Scottish Burgh Survey), Glasgow: University of Glasgow.

Simpson, Jacqueline (1995) '"The Weird Sisters Wandering": Burlesque Witchery in Montgomerie's *Flyting*', *Folklore* 106: 9–20.

Sinclair, George (1871) *Satan's Invisible World Discovered* [1685], Edinburgh.

Smailes, Helen (compiler) (1990) *The Concise Catalogue of the Scottish National Portrait Gallery*, Edinburgh: National Galleries of Scotland.

Smelik, K.A.D. (1977) 'The Witch of Endor: 1 Samuel 28 in Rabbinic and Christian Exegesis till 800 AD', *Vigilae Christianae* 33: 160ff.

Smith, A. G. R. (ed.) (1973) *The Reign of James VI and I* (Problems in Focus), London and Basingstoke: Macmillan.

Smith, J. Irvine (1972) 'Introduction' to *Selected Justiciary Cases 1624–1650*, vol. 2, 2 vols, Edinburgh: Stair Society.

—— (1958a) 'The Transition to the Modern Law', in G. C. H. Paton (ed.), *An Introduction to Scottish Legal History* (Stair Society, vol. 20), Edinburgh: Stair Society, 25–43.

—— (1958b) 'Criminal Procedure', in G. C. H. Paton (ed.), *An Introduction to Scottish Legal History* (Stair Society, vol. 20), Edinburgh: Stair Society, 426–48.

Smout, Christopher (1972) *A History of the Scottish People, 1560–1830*, London: Fontana.

—— (1995) 'The Culture of Migration: Scots as Europeans 1500–1800', *History Workshop Journal* 40: 108–17.

SND (1931–) *The Scottish National Dictionary*, ed. William Grant *et al.*, 10 vols, Edinburgh: Scottish National Dictionary Association.

Snyder, Jon R. (1989) *Writing the Scene of Speaking: Theories of Dialogue in the Late Italian Renaissance*, Stanford: Stanford University Press.

Spierenburg, Pieter (1984) *The Spectacle of Suffering: Executions and the Evolution of Repression from a Preindustrial Metropolis to the European Experience*, Cambridge, New York and Melbourne: Cambridge University Press.

Spottiswoode, John (1668) *The History of the Church of Scotland*, 3rd edn, R. Royston.

—— (1847–51) *History of the Church and State of Scotland*, 3 vols, Edinburgh: Spottiswoode Society.

Stafford, Helen (1953) 'Notes on Scottish Witchcraft Cases, 1590–91', in Norton Downs (ed.), *Essays in Honour of Conyers Read*, Chicago: University of Chicago Press, 96–118.

STC (1991) *A Short-Title Catalogue of Books Printed in England, Scotland and Ireland and of Books Printed Abroad 1475–1640*, first compiled by A. W. Pollard and G. R. Redgrave, vol. 3, A Printers' and Publishers' Index by K. F. Pantzer, London: Bibliographical Society.

Stearne, John (1648) *A Confirmation and Discovery of Witch-craft*.

Stevenson, David (1997) *Scotland's Last Royal Wedding: The Marriage of James VI and Anne of Denmark*, Edinburgh: John Donald.

Teall, John L. (1962) 'Witchcraft and Calvinism in Elizabethan England: Divine Power and Human Agency', *Journal of the History of Ideas* 23: 21–36.

Tedeschi, John (1993) 'Inquisitorial Law and the Witch', in Bengt Ankarloo and Gustav Henningsen (eds), *Early Modern European Witchcraft: Centres and Peripheries*, Oxford: Clarendon, 83–118.

Thomas, Keith (1973) *Religion and the Decline of Magic: Studies in Popular Beliefs in Sixteenth- and Seventeenth-century England*, Harmondsworth: Penguin.

Thorndike, Lynn (1915) 'Some Medieval Conceptions of Magic', *The Monist* 25: 107–39.

—— (1923–58) *A History of Magic and Experimental Science*, 8 vols, New York and London: Macmillan.

Tilley, M. P. (1950) *A Dictionary of the Proverbs in England in the Sixteenth and Seventeenth Centuries*, Ann Arbor, Michigan: University of Michigan Press.

Underdown, D. E. (1985) 'The Taming of the Scold', in Anthony Fletcher and John

Stevenson (eds), *Order and Disorder in Early Modern England*, Cambridge: Cambridge University Press, 116–36.

Unsworth, C. R. (1989) 'Witchcraft Beliefs and Criminal Procedure in Early Modern England', in Thomas G. Watkin (ed.), *Legal Record and Historical Reality*, London: Hambledon.

Walker, D. P. (1981) *Unclean Spirits: Possession and Exorcism in France and England in the Late Sixteenth and Early Seventeenth Centuries*, London: Scolar Press.

—— (1982) 'Demonic Possession Used as Propaganda in the Later Sixteenth Century', in *Scienze, Credenze Occulte, Livelli di Cultura*, Firenze: Leo S. Olschki, 237–48.

—— (1983) 'Le Cessazione dei Miracoli', *Intersezioni* 3: 285–310.

Wallace Jr., D. D. (1978) 'George Gifford, Puritan Propaganda and Popular Religion in Elizabethan England', *Sixteenth Century Journal* 9: 27–49.

Warner, G. F. (1893) 'The Library of James VI, 1573–1583', *Miscellany of the Scottish History Society*, Edinburgh: Scottish History Society, vol. 1: xi–lxxv.

Warrender Papers (1931–2) *The Warrender Papers*, ed. Annie I. Cameron, 2 vols, Edinburgh: Scottish History Society.

Webster, Charles (1982) 'Paracelsus and Demons: Science as a Synthesis of Popular Belief', in *Scienze, Credenze Occulte, Livelli di Cultura*, Firenze: Leo S. Olschki, 3–20.

Webster, John (1677) *The Displaying of Supposed Witchcraft*.

Weyer, Johann (1991) *Witches, Devils, and Doctors in the Renaissance: Johann Weyer, 'De Praestigiis Daemonum'*, trans. John Shea, Binghampton, New York: Medieval and Renaissance Texts and Studies.

Whyte, Ian D. (1995) *Scotland Before the Industrial Revolution: An Economic and Social History c.1050–c.1750*, London and New York: Longman.

—— (1997) *Scotland's Society and Economy in Transition, c.1500–c.1760*, Basingstoke: Macmillan Press; New York: St Martin's Press.

Whyte, Ian and Whyte, Kathleen (1988) *Discovering East Lothian*, Edinburgh: John Donald.

Wiesner, Merry E. (1993) *Women and Gender in Early Modern Europe* (New Approaches to European History), Cambridge: Cambridge University Press.

Williamson, Arthur H. (1979) *Scottish National Consciousness in the Age of James VI: The Apocalypse, the Union and the Shaping of Scotland's Public Culture*, Edinburgh: John Donald.

Willis, Deborah (1995) *Malevolent Nurture: Witch-hunting and Maternal Power in Early Modern England*, Ithaca and London: Cornell University Press.

Willock, Ian D. (1966) *The Origins and Development of the Jury in Scotland* (Stair Society, vol. 23), Edinburgh: Stair Society.

Willson, D. H. (1965) *King James VI and I*, London: Jonathan Cape.

Wormald, Jenny (1981) *Court, Kirk, and Community: Scotland 1470–1625* (New History of Scotland, vol. 4), London: Edward Arnold.

—— (1983) '"Princes" and the Regions in the Scottish Reformation', in N. MacDougall (ed.), *Church, Politics and Society: Scotland 1408–1929*, Edinburgh: John Donald, 65–84.

—— (1985) *Lords and Men in Scotland: Bonds of Manrent 1442–1603*, Edinburgh: John Donald.

—— (ed.) (1991a) *Scotland Revisited*, London: Collins and Brown.

—— (1991b) 'James VI and I, "Basilikon Doron" and "The Trew Law of Free Monarchies": The Scottish Context and the English Translation', in Linda Levy Peck (ed.), *The Mental World of the Jacobean Court*, Cambridge: Cambridge University Press, 36–54.

—— (1995) 'Ecclesiastical Vitriol: The Kirk, the Puritans and the Future King', in John Guy (ed.), *The Reign of Elizabeth I: Court and Culture in the Last Decade*, Cambridge: Cambridge University Press.

—— (2000) 'The Witches, the Devil and the King', in Terry Brotherstone and David Ditchburn (eds), *Freedom and Authority: Scotland c.1050–c.1650: Historical and Historiographical Essays Presented to Grant G. Simpson*, East Linton: Tuckwell Press, 165–80.

Wright, Thomas (1851) *Narratives of Sorcery and Magic*, 2 vols, London: Richard Bentley.

Yeoman, L. A. 'Hunting the Rich Witch in Scotland: High Status Witch Suspects and their Persecutors, 1590–1650', in J. Goodare (ed.), *The Scottish Witch-Hunt in Context*, Manchester: Manchester University Press, 2001 forthcoming.

Zika, Charles (1989/90) 'Fears of Flying: Representations of Witchcraft and Sexuality in Early Sixteenth-Century Germany', *Australian Journal of Art* 8: 19–47.

INDEX